ORION BLUE BOOK

VINTAGE GUITARS
&
COLLECTIBLES
2003

FOURTH QUARTER
FALL EDITION

ORION RESEARCH CORPORATION
14555 N. Scottsdale Rd. Suite 330
Scottsdale, Arizona 85254
voice: 480.951.1114   fax: 480.951.1117
email: sales@orionbluebook.com
web site: www.orionbluebook.com

2003 Fall Edition

Roger Rohrs
Publisher

ORION'S PUBLISHER, ROGER ROHRS

Listed in Who's Who in American Colleges and Universities, Mr. Rohrs graduated from Polytechnic State University in San Luis Obispo, California. He received a B.A. in Business with a concentration in Marketing in 1969. Following graduation, Mr. Rohrs served as an Army officer in Vietnam where he received an Air Combat Medal and Purple Heart.

Mr. Rohrs returned to California to resume his business career with Warehouse Sound Company and a chain of retail stereo stores named Stereo West. These two businesses evolved from a stereo store Mr. Rohrs and two partners had begun during their college years. The annual sales volume of these businesses reached eight million dollars within four years of operation.

The original Orion Blue Book began in 1973 during Mr. Rohrs' ownership of the stereo retail stores. Seeing a need for his salespeople to have a uniform reference for pricing used equipment, Mr. Rohrs compiled the Orion Trade-In Guide. It also served as a training guide for new salespeople who were unfamiliar with product lines and retail pricing.

In 1977, Mr. Rohrs cofounded Nautilus Recordings. Nautilus Recordings became well known as a producer and distributor of audiophile recordings.

In 1979, Mr. Rohrs exchanged his interest in Nautilus Recordings for exclusive ownership of the Orion Trade-In Guide. Since then, he and his wife, Marty Rohrs, who is responsible for Orion's Public Relations have developed this single book into a product line containing eleven separate Blue Books: Audio, Camera, Car Stereo, Computer, Copier, Guitars and Musical Instruments, Gun, Power Tool, Professional Sound, Video and Television, and Vintage Guitar and Collectibles. Marty also developed an integral part of our research-The Board of Advisor Program.

In addition to the above business ventures, Mr. Rohrs has owned restaurants, a retail clothing store, and a graphic arts and printing establishment. He is a licensed California Real Estate Broker and business consultant. In 1995, Mr. Rohrs saw that the Internet was fast becoming the marketplace of the world. Early that year, Orion became Internet certified, and now Mr. Rohrs consults with businesses on providing an Internet presence.
Mr. Rohrs's personal e-mail address is: rrohrs99@hotmail.com

ISBN 0-932089-66-6 (ANNUAL)
ISBN 0-932089-67-4 (Fall)
ISSN 1056-8581
Copyright © 1990-2003 Orion Research Corporation   **2003 Fall Edition**
First Printing October 2003

CONTENTS

Save $20 on your next Orion Blue Book Purchase.

PROFIT   Accept only those products which will yield a profit margin within a reasonable time in your region. The prices within the Orion Blue Book reflect a national average price that a dealer will be able to obtain within 30 days. Dealers often make more profit on used equipment than on the sale of new equipment. If you over-allow on trade-ins, your ability to resell the product at a profitable price is diminished.

CAUTION: Fluctuations in the value of the dollar against foreign currencies have an impact on the value of imported equipment. Values are based on the exchange rate of 2003.

REGIONAL PRICING   Evaluate your local or regional demand for certain product lines or even individual products within the line. The values in the Orion Blue Book are based on national averages determined by dealer surveys.

TEST   All equipment should be carefully tested before allowing a trade-in. Scrutinize all mechanical equipment. The color and paint should be original as well as the pickup. It is advisable to play the guitar and listen for good sound quality. You should also check amplifiers for damaged speakers etc.

COSMETIC CONDITION   Consideration of the unit's cosmetic condition is a good indication of the kind of care the unit has received. Scratches and dents would be more reflective of condition than the age of the product. If any items are missing you should deduct a reasonable amount from the determined value. Any modifications will also have an effect on its value.

PRODUCT REQUEST FILE   Keep a current file list of those products not in your used department which customers are requesting. Ask the customer for the price range they are willing to pay. This will help you determine local demand.

DISPLAY   Make the Orion Blue Book accessible to your customers. Some dealers chain the book to the counter. The customer can then determine the used value of the products without taking the salesperson away from another customer.

ADVERTISING   The Orion Blue Book has been used as a promotional tool by many dealers. Advertisements are placed offering 150% of the Orion Blue Book's "average" trade-in value for a specific product line. For example: "this week only, trade in your AMPEG products and receive 150% of the Orion Blue Book's average price."

YOUR STORE NAME

TRADE-IN DAYS
150% TRADE-IN VALUE TOWARDS PURCHASE

Get 150% of the Orion Blue Book used average trade-in value on your Ampeg equipment towards the purchase of Ampeg equipment. Your store reserves the right to inspect and refuse certain trades.

CAUTION: Be sure to qualify which manufacturers' products you want. In failing to specify, you will wind up paying too much for products you don't want and will have trouble reselling them. For this promotion, use quality lines which you carry in your store. It is also advisable to limit your promotion to a specific time period.

Free Radio Time: Radio talk shows always need interesting, knowledgeable guests. Many dealers contact local radio stations and volunteer to be on a talk show. Listeners are invited to call in and find out the value of their used equipment from an expert, the dealer. By using the Blue Books, the dealer can send any of his salespeople to offer this service to the radio listeners, you are not only receiving free advertising, you are demonstrating that you are an expert in your area.

SURVEY PARTICIPATION   Orion has an active dealer survey program. By completing the survey, which is located in the back of the book, you will receive a $20 coupon towards the purchase of an Orion Blue Book.

TYPE	YR	MFG	MODEL	SELL EXC	SELL AVG	BUY EXC	BUY AVG
MIC	57-64	AKG	**C-12 TUBE MULTI-PATTERN**	5685	**4860**	4285	3690
GTAMP	60	FENDER	**CONCERT/4x10"/BRN**	1500	**1290**	1130	975
ELGUIT	62	GIBSON	**SUPER 400 CES/SUNBURST/POINTED CUT**	11370	**9470**	8200	5080
GUITAR	59	MARTIN	**D-28E/FLATTOP/2 PU** SERIAL #165577-171047	3150	**2710**	2375	2045
ELGUIT	59	RICKENBAC	**4000 BASS/AUTUMN GLO**	1830	**1575**	1370	1180
BANJO	11	VEGA	**FAIRBANKS WHYTE LADY #2/OPEN BACK**	1780	**1530**	1340	1155
SYNTH	78-82	YAMAHA	**CS-80 ANALOG**	630	**550**	480	415

TYPE   Category of unit: Banjo, Electric Guitar, Guitar, Guitar Amp, Mandolin, Mandola, Microphone, Power Amplifier, Preamplifier, Receiver, Steel Guitar, Synthesizer, Test Equipment, Tuner, and Ukulele.

YR   Year the unit was released for sale.

MFG   Manufacturer of unit. The full name of each manufacturer appears before each grouping.

MODEL   Identification of product by model number and/or name.

SELL EXC   The selling price if all original parts and in excellent condition.

SELL AVG   The selling price if all original parts and in average condition.

BUY EXC   Price paid to the customer if the unit is in excellent working order and appearance. All original with no modifications.

BUY AVG   Average price paid to the customer for a product. Might show some wear.

SAVE $20.00 ON YOUR NEXT ORDER
FILL OUT THE SURVEY IN THE BACK OF THE BOOK

ANT	ANTIGUA	OP-BK	OPEN BACK
BDY	BODY	PRE	PREAMPLIFIER
BLK	BLACK	PU	PICKUP
BLND	BLOND	PWR	POWER AMPLIFIER
B&S	BACK & SIDES	R&W	RED & WHITE
B&W	BLACK & WHITE	RCV	RECEIVER
BR/BRN	BROWN	REG	REGULATOR
BRD	BURGUNDY	RESON	RESONATOR
CAB	CABINET	REV	REVERB
CH	CHANNEL	RND	ROUND
CHY	CHERRY	RSWD	ROSEWOOD
CNDY	CANDY	SGL	SINGLE
CONCRT	CONCERT	SHLDR	SHOULDER
CON	CONTROL	SG	SOLID GUITAR
CRE	CREAM	SLD	SOLID
CRLY	CURLY	SLVR	SILVER
CUT/CA	CUTAWAY	SM	SMALL
DAK	DAKOTA	SMK	SMOKE
DK	DARK	SPKR/SPKRS	SPEAKER
DBL	DOUBLE	SPRU	SPRUCE
EBO	EBONY	SQ	SQUARE
EFFECTS	EFFECTS	STDBY	STANDBY
ELGUIT	ELECTRIC GUITAR	STGUIT	STEEL GUITAR
ES	ELECTRIC SPANISH	STRG	STRING
FGRBD	FINGERBOARD	SUBST/SBRST/SB	SUNBURST
FLM	FLAME	SW	SWITCHMASTER
GLD	GOLD	SWTCH	SWITCH
GR/GRN	GREEN	SYNTH	SYNTHESIZER
GTAMP	GUITAR AMPLIFIER	T	THIN BODY
GUITAR	ACOUSTIC GUITAR	TBL	TURNTABLE
HMBKR	HUMBUCKER	TH	THIN HOLLOWBODY
HB	HUMBUCKING	TENN	TENNESSEAN
HRDWARE/HDWA	HARDWARE	TEST	TEST EQUIPMENT
JEN	JENSEN	TNR	TUNER
MAHG/MHGY	MAHOGANY	TRAN	TRANSPARENT
MANDOL	MANDOLINS	TREM	TREMOLO
MANDOLA	MANDOLA	TW	TWEED
MIC	MICROPHONE	TX	TOLEX
MID	MID-RANGE	UKE	UKULELE
MPL	MAPLE	UPRIGHT	UPRIGHT BASS
NA/NAT	NATURAL	VI/VIB	VIBRATO
NK/NCK	NECK	WAL	WALNUT
NAR	NARROW	WHT	WHITE
NP	NAMEPLATE		

BOARD OF ADVISORS

Orion Research Corporation is proud to introduce our Board of Advisors. During the past year, these Board members have completed an extensive review of data projected for this years edition of the Orion Blue Book. The Board has been a valued addition to the existing Dealer Survey Program in providing the most accurate pricing possible. Our thanks to these board members for sharing their time and expertise.

History of AKG and Neumann Microphone Consultants

Christina Burkhardt
AKG Acoustics
Lembockgasse 21-25
PO Box 158
A-1230
Vienna, Austria

Kevin Madden
AKG Acoustics
1449 Donelson Pike suite #12
Nashville, TN 37217-2640
(615) 360-0499
fax (615) 360-0275

Karl Winkler
Sennheiser / Neumann Electronics
1 Enterprise Drive
Old Lyme, CT 06371
(860) 434-9190
fax (860) 434-9022

Hirsh Gardner
Daddy's Used Gear By Mail
165 Massachusetts Avenue
Boston, MA 02215
(617) 247-0909
email: hag111@aol.com
-Drummer with MCA, Electra Recording Artist "New England".
-Record Producer: winner of the "Boston-Phoenix Best Poll" producer of the year.
-Sales Rep Daddy's since 1990, winner of "Used Gear Salesman of The Year" award 1992-1996
-Employee of the The Year 1992

Combining his expert knowledge of vintage recording equipment studio gear, his years of recording and touring experience, five years of being the top salesman at Daddy's Junky Music, Hirsh brings a wealth of knowledge and experience to his customers.

Daddy's has 19 retail stores and is celebrating its 30th anniversary this year.

Mario Campa
John DeSilva
Toys From The Attic
203 Mamaroneck Ave.
White Plains, NY 10601
voice: 914.421.0069
fax: 914.328.3852
email: info@tfta.com
url: www.tfta.com

John and Mario first met in college in 1981 in front of a stereo. Their mutual love of guitar and music secured what has been a long standing friendship which in 1995 developed into a business known as **Toys From The Attic**. Their unique and diverse approach, half of the business specializing in high-end musical instruments and the other half high-end audio, has been very well received. It truly shows their love and dedication to music. Their strict grading policies and dedication to customer satisfaction have been their keys to success.

Both sides of the business specialize in pre-owned gear, as well as several new lines specially selected for their extraordinary quality and value. All pre-owned items are tested and serviced when necessary. High quality repair services remains another of their specialities.

Every item is sold with a money back guarantee and their showroom is a must see when traveling in the Northeast.

They are members of the Academy for the Advancement of High-End Audio and the Mail Order Merchants Association.

Clay Harrel
url: clay.by.net
email: hag111@adl.com
Clay is a private guitar collector. He buys guitars made from 1920 to 1970 by Gibson, Fender, Martin, Gretsch, Epiphone, National, Dobro, and Rickenbacker.

Fletcher
Mercenary Audio
131 Morse St.
Foxboro, MA 02035
(508) 543-0069
fax (508) 543-9670
url: www.mecenary.com

Fletcher, as he is known in the industry, brings 24 years of professional audio experience to **Mercenary Audio**. Starting in 1973, as a live sound mixer for local New York bands, Fletcher combined his technical and business abilities by opening a sound reinforcement company in 1975. Fletcher is a graduate of Emerson College with a BS degree in Mass Communications.

His hands on live audio and recording experience ranges from several years as a program producer for radio stations WLIR in New York, WERS and WCOZ in Boston, to national tours with nationally known recording artists. Fletcher also has practical business experience in the industry, having been the studio manager for World Class Studio for Normandy Sound.

Since the opening of **Mercenary Audio** in 1989, Fletcher has continued to work as a recording engineer/producer on current projects with artists such as Benn Orr of the Cars, Peter Wolf of the J. Geils Band, and local artist Black Number Line. He feels it is vitally important that he and his staff continue in the recording field, in order to keep abreast of the technology and intelligently share this information with Mercenary's clients. This is the key to keeping Mercenary separate and above its competitors.

Tim Becker
Martin Music
910 N. 21st Street
Newark, OH 43055
(740) 366-2344
fax (740) 366-2345
Tim is the owner of **Martin Music**, founded in 1948. He was a 15 year employee of Coyle Music. As a clarinet, guitar and sax player he collects band instruments, especially clarinets.

Tim is also a Music Business Historian and Member of A.M.I.S.; he is a professional appraisor and buyer of guitars, pianos, and band instruments.

HISTORY OF VINTAGE AKG MICROPHONES

Courtesy of Christina Burkhardt

AKG – Vienna, Austria

1946   AKG DYN Series – including Dyn 60, Dyn 60G, Dyn 60K, Dyn 60K-Studio, etc. All parts are hand made. Annual output 500 to 600 units.

1947   First AKG condenser Tube Microphone. The capsule is a predecessor of the CK12. The diaphragm is made from Styroflex foil, gold sputtered by Goerz.

1950   AKG starts designing the world's first high quality dynamic microphone, the D12 with its "mass-loaded tube".

1951   Dual-diaphragm microphone is developed and called the "C2". About 500 units are made.

1953   Breakthrough of the D12, a large-diaphragm mic that not only provides the first true cardioid polar pattern but introduces engineering innovations such as the mass-loaded tube and "deep-drawn" diaphragm. Film sound engineers too praise the directivity and remarkable low susceptibility to wind noise. The same year also sees the birth of another legendary AKG product: the C12, the first remote controlled multipattern capacitor microphone. The C12 was originally made in runs of 50 units per month and became an international best-seller.

1954   Under water loudspeakers and microphones (Dyn 120 UWS) are developed, the latter derived from the Dyn 60K. The specifications are impressive: Watertight down to 330 ft. at a diving rate of 25 ft./minute: frequency range 30 to 20,000 Hz; sensitivity 0.2 M/Ybar; seawater-proof, chrome plated brass case; weight 15 lbs.; size: 9.8 x 5.5 dia. in. The total output of 20 units was sold to scientists and port authorities. Hans Hass uses a Dyn 120 UWS in shooting his first underwater sound movie, "Abenteuer im Roten Meer" (Adventures in the Red Sea) which won first prize at the "Biennale" biannual film festival at Venice, Italy.

1955   The first postwar Salzburg Festival uses AKG microphones. A unidirectional microphone is specifically designed for Herbert von Karajan. Unlike in his later years, Karajan rejected all audio equipment. When he conducted a performance, he allowed no microphones to be visible to the audience. So AKG had to design a special shotgun microphone that could be set up far from the musicians, in the wings or in the orchestra pit.
D36: The world's first dynamic microphone with remotely selectable polar patterns.
C28: A small-diaphragm condenser microphone.

1956   D11: Unidirectional dynamic microphone for amateur tape recordists.
Introduction of professional cardioid microphones with adjustable rear sound entries for reduced proximity effect. (D24, D19)
Introduction of the Dyn 200 Series of dynamic microphones including gooseneck models and M410, M411 OEM microphones for Telefunken. The east bloc business grows significantly.

1957   The "sheet metal capsule", a dynamic capsule in a tight sheet-metal case, is developed and used over the following years in many AKG microphones including the D9, D11, and D14 as well as OEM microphones for Saba, Korting, Telefunken, Stuzzi, and Eumig.

1958   D15: First dynamic reporters' microphone with a tight unidirectional pattern.
D25: Shock mounted, unidirectional dynamic microphone for use on a fishpole in radio, TV, and film work.
D30: First dynamic studio microphone with four selectable polar patterns.

1959   D45—as D30, except with shock mount and remotely selectable polar patterns.

1960   AKG designs and manufactures for Telefunken, the ELA M250 and ELA M251, two extremely rare thus much sought-after collector's items.
Rerun of the C12 and several other versions for Telefunken and Siemens using the then advanced GE 6072 double triode.
Design of the first professional small-diaphragm condenser microphone with miniature tube (Nuvistor), the AKG C60.

HISTORY OF VINTAGE AKG MICROPHONES
continued

1960/61 The c26 and c30 capacitor microphones are developed further into the c60 with Nuvistor miniature tube (the name is derived from "nueva vista" – a new vision).

1962 A v-shaped dual microphone for interviewing (ENG) use is built and later continued by another company that even applies for a patent assigned by one Mr. Hagopian.
The C12A Nuvistor condenser microphone is developed as a predecessor of today's C414.

1963 The DX11 reverb microphone is a innovative idea which, however, is not accepted by the market. This is one of the few flops in AKG's history of success.

1964 The "CMS" modular capacitor microphone system with the C451 with FET preamp and CK1, CK2, etc. is developed and later becomes famous all over the world. After initial problems have been solved, it strengthens AKG's monopoly with BBX. The capsules originally had embossed metal diaphragms that were susceptible to humidity and therefore later replaced with plastic diaphragms.

1970 The C412, a solid-state version of the C12A with three polar patterns and a preattenuation pad selectable on the microphone is designed.

1971 A high quality electret capsule for use in a new, professional small cassette recorder from UHER is developed (OEM order). The C412 is further improved and renamed C414.

1972 The C24 is relaunched as the C24-cb large-diaphragm stereo capacitor microphone with separately, remotely selectable polar patterns for each channel.

1973 The first production runs of electret microphones are made.
The first AKG dummy head microphone, made by AKG Munich, is used for head related stereo (binaural) recording.

1975 The D140 is a small, top quality dynamic studio microphone with virtually no competition at the time.

1977 C414 EB: First C414 version with improved circuitry and integrated XLR connector.
The C303 line level microphone with built-in compressor and headphone monitor amplifier for the newly created ORF regional TV stations is designed and made in small runs
The C414 is retouched again, specifically the housing, and fitted with an XLR connector. The designation is changed to C414EB.

1978 The first true vocal microphone line is developed. Originally planned as "Alpha", "Beta", and "Gamma", they are later renamed D310, D320, and D330. The first endorsement contracts are concluded with Jon Hiseman, Roger Whittaker, and other artists.

1979 C422 eb: Large diaphragm stereo condenser microphone with advanced solid-state electronics.

1983 New CMS system comprising a C460 electronic preamp and CK61, CK62, and CK63 capsules also includes remote capsules CK1X, CK2X that can be connected to the preamp with cables up to 200 ft. long.
The AKG Tube: Black market prices for C12 microphones skyrocket. Responding to the market situation, AKG makes the first rerun of a large-diaphragm tube microphone using the same 6072 tube as the original C12.

HISTORY OF VINTAGE NEUMANN MICROPHONES

Courtesy of Karl Winkler, Neumann, USA

U 47   (Large diaphragm tube mic made from 1949 through 1965. Features two polar patterns – cardioid and omni. Uses VF14 tube.)

M 49   (Large diaphragm tube mic made from 1951 through 1974. Features remote controlled variable polar patterns. Uses AC701k tube.)

M 50   (Small diaphragm tube mic made from 1951 through 1971. Omni polar pattern only with capsule mounted in sphere. Uses AC701k tube.)

KM 53   (Small diaphragm tube mic made from 1953 through 1968. Omni polar pattern only. Uses AC701k tube.)

KM 54   (Small diaphragm tube mic made from 1953 through 1969. Cardioid polar pattern only. Uses AC701k tube.)

KM 56   (Small diaphragm tube mic made from 1955 through 1970. Three polar patterns – omni, cardioid and figure 8. Uses AC701k tube.)

U 48   (Large diaphragm tube mic made from 1957 through 1965. Features two polar patterns – figure 8 and omni. Uses VF14 tube.)

SM 2   (Small diaphragm stereo tube mic made from 1957 through 1966. Features remote polar pattern control. Uses two AC701k tubes.)

KM 253   (Small diaphragm tube mic made from 1960 through 1967. Omni polar pattern only, connectors with high RF immunity for broadcast environment. Uses AC701k tube.)

KM 253   (Small diaphragm tube mic made from 1960 through 1969. Cardioid polar pattern only, connectors with high RF immunity for broadcast environment. Uses AC701k tube.)

U 67   (Large diaphragm tube mic made from 1960 through 1971 with "revival issue" of 400 units in 1992. Features three polar patterns – cardioid, omni and figure 8 high pass filter and 14-dB pad. Uses EF86 tube.)

M 249   (Large diaphragm tube mic made from 1960 through 1969. Features remote controlled variable polar patterns and connectors with high immunity to RF for broadcast environment. Uses AC701k tube.)

M 250   (Small diaphragm tube mic made from 1960 through 1969. Omni polar pattern only with capsule mounted in sphere; utilizes connectors with high immunity to RF for broadcast environment. Uses AC701k tube.)

KM 256   (Small diaphragm tube mic made from 1961 through 1970. Features three polar patterns – cardioid, omni and figure 8. Connectors with high immunity to RF used for broadcast environment. Uses AC701k tube.)

SM 23   (Small diaphragm stereo tube mic made from 1961 through 1966. Features remote polar pattern control. Uses two AC701k tubes.)

M 269   (Large diaphragm tube mic made from 1962 through 1973. Features three polar patterns – cardioid, omni and figure 8, high pass filter and 14-dB pad. Uses AC701k tube to be compatible with broadcast facility power supplies.)

SM 69   (Large diaphragm stereo tube mic made from 1964 through 1973. Features remote control of polar patterns. Uses two AC701k tubes.)

HISTORY OF VINTAGE NEUMANN MICROPHONES

continued

KM 63   (Small diaphragm tube mic made from 1964 through 1971. Omni polar pattern only. Uses AC701k tube.)

KM 64   (Small diaphragm tube mic made from 1964 through 1971. Cardioid polar pattern only. Uses AC701 tube.)

KM 65   (Small diaphragm tube mic made from 1964 through 1971. Cardioid polar pattern only with bass rolloff. Uses AC701k tube.)

U 64   (Small diaphragm tube mic made from 1964 through 1971. Cardioid polar pattern only. Uses 7586 nuvistor.)

KM 66   (Small diaphragm tube mic made in 1966 only. Three polar patterns – omni, cardioid, figure 8. Uses AC701k tube.)

KM 83   (Small diaphragm FET mic made from 1966 through 1988. Omni polar pattern only. Phantom 48V powered.)

KM 84   (Small diaphragm FET mic made from 1966 through 1988. Cardioid polar pattern only. Phantom 48V powered.)

KM 85   (Small diaphragm FET mic made from 1966 through 1988. Cardioid polar pattern with bass rolloff. Phantom 48V powered.)

U 87   (Large diaphragm FET mic made from 1967 through 1986. Three polar patterns – cardioid, omni and figure 8. Phantom 48V powered plus optional internal battery.)

KM 86   (Small diaphragm FET mic made from 1968 through 1986. Three polar patterns – cardioid, omni and figure 8 plus high pass filter and pad switch. Phantom 48V powered.)

U 47   (Large diaphragm FET mic made from 1969 through 1986. Cardioid polar pattern only. Includes high pass filter and pad switch. Phantom 48v powered.)

KM 88   (Small diaphragm FET mic made from 1968 through 1986. Three polar patterns - cardioid, omni and figure 8 plus high pass filter and pad switch. Phantom 48V powered.)

SM 69   (Large diaphragm stereo mic made from 1969 through present. Features remote control of polar patterns. Requires external pattern switch/power supply unit.)

KMS 85   (Small diaphragm vocalist mic made from 1971 to ?? [probably mid 1970s]. Cardioid pattern only. Phantom 48V powered.)

KU 80   (Artificial head mic made from 1973 to ?? [probably late 1970s]. Two omni microphones installed in simulated ears. Phantom 48V powered.)

A Few Words About Vintage Guitars
by Clay Harrell

What is a Vintage Guitar?

"Vintage" is a term that has acquired a new meaning apart from its original usage. The term is a combination of Vint (of the vine) and Age (time of creation). This term is used in the wine industry to indicate a wine's harvest date. The use of "vintage" has been modified by collectors to mean old, such as a "vintage car" or "vintage clothing". This extension of the meaning is used in guitar terminology to mean "an original, older guitar."

The most collectible guitars are those made from the mid 1920's to 1969. Guitars made prior to the mid 1920's are generally too primitive in design to have collectible value (of course there are some exceptions, but 99% of the time this holds true). Guitars after 1969, even though they may be over 25 years old, generally have no collectibility. All the major guitar manufacturers were in dire straits during the 1970's. They were either bought out by larger conglomerates looking to make guitars as quickly as possible, and/or their quality and choice of materials had become substandard.

Many people ask if their new guitar will be valuable in the future. Frankly, no one knows. But my off-the-cuff response would be, "no". The materials, environment and society of pre-1970 was much different, thus producing different instruments which I feel can not be duplicated today. However all the major guitar manufacturers are certainly trying to recapture the past with their "vintage reissue" guitars. But just remember, when you are buying a new guitar and the dealer says, "you know some day this will be a very collectible guitar", don't believe it. He doesn't have a crystal ball.

What makes a guitar collectible/valuable?

As with baseball cards, Barbie dolls, and other collectibles, condition is very important. Instruments in "mint" condition are always worth more than instruments in excellent condition. Also, we need to explain the term "mint", as it is constantly misrepresented. "Mint" means in the same condition as if you purchased the item new today. There is no such thing as "mint for its age". Either an item is mint (brand new condition) or it's not.

Guitars must also meet several other criteria to be collectible. One of the most important aspects is originality. Any modifications, replaced parts or repairs, no matter how practical, will decrease the value of an instrument. Even replacing the original case or re-fretting the guitar (the equivalent to replacing a car's tires) will decrease its value. Originality is even more important to a guitar's collectibility than condition. For example, a "beat-up" original finish guitar will always be worth more than a perfectly refinished one. Even if the new finish is done professionally and looks perfect, it will be worth approximately half the price of an original finish guitar or maybe even less.

Another thing that effects value is demand. The Fender electric mandolin, although very rare, is not worth very much. The reason is demand, or "who wants it?". If the instrument has limited popularity, for whatever reason, it will appeal to a limited crowd. Hence, it will not be worth as much as a popular instrument that has greater demand.

To some extent, rarity has only limited connection to value. For example, the Fender Telecaster is collectible and valuable, even though Fender made tens of thousands of them from 1950 to 1965 (Fender's most collectible era). The reason again is demand. Although the Telecaster is not rare compared to their electric mandolin, it is a very popular guitar today (the key word here is **today**). Hence, it is worth considerably more than the electric mandolin since it appeals to more people.

To summarize, for an instrument to be valuable there must be:
- Originality (stock, unmodified, no repairs).
- Condition. The better the condition, the more valuable it is.
- Demand for the model and year.

Without the above three items you merely have a used guitar, not a vintage guitar.

Clay Harrell is a private guitar collector. He buys guitars made from 1920 to 1970 by Gibson, Fender, Martin, Gretsch, Epiphone, National, Dobro, and Rickenbacker. His Internet web site is **http://clay.by.net**. He can be reached by e-mail at **harrelc@aa.wl.com**

ALEMBIC, INC.
3005 WILJAN COURT
SANTA ROSA, CA 95407-5702
(707) 523-2611
Fax (707) 523-2935

ALTEC LANSING
C/O ELECTRO-VOICE
BURNSVILLE, MN 55337
(952) 884-4051
Fax (952) 884-0043

AMPEG
SEE ST. LOUIS MUSIC INC.

DOBRO
SEE GIBSON GUITAR CORP.

D'AQUISTO
20 E. INDUSTRY CT.
DEER PARK, NY 11729
(516)586-4426
Fax (516)586-4472

EPIPHONE COMPANY
645 MASSMAN DR.
NASHVILLE, TN 37210
(615) 871-4500
Fax (615) 872-7768

FENDER MUSICAL INST.
8860 E. CHAPARREL RD. STE 100
SCOTTSDALE, AZ 85250
(480)596-9690
Fax (480) 596-1384

GIBSON GUITAR CORP.
309 PLUS PARK BLVD.
NASHVILLE, TN 37217
(615) 871-4500
Fax (615) 884-7219

GOYA
SEE MARTIN GUITAR CO.

GRETSCH
P.O. BOX 2468
SAVANNAH, GA 31402
(912) 748-7070
Fax (912) 748-6005

GUILD MUSIC CORP.
SEE FENDER MUSICAL INST.

HIWATT AMPLIFICATION
8163 LANKERSHIM BLVD.
NORTH HOLLYWOOD, CA 91605
(818) 764-8383
Fax (818) 764-0080

IBANEZ
1726 WINCHESTER RD
BENSALEM, PA 19020
(215) 638-8670
Fax (215) 245-8583

KAY GUITAR COMPANY
C/O ASIAN-AMER. MFG.
17091 DAILMLER ST
IRVINE, CA 92614
(949) 752-0050
Fax (949) 752-0056

MARSHALL AMPS
316 SERVICE RD.
MELVILLE, NY 11747

MARTIN GUITAR CO.
P.O. BOX 329
NAZARETH, PA 18064
(610) 759-2837
Fax (610) 759-5757

McINTOSH LAB., INC.
2 CHAMBERS STREET
BINGHAMTON, NY 13903-2699
(307) 723-3512
Fax (607) 724-0549

MUSICMAN/ERNIE BALL
151 SUBURBAN ROAD
SAN LOUIS OBISPO, CA 93401
(800) 544-7726
Fax (805) 544-7275

NATIONAL RESO-PHONIC GUITARS
871 C VIA ESTEBAN
SAN LUIS OBISPO, CA. 93401
(805) 546-8442
Fax (805) 546-8430

OVATION INSTRUMENTS
C/O KAMAN MUSIC CORP.
20 OLD WINDSOR ROAD
BLOOMFIELD, CT 06002-0507
(860) 509-8888
Fax (860) 509-8890

RAMIREZ
C/O DAVID PERRY GUITAR IMPORTS
PO BOX 188
LEESBURG, VA 20175
(800) 593-1331
Fax (703) 771-8170

RECORDING KING
SEE GIBSON GUITAR CORP

B.C. RICH INT'L, INC.
4940 DELHI PIKE
CINCINNATI, OH 45238
(513) 451-5000
Fax (513) 347-2298

RICKENBACKER INT'L
3895 S. MAIN STREET
SANTA ANA, CA 92707-5710
(714) 545-5574
Fax (714) 754-0135

SENNHEISER ELECTRONICS CORP.
1 ENTERPRISE DRIVE
OLD LYME, CT 06371
(860) 434-9190
Fax (860) 434-1759

ST. LOUIS MUSIC, INC.
1400 FERGUSON AVE.
ST. LOUIS, MO 63133
(314) 727-4512
Fax (314) 727-8929

VOX AMPLIFIERS
316 S. SERVICE RD.
MELVILLE, NY 11747
(516) 333-9100

WASHBURN INT'L
444 E. COURTLAND ST
MUNDELEIN, IL 60060
(847) 949-0444
Fax (847) 949-8444

YAMAHA CORP OF AMER.
6600 ORANGETHORPE AVE.
BUENA PARK, CA 90620
(714) 522-9011

2004 ORDER FORM
ORION BLUE BOOKS

2004 AUDIO   TOTAL

64,277 products from over 1,400 manufacturers. Hardbound, listing the following: Cassettes, 4&8-track Cartridges, CD players, Digital Audio Tape Players, Equalizers, Integrated and Power Amplifiers, Preamplifiers, Speakers, Receivers, Reel-to-Reels, Signal Processors, Systems, Turntables, and more. ....**$179 per book** _____

2004 CAMERA

24,122 products from over 400 manufacturers. Hardbound, listing the following: 35mm Cameras, Medium Format, Press View, Instamatic, Disk, TLR & Self Processing Cameras, Lenses, Back, Bellows, Viewfinders, Enlargers, Exposure Meters, Slide Projectors & Viewers, Movie Cameras, Projectors, and more. ....**$144 per book** _____

2004 CAR STEREO

43,749 products from over 200 manufacturers. Hardbound, listing the following: Cassette Receivers, CD Players, Digital Audio Tape Players, Equalizers, Power Amplifiers, Speakers, and more. ....**$144 per book** _____

2004 COMPUTER (Quarterly)

60,675 hardware products from over 1000 manufacturers. Hardbound, listing the following: Systems, Fax Machines, Monitors, Printers, Plotters, Scanners, Modems, Disk Drives, Tape Backups, Terminals, and more. .... **$129 per book** _____
.... **$516 annual subscription** _____

2004 COPIER

3,603 Copiers, Typewriters and Duplicators are listed in this softbound volume. ....**$39 per book** _____

2004 GUITARS & MUSICAL INSTRUMENTS

72,324 products from over 450 manufacturers. Hardbound, listing the following: Guitars, Guitar Amps, Tuners, Drums, Cymbals, Banjos, Brass Winds, Wood Winds, Cellos, Harps, Dulcimers, Keyboards, Keyboard Amps, Mandolins, Marimbas, Synthesizers, Violins, Xylophones, and more.**$179 per book** _____

22nd Issue GUN & SCOPES   TOTAL

17,756 products from over 300 manufacturers. Softbound, listing the following: Handguns, Rifles, Shotguns, and Black Powder Firearms. ....**$45 per book** _____

2004 POWER TOOL (APRIL)

18,540 products from over 120 manufacturers. Hardbound, listing the following: Compressors, Pumps, Generators, Saws, including Circular, Reciprocal, Sabre, etc., Power Screwdrivers, Demolition Tools, Planers, Chisels, Scalers, Boring Drills, Nailers, and more. ....**$94 per book** _____

2004 PROFESSIONAL SOUND

46,977 products from over 350 manufacturers. Hardbound, listing the following: Monitors, MIDIs, Microphones, Equalizers, Enclosures, Mixers, Reel-to-Reels, Signal Processors, Wireless Systems, Crossover networks, Integrated and Power Amplifiers, Raw Speaker Components, PA Systems, and more. .... **$144 per book** _____

2004 VIDEO & TELEVISION

34,721 products from over 200 manufacturers. Hardbound, listing the following: TVs, VCRs, Camcorders, Laser Videodisc Players, B&W Cameras, Color Video Cameras, Broadcast Cameras, Electronic Still Video Cameras, Lenses, Umatic Recorder/Players, and more. .... **$144 per book** _____

2004 VINTAGE GUITARS & COLLECTIBLES (Quarterly)

11,178 Vintage Guitars listed in this quarterly hardbound volume. Also available on an annual subscription of 4 issues. ....**$54 per book** _____
.... **$216 annual subscription** _____

ALL BOOKS AVAILABLE ON CD
WINDOWS 95/98/2000/NT 4.0/XP
☐ **BOOK**   ☐ **CD**

Name: _____ Method of Payment: ☐ Enclosed check ☐ C.O.D. ☐ Credit Card

Shipping Address (no P.O. Boxes): Street _____

City _____ State _____ Zip _____ Phone _____

If paying by Credit Card: ☐ American Express   ☐ Discover   ☐ Mastercard   ☐ Visa

Name on Card: _____ Card Number: _____

Expiration Date: _____ Signature: _____

SATISFACTION GUARANTEED

You will receive a full refund (less shipping) if the Orion Blue Book is returned within 20 days.

Orion Research Corporation

14555 N. Scottsdale Rd. #330
Scottsdale, AZ 85254-3487
voice: (480) 951-1114 fax: (480) 951-1117
email: sales@orionbluebook.com

ORDER HOTLINE
1-800-844-0759

FAX HOTLINE
1-800-375-1315

Subtotal _____
Less Survey Discount _____
Sales Tax (7.2% Arizona only) _____
Shipping & Handling (**$9.00 per book**) _____
COD (USA ONLY) $7.50 per order _____
Total _____

DATING YOUR GUITAR

Date your guitar! That's right, find out when your guitar was made.

ALEMBIC

The first 2 numbers of the serial number correspond to the year it was built. There may also be present a letter code designating a certain model. The latter digits indicate the individual instrument and its place in production.

AMERICAN ARCHTOPS

The digits after the dash in the serial number are the year that the guitar was made in.

TOM ANDERSON

The neck plate of each guitar has the date it was completed along with the letters A,N or P which stands for a.m., noon or p.m.

ARPEGGIO KORINA

The first 2 numbers (they will have a space between them) are the year of manufacture, then a 0, then the production number for that year.

BENEDETTO

Benedetto archtops have a 4 or 5 digit serial number ..the last 2 digits in the # are the year in which the instrument was made .. the digits in front of the last 2 are the instruments place in production...

G. S. BRANDT

The year is on the label inside of the guitar - you can also use a mirror to read the inside of the top of the guitar which is signed and dated...

BREEDLOVE

On the label, inside of the guitar - the first two numbers of the serial number is the year the instrument was made.

BUSCARINO

The last two digits of the serial number is the year in which the guitar was made in.

M. CAMPELLONE

The first three digits of the serial number are the sequence of production - the next two are the month - the last two are the year in which the guitar was made.

CARVIN

From 1964 thru 1968 Carvin Guitars DO NOT HAVE serial numbers...then in 1970 they started off with number 5000...

Year Serial #
1970 5000
1980-1983 11,000 - 13,000
1983-1984 13,001 - 15,000
1985-1986 17,000 - 20,000
1988-1989 22,000 - 25,000
1989-1991 26,000 - 33,000
1992-???? 35,000- ????

CITRON

The first two digits of the serial number is the month in which the guitar was made...the second two digits are the year in which the guitar was made.

COLLINGS

The date is on the label on the inside of the guitar.

COMINS

The date is on the label on the inside of the guitar.

CHARLES COTE' BASSES

Before 1995 Charles Cote' Basses Do Not Have Serial Numbers...starting in 1995 each bass has a 5 digit serial # ..the first 2 #'s are the year in which it was manufactured .. the last three #'s are the sequence in manufacturing of that year.

DANELECTRO

Most Danelectro serial #'s have 4 digits .. the first 2 are the week of completion. The last digit is the year.

D'ANGELICO

John D'Angelico built 1,164 guitars, all by hand .. the first few had no serial #'s.

Year - Serial #

1932- 1005-1097	1934	1936- 1105-1235	1937 - 1234-1317
1938 - 1318-1385	1939 - 1388-1456	1940 - 1457-1508	1941 - 1509-1562
1942 – 1563-1621	1943 – 1922-1658	1944 – 1659-1681	1945 – 1982-1702
1946 – 1703-1740	1947 – 1738-1781	1948 – 1782-1804	1949 – 1805-1831
1950 – 1832-1855	1951 – 1886-1908	1952 – 1886-1908	1953 – 1909-1936
1954 – 1933-1962	1955 – 1989-2017	1956 – 1989-2017	1957 – 2018-2040
1958 – 2041-2067	1959 – 2068-2098	1960 – 2099-2122	1961-64 – 2123-2164
1965-66 – 2212-2214			

D'AQUISTO

Year - Serial #

1965 - 1001-1005	1966 - 1006-1014	1967 - 1015-1022	1968 - 1023-1029
1969 - 1030-1036	1970 - 1037-1043	1971 - 1044-1050	1972 - 1051-1063
1973 - 1064-1073	1974 - 1074-1084	1975 - 1085-1094	1976 - 1095-1102
1977 - 1103-1112	1978 - 1113-1125	1979 - 1126-1133	1980 - 1134-1142
1981 - 1143-1151	1982 - 1152-1160	1983 - 1161-1164	1984 - 1166-1175
1985 - 1176-1183	1986 - 1185-1192	1987 - 1193-1202	1988 - 1201-1210
1989 - 1211-1217	1990 - 1218-1228		

DEAN

Dean guitars made in the USA have a 7 digit serial number .. the first 2 numbers are the year of manufacture ..the remaining numbers are the production numbers. ..this does not apply to Dean imported guitars (no year in the serial number..consult an expert or call Dean for the year of manufacture).

DOBRO / REGAL

Year - Serial #
1928 - 900-1700
1929 - 1800-2000
1930-1931 - 3000
1932-1933 - 5000-5500
1934-1936 - 5700-7600
1937 - 8000-9000

B prefix on most 1931-1932 Cyclops models. Regal (OMI - 1970 on) .. 1970-1979 "D" or "B" followed by 3 or 4 digits (ranking) & last number (year) .. "B" = Metal .. "D"= Wood

1980-1987 the number before the letter is the year. 1988 on the last 2 numbers are the year.

EISELE

Get a mirror and look at the underside of the top of the guitar for the date.

ENGLISH

The date is on the label on the inside of the guitar.

EPIPHONE

Epiphone started in 1928 making banjos and was family owned for years .. then it was sold to C.G.Conn company .. then back to the original family .. then were made by Gibson Guitar ...and were American made until approx. 1970 ..then production was moved to Japan and later Korea.

Year - Serial #

1930-1932 - 10,000 series	1932 - 5000	1933 - 6000	1934 - 7000
1935 - 8000-9000	1936 - 10,000	1937 - 11,000	1938 - 12,000
1939-1940 - 13,000	1941-1942 - 14,000	1943 - 18,000	1944 - 19,000; 51,000-52,000
1945 - 52,000-54,000	1946 - 54,000-55,000	1947 - 56,000	1948 - 57,000
1949 - 58,000	1950 - 59,000	1951 and some 1930's - 60,000-63,000	1952 - 64,000
1953 - 64,000-66,000	1954 - 68,000	1955-1957 - 69,000	

EPIPHONE MADE BY GIBSON 1958-1961

Year - Serial #
1958 - A-1000
1959 - A-2000
1960-1961 - A3000/A4000

FENDER

Year - Serial #

1950-1954 - Up to 6,000	1954-1956 - Up to 10,000- 4 or 5 digits (inc 0 or – prefix)	1955-1956 - 10,000 -" " " "	1957 - 10,000-20,000-5 or 6 digits (inc 0 or – prefix)
1958 - 20,000-30,000 -" "	1959 - 30,000-40,000	1960 - 40,000-50,000	1961 - 50.000-70,000
1962 - 60,000-90,000	1963 - 80,000-90,000	1963 - Up to L10,000 L + 5 digits...(beginning of the infamous "L" Series)	1963 - L10,000-L20,000
1964 - L20,000-L50,000	1965 - L50,000-L90,000	1965 - 100,000	1966-1967 - 100,000-200,000
1968 - 200,000	1969-1970 - 200,000-300,000	1971-1972 - 300,000	1973 - 300,000-500,000
1974-1975 - 400,000-500,000	1976 - 500,000-700,000	1976 - 76 or S6 + 5 digits	1977 - S7 or S8 + 5 digits
1978 - S7, S8 or S9 + 5 digits	1979 - S9 or E0 + 5 digits	1980-1981 - S9, E0 or E1 + 5 digits	1982 - E1,E2 or E3 + 5 digits
1983 - E2 or E3 + 5 digits	1984 - E3 or E4 + 5 digits	1987 - E4 + 5 digits	1988 - E4 or E8 + 5 digits
1989 - E4 or E8 + 5 digits	1990 - E8 or N9 + 5 digits	1990 - N0 + 5 digits	1991 - N1 + 5/6 digits
1992 - N2 + 5/6 digits			

FROGGY BOTTOM

The month and year that the guitar was made will be on the label on the inside of the guitar.

G & L

"G" is for Guitar..."B" is for Bass..."BC" is for Broadcaster.

Year - Serial #

1980 - G000530 -B000518	1981 - G003122 -B001917
1982 - G009886 -B008525	1983 - G011654 -B010382
1984 - G013272 -B014266	1985 - G014690 -B016018
1986 - G017325 -B017691	1987 - G020241 -B018063
1988 - G023725 -B019627	1989 - G024983 -B020106
1990 - G026344 -B021788	1991 - G027163 -B023013
1992 - G029962 -B024288	

GIBSON

Year - Serial #

1903 - 1500	1904 - 2500	1905 - 3500	1906 - 5500
1907 - 8300	1908 - 9700	1909 - 10,100	1910 - 10,600
1911 - 10,850	1912 - 13,350	1913 - 16,100	1914 - 20,150
1915 - 25,150	1916 - 32,000	1917 - 39,500	1918 - 47,900
1919 - 53,800	1920 - 63,650	1921 - 69,300	1922 - 71,400
1923 - 74,900	1924 - 81,200	1925 - 82,700	1926 - 83,600
1927 - 85,400	1928 - 87,300	1929 - 89,750	1930 - 90,200
1931 - 90,450	1932 - 90,700	1933 - 91,400	1934 - 92,300
1935 - 92,800	1936 - 94,100	1937 - 95,200	1938 - 95,750
1939 - 96,050	1940 - 96,600	1941 - 97,400	1942 - 97,700
1943 - 97,850	1944 - 98,250	1945 - 98,650	1946 - 99,300
1947 - 99,999			

(A-Series from 1947-1961)

Year - Serial #

1947 - A1304	1948 - A2665
1949 - A4413	1950 - A6597
1951 - A9419	1952 - A12,462
1953 - A16,101	1954 - A18,667
1955 - A21,909	1956 - A24,755
1957 - A26,819	1958 - A28,880
1959 - A32,284	1960 - A35,645
1961 - A36,147	

EPIPHONE A-SERIES ..1958-1961 (see section of the Dating Service)

Year - Serial #
1958 - A1000
1959 - A2000
1960-1961 - A3000-A4222

GIBSON-SERIAL #'s 1961-1969...(various models)

Year - Serial #

1961 - 100-42,440	1962 - 42,441-61,180
1963 - 61,450-64,222	1964 - 64,240-70,501
1962 - 71,180-96,600	1963 - 96,601-99,999
1967 - 000001-099999	1963-1967 -100,000-106,099
1963 - 106,100-106,899	1963-1967 -109,000-1,099,999
1963 - 110,000-111,549	1963-1967 - 111,550-115,799
1963 - 115,800-118,299	1963-1967 - 118,300-120,999
1963 - 121,000-139,999	

Gibsons 1960-1975 serial numbers overlap depending on the various models ..it is best to contact an expert or Gibson with the model, color and serial # for accurate dating .. a
simi-coherent serial# system returns in 1975 but still has a lot of overlapping depending
on the year and the model.

GIBSON SERIAL NUMBERS 1975-1977... (1975 still has many overlaps)

Year - Serial # Prefix
1975 - 99
1976 - 00
1977 - 06

GIBSON SERIAL NUMBERS 1977 TO NOW
8 digit number : ydddynnn

yy (1st. & 5th. digit)= year of manufacture
dd. (digits 2-4)= day of year
nnn (digits 6-8)=daily # rank

Some Heritage and Vintage reissue have the vintage style serial number.

GOODALL

Look on the label inside of the sound hole for the date the guitar was made.

GRETSCH

Years 1965-1972 = the first 1 or 2 numbers = the month (1-12)...the next number = the last number of the year...the rest of the numbers are the instruments number.

Years 1973-1981 = 1 or 2 numbers before the hyphen = the month (1-12)...the first number after the hyphen = the last number of the year ... the rest of the numbers are the instruments number.

Syncromatic Serial Numbers ... 1940-1949 = 007 - 900

Year - Serial #

1949-1950 - 3000	1951 - 4000-5000
1952 - 5000-8000	1953 - 9000-12,000
1954 - 12,000-16,000	1955 - 17,000-21,000
1957 - 22,000-26,000	1958 - 27,000-30,000
1959 - 30,000-34,000	1960 - 34,000-39,000
1961 - 39,000-45,000	1962 - 46,000-52,000
1963 - 53,000-63,000	1964 - 63,000-77,000
1964-early 1965 - 77,000-84,000	

GUILD

Year - Serial #

1952 - 350	1953 - 840
1954 - 1526	1955 - 2468
1956 - 3830	1957 - 5712
1958 - 8348	1959 - 12035
1960 - 14713	1961 - 18419
1962 - 22722	1963 - 28943
1964 - 38636	

From 1965 thru 1969 Guild Guitars had different serial numbers for different models of instruments...then in 1970 they changed back to the original system or serial numbers.

Year - Serial #

1970 - 50978	1971 - 61463
1972 - 75602	1973 - 95496
1974 - 112803	1975 - 130304
1976 - 149625	1977 - 169867
1978 - 195067	

1979 - 211877... up until 9-30-79...then they changed back to a different series of serial numbers per model again.

HOLLENBECK

Read the label on the inside of the guitar for the date.

IBANEZ

In dating Ibanez guitars made before 1987 .. the first letter is the month (A is Jan., B is Feb, C is March..etc) the next two numbers are the year .. the next four numbers are the production number that month (they only produced 9999 pieces each month)..(example) ...C760287 = March 1976 the 287th. piece made.

In dating Ibanez guitars made after 1987 .. the letter is now the factory designation .. the first number is the year built ... the next five numbers are the production number of the piece for the year ..(example) .. F700015 = the 15th. guitar made in 1987.

LACEY

The date that the guitar was made will be on the truss rod cover.

LANGEJANS

The date that the guitar was made is on the label inside of the sound hole.

BILL LAWRENCE

The first two numbers of the serial number are the year that the guitar was made in - then a letter for the month (A=Jan., B=Feb., C=March, etc) then comes the guitars place in production.

C. F. MARTIN

Year - Serial #

1898 - 8343	1899 - 8716	1900 - 9125	1901 - 9310
1902 - 9528	1903 - 9810	1904 - 9988	1905 - 10,120
1906 - 10,329	1907 - 10,727	1908 - 10,883	1909 - 11,018
1910 - 11,203	1911 - 11,413	1912 - 11,565	1913 - 11,821
1914 - 12,047	1915 - 12,209	1916 - 12,390	1917 - 12,988
1918 - 13,450	1919 - 14,512	1920 - 15,848	1921 - 16,758
1922 - 17,839	1923 - 19,891	1924 - 22,008	1925 - 24,116
1926 - 28,689	1927 - 34,435	1928 - 37,568	1929 - 40,843
1930 - 45,317	1931 - 49,589	1932 - 52,590	1933 - 55,084
1934 - 58,679	1935 - 61,947	1936 - 65,176	1937 - 68,865
1938 - 71,667	1939 - 74,061	1940 - 76,734	1941 - 80,013
1942 - 83,107	1943 - 86,724	1944 - 90,149	1945 - 93,623
1946 - 98,158	1947 - 103,468	1948 - 108,269	1949 - 112,961
1950 - 117,961	1951 - 122,799	1952 - 128,436	1953 - 134,501
1954 - 141,345	1955 - 147,328	1956 - 152,775	1957 - 159,061
1958 - 165,576	1959 - 171,047	1960 - 175,689	1961 - 181,297
1962 - 187,384	1963 - 193,327	1964 - 199,626	1965 - 207,030
1966 - 217,215	1967 - 230,095	1968 - 241,925	1969 - 256,003
1970 - 271,633	1971 - 294,270	1972 - 313,302	1973 - 333,873
1974 - 353,387	1975 - 371,828	1976 - 388,800	1977 - 399,625
1978 - 407,800	1979 - 419,900	1980 - 430,300	1981 - 436,474
1982 - 439,627	1983 - 446,101	1984 - 453,300	1985 - 460,575
1986 - 468,175	1987 - 476,216	1988 - 483,952	1989 - 493,279
1990 - 503,309	1991 - 512,487	1992 - 522,655	1993 - 535,223
1994 - 551,696	1995 - 570,434		

McCOLLUM

Look at the inside of the top for the date of the guitar with a mirror.

McKERRIHAN ARCHTOPS

Look on the inside of the guitar ...it will be signed and dated ...on solid bodys look under the neck pickup.

MEGAS

The date is on the label inside of the guitar.

MORTORO

The last two numbers in the serial number are the year of the guitar- unless the guitar is a 7 or 8 string in which case there will be an extra number on the end of the serial number (the second and third numbers from the end of the serial number would be the year of the guitar if its a 7 or 8 string).

PSR/PAUL REED SMITH

The first digit of the serial number is the last digit of the year in which the guitar was made.

RAREBIRD

Beginning in 1976, some of the early models have an eagle on the headstock with a 6 digit serial number that stands for the "Day-Month-Year" of the instrument (DDMMYY).

In 1988 they switched to a 4 digit serial number .. the first 2 numbers are the sequence in production the last 2 numbers are the year of manufacture.

RIBBECKE

Look on the label for the date + the first two digits of the serial number are usually the year.

RICKENBACKER

Serial numbers 1960 - 1986 = the year is the first letter, the month is the second letter...

Serial numbers 1986-1995 = the year is the number after the letter..the letter is the month ...

Year - Letter

1961 -A	1962 -B
1963 -C	1964 -D
1965 -E	1966 -F
1967 -G	1968 -H
1969 –I	1970 -J
1971 -K	1972 -L
1973 -M	1974 -N
1975 -O	1976 -P
1977 -Q	1978 –R
1979 -S	1980 -T
1981 -U	1982 -V
1983 -W	1984 -X
1985 -Y	1986 –Z

Month - Code

Jan- A	Feb- B
Mar.- C	April- D
May- E	June- F
July- G	Aug- H
Sept- I	Oct- J
Nov- K	Dec- L

Year - Number
1987- 0
1988 -1
1989 -2
1990 -3
1991 -4
1992 -5
1993 -6
1994 -7

SADOWSKI

Inside of the control panel is the date in which the guitar was made.

SHANTI

Use a mirror to read just behind the last tone bar on the inside of the top of the instrument which is signed and dated.

STROMBERG

The Strombergs (Charles and Elmer) made approximately 640 instruments up until 1955 when they both died. They used their business cards as labels in the guitars, the telephone number on the card helps to determine the approximate year the instrument was made.

Year - Phone # on the Card
1920-1927...Bowdoin 1728R or 1728M
1927-1929...Bowdoin 6559W or 1242W
1929-1932...Bowdoin 1878R
1932-1945...CA 3174
1949-1955...CA 7-3174

TAYLOR

Starting in 1974 ...the first two digits in the serial number is the year that the instrument was manufactured.

RICK TURNER

The first two digits in the serial number is the year in which the guitar was made.

WASHBURN

George Washburn started making guitars in 1864 .. the company has changed hands many times since then ..Washburn guitars had a fire sometime in the 1920's that destroyed everything, including all records and paperwork that they had prior to the day of the fire ... then the same thing happened again in the 1950's !!

From 1988 on ... on some models (but not all) - the first two digits of the serial number is the year the guitar was made.

On all limited editions ..the year will be in the "Model Name" of the guitar ... (example) ..."D-95 LTD" = 1995 ..."D-92LTD" = 1992 ...etc...

XOTIC

The first digit of the serial number is the year in which the guitar was made.

Our sincere thanks to John at Ducks Deluxe who provided all the information for dating your guitars. For further information, please e-mail ducks@ducksdeluxe.com or go to their web-site, www.ducksdeluxe.com.

TYPE	YR	MFG	PRICES--BASED ON 100% ORIGINAL MODEL	SELL EXC	SELL AVG	BUY EXC	BUY AVG
			ABBOTT MUSICAL INSTRUMENTS				
MANDOLIN	33	ABBOTT	**MODEL 1** FLATBACK	384	**284**	244	204
MANDOL	34	ABBOTT	**MODEL F** ARCHED	384	**284**	244	204
UKULELE	27	ABBOTT	**SILVER DOLLAR**	240	**177**	152	127
UKE	28	ABBOTT	**SILVER DOLLAR**	349	**258**	222	185
UKE	29	ABBOTT	**SILVER DOLLAR**	316	**234**	201	168
			ACOUSTIC				
ELEC. GUITAR	72	ACOUSTIC	**BLACK WIDOW** BLACK, SOLID BODY	813	**601**	516	431
ELGUIT	73	ACOUSTIC	**BLACK WIDOW** BLACK, ROSEWOOD, 24-FRET, 2 HB	892	**660**	567	474
ELGUIT	74	ACOUSTIC	**BLACK WIDOW** BLACK, 20-FRET, 1 HB	432	**319**	274	229
ELGUIT	75	ACOUSTIC	**BLACK WIDOW** BLACK, SOLID BODY	441	**326**	280	234
GUITAR AMP	71	ACOUSTIC	**134 LEAD** 4x10" SPEAKERS	312	**230**	198	165
GTAMP	71	ACOUSTIC	**135 LEAD** 12" SPEAKER	230	**170**	146	122
GTAMP	71	ACOUSTIC	**360**	192	**142**	122	102
GTAMP	74	ACOUSTIC	**370 BASS** 200 WATT, 406 CABINET, EQ	478	**353**	303	253
			AKG ACOUSTICS				
ELEC. GUITAR	67	AKG	**ES-335** BURGUNDY MIST	4,080	**3,017**	2,592	2,167
MIC	57-64	AKG	**C-12** TUBE, MULTI-PATTERN	8,414	**6,223**	5,346	4,470
MIC	64-73	AKG	**C-12A** TUBE, MULTI-PATTERN	1,912	**1,414**	1,215	1,015
MIC	64	AKG	**C-12VR** TUBE, MONO CONDENSER	2,071	**1,532**	1,316	1,100
MIC	59-78	AKG	**C-24** MULTI-PATTERN CONDENSER	10,357	**7,660**	6,581	5,502
MIC	55	AKG	**C-28** SMALL DIAPHRAGM CONDENSER	1,624	**1,201**	1,032	862
MIC	65-67	AKG	**C-60** TUBE, CONDENSER	744	**550**	473	395
MIC	65	AKG	**C-61** TUBE	956	**707**	607	507
MIC	88	AKG	**C-401B** FIGURE 8, MICRO CONDENSER	299	**221**	190	159
MIC	70	AKG	**C-412** SOLID STATE	1,274	**942**	810	677
MIC	82	AKG	**C-414E1** MULTI-PATTERN, REMOTE	805	**595**	511	427
MIC	68	AKG	**C-414EB** CONDENSER	867	**641**	551	461
MIC	77-82	AKG	**C-414EB** MULTI-PATTERN CONDENSER	1,460	**1,079**	927	775
MIC	74	AKG	**C-414ULS**	774	**572**	492	411
MIC	64	AKG	**C-451** MODULAR CAPACITOR, FET	498	**368**	316	264
MIC	68	AKG	**C-451E** NICKEL CARDIOID COMBO	502	**371**	319	266
MIC	77	AKG	**C-452EB** BLACK, COMBO CONDENSER	495	**366**	314	263
MIC	78	AKG	**CK-1S** CARDIOID NICKEL CAPSULE	158	**117**	100	84
MIC	84	AKG	**CK-2X** OMNI BLACK CAPSULE	264	**195**	167	140
MIC	78	AKG	**CK-22** OMNI BLACK CAPSULE	264	**195**	167	140
MIC	98	AKG	**CK-31 DISCREET CARDIOID CAPSULE**	147	**109**	93	78
MIC	98	AKG	**CK-32 DISCREET OMNI**	146	**108**	93	78
MIC	98	AKG	**CK-33 HYPERCARDIOID CAPSULE**	146	**108**	93	78
MIC	64	AKG	**D-12E** CARDIOID DYNAMIC	341	**252**	217	181
			ALAMO				
ELEC. GUITAR	61	ALAMO	**FIESTA**	216	**159**	137	114
ELGUIT	63	ALAMO	**TITAN MARK I SPANISH**	288	**213**	183	153
GUITAR AMP	62	ALAMO	**CAPRI MODEL 2560**	192	**142**	122	102
GTAMP	65	ALAMO	**MONTCLAIR REVERB** 1x12" SPEAKER	240	**177**	152	127
GTAMP	64	ALAMO	**PARAGON PIGGYBACK BASS** 1x15" SPEAKER	384	**284**	244	204
			ALEMBIC, INC				
ELEC. GUITAR	79	ALEMBIC	**PICCOLO BASS**	996	**736**	633	529

TYPE	YR	MFG	PRICES--BASED ON 100% ORIGINAL MODEL	SELL EXC	SELL AVG	BUY EXC	BUY AVG
ELGUIT	71	ALEMBIC	**SERIES 1 BASS**	1,811	**1,339**	1,151	962
ELGUIT	74	ALEMBIC	**SERIES 1 BASS**	1,992	**1,473**	1,265	1,058
ELGUIT	74	ALEMBIC	**STANLEY CLARKE BASS**	1,309	**968**	832	695

ALTEC LANSING TECHNOLOGIES, INC.

TYPE	YR	MFG	MODEL	SELL EXC	SELL AVG	BUY EXC	BUY AVG
ENCL	62	ALTEC	**609**	158	**117**	100	84
ENCL	78	ALTEC	**612 CABINET ONLY**	264	**195**	167	140
MIC	47	ALTEC	**21B ANTIQUE CONDENSER** "COKE BOTTLE"	585	**433**	372	311
MIC	39-60	ALTEC	**639A or B "BIRD CAGE" DYNAMIC** RIBBON	1,754	**1,297**	1,115	932
MIC	56	ALTEC	**660A DYNAMIC**	336	**248**	213	178
PRE	55	ALTEC	**1588B**	348	**257**	221	185
PRE	62	ALTEC	**A-333A MONO** 2x6L6G TUBES	246	**182**	156	131
PRE	62	ALTEC	**A-433A**	154	**114**	98	82
PWR	73-78	ALTEC	**340A**	211	**156**	134	112
PWR	62	ALTEC	**A-127B** 2x6L6G TUBES	413	**306**	262	219
PWR	62	ALTEC	**A-287F** 2x845 or 284 TUBES, 75 WATT	678	**501**	431	360
PWR	62	ALTEC	**A-287W** 2x805 TUBES	768	**568**	488	408
PWR	62	ALTEC	**A-340A** 35 WATT	432	**319**	274	229
PWR	62	ALTEC	**A-350A** 2x6550 TUBES, 40 WATT	426	**315**	270	226
PWR	62	ALTEC	**A-1530A** 70 WATT	518	**383**	329	275
RAW	62	ALTEC	**288A/B/C** DRIVER, 24, 20, 16 OHMS	240	**178**	153	128
RAW	62	ALTEC	**290A/B/C** DRIVER	157	**116**	100	83
RAW	74-79	ALTEC	**406-8C PAIR**	441	**326**	280	234
RAW	62	ALTEC	**515** 15", 16 0HM	240	**177**	152	127
RAW	62	ALTEC	**515B** 15", 16 OHM	298	**220**	189	158
RAW	62	ALTEC	**600B** 12" CONE	159	**117**	101	84
RAW	73	ALTEC	**601A/B** 12" CONE	148	**110**	94	79
RAW	73-78	ALTEC	**601C/D** 12" CONE	168	**124**	106	89
RAW	73-78	ALTEC	**602A/B/C/D** 14" CONE	147	**109**	93	78
RAW	73-78	ALTEC	**603A/B** 15" CONE	183	**135**	116	97
RAW	62	ALTEC	**603B** 15" CONE	139	**102**	88	73
RAW	48-53	ALTEC	**604** 15" CONE, COAXIAL HORN TWEETER, CROSSOVER	286	**211**	181	151
RAW	53	ALTEC	**604B** 15", CROSSOVER	331	**244**	210	175
RAW	65	ALTEC	**604B** CROSSOVER	369	**273**	234	196
RAW	65-70	ALTEC	**604C/D** 15" CONE, CROSSOVER	344	**254**	218	183
RAW	53-58	ALTEC	**604E** 15" CONE, CROSSOVER	258	**190**	164	137
RAW	55-60	ALTEC	**605A** 15" CONE, CROSSOVER	297	**220**	189	158
RAW	62	ALTEC	**605A** 15" CONE, CROSSOVER	348	**257**	221	185
RAW	60-65	ALTEC	**605B** 15" CONE, CROSSOVER	264	**195**	168	140
RAW	62	ALTEC	**606A**	158	**117**	100	84
RAW	62	ALTEC	**606A** 15" CONE	184	**136**	117	97
RAW	62	ALTEC	**606B** 12" CONE	139	**102**	88	73
RAW	73	ALTEC	**682A**	90	**66**	57	47
RAW	74	ALTEC	**683A**	90	**66**	57	47
RAW	62	ALTEC	**702A** DRIVER	231	**171**	147	122
RAW	62	ALTEC	**720A** DRIVER	303	**224**	192	161
RAW	62	ALTEC	**728B** 12" CONE	608	**450**	386	323
RAW	60	ALTEC	**755C 12" PAIR**	356	**263**	226	189
RAW	74-79	ALTEC	**802A/B/C/D** DRIVER	225	**166**	143	119

	TYPE	YR	MFG	PRICES--BASED ON 100% ORIGINAL MODEL	SELL EXC	SELL AVG	BUY EXC	BUY AVG
	RAW	74	ALTEC	**802B** DRIVER	182	**134**	115	96
	RAW	60	ALTEC	**803B 15" PAIR**	345	**255**	219	183
	RAW	73	ALTEC	**805** 15" CONE	180	**133**	114	95
	RAW	76-81	ALTEC	**806A** DRIVER	303	**224**	192	161
	RAW	73-78	ALTEC	**811B** HIGH FREQUENCY HORN	327	**242**	208	173
	RAW	60	ALTEC	**3000B HORN TWEETER**	321	**237**	204	170
	RAW	62	ALTEC	**A-31 HORN** HAS 720A DRIVER	598	**442**	380	317
	RAW	62	ALTEC	**H-803** 2x4" CELLS	162	**119**	103	86
	RAW	62	ALTEC	**H-805** 2x4" CELLS	230	**170**	146	122
	RAW	62	ALTEC	**H-1003** 2x5" CELLS	231	**171**	147	122
	RAW	62	ALTEC	**H-1803** 3x6" CELLS	309	**228**	196	164
SPKR		62	ALTEC	**607** 15" or 12", MAHOGANY or WALNUT	185	**137**	117	98
	SPKR	62	ALTEC	**608A** 15", ALDER or WALNUT	274	**203**	174	145
	SPKR	62	ALTEC	**609B** 12" 412A	182	**134**	115	96
	SPKR	62	ALTEC	**609CC** 8" 408A	177	**131**	112	94
	SPKR	62	ALTEC	**815** 288C 1505, 2x515	601	**445**	382	319
	SPKR	74-79	ALTEC	**819AI STONEHENGE PAIR**	927	**685**	589	492
	SPKR	47	ALTEC	**820A** 802B, H802, 2x803A, H-800D	760	**562**	483	403
	SPKR	74	ALTEC	**820C** 802B, H-811. 2x803A, N-800D	752	**556**	478	399
	SPKR	62	ALTEC	**824A** 12", 412A, 3000A	186	**137**	118	98
	SPKR	62	ALTEC	**826A** ICONIC 801A, H-811A, 803A	370	**274**	235	196
	SPKR	62-65	ALTEC	**830A LAGUNA PAIR**	1,513	**1,119**	961	804
	SPKR	64-69	ALTEC	**831A CAPISTRANO PAIR**	855	**632**	543	454
	SPKR	64-69	ALTEC	**836A LIDO PAIR**	251	**186**	159	133
	SPKR	64-69	ALTEC	**837A AVALON PAIR**	526	**389**	334	279
	SPKR	74-79	ALTEC	**843A MALIBU PAIR**	808	**597**	513	429
	SPKR	73-78	ALTEC	**873A BARCELONA PAIR**	1,764	**1,304**	1,121	937
	SPKR	79-81	ALTEC	**893C PAIR**	204	**151**	129	108
	SPKR	76	ALTEC	**A-7 UTILITY VOICE OF THE THEATER**	336	**249**	214	179
	SPKR	77-82	ALTEC	**SANTANA II PAIR**	661	**489**	420	351

ALVAREZ/ALVAREZ YAIRI

	TYPE	YR	MFG	MODEL	SELL EXC	SELL AVG	BUY EXC	BUY AVG
GUITAR (ACOUSTIC)		75	ALVAREZ	**ARTIST** SUNBURST, FLATTOP ACOUSTIC	384	**284**	244	204
	GUITAR	76	ALVAREZ	**CX-120** ROSEWOOD, BUTTERFLY TUNERS	336	**248**	213	178
	GUITAR	70	ALVAREZ	**CY-140 CLASSICAL** CEDAR TOP, JACARANDA BACK/SIDES	478	**353**	303	253
	GUITAR	85	ALVAREZ	**DY-51 DREADNOUGHT** NATURAL	438	**324**	278	233
	GUITAR	80	ALVAREZ	**DY-58** FLAT TOP, 9-STRINGS, DOUBLES ON THE THREE HIGH STRINGS	480	**355**	305	255
	GUITAR	82	ALVAREZ	**DY-60**	465	**344**	295	247
	GUITAR	77	ALVAREZ	**DY-77** NATURAL	637	**471**	405	338
	GUITAR	80	ALVAREZ	**DY-80 CANYON CREEK** 12-STRING, FLAMED CORAL ROSEWOOD BODY	478	**353**	303	253
	GUITAR	70	ALVAREZ	**DY-90 DREADNOUGHT** ROSEWOOD BACK/SIDES	717	**530**	455	380
	GUITAR	77	ALVAREZ	**MODEL 5056** ROSEWOOD, "TREE OF LIFE" INLAY	696	**515**	442	370
	GUITAR	89	ALVAREZ	**MODEL 5063**	384	**284**	244	204
	GUITAR	89	ALVAREZ	**MODEL 5414** 12-STRING	362	**268**	230	192
STEEL GUITAR		60	ALVAREZ	**MODEL 5010** KOA	384	**284**	244	204

AMPEG by ST LOUIS MUSIC, INC

	TYPE	YR	MFG	MODEL	SELL EXC	SELL AVG	BUY EXC	BUY AVG
ELEC. GUITAR		60	AMPEG	**AEB-1 BASS** SOLID BODY	615	**455**	391	326
	ELGUIT	65	AMPEG	**AEB-1 BASS** SOLID BODY	606	**448**	385	322
	ELGUIT	66	AMPEG	**AEB-1 BASS** SUNBURST	478	**353**	303	253
	ELGUIT	67	AMPEG	**AEB-1 BASS**	499	**369**	317	265

TYPE	YR	MFG	PRICES--BASED ON 100% ORIGINAL MODEL	SELL EXC	SELL AVG	BUY EXC	BUY AVG
ELGUIT	62	AMPEG	**ASB BASS** SOLID BODY, HORNS	466	**345**	296	247
ELGUIT	68	AMPEG	**ASB BASS** SOLID BODY, HORNS	457	**338**	290	243
ELGUIT	67	AMPEG	**ASB-1 DEVIL BASS** FIREBURST, LONG HORN	1,990	**1,471**	1,264	1,057
ELGUIT	67	AMPEG	**AUB-1 BASS** FRETLESS	880	**651**	559	467
ELGUIT	68	AMPEG	**AUB-1 BASS** FRETLESS	861	**636**	547	457
ELGUIT	69	AMPEG	**AUB-1 BASS** FRETLESS	832	**615**	528	442
ELGUIT	63	AMPEG	**AUSB** FRETLESS, HORNS	723	**535**	459	384
ELGUIT	63	AMPEG	**BABY BASS** RED BODY/NECK	2,065	**1,527**	1,312	1,097
ELGUIT	64	AMPEG	**BABY BASS** CREAM, WHITE NECK	1,912	**1,414**	1,215	1,015
ELGUIT	65	AMPEG	**BABY BASS** RED BODY/NECK	1,832	**1,355**	1,164	973
ELGUIT	66	AMPEG	**BABY BASS** SUNBURST	1,554	**1,149**	987	825
ELGUIT	68	AMPEG	**BABY BASS** SUNBURST	1,513	**1,119**	961	804
ELGUIT	68	AMPEG	**BABY BASS** RED BODY/NECK	1,811	**1,339**	1,151	962
ELGUIT	60	AMPEG	**BABY BASS 4** FIBERGLASS	1,185	**876**	753	629
ELGUIT	62	AMPEG	**BABY BASS 4** FIBERGLASS	1,333	**986**	847	708
ELGUIT	68	AMPEG	**BABY BASS 4** WHITE, FIBERGLASS	1,395	**1,032**	886	741
ELGUIT	69	AMPEG	**BABY BASS 4** BLACK, FIBERGLASS	780	**577**	495	414
ELGUIT	70	AMPEG	**BABY BASS 4** SUNBURST, FIBERGLASS	876	**648**	556	465
ELGUIT	65	AMPEG	**BABY BASS 5** SUNBURST, 5-STRING	709	**524**	450	376
ELGUIT	69	AMPEG	**DAN ARMSTRONG LUCITE**	1,378	**1,019**	875	732
ELGUIT	70	AMPEG	**DAN ARMSTRONG LUCITE** RT PU	1,344	**994**	854	714
ELGUIT	71	AMPEG	**DAN ARMSTRONG LUCITE**	1,330	**984**	845	706
ELGUIT	69	AMPEG	**LONG HORN BASS** RED & BLACK SUNBURST	478	**353**	303	253
ELGUIT	60	AMPEG	**SCROLL BASS** RED SUNBURST, LEFT-HANDED	621	**459**	394	329
ELGUIT	66	AMPEG	**SCROLL BASS**	648	**479**	412	344
ELGUIT	63	AMPEG	**SONIC SIX by BURNS** CHERRY, SOLID BODY, TREMOLO, 2 PU's	289	**214**	184	154
ELGUIT	67	AMPEG	**SSB BASS** SMALL SOLID BODY	301	**222**	191	160
ELGUIT	66	AMPEG	**SSUB-1 BASS** FRETLESS	275	**203**	175	146
ELGUIT	72	AMPEG	**SUPER STUD** SOLID BODY	212	**156**	134	112
ELGUIT	63	AMPEG	**THINLINE by BURNS** DOUBLE CUTAWAY, 2 PU's	422	**312**	268	224
ELGUIT	64	AMPEG	**THINLINE by BURNS** SEMI-HOLLOW BODY, TWO F-HOLES,DOUBLE CUTAWAY,TREMOLO	403	**298**	256	214
ELGUIT	63	AMPEG	**WILD DOG by BURNES** SUNBURST, TREMOLO, 3 PU's	438	**324**	278	233
ELGUIT	63	AMPEG	**WILD DOG DELUXE by BURNS** SUNBURST, SOLID BODY, BOUND NECK, TREMOLO	518	**383**	329	275
ELGUIT	64	AMPEG	**WILD DOG DELUXE by BURNS** SUNBURST, SOLID BODY, BOUND NECK, TREMOLO	478	**353**	303	253
GUITAR AMP	57	AMPEG	**5-18D** BLUE SPECKLE, P12N SPEAKER	245	**181**	156	130
GTAMP	66	AMPEG	**B-15N BASS** BLACK TOLEX FLIPTOP	355	**262**	225	188
GTAMP	70	AMPEG	**B-15N BASS**	350	**259**	222	186
GTAMP	73	AMPEG	**B-15N BASS** BLACK TOLEX FLIPTOP	337	**249**	214	179
GTAMP	75	AMPEG	**B-15N BASS** BLACK TOLEX FLIPTOP	285	**210**	181	151
GTAMP	69	AMPEG	**B-18 BASS** FLIPTOP	373	**276**	237	198
GTAMP	69	AMPEG	**B-25 TUBE** RED-BLACK PAISLEY	248	**183**	157	132
GTAMP	70	AMPEG	**B-25 TUBE** 2-CHANNEL, 50 WATT	246	**182**	156	131
GTAMP	63	AMPEG	**ECHO TWIN** 2x12" SPEAKERS	162	**119**	103	86
GTAMP	64	AMPEG	**ECHO TWIN SUPER ET-2**	260	**192**	165	138

TYPE	YR	MFG	MODEL	SELL EXC	SELL AVG	BUY EXC	BUY AVG
			PRICES--BASED ON 100% ORIGINAL				
GTAMP	70	AMPEG	**G-110** 10" SPEAKER, REVERB, TREMOLO	89	**66**	56	47
GTAMP	64	AMPEG	**GEMINI I** BLUE, 12" SPEAKER	187	**138**	118	99
GTAMP	65	AMPEG	**GEMINI I** 12" SPEAKER	176	**130**	112	93
GTAMP	69	AMPEG	**GEMINI I** 12" SPEAKER	195	**144**	124	104
GTAMP	63	AMPEG	**GEMINI II** TUBE, TREMOLO, VIBRATO	451	**333**	286	239
GTAMP	66	AMPEG	**GEMINI II** 15" COMBO	423	**313**	269	224
GTAMP	58	AMPEG	**JET 12** GREY SPARKLE	148	**110**	94	79
GTAMP	60	AMPEG	**JET 12** COPPER, 1x12"	144	**106**	91	76
GTAMP	63	AMPEG	**JET 12**	131	**97**	83	69
GTAMP	64	AMPEG	**JET 12** GREY TOLEX	129	**95**	82	68
GTAMP	65	AMPEG	**JET 12** BLUE DIAMOND	122	**90**	78	65
GTAMP	66	AMPEG	**JET 12** GREY	118	**87**	75	62
GTAMP	68	AMPEG	**JET 12** BLUE, 1x12"	111	**82**	70	59
GTAMP	52	AMPEG	**M-12** 1x12" JENSEN, 2-CHANNEL & VIB	192	**142**	122	102
GTAMP	60	AMPEG	**M-12** 1x12" JENSEN, P12-R SPEAKER	161	**119**	102	85
GTAMP	63	AMPEG	**M-15** 15" SPEAKER, 2-CHANNEL, VIBRATO	146	**108**	93	78
GTAMP	58	AMPEG	**PORTAFLEX BASS** 35 WATT COMBO	259	**191**	164	137
GTAMP	60	AMPEG	**PORTAFLEX B-12** 12" JBL	312	**230**	198	165
GTAMP	65	AMPEG	**PORTAFLEX B-12**	286	**211**	181	151
GTAMP	67	AMPEG	**PORTAFLEX B-12XT**	371	**274**	236	197
GTAMP	64	AMPEG	**PORTAFLEX B-15** 15" SPEAKER	377	**279**	239	200
GTAMP	65	AMPEG	**PORTAFLEX B-15 BASS**	317	**235**	201	168
GTAMP	69	AMPEG	**PORTAFLEX SB-12**	168	**124**	106	89
GTAMP	61	AMPEG	**REVERBEROCKET**	402	**297**	255	213
GTAMP	62	AMPEG	**REVERBEROCKET**	300	**222**	190	159
GTAMP	64	AMPEG	**REVERBEROCKET** BLUE DIAMOND	293	**217**	186	156
GTAMP	66	AMPEG	**REVERBEROCKET**	283	**209**	179	150
GTAMP	68	AMPEG	**REVERBEROCKET**	264	**195**	168	140
GTAMP	67	AMPEG	**REVERBEROCKET II**	271	**200**	172	144
GTAMP	69	AMPEG	**REVERBEROCKET II**	293	**217**	186	156
GTAMP	70	AMPEG	**REVERBEROCKET II**	289	**214**	184	154
GTAMP	72	AMPEG	**REVERBEROCKET II**	198	**146**	126	105
GTAMP	60	AMPEG	**STEREO 435-S** 2x12" SPEAKERS	196	**145**	125	104
GTAMP	58	AMPEG	**STEREO TWIN** 2x12" SPEAKERS, VIBRATO	198	**146**	126	105
GTAMP	69	AMPEG	**SVT** HEAD CABINET	498	**368**	316	264
GTAMP	69	AMPEG	**SVT BASS**	495	**366**	314	263
GTAMP	72	AMPEG	**SVT BASS** 8x10" CABINET	474	**350**	301	251
GTAMP	79	AMPEG	**SVT BASS**	492	**364**	312	261
GTAMP	74	AMPEG	**V-2** 4x12" CABINET	269	**199**	171	143
GTAMP	72	AMPEG	**V-4** STACK (2)4x12" CABINETS	590	**436**	375	313
GTAMP	74	AMPEG	**V-4** STACK (2)4x12" CABINETS	588	**435**	373	312
GTAMP	76	AMPEG	**VT-22**	384	**284**	244	204
GTAMP	74	AMPEG	**VT-40** 4x10" SPEAKERS, COMBO	213	**157**	135	113
GTAMP	76	AMPEG	**VT-40** 4x10" SPEAKERS, COMBO	211	**156**	134	112
SIGNAL PROCESSOR	81	AMPEG	**A-1 DISTORTION**	114	**84**	72	60
SGNPRO	81	AMPEG	**A-2 COMPRESSOR**	110	**81**	70	58
SGNPRO	81	AMPEG	**A-3 OVERDRIVE**	112	**83**	71	59
SGNPRO	81	AMPEG	**A-4 PHASER**	113	**83**	71	60
UPRIG	60	AMPEG	**UPRIGHT BABY BASS** SUNBURST	1,226	**907**	779	651
UPRIGHT	63	AMPEG	**UPRIGHT BABY BASS** WHITE	1,394	**1,031**	886	741
UPRIGHT	65	AMPEG	**UPRIGHT BABY BASS** SUNBURST	827	**612**	525	439

TYPE	YR	MFG	PRICES--BASED ON 100% ORIGINAL MODEL	SELL EXC	SELL AVG	BUY EXC	BUY AVG
UPRIGHT	70	AMPEG	**UPRIGHT BABY BASS** BROWN SUNBURST	1,043	**771**	663	554
UPRIGHT	59	AMPEG	**UPRIGHT BASS** FIBERGLASS	780	**577**	495	414

ARGONE

MIC		48	ARGONE	**AR-57 CAPSULE** CHROME	144	**106**	91	76

ARP INSTRUMENTS

SYNTHESIZER	79	ARP	**1623** SEQUENCER	243	**180**	154	129
SYNTH	80	ARP	**2353** SOLUS ANALOG	402	**297**	255	213
SYNTH	70	ARP	**2500** MODULAR	1,200	**888**	763	638
SYNTH	71	ARP	**2600**	1,973	**1,459**	1,254	1,048
SYNTH	71	ARP	**2601** KEYBOARD ANALOG	1,513	**1,119**	961	804
SYNTH	72	ARP	**2823** ODYSSEY ANALOG	478	**353**	303	253
SYNTH	76	ARP	**AVATAR**	261	**193**	165	138
SYNTH	70	ARP	**AXXE I** ANALOG	518	**383**	329	275
SYNTH	75	ARP	**AXXE I**	432	**320**	275	230
SYNTH	78	ARP	**QUADRA**	683	**505**	434	363

AUDIO RESEARCH CORPORATION

PRE		69	AUDIORES	**SP-2 TUBE**	216	**159**	137	114
XOVER		72	AUDIORES	**EC-2 TUBE**	504	**372**	320	267

B & O

MIC		55	B & O	**FENTONE BIDIRECTIONAL RIBBON**	757	**560**	481	402

BACON & DAY

BANJO		20	BACON	**A-1** TENOR	478	**353**	303	253
	BANJO	25	BACON	**A-1 SUPER** TENOR	472	**349**	300	250
	BANJO	30	BACON	**BELMONT** 5-STRING, RESONATOR	708	**523**	450	376
	BANJO	58	BACON	**BELMONT** 5-STRING	594	**439**	377	315
	BANJO	64	BACON	**BELMONT** 5-STRING, RESONATOR	796	**589**	506	423
	BANJO	22	BACON	**BLUE BELL** TENOR, RESONATOR	888	**656**	564	471
	BANJO	21	BACON	**BLUE BELL BANJO-MANDOLIN** OPEN BACK	441	**326**	280	234
	BANJO	20	BACON	**BLUE RIBBON** TENOR, OPEN BACK	612	**452**	389	325
	BANJO	20	BACON	**BLUE RIBBON** STYLE A, SUPER 5-STRING	799	**591**	508	424
	BANJO	24	BACON	**CELLO BANJO**	4,454	**3,294**	2,830	2,366
	BANJO	38	BACON	**CELLO BANJO**	1,431	**1,058**	909	760
	BANJO	40	BACON	**CELLO BANJO** 4-STRING, F-HOLE FLANGE	1,352	**1,000**	859	718
	BANJO	15	BACON	**FF PROFESSIONAL #1**	2,011	**1,487**	1,277	1,068
	BANJO	25	BACON	**MONTANA SILVER BELL #1 SPECIAL**	1,652	**1,221**	1,049	877
	BANJO	26	BACON	**MONTANA SILVER BELL #1 SPECIAL**	1,651	**1,221**	1,049	877
	BANJO	28	BACON	**MONTANA SILVER BELL #1 SPECIAL** PLECTRUM	1,646	**1,217**	1,046	874
	BANJO	28	BACON	**MONTANA SILVER BELL #1 SPECIAL**	1,650	**1,220**	1,048	876
	BANJO	29	BACON	**MONTANA SILVER BELL #1 SPECIAL** TENOR	1,643	**1,215**	1,044	873
	BANJO	30	BACON	**MONTANA SILVER BELL #1 SPECIAL**	1,642	**1,214**	1,043	872
	BANJO	30	BACON	**MONTANA SILVER BELL #3** TENOR	2,229	**1,648**	1,416	1,184
	BANJO	40	BACON	**NE PLUS ULTRA SILVER BELL** TENOR	3,496	**2,585**	2,221	1,857
	BANJO	46	BACON	**NE PLUS ULTRA SILVER BELL** TENOR	4,032	**2,982**	2,562	2,142
	BANJO	60	BACON	**NE PLUS ULTRA SILVER BELL** PLECTRUM	1,992	**1,473**	1,265	1,058
	BANJO	72	BACON	**ODE STYLE 25R** MAHOGANY RIM/RESONATOR	480	**355**	305	255
	BANJO	20	BACON	**PEERLESS MANDOLIN-BANJO**	578	**428**	367	307
	BANJO	25	BACON	**PEERLESS MANDOLIN-BANJO** PLECTRUM	438	**324**	278	233
	BANJO	26	BACON	**PEERLESS MANDOLIN-BANJO** PLECTRUM	422	**312**	268	224
	BANJO	27	BACON	**PEERLESS MANDOLIN-BANJO** PLECTRUM	504	**372**	320	267

TYPE	YR	MFG	PRICES--BASED ON 100% ORIGINAL MODEL	SELL EXC	SELL AVG	BUY EXC	BUY AVG
BANJO	30	BACON	**PEERLESS MANDOLIN-BANJO**	449	**332**	285	238
BANJO	36	BACON	**RHYTHM KING** TENOR, 19-FRET	470	**347**	298	249
BANJO	28	BACON	**SENORITA** TENOR, RESONATOR	829	**613**	527	440
BANJO	30	BACON	**SENORITA** TENOR, SUNBURST	746	**552**	474	396
BANJO	35	BACON	**SENORITA** TENOR, SUNBURST	735	**543**	467	390
BANJO	40	BACON	**SENORITA** TENOR, 19-FRET	876	**648**	556	465
BANJO	41	BACON	**SENORITA** TENOR, 19-FRET	868	**642**	552	461
BANJO	48	BACON	**SENORITA** 5-STRING RESONATOR	829	**613**	527	440
BANJO	50	BACON	**SENORITA** PLECTRUM	668	**494**	424	354
BANJO	22	BACON	**SILVER BELL 1** TENOR	1,465	**1,084**	931	778
BANJO	23	BACON	**SILVER BELL 1** TENOR	1,421	**1,051**	903	755
BANJO	24	BACON	**SILVER BELL 1** PLECTRUM	1,353	**1,001**	860	719
BANJO	24	BACON	**SILVER BELL 1** TENOR	1,477	**1,092**	938	784
BANJO	25	BACON	**SILVER BELL 1** TENOR	1,394	**1,031**	886	741
BANJO	26	BACON	**SILVER BELL 1** TENOR	1,382	**1,022**	878	734
BANJO	27	BACON	**SILVER BELL 1** TENOR	1,363	**1,008**	866	724
BANJO	27	BACON	**SILVER BELL 1** PLECTRUM, F-HOLE	1,460	**1,079**	927	775
BANJO	28	BACON	**SILVER BELL 1** TENOR	1,344	**994**	854	714
BANJO	29	BACON	**SILVER BELL 1** TENOR	1,273	**942**	809	676
BANJO	30	BACON	**SILVER BELL 1** TENOR, F-HOLE FLANGE	1,340	**991**	851	711
BANJO	34	BACON	**SILVER BELL 1** TENOR, F-HOLE FLANGE	1,024	**757**	650	544
BANJO	37	BACON	**SILVER BELL 1** TENOR	1,052	**778**	668	558
BANJO	24	BACON	**SILVER BELL 2** TENOR	2,022	**1,495**	1,285	1,074
BANJO	28	BACON	**SILVER BELL 2** TENOR	2,008	**1,485**	1,276	1,066
BANJO	36	BACON	**SILVER BELL 2** TENOR	1,648	**1,219**	1,047	875
BANJO	25	BACON	**SILVER BELL 3** TENOR	4,031	**2,981**	2,561	2,141
BANJO	26	BACON	**SILVER BELL 3** TENOR	3,936	**2,911**	2,501	2,091
BANJO	28	BACON	**SILVER BELL 3** TENOR	3,840	**2,840**	2,440	2,040
BANJO	30	BACON	**SILVER BELL SERENADER** TENOR	891	**659**	566	473
BANJO	32	BACON	**SILVER BELL SERENADER** TENOR, F-HOLE	897	**663**	570	476
BANJO	55	BACON	**SILVER BELL SERENADER** PLECTRUM	829	**613**	527	440
BANJO	30	BACON	**SPECIAL I** TENOR, WALNUT NECK, RESONATOR	709	**524**	450	376
BANJO	33	BACON	**SPECIAL I** TENOR, RESONATOR	681	**504**	433	362
BANJO	38	BACON	**SPECIAL I** TENOR, CLOVER LEAF FLANGES	713	**527**	453	378
BANJO	67	BACON	**SPECIAL I** TENOR, WALNUT NECK	478	**353**	303	253
BANJO	30	BACON	**SPECIAL II** TENOR	447	**330**	284	237
BANJO	33	BACON	**STYLE 0** TENOR, TULIP FLANGE, 17-FRET	484	**358**	308	257
BANJO	30	BACON	**STYLE 1** PLECTRUM, ROSEWOOD	2,073	**1,533**	1,317	1,101
BANJO	29	BACON	**STYLE 2** TENOR	1,354	**1,001**	860	719
BANJO	20	BACON	**STYLE C MANDOLIN-BANJO**	387	**286**	246	206
BANJO	22	BACON	**STYLE C MANDOLIN-BANJO**	362	**268**	230	192
BANJO	24	BACON	**STYLE C MANDOLIN-BANJO**	342	**253**	217	182
BANJO	25	BACON	**STYLE C MANDOLIN-BANJO**	336	**248**	213	178
BANJO	28	BACON	**SULTANA 1 SILVER BELL** TENOR	2,033	**1,503**	1,291	1,080

TYPE	YR	MFG	PRICES--BASED ON 100% ORIGINAL MODEL	SELL EXC	SELL AVG	BUY EXC	BUY AVG
BANJO	30	BACON	**SULTANA 1 SILVER BELL** TENOR	2,017	**1,492**	1,282	1,072
BANJO	35	BACON	**SULTANA 1 SILVER BELL** TENOR	2,018	**1,493**	1,282	1,072
BANJO	40	BACON	**SULTANA 1 SILVER BELL** TENOR	2,014	**1,489**	1,279	1,069
BANJO	30	BACON	**SULTANA 3 SILVER BELL** PLECTRUM	3,435	**2,541**	2,183	1,825
BANJO	38	BACON	**SULTANA 7 SILVER BELL** TENOR	5,280	**3,905**	3,355	2,805
BANJO	25	BACON	**SUPER A** TENOR	694	**513**	441	368
BANJO	20	BACON	**SUPER A-1** TENOR, SNAP-IN RESONATOR	446	**330**	283	237
BANJO	39	BACON	**SUPERTONE** 5-STRING	598	**442**	380	317
BANJO	40	BACON	**SYMPHONIE** TENOR, PERALOID FINGERBOARD	1,593	**1,178**	1,012	846
BANJO	24	BACON	**TENOR LUTE** 4-STRING	1,063	**786**	675	565
GUITAR (ACOUSTIC)	38	BACON	**RAMONA** ARCHTOP	533	**394**	339	283
GUITAR	40	BACON	**RAMONA** ARCHTOP	478	**353**	303	253
GUITAR	40	BACON	**SENORITA** SUNBURST, MAHOGANY BACK/SIDES	876	**648**	556	465
STEEL GUITAR	50	BACON	**BELMONT** 5-STRING	288	**213**	183	153

BALDWIN

TYPE	YR	MFG	MODEL	SELL EXC	SELL AVG	BUY EXC	BUY AVG
BANJO	70	BALDWIN	**2SR ELECTRIC** 5-STRING	423	**313**	269	224
BANJO	73	BALDWIN	**ODE STYLE B** DOT FINGERBOARD INLAY	971	**718**	617	516
BANJO	74	BALDWIN	**ODE STYLE B** DOT FINGERBOARD INLAY	961	**711**	611	511
BANJO	70	BALDWIN	**ODE STYLE C**	970	**717**	616	515
BANJO	75	BALDWIN	**ODE STYLE C**	1,141	**844**	725	606
BANJO	79	BALDWIN	**ODE STYLE C** 5-STRING, NICKEL HARDWARE	1,274	**942**	810	677
BANJO	76	BALDWIN	**ODE STYLE D** 5-STRING, GOLD HARDWARE	974	**720**	619	517
BANJO	77	BALDWIN	**ODE STYLE D** 5-STRING, GOLD HARDWARE	977	**722**	620	519
BANJO	60	BALDWIN	**RB-175** 5-STRING, LONG NECK, OPEN BACK	644	**476**	409	342
BANJO	65	BALDWIN	**RB-175** 5-STRING, LONG NECK, OPEN BACK	552	**408**	351	293
ELEC. GUITAR	69	BALDWIN	**706** DOUBLE CUTAWAY,SEMI-HOLLOW BODY,2 F-HOLES, 2 PU's	480	**355**	305	255
ELGUIT	68	BALDWIN	**706V** DOUBLE CUTAWAY,SEMI-HOLLOW BODY,VIBRATO,2 F-HOLES, 2 PU's	1,060	**784**	674	563
ELGUIT	67	BALDWIN	**712R** 12-STRING,DOUBLE CUTAWAY,SEMI-HOLLOW BODY,2 PU's	480	**355**	305	255
ELGUIT	66	BALDWIN	**BABY BISON** BLACK	583	**431**	370	310
ELGUIT	66	BALDWIN	**BABY BISON** SUNBURST	693	**512**	440	368
ELGUIT	67	BALDWIN	**BABY BISON** CHERRY	722	**534**	459	384
ELGUIT	67	BALDWIN	**BABY BISON** TRANSPARENT RED	722	**534**	459	384
ELGUIT	68	BALDWIN	**BABY BISON** NATURAL	711	**526**	452	377
ELGUIT	68	BALDWIN	**BABY BISON** SUNBURST	723	**535**	459	384
ELGUIT	69	BALDWIN	**BABY BISON** CHERRY	722	**534**	459	384
ELGUIT	64	BALDWIN	**BISON** BLACK	593	**438**	376	315
ELGUIT	65	BALDWIN	**BISON** BLACK	757	**560**	481	402
ELGUIT	68	BALDWIN	**BISON** BLACK	1,063	**786**	675	565
ELGUIT	69	BALDWIN	**BISON** JAZZ WHITE	1,157	**856**	735	615
ELGUIT	65	BALDWIN	**DOUBLE SIX** SUNBURST, 12-STRING	935	**691**	594	496
ELGUIT	67	BALDWIN	**DOUBLE SIX** GREEN SUNBURST, 12-STRING	637	**471**	405	338
ELGUIT	67	BALDWIN	**DOUBLE SIX** BLACK, 12-STRING	776	**574**	493	412
ELGUIT	70	BALDWIN	**DOUBLE SIX** SUNBURST, 12-STRING	694	**513**	441	368

TYPE	YR	MFG	PRICES--BASED ON 100% ORIGINAL MODEL	SELL EXC	SELL AVG	BUY EXC	BUY AVG
ELGUIT	67	BALDWIN	**GB-66 DELUXE** SUNBURST, DOUBLE CUT, 2 PU's	467	**345**	297	248
ELGUIT	68	BALDWIN	**HANK MARVIN** WHITE	1,630	**1,205**	1,035	865
ELGUIT	65	BALDWIN	**JAZZ SPLIT SOUND** OFFSET DOUBLE CUTAWAY, SOLIDBODY, TREMOLO, 3 PU's	518	**383**	329	275
ELGUIT	66	BALDWIN	**MARVIN** OFFSET DOUBLE CUTAWAY, SOLIDBODY, TREMOLO, 3 PU's	537	**397**	341	285
ELGUIT	65	BALDWIN	**VIBRASLIM** DOUBLE CUTAWAY, SEMI-HOLLOW BODY, TREMOLO, 2 PU's	801	**592**	509	425
ELGUIT	66	BALDWIN	**VIBRASLIM** SUNBURST	478	**353**	303	253
ELGUIT	68	BALDWIN	**VIBRASLIM** THIN HOLLOW BODY, 2 PU's	644	**476**	409	342
ELGUIT	65	BALDWIN	**VIRGINIAN** NATURAL	573	**423**	364	304
ELGUIT	66	BALDWIN	**VIRGINIAN** NATURAL	560	**414**	356	297
ELGUIT	67	BALDWIN	**VIRGINIAN** NATURAL	502	**371**	319	266
ELGUIT	68	BALDWIN	**VIRGINIAN** NATURAL	479	**354**	304	254
ELGUIT	69	BALDWIN	**VIRGINIAN** NATURAL	485	**359**	308	258
ELGUIT	70	BALDWIN	**VIRGINIAN** NATURAL	461	**341**	293	245

BENEDETTO GUITARS by FENDER MUSICAL INSTRUMENTS

GUITAR (ACOUSTIC)	80	BENEDETTO	**FRATELLO** ARCHTOP, MAPLE BACK/SIDES, INLAYS, GOLD TUNERS	10,800	**7,987**	6,862	5,737
GUITAR	93	BENEDETTO	**LA VENEZIA** ARCHTOP, EUROPEAN WOODS, BLACK TUNERS	12,373	**9,151**	7,862	6,573

BEYER

MIC	89	BEYER	**M-500STG HYPERCARDIOID DYNAMIC**	586	**433**	372	311
MIC	89	BEYER	**M-500TG HYPERCARDIOID DYNAMIC**	586	**433**	372	311

BIGSBY

ELEC. GUITAR	48	BIGSBY	**SOLID BODY** SINGLE PU	8,385	**6,201**	5,328	4,454
ELGUIT	50	BIGSBY	**SOLID BODY** DOUBLE PU	18,168	**13,437**	11,544	9,652
ELGUIT	52	BIGSBY	**SOLID BODY** DOUBLE PU	18,118	**13,399**	11,512	9,625

BRUNO

GUITAR (ACOUSTIC)	24	BRUNO	**HARP GUITAR** 12-STRING+4-STRING BASS, MAHOGANY/SPRUCE TOP	1,203	**890**	764	639
MANDOLIN	24	BRUNO	**BANJO-MANDOLIN** 10", OPEN BACK	288	**213**	183	153
MANDOL	22	BRUNO	**BOWL BACK** BRAZILIAN ROSEWOOD	480	**355**	305	255
UKULELE	20	BRUNO	**SOPRANO** CURLY KOA, SOUND HOLE INLAY	288	**213**	183	153

BUCHLA

SYNTHESIZER	80	BUCHLA	**100 MODULAR**	1,414	**1,045**	898	751
SYNTH	80	BUCHLA	**TOUCHE'**	1,394	**1,031**	886	741

BURNS/BALDWIN

ELEC. GUITAR	67	BURNS	**FLYTE**	457	**338**	290	243
ELGUIT	74	BURNS	**FLYTE**	478	**353**	303	253
ELGUIT	62	BURNS	**JAZZ** SUNBURST, SPLIT-SOUND	574	**424**	364	304
ELGUIT	64	BURNS	**JAZZ** SUNBURST, SPLIT-SOUND	478	**353**	303	253
ELGUIT	65	BURNS	**JAZZ** SUNBURST, SPLIT-SOUND	495	**366**	314	263
ELGUIT	66	BURNS	**JAZZ** SUNBURST, SPLIT-SOUND	484	**358**	308	257
ELGUIT	67	BURNS	**JAZZ** SUNBURST, SPLIT-SOUND	449	**332**	285	238
ELGUIT	68	BURNS	**JAZZ** SUNBURST, SPLIT-SOUND	440	**325**	279	234
ELGUIT	69	BURNS	**JAZZ** SUNBURST, SPLIT-SOUND	486	**359**	309	258
ELGUIT	64	BURNS	**MARVIN**	598	**442**	380	317
ELGUIT	65	BURNS	**NU-SONIC** WHITE, TREMOLO	384	**284**	244	204
ELGUIT	66	BURNS	**NU-SONIC** WHITE	373	**276**	237	198
ELGUIT	68	BURNS	**NU-SONIC BASS** BLACK, 2 PU's	367	**271**	233	195
ELGUIT	68	BURNS	**SINGLE 6** SEMI-HOLLOW, VIBRATO, 2 PU's	348	**257**	221	185

	TYPE	YR	MFG	MODEL	SELL EXC	SELL AVG	BUY EXC	BUY AVG
				PRICES--BASED ON 100% ORIGINAL				
	ELGUIT	63	BURNS	**SPLITSONIC** RED SUNBURST, 3 PU's	478	**353**	303	253
	ELGUIT	64	BURNS	**SPLITSONIC** RED SUNBURST, 3 PU's	438	**324**	278	233
	ELGUIT	67	BURNS	**SPLITSONIC** RED SUNBURST, 3 PU's	504	**372**	320	267

CARVIN

	TYPE	YR	MFG	MODEL	SELL EXC	SELL AVG	BUY EXC	BUY AVG
ELEC. GUITAR		72	CARVIN	**DBS-98B** NATURAL, DOUBLE NECK, 3 PU's, SERIAL #5000-9999	384	**284**	244	204
GUITAR AMP		79	CARVIN	**VT- 112** TUBE, 1x12" SPEAKER	144	**106**	91	76
	GTAMP	78	CARVIN	**VT-1500** TUBE AMP HEAD, CABINET	120	**88**	76	63

CHAMBERLIN

	TYPE	YR	MFG	MODEL	SELL EXC	SELL AVG	BUY EXC	BUY AVG
SYNTHESIZER		61	CHAMBER	**CHAMBERLIN**	2,359	**1,745**	1,499	1,253

CHURCH/MGM

	TYPE	YR	MFG	MODEL	SELL EXC	SELL AVG	BUY EXC	BUY AVG
MIC		52	CHURCH	**CHURCH MIKE TUBE** NEUMANN CAPSULE	7,200	**5,325**	4,575	3,825

CLASSIC GUITAR, LTD.

	TYPE	YR	MFG	MODEL	SELL EXC	SELL AVG	BUY EXC	BUY AVG
ELEC. GUITAR		62	CLASSIC	**GONZALES BASS**	599	**443**	380	318
GUITAR (ACOUSTIC)		64	CLASSIC	**ESTRALITA** ARCHTOP	288	**213**	183	153
	GUITAR	55	CLASSIC	**GONZALES** FLATTOP	384	**284**	244	204
	GUITAR	66	CLASSIC	**LATINO** FLATTOP	996	**736**	633	529

COLE

	TYPE	YR	MFG	MODEL	SELL EXC	SELL AVG	BUY EXC	BUY AVG
BANJO		81	COLE	**1881 ECLIPSE** 5-STRING, OPEN BACK	1,326	**981**	843	704

COLEY

	TYPE	YR	MFG	MODEL	SELL EXC	SELL AVG	BUY EXC	BUY AVG
MANDOLIN		75	COLEY	**COLEMAN MANDOLIN**	1,593	**1,178**	1,012	846

CORAL by DANELECTRO

	TYPE	YR	MFG	MODEL	SELL EXC	SELL AVG	BUY EXC	BUY AVG
ELEC. GUITAR		67	CORAL	**COMBO** SUNBURST, ARCHTOP, ROUND HOLE	335	**247**	212	177
	ELGUIT	60	CORAL	**FIREFLY**	356	**263**	226	189
	ELGUIT	65	CORAL	**FIREFLY**	363	**269**	231	193
	ELGUIT	68	CORAL	**FIREFLY** TWIN PU's	320	**237**	203	170
	ELGUIT	67	CORAL	**FIREFLY BASS** HOLLOW BODY	478	**353**	303	253
	ELGUIT	67	CORAL	**FIREFLY-12** 12-STRING, HOLLOW BODY	467	**345**	297	248
	ELGUIT	60	CORAL	**HORNET** RED, 2 PU's	384	**284**	244	204
	ELGUIT	67	CORAL	**SCORPION-12** SUNBURST	475	**351**	301	252
	ELGUIT	64	CORAL	**SITAR** 13-STRING	1,180	**873**	750	627
	ELGUIT	64	CORAL	**SITAR** 19-STRING, 3 PU's	1,307	**967**	830	694
	ELGUIT	65	CORAL	**SITAR** 19-STRING, 3 PU's	1,389	**1,027**	882	737
	ELGUIT	67	CORAL	**SITAR** 6-STRING, GOURD SHAPED, 1 PU	912	**674**	579	484
	ELGUIT	67	CORAL	**SITAR** 13-STRING	1,223	**904**	777	649
	ELGUIT	67	CORAL	**SITAR** 19-STRING, 3 PU's	1,345	**995**	855	715
	ELGUIT	68	CORAL	**SITAR** 13-STRING	1,258	**930**	799	668
	ELGUIT	68	CORAL	**SITAR** 19-STRING, 3 PU's	1,511	**1,117**	960	802
GUITAR (ACOUSTIC)		68	CORAL	**LONG-HORN** HOLLOW BODY	1,104	**817**	702	587

CRAFTSMEN

	TYPE	YR	MFG	MODEL	SELL EXC	SELL AVG	BUY EXC	BUY AVG
PWR		50	CRAFT	**C-500 TUBE** MONO, CLASS A TRIODE	247	**183**	157	131
	PWR	73	CRAFT	**C-500 WILLIAMSON AMP** 12 WATT	307	**227**	195	163

CRUMAR

	TYPE	YR	MFG	MODEL	SELL EXC	SELL AVG	BUY EXC	BUY AVG
SYNTHESIZER		80	CRUMAR	**BIT ONE**	385	**285**	245	205

DAN ARMSTRONG

	TYPE	YR	MFG	MODEL	SELL EXC	SELL AVG	BUY EXC	BUY AVG
EFFECTS		76	DAN ARMST	**GREEN RINGER**	275	**203**	175	146
	EFFECTS	77	DAN ARMST	**RED RINGER**	253	**187**	161	134
ELEC. GUITAR		75	DAN ARMST	**DAN ARMSTRONG LUCITE BASS**	1,512	**1,118**	960	803

DANELECTRO, SEE ALSO CORAL, SILVERTONE

TYPE	YR	MFG	MODEL (PRICES--BASED ON 100% ORIGINAL)	SELL EXC	SELL AVG	BUY EXC	BUY AVG
ELEC. GUITAR	56	DANELECTR	**BASS** 4-STRING, SINGLE CUTAWAY	653	**483**	415	347
ELGUIT	57	DANELECTR	**BASS** BRONZE, 6-STRING, SINGLE CUTAWAY	796	**589**	506	423
ELGUIT	58	DANELECTR	**BASS** BRONZE, 6-STRING	790	**584**	502	419
ELGUIT	59	DANELECTR	**BASS** 6-STRING	785	**580**	498	417
ELGUIT	60	DANELECTR	**BASS** BLACK, 6-STRING	780	**577**	495	414
ELGUIT	60	DANELECTR	**BASS** BRONZE, 6-STRING	782	**578**	497	415
ELGUIT	60	DANELECTR	**BELLZOUKI 12**	956	**707**	607	507
ELGUIT	61	DANELECTR	**BELLZOUKI 12** 1 PU	796	**589**	506	423
ELGUIT	63	DANELECTR	**BELLZOUKI 12**	876	**648**	556	465
ELGUIT	65	DANELECTR	**BELLZOUKI 12** SUNBURST, 1 PU	855	**632**	543	454
ELGUIT	66	DANELECTR	**BELLZOUKI 12** 2 PU's	752	**556**	478	399
ELGUIT	67	DANELECTR	**BELLZOUKI 12** HORN BODY SHAPE, 2 PU's	935	**691**	594	496
ELGUIT	68	DANELECTR	**COBRA XII** 12-STRING	432	**319**	274	229
ELGUIT	58	DANELECTR	**CONVERTIBLE** DOUBLE CUTAWAY	430	**318**	273	228
ELGUIT	59	DANELECTR	**CONVERTIBLE** DOUBLE CUTAWAY, THIN BODY	480	**355**	305	255
ELGUIT	60	DANELECTR	**CONVERTIBLE** DOUBLE CUTAWAY, HOLLOW BODY	580	**429**	369	308
ELGUIT	62	DANELECTR	**CONVERTIBLE** 1 PU	497	**367**	315	264
ELGUIT	67	DANELECTR	**CONVERTIBLE**	433	**320**	275	230
ELGUIT	68	DANELECTR	**CONVERTIBLE** DOUBLE CUTAWAY	426	**315**	270	226
ELGUIT	67	DANELECTR	**CORAL HORNET 2** 2 PU's	470	**347**	298	249
ELGUIT	68	DANELECTR	**CORAL HORNET 2** 2 PU's	557	**412**	354	296
ELGUIT	69	DANELECTR	**CORAL HORNET 2** 2 PU's	536	**396**	340	285
ELGUIT	67	DANELECTR	**DRAGON** WALNUT, SINGLE CUTAWAY, ARCHTOP	384	**284**	244	204
ELGUIT	60	DANELECTR	**GUITARALIN LONG-HORN**	1,205	**891**	766	640
ELGUIT	61	DANELECTR	**GUITARALIN LONG-HORN**	956	**707**	607	507
ELGUIT	63	DANELECTR	**GUITARALIN LONG-HORN**	1,115	**825**	708	592
ELGUIT	71	DANELECTR	**LANCER XII** 12-STRING	390	**288**	248	207
ELGUIT	59	DANELECTR	**LONG-HORN BASS** SUNBURST, 6-STRING	962	**712**	611	511
ELGUIT	60	DANELECTR	**LONG-HORN BASS** SUNBURST, 6-STRING	921	**681**	585	489
ELGUIT	62	DANELECTR	**LONG-HORN BASS** BRONZE SUNBURST, 4-STRING	864	**639**	549	459
ELGUIT	63	DANELECTR	**LONG-HORN BASS** 6-STRING	848	**627**	539	450
ELGUIT	64	DANELECTR	**LONG-HORN BASS** SUNBURST, 4-STRING	762	**563**	484	404
ELGUIT	65	DANELECTR	**LONG-HORN BASS** SUNBURST, 6-STRING	885	**654**	562	470
ELGUIT	56	DANELECTR	**MODEL C** SINGLE CUTAWAY	340	**252**	216	181
ELGUIT	57	DANELECTR	**PRO 1** BROWN	478	**353**	303	253
ELGUIT	60	DANELECTR	**PRO 1**	439	**325**	279	233
ELGUIT	63	DANELECTR	**PRO 1** BROWN	391	**289**	248	208
ELGUIT	64	DANELECTR	**PRO 1**	480	**355**	305	255
ELGUIT	58	DANELECTR	**SHORT-HORN** BLACK, 1 PU	491	**363**	312	261
ELGUIT	60	DANELECTR	**SHORT-HORN** BRONZE, 1 PU	481	**356**	306	256
ELGUIT	60	DANELECTR	**SHORT-HORN** DOUBLE NECK	1,155	**854**	734	614
ELGUIT	61	DANELECTR	**SHORT-HORN** JIMMY PAGE BLACK	791	**585**	502	420
ELGUIT	61	DANELECTR	**SHORT-HORN** DOUBLE NECK	1,155	**854**	734	614
ELGUIT	62	DANELECTR	**SHORT-HORN** BLOND, CONVERTIBLE	491	**363**	312	261

TYPE	YR	MFG	PRICES--BASED ON 100% ORIGINAL MODEL	SELL EXC	SELL AVG	BUY EXC	BUY AVG
ELGUIT	62	DANELECTR	**SHORT-HORN** DOUBLE NECK	1,155	**854**	734	614
ELGUIT	63	DANELECTR	**SHORT-HORN** BLACK, 1 PU	426	**315**	270	226
ELGUIT	63	DANELECTR	**SHORT-HORN** JIMMY PAGE BLACK	893	**661**	567	474
ELGUIT	64	DANELECTR	**SHORT-HORN** BLOND, CONVERTIBLE	499	**369**	317	265
ELGUIT	65	DANELECTR	**SHORT-HORN** BLACK, 2 PU's	533	**394**	339	283
ELGUIT	66	DANELECTR	**SHORT-HORN** BLACK, VIBRATO, 1 PU	446	**330**	283	237
ELGUIT	60	DANELECTR	**SHORT-HORN BASS** COPPER, 6-STRING	561	**415**	356	298
ELGUIT	62	DANELECTR	**SHORT-HORN BASS** BRONZE, 4-STRING	571	**422**	362	303
ELGUIT	63	DANELECTR	**SHORT-HORN BASS** DOUBLE NECK	1,164	**861**	739	618
ELGUIT	64	DANELECTR	**SHORT-HORN BASS** 15-FRET	426	**315**	270	226
ELGUIT	65	DANELECTR	**SHORT-HORN BASS** BRONZE, 6-STRING	533	**394**	339	283
ELGUIT	66	DANELECTR	**SHORT-HORN BASS** BRONZE, 6-STRING	518	**383**	329	275
ELGUIT	63	DANELECTR	**SHORT-HORN DELUXE** DARK WALNUT, 3 PU's	551	**407**	350	292
ELGUIT	58	DANELECTR	**SILVERTONE** BLACK, WHITE SIDES, 2 PU's	323	**239**	205	171
ELGUIT	58	DANELECTR	**SILVERTONE** BLACK & WHITE, SINGLE CUTAWAY	384	**284**	244	204
ELGUIT	59	DANELECTR	**SILVERTONE** BROWN, WHITE SIDES, 1 PU	413	**306**	262	219
ELGUIT	60	DANELECTR	**SILVERTONE** RED & BLACK SUNBURST	317	**235**	201	168
ELGUIT	60	DANELECTR	**SILVERTONE** RED & WHITE	371	**274**	236	197
ELGUIT	60	DANELECTR	**SILVERTONE** BLACK, 1 PU	384	**284**	244	204
ELGUIT	60	DANELECTR	**SILVERTONE** RED & BLACK SUNBURST, 2 PU's	432	**319**	274	229
ELGUIT	61	DANELECTR	**SILVERTONE** BROWN, SINGLE CUTAWAY, 1 PU	384	**284**	244	204
ELGUIT	62	DANELECTR	**SILVERTONE** 2 PU's	315	**233**	200	167
ELGUIT	62	DANELECTR	**SILVERTONE** 1 PU	384	**284**	244	204
ELGUIT	64	DANELECTR	**SILVERTONE** BLACK SPARKLE, 1 PU	384	**284**	244	204
ELGUIT	65	DANELECTR	**SILVERTONE** RED & BLACK SUNBURST, DOUBLE CUTAWAY	384	**284**	244	204
ELGUIT	67	DANELECTR	**SILVERTONE** BLACK & WHITE, BUILT IN AMP, SINGLE LIPSTICK PU	360	**266**	228	191
ELGUIT	60	DANELECTR	**SILVERTONE BASS** 6-STRING	478	**353**	303	253
ELGUIT	67	DANELECTR	**SLIMLINE SL 2V** VIBROLA, 2 PU's	322	**238**	204	171
ELGUIT	67	DANELECTR	**SLIMLINE SL 3N** GATOR FINISH, 3 PU's	323	**239**	205	171
ELGUIT	67	DANELECTR	**SLIMLINE SL12N** 12-STRING	346	**256**	220	184
ELGUIT	60	DANELECTR	**STANDARD** BLACK, DOUBLE CUTAWAY, 2 PU's	753	**557**	478	400
ELGUIT	63	DANELECTR	**STANDARD** DOUBLE CUTAWAY, 1 PU	446	**330**	283	237
ELGUIT	56	DANELECTR	**U-1** BRONZE, SINGLE CUTAWAY	480	**355**	305	255
ELGUIT	57	DANELECTR	**U-1** COPPER, 1 PU	447	**330**	284	237
ELGUIT	58	DANELECTR	**U-1** COPPER, 1 PU	457	**338**	290	243
ELGUIT	59	DANELECTR	**U-1** COPPER, 1 PU	469	**347**	298	249
ELGUIT	60	DANELECTR	**U-1** 1 PU	460	**340**	292	244
ELGUIT	61	DANELECTR	**U-1** 1 PU	369	**273**	234	196
ELGUIT	62	DANELECTR	**U-1** 1 PU	378	**279**	240	200
ELGUIT	57	DANELECTR	**U-2** BLACK, SINGLE CUTAWAY, 2 PU's	575	**425**	365	305
ELGUIT	59	DANELECTR	**U-2** 2 PU's	568	**420**	361	301
ELGUIT	65	DANELECTR	**U-2** 2 PU's	637	**471**	405	338

TYPE	YR	MFG	PRICES--BASED ON 100% ORIGINAL MODEL	SELL EXC	SELL AVG	BUY EXC	BUY AVG
ELGUIT	58	DANELECTR	**U-3** BLACK, 3 PU's	639	**472**	406	339
ELGUIT	58	DANELECTR	**UB-2** SINGLE CUTAWAY, 6-STRING, 2 PU's	717	**530**	455	380
GUITAR AMP	60	DANELECTR	**CADET**	144	**106**	91	76
GTAMP	55	DANELECTR	**CADET 120** 1x6" GEFCO SPEAKER	240	**177**	152	127
GTAMP	59	DANELECTR	**CENTURION 275**	288	**213**	183	153
GTAMP	60	DANELECTR	**CENTURION 275**	432	**319**	274	229
GTAMP	63	DANELECTR	**DM-10** BLUE, 1x8" JENSEN	117	**86**	74	62
GTAMP	66	DANELECTR	**DM-10** 1x8" SPEAKER, VIBRATO, TUBE	216	**159**	137	114
GTAMP	64	DANELECTR	**DM-25** 35 WATT	288	**213**	183	153
GTAMP	65	DANELECTR	**DM-25** REVERB, TREMOLO	281	**208**	178	149
GTAMP	57	DANELECTR	**LEADER DELUXE SIZE** 12" SPEAKER	134	**99**	85	71
GTAMP	65	DANELECTR	**REVERB UNIT**	216	**159**	137	114
GTAMP	60	DANELECTR	**SILVERTONE** 2x12" SPEAKERS, TREMOLO, REVERB	330	**244**	209	175
GTAMP	50	DANELECTR	**SPECIAL** BROWN, SINGLE CHANNEL. 12" SPEAKER AND VIBRATO	144	**106**	91	76
GUITAR (ACOUSTIC)	45	DANELECTR	**SILVERTONE** SUNBURST, ARCHTOP, MAPLE BACK/SIDES	350	**259**	222	186
GUITAR	54	DANELECTR	**SILVERTONE** SUNBURST, ARCHTOP, SINGLE CUTAWAY	341	**252**	217	181
GUITAR	67	DANELECTR	**TEARDROP** SUNBURST, SPRUCE, SEMI-HOLLOW	264	**195**	167	140

D'ANGELICO

TYPE	YR	MFG	MODEL	SELL EXC	SELL AVG	BUY EXC	BUY AVG
GUITAR (ACOUSTIC)	51	DANGELICO	**"SPECIAL"** BLOND, NON-CUTAWAY, 17 1/2", SERIAL # 1856-1885	12,868	**9,517**	8,177	6,836
GUITAR	36	DANGELICO	**EXCEL** SUNBURST, EARLY STYLE STRAIGHT "F" HOLES, SERIAL # 1105-1235	11,914	**8,811**	7,570	6,329
GUITAR	37	DANGELICO	**EXCEL** SUNBURST, SERIAL # 1236-1317	11,811	**8,735**	7,505	6,275
GUITAR	37	DANGELICO	**EXCEL** BLOND, ARCHTOP, SERIAL # 1236-1317	16,829	**12,447**	10,693	8,940
GUITAR	39	DANGELICO	**EXCEL** SUNBURST, NON-CUTAWAY, SERIAL # 1318-1385	18,816	**13,916**	11,956	9,996
GUITAR	40	DANGELICO	**EXCEL** SUNBURST, SERIAL # 1457-1508	12,691	**9,386**	8,064	6,742
GUITAR	43	DANGELICO	**EXCEL** SUNBURST, CURLY MAPLE, SERIAL # 1622-1658	11,573	**8,559**	7,354	6,148
GUITAR	45	DANGELICO	**EXCEL** SUNBURST, SPRUCE, EBONY BOARD, SERIAL # 1682-1702	17,870	**13,216**	11,355	9,493
GUITAR	47	DANGELICO	**EXCEL** SUNBURST, NON-CUTAWAY, SERIAL # 1738-1781	14,400	**10,650**	9,150	7,650
GUITAR	50	DANGELICO	**EXCEL** BLOND, FULL BODY, SERIAL # 1832-1855	21,120	**15,620**	13,420	11,220
GUITAR	50	DANGELICO	**EXCEL** SUNBURST, CUTAWAY, SERIAL # 1832-1855	33,600	**24,850**	21,350	17,850
GUITAR	50	DANGELICO	**EXCEL** BLOND, CUTAWAY, SEROA; # 1832-1855	37,200	**27,513**	23,638	19,763
GUITAR	52	DANGELICO	**EXCEL** BLOND, NON-CUTAWAY, SERIAL # 1886-1908	15,484	**11,452**	9,839	8,226
GUITAR	52	DANGELICO	**EXCEL** NATURAL, JAZZ, LEFT-HANDED, SERIAL # 1886-1908	22,837	**16,890**	14,511	12,132
GUITAR	53	DANGELICO	**EXCEL** BLOND, CUTAWAY, SERIAL # 1909-1936	27,040	**19,998**	17,181	14,365
GUITAR	56	DANGELICO	**EXCEL** NATURAL, CUTAWAY, SERIAL # 1989-2017	43,200	**31,950**	27,450	22,950
GUITAR	56	DANGELICO	**EXCEL** SUNBURST, FULL BODY, SERIAL # 1989-2017	45,297	**33,501**	28,782	24,064
GUITAR	57	DANGELICO	**EXCEL** BLOND, CUTAWAY, SERIAL # 2018-2040	27,041	**19,999**	17,182	14,365
GUITAR	59	DANGELICO	**EXCEL** NON-CUTAWAY, SERIAL # 2068-2098	18,828	**13,925**	11,963	10,002
GUITAR	59	DANGELICO	**EXCEL** SUNBURST, CUTAWAY, SERIAL # 2068-2098	31,139	**23,030**	19,786	16,542
GUITAR	59	DANGELICO	**EXCEL** BLOND, CUTAWAY, SERIAL # 2068-2098	31,490	**23,290**	20,009	16,729
GUITAR	59	DANGELICO	**EXCEL** NY SUNBURST, CUTAWAY, SERIAL # 2068-2098	35,496	**26,252**	22,555	18,857
GUITAR	60	DANGELICO	**EXCEL** FLAME MAPLE, SERIAL # 2099-2122	16,385	**12,118**	10,411	8,704
GUITAR	60	DANGELICO	**EXCEL** NATURAL, CUTAWAY, SERIAL # 2099-2122	38,400	**28,400**	24,400	20,400
GUITAR	60	DANGELICO	**EXCEL** SUNBURST, CUTAWAY, SERIAL # 2099-2122	57,600	**42,600**	36,600	30,600
GUITAR	61	DANGELICO	**EXCEL** NY BLOND, CUTAWAY, SERIAL # 2123-2164	45,815	**33,884**	29,111	24,339

TYPE	YR	MFG	PRICES--BASED ON 100% ORIGINAL MODEL	SELL EXC	SELL AVG	BUY EXC	BUY AVG
GUITAR	63	DANGELICO	**EXCEL** BLOND, CUTAWAY, LEFT-HANDED, SERIAL # 2123-2164	37,704	**27,885**	23,957	20,030
GUITAR	60	DANGELICO	**EXCEL SPECIAL** BLOND, 2 PU's, SERIAL # 2099-2122	22,550	**16,677**	14,328	11,979
GUITAR	46	DANGELICO	**EXCEL TENOR** BLOND, FULL BODY, SERIAL # 1703-1740	17,413	**12,878**	11,064	9,250
GUITAR	52	DANGELICO	**MEL BAY** BLOND, FULL BODY, SERIAL # 1886-1908	20,165	**14,914**	12,813	10,713
GUITAR	38	DANGELICO	**NEW YORKER** SUNBURST, SERIAL # 1318-1385	24,000	**17,750**	15,250	12,750
GUITAR	38	DANGELICC	**NEW YORKER** SUNBURST, STRAIGHT F-HOLE, SERIAL # 1318-1385	39,048	**28,879**	24,811	20,744
GUITAR	39	DANGELICO	**NEW YORKER** SUNBURST, NON-CUTAWAY, SERIAL # 1388-1456	16,477	**12,186**	10,470	8,753
GUITAR	39	DANGELICO	**NEW YORKER** BLOND, NON-CUTAWAY, SERIAL # 1388-1456	37,872	**28,010**	24,065	20,120
GUITAR	43	DANGELICC	**NEW YORKER** BLOND, CUTAWAY, 18", SERIAL # 1622-1658	64,034	**47,359**	40,688	34,018
GUITAR	47	DANGELICC	**NEW YORKER** BLOND, CUTAWAY, SERIAL # 1738-1781	63,341	**46,846**	40,248	33,650
GUITAR	48	DANGELICO	**NEW YORKER** SUNBURST, CUTAWAY, SERIAL # 1782-1804	50,032	**37,003**	31,791	26,579
GUITAR	50	DANGELICO	**NEW YORKER** NATURAL, SERIAL # 1832-1855	48,000	**35,500**	30,500	25,500
GUITAR	51	DANGELICO	**NEW YORKER** BLOND, CUTAWAY, SERIAL # 1856-1885	49,863	**36,878**	31,684	26,489
GUITAR	53	DANGELICO	**NEW YORKER** BLOND, CUTAWAY, SERIAL # 1909-1936	48,040	**35,529**	30,525	25,521
GUITAR	54	DANGELICO	**NEW YORKER** SUNBURST, FULL BODY, SERIAL # 1933-1962	49,419	**36,550**	31,402	26,254
GUITAR	54	DANGELICO	**NEW YORKER** BLOND, CUTAWAY, SDRIAL # 1933-1962	66,652	**49,295**	42,352	35,409
GUITAR	55	DANGELICO	**NEW YORKER** SUNBURST, CUTAWAY, SERIAL # 1961-1988	46,542	**34,422**	29,574	24,725
GUITAR	56	DANGELICO	**NEW YORKER** BLOND, CUTAWAY, SERIAL # 1989-2017	47,183	**34,895**	29,980	25,065
GUITAR	57	DANGELICO	**NEW YORKER** SUNBURST, CUTAWAY, SERIAL # 2018-2040	53,113	**39,282**	33,749	28,216
GUITAR	58	DANGELICO	**NEW YORKER** NATURAL, CUTAWAY, SERIAL # 2041-2067	67,200	**49,700**	42,700	35,700
GUITAR	59	DANGELICO	**NEW YORKER** SUNBURST, NON-CUTAWAY, SERIAL # 2068-2098	45,577	**33,708**	28,960	24,213
GUITAR	62	DANGELICO	**NEW YORKER** BLOND, CUTAWAY, SERIAL # 2123-2164	34,023	**25,163**	21,619	18,074
GUITAR	63	DANGELICO	**NEW YORKER** NATURAL, CUTAWAY, INLAY, SERIAL # 2123-2164	64,593	**47,772**	41,043	34,315
GUITAR	64	DANGELICO	**NEW YORKER** BLOND, CUTAWAY, SERIAL # 2123-2164	34,023	**25,163**	21,619	18,074
GUITAR	49	DANGELICC	**NEW YORKER DELUXE** BLOND, CUTAWAY, 17", SERIAL # 1805-1831	48,352	**35,760**	30,723	25,687
GUITAR	60	DANGELICO	**NEW YORKER SPECIAL** SUNBURST, SERIAL # 2099-2122	22,591	**16,708**	14,355	12,001
GUITAR	64	DANGELICO	**NEW YORKER SPECIAL** SUNBURST, SERIAL # 2123-2164	48,000	**35,500**	30,500	25,500
GUITAR	33	DANGELICO	**SELMER CUSTOM** CUTAWAY, 16", SERIAL # 1005-1097	12,864	**9,514**	8,174	6,834
GUITAR	36	DANGELICO	**STYLE A** SUNBURST, SERIAL # 1105-1235	8,102	**5,992**	5,148	4,304
GUITAR	37	DANGELICO	**STYLE A** SUNBURST, SERIAL # 1234-1317	8,094	**5,986**	5,143	4,300
GUITAR	39	DANGELICO	**STYLE A** SUNBURST, ARCHTOP, SERIAL # 1388-1456	8,006	**5,921**	5,087	4,253
GUITAR	42	DANGELICO	**STYLE A** SUNBURST, SERIAL # 1563-1621	7,638	**5,649**	4,853	4,058
GUITAR	39	DANGELICO	**STYLE A-1** SUNBURST, SERIAL # 1388-1456	7,680	**5,680**	4,880	4,080
GUITAR	40	DANGELICO	**STYLE A-1** SUNBURST, SERIAL # 1457-1508	8,605	**6,364**	5,468	4,571
GUITAR	42	DANGELICO	**STYLE A-1** SUNBURST, SERIAL # 1563-1621	8,845	**6,541**	5,620	4,699
GUITAR	49	DANGELICO	**STYLE A-1** SUNBURST, SERIAL # 1805-1831	8,120	**6,005**	5,159	4,314
GUITAR	36	DANGELICO	**STYLE B** SERIAL # 1105-1235	13,828	**10,227**	8,787	7,346
GUITAR	38	DANGELICO	**STYLE B** BLOND, SERIAL # 1318-1385	11,227	**8,303**	7,133	5,964
GUITAR	38	DANGELICO	**STYLE B** SUNBURST, SERIAL # 1318-1385	12,802	**9,468**	8,134	6,801
GUITAR	42	DANGELICO	**STYLE B** SUNBURST, SERIAL # 1563-1621	12,000	**8,875**	7,625	6,375
MANDOLIN	42	DANGELICO	**A-STYLE PLAIN** SERIAL # 1563-1621	10,055	**7,436**	6,389	5,341
MANDOL	39	DANGELICO	**DELUXE 2-POINT** SERIAL # 1388-1456	6,455	**4,774**	4,101	3,429

TYPE	YR	MFG	PRICES--BASED ON 100% ORIGINAL MODEL	SELL EXC	SELL AVG	BUY EXC	BUY AVG
D'AQUISTO							
ELEC. GUITAR	78	DAQUISTO	**EXCEL SOLIDBODY** SUNBURST, SERIAL # 1113-1125	16,320	**12,070**	10,370	8,670
ELGUIT	88	DAQUISTO	**EXCEL SOLIDBODY** SUNBURST, MAPLE TOP, 2 PU's, SERIAL # 1201-1210	15,360	**11,360**	9,760	8,160
GUITAR (ACOUSTIC)	78	DAQUISTO	**10-STRING SPECIAL** HONEY SUNBURST, MARK LEAF CASE, SERIAL # 1113-1125	43,204	**31,953**	27,453	22,952
GUITAR	68	DAQUISTO	**EXCEL** SUNBURST, CUTAWAY, SERIAL # 1023-1029	35,520	**26,270**	22,570	18,870
GUITAR	78	DAQUISTO	**EXCEL DELUXE** BLOND, SERIAL # 1113-1125	32,050	**23,704**	20,365	17,026
GUITAR	66	DAQUISTO	**NEW YORKER** SUNBURST, CUTAWAY, 18", SERIAL # 1006-1014	55,200	**40,825**	35,075	29,325
GUITAR	69	DAQUISTO	**NEW YORKER** SUNBURST, CUTAWAY, SERIAL # 1030-1036	46,775	**34,594**	29,721	24,849
GUITAR	77	DAQUISTO	**NEW YORKER** VIOLIN FINISH, CUTAWAY, SERIAL # 1103-1112	47,014	**34,770**	29,873	24,976
GUITAR	77	DAQUISTO	**NEW YORKER** CARVED EBONY,VIOLIN FINISH,17",ARCHTOP,SERIAL # 1103-1112	48,000	**35,500**	30,500	25,500
GUITAR	81	DAQUISTO	**NEW YORKER** SUNBURST, CUTAWAY, SERIAL # 1143-1151	24,000	**17,750**	15,250	12,750
GUITAR	85	DAQUISTO	**NEW YORKER** SUNBURST, SERIAL # 1176-1183	47,808	**35,358**	30,378	25,398
GUITAR	87	DAQUISTO	**NEW YORKER** BLOND, CUTAWAY, SERIAL # 1193-1202	43,200	**31,950**	27,450	22,950
GUITAR	66	DAQUISTO	**NEW YORKER DELUXE** BLOND, SERIAL # 1006-1014	52,835	**39,076**	33,572	28,068
GUITAR	70	DAQUISTO	**NEW YORKER DELUXE** SUNBURST, SERIAL # 1037-1043	51,655	**38,203**	32,822	27,442
GUITAR	72	DAQUISTO	**NEW YORKER DELUXE** SUNBURST, SERIAL # 1051-1063	50,771	**37,549**	32,261	26,972
GUITAR	72	DAQUISTO	**NEW YORKER DELUXE** BLOND, SERIAL # 1051-1063	54,701	**40,456**	34,758	29,060
GUITAR	75	DAQUISTO	**NEW YORKER DELUXE** SUNBURST, SERIAL # 1085-1094	51,060	**37,763**	32,444	27,125
GUITAR	78	DAQUISTO	**NEW YORKER DELUXE** SUNBURST, SERIAL # 1113-1125	48,552	**35,908**	30,850	25,793
GUITAR	76	DAQUISTO	**NEW YORKER SPECIAL** VIOLIN FINISH, SERIAL # 1095-1102	46,174	**34,149**	29,339	24,529
GUITAR	78	DAQUISTO	**NEW YORKER SPECIAL** SUNBURST, SERIAL # 1113-1125	41,616	**30,779**	26,444	22,109
GUITAR	79	DAQUISTO	**SOLID BODY** 7-STRING, SERIAL # 1126-1133	33,600	**24,850**	21,350	17,850
GUITAR	80	DAQUISTO	**SOLID BODY** 7-STRING, SERIAL # 1134-1142	30,624	**22,649**	19,459	16,269
MANDOLIN	72	DAQUISTO	**MANDOLIN ASYMMETRICAL** 2-POINT BODY	15,190	**11,234**	9,652	8,069
DAY SEQUERRA							
TUNER	73	DAY	**MODEL 1 FM TUNER**	3,936	**2,911**	2,501	2,091
DEARMOND							
EFFECTS	77	DEARMOND	**THUNDERBOLT B** 5 OCTAVE WAH	141	**104**	89	74
EFFECTS	76	DEARMOND	**VOLUME PEDAL 1602**	104	**77**	66	55
EFFECTS	78	DEARMOND	**VOLUME PEDAL 1602**	96	**71**	61	51
DELVECCHIO DINAMICO							
BANJO	68	DELVECCHI	**DINAMICO**	480	**355**	305	255
BANJO	75	DELVECCHI	**DINAMICO**	438	**324**	278	233
UKULELE	55	DELVECCHI	**DINAMICO** RESONATOR	425	**314**	270	225
UKE	60	DELVECCHI	**DINAMICO**	480	**355**	305	255
DOBRO, SEE ALSO MOSRITE, REGAL							
GUITAR (ACOUSTIC)	35	DOBRO	**14 METAL BODY** SQUARE NECK, 14-FRET, SERIAL # 5700-7600	885	**654**	562	470
GUITAR	37	DOBRO	**14 STEEL BODY** VIOLIN EDGE, SERIAL # 8000-9000	881	**651**	559	468
GUITAR	36	DOBRO	**15 METAL BODY** VIOLIN EDGE, NICKLE-PLATED, SERIAL # 5700-7600	1,475	**1,091**	937	783
GUITAR	37	DOBRO	**15 METAL BODY** VIOLIN EDGE, NICKLE-PLATED, SERIAL # 8000-9000	1,464	**1,083**	930	778
GUITAR	35	DOBRO	**16 METAL BODY** VIOLIN EDGE,ENGRAVED,NICKLE-PLATED,SERIAL # 5700-7600	1,597	**1,181**	1,015	848
GUITAR	30	DOBRO	**19** SERIAL # 3000-	876	**648**	556	465
GUITAR	36	DOBRO	**19** SERIAL # 5700-7600	834	**616**	530	443
GUITAR	37	DOBRO	**19** SERIAL # 8000-9000	885	**654**	562	470
GUITAR	28	DOBRO	**27** DARK WALNUT, ROUND NECK, SERIAL # 900-1700	1,598	**1,182**	1,015	849

TYPE	YR	MFG	PRICES--BASED ON 100% ORIGINAL MODEL	SELL EXC	SELL AVG	BUY EXC	BUY AVG
GUITAR	28	DOBRO	27 ROUND NECK, 12-FRET, SERIAL # 900-1700	1,652	**1,221**	1,049	877
GUITAR	29	DOBRO	27 ROUND NECK, 12-FRET, SLOT HEAD, SERIAL # 1800-2000	1,445	**1,069**	918	768
GUITAR	29	DOBRO	27 BROWN SUNBURST, ROUND NECK, SERIAL # 1800-2000	1,512	**1,118**	961	803
GUITAR	29	DOBRO	27 WALNUT, ROUND NECK, SERIAL # 1800-2000	1,584	**1,172**	1,007	842
GUITAR	30	DOBRO	27 BROWN FINISH, SQUARE NECK, SERIAL # 3000-	1,227	**908**	780	652
GUITAR	32	DOBRO	27 SQUARE NECK, SERIAL # 5000-5500	1,109	**820**	705	589
GUITAR	34	DOBRO	27 SUNBURST, ROUND NECK, SERIAL # 5700-7600	1,205	**891**	766	640
GUITAR	35	DOBRO	27 ROUND NECK, 14-FRET, SERIAL # 5700-7600	878	**649**	558	466
GUITAR	35	DOBRO	27 SUNBURST, SQUARE NECK, SERIAL # 5700-7600	1,195	**883**	759	634
GUITAR	36	DOBRO	27 SUNBURST, RESONATOR, SERIAL # 5700-7600	1,164	**861**	739	618
GUITAR	37	DOBRO	27 SUNBURST, ROUND NECK, HAWAIIAN, SERIAL # 8000-9000	842	**623**	535	447
GUITAR	40	DOBRO	27 SUNBURST, SQUARE NECK	1,445	**1,069**	918	768
GUITAR	70	DOBRO	27 SUNBURST, SQUARE NECK	2,314	**1,711**	1,470	1,229
GUITAR	29	DOBRO	27 G DARK WALNUT, SERIAL # 1800-2000	1,136	**840**	722	603
GUITAR	30	DOBRO	27 G HARDWOOD BODY, SERIAL # 3000-	1,136	**840**	722	603
GUITAR	32	DOBRO	27 G SUNBURST, WHITE BINDING TOP, SERIAL # 5000-5500	1,115	**825**	708	592
GUITAR	36	DOBRO	27 G SUNBURST, ROUND NECK, RESONATOR, SERIAL # 5700-7600	877	**648**	557	466
GUITAR	30	DOBRO	27.50 REGAL TENOR SERIAL # 3000-	598	**442**	380	317
GUITAR	36	DOBRO	30 SUNBURST, ROUND NECK, 12-FRET, SERIAL # 5700-7600	799	**591**	508	424
GUITAR	30	DOBRO	32 SUNBURST, ROUND NECK, SERIAL # 3000-	1,474	**1,090**	936	783
GUITAR	37	DOBRO	32 METAL BODY, VIOLIN EDGE, SERIAL # 8000-9000	640	**473**	406	340
GUITAR	38	DOBRO	32 SUNBURST, ROUND NECK, 14-FRET	829	**613**	527	440
GUITAR	76	DOBRO	33 ROUND NECK	670	**495**	425	355
GUITAR	70	DOBRO	33D	750	**555**	477	398
GUITAR	71	DOBRO	33D ROUND NECK	757	**560**	481	402
GUITAR	75	DOBRO	33D ROUND NECK	708	**523**	450	376
GUITAR	75	DOBRO	33H	992	**734**	630	527
GUITAR	30	DOBRO	36 ROUND NECK, SERIAL # 3000-	1,195	**883**	759	634
GUITAR	75	DOBRO	36S 8-STRING	657	**486**	417	349
GUITAR	30	DOBRO	37 SERIAL # 3000-	1,661	**1,229**	1,055	882
GUITAR	30	DOBRO	37 MAHOGANY, SERIAL # 3000-	1,678	**1,241**	1,066	891
GUITAR	30	DOBRO	37 MAHOGANY, SQUARE NECK, SERIAL # 3000-	1,763	**1,304**	1,120	936
GUITAR	31	DOBRO	37 MAHOGANY, ROUND NECK, RESONATOR, SERIAL # 3000-	1,725	**1,275**	1,096	916
GUITAR	32	DOBRO	37 SUNBURST, SQUARE NECK,14-FRET, SERIAL # 5000-5500	1,465	**1,084**	931	778
GUITAR	32	DOBRO	37 RESONATOR, SERIAL # 5000-5500	1,694	**1,253**	1,076	900
GUITAR	33	DOBRO	37 SUNBURST, SQUARE NECK, SERIAL # 5000-5500	1,506	**1,113**	957	800
GUITAR	34	DOBRO	37 SUNBURST, SQUARE NECK, SERIAL # 5700-7600	1,434	**1,060**	911	761
GUITAR	35	DOBRO	37 SUNBURST, SQUARE NECK, 12-FRET, SERIAL # 5700-7600	1,390	**1,028**	883	738
GUITAR	36	DOBRO	37 SUNBURST, SQUARE NECK, SERIAL # 5700-7600	1,388	**1,026**	882	737
GUITAR	37	DOBRO	37 MAHOGANY, ROUND NECK, SERIAL # 8000-9000	1,169	**864**	742	621
GUITAR	37	DOBRO	37 SUNBURST, SQUARE NECK, SERIAL # 8000-9000	1,201	**888**	763	638
GUITAR	38	DOBRO	37 SUNBURST, SQUARE NECK	1,169	**864**	742	621
GUITAR	39	DOBRO	37 SUNBURST, SQUARE NECK	1,187	**878**	754	630

TYPE	YR	MFG	PRICES--BASED ON 100% ORIGINAL MODEL	SELL EXC	SELL AVG	BUY EXC	BUY AVG
GUITAR	40	DOBRO	37 SUNBURST, SQUARE NECK, 12-FRET	1,090	806	692	579
GUITAR	28	DOBRO	37G MAHOGANY, ROUND NECK, SERIAL # 900-1700	1,320	976	839	701
GUITAR	30	DOBRO	37G SQUARE NECK, SERIAL # 3000-	967	715	614	514
GUITAR	33	DOBRO	37G MAHOGANY, ROUND NECK, SERIAL # 5000-5500	1,255	928	797	667
GUITAR	34	DOBRO	37G SQUARE NECK, SERIAL # 5700-7600	1,418	1,049	901	753
GUITAR	33	DOBRO	45 SPRUCE TOP, MAHOGANY BODY, F-HOLES, SERIAL # 5000-5500	1,230	910	782	653
GUITAR	35	DOBRO	45G SPRUCE TOP, SQUARE NECK, SERIAL # 5700-7600	1,206	892	766	641
GUITAR	36	DOBRO	45G BLOND, SERIAL # 5700-7600	1,061	785	674	564
GUITAR	38	DOBRO	46 METAL BODY, VIOLIN EDGE, ALUMALITE	950	702	603	504
GUITAR	39	DOBRO	46 ROUND NECK, 14-FRET, ALUMALITE	893	661	567	474
GUITAR	40	DOBRO	46 ROUND NECK	956	707	607	507
GUITAR	40	DOBRO	47 REGAL ROUND	1,191	881	757	632
GUITAR	37	DOBRO	55 SUNBURST, 12-FRET, DOT INLAY, SERIAL # 8000-9000	796	589	506	423
GUITAR	35	DOBRO	60 SERIAL # 5700-7600	1,414	1,045	898	751
GUITAR	36	DOBRO	60 SERIAL # 5700-7600	1,220	929	790	604
GUITAR	70	DOBRO	60D NATURAL, SQUARE NECK, RESONATOR	756	559	480	401
GUITAR	75	DOBRO	60D SUNBURST, ROUND NECK	498	368	316	264
GUITAR	75	DOBRO	60D NATURAL, SQUARE NECK, RESONATOR	692	511	439	367
GUITAR	77	DOBRO	60D SUNBURST, SQUARE NECK	641	474	407	340
GUITAR	78	DOBRO	60D BROWN SUNBURST, SQUARE NECK	536	396	340	285
GUITAR	80	DOBRO	60D SUNBURST, SQUARE NECK	518	383	329	275
GUITAR	76	DOBRO	60DN NATURAL, MAPLE, SQUARE NECK, SERIAL #D11296	522	398	338	258
GUITAR	78	DOBRO	60DN NATURAL, SQUARE NECK	534	395	339	284
GUITAR	75	DOBRO	60S SUNBURST	623	460	395	330
GUITAR	38	DOBRO	62 VIOLIN EDGE, SPANISH DANCE	721	533	458	383
GUITAR	28	DOBRO	65 RESONATOR, SANDBLASTED PATTERN, SERIAL # 900-1700	1,847	1,366	1,173	981
GUITAR	29	DOBRO	65 ROUND NECK, SERIAL # 1800-2000	1,493	1,104	949	793
GUITAR	30	DOBRO	65 WOOD BODY, SERIAL # 3000-	1,392	1,030	885	740
GUITAR	33	DOBRO	65 FRENCH SCROLL PATTERN, SERIAL # 5000-5500	1,832	1,355	1,164	973
GUITAR	40	DOBRO	65 LATTICE TOP DESIGN	1,992	1,473	1,265	1,058
GUITAR	29	DOBRO	65 TENOR SERIAL # 1800-2000	1,437	1,062	913	763
GUITAR	78	DOBRO	66 SUNBURST	623	460	395	330
GUITAR	70	DOBRO	90 METAL BODY, SQUARE NECK, SERIAL #B285 9	561	415	356	298
GUITAR	28	DOBRO	100 DELUXE WALNUT, ROUND NECK, SERIAL # 900-1700	4,800	3,550	3,050	2,550
GUITAR	32	DOBRO	125 ROUND NECK, HEART INLAY, SERIAL # 5000-5500	2,390	1,767	1,518	1,269
GUITAR	29	DOBRO	126T WALNUT, SERIAL # 1800-2000	1,430	1,057	908	759
GUITAR	28	DOBRO	156 ROUND NECK, SERIAL # 900-1700	12,000	8,875	7,625	6,375
GUITAR	35	DOBRO	ANGELUS HAWAIIAN STYLE SERIAL # 5700-7600	724	536	460	385
GUITAR	36	DOBRO	ANGELUS HAWAIIAN STYLE SERIAL # 5700-7600	624	462	397	332
GUITAR	37	DOBRO	ANGELUS HAWAIIAN STYLE SERIAL # 8000-9000	589	435	374	313
GUITAR	56	DOBRO	BABY BASS COPPER FLAKE ZORKO	1,287	952	818	683
GUITAR	35	DOBRO	DOBRO JR FLATTOP, SERIAL # 5700-7600	433	320	275	230

TYPE	YR	MFG	PRICES--BASED ON 100% ORIGINAL MODEL	SELL EXC	SELL AVG	BUY EXC	BUY AVG
GUITAR	68	DOBRO	**HOUND DOG** SUNBURST, RESONATOR	444	**328**	282	236
GUITAR	30	DOBRO	**MAGNATONE CYCLOPS** RESONATOR, SERIAL # 3000-	878	**649**	558	466
GUITAR	31	DOBRO	**MAGNATONE CYCLOPS** ROUND NECK, SERIAL # 3000-	996	**736**	633	529
GUITAR	30	DOBRO	**PROFESSIONAL M-15 REGAL** NICKEL BODY, SERIAL # 3000-	1,832	**1,355**	1,164	973
GUITAR	74	DOBRO	**RESONATOR** ROSEWOOD, SQUARE NECK	1,992	**1,473**	1,265	1,058
GUITAR	76	DOBRO	**RESONATOR** SUNBURST, ROUND NECK	1,164	**861**	739	618
GUITAR	79	DOBRO	**RESONATOR** GOLD-PLATED, SQUARE NECK	696	**515**	442	370
MANDOLIN	29	DOBRO	**MANDOLIN** WALNUT NECK/SIDES, INLAY	2,073	**1,533**	1,317	1,101
MANDOL	34	DOBRO	**MANDOLIN** SUNBURST, F-HOLES	750	**555**	477	398
MANDOL	35	DOBRO	**MANDOLIN** WOOD BODY	956	**707**	607	507
MANDOL	68	DOBRO	**RESONATOR** WOOD BODY	657	**486**	417	349
STEEL GUITAR	39	DOBRO	**METAL** 6-STRING	1,175	**869**	746	624
UKULELE	31	DOBRO	**CYCLOPS** ROSEWOOD, ROUND NECK	1,652	**1,221**	1,049	877
UKE	31	DOBRO	**CYCLOPS** EBONY, FRENCH SCROLL	2,983	**2,206**	1,895	1,585
UKE	37	DOBRO	**CYCLOPS** WOOD BODY, SQUARE HEAD SLOTS	1,257	**930**	799	668
UKE	32	DOBRO	**DOUBLE CYCLOPS** ROSEWOOD TOP/FINGERBOARD	957	**707**	608	508
UKE	32	DOBRO	**DOUBLE CYCLOPS** SQUARE NECK	1,273	**942**	809	676
UKE	33	DOBRO	**F-HOLES** WOOD BODY, INLAYS	1,195	**883**	759	634

DYNACO ELECTRONICS

TYPE	YR	MFG	MODEL	SELL EXC	SELL AVG	BUY EXC	BUY AVG
PRE	64	DYNACO	**PAS-1**	141	**104**	89	74
PRE	64-69	DYNACO	**PAS-2 KIT**	137	**101**	87	72
PRE	64-69	DYNACO	**PAS-2A ASSEMBLED**	120	**88**	76	63
PRE	64-69	DYNACO	**PAS-3 KIT**	190	**140**	120	100
PRE	64-69	DYNACO	**PAS-3A ASSEMBLED**	168	**124**	106	89
PRE	69-74	DYNACO	**PAS-3X/A ASSEMBLED**	144	**106**	91	76
PWR	54-60	DYNACO	**MARK II** 50 WATT	287	**212**	182	152
PWR	64-69	DYNACO	**MARK III KIT** MONO, TUBE, AMP, 60 WATTS, PAIR	214	**158**	136	113
PWR	64-69	DYNACO	**MARK IIIA ASSEMBLED** MONO, 60 WATT	446	**330**	283	237
PWR	64-69	DYNACO	**MARK IV KIT** 40 WATT	373	**276**	237	198
PWR	78	DYNACO	**MARK VI KIT** 100 WATTS	168	**124**	106	89
PWR	64	DYNACO	**ST-70**	187	**138**	118	99
PWR	64-69	DYNACO	**STEREO 35** 17 WATT	267	**198**	170	142
PWR	72-77	DYNACO	**STEREO 70 ASSEMBLED** 35 WATT	322	**238**	204	171
PWR	64-69	DYNACO	**STEREO 70 KIT** 35 WATT	256	**189**	162	136
TUNER	64-69	DYNACO	**FM-3 ASSEMBLED**	185	**137**	117	98
TUNER	73	DYNACO	**FM-3 KIT**	190	**140**	120	100
TUNER	64	DYNACO	**FM-3A ASSEMBLED**	191	**141**	121	101

EARTHWOOD BASS by ERNIE BALL

TYPE	YR	MFG	MODEL	SELL EXC	SELL AVG	BUY EXC	BUY AVG
GUITAR AMP	77	EARTH	**MV-10**	168	**124**	106	89
GUITAR (ACOUSTIC)	75	EARTH	**EARTHWOOD BASS**	656	**485**	417	348
GUITAR	76	EARTH	**EARTHWOOD BASS E**	1,104	**816**	701	586

EICO

TYPE	YR	MFG	MODEL	SELL EXC	SELL AVG	BUY EXC	BUY AVG
PRE	60	EICO	**HF-85 ASSEMBLED** TUBE	177	**131**	112	94
PWR	73	EICO	**HF-20 KIT**	99	**73**	63	53
PWR	60	EICO	**HF-30** MONO TUBE	170	**126**	108	90
PWR	73-78	EICO	**HF-50 KIT**	226	**167**	143	120
PWR	73-78	EICO	**HF-60 KIT**	428	**316**	272	227
PWR	61-63	EICO	**HF-86 KIT** STEREO TUBE	277	**205**	176	147
PWR	61-63	EICO	**HF-87 KIT** STEREO TUBE	290	**215**	184	154

TYPE	YR	MFG	PRICES--BASED ON 100% ORIGINAL MODEL	SELL EXC	SELL AVG	BUY EXC	BUY AVG
PWR	60	EICO	**HF-89 ASSEMBLED** TUBE	417	**308**	265	221
PWR	60	EICO	**HF-89 KIT** TUBE	360	**266**	228	191

EKO, MADE IN ITALY

TYPE	YR	MFG	MODEL	SELL EXC	SELL AVG	BUY EXC	BUY AVG
ELEC. GUITAR	63	EKO	**500-4V**	429	**317**	272	227
ELGUIT	64	EKO	**700 4V**	480	**355**	305	255
ELGUIT	69	EKO	**955/2 VIOLIN BASS**	336	**248**	213	178
ELGUIT	67	EKO	**995 VIOLIN BASS** 2 PU's	449	**332**	285	238
ELGUIT	67	EKO	**BARRACUDA**	336	**248**	213	178
ELGUIT	71	EKO	**BARRACUDA**	405	**299**	257	215
ELGUIT	75	EKO	**BARRACUDA**	271	**200**	172	144
ELGUIT	66	EKO	**COBRA**	403	**298**	256	214
ELGUIT	69	EKO	**COBRA**	360	**266**	228	191
ELGUIT	69	EKO	**COBRA BASS II**	288	**213**	183	153
ELGUIT	75	EKO	**COBRA BASS II**	340	**252**	216	181
ELGUIT	67	EKO	**COBRA XII** 12-STRING	302	**223**	192	160
ELGUIT	64	EKO	**CONDOR**	336	**248**	213	178
ELGUIT	68	EKO	**CONDOR** 3 PU's	268	**198**	170	142
ELGUIT	68	EKO	**CONDOR BASS** 2 PU's	321	**237**	204	170
ELGUIT	64	EKO	**CRESTLINE** RED SPARKLE	456	**337**	289	242
ELGUIT	65	EKO	**DRAGON**	408	**301**	259	216
ELGUIT	67	EKO	**DRAGON**	384	**284**	244	204
ELGUIT	67	EKO	**FLORENTINE** DOUBLE CUTAWAY	432	**319**	274	229
ELGUIT	68	EKO	**KADETT** ORANGE, DOUBLE CUTAWAY, SOLID, 3 PU's	375	**277**	238	199
ELGUIT	70	EKO	**KADETT** SOLID BODY	350	**259**	222	186
ELGUIT	67	EKO	**KADETT XII**	432	**319**	274	229
ELGUIT	68	EKO	**KADETT XII**	372	**275**	236	197
ELGUIT	67	EKO	**LANCER**	456	**337**	289	242
ELGUIT	71	EKO	**LARK I** SUNBURST	293	**217**	186	156
ELGUIT	70	EKO	**LARK II** SUNBURST	330	**244**	209	175
ELGUIT	76	EKO	**MANTA** 2 PU's	332	**245**	211	176
ELGUIT	67	EKO	**ROK** ROCKET SHAPED	427	**315**	271	226
ELGUIT	70	EKO	**ROK IV** A.K.A. ROCKET	504	**372**	320	267
ELGUIT	67	EKO	**ROK VI**	498	**368**	316	264
ELGUIT	70	EKO	**ROK XII** 12-STRING	465	**344**	295	247
ELGUIT	64	EKO	**TONEMASTER** SQUARE NECK, LAP GUITAR	497	**367**	315	264
ELGUIT	76	EKO	**X 27** SOLID BODY, 2 PU's	270	**200**	172	143
GUITAR (ACOUSTIC)	71	EKO	**CLASSICAL** SPANISH ROSEWOOD	280	**207**	178	148
GUITAR	64	EKO	**EL DORADO 1101** 12-STRING	453	**335**	287	240
GUITAR	64	EKO	**EL DORADO 1102** 6-STRING	288	**213**	183	153
GUITAR	60	EKO	**RANCHERO FOLK BASS** NATURAL	192	**142**	122	102
GUITAR	66	EKO	**RANGER IV DREADNOUGHT** MAHOGANY BODY	303	**224**	192	161
GUITAR	70	EKO	**RANGER XII** 12-STRING	278	**205**	176	147

ELECTRO HARMONIX

TYPE	YR	MFG	MODEL	SELL EXC	SELL AVG	BUY EXC	BUY AVG
EFFECTS	78	ELECHARM	**10-BAND GRAPHIC EQUALIZER**	57	**42**	36	30
EFFECTS	79	ELECHARM	**16 SECOND DELAY FRONT CONTROLLER**	115	**85**	73	61
EFFECTS	74	ELECHARM	**BAD STONE PHASER** 2 KNOBS	81	**60**	51	43
EFFECTS	77	ELECHARM	**BAD STONE PHASER** 3 KNOBS	64	**47**	40	34
EFFECTS	79	ELECHARM	**BIG MUFF**	97	**72**	62	52
EFFECTS	74	ELECHARM	**BIG MUFF II**	87	**64**	55	46
EFFECTS	71	ELECHARM	**BIG MUFF FUZZ DELUXE** BLACK, GRAPHICS	134	**99**	85	71
EFFECTS	75	ELECHARM	**BIG MUFF FUZZ DELUXE** COMPRESSOR	92	**68**	58	48
EFFECTS	72	ELECHARM	**BLACK FINGER SUSTAINER**	95	**70**	60	50

TYPE	YR	MFG	MODEL	PRICES--BASED ON 100% ORIGINAL	SELL EXC	SELL AVG	BUY EXC	BUY AVG
EFFECTS	78	ELECHARM	CLONE THEORY		130	96	82	69
EFFECTS	74	ELECHARM	CRYING TONE WAH WAH		59	44	37	31
EFFECTS	78	ELECHARM	DELUXE ELECTRIC MISTRESS		146	108	93	78
EFFECTS	79	ELECHARM	DELUXE MEMORY MAN		159	117	101	84
EFFECTS	76	ELECHARM	DR. Q FOLLOWER		96	71	61	51
EFFECTS	78	ELECHARM	ECHO FLANGER		62	46	39	33
EFFECTS	76	ELECHARM	ELECTRIC MISTRESS		94	69	59	49
EFFECTS	74	ELECHARM	FREQUENCY ANALYZER		292	216	186	155
EFFECTS	79	ELECHARM	FULL DOUBLE TRACKER SILVER, ANALOG		192	142	122	102
EFFECTS	76	ELECHARM	GOLDEN THROAT TALK BOX		93	68	59	49
EFFECTS	75	ELECHARM	HOT TUBES		118	87	75	62
EFFECTS	76	ELECHARM	HOT TUBES OVERDRIVE		120	89	76	64
EFFECTS	77	ELECHARM	INSTANT REPLAY		336	248	213	178
EFFECTS	76	ELECHARM	LITTLE BIG MUFF FUZZ		96	71	61	51
EFFECTS	74	ELECHARM	LPB-2 POWER BOOSTER		98	73	62	52
EFFECTS	77	ELECHARM	MEMORY MAN DELAY		96	71	61	51
EFFECTS	74	ELECHARM	MOLE BASS BOOSTER		79	58	50	42
EFFECTS	76	ELECHARM	OCTAVE MULTIPLEXER		240	177	152	127
EFFECTS	80	ELECHARM	POLY PHASE		144	106	91	76
EFFECTS	76	ELECHARM	QUEEN TRIGGERED WAH		168	124	106	89
EFFECTS	73	ELECHARM	SCREAMING BIRD		99	73	63	53
EFFECTS	72	ELECHARM	SCREAMING TREE		192	142	122	102
EFFECTS	76	ELECHARM	SCREAMING TREE TREBLE BOOST		144	106	91	76
EFFECTS	77	ELECHARM	SILENCER NOISE GATE		79	58	50	42
EFFECTS	78	ELECHARM	SLAP BACK ECHO		91	67	57	48
EFFECTS	75	ELECHARM	SMALL STONE CHORUS		109	80	69	58
EFFECTS	75	ELECHARM	SMALL STONE PHASOR		96	71	61	51
EFFECTS	78	ELECHARM	SOUL PREACHER COMPRESSOR		56	41	35	30
EFFECTS	78	ELECHARM	SPACE DRUM		115	85	73	61
EFFECTS	77	ELECHARM	SWITCHABLE A/B BOX		50	37	32	27
EFFECTS	77	ELECHARM	SWITCHBLADE		81	60	51	43
EFFECTS	78	ELECHARM	TALKING PEDAL		175	129	111	93
EFFECTS	80	ELECHARM	VOCORDER (RACK)		598	442	380	317
EFFECTS	78	ELECHARM	Y-TRIGGER FILTER SWEEP		148	110	94	79
EFFECTS	77	ELECHARM	ZIPPER ENVELOPE FOLLOWER		105	78	67	56

ELECTRA

TYPE	YR	MFG	MODEL		SELL EXC	SELL AVG	BUY EXC	BUY AVG
ELEC. GUITAR	76	ELECTRA	ELVIN BISHOP		557	412	354	296
ELGUIT	77	ELECTRA	ELVIN BISHOP		528	390	335	280
ELGUIT	78	ELECTRA	MPC OUTLAW BACK HOLE EFFECTS		336	248	213	178
ELGUIT	77	ELECTRA	MPC OUTLAW BASS BACK HOLE EFFECTS		312	230	198	165
ELGUIT	72	ELECTRA	ROCK		288	213	183	153
ELGUIT	71	ELECTRA	ROCK LES PAUL COPY		310	229	197	164
ELGUIT	75	ELECTRA	SUPER ROCK LES PAUL COPY		307	227	195	163

ELECTRO VOICE

TYPE	YR	MFG	MODEL		SELL EXC	SELL AVG	BUY EXC	BUY AVG
MIC	61	ELECTRO V	950 CARDAX "MERCURY MIC"		96	71	61	51
RAW	60-77	ELECTRO V	15W 15" PAIR		217	161	138	115
RAW	60-77	ELECTRO V	18W/K		296	219	188	157
RAW	60	ELECTRO V	BB- MID HORN & XOVER PAIR		216	159	137	114
RAW	60	ELECTRO V	BB-1 HORN TWEETER & XOVER PAIR		216	159	137	114
RAW	60	ELECTRO V	BB-2 HORN TWEETER & XOVER PAIR		216	159	137	114
RAW	60	ELECTRO V	BB-5 HORN TWEETER & XOVER PAIR		217	161	138	115
RAW	60	ELECTRO V	HF-1 HORN TWEETER & XOVER PAIR		217	161	138	115
RAW	60	ELECTRO V	LS-15 15" PAIR		217	161	138	115
RAW	68	ELECTRO V	LT- 8 8" PAIR		217	161	138	115
RAW	68	ELECTRO V	LT-12 12" PAIR		217	161	138	115
RAW	60	ELECTRO V	MF-1 MID HORN & XOVER PAIR		217	161	138	115
RAW	60	ELECTRO V	SP-8B 8" PAIR		217	161	138	115
RAW	74	ELECTRO V	ST-350 HORN TWEETER PAIR		217	161	138	115
RAW	60	ELECTRO V	T- 10A HORN MID RANGE DRVR PAIR		217	161	138	115
RAW	60	ELECTRO V	T- 35 HORN TWEETER PAIR		147	109	93	78
RAW	60	ELECTRO V	T-250 HORN MID RANGE DRVR PAIR		217	161	138	115
RAW	60	ELECTRO V	T-350 HORN TWEETER PAIR		216	159	137	114
XOVER	60	ELECTRO V	X- 8 PAIR		658	487	418	349
XOVER	60	ELECTRO V	X-325 PAIR		657	486	417	349

EMP

TYPE	YR	MFG	MODEL		SELL EXC	SELL AVG	BUY EXC	BUY AVG
SPKR	68	EMP	9000-M GRENADIER		796	589	506	423

ELECTRONIC MUSIC STUDIOS OF AMERICA

TYPE	YR	MFG	MODEL		SELL EXC	SELL AVG	BUY EXC	BUY AVG
SYNTHESIZER	73	EMSA	SYNTHI A		996	736	633	529
SYNTH	74	EMSA	SYNTHI AKS		1,076	795	683	571
SYNTH	72	EMSA	VCS3 MK II		637	471	405	338

	TYPE	YR	MFG	PRICES--BASED ON 100% ORIGINAL MODEL	SELL EXC	SELL AVG	BUY EXC	BUY AVG
	SYNTH	71	EMSA	VCS3 THE "PUTNEY"	1,015	751	645	539
				EPIPHONE by EPIPHONE PRE-1957				
BANJO		28	EPI	ARTIST PLECTRUM	1,341	991	852	712
	BANJO	28	EPI	ARTIST TENOR	1,598	1,182	1,015	849
	BANJO	30	EPI	ARTIST TENOR SERIAL # 10000-	1,593	1,178	1,012	846
	BANJO	28	EPI	CONCERT SPECIAL RECORDING TENOR	1,455	1,076	924	773
	BANJO	29	EPI	CONCERT SPECIAL RECORDING TENOR	1,334	986	847	708
	BANJO	30	EPI	CONCERT SPECIAL RECORDING TENOR SERIAL # 10000-	1,354	1,001	860	719
	BANJO	28	EPI	DELUXE RECORDING TENOR	4,339	3,209	2,757	2,305
	BANJO	40	EPI	ELECTAR SUNBURST, NO SOUND HOLE, 1 PU, SERIAL # 13000-	666	492	423	353
	BANJO	28	EPI	POT GOLD-PLATED ENGRAVED HARDWARE	669	494	425	355
	BANJO	30	EPI	RIALTO PLECTRUM WALNUT NECK, RESONATOR, SERIAL # 10000-	478	353	303	253
	BANJO	28	EPI	STYLE B TENOR	1,552	1,148	986	824
ELEC. GUITAR		39	EPI	CENTURY WALNUT, NON-CUTAWAY, 1 PU, SERIAL # 13000-	921	681	585	489
	ELGUIT	52	EPI	CENTURY MAHOGANY, NON-CUTAWAY, 1 PU, SERIAL # 64000-	498	368	316	264
	ELGUIT	53	EPI	CENTURY MAHOGANY, NON-CUTAWAY, 1 PU, SERIAL # 64000-66000	494	365	314	262
	ELGUIT	54	EPI	CENTURY MAHOGANY, NON-CUTAWAY, 1 PU, SERIAL #68000-	490	362	311	260
	ELGUIT	53	EPI	ELECTROMATIC NATURAL, SERIAL # 64000-66000	1,589	1,175	1,010	844
	ELGUIT	38	EPI	EMPEROR NATURAL, ARCHTOP, SERIAL # 12000-	1,673	1,237	1,063	888
	ELGUIT	38	EPI	EMPEROR NATURAL, FLAME BACK/SIDES, SERIAL # 12000-	1,673	1,237	1,063	888
	ELGUIT	39	EPI	EMPEROR SUNBURST, SERIAL # 13000-	2,390	1,767	1,518	1,269
	ELGUIT	40	EPI	EMPEROR BLOND, NON-CUTAWAY, ARCHTOP, SERIAL # 13000-	1,535	1,135	975	815
	ELGUIT	41	EPI	EMPEROR BLOND, SERIAL # 14000-	1,520	1,124	966	807
	ELGUIT	42	EPI	EMPEROR SUNBURST, SERIAL # 14000-	1,054	779	669	559
	ELGUIT	43	EPI	EMPEROR NATURAL, SERIAL # 18000-	1,015	751	645	539
	ELGUIT	43	EPI	EMPEROR SUNBURST, SERIAL # 18000-	1,015	751	645	539
	ELGUIT	45	EPI	EMPEROR NATURAL, NON-CUTAWAY, SERIAL # 52000-54000	961	711	611	511
	ELGUIT	45	EPI	EMPEROR SUNBURST, NEW YORK ARCHTOP. SERIAL # 52000-54000	1,027	759	652	545
	ELGUIT	46	EPI	EMPEROR NATURAL, NON-CUTAWAY, SERIAL # 54000-55000	1,018	753	647	541
	ELGUIT	46	EPI	EMPEROR SUNBURST, SERIAL # 54000-55000	1,018	753	647	541
	ELGUIT	47	EPI	EMPEROR SUNBURST, ERIAL # 56000-	2,075	1,535	1,318	1,102
	ELGUIT	48	EPI	EMPEROR BLOND, NEW YORK ARCHTOP, SERIAL # 57000-	1,661	1,229	1,055	882
	ELGUIT	49	EPI	EMPEROR NATURAL, NON-CUTAWAY, SERIAL # 58000-	1,867	1,380	1,186	991
	ELGUIT	50	EPI	EMPEROR NATURAL, ARCHTOP, CUTAWAY, SERIAL # 59000-	1,860	1,375	1,182	988
	ELGUIT	50	EPI	EMPEROR SUNBURST. ARCHTOP CUTAWAY, SERIAL # 59000-	1,860	1,375	1,182	988
	ELGUIT	51	EPI	EMPEROR NATURAL, NON-CUTAWAY, SERIAL # 60000-63000	1,867	1,380	1,186	991
	ELGUIT	51	EPI	EMPEROR NATURAL, VARITONE, SERIAL # 60000-63000	2,390	1,767	1,518	1,269
	ELGUIT	51	EPI	EMPEROR SUNBURST, CUTAWAY, SERIAL # 60000-63000	2,944	2,177	1,870	1,564
	ELGUIT	54	EPI	EMPEROR NEW YORK ARCHTOP, SERIAL # 68000-	2,884	2,133	1,833	1,532
	ELGUIT	54	EPI	EMPEROR SUNBURST, SERIAL # 68000-	3,072	2,272	1,952	1,632
	ELGUIT	54	EPI	EMPEROR NATURAL, ARCHTOP, CUTAWAY, SERIAL # 68000-	4,398	3,253	2,795	2,336
	ELGUIT	55	EPI	EMPEROR NATURAL, SERIAL # 69000-	1,990	1,471	1,264	1,057
	ELGUIT	55	EPI	EMPEROR SUNBURST, SERIAL # 69000-	3,840	2,840	2,440	2,040
	ELGUIT	49	EPI	EMPEROR REGENT NEW YORK ARCHTOP, SERIAL # 58000-	1,493	1,104	949	793
	ELGUIT	50	EPI	EMPEROR REGENT NATURAL, CUTAWAY, QUILTED MAPLE, SERIAL # 59000-	2,391	1,768	1,519	1,270

TYPE	YR	MFG	PRICES--BASED ON 100% ORIGINAL MODEL	SELL EXC	SELL AVG	BUY EXC	BUY AVG
ELGUIT	51	EPI	**EMPEROR REGENT** BLOND, FLAME MAPLE, SERIAL # 60000-63000	2,387	**1,765**	1,517	1,268
ELGUIT	51	EPI	**EMPEROR REGENT** NATURAL, CUTAWAY, ARCHTOP, SERIAL # 60000-63000	2,387	**1,765**	1,517	1,268
ELGUIT	53	EPI	**EMPEROR REGENT** BLOND, CUTAWAY, SERIAL # 64000-66000	2,381	**1,761**	1,513	1,265
ELGUIT	55	EPI	**HARRY VOLPE** SUNBURST, DOT INLAY, NON-CUTAWAY, SERIAL # 69000-	1,545	**1,143**	982	821
ELGUIT	39	EPI	**ZEPHYR** SERIAL # 13000-	876	**648**	556	465
ELGUIT	40	EPI	**ZEPHYR** BLOND, SERIAL # 13000-	1,274	**942**	810	677
ELGUIT	42	EPI	**ZEPHYR** BLOND, SERIAL # 14000-	1,195	**883**	759	634
ELGUIT	43	EPI	**ZEPHYR** BLOND	1,193	**882**	758	633
ELGUIT	44	EPI	**ZEPHYR** BLOND	1,213	**897**	771	644
ELGUIT	49	EPI	**ZEPHYR** SUNBURST	1,328	**982**	844	705
ELGUIT	51	EPI	**ZEPHYR** SUNBURST	1,431	**1,058**	909	760
ELGUIT	54	EPI	**ZEPHYR** SUNBURST, CUTAWAY	1,245	**920**	791	661
ELGUIT	41	EPI	**ZEPHYR DELUXE** BLOND	3,072	**2,272**	1,952	1,632
ELGUIT	42	EPI	**ZEPHYR DELUXE** BLOND	2,976	**2,201**	1,891	1,581
ELGUIT	45	EPI	**ZEPHYR DELUXE** BLOND	2,390	**1,767**	1,518	1,269
ELGUIT	51	EPI	**ZEPHYR DELUXE** BLOND	2,386	**1,765**	1,516	1,267
ELGUIT	41	EPI	**ZEPHYR DELUXE REGENT** SUNBURST	3,132	**2,316**	1,990	1,664
ELGUIT	42	EPI	**ZEPHYR DELUXE REGENT** NATURAL	3,144	**2,325**	1,998	1,670
ELGUIT	46	EPI	**ZEPHYR DELUXE REGENT** SUNBURST	3,228	**2,387**	2,051	1,715
ELGUIT	48	EPI	**ZEPHYR DELUXE REGENT** NATURAL	3,172	**2,346**	2,016	1,685
ELGUIT	49	EPI	**ZEPHYR DELUXE REGENT** NATURAL	2,125	**1,571**	1,350	1,129
ELGUIT	49	EPI	**ZEPHYR DELUXE REGENT** SUNBURST	3,143	**2,324**	1,997	1,669
ELGUIT	50	EPI	**ZEPHYR DELUXE REGENT** SUNBURST	2,071	**1,532**	1,316	1,100
ELGUIT	50	EPI	**ZEPHYR DELUXE REGENT** NATURAL	2,109	**1,559**	1,340	1,120
ELGUIT	51	EPI	**ZEPHYR DELUXE REGENT** SUNBURST	1,992	**1,473**	1,265	1,058
ELGUIT	51	EPI	**ZEPHYR DELUXE REGENT** NATURAL	2,032	**1,503**	1,291	1,079
ELGUIT	52	EPI	**ZEPHYR DELUXE REGENT** NATURAL	2,071	**1,532**	1,316	1,100
ELGUIT	52	EPI	**ZEPHYR DELUXE REGENT** BLOND	3,063	**2,265**	1,946	1,627
ELGUIT	53	EPI	**ZEPHYR DELUXE REGENT** SUNBURST	2,376	**1,757**	1,510	1,262
ELGUIT	53	EPI	**ZEPHYR DELUXE REGENT** NATURAL	2,388	**1,766**	1,517	1,268
ELGUIT	54	EPI	**ZEPHYR DELUXE REGENT** SUNBURST	2,374	**1,755**	1,508	1,261
ELGUIT	51	EPI	**ZEPHYR EMPEROR REGENT** BLOND, 3 PU's, SERIAL #61688	4,108	**3,038**	2,610	2,182
ELGUIT	52	EPI	**ZEPHYR EMPEROR REGENT** SUNBURST, 3 PU's	3,941	**2,915**	2,504	2,094
ELGUIT	53	EPI	**ZEPHYR EMPEROR REGENT** SUNBURST, 3 PU's	3,759	**2,780**	2,388	1,997
ELGUIT	53	EPI	**ZEPHYR EMPEROR REGENT** BLOND	3,835	**2,836**	2,436	2,037
ELGUIT	54	EPI	**ZEPHYR EMPEROR REGENT** BLOND	3,956	**2,925**	2,513	2,101
ELGUIT	51	EPI	**ZEPHYR REGENT** SUNBURST	1,432	**1,059**	910	760
ELGUIT	52	EPI	**ZEPHYR REGENT** SUNBURST, NEW YORK ARCHTOP	1,463	**1,082**	929	777
ELGUIT	53	EPI	**ZEPHYR REGENT** SUNBURST	1,661	**1,229**	1,055	882
ELGUIT	54	EPI	**ZEPHYR REGENT** SUNBURST, CUTAWAY, 1-DeARMOND PU	1,637	**1,211**	1,040	870
ELGUIT	49	EPI	**ZEPHYR TENOR** NATURAL, NON-CUTAWAY, 1-17" WIDE PICKUP (RARE MODEL)	1,158	**856**	736	615
GUITAR (ACOUSTIC)	33	EPI	**BEVERLY** DARK BROWN, FLATTOP	357	**264**	226	189

TYPE	YR	MFG	PRICES--BASED ON 100% ORIGINAL MODEL	SELL EXC	SELL AVG	BUY EXC	BUY AVG
GUITAR	32	EPI	**BLACKSTONE** SUNBURST	696	**515**	442	370
GUITAR	33	EPI	**BLACKSTONE** SUNBURST	1,001	**740**	636	531
GUITAR	34	EPI	**BLACKSTONE** SUNBURST	962	**712**	611	511
GUITAR	35	EPI	**BLACKSTONE** SUNBURST	737	**545**	468	391
GUITAR	38	EPI	**BLACKSTONE** SUNBURST	823	**609**	523	437
GUITAR	41	EPI	**BLACKSTONE** SUNBURST	772	**571**	491	410
GUITAR	42	EPI	**BLACKSTONE** SUNBURST, LEFT-HANDED	783	**579**	497	416
GUITAR	43	EPI	**BLACKSTONE** BLOND	812	**600**	516	431
GUITAR	45	EPI	**BLACKSTONE** BLOND	832	**615**	528	442
GUITAR	46	EPI	**BLACKSTONE** SUNBURST	748	**553**	475	397
GUITAR	48	EPI	**BLACKSTONE** SUNBURST	699	**517**	444	371
GUITAR	49	EPI	**BLACKSTONE** SUNBURST	796	**589**	506	423
GUITAR	32	EPI	**BROADWAY** SUNBURST	2,062	**1,525**	1,310	1,095
GUITAR	34	EPI	**BROADWAY** SUNBURST	2,040	**1,509**	1,296	1,084
GUITAR	35	EPI	**BROADWAY** SUNBURST	1,493	**1,104**	949	793
GUITAR	36	EPI	**BROADWAY** NATURAL	1,474	**1,090**	936	783
GUITAR	37	EPI	**BROADWAY** NATURAL	1,434	**1,060**	911	761
GUITAR	37	EPI	**BROADWAY** SUNBURST	2,024	**1,497**	1,286	1,075
GUITAR	39	EPI	**BROADWAY** TENOR, SUNBURST	695	**514**	441	369
GUITAR	44	EPI	**BROADWAY** NATURAL	1,417	**1,048**	900	753
GUITAR	45	EPI	**BROADWAY** NATURAL	1,372	**1,015**	872	729
GUITAR	46	EPI	**BROADWAY** SUNBURST	1,352	**1,000**	859	718
GUITAR	46	EPI	**BROADWAY** NATURAL	1,352	**1,000**	859	718
GUITAR	48	EPI	**BROADWAY** SUNBURST	1,312	**970**	833	697
GUITAR	49	EPI	**BROADWAY** NATURAL	1,275	**943**	810	677
GUITAR	50	EPI	**BROADWAY** TENOR, SUNBURST	673	**498**	428	358
GUITAR	50	EPI	**BROADWAY** NATURAL	1,257	**930**	799	668
GUITAR	51	EPI	**BROADWAY** SUNBURST	1,558	**1,152**	990	827
GUITAR	53	EPI	**BROADWAY** SUNBURST	1,555	**1,150**	988	826
GUITAR	50	EPI	**BROADWAY REGENT** SUNBURST	1,450	**1,072**	921	770
GUITAR	51	EPI	**BROADWAY REGENT** SUNBURST	1,438	**1,063**	913	763
GUITAR	55	EPI	**BROADWAY REGENT** SUNBURST	1,466	**1,084**	932	779
GUITAR	51	EPI	**BYRON** SUNBURST	594	**439**	377	315
GUITAR	55	EPI	**BYRON** SUNBURST	515	**381**	327	273
GUITAR	41	EPI	**CORONET** ARCHTOP, HOLLOW BODY	796	**589**	506	423
GUITAR	35	EPI	**DELUXE** SUNBURST, ARCHTOP	2,390	**1,767**	1,518	1,269
GUITAR	38	EPI	**DELUXE** SUNBURST, ARCHTOP	2,271	**1,679**	1,443	1,206
GUITAR	39	EPI	**DELUXE** SUNBURST, ARCHTOP	3,252	**2,405**	2,066	1,727
GUITAR	42	EPI	**DELUXE** BLOND	3,404	**2,517**	2,163	1,808
GUITAR	43	EPI	**DELUXE** NATURAL	1,912	**1,414**	1,215	1,015
GUITAR	46	EPI	**DELUXE** SUNBURST, ARCHTOP	3,840	**2,840**	2,440	2,040
GUITAR	48	EPI	**DELUXE** NEW YORK ARCHTOP	1,593	**1,178**	1,012	846

TYPE	YR	MFG	PRICES--BASED ON 100% ORIGINAL MODEL	SELL EXC	SELL AVG	BUY EXC	BUY AVG
GUITAR	50	EPI	**DELUXE** BLOND	1,591	**1,177**	1,011	845
GUITAR	51	EPI	**DELUXE** SUNBURST, ARCHTOP	1,975	**1,461**	1,255	1,049
GUITAR	51	EPI	**DELUXE** NATURAL, CUTAWAY	3,060	**2,263**	1,944	1,625
GUITAR	52	EPI	**DELUXE** SUNBURST	1,584	**1,171**	1,006	841
GUITAR	53	EPI	**DELUXE** SUNBURST	1,591	**1,177**	1,011	845
GUITAR	55	EPI	**DELUXE** NATURAL	1,586	**1,173**	1,008	843
GUITAR	55	EPI	**DELUXE** SUNBURST, ARCHTOP	1,992	**1,473**	1,265	1,058
GUITAR	55	EPI	**DELUXE** NATURAL, CUTAWAY	2,989	**2,210**	1,899	1,588
GUITAR	50	EPI	**DEVON** SUNBURST, NEW YORK ARCHTOP	1,688	**1,248**	1,072	897
GUITAR	50	EPI	**DEVON** BLOND, NEW YORK ARCHTOP	1,938	**1,433**	1,231	1,029
GUITAR	51	EPI	**DEVON** OVAL FINGERBOARD INLAY	1,765	**1,305**	1,121	937
GUITAR	53	EPI	**DEVON** SUNBURST, NEW YORK ARCHTOP	1,426	**1,055**	906	757
GUITAR	54	EPI	**DEVON** SUNBURST	717	**530**	455	380
GUITAR	55	EPI	**DEVON** SUNBURST, NEW YORK ARCHTOP, OVAL FINGERBOARD INLAY	1,193	**882**	758	633
GUITAR	50	EPI	**DOUBLE ARCHTOP** F-HOLE	522	**386**	331	277
GUITAR	38	EPI	**ELECTAR** FLATTOP, F-HOLE	518	**383**	329	275
GUITAR	36	EPI	**ELECTAR SPANISH** BLOND	1,191	**881**	757	632
GUITAR	37	EPI	**ELECTAR SPANISH** ELECTRIC ARCHTOP	534	**395**	339	284
GUITAR	39	EPI	**EMPEROR** SUNBURST, ARCHTOP	4,560	**3,372**	2,897	2,422
GUITAR	40	EPI	**EMPEROR** SUNBURST	3,739	**2,765**	2,375	1,986
GUITAR	51	EPI	**EMPEROR** NATURAL, ARCHTOP	3,696	**2,733**	2,348	1,963
GUITAR	54	EPI	**EMPEROR** NATURAL, CUTAWAY, ARCHTOP	4,512	**3,337**	2,867	2,397
GUITAR	54	EPI	**EMPEROR** NATURAL, CUTAWAY, ARCHTOP, NEW YORK PU's	4,678	**3,459**	2,972	2,485
GUITAR	52	EPI	**ESTRELLA** BLOND, SPRUCE TOP	677	**501**	430	360
GUITAR	44	EPI	**FT- 30** MAHOGANY BROWN	557	**412**	354	296
GUITAR	44	EPI	**FT- 45** NATURAL	955	**706**	606	507
GUITAR	45	EPI	**FT- 75** NEW YORK FLATTOP	751	**555**	477	399
GUITAR	44	EPI	**FT- 79 TEXAN** MAPLE BACK/SIDES, FLATTOP	1,981	**1,465**	1,259	1,052
GUITAR	48	EPI	**FT- 79 TEXAN** MAPLE BACK/SIDES, FLATTOP	1,131	**837**	719	601
GUITAR	49	EPI	**FT- 79 TEXAN** MAPLE BACK/SIDES, FLATTOP	1,887	**1,395**	1,199	1,002
GUITAR	53	EPI	**FT- 79 TEXAN** MAPLE BACK/SIDES, FLATTOP	998	**738**	634	530
GUITAR	44	EPI	**FT-110** NATURAL	1,115	**825**	708	592
GUITAR	50	EPI	**FT-110** FLATTOP	1,492	**1,104**	948	793
GUITAR	51	EPI	**FT-110** FLATTOP	1,451	**1,073**	922	771
GUITAR	52	EPI	**FT-110** FLATTOP	1,319	**975**	838	700
GUITAR	53	EPI	**FT-110** FLATTOP	1,309	**968**	832	695
GUITAR	52	EPI	**FT-210 DELUXE** CUTAWAY, NEW YORK FLATTOP	1,993	**1,474**	1,266	1,059
GUITAR	38	EPI	**MADRID** SUNBURST, NEW YORK FLATTOP	1,331	**984**	846	707
GUITAR	39	EPI	**MADRID** SUNBURST, NEW YORK FLATTOP	1,328	**982**	844	705
GUITAR	36	EPI	**NAVARRE** HAWAIIAN, MASTERBUILT LABEL	871	**664**	564	431
GUITAR	38	EPI	**NAVARRE** SUNBURST, NEW YORK FLATTOP	705	**537**	456	349
GUITAR	32	EPI	**OLYMPIC** MAHOGANY, ARCHTOP	576	**426**	366	306

TYPE	YR	MFG	PRICES--BASED ON 100% ORIGINAL MODEL	SELL EXC	SELL AVG	BUY EXC	BUY AVG
GUITAR	33	EPI	**OLYMPIC** SUNBURST, ARCHTOP	674	**499**	428	358
GUITAR	35	EPI	**OLYMPIC** MAHOGANY, ARCHTOP	664	**491**	422	352
GUITAR	39	EPI	**OLYMPIC** SUNBURST, ARCHTOP	650	**481**	413	345
GUITAR	40	EPI	**OLYMPIC** SUNBURST, ARCHTOP	604	**447**	384	321
GUITAR	41	EPI	**OLYMPIC** SUNBURST, ARCHTOP	569	**421**	361	302
GUITAR	43	EPI	**OLYMPIC** TENOR, SUNBURST, ARCHTOP	536	**396**	340	285
GUITAR	44	EPI	**OLYMPIC** SUNBURST, ARCHTOP	495	**366**	314	263
GUITAR	27	EPI	**RECORDING A** NEW YORK FLATTOP	851	**648**	551	421
GUITAR	28	EPI	**RECORDING A** NEW YORK FLATTOP	992	**734**	630	527
GUITAR	24	EPI	**RECORDING D** NEW YORK ARCHTOP	1,116	**825**	709	593
GUITAR	27	EPI	**RECORDING D** NEW YORK ARCHTOP	790	**602**	512	391
GUITAR	28	EPI	**RECORDING D** NEW YORK ARCHTOP	939	**695**	597	499
GUITAR	28	EPI	**RECORDING E** SUNBURST	2,231	**1,650**	1,417	1,185
GUITAR	44	EPI	**RITZ** NATURAL, TORTOISE SHELL BINDING	599	**443**	380	318
GUITAR	33	EPI	**ROYAL MASTERBILT** SUNBURST, MAHOGANY BACK/SIDES	677	**501**	430	360
GUITAR	34	EPI	**ROYAL MASTERBILT** SUNBURST, WALNUT BACK/SIDES	528	**391**	336	281
GUITAR	34	EPI	**SPARTAN** SUNBURST	781	**577**	496	415
GUITAR	35	EPI	**SPARTAN** SUNBURST	637	**471**	405	338
GUITAR	38	EPI	**SPARTAN** SUNBURST	681	**504**	433	362
GUITAR	44	EPI	**SPARTAN** SUNBURST, ARCHTOP, WALNUT BACK/SIDES,GREACIAN COLUMN INLAY	757	**560**	481	402
GUITAR	45	EPI	**SPARTAN** SUNBURST, NEW YORK ARCHTOP	653	**483**	415	347
GUITAR	47	EPI	**SPARTAN** BLOND	653	**483**	415	347
GUITAR	33	EPI	**TRIUMPH** SUNBURST, NON-CUTAWAY	2,305	**1,705**	1,465	1,225
GUITAR	34	EPI	**TRIUMPH** SUNBURST, NON-CUTAWAY	1,874	**1,386**	1,191	996
GUITAR	35	EPI	**TRIUMPH** SUNBURST, NON-CUTAWAY	1,809	**1,338**	1,149	961
GUITAR	38	EPI	**TRIUMPH** SUNBURST, NON-CUTAWAY	1,746	**1,291**	1,109	927
GUITAR	41	EPI	**TRIUMPH** SUNBURST, NON-CUTAWAY	1,696	**1,254**	1,077	901
GUITAR	43	EPI	**TRIUMPH** SUNBURST, NON-CUTAWAY	1,614	**1,194**	1,026	857
GUITAR	44	EPI	**TRIUMPH** SUNBURST, NON-CUTAWAY	1,568	**1,160**	996	833
GUITAR	45	EPI	**TRIUMPH** SUNBURST, NON-CUTAWAY	1,502	**1,111**	954	798
GUITAR	46	EPI	**TRIUMPH** SUNBURST, NON-CUTAWAY	1,441	**1,066**	916	766
GUITAR	46	EPI	**TRIUMPH** NATURAL BLOND, NON-CUTAWAY	1,797	**1,329**	1,141	954
GUITAR	47	EPI	**TRIUMPH** SUNBURST, NON-CUTAWAY	1,412	**1,044**	897	750
GUITAR	47	EPI	**TRIUMPH** NATURAL BLOND, NON-CUTAWAY	1,759	**1,301**	1,118	934
GUITAR	48	EPI	**TRIUMPH** SUNBURST, NON-CUTAWAY	1,368	**1,011**	869	726
GUITAR	49	EPI	**TRIUMPH** NATURAL BLOND, NON-CUTAWAY	1,649	**1,219**	1,047	876
GUITAR	51	EPI	**TRIUMPH** SUNBURST, NON-CUTAWAY	1,310	**969**	832	696
GUITAR	53	EPI	**TRIUMPH** SUNBURST, NON-CUTAWAY	1,533	**1,133**	974	814
GUITAR	55	EPI	**TRIUMPH** TENOR, NATURAL BLOND	705	**521**	448	374
GUITAR	50	EPI	**TRIUMPH REGENT** NATURAL BLOND, CUTAWAY	2,076	**1,535**	1,319	1,103
GUITAR	51	EPI	**TRIUMPH REGENT** SUNBURST, CUTAWAY	2,045	**1,513**	1,299	1,086
GUITAR	51	EPI	**TRIUMPH REGENT** NATURAL BLOND, CUTAWAY	2,055	**1,520**	1,306	1,091

TYPE	YR	MFG	PRICES--BASED ON 100% ORIGINAL MODEL	SELL EXC	SELL AVG	BUY EXC	BUY AVG
GUITAR	52	EPI	**TRIUMPH REGENT** NATURAL BLOND, CUTAWAY	2,038	**1,507**	1,295	1,082
GUITAR	53	EPI	**TRIUMPH REGENT** SUNBURST, CUTAWAY	2,908	**2,151**	1,848	1,545
GUITAR	30	EPI	**ZENITH** SUNBURST	750	**555**	477	398
GUITAR	32	EPI	**ZENITH** SUNBURST	735	**543**	467	390
GUITAR	33	EPI	**ZENITH** SUNBURST	719	**531**	456	381
GUITAR	34	EPI	**ZENITH** SUNBURST	698	**516**	444	371
GUITAR	35	EPI	**ZENITH** SUNBURST	688	**509**	437	365
GUITAR	36	EPI	**ZENITH** SUNBURST, LEFT-HANDED	657	**486**	417	349
GUITAR	36	EPI	**ZENITH** SUNBURST	677	**501**	430	360
GUITAR	37	EPI	**ZENITH** SUNBURST	663	**490**	421	352
GUITAR	42	EPI	**ZENITH** SUNBURST	630	**466**	400	335
GUITAR	43	EPI	**ZENITH** SUNBURST	633	**468**	402	336
GUITAR	44	EPI	**ZENITH** SUNBURST	618	**457**	392	328
GUITAR	47	EPI	**ZENITH** SUNBURST	597	**441**	379	317
GUITAR	48	EPI	**ZENITH** SUNBURST	588	**435**	373	312
GUITAR	49	EPI	**ZENITH** SUNBURST	576	**426**	366	306
GUITAR	50	EPI	**ZENITH** SUNBURST	564	**417**	358	299
GUITAR	51	EPI	**ZENITH** SUNBURST	555	**411**	353	295
GUITAR	52	EPI	**ZENITH** SUNBURST	549	**406**	348	291
GUITAR	53	EPI	**ZENITH** SUNBURST	535	**396**	340	284
MANDOLIN	35	EPI	**ADELPHI** SUNBURST, F-HOLES	796	**589**	506	423
MANDOL	39	EPI	**ADELPHI** SUNBURST, F-HOLES	757	**560**	481	402
MANDOL	44	EPI	**ADELPHI** SUNBURST, F-HOLES	748	**553**	475	397
MANDOL	45	EPI	**ADELPHI** SUNBURST, F-HOLES	876	**648**	556	465
MANDOL	47	EPI	**ADELPHI** SUNBURST, F-HOLES	715	**528**	454	379
MANDOL	44	EPI	**RIVOLI** SUNBURST, A STYLE	795	**588**	505	422
MANDOL	51	EPI	**RIVOLI** SUNBURST, OVAL SOUND HOLE	480	**355**	305	255
MANDOL	34	EPI	**STRAND** SUNBURST, MASTERBUILT PEGHEAD	1,155	**854**	734	614
MANDOL	44	EPI	**STRAND** SUNBURST, CENTER-DIP PEGHEAD	677	**501**	430	360
STEEL GUITAR	40	EPI	**CENTURY LAP STEEL** BLACK, 6-STRING	410	**303**	261	218
STGUIT	51	EPI	**CENTURY LAP STEEL** SUNBURST	432	**320**	275	230
STGUIT	52	EPI	**CENTURY LAP STEEL** BLACK	478	**353**	303	253
STGUIT	41	EPI	**CORONET** BLACK, 6-STRING, BLADE PU	598	**442**	380	317
STGUIT	37	EPI	**ELECTAR C** SUNBURST	478	**353**	303	253
STGUIT	37	EPI	**ELECTAR M** BLACK	470	**347**	298	249
STGUIT	38	EPI	**ELECTAR M** BLUE ART DECO	401	**296**	254	213
STGUIT	39	EPI	**ELECTAR M** BLACK	489	**362**	311	260
STGUIT	43	EPI	**ELECTAR ZEPHYR LAP STEEL** 8-STRING	474	**350**	301	251
UKULELE	50	EPI	**BARITONE**	240	**177**	152	127

EPIPHONE

BANJO	68	EPIPHONE	**ARTIST TENOR**	737	**545**	468	391
BANJO	63	EPIPHONE	**CAMPUS LONGNECK**	447	**330**	284	237
BANJO	64	EPIPHONE	**LONG NECK PETE SEEGER STYLE** 5-STRING	445	**329**	283	236

TYPE	YR	MFG	PRICES--BASED ON 100% ORIGINAL MODEL	SELL EXC	SELL AVG	BUY EXC	BUY AVG
BANJO	65	EPIPHONE	**LONG NECK POT** 5-STRING	443	**328**	281	235
BANJO	67	EPIPHONE	**MINISTREL**	637	**471**	405	338
BANJO	65	EPIPHONE	**MINSTREL** FLAT HEAD MASTERTONE STYLE TONE RING	447	**330**	284	237
BANJO	65	EPIPHONE	**MINSTREL**	717	**530**	455	380
BANJO	67	EPIPHONE	**MINSTREL** EB-88 1 PIECE FLANGE, SERIAL #056285	832	**615**	528	442
ELEC. GUITAR	58	EPIPHONE	**BROADWAY** NATURAL, 1 ROUNDED CUTAWAY	947	**700**	602	503
ELGUIT	59	EPIPHONE	**BROADWAY** SUNBURST, 1 ROUNDED CUTAWAY	836	**618**	531	444
ELGUIT	61	EPIPHONE	**BROADWAY** BLOND, 1 ROUNDED CUTAWAY	687	**508**	436	365
ELGUIT	63	EPIPHONE	**BROADWAY** NATURAL, 1 ROUNDED CUTAWAY	647	**478**	411	343
ELGUIT	63	EPIPHONE	**BROADWAY** SUNBURST, 1 ROUNDED CUTAWAY	738	**545**	469	392
ELGUIT	64	EPIPHONE	**BROADWAY** SUNBURST, 1 ROUNDED CUTAWAY	732	**541**	465	389
ELGUIT	65	EPIPHONE	**BROADWAY** SUNBURST, 1 ROUNDED CUTAWAY	662	**489**	420	351
ELGUIT	65	EPIPHONE	**BROADWAY** BLOND, HOLLOW BODY	768	**568**	488	408
ELGUIT	66	EPIPHONE	**BROADWAY** SUNBURST, 1 ROUNDED CUTAWAY	776	**574**	493	412
ELGUIT	66	EPIPHONE	**BROADWAY** BLOND, HOLLOW BODY	803	**594**	510	426
ELGUIT	67	EPIPHONE	**BROADWAY** SUNBURST, 1 ROUNDED CUTAWAY	621	**459**	394	329
ELGUIT	67	EPIPHONE	**BROADWAY** CHERRY, HOLLOW BODY	745	**551**	473	396
ELGUIT	68	EPIPHONE	**BROADWAY** SUNBURST, HOLLOW BODY	497	**367**	315	264
ELGUIT	68	EPIPHONE	**BROADWAY** NATURAL, 1 ROUNDED CUTAWAY	517	**382**	328	274
ELGUIT	69	EPIPHONE	**BROADWAY** SUNBURST, 1 ROUNDED CUTAWAY	491	**363**	312	261
ELGUIT	69	EPIPHONE	**BROADWAY** SUNBURST	756	**559**	480	401
ELGUIT	67	EPIPHONE	**CAIOLA CUSTOM** YELLOW SUNBURST	1,180	**873**	750	627
ELGUIT	68	EPIPHONE	**CAIOLA CUSTOM** WALNUT, 2 MINI HUMBUCKERS	1,213	**897**	771	644
ELGUIT	68	EPIPHONE	**CAIOLA CUSTOM** CHERRY, 2 MINI HUMBUCKERS	1,214	**898**	771	645
ELGUIT	69	EPIPHONE	**CAIOLA CUSTOM** WALNUT, 2 MINI HUMBUCKERS	1,172	**866**	744	622
ELGUIT	64	EPIPHONE	**CAIOLA ROYAL** TAN, 2 MINI HUMBUCKERS	885	**654**	562	470
ELGUIT	65	EPIPHONE	**CAIOLA ROYAL** TAN, 2 MINI HUMBUCKERS	882	**652**	560	468
ELGUIT	65	EPIPHONE	**CAIOLA STANDARD** WALNUT, 2 MINI HUMBUCKERS	879	**650**	558	467
ELGUIT	65	EPIPHONE	**CAIOLA STANDARD** SUNBURST, 2 P-90's	881	**651**	559	468
ELGUIT	66	EPIPHONE	**CAIOLA STANDARD** CHERRY, 2 P-90's	880	**651**	559	467
ELGUIT	67	EPIPHONE	**CAIOLA STANDARD** CHERRY, 2 P-90's	878	**649**	558	466
ELGUIT	67	EPIPHONE	**CAIOLA STANDARD** SUNBURST, 2 P-90's	878	**649**	558	466
ELGUIT	68	EPIPHONE	**CAIOLA STANDARD** SUNBURST, 2 P-90's	1,003	**741**	637	532
ELGUIT	69	EPIPHONE	**CAIOLA STANDARD** CHERRY, 2 P-90's	877	**648**	557	466
ELGUIT	61	EPIPHONF	**CASINO** SUNBURST, DOUBLE CUTAWAY, 2 PU's, NON-VIB	851	**629**	541	452
ELGUIT	62	EPIPHONE	**CASINO** SUNBURST, DOUBLE CUTAWAY, 1 PU	564	**417**	358	299
ELGUIT	63	EPIPHONE	**CASINO** SUNBURST, DOUBLE CUTAWAY, 1 PU, VIBRATO	525	**388**	333	278
ELGUIT	63	EPIPHONE	**CASINO** SUNBURST, DOUBLE CUTAWAY, 1 PU, LEFT-HANDED	556	**411**	353	295
ELGUIT	64	EPIPHONE	**CASINO** CHERRY, DOUBLE CUTAWAY, 1 PU	469	**347**	298	249
ELGUIT	65	EPIPHONE	**CASINO** SUNBURST, DOUBLE CUTAWAY, 2 PU's	628	**465**	399	334
ELGUIT	65	EPIPHONE	**CASINO** CHERRY, DOUBLE CUTAWAY, 2 PU's	956	**707**	607	507
ELGUIT	66	EPIPHONE	**CASINO** SUNBURST, DOUBLE CUTAWAY, 1 PU, VIBRATO	586	**433**	372	311
ELGUIT	66	EPIPHONE	**CASINO** SUNBURST, DOUBLE CUTAWAY, 2 PU's	895	**662**	569	475

TYPE	YR	MFG	PRICES--BASED ON 100% ORIGINAL MODEL	SELL EXC	SELL AVG	BUY EXC	BUY AVG
ELGUIT	67	EPIPHONE	**CASINO** CHERRY, DOUBLE CUTAWAY, 1 PU, VIBRATO	469	**347**	298	249
ELGUIT	67	EPIPHONE	**CASINO** SUNBURST, DOUBLE CUTAWAY, 1 PU	506	**374**	322	269
ELGUIT	67	EPIPHONE	**CASINO** SUNBURST, DOUBLE CUTAWAY, 2 PU's	540	**399**	343	287
FLGUIT	68	EPIPHONE	**CASINO** SUNBURST, DOUBLE CUTAWAY, 2 PU's	438	**324**	278	233
ELGUIT	68	EPIPHONE	**CASINO** SUNBURST, 1 PU	469	**347**	298	249
ELGUIT	68	EPIPHONE	**CASINO** CHERRY, 2 PU's	484	**358**	308	257
ELGUIT	69	EPIPHONE	**CASINO** CHERRY, DOUBLE CUTAWAY, 1 PU, VIBRATO	478	**353**	303	253
ELGUIT	58	EPIPHONE	**CENTURY** SUNBURST, NON-CUTAWAY, 1 PU	577	**427**	367	307
ELGUIT	59	EPIPHONE	**CENTURY** SUNBURST, NON-CUTAWAY, 1 PU	490	**362**	311	260
ELGUIT	60	EPIPHONE	**CENTURY** BURGUNDY, NON-CUTAWAY, 1 PU	532	**394**	338	283
ELGUIT	60	EPIPHONE	**CENTURY** SUNBURST, NON-CUTAWAY, 1 PU	533	**394**	339	283
ELGUIT	61	EPIPHONE	**CENTURY** BURGUNDY, NON-CUTAWAY, 1 PU	519	**384**	330	275
ELGUIT	64	EPIPHONE	**CENTURY** BURGUNDY	529	**391**	336	281
ELGUIT	65	EPIPHONE	**CENTURY** BURGUNDY, NON-CUTAWAY, 1 PU	518	**383**	329	275
ELGUIT	66	EPIPHONE	**CENTURY** SUNBURST, NON-CUTAWAY, 1 PU	533	**394**	339	283
ELGUIT	68	EPIPHONE	**CENTURY** SUNBURST, NON-CUTAWAY, 1 PU	498	**368**	316	264
ELGUIT	58	EPIPHONE	**CORONET** SUNBURST, 1 PU	364	**269**	231	193
ELGUIT	59	EPIPHONE	**CORONET** BLACK, 1 PU	357	**264**	226	189
ELGUIT	61	EPIPHONE	**CORONET** CHERRY, 1 PU	352	**260**	223	187
ELGUIT	62	EPIPHONE	**CORONET** CHERRY, 1 PU	328	**242**	208	174
ELGUIT	63	EPIPHONE	**CORONET** CHERRY, 1 PU	311	**230**	197	165
ELGUIT	63	EPIPHONE	**CORONET** GREEN, 1 PU	312	**230**	198	165
ELGUIT	64	EPIPHONE	**CORONET** CHERRY, 1 PU	289	**214**	184	154
ELGUIT	65	EPIPHONE	**CORONET** CHERRY, 1 PU	277	**205**	176	147
ELGUIT	65	EPIPHONE	**CORONET** TRANSPARENT GREEN, 1 PU	277	**205**	176	147
ELGUIT	66	EPIPHONE	**CORONET** CHERRY, 1 PU	264	**195**	168	140
ELGUIT	61	EPIPHONE	**CRESTWOOD CUSTOM** WHITE, 2 MINI HUMBUCKERS	535	**396**	340	284
ELGUIT	65	EPIPHONE	**CRESTWOOD CUSTOM** RED, 2 MINI HUMBUCKERS, VIB	422	**312**	268	224
ELGUIT	67	EPIPHONE	**CRESTWOOD CUSTOM** WHITE, 2 MINI HUMBUCKERS, VIB	362	**268**	230	192
ELGUIT	68	EPIPHONE	**CRESTWOOD CUSTOM** RED, 2 MINI HUMBUCKERS, VIB	347	**257**	220	184
ELGUIT	63	EPIPHONE	**CRESTWOOD DELUXE** RED, 3 MINI HUMBUCKERS, VIB	499	**369**	317	265
ELGUIT	65	EPIPHONE	**CRESTWOOD DELUXE** WHITE, 3 MINI HUMBUCKERS, VIB	420	**310**	267	223
ELGUIT	65	EPIPHONE	**CRESTWOOD DELUXE** RED, 3 MINI HUMBUCKERS, VIB	432	**319**	274	229
ELGUIT	66	EPIPHONE	**CRESTWOOD DELUXE** RED, 3 MINI HUMBUCKERS, VIB	478	**353**	303	253
ELGUIT	59	EPIPHONE	**DELUXE CUTAWAY MODEL A-212** SUNBURST	5,525	**4,086**	3,511	2,935
ELGUIT	50	EPIPHONE	**DELUXE REGENT** SUNBURST, NEW YORK ARCHTOP	887	**656**	563	471
ELGUIT	66	EPIPHONE	**DWIGHT** CHERRY, SOLID BODY, 1 PU	552	**408**	351	293
ELGUIT	67	EPIPHONE	**DWIGHT** CHERRY, SOLID BODY, 1 PU	542	**401**	344	288
ELGUIT	64	EPIPHONE	**EMBASSY DELUXE BASS** RED, SOLID BODY	955	**706**	606	507
ELGUIT	65	EPIPHONE	**EMBASSY DELUXE BASS** RED, SOLID BODY	678	**501**	431	360
ELGUIT	68	EPIPHONE	**EMBASSY DELUXE BASS** RED, SOLID BODY	721	**533**	458	383
ELGUIT	61	EPIPHONE	**EMPEROR** NATURAL	1,354	**1,001**	860	719

TYPE	YR	MFG	PRICES--BASED ON 100% ORIGINAL MODEL	SELL EXC	SELL AVG	BUY EXC	BUY AVG
ELGUIT	62	EPIPHONE	**EMPEROR** SUNBURST	1,313	**971**	834	697
ELGUIT	63	EPIPHONE	**EMPEROR** CURLY MAPLE, 18 1/2" WIDE	1,304	**964**	828	693
ELGUIT	64	EPIPHONE	**EMPEROR** SUNBURST	1,330	**984**	845	706
ELGUIT	78	EPIPHONE	**EMPEROR JAZZ BOX** BLOND,SPRUCE TOP,FLAMED MAPLE GACK/SIDES/NECK,HB's	451	**333**	286	239
ELGUIT	68	EPIPHONE	**ENTRADA EC-90**	220	**168**	142	109
ELGUIT	60	EPIPHONE	**GRANADA** SUNBURST, DOT INLAY, NON-CUTAWAY	451	**333**	286	239
ELGUIT	64	EPIPHONE	**GRANADA** SUNBURST, DOT INLAY, NON-CUTAWAY	433	**320**	275	230
ELGUIT	65	EPIPHONE	**GRANADA** SUNBURST, VINE INLAY	557	**412**	354	296
ELGUIT	67	EPIPHONE	**GRANADA** SUNBURST, DOT INLAY, CUTAWAY	605	**448**	384	321
ELGUIT	68	EPIPHONE	**GRANADA** SUNBURST, DOT INLAY, CUTAWAY	641	**474**	407	340
ELGUIT	64	EPIPHONE	**HOWARD ROBERTS** SUNBURST, HOLLOW	1,424	**1,053**	905	756
ELGUIT	65	EPIPHONE	**HOWARD ROBERTS** SUNBURST	1,193	**882**	758	633
ELGUIT	65	EPIPHONE	**HOWARD ROBERTS** BLOND, HOLLOW	1,507	**1,114**	957	800
ELGUIT	66	EPIPHONE	**HOWARD ROBERTS** WALNUT, HOLLOW	1,169	**864**	742	621
ELGUIT	68	EPIPHONE	**HOWARD ROBERTS**	1,084	**802**	689	576
ELGUIT	68	EPIPHONE	**HOWARD ROBERTS** NATURAL	1,174	**868**	746	623
ELGUIT	65	EPIPHONE	**HOWARD ROBERTS CUSTOM** BLACK, TUN-O-MAT	1,228	**908**	780	652
ELGUIT	67	EPIPHONE	**HOWARD ROBERTS SE** SUNBURST, HOLLOW	1,164	**861**	739	618
ELGUIT	61	EPIPHONE	**NEWPORT BASS** SOLID CHERRY, 1 PU	472	**349**	300	250
ELGUIT	62	EPIPHONE	**NEWPORT BASS** SOLID CHERRY, 1 PU	469	**347**	298	249
ELGUIT	63	EPIPHONE	**NEWPORT BASS** 2 PU's	459	**340**	292	244
ELGUIT	63	EPIPHONE	**NEWPORT BASS** SOLID CHERRY, 1 PU	462	**342**	294	245
ELGUIT	63	EPIPHONE	**NEWPORT BASS** CHERRY, 2 PU's	497	**367**	315	264
ELGUIT	65	EPIPHONE	**NEWPORT BASS** SOLID CHERRY, 1 PU,BAT WING HEADSTOCK	427	**315**	271	226
ELGUIT	67	EPIPHONE	**NEWPORT BASS** SOLID CHERRY, 1 PU	424	**313**	269	225
ELGUIT	68	EPIPHONE	**NEWPORT BASS** SOLID CHERRY, 1 PU	461	**341**	293	245
ELGUIT	60	EPIPHONE	**OLYMPIC** SUNBURST, 1 PU, SINGLE CUTAWAY	460	**340**	292	244
ELGUIT	61	EPIPHONE	**OLYMPIC** SUNBURST, 1 PU, SINGLE CUTAWAY	448	**331**	284	238
ELGUIT	62	EPIPHONE	**OLYMPIC** SUNBURST, 1 PU, 3/4 SCALE	440	**325**	279	234
ELGUIT	64	EPIPHONE	**OLYMPIC** SUNBURST, 1 PU, DOUBLE CUTAWAY	422	**312**	268	224
ELGUIT	65	EPIPHONE	**OLYMPIC** CHERRY, 1 PU	403	**298**	256	214
ELGUIT	65	EPIPHONE	**OLYMPIC** INVERNESS GREEN, 2 PU's	403	**298**	256	214
ELGUIT	65	EPIPHONE	**OLYMPIC** CALIFORNIA CORAL, 1 PU	415	**307**	264	220
ELGUIT	65	EPIPHONE	**OLYMPIC** SUNBURST, 1 PU	429	**317**	272	227
ELGUIT	65	EPIPHONE	**OLYMPIC** CHERRY, 2 PU's	478	**353**	303	253
ELGUIT	66	EPIPHONE	**OLYMPIC** SUNBURST, 1 PU, VIBRATO	488	**361**	310	259
ELGUIT	67	EPIPHONE	**OLYMPIC** CHERRY, 1 PU	478	**353**	303	253
ELGUIT	68	EPIPHONE	**OLYMPIC** CHERRY, BATWING	379	**280**	240	201
ELGUIT	68	EPIPHONE	**OLYMPIC** SUNBURST, 1 PU, BATWING PEGHEAD	458	**339**	291	243
ELGUIT	69	EPIPHONE	**OLYMPIC** CHERRY, 1 PU, VIBRATO	433	**320**	275	230
ELGUIT	60	EPIPHONE	**OLYMPIC 3/4** SUNBURST, SINGLE CUTAWAY	486	**359**	309	258
ELGUIT	60	EPIPHONE	**OLYMPIC DOUBLE** SINGLE CUTAWAY	457	**338**	290	243
ELGUIT	64	EPIPHONE	**OLYMPIC DOUBLE** SUNBURST, 2 PU's	480	**355**	305	255

TYPE	YR	MFG	PRICES--BASED ON 100% ORIGINAL MODEL	SELL EXC	SELL AVG	BUY EXC	BUY AVG
ELGUIT	65	EPIPHONE	**OLYMPIC DOUBLE** SUNBURST, 2 PU's	469	**347**	298	249
ELGUIT	65	EPIPHONE	**OLYMPIC DOUBLE** CHERRY, 2 PU's	472	**349**	300	250
ELGUIT	66	EPIPHONE	**OLYMPIC DOUBLE** CHERRY, 2 PU's	488	**361**	310	259
ELGUIT	67	EPIPHONE	**OLYMPIC DOUBLE** SPARKLING BURGUNDY	494	**365**	314	262
ELGUIT	68	EPIPHONE	**OLYMPIC DOUBLE** CHERRY	489	**362**	311	260
ELGUIT	69	EPIPHONE	**OLYMPIC DOUBLE** DOUBLE CUTAWAY	480	**355**	305	255
ELGUIT	62	EPIPHONE	**OLYMPIC SPECIAL** SUNBURST	496	**367**	315	263
ELGUIT	63	EPIPHONE	**OLYMPIC SPECIAL** SUNBURST	493	**364**	313	262
ELGUIT	64	EPIPHONE	**OLYMPIC SPECIAL** SUNBURST, DOUBLE CUTAWAY	489	**362**	311	260
ELGUIT	65	EPIPHONE	**OLYMPIC SPECIAL** SUNBURST, DOUBLE CUTAWAY	496	**367**	315	263
ELGUIT	67	EPIPHONE	**OLYMPIC SPECIAL** SUNBURST	494	**365**	314	262
ELGUIT	62	EPIPHONE	**PROFESSIONAL** CHERRY, 1 PU	885	**654**	562	470
ELGUIT	65	EPIPHONE	**PROFESSIONAL** CHERRY	884	**653**	561	469
ELGUIT	63	EPIPHONE	**PROFESSIONAL THIN** SUNBURST, DOUBLE CUTAWAY	883	**653**	561	469
ELGUIT	65	EPIPHONE	**PROFESSIONAL THIN** CHERRY, DOUBLE CUTAWAY	883	**653**	561	469
ELGUIT	62	EPIPHONE	**RIVIERA**	1,434	**1,060**	911	761
ELGUIT	65	EPIPHONE	**RIVIERA** CHERRY, 12-STRING, FREQUENSATOR	459	**340**	292	244
ELGUIT	66	EPIPHONE	**RIVIERA** CHERRY, 12-STRING, FREQUENSATOR	494	**365**	314	262
ELGUIT	67	EPIPHONE	**RIVIERA** CHERRY, 12-STRING, FREQUENSATOR	432	**319**	274	229
ELGUIT	68	EPIPHONE	**RIVIERA** CHERRY, 12-STRING, FREQUENSATOR	509	**377**	323	270
ELGUIT	62	EPIPHONE	**RIVIERA THIN** TAN, FREQUENSATOR	500	**369**	317	265
ELGUIT	62	EPIPHONE	**RIVIERA THIN** SUNBURST, FREQUENSATOR	518	**383**	329	275
ELGUIT	63	EPIPHONE	**RIVIERA THIN** CHERRY, FREQUENSATOR	505	**374**	321	268
ELGUIT	64	EPIPHONE	**RIVIERA THIN** CHERRY, FREQUENSATOR	478	**353**	303	253
ELGUIT	65	EPIPHONE	**RIVIERA THIN** SUNBURST, FREQUENSATOR	476	**352**	302	252
ELGUIT	66	EPIPHONE	**RIVIERA THIN** SUNBURST, FREQUENSATOR	473	**350**	300	251
ELGUIT	66	EPIPHONE	**RIVIERA THIN** CHERRY, FREQUENSATOR	494	**365**	314	262
ELGUIT	67	EPIPHONE	**RIVIERA THIN** SUNBURST, FREQUENSATOR	477	**352**	303	253
ELGUIT	67	EPIPHONE	**RIVIERA THIN** CHERRY, FREQUENSATOR	478	**353**	303	253
ELGUIT	67	EPIPHONE	**RIVIERA THIN** GREEN, FREQUENSATOR	480	**355**	305	255
ELGUIT	68	EPIPHONE	**RIVIERA THIN** SUNBURST, FREQUENSATOR	460	**340**	292	244
ELGUIT	68	EPIPHONE	**RIVIERA THIN** CHERRY, FREQUENSATOR	463	**342**	294	246
ELGUIT	64	EPIPHONE	**RIVIERA THIN ROYAL** TAN, FREQUENSATOR	478	**353**	303	253
ELGUIT	64	EPIPHONE	**RIVOLI BASS** SUNBURST, SYMETR, DOUBLE CUTAWAY, 1 PU	847	**626**	538	450
ELGUIT	65	EPIPHONE	**RIVOLI BASS** SUNBURST, SYMETR, DOUBLE CUTAWAY, 1 PU	713	**527**	453	378
ELGUIT	67	EPIPHONE	**RIVOLI BASS** SUNBURST, SYMETR, DOUBLE CUTAWAY, 1 PU	810	**599**	514	430
ELGUIT	67	EPIPHONE	**RIVOLI BASS** NATURAL, SYMETR, DOUBLE CUTAWAY, 1 PU	811	**599**	515	430
ELGUIT	68	EPIPHONE	**RIVOLI BASS** SUNBURST, SYMETR, DOUBLE CUTAWAY, 1 PU	674	**499**	428	358
ELGUIT	58	EPIPHONE	**SHERATON** NATURAL, 2 NEW YORK PU's	5,520	**4,082**	3,507	2,932
ELGUIT	58	EPIPHONE	**SHERATON** NATURAL, 3 PU's	1,661	**1,229**	1,055	882
ELGUIT	61	EPIPHONE	**SHERATON** SUNBURST	684	**506**	434	363
ELGUIT	61	EPIPHONE	**SHERATON** NATURAL, 3 PU's	757	**560**	481	402

TYPE	YR	MFG	PRICES--BASED ON 100% ORIGINAL MODEL	SELL EXC	SELL AVG	BUY EXC	BUY AVG
ELGUIT	63	EPIPHONE	**SHERATON** SUNBURST	684	**506**	434	363
ELGUIT	64	EPIPHONE	**SHERATON** SUNBURST	613	**453**	389	325
ELGUIT	64	EPIPHONE	**SHERATON** NATURAL	684	**506**	434	363
ELGUIT	65	EPIPHONE	**SHERATON** GOLD-NATURAL, VIBRATO	533	**394**	339	283
ELGUIT	66	EPIPHONE	**SHERATON** NATURAL	522	**386**	331	277
ELGUIT	66	EPIPHONE	**SHERATON** CHERRY	531	**393**	337	282
ELGUIT	67	EPIPHONE	**SHERATON** CHERRY	456	**337**	290	242
ELGUIT	67	EPIPHONE	**SHERATON** SUNBURST	461	**341**	293	245
ELGUIT	67	EPIPHONE	**SHERATON** NATURAL	474	**350**	301	251
ELGUIT	68	EPIPHONE	**SHERATON** SUNBURST	467	**345**	297	248
ELGUIT	62	EPIPHONE	**SORRENTO** 2 PU's	757	**560**	481	402
ELGUIT	61	EPIPHONE	**SORRENTO THIN** SUNBURST	657	**486**	417	349
ELGUIT	62	EPIPHONE	**SORRENTO THIN**	650	**481**	413	345
ELGUIT	64	EPIPHONE	**SORRENTO THIN**	644	**476**	409	342
ELGUIT	65	EPIPHONE	**SORRENTO THIN** SUNBURST, 1 PU	637	**471**	405	338
ELGUIT	65	EPIPHONE	**SORRENTO THIN** NATURAL	639	**472**	406	339
ELGUIT	66	EPIPHONE	**SORRENTO THIN** SUNBURST	629	**465**	400	334
ELGUIT	67	EPIPHONE	**SORRENTO THIN** SUNBURST	624	**461**	396	331
ELGUIT	60	EPIPHONE	**WILSHIRE** SUNBURST	1,223	**904**	777	649
ELGUIT	61	EPIPHONE	**WILSHIRE** CHERRY	876	**648**	556	465
ELGUIT	62	EPIPHONE	**WILSHIRE** CHERRY	738	**545**	469	392
ELGUIT	63	EPIPHONE	**WILSHIRE** CHERRY	723	**535**	459	384
ELGUIT	63	EPIPHONE	**WILSHIRE** SUNBURST, 12-STRING	941	**696**	598	500
ELGUIT	64	EPIPHONE	**WILSHIRE** CHERRY	704	**521**	447	374
ELGUIT	65	EPIPHONE	**WILSHIRE** CHERRY	813	**601**	516	431
ELGUIT	66	EPIPHONE	**WILSHIRE** SUNBURST, 12-STRING	631	**467**	401	335
ELGUIT	66	EPIPHONE	**WILSHIRE** CHERRY, BATWING PEGHEAD	654	**484**	416	347
ELGUIT	67	EPIPHONE	**WILSHIRE** CHERRY	649	**480**	412	345
ELGUIT	68	EPIPHONE	**WILSHIRE** PACIFIC BLUE METALLIC	663	**490**	421	352
ELGUIT	68	EPIPHONE	**WILSHIRE** CHERRY, 12-STRING	796	**589**	506	423
ELGUIT	60	EPIPHONE	**WINDSOR** SUNBURST	760	**562**	483	403
ELGUIT	61	EPIPHONE	**WINDSOR** NATURAL	795	**588**	505	422
ELGUIT	60	EPIPHONE	**ZEPHYR** THINLINE	956	**707**	607	507
ELGUIT	65	EPIPHONE	**ZEPHYR EMPEROR REGENT** NATURAL, 3 ON-OFF TOGGLES	1,307	**967**	830	694
FLGUIT	58	EPIPHONE	**ZEPHYR REGENT** SUNBURST	1,115	**825**	708	592
ELGUIT	58	EPIPHONE	**ZEPHYR THIN** SUNBURST, CUTAWAY, 2 PU's	2,345	**1,734**	1,490	1,245
ELGUIT	59	EPIPHONE	**ZEPHYR THIN** SUNBURST, CUTAWAY, 2 PU's	1,483	**1,096**	942	787
ELGUIT	60	EPIPHONE	**ZEPHYR THIN** SUNBURST, CUTAWAY, 2 PU's	1,449	**1,072**	921	770
ELGUIT	61	EPIPHONE	**ZEPHYR THIN** NATURAL, CUTAWAY, 2 PU's	1,398	**1,034**	888	743
ELGUIT	61	EPIPHONE	**ZEPHYR THIN** SUNBURST, CUTAWAY, 2 PU's	1,421	**1,051**	903	755
GUITAR AMP	62	EPIPHONE	**CENTURY** 15" JENSEN	432	**319**	274	229
GTAMP	62	EPIPHONE	**DEVON** 10" SPEAKER	312	**230**	198	165
GTAMP	74	EPIPHONE	**E-65** 1x10", 5 WATT	95	**70**	60	50

TYPE	YR	MFG	PRICES--BASED ON 100% ORIGINAL MODEL	SELL EXC	SELL AVG	BUY EXC	BUY AVG
GTAMP	65	EPIPHONE	**GA-50**	242	**179**	154	129
GTAMP	63	EPIPHONE	**GALAXY** GREY, 1x10" JENSEN, REV TREM	242	**179**	154	129
GTAMP	65	EPIPHONE	**JMF H-25 HEAD**	240	**177**	152	127
GTAMP	66	EPIPHONE	**MAXIMA** 100 WATTS, 2 SPEAKER BOTTOMS,2x10" SPEAKERS IN EACH BOTTOM	168	**124**	106	89
GTAMP	62	EPIPHONE	**PACEMAKER**	186	**137**	118	98
GTAMP	64	EPIPHONE	**PACEMAKER**	168	**124**	107	89
GTAMP	65	EPIPHONE	**PACEMAKER** 1x8" SPEAKER	144	**106**	91	76
GTAMP	61	EPIPHONE	**PROFESSIONAL** CHERRY	577	**427**	367	307
GTAMP	60	EPIPHONE	**ZEPHYR**	196	**145**	125	104
GTAMP	61	EPIPHONE	**ZEPHYR** EA-15RV	480	**355**	305	255
GUITAR (ACOUSTIC)	66	EPIPHONE	**BARCELONA CLASSICAL** MAPLE BACK/SIDES	309	**228**	196	164
GUITAR	62	EPIPHONE	**BARD FT-112** NATURAL, 12-STRING, MAHOGANY	648	**479**	412	344
GUITAR	63	EPIPHONE	**BARD FT-112** NATURAL, 12-STRING, MAHOGANY	576	**426**	366	306
GUITAR	64	EPIPHONE	**BARD FT-112** NATURAL, 12-STRING	518	**383**	329	275
GUITAR	64	EPIPHONE	**BARD FT-112** NATURAL, 12-STRING, MAHOGANY	574	**424**	364	304
GUITAR	65	EPIPHONE	**BARD FT-112** NATURAL, 12-STRING	526	**389**	334	279
GUITAR	65	EPIPHONE	**BARD FT-112** NATURAL, 12-STRING, MAHOGANY	562	**416**	357	298
GUITAR	66	EPIPHONE	**BARD FT-112** NATURAL, 12-STRING, MAHOGANY	565	**418**	359	300
GUITAR	67	EPIPHONE	**BARD FT-112** NATURAL, 12-STRING	518	**383**	329	275
GUITAR	67	EPIPHONE	**BARD FT-112** NATURAL, 12-STRING, MAHOGANY	563	**416**	358	299
GUITAR	67	EPIPHONE	**BARD FT-112** SUNBURST, 12-STRING	574	**424**	364	304
GUITAR	61	EPIPHONE	**CABALLERO FT- 30** MAHOGANY, FLATTOP	285	**210**	181	151
GUITAR	63	EPIPHONE	**CABALLERO FT- 30** MAHOGANY, FLATTOP	276	**204**	175	146
GUITAR	64	EPIPHONE	**CABALLERO FT- 30** MAHOGANY, FLATTOP	249	**184**	158	132
GUITAR	65	EPIPHONE	**CABALLERO FT- 30** TENOR, MAHOGANY, FLATTOP	277	**205**	176	147
GUITAR	66	EPIPHONE	**CABALLERO FT- 30** MAHOGANY, FLATTOP	288	**213**	183	153
GUITAR	67	EPIPHONE	**CABALLERO FT- 30** MAHOGANY, FLATTOP	268	**198**	170	142
GUITAR	68	EPIPHONE	**CABALLERO FT- 30** MAHOGANY, FLATTOP	256	**189**	162	136
GUITAR	72	EPIPHONE	**CABALLERO FT- 30** MAHOGANY, FLATTOP	207	**153**	131	110
GUITAR	58	EPIPHONE	**CORTEZ FT- 45**	581	**430**	369	309
GUITAR	61	EPIPHONE	**CORTEZ FT- 45** SUNBURST, FLATTOP	557	**412**	354	296
GUITAR	64	EPIPHONE	**CORTEZ FT- 45** SUNBURST, FLATTOP	552	**408**	350	293
GUITAR	66	EPIPHONE	**CORTEZ FT- 45** SUNBURST, FLATTOP	547	**404**	347	290
GUITAR	67	EPIPHONE	**CORTEZ FT- 45**	542	**401**	344	288
GUITAR	65	EPIPHONE	**CORTEZ FT- 45N** NATURAL, FLATTOP	598	**442**	380	317
GUITAR	66	EPIPHONE	**CORTEZ FT- 45N** NATURAL, FLATTOP	591	**437**	375	314
GUITAR	67	FPIPHONE	**CORTEZ FT- 45N** BLOND, FLATTOP	586	**433**	372	311
GUITAR	68	EPIPHONE	**CORTEZ FT- 45N** BLOND, FLATTOP	557	**412**	354	296
GUITAR	59	EPIPHONE	**DELUXE REGENT** SUNBURST, ARCHTOP	3,628	**2,683**	2,305	1,927
GUITAR	63	EPIPHONE	**ELDORADO FT- 90** BLOND	943	**697**	599	501
GUITAR	65	EPIPHONE	**ELDORADO FT- 90** NATURAL, SERIAL #541164	863	**638**	548	458
GUITAR	65	EPIPHONE	**ELDORADO FT- 90** CHERRY SUNBURST	878	**649**	558	466
GUITAR	66	EPIPHONE	**ELDORADO FT- 90** CHERRY SUNBURST	856	**633**	544	454
GUITAR	68	EPIPHONE	**ELDORADO FT- 90** SUNBURST	649	**480**	412	345
GUITAR	69	EPIPHONE	**ELDORADO FT- 90** SUNBURST	624	**462**	397	332

TYPE	YR	MFG	PRICES--BASED ON 100% ORIGINAL MODEL	SELL EXC	SELL AVG	BUY EXC	BUY AVG
GUITAR	68	EPIPHONE	ELDORADO FT- 90N BLOND	574	424	364	304
GUITAR	59	EPIPHONE	EMPEROR SUNBURST, THINLINE	2,184	1,615	1,387	1,160
GUITAR	63	EPIPHONE	EMPEROR NATURAL, CURLY MAPLE	2,297	1,699	1,459	1,220
GUITAR	68	EPIPHONE	EMPEROR A-112 SUNBURST	1,031	762	655	547
GUITAR	63	EPIPHONE	EMPEROR A-112N BLOND	2,234	1,652	1,420	1,187
GUITAR	59	EPIPHONE	EMPEROR E-112T SUNBURST	4,268	3,156	2,712	2,267
GUITAR	65	EPIPHONE	EMPEROR E-112T BLOND	2,323	1,718	1,476	1,234
GUITAR	66	EPIPHONE	EMPEROR E-112T SUNBURST	3,227	2,387	2,050	1,714
GUITAR	59	EPIPHONE	EXCELLENTE FT-120 ROSEWOOD, FLATTOP	956	707	607	507
GUITAR	64	EPIPHONE	EXCELLENTE FT-120 ROSEWOOD, FLATTOP	949	702	603	504
GUITAR	66	EPIPHONE	EXCELLENTE FT-120 ROSEWOOD, FLATTOP	943	697	599	501
GUITAR	68	EPIPHONE	EXCELLENTE FT-120 ROSEWOOD, FLATTOP	876	648	556	465
GUITAR	63	EPIPHONE	EXCELLENTE FT-350	1,035	766	658	550
GUITAR	66	EPIPHONE	F- 20NT NATURAL, MAHOGANY BACK/SIDES	283	209	179	150
GUITAR	64	EPIPHONE	F- 25 WHITE PICKGUARDS, FLATTOP	439	325	279	233
GUITAR	64	EPIPHONE	F- 25 SPRUCE TOP, MAHOGANY BACK/SIDES	439	325	279	233
GUITAR	64	EPIPHONE	F- 25 NATURAL, FLATTOP	455	336	289	241
GUITAR	67	EPIPHONE	F- 25 SPRUCE TOP, MAHOGANY BACK/SIDES	428	316	272	227
GUITAR	66	EPIPHONE	F- 25 000 SIZE NATURAL, SPRUCE TOP	289	214	184	154
GUITAR	68	EPIPHONE	FOLKSTER FT- 95 FLATTOP	290	221	188	144
GUITAR	63	EPIPHONE	FRONTIER FT-110 NATURAL	453	335	287	240
GUITAR	64	EPIPHONE	FRONTIER FT-110 NATURAL	451	333	286	239
GUITAR	65	EPIPHONE	FRONTIER FT-110 NATURAL	448	331	284	238
GUITAR	66	EPIPHONE	FRONTIER FT-110 SUNBURST	444	328	282	236
GUITAR	66	EPIPHONE	FRONTIER FT-110 NATURAL	446	330	283	237
GUITAR	67	EPIPHONE	FRONTIER FT-110 SUNBURST	429	317	272	227
GUITAR	68	EPIPHONE	FRONTIER FT-110 NATURAL	487	360	309	259
GUITAR	68	EPIPHONE	FRONTIER FT-110 SUNBURST	491	363	312	261
GUITAR	64	EPIPHONE	FT- 28 TENOR, MAHOGANY	433	320	275	230
GUITAR	70	EPIPHONE	FT-165 ROSEWOOD BACK/SIDES, 12-STRING	339	251	215	180
GUITAR	64	EPIPHONE	HOWARD ROBERTS	1,713	1,267	1,088	910
GUITAR	66	EPIPHONE	HOWARD ROBERTS STANDARD SUNBURST	1,394	1,031	886	741
GUITAR	65	EPIPHONE	MADRID EC-30 CLASSICAL	384	284	244	204
GUITAR	66	EPIPHONE	NEWPORT BASS SOLID CHERRY, 1 PU	427	315	271	226
GUITAR	64	EPIPHONE	SERENADER NATURAL	518	383	329	275
GUITAR	63	EPIPHONE	SERENADER FT- 85 12-STRING, FLATTOP	474	350	301	251
GUITAR	64	EPIPHONE	SERENADER FT- 85 12-STRING, FLATTOP	451	333	286	239
GUITAR	67	EPIPHONE	SERENADER FT- 85 12-STRING, FLATTOP	447	330	284	237
GUITAR	67	EPIPHONE	SEVILLE	336	248	213	178
GUITAR	63	EPIPHONE	SORRENTO E452 THIN SUNBURST, CUTAWAY, 1 PU	728	538	462	387
GUITAR	63	EPIPHONE	SORRENTO E452 THIN NATURAL, CUATAWY, 1 PU	733	542	466	389
GUITAR	64	EPIPHONE	SORRENTO E452 THIN NATURAL, CUTAWAY, 2 PU's	757	560	481	402
GUITAR	66	EPIPHONE	SORRENTO E452 THIN SUNBURST, CUTAWAY, 1 PU	737	545	468	391
GUITAR	67	EPIPHONE	SORRENTO E452 THIN SUNBURST, CUTAWAY, 2 PU's	711	526	452	377

TYPE	YR	MFG	PRICES--BASED ON 100% ORIGINAL MODEL	SELL EXC	SELL AVG	BUY EXC	BUY AVG
GUITAR	68	EPIPHONE	SORRENTO E452 THIN SUNBURST, CUTAWAY, 2 PU's	691	511	439	367
GUITAR	58	EPIPHONE	TEXAN FT-79 NATURAL	1,394	1,031	886	741
GUITAR	63	EPIPHONE	TEXAN FT-79 NATURAL	1,183	875	752	628
GUITAR	64	EPIPHONE	TEXAN FT-79 SUNBURST	1,364	1,008	866	724
GUITAR	66	EPIPHONE	TEXAN FT-79 SUNBURST	1,128	860	731	559
GUITAR	67	EPIPHONE	TEXAN FT-79 SUNBURST	1,354	1,001	860	719
GUITAR	68	EPIPHONE	TEXAN FT-79 SUNBURST	1,068	790	678	567
GUITAR	69	EPIPHONE	TEXAN FT-79	1,076	795	683	571
GUITAR	60	EPIPHONE	TEXAN FT-79N NATURAL BLOND	1,493	1,104	949	793
GUITAR	62	EPIPHONE	TEXAN FT-79N NATURAL BLOND	1,211	896	769	643
GUITAR	64	EPIPHONE	TEXAN FT-79N NATURAL BLOND	1,201	888	763	638
GUITAR	65	EPIPHONE	TEXAN FT-79N NATURAL BLOND	1,163	860	739	618
GUITAR	67	EPIPHONE	TEXAN FT-79N NATURAL BLOND	1,159	857	736	616
GUITAR	69	EPIPHONE	TEXAN FT-79N NATURAL BLOND	1,265	935	803	672
GUITAR	67	EPIPHONE	TRIUMPH SUNBURST, CUTAWAY	1,260	932	800	669
GUITAR	59	EPIPHONE	TRIUMPH REGENT SUNBURST, CUTAWAY	1,649	1,219	1,047	876
GUITAR	60	EPIPHONE	TRIUMPH REGENT SUNBURST, CUTAWAY	1,593	1,178	1,012	846
GUITAR	61	EPIPHONE	TRIUMPH REGENT NATURAL BLOND, CUTAWAY	1,206	892	766	641
GUITAR	63	EPIPHONE	TRIUMPH REGENT SUNBURST, CUTAWAY	1,460	1,079	927	775
GUITAR	64	EPIPHONE	TRIUMPH REGENT SUNBURST, CUTAWAY	1,449	1,072	921	770
GUITAR	65	EPIPHONE	TRIUMPH REGENT SUNBURST, CUTAWAY, SERIAL #407167	1,195	883	759	634
GUITAR	66	EPIPHONE	TRIUMPH REGENT SUNBURST, LEFT-HANDED	1,752	1,296	1,113	931
GUITAR	67	EPIPHONE	TRIUMPH REGENT NATURAL BLOND, CUTAWAY	1,132	863	733	561
GUITAR	67	EPIPHONE	TRIUMPH REGENT SUNBURST, OVAL HOLE, (RARE) FLOATING JOHNNY SMITH TYPE PU	1,752	1,296	1,113	931
GUITAR	68	EPIPHONE	TRIUMPH REGENT SUNBURST, CUTAWAY	1,749	1,293	1,111	929
GUITAR	58	EPIPHONE	ZENITH SUNBURST	777	575	494	413
GUITAR	62	EPIPHONE	ZENITH SUNBURST	770	570	489	409
GUITAR	64	EPIPHONE	ZENITH SUNBURST	557	412	354	296
GUITAR	66	EPIPHONE	ZENITH SUNBURST	598	442	380	317
GUITAR	67	EPIPHONE	ZENITH SUNBURST	586	433	372	311
MANDOLIN	70	EPIPHONE	A-5 COPY FLORENTINE CUTAWAY, MADE IN JAPAN	593	438	376	315
MANDOL	66	EPIPHONE	VENETIAN ELECTRIC by GIBSON HIGHLY FIGURED CURLY MAPLE,1 P-90 SINGLE COIL PU	518	383	329	275
STEEL GUITAR	64	EPIPHONE	TROUBADOUR FLATTOP	615	455	391	326
STGUIT	66	EPIPHONE	TROUBADOUR FLATTOP	555	411	353	295
STGUIT	67	EPIPHONE	TROUBADOUR FLATTOP	491	363	312	261

FAIRCHILD

TYPE	YR	MFG	MODEL	SELL EXC	SELL AVG	BUY EXC	BUY AVG
PWR	62-69	FAIRCHILD	255 TUBE MONO	179	132	114	95
PWR	73-77	FAIRCHILD	260	144	107	92	77
PWR	61	FAIRCHILD	HF-87 KIT STEREO, TUBE, 35 WATTS	168	124	106	89
SIGNAL PROCESSOR	61	FAIRCHILD	660 MONO LIMITER	96	71	61	51
SGNPRO	61	FAIRCHILD	661TL NOISE GATE	537	397	341	285
SGNPRO	61	FAIRCHILD	663 COMPRESSOR	537	397	341	285
SGNPRO	61	FAIRCHILD	666 MONO COMPRESSOR	6,720	4,970	4,270	3,570
SGNPRO	61	FAIRCHILD	670 STEREO LIMITER	12,840	9,496	8,158	6,821

TYPE	YR	MFG	PRICES--BASED ON 100% ORIGINAL MODEL	SELL EXC	SELL AVG	BUY EXC	BUY AVG
			FAIRLIGHT INSTRUMENTS				
SYNTHESIZER	80	FAIRLI	**FAIRLIGHT CMI**	1,430	**1,057**	908	759
			FARFISA				
SYNTHESIZER	67	FARFISA	**COMPACT DELUXE**	206	**152**	131	109
SYNTH	66	FARFISA	**VIP-233 DOUBLE KEYBOARD**	288	**213**	183	153
			FAVILLA BROTHERS				
GUITAR (ACOUSTIC)	31	FAVILLA	**6/8 NEW YORK** DOUBLE NECK	1,455	**1,076**	924	773
GUITAR	29	FAVILLA	**00 NEW YORK** FLATTOP	1,313	**971**	834	697
GUITAR	34	FAVILLA	**DETROIT** FLATTOP	1,154	**854**	733	613
GUITAR	38	FAVILLA	**DETROIT** ARCHTOP, 16"	1,569	**1,160**	997	833
UKULELE	55	FAVILLA	**BARITONE**	309	**228**	196	164
			FENDER MUSICAL CORP.				
BANJO	70	FENDER	**ALLEGRO** TENOR	538	**398**	342	286
BANJO	71	FENDER	**ALLEGRO** 5-STRING	464	**343**	295	246
BANJO	68	FENDER	**ARTIST** PLECTRUM	466	**345**	296	247
BANJO	68	FENDER	**ARTIST** TENOR	516	**381**	328	274
BANJO	70	FENDER	**ARTIST** TENOR	489	**362**	311	260
BANJO	70	FENDER	**ARTIST DELUXE**	987	**730**	627	524
BANJO	70	FENDER	**CONCERT TONE**	976	**722**	620	518
BANJO	74	FENDER	**CONCERT TONE** PLECTRUM	763	**564**	484	405
BANJO	74	FENDER	**CONCERT TONE** TENOR	808	**597**	513	429
BANJO	82	FENDER	**LEO** 5-STRING,CLEAR HEAD, RESONATOR	751	**555**	477	399
EFFECTS	70	FENDER	**DIMENSION IV** SOUND EXPANDER	96	**71**	61	51
EFFECTS	64	FENDER	**ELECTRONIC ECHO CHAMBER** TAPE ECHO	285	**210**	181	151
EFFECTS	65	FENDER	**FE-1000** ELECTRONIC ECHO CHAMBER	489	**362**	311	260
EFFECTS	76	FENDER	**FUZZ-WAH**	106	**78**	67	56
EFFECTS	64	FENDER	**REVERB TANK** TUBE, BLACK, WHITE KNOBS	609	**450**	387	323
EFFECTS	68	FENDER	**VOLUME PEDAL** CHROME	109	**80**	69	58
ELEC. GUITAR	65	FENDER	**BASS V** SUNBURST, 5-STRING	1,195	**883**	759	634
ELGUIT	65	FENDER	**BASS V** LAKE PLACID BLUE, 5-STRING	1,555	**1,150**	988	826
ELGUIT	66	FENDER	**BASS V** SUNBURST, 5-STRING	1,206	**892**	766	641
ELGUIT	66	FENDER	**BASS V** CANDY APPLE RED, 5-STRING	1,520	**1,124**	966	807
ELGUIT	66	FENDER	**BASS V** OCEAN TURQUOISE, 5-STRING	1,985	**1,468**	1,261	1,054
ELGUIT	67	FENDER	**BASS V** LAKE PLACID BLUE, 5-STRING	1,208	**893**	767	642
ELGUIT	68	FENDER	**BASS V** SUNBURST, 5-STRING	1,112	**822**	706	591
ELGUIT	69	FENDER	**BASS V** SUNBURST, 5-STRING	1,109	**820**	705	589
ELGUIT	70	FENDER	**BASS V** SUNBURST, 5-STRING	1,032	**763**	656	548
ELGUIT	71	FENDER	**BASS V** SUNBURST, 5-STRING	1,158	**856**	736	615
ELGUIT	62	FENDER	**BASS VI** 3-TONE SUNBURST, 6-STRING, 3 PU's, TREM, CLAY DOTS	2,389	**1,767**	1,518	1,269
ELGUIT	63	FENDER	**BASS VI** SUNBURST, 6-STRING	1,735	**1,283**	1,102	922
ELGUIT	63	FENDER	**BASS VI** LAKE PLACID BLUE, 6-STRING	3,369	**2,492**	2,141	1,790
ELGUIT	63	FENDER	**BASS VI** BLACK, 6-STRING	3,380	**2,499**	2,147	1,795
ELGUIT	64	FENDER	**BASS VI** SUNBURST, 6-STRING	1,735	**1,283**	1,102	922
ELGUIT	64	FENDER	**BASS VI** LAKE PLACID BLUE, 6-STRING	3,219	**2,381**	2,045	1,710
ELGUIT	65	FENDER	**BASS VI** SUNBURST, 6-STRING	1,834	**1,356**	1,165	974

TYPE	YR	MFG	MODEL	SELL EXC	SELL AVG	BUY EXC	BUY AVG
			PRICES--BASED ON 100% ORIGINAL				
ELGUIT	65	FENDER	**BASS VI** LAKE PLACID BLUE, 6-STRING	3,211	**2,374**	2,040	1,705
ELGUIT	66	FENDER	**BASS VI** SUNBURST, 6-STRING	1,979	**1,464**	1,257	1,051
ELGUIT	67	FENDER	**BASS VI** SUNBURST, 6-STRING	1,605	**1,187**	1,019	852
ELGUIT	68	FENDER	**BASS VI** SUNBRUST, 6-STRING	1,582	**1,170**	1,005	840
ELGUIT	70	FENDER	**BASS VI** SUNBURST, 6-STRING	1,464	**1,082**	930	777
ELGUIT	73	FENDER	**BASS VI** SUNBURST, 6-STRING	1,354	**1,001**	860	719
ELGUIT	50	FENDER	**BROADCASTER**	25,056	**18,531**	15,921	13,311
ELGUIT	51	FENDER	**BROADCASTER**	17,318	**12,808**	11,004	9,200
ELGUIT	67	FENDER	**BRONCO** RED, 1 PU, 24" SCALE	287	**212**	182	152
ELGUIT	68	FENDER	**BRONCO** RED, 1 PU, 24" SCALE, SERIAL #206453	284	**210**	180	150
ELGUIT	69	FENDER	**BRONCO** RED. 1 PU, 24" SCALE	283	**209**	179	150
ELGUIT	70	FENDER	**BRONCO** RED	250	**185**	159	133
ELGUIT	73	FENDER	**BRONCO** RED, 1 PU, 24" SCALE, SERIAL #376380	248	**183**	157	132
ELGUIT	76	FENDER	**BRONCO** RED, 1 PU, 24" SCALE	246	**182**	156	131
ELGUIT	81	FENDER	**BULLET**	189	**139**	120	100
ELGUIT	66	FENDER	**CORONADO BASS** LAKE PLACID BLUE	967	**715**	614	514
ELGUIT	66	FENDER	**CORONADO I** SUNBURST, 1 PU, TREMOLO, SERIAL #200865	478	**353**	303	253
ELGUIT	67	FENDER	**CORONADO I** CHERRY RED, 1 PU	489	**362**	311	260
ELGUIT	68	FENDER	**CORONADO I** SUNBURST, 1 PU, SERIAL #622740	476	**352**	302	252
ELGUIT	69	FENDER	**CORONADO I** SUNBURST	459	**340**	292	244
ELGUIT	66	FENDER	**CORONADO I BASS** SUNBURST, 1 PU	425	**314**	270	225
ELGUIT	68	FENDER	**CORONADO I BASS** SUNBURST	443	**328**	281	235
ELGUIT	68	FENDER	**CORONADO I BASS** WHITE, 1 PU	443	**328**	281	235
ELGUIT	65	FENDER	**CORONADO II** SUNBURST. 2 PU's	509	**377**	323	270
ELGUIT	66	FENDER	**CORONADO II** SUNBURST, 2 PU's, SERIAL #500641	490	**362**	311	260
ELGUIT	66	FENDER	**CORONADO II** TRANSPARENT ORANGE	494	**365**	314	262
ELGUIT	66	FENDER	**CORONADO II** CHERRY RED, 2 PU's	497	**367**	315	264
ELGUIT	67	FENDER	**CORONADO II** CHERRY RED, 2 PU's, SERIAL #180882-201286	434	**321**	276	231
ELGUIT	67	FENDER	**CORONADO II** ANTIGUA, 2 PU's	449	**332**	285	238
ELGUIT	67	FENDER	**CORONADO II** SUNBURST, 2 PU's, SERIAL #180882-201286	455	**336**	289	241
ELGUIT	67	FENDER	**CORONADO II** WILDWOOD GOLD, 2 PU's, SERIAL #180882-201286	795	**588**	505	422
ELGUIT	68	FENDER	**CORONADO II** ANTIGUA, 2 PU's, SERIAL #503008	419	**310**	266	222
ELGUIT	68	FENDER	**CORONADO II** SUNBURST, 2 PU's, SERIAL #503008	432	**319**	274	229
ELGUIT	68	FENDER	**CORONADO II** LAKE PLACID BLUE	514	**380**	326	273
ELGUIT	68	FENDER	**CORONADO II** ORANGE	566	**418**	359	300
ELGUIT	68	FENDER	**CORONADO II** RED	598	**442**	380	317
ELGUIT	68	FENDER	**CORONADO II** WILDWOOD	717	**530**	455	380
ELGUIT	69	FENDER	**CORONADO II** ANTIGUA, 2 PU's	637	**471**	405	338
ELGUIT	69	FENDER	**CORONADO II** SUNBURST, 2 PU's	637	**471**	405	338
ELGUIT	70	FENDER	**CORONADO II** ANTIGUA, 2 PU's	632	**467**	401	336
ELGUIT	71	FENDER	**CORONADO II** ANTIGUA, 2 PU's	629	**465**	400	334
ELGUIT	73	FENDER	**CORONADO II** SUNBURST, 2 PU's	625	**462**	397	332
ELGUIT	74	FENDER	**CORONADO II** CHERRY RED, 2 PU's	622	**460**	395	330

TYPE	YR	MFG	PRICES--BASED ON 100% ORIGINAL MODEL	SELL EXC	SELL AVG	BUY EXC	BUY AVG
ELGUIT	67	FENDER	**CORONADO II BASS** SUNBURST, 2 PU's	434	**321**	276	231
ELGUIT	68	FENDER	**CORONADO II BASS** SUNBURST, 2 PU's	497	**367**	315	264
ELGUIT	69	FENDER	**CORONADO II BASS** SUNBURST, 2 PU's	427	**315**	271	226
ELGUIT	71	FENDER	**CORONADO II BASS** ANTIGUA	414	**306**	263	220
ELGUIT	66	FENDER	**CORONADO XII** SUNBURST, 12-STRING	475	**351**	301	252
ELGUIT	67	FENDER	**CORONADO XII** SUNBURST, 12-STRING	477	**352**	303	253
ELGUIT	67	FENDER	**CORONADO XII**	540	**399**	343	287
ELGUIT	67	FENDER	**CORONADO XII** ORANGE, 12-STRING	695	**514**	441	369
ELGUIT	68	FENDER	**CORONADO XII** WILDWOOD GOLD, 12-STRING	527	**389**	334	279
ELGUIT	68	FENDER	**CORONADO XII** RAINBOW GOLD	709	**524**	450	376
ELGUIT	69	FENDER	**CORONADO XII** SUNBURST, 12-STRING	422	**312**	268	224
ELGUIT	69	FENDER	**CORONADO XII** ANTIGUA, 12-STRING	455	**336**	289	241
ELGUIT	58	FENDER	**DUO-SONIC** DESERT SAND, ANODIZED PICKGUARD	783	**579**	497	416
ELGUIT	62	FENDER	**DUO-SONIC** SUNBURST	549	**406**	348	291
ELGUIT	57	FENDER	**DUO-SONIC 3/4** TAN, SERIAL #19459-21921	556	**411**	353	295
ELGUIT	58	FENDER	**DUO-SONIC 3/4** TAN, SERIAL #15642-28853	657	**486**	417	349
ELGUIT	59	FENDER	**DUO-SONIC 3/4** TAN, SERIAL #31988-91408	429	**317**	272	227
ELGUIT	60	FENDER	**DUO-SONIC 3/4** SUNBURST, SERIAL #44142-58544	444	**328**	282	236
ELGUIT	60	FENDER	**DUO-SONIC 3/4** TAN, SERIAL #44142-58544	504	**372**	320	267
ELGUIT	61	FENDER	**DUO-SONIC 3/4** SUNBURST	470	**347**	298	249
ELGUIT	62	FENDER	**DUO-SONIC 3/4** SUNBURST, SERIAL #77201-87360	284	**210**	180	150
ELGUIT	63	FENDER	**DUO-SONIC 3/4** WHITE, SERIAL #89686-99155/L14848	277	**205**	176	147
ELGUIT	63	FENDER	**DUO-SONIC 3/4** SUNBURST	282	**208**	179	149
ELGUIT	64	FENDER	**DUO-SONIC 3/4** TAN, SERIAL #L27092-L54517	456	**337**	289	242
ELGUIT	65	FENDER	**DUO-SONIC 3/4** TAN, SERIAL #119359/L74879-L86654	446	**330**	283	237
ELGUIT	66	FENDER	**DUO-SONIC 3/4** RED, SERIAL #105288-148942	284	**210**	180	150
ELGUIT	69	FENDER	**DUO-SONIC 3/4** SUNBURST	379	**280**	240	201
ELGUIT	69	FENDER	**DUO-SONIC 3/4** TAN, SERIAL #44142-58544	431	**318**	273	228
ELGUIT	64	FENDER	**DUO-SONIC II** RED, 24", SERIAL #L5225-L55651	428	**316**	272	227
ELGUIT	64	FENDER	**DUO-SONIC II** WHITE	494	**365**	314	262
ELGUIT	65	FENDER	**DUO-SONIC II** WHITE	441	**326**	280	234
ELGUIT	65	FENDER	**DUO-SONIC II** RED, 24"	458	**339**	291	243
ELGUIT	66	FENDER	**DUO-SONIC II** WHITE, 24", SERIAL #105579-133083	413	**306**	262	219
ELGUIT	66	FENDER	**DUO-SONIC II** RED, 24", SERIAL #105579-133083	414	**306**	263	220
ELGUIT	65	FENDER	**ELECTRIC XII** 3-TONE SUNBURST, 12-STRING, TORTOISE GUARD, SPLIT PU's	1,219	**901**	774	647
ELGUIT	66	FENDER	**ELECTRIC XII** SUNBURST,12-STRING,SPLIT PU's, SERIAL #117648-194134/L78314	967	**715**	614	514
ELGUIT	66	FENDER	**ELECTRIC XII** RED, 12-STRING, SPLIT PU's	1,125	**832**	714	597
ELGUIT	66	FENDER	**ELECTRIC XII** WHITE, 12-STRING, SPLIT PU's, SERIAL #117648-194134/L78314	1,278	**945**	812	679
ELGUIT	66	FENDER	**ELECTRIC XII** LAKE PLACID BLUE, 12-STRING	1,589	**1,175**	1,010	844
ELGUIT	66	FENDER	**ELECTRIC XII** CANDY APPLE RED	1,680	**1,243**	1,068	893
ELGUIT	66	FENDER	**ELECTRIC XII** SHORELINE GOLD, 12-STRING	2,880	**2,130**	1,830	1,530
ELGUIT	69	FENDER	**ELECTRIC XII** CANDY APPLE RED	1,276	**944**	811	678

TYPE	YR	MFG	PRICES--BASED ON 100% ORIGINAL MODEL	SELL EXC	SELL AVG	BUY EXC	BUY AVG
ELGUIT	69	FENDER	**ELECTRIC XII** SUNBURST, 12-STRING, SPLIT PU's	1,302	963	827	692
ELGUIT	51	FENDER	**ESQUIRE** BLOND, 1 PU, SERIAL #0210-4941	7,684	5,683	4,883	4,082
ELGUIT	52	FENDER	**ESQUIRE** BLOND, 1 PU	7,518	5,560	4,777	3,994
ELGUIT	52	FENDER	**ESQUIRE** BLOND, 1 PU, SERIAL #546-4782	9,038	6,684	5,743	4,801
ELGUIT	53	FENDER	**ESQUIRE** BLOND, 1 PU	7,788	5,760	4,948	4,137
ELGUIT	54	FENDER	**ESQUIRE** BLOND, 1 PU, SERIAL #0612-09326	8,738	6,463	5,552	4,642
ELGUIT	55	FENDER	**ESQUIRE** BLOND, 1 PU, SERIAL #7045-12842/21616	5,190	3,838	3,298	2,757
ELGUIT	56	FENDER	**ESQUIRE** BLOND, 1 PU, SERIAL #11257-66675	5,164	3,819	3,281	2,743
ELGUIT	56	FENDER	**ESQUIRE** TWEED, MAPLE NECK	6,143	4,543	3,903	3,263
ELGUIT	57	FENDER	**ESQUIRE** BLOND, 1 PU, SERIAL #7970-025167/19418-21803	5,057	3,740	3,213	2,686
ELGUIT	58	FENDER	**ESQUIRE** BLOND, 1 PU, SERIAL #30134-027885	6,075	4,493	3,860	3,227
ELGUIT	59	FENDER	**ESQUIRE** BLOND, 1 PU, ROSEWOOD, SERIAL #37659	4,731	3,499	3,006	2,513
ELGUIT	59	FENDER	**ESQUIRE** DAKOTA RED, ROSEWOOD BRD, SERIAL #37659	8,523	6,304	5,416	4,528
ELGUIT	60	FENDER	**ESQUIRE** BLOND, 1 PU, SINGLE CUT, SERIAL #45122-59002	4,677	3,459	2,971	2,484
ELGUIT	60	FENDER	**ESQUIRE** BLOND, ROSEWOOD, CURLY MAPLE NECK	7,515	5,558	4,775	3,992
ELGUIT	60	FENDER	**ESQUIRE** BURGUNDY MIST, 1 PU, SERIAL #45122-59002	7,518	5,560	4,777	3,994
ELGUIT	61	FENDER	**ESQUIRE** BLOND, 1 PU, SERIAL #55953-66449	4,619	3,416	2,935	2,454
ELGUIT	62	FENDER	**ESQUIRE** DAKOTA RED, LEFT-HANDED	5,931	4,387	3,769	3,151
ELGUIT	63	FENDER	**ESQUIRE** WHITE, 1 PU	3,290	2,433	2,091	1,748
ELGUIT	63	FENDER	**ESQUIRE** BLOND, 1 PU, SERIAL #L03475-L37511	4,428	3,275	2,813	2,352
ELGUIT	63	FENDER	**ESQUIRE** SUNBURST, 1 PU	5,166	3,821	3,283	2,744
ELGUIT	64	FENDER	**ESQUIRE** BURGUNDY MIST, 1 PU, SERIAL #L36733-L58702	5,201	3,846	3,304	2,763
ELGUIT	65	FENDER	**ESQUIRE** LAKE PLACID BLUE, SERIAL #115147/L12425	4,620	3,417	2,935	2,454
ELGUIT	66	FENDER	**ESQUIRE** BLOND, 1 PU, SERIAL #115118-193463	2,073	1,533	1,317	1,101
ELGUIT	67	FENDER	**ESQUIRE** BLOND, 1 PU, MAPLE NECK	1,923	1,422	1,222	1,022
ELGUIT	67	FENDER	**ESQUIRE** WHITE, 1 PU	3,753	2,776	2,385	1,994
ELGUIT	67	FENDER	**ESQUIRE** CANDY APPLE RED, 1 PU	5,184	3,834	3,294	2,754
ELGUIT	68	FENDER	**ESQUIRE** BLOND, 1 PU	1,629	1,204	1,035	865
ELGUIT	68	FENDER	**ESQUIRE** SUNBURST, 1 PU	3,664	2,710	2,328	1,946
ELGUIT	70	FENDER	**ESQUIRE** BLOND, 1 PU	1,366	1,010	868	725
ELGUIT	35	FENDER	**ESQUIRE** BLOND, 1 PU	4,392	3,248	2,790	2,333
ELGUIT	59	FENDER	**ESQUIRE CUSTOM** SUNBURST, ROSEWOOD BOARD, SERIAL #37659	6,065	4,485	3,853	3,222
ELGUIT	62	FENDER	**ESQUIRE CUSTOM** SUNBURST, ROSEWOOD BOARD	5,387	3,984	3,423	2,862
ELGUIT	63	FENDER	**ESQUIRE CUSTOM** SUNBURST, ROSEWOOD BOARD, SERIAL #L16550-L42308	5,676	4,198	3,606	3,015
ELGUIT	65	FENDER	**ESQUIRE CUSTOM** SUNBURST, ROSEWOOD BOARD, LEFT-HANDED	6,120	4,526	3,889	3,251
ELGUIT	65	FENDER	**ESQUIRE CUSTOM** SUNBURST, LEFT-HANDED	7,362	5,444	4,678	3,911
ELGUIT	66	FENDER	**ESQUIRE CUSTOM** SUNBURST, ROSEWOOD BOARD, SERIAL #115118-193463	4,446	3,288	2,825	2,362
ELGUIT	67	FENDER	**ESQUIRE CUSTOM** SUNBURST, ROSEWOOD BOARD, SERIAL #208410	4,394	3,250	2,792	2,334
ELGUIT	68	FENDER	**ESQUIRE CUSTOM** SUNBURST, ROSEWOOD BOARD	3,947	2,919	2,508	2,097
ELGUIT	69	FENDER	**ESQUIRE CUSTOM** SUNBURST, ROSEWOOD BROAD	3,825	2,829	2,430	2,032
ELGUIT	61	FENDER	**JAGUAR** SUNBURST	2,390	1,767	1,518	1,269
ELGUIT	62	FENDER	**JAGUAR** OLYMPIC WHITE	1,554	1,149	987	825

TYPE	YR	MFG	PRICES--BASED ON 100% ORIGINAL MODEL	SELL EXC	SELL AVG	BUY EXC	BUY AVG
ELGUIT	62	FENDER	JAGUAR BLACK	1,703	1,259	1,082	904
ELGUIT	62	FENDER	JAGUAR LAKE PLACID BLUE	1,847	1,366	1,173	981
ELGUIT	62	FENDER	JAGUAR DAPHNE BLUE	2,126	1,572	1,351	1,129
ELGUIT	62	FENDER	JAGUAR SUNBURST, GREEN GUARD, CLAY DOTS	2,378	1,759	1,511	1,263
ELGUIT	62	FENDER	JAGUAR FIESTA RED	2,928	2,165	1,860	1,555
ELGUIT	62	FENDER	JAGUAR CANDY APPLE RED	2,976	2,201	1,891	1,581
ELGUIT	63	FENDER	JAGUAR BLACK	1,380	1,020	877	733
ELGUIT	63	FENDER	JAGUAR SEE-THRU BLOND, ASH	1,445	1,069	918	768
ELGUIT	63	FENDER	JAGUAR OLYMPIC WHITE, SERIAL #20631-158483/L01083-L35810	1,477	1,092	938	784
ELGUIT	63	FENDER	JAGUAR FIESTA RED, SERIAL #20631-158483/L01083-L35810	1,985	1,468	1,261	1,054
ELGUIT	63	FENDER	JAGUAR SUNBURST, SERIAL #20631-158483/L01083-L35810	2,377	1,758	1,510	1,263
ELGUIT	63	FENDER	JAGUAR CANDY APPLE RED	2,972	2,198	1,888	1,578
ELGUIT	64	FENDER	JAGUAR OLYMPIC WHITE	1,024	757	650	544
ELGUIT	64	FENDER	JAGUAR CANDY APPLE RED, SERIAL #1037171/L18181-L64673	1,368	1,012	869	727
ELGUIT	64	FENDER	JAGUAR LAKE PLACID BLUE, SERIAL #103717/L18181-L64673	1,746	1,291	1,109	927
ELGUIT	64	FENDER	JAGUAR CANDY APPLE RED, LEFT-HANDED	2,390	1,767	1,518	1,269
ELGUIT	64	FENDER	JAGUAR SUNBURST, SERIAL #103717/L18181-L64673	2,390	1,767	1,518	1,269
ELGUIT	65	FENDER	JAGUAR BLACK	1,292	955	821	686
ELGUIT	65	FENDER	JAGUAR OLYMPIC WHITE, SERIAL #89376-209297/L16891-L97962	1,475	1,091	937	783
ELGUIT	65	FENDER	JAGUAR SHORE LINE GOLD, GOLD HARDWARE	1,602	1,184	1,018	851
ELGUIT	65	FENDER	JAGUAR LAKE PLACID BLUE	1,673	1,237	1,063	888
ELGUIT	65	FENDER	JAGUAR SONIC BLUE GREEN GUARD	1,900	1,405	1,207	1,009
ELGUIT	65	FENDER	JAGUAR FIREMIST GOLD	2,147	1,588	1,364	1,140
ELGUIT	65	FENDER	JAGUAR SUNBURST	2,376	1,757	1,510	1,262
ELGUIT	65	FENDER	JAGUAR CANDY APPLE RED, SERIAL #89376-209297/L16891-L97962	2,952	2,183	1,876	1,568
ELGUIT	66	FENDER	JAGUAR SUNBURST	1,011	748	642	537
ELGUIT	66	FENDER	JAGUAR BLACK, DOT INLAY, BINDING	1,115	825	708	592
ELGUIT	66	FENDER	JAGUAR OLYMPIC WHITE, DOT INLAY, SERIAL #113301-240568/L27443-L892	1,210	895	769	643
ELGUIT	66	FENDER	JAGUAR CANDY APPLE RED, DOT INLAY, SERIAL #113301-240568/L27443-L8	1,263	934	802	671
ELGUIT	66	FENDER	JAGUAR LAKE PLACID BLUE, DOT INLAY	1,403	1,038	891	745
ELGUIT	66	FENDER	JAGUAR SUNBURST, LEFT-HANDED, SERIAL #113301-240568/L27443-L89246	1,521	1,125	966	808
ELGUIT	66	FENDER	JAGUAR FIESTA RED, DOT INLAY, SERIAL #113301-240568/L27443-L89246	1,806	1,336	1,148	959
ELGUIT	67	FENDER	JAGUAR SUNBURST, SERIAL #22074-705980/L62623	987	730	627	524
ELGUIT	67	FENDER	JAGUAR BLACK, SERIAL #22074-705980/L62623	1,066	788	677	566
ELGUIT	67	FENDER	JAGUAR LAKE PLACID BLUE	1,375	1,017	874	730
ELGUIT	68	FENDER	JAGUAR SUNBURST, SERIAL #214627-237386	956	707	607	507
ELGUIT	68	FENDER	JAGUAR LAKE PLACID BLUE, SERIAL #214627-237386	1,315	972	835	698
ELGUIT	68	FENDER	JAGUAR TEAL GREEN METALLIC	1,440	1,065	915	765
ELGUIT	68	FENDER	JAGUAR WHITE	1,664	1,231	1,057	884
ELGUIT	69	FENDER	JAGUAR SUNBURST	957	707	608	508
ELGUIT	69	FENDER	JAGUAR OLYMPIC WHITE	1,108	820	704	589
ELGUIT	69	FENDER	JAGUAR SUNBURST, LEFT-HANDED	1,620	1,198	1,029	860

TYPE	YR	MFG	PRICES--BASED ON 100% ORIGINAL MODEL	SELL EXC	SELL AVG	BUY EXC	BUY AVG
ELGUIT	71	FENDER	**JAGUAR** SUNBURST	970	**717**	616	515
ELGUIT	71	FENDER	**JAGUAR** LAKE PLACID BLUE	1,067	**789**	678	567
ELGUIT	71	FENDER	**JAGUAR** BLACK	1,104	**816**	701	586
ELGUIT	73	FENDER	**JAGUAR** SUNBURST	920	**680**	584	489
ELGUIT	74	FENDER	**JAGUAR** SUNBURST	915	**677**	581	486
ELGUIT	60	FENDER	**JAZZ BASS** SUNBURST, STACK KNOB, SERIAL #44043-66626	8,856	**6,550**	5,627	4,705
ELGUIT	60	FENDER	**JAZZ BASS** WHITE, STACK KNOB, SERIAL #44043-66626	9,453	**6,991**	6,006	5,021
ELGUIT	61	FENDER	**JAZZ BASS** SUNBURST, CONCENTRIC KNOB, SERIAL #56017-74757	8,630	**6,382**	5,483	4,584
ELGUIT	61	FENDER	**JAZZ BASS** FIESTA RED, CONCENTRIC KN, SERIAL #56017-74757	9,604	**7,103**	6,103	5,102
ELGUIT	62	FENDER	**JAZZ BASS** OLYMPIC WHITE, 3 KNOBS, SERIAL #75765-95570/L49923	5,407	**3,999**	3,436	2,872
ELGUIT	62	FENDER	**JAZZ BASS** SUNBURST, SERIAL #75765-95570/L49923	6,216	**4,597**	3,949	3,302
ELGUIT	62	FENDER	**JAZZ BASS** FIESTA RED, CONCENTRIC KN	7,608	**5,626**	4,834	4,041
ELGUIT	63	FENDER	**JAZZ BASS** SUNBURST, SERIAL #57263-97989/L01885-L59792	5,209	**3,853**	3,310	2,767
ELGUIT	63	FENDER	**JAZZ BASS** OLYMPIC WHITE, SERIAL #57263-97989/L01885-L59792	6,240	**4,615**	3,965	3,315
ELGUIT	63	FENDER	**JAZZ BASS** CORAL PINK, MATCHING HEADSTOCK, 3 KNOB	7,680	**5,680**	4,880	4,080
ELGUIT	64	FENDER	**JAZZ BASS** SUNBURST, SERIAL #L16100-L85607	4,582	**3,388**	2,911	2,434
ELGUIT	64	FENDER	**JAZZ BASS** LAKE PLACID BLUE, SERIAL #L16100-L85607	4,869	**3,601**	3,093	2,586
ELGUIT	64	FENDER	**JAZZ BASS** SUNBURST, LEFT-HANDED, SERIAL #L16100-L85607	5,566	**4,116**	3,536	2,956
ELGUIT	65	FENDER	**JAZZ BASS** SUNBURST, SERIAL #91213-129012/L05549-L99849	4,473	**3,308**	2,842	2,376
ELGUIT	65	FENDER	**JAZZ BASS** OLYMPIC WHITE, SERIAL #11746-117472/L05549-L99849	5,354	**3,960**	3,402	2,844
ELGUIT	65	FENDER	**JAZZ BASS** BLACK	5,647	**4,176**	3,588	3,000
ELGUIT	65	FENDER	**JAZZ BASS** FIESTA RED, SERIAL #91213-129012/L05549-L99849	5,729	**4,237**	3,640	3,043
ELGUIT	65	FENDER	**JAZZ BASS** LAKE PLACID BLUE	5,858	**4,333**	3,722	3,112
ELGUIT	65	FENDER	**JAZZ BASS** SONIC BLUE, MATCHING HEADSTOCK	6,240	**4,615**	3,965	3,315
ELGUIT	66	FENDER	**JAZZ BASS** SUNBURST, SERIAL #12050-210867/L09298-L66240	2,320	**1,716**	1,474	1,232
ELGUIT	66	FENDER	**JAZZ BASS** OLYMPIC WHITE	3,141	**2,323**	1,995	1,668
ELGUIT	66	FENDER	**JAZZ BASS** CANDY APPLE RED	3,287	**2,431**	2,088	1,746
ELGUIT	66	FENDER	**JAZZ BASS** BLACK, DOT INLAY	3,905	**2,888**	2,481	2,074
ELGUIT	66	FENDER	**JAZZ BASS** OCEAN TURQUOISE, DOT INLAY	5,609	**4,148**	3,564	2,979
ELGUIT	67	FENDER	**JAZZ BASS** SUNBURST, SERIAL #200294-219686	1,732	**1,281**	1,101	920
ELGUIT	68	FENDER	**JAZZ BASS** SUNBURST, SERIAL #18565-249563	1,675	**1,238**	1,064	889
ELGUIT	68	FENDER	**JAZZ BASS** FIREMIST SILVER, SERIAL #185656-249563	2,135	**1,579**	1,356	1,134
ELGUIT	68	FENDER	**JAZZ BASS** 3-TONE SUNBURST, ROSEWOOD BOARD	2,389	**1,767**	1,518	1,269
ELGUIT	69	FENDER	**JAZZ BASS** CANDY APPLE RED, 4-BOLT, SERIAL #224160-282725	1,445	**1,069**	918	768
ELGUIT	69	FENDER	**JAZZ BASS** SUNBURST, SERIAL #224160-282725	1,515	**1,121**	963	805
ELGUIT	69	FENDER	**JAZZ BASS** LAKE PLACID BLUE	4,128	**3,053**	2,623	2,193
ELGUIT	70	FENDER	**JAZZ BASS** BLACK, 4-BOLT NECK, SERIAL #295831-599166	1,336	**988**	849	709
ELGUIT	70	FENDER	**JAZZ BASS** OLYMPIC WHITE	1,354	**1,001**	860	719
ELGUIT	70	FENDER	**JAZZ BASS** SUNBURST	1,910	**1,412**	1,213	1,014
ELGUIT	71	FENDER	**JAZZ BASS** SUNBURST, MAPLE NECK	1,192	**881**	757	633
ELGUIT	71	FENDER	**JAZZ BASS** BLACK	1,200	**887**	762	637
ELGUIT	72	FENDER	**JAZZ BASS** SUNBURST, SERIAL #271353-403365	1,185	**876**	753	629

TYPE	YR	MFG	PRICES--BASED ON 100% ORIGINAL MODEL	SELL EXC	SELL AVG	BUY EXC	BUY AVG
ELGUIT	72	FENDER	**JAZZ BASS** BLACK	1,494	**1,105**	949	794
ELGUIT	73	FENDER	**JAZZ BASS** BROWN, MAPLE FINGERBOARD	839	**620**	533	445
ELGUIT	73	FENDER	**JAZZ BASS** BLACK, MAPLE NECK	1,006	**744**	639	534
ELGUIT	73	FENDER	**JAZZ BASS** BLOND, SERIAL #387485-551463	1,047	**774**	665	556
ELGUIT	73	FENDER	**JAZZ BASS** NATURAL, MAPLE NECK, SERIAL #387485-551463	1,169	**864**	742	621
ELGUIT	73	FENDER	**JAZZ BASS** SUNBURST	1,255	**928**	797	667
ELGUIT	74	FENDER	**JAZZ BASS** BROWN, MAPLE NECK, SERIAL #547912-647445	830	**614**	527	441
ELGUIT	74	FENDER	**JAZZ BASS** BLACK, MAPLE NECK, SERIAL #547912-647445	986	**729**	627	524
ELGUIT	74	FENDER	**JAZZ BASS** BLOND	1,038	**768**	660	551
ELGUIT	74	FENDER	**JAZZ BASS** SUNBURST	1,136	**840**	722	603
ELGUIT	74	FENDER	**JAZZ BASS** NATURAL, SERIAL #547912-647445	1,370	**1,013**	871	728
ELGUIT	75	FENDER	**JAZZ BASS** BLACK, SERIAL #614166-688002	912	**675**	580	485
ELGUIT	75	FENDER	**JAZZ BASS** SUNBURST, MAPLE NECK, SERIAL #353388-371828	1,061	**785**	674	564
ELGUIT	75	FENDER	**JAZZ BASS** BLOND, PEARLOID INLAYS, MARCUS MILLER STYLE	1,071	**792**	680	569
ELGUIT	75	FENDER	**JAZZ BASS** NATURAL, SERIAL #614166-688002	1,298	**960**	825	690
ELGUIT	76	FENDER	**JAZZ BASS** OLYMPIC WHITE, MAPLE NECK	816	**604**	519	434
ELGUIT	76	FENDER	**JAZZ BASS** NATURAL	1,276	**944**	811	678
ELGUIT	77	FENDER	**JAZZ BASS** BLACK, MAPLE NECK	818	**605**	520	435
ELGUIT	77	FENDER	**JAZZ BASS** BROWN, MAPLE NECK	906	**670**	575	481
ELGUIT	77	FENDER	**JAZZ BASS** WHITE, MAPLE NECK	980	**724**	622	520
ELGUIT	77	FENDER	**JAZZ BASS** SUNBURST, MAPLE NECK	1,005	**743**	638	533
ELGUIT	77	FENDER	**JAZZ BASS** NATURAL, MAPLE NECK	1,056	**781**	671	561
ELGUIT	78	FENDER	**JAZZ BASS** WINE RED, SLAB FRETBOARD	784	**580**	498	416
ELGUIT	78	FENDER	**JAZZ BASS** OLYMPIC WHITE	816	**603**	518	433
ELGUIT	78	FENDER	**JAZZ BASS** BLACK, MAPLE NECK	817	**604**	519	434
ELGUIT	78	FENDER	**JAZZ BASS** NATURAL, MAPLE NECK, SERIAL #S731966	901	**666**	572	478
ELGUIT	78	FENDER	**JAZZ BASS** SUNBURST, MAPLE NECK, SERIAL #S731966	902	**667**	573	479
ELGUIT	78	FENDER	**JAZZ BASS** ANTIGUA, SERIAL #S731966	956	**707**	607	507
ELGUIT	78	FENDER	**JAZZ BASS** BROWN, MAPLE NECK, SERIAL #S731966	956	**707**	607	507
ELGUIT	80	FENDER	**JAZZ BASS** ANTIGUA	916	**678**	582	487
ELGUIT	84	FENDER	**JAZZ BASS** BLACK	657	**486**	417	349
ELGUIT	58	FENDER	**JAZZMASTER** SUNBURST, SERIAL #31474-40403	2,341	**1,731**	1,487	1,243
ELGUIT	58	FENDER	**JAZZMASTER** SAN MARINO BLUE	5,153	**3,811**	3,274	2,737
ELGUIT	59	FENDER	**JAZZMASTER** SUNBURST, ANODIZED PICKGUARD, SERIAL #31734-101396	2,102	**1,554**	1,335	1,116
ELGUIT	59	FENDER	**JAZZMASTER** BLOND, GOLD HARDWARE	3,672	**2,715**	2,333	1,950
ELGUIT	60	FENDER	**JAZZMASTER** OLYMPIC WHITE	1,816	**1,343**	1,154	964
ELGUIT	60	FENDER	**JAZZMASTER** SUNBURST	2,215	**1,638**	1,407	1,177
ELGUIT	60	FENDER	**JAZZMASTER** BLOND SEE-THROUGH	2,227	**1,647**	1,415	1,183
ELGUIT	61	FENDER	**JAZZMASTER** SUNBURST, SERIAL #56090-70445	1,434	**1,060**	911	761
ELGUIT	61	FENDER	**JAZZMASTER** BLOND, LEFT-HANDED	3,144	**2,325**	1,998	1,670
ELGUIT	62	FENDER	**JAZZMASTER** SUNBURST, SERIAL #70860-96846/L05540-L27818	1,433	**1,060**	910	761
ELGUIT	62	FENDER	**JAZZMASTER** OLYMPIC WHITE, SERIAL #70860-96846/L05540-L27818	1,736	**1,284**	1,103	922

TYPE	YR	MFG	**PRICES--BASED ON 100% ORIGINAL** MODEL	SELL EXC	SELL AVG	BUY EXC	BUY AVG
ELGUIT	62	FENDER	**JAZZMASTER** FIESTA RED, SERIAL #70860-96846/L05540-L27818	2,330	**1,723**	1,481	1,238
ELGUIT	62	FENDER	**JAZZMASTER** BURGUNDY MIST	3,158	**2,335**	2,006	1,677
ELGUIT	63	FENDER	**JAZZMASTER** OLYMPIC WHITE	1,765	**1,305**	1,121	937
ELGUIT	63	FENDER	**JAZZMASTER** CANDY APPLE RED	1,787	**1,322**	1,135	949
ELGUIT	63	FENDER	**JAZZMASTER** BLONDE, SERIAL #66908-121637/L00446-L38685	1,792	**1,325**	1,138	952
ELGUIT	63	FENDER	**JAZZMASTER** SUNBURST, SERIAL #66908-121637/L00446-L38685	1,844	**1,363**	1,171	979
ELGUIT	63	FENDER	**JAZZMASTER** LAKE PLACID BLUE, SERIAL #66908-121637/L00446-L38685	2,014	**1,489**	1,279	1,069
ELGUIT	64	FENDER	**JAZZMASTER** OLYMPIC WHITE, SERIAL #L07397-L68238	1,654	**1,223**	1,051	878
ELGUIT	64	FENDER	**JAZZMASTER** SUNBURST, SERIAL #L07397-L68238	1,727	**1,277**	1,097	917
ELGUIT	64	FENDER	**JAZZMASTER** CANDY APPLE RED	1,847	**1,366**	1,173	981
ELGUIT	64	FENDER	**JAZZMASTER** LAKE PLACID BLUE, SERIAL #L07397-L68238	2,018	**1,493**	1,282	1,072
ELGUIT	64	FENDER	**JAZZMASTER** DAKOTA RED	2,143	**1,585**	1,362	1,138
ELGUIT	64	FENDER	**JAZZMASTER** SONIC BLUE, SERIAL #L07397-L68238	3,050	**2,256**	1,938	1,620
ELGUIT	64	FENDER	**JAZZMASTER** BURGUNDY MIST, SERIAL #L07397-L68238	3,530	**2,611**	2,243	1,875
ELGUIT	65	FENDER	**JAZZMASTER** OLYMPIC WHITE, SERIAL #38862-145681/L06727-L99227	1,583	**1,170**	1,005	840
ELGUIT	65	FENDER	**JAZZMASTER** CANDY APPLE RED, SERIAL #38862-145681/L06727-L99227	1,605	**1,187**	1,019	852
ELGUIT	65	FENDER	**JAZZMASTER** SUNBURST, BOUND FRETBRD WITH DOTS, TORTOISE PICKGUARD	1,628	**1,204**	1,034	864
ELGUIT	65	FENDER	**JAZZMASTER** SONIC BLUE	1,817	**1,344**	1,154	965
ELGUIT	65	FENDER	**JAZZMASTER** OLYMPIC WHITE, LEFT-HANDED, SERIAL #38862-145681/L06727-L99	1,982	**1,466**	1,259	1,053
ELGUIT	65	FENDER	**JAZZMASTER** BLOND, SERIAL #38862-145681/L06727-L99227	2,033	**1,503**	1,291	1,080
ELGUIT	65	FENDER	**JAZZMASTER** LAKE PLACID BLUE	2,103	**1,555**	1,336	1,117
ELGUIT	65	FENDER	**JAZZMASTER** FIREMIST GOLD	3,336	**2,467**	2,119	1,772
ELGUIT	66	FENDER	**JAZZMASTER** SUNBURST, DOT INLAY, SERIAL #119049-501282	1,410	**1,042**	896	749
ELGUIT	66	FENDER	**JAZZMASTER** CANDY APPLE RED, DOT INLAY, SERIAL #119049-501282	1,579	**1,167**	1,003	838
ELGUIT	66	FENDER	**JAZZMASTER** LAKE PLACID BLUE, DOT INLAY	1,691	**1,251**	1,074	898
ELGUIT	67	FENDER	**JAZZMASTER** SUNBURST, BLOCK INLAY, SERIAL #149078-502479	1,297	**959**	824	689
ELGUIT	68	FENDER	**JAZZMASTER** SUNBURST, SERIAL #185186	1,263	**934**	802	671
ELGUIT	69	FENDER	**JAZZMASTER** SUNBURST, BOUND ROSEWOOD BOARD, BLOCK INLAY	826	**611**	525	439
ELGUIT	70	FENDER	**JAZZMASTER** SUNBURST	708	**523**	450	376
ELGUIT	71	FENDER	**JAZZMASTER** SUNBURST	705	**521**	448	374
ELGUIT	72	FENDER	**JAZZMASTER** SUNBURST	648	**479**	412	344
ELGUIT	72	FENDER	**JAZZMASTER** CANDY APPLE RED, SERIAL #391167	1,037	**767**	659	551
ELGUIT	74	FENDER	**JAZZMASTER** SUNBURST	471	**348**	299	250
ELGUIT	76	FENDER	**JAZZMASTER** SUNBURST	470	**347**	298	249
ELGUIT	77	FENDER	**JAZZMASTER** SUNBURST	467	**345**	297	248
ELGUIT	78	FENDER	**JAZZMASTER** SUNBURST	466	**345**	296	247
ELGUIT	80	FENDER	**JAZZMASTER** SUNBURST	498	**368**	316	264
ELGUIT	79	FENDER	**LEAD I**	284	**210**	180	150
ELGUIT	81	FENDER	**LEAD I**	280	**207**	178	148
ELGUIT	68	FENDER	**LTD** HOLLOW BODY, QUILTED MAPLE	1,992	**1,473**	1,265	1,058
ELGUIT	70	FENDER	**LTD** HOLLOW BODY, QUILTED MAPLE	1,624	**1,201**	1,032	862
ELGUIT	71	FENDER	**LTD** HOLLOW BODY, QUILTED MAPLE	1,536	**1,136**	976	816
ELGUIT	57	FENDER	**MANDO ELECTRIC** BLOND	2,027	**1,499**	1,288	1,077

TYPE	YR	MFG	PRICES--BASED ON 100% ORIGINAL MODEL	SELL EXC	SELL AVG	BUY EXC	BUY AVG
ELGUIT	58	FENDER	**MANDO ELECTRIC** SUNBURST 3-TONE	1,606	**1,187**	1,020	853
ELGUIT	65	FENDER	**MARAUDER** SUNBURST	7,099	**5,250**	4,510	3,771
ELGUIT	66	FENDER	**MARAUDER** SUNBURST	7,003	**5,179**	4,449	3,720
ELGUIT	70	FENDER	**MAVERICK** SUNBURST	916	**678**	582	487
ELGUIT	71	FENDER	**MAVERICK** SUNBURST	796	**589**	506	423
ELGUIT	68	FENDER	**MONTEGO I** SUNBURST, HOLLOW BODY, 1 PU	1,083	**801**	688	575
ELGUIT	71	FENDER	**MONTEGO I** SUNBURST, HOLLOW BODY, 1 PU	959	**709**	609	509
ELGUIT	75	FENDER	**MONTEGO I** SUNBURST	796	**589**	506	423
ELGUIT	69	FENDER	**MONTEGO II** SUNBURST, HOLLOW BODY, 2 PU's	1,248	**923**	793	663
ELGUIT	71	FENDER	**MONTEGO II** SUNBURST, HOLLOW BODY, 2 PU's	1,137	**841**	722	604
ELGUIT	75	FENDER	**MONTEGO II** SUNBURST	996	**736**	633	529
ELGUIT	69	FENDER	**MUSICLANDER** LAKE PLACID BLUE	979	**724**	622	520
ELGUIT	69	FENDER	**MUSICLANDER SWINGER**	710	**525**	451	377
ELGUIT	70	FENDER	**MUSICLANDER SWINGER** SERIAL #255017-272793	708	**523**	450	376
ELGUIT	71	FENDER	**MUSICLANDER SWINGER** SERIAL #256809-271956	706	**522**	448	375
ELGUIT	57	FENDER	**MUSICMASTER** BLOND, SERIAL #12717-22598/-18916--22214	472	**349**	300	250
ELGUIT	57	FENDER	**MUSICMASTER** TAN	475	**351**	301	252
ELGUIT	58	FENDER	**MUSICMASTER** TAN	496	**367**	315	263
ELGUIT	58	FENDER	**MUSICMASTER** BLOND	500	**369**	317	265
ELGUIT	59	FENDER	**MUSICMASTER** BLOND, SERIAL #31563-022878/-23611	467	**345**	297	248
ELGUIT	60	FENDER	**MUSICMASTER** BLOND, SERIAL #42216-58644	428	**316**	272	227
ELGUIT	61	FENDER	**MUSICMASTER** SUNBURST	426	**315**	270	226
ELGUIT	62	FENDER	**MUSICMASTER** SUNBURST	424	**313**	269	225
ELGUIT	62	FENDER	**MUSICMASTER** WHITE, SERIAL #73457-92718/L08931	424	**313**	269	225
ELGUIT	63	FENDER	**MUSICMASTER** WHITE, SERIAL #15682-98685/L00186-L24179	352	**260**	223	187
ELGUIT	63	FENDER	**MUSICMASTER** SUNBURST. SERIAL #15682-98685/L00186-L24179	355	**262**	225	188
ELGUIT	65	FENDER	**MUSICMASTER** BLUE	319	**236**	203	169
ELGUIT	65	FENDER	**MUSICMASTER** RED	319	**236**	203	169
ELGUIT	65	FENDER	**MUSICMASTER** WHITE	322	**238**	204	171
ELGUIT	66	FENDER	**MUSICMASTER** RED, SERIAL #158057-160133	318	**235**	202	169
ELGUIT	66	FENDER	**MUSICMASTER** BLUE	320	**237**	203	170
ELGUIT	67	FENDER	**MUSICMASTER** WHITE, SERIAL #203956	317	**235**	201	168
ELGUIT	68	FENDER	**MUSICMASTER** WHITE	317	**235**	201	168
ELGUIT	68	FENDER	**MUSICMASTER** RED	319	**236**	203	169
ELGUIT	69	FENDER	**MUSICMASTER** SONIC BLUE, SOLID BODY	319	**236**	203	169
ELGUIT	69	FENDER	**MUSICMASTER** RED, SERIAL #271329-296111	320	**237**	203	170
ELGUIT	70	FENDER	**MUSICMASTER** RED	286	**211**	181	151
ELGUIT	71	FENDER	**MUSICMASTER** BLUE-GREEN	285	**210**	181	151
ELGUIT	71	FENDER	**MUSICMASTER** WHITE	285	**210**	181	151
ELGUIT	73	FENDER	**MUSICMASTER** BLUE	284	**210**	180	150
ELGUIT	73	FENDER	**MUSICMASTER** WHITE	284	**210**	180	150
ELGUIT	74	FENDER	**MUSICMASTER** CREAM	250	**185**	159	133

TYPE	YR	MFG	PRICES--BASED ON 100% ORIGINAL MODEL	SELL EXC	SELL AVG	BUY EXC	BUY AVG
ELGUIT	74	FENDER	**MUSICMASTER** RED	283	**209**	179	150
ELGUIT	75	FENDER	**MUSICMASTER** BLUE	234	**173**	148	124
ELGUIT	75	FENDER	**MUSICMASTER** BLACK	240	**177**	152	127
ELGUIT	75	FENDER	**MUSICMASTER** RED	248	**183**	157	132
ELGUIT	78	FENDER	**MUSICMASTER** WHITE	239	**176**	151	126
ELGUIT	67	FENDER	**MUSICMASTER BASS** RED	358	**264**	227	190
ELGUIT	70	FENDER	**MUSICMASTER BASS** SONIC BLUE	353	**261**	224	187
ELGUIT	70	FENDER	**MUSICMASTER BASS** SONIC BLUE	356	**263**	226	189
ELGUIT	71	FENDER	**MUSICMASTER BASS** WHITE	352	**260**	223	187
ELGUIT	73	FENDER	**MUSICMASTER BASS** RED	348	**257**	221	185
ELGUIT	78	FENDER	**MUSICMASTER BASS** BLACK	284	**210**	180	150
ELGUIT	65	FENDER	**MUSICMASTER II** RED	319	**236**	203	169
ELGUIT	65	FENDER	**MUSICMASTER II** DAPHNE BLUE	424	**313**	269	225
ELGUIT	66	FENDER	**MUSICMASTER II** WHITE, SERIAL #118372-203501	316	**234**	201	168
ELGUIT	67	FENDER	**MUSICMASTER II** RED	367	**271**	233	195
ELGUIT	67	FENDER	**MUSICMASTER II** LONG SCALE	432	**319**	274	229
ELGUIT	64	FENDER	**MUSTANG** WHITE, SERIAL #L41937-L63050	509	**377**	323	270
ELGUIT	65	FENDER	**MUSTANG** WHITE	507	**375**	322	269
ELGUIT	65	FENDER	**MUSTANG** DAKOTA RED	629	**465**	400	334
ELGUIT	65	FENDER	**MUSTANG** SONIC BLUE, SERIAL #102526-124001/L23537-L99089	696	**515**	442	370
ELGUIT	66	FENDER	**MUSTANG** BLUE, SERIAL #105853-501486	489	**362**	311	260
ELGUIT	66	FENDER	**MUSTANG** RED, SERIAL #105853-501486	489	**362**	311	260
ELGUIT	66	FENDER	**MUSTANG** WHITE	490	**362**	311	260
ELGUIT	67	FENDER	**MUSTANG** WHITE	482	**357**	306	256
ELGUIT	67	FENDER	**MUSTANG** RED, SERIAL #175239-208631	483	**357**	307	257
ELGUIT	67	FENDER	**MUSTANG** COMP YELLOW, RACING STRIPES	489	**362**	311	260
ELGUIT	67	FENDER	**MUSTANG** BLUE, LEFT-HANDED	1,035	**766**	658	550
ELGUIT	68	FENDER	**MUSTANG** BLUE	467	**345**	297	248
ELGUIT	68	FENDER	**MUSTANG** WHITE	480	**355**	305	255
ELGUIT	68	FENDER	**MUSTANG** RED	545	**403**	346	289
ELGUIT	69	FENDER	**MUSTANG** COMP RED, RACING STRIPES, SERIAL #269928	479	**354**	304	254
ELGUIT	69	FENDER	**MUSTANG** RED	528	**391**	336	281
ELGUIT	70	FENDER	**MUSTANG** COMP RED, RACING STRIPES	459	**340**	292	244
ELGUIT	70	FENDER	**MUSTANG** BLACK, SERIAL #301922	535	**396**	340	284
ELGUIT	70	FENDER	**MUSTANG** BLUE, SERIAL #301922	602	**445**	383	320
ELGUIT	71	FENDER	**MUSTANG** COMP CANDY APPLE RED	461	**341**	293	245
ELGUIT	71	FENDER	**MUSTANG** WHITE, SERIAL #317799-588161	478	**353**	303	253
ELGUIT	71	FENDER	**MUSTANG** SUNBURST, SERIAL #317526-335966	487	**360**	309	259
ELGUIT	71	FENDER	**MUSTANG** CANDY APPLE RED, STRIPES	603	**446**	383	320
ELGUIT	71	FENDER	**MUSTANG** COMP RED, RACING STRIPES	621	**459**	394	329
ELGUIT	71	FENDER	**MUSTANG** COMP YELLOW, RACING STRIPES	621	**459**	394	329
ELGUIT	72	FENDER	**MUSTANG** CANDY APPLE RED	424	**313**	269	225

TYPE	YR	MFG	PRICES--BASED ON 100% ORIGINAL MODEL	SELL EXC	SELL AVG	BUY EXC	BUY AVG
ELGUIT	72	FENDER	**MUSTANG** COMP BLUE, RACING STRIPES, SERIAL #359003-360239	426	**315**	270	226
ELGUIT	72	FENDER	**MUSTANG** COMP RED, RACING STRIPES, SERIAL #359003-360239	429	**317**	272	227
ELGUIT	72	FENDER	**MUSTANG** SUNBURST	483	**357**	307	257
ELGUIT	72	FENDER	**MUSTANG** SUNBURST, LEFT-HANDED	494	**365**	314	262
ELGUIT	72	FENDER	**MUSTANG** YELLOW, SERIAL #359003-360239	499	**369**	317	265
ELGUIT	72	FENDER	**MUSTANG** BLUE, SERIAL #359003-360239	551	**407**	350	292
ELGUIT	73	FENDER	**MUSTANG** SUNBURST, LEFTHANDED	422	**312**	268	224
ELGUIT	73	FENDER	**MUSTANG** RED, SERIAL #411526	437	**323**	278	232
ELGUIT	73	FENDER	**MUSTANG** WHITE	439	**325**	279	233
ELGUIT	73	FENDER	**MUSTANG** SUNBURST, SERIAL #411526	440	**325**	279	234
ELGUIT	73	FENDER	**MUSTANG** BLACK	443	**328**	281	235
ELGUIT	73	FENDER	**MUSTANG** COMP LAKE PLACID BLUE	541	**400**	344	287
ELGUIT	74	FENDER	**MUSTANG** SUNBURST	380	**281**	241	201
ELGUIT	74	FENDER	**MUSTANG** RED	383	**283**	243	203
ELGUIT	74	FENDER	**MUSTANG** BLUE	437	**323**	278	232
ELGUIT	75	FENDER	**MUSTANG** BLACK	355	**262**	225	188
ELGUIT	75	FENDER	**MUSTANG** SUNBURST	355	**262**	225	188
ELGUIT	75	FENDER	**MUSTANG** WHITE	357	**264**	226	189
ELGUIT	75	FENDER	**MUSTANG** BROWN	476	**352**	302	252
ELGUIT	76	FENDER	**MUSTANG** WHITE, LEFT-HANDED	347	**257**	220	184
ELGUIT	76	FENDER	**MUSTANG** SUNBURST	349	**258**	222	185
ELGUIT	76	FENDER	**MUSTANG** NATURAL	350	**259**	222	186
ELGUIT	76	FENDER	**MUSTANG** BLUE	502	**371**	319	266
ELGUIT	76	FENDER	**MUSTANG** SEA FOAM GREEN	512	**379**	325	272
ELGUIT	77	FENDER	**MUSTANG** BLACK	353	**261**	224	187
ELGUIT	77	FENDER	**MUSTANG** WHITE	355	**262**	225	188
ELGUIT	77	FENDER	**MUSTANG** SUNBURST	564	**417**	358	299
ELGUIT	77	FENDER	**MUSTANG** CHERRY	565	**418**	359	300
ELGUIT	78	FENDER	**MUSTANG** RED	281	**208**	178	149
ELGUIT	78	FENDER	**MUSTANG** BROWN	284	**210**	180	150
ELGUIT	78	FENDER	**MUSTANG** ANTIGUA	355	**262**	225	188
ELGUIT	78	FENDER	**MUSTANG** NATURAL	474	**350**	301	251
ELGUIT	78	FENDER	**MUSTANG** BLUE	553	**409**	351	294
ELGUIT	79	FENDER	**MUSTANG** BROWN	319	**236**	203	169
ELGUIT	79	FENDER	**MUSTANG** ANTIGUA	464	**343**	295	246
ELGUIT	81	FENDER	**MUSTANG** RED	317	**235**	201	168
ELGUIT	67	FENDER	**MUSTANG BASS** NATURAL	626	**463**	398	333
ELGUIT	71	FENDER	**MUSTANG BASS** COMPETITION RED	557	**412**	354	296
ELGUIT	76	FENDER	**MUSTANG BASS** SUNBRUST	518	**383**	329	275
ELGUIT	52	FENDER	**PRECISION BASS** BUTTERSCOTCH, SLAB BODY	5,452	**4,032**	3,464	2,896
ELGUIT	52	FENDER	**PRECISION BASS** BLOND, SLAB BODY ONLY, SERIAL #299-1351	6,441	**4,764**	4,093	3,422
ELGUIT	53	FENDER	**PRECISION BASS** BUTTERSCOTCH	5,241	**3,876**	3,330	2,784

TYPE	YR	MFG	PRICES--BASED ON 100% ORIGINAL MODEL	SELL EXC	SELL AVG	BUY EXC	BUY AVG
ELGUIT	53	FENDER	**PRECISION BASS** BLOND, SERIAL #0608-1632	6,404	**4,736**	4,069	3,402
ELGUIT	54	FENDER	**PRECISION BASS** BUTTERSCOTCH, SLAB BODY	5,009	**3,704**	3,182	2,661
ELGUIT	54	FENDER	**PRECISION BASS** SUNBURST	5,025	**3,716**	3,193	2,669
ELGUIT	54	FENDER	**PRECISION BASS** BLOND	6,436	**4,760**	4,090	3,419
ELGUIT	55	FENDER	**PRECISION BASS** SUNBURST	4,800	**3,550**	3,050	2,550
ELGUIT	55	FENDER	**PRECISION BASS** BLOND, SERIAL #0534-11255	5,675	**4,197**	3,606	3,015
ELGUIT	56	FENDER	**PRECISION BASS** SUNBURST	5,666	**4,191**	3,600	3,010
ELGUIT	56	FENDER	**PRECISION BASS** SUNBURST 2-TONE, SERIAL #1341-75820/CONTURED BODY	6,443	**4,765**	4,094	3,423
ELGUIT	57	FENDER	**PRECISION BASS** SUNBURST 2-TONE, SPLIT PICKUPS/ANODIZED GUARD	6,624	**4,899**	4,209	3,519
ELGUIT	58	FENDER	**PRECISION BASS** OLYMPIC WHITE	3,761	**2,781**	2,389	1,998
ELGUIT	58	FENDER	**PRECISION BASS** SUNBURST	4,721	**3,491**	2,999	2,508
ELGUIT	58	FENDER	**PRECISION BASS** SUNBURST 3-TONE, SERIAL #26150-028058/-24233, SPLIT PICKUPS	4,816	**3,562**	3,060	2,558
ELGUIT	58	FENDER	**PRECISION BASS** BLOND, SERIAL #26150-028058/-24233	5,095	**3,768**	3,237	2,707
ELGUIT	59	FENDER	**PRECISION BASS** OLYMPIC WHITE, SLAB BOARD	4,538	**3,356**	2,884	2,411
ELGUIT	59	FENDER	**PRECISION BASS** SUNBURST 3-TONE, SERIAL #32573-95325	4,818	**3,563**	3,061	2,559
ELGUIT	59	FENDER	**PRECISION BASS** SUNBURST, ROSEWOOD SLAB BOARD	5,157	**3,814**	3,276	2,739
ELGUIT	60	FENDER	**PRECISION BASS** OLYMPIC WHITE	3,483	**2,576**	2,213	1,850
ELGUIT	60	FENDER	**PRECISION BASS** SUNBURST	4,142	**3,063**	2,632	2,200
ELGUIT	60	FENDER	**PRECISION BASS** BLONDE SEE-THRU	4,542	**3,359**	2,886	2,413
ELGUIT	61	FENDER	**PRECISION BASS** OLYMPIC WHITE	4,252	**3,145**	2,702	2,259
ELGUIT	62	FENDER	**PRECISION BASS** SEA FOAM GREEN, SERIAL #70856-306266/L00938	3,566	**2,637**	2,266	1,894
ELGUIT	62	FENDER	**PRECISION BASS** SUNBURST, SERIAL #70856-306266/L00938	4,091	**3,026**	2,599	2,173
ELGUIT	63	FENDER	**PRECISION BASS** SUNBURST	4,066	**3,007**	2,583	2,160
ELGUIT	63	FENDER	**PRECISION BASS** CANDY APPLE RED	4,220	**3,121**	2,681	2,241
ELGUIT	63	FENDER	**PRECISION BASS** OLYMPIC WHITE, SERIAL #22520-98462/L0827-L80387	4,433	**3,278**	2,816	2,355
ELGUIT	64	FENDER	**PRECISION BASS** SUNBURST 3-TONE, SERIAL #34654-76736/L01734-L85182	2,246	**1,661**	1,427	1,193
ELGUIT	64	FENDER	**PRECISION BASS** OLYMPIC WHITE, SERIAL #34854-76736/L01734-L85182	3,275	**2,422**	2,081	1,740
ELGUIT	64	FENDER	**PRECISION BASS** CANDY APPLE RED	3,903	**2,886**	2,480	2,073
ELGUIT	64	FENDER	**PRECISION BASS** SHORELINE GOLD, LEFT-HANDED	4,207	**3,111**	2,673	2,235
ELGUIT	64	FENDER	**PRECISION BASS** SUNBURST	4,656	**3,443**	2,958	2,473
ELGUIT	64	FENDER	**PRECISION BASS** LAKE PLACID BLUE	4,714	**3,486**	2,995	2,504
ELGUIT	64	FENDER	**PRECISION BASS** BURGUNDY MIST, SERIAL #34654-76736/L01734-L85182	4,718	**3,489**	2,998	2,506
ELGUIT	65	FENDER	**PRECISION BASS** SUNBURST	3,199	**2,366**	2,033	1,699
ELGUIT	65	FENDER	**PRECISION BASS** OLYMPIC WHITE	3,371	**2,493**	2,142	1,791
ELGUIT	65	FENDER	**PRECISION BASS** CANDY APPLE RED, SERIAL #100339-176651/L32519-L99751	3,839	**2,839**	2,439	2,039
ELGUIT	65	FENDER	**PRECISION BASS** SHERWOOD GREEN, SERIAL #100339-176651/L32519-L99751	3,846	**2,844**	2,444	2,043
ELGUIT	65	FENDER	**PRECISION BASS** LAKE PLACID BLUE	3,995	**2,955**	2,538	2,122
ELGUIT	65	FENDER	**PRECISION BASS** BLOND SEE-THRU	4,326	**3,199**	2,749	2,298
ELGUIT	65	FENDER	**PRECISION BASS** BLACK	4,348	**3,216**	2,763	2,310
ELGUIT	66	FENDER	**PRECISION BASS** SUNBURST, SERIAL #73159-247551	2,266	**1,676**	1,440	1,204
ELGUIT	66	FENDER	**PRECISION BASS** OLYMPIC WHITE	2,361	**1,746**	1,500	1,254
ELGUIT	66	FENDER	**PRECISION BASS** LAKE PLACID BLUE, SERIAL #73159-247551	3,377	**2,497**	2,145	1,794

TYPE	YR	MFG	PRICES--BASED ON 100% ORIGINAL MODEL	SELL EXC	SELL AVG	BUY EXC	BUY AVG
ELGUIT	66	FENDER	**PRECISION BASS** CANDY APPLE RED, SERIAL #73159-247551	3,653	**2,702**	2,321	1,941
ELGUIT	66	FENDER	**PRECISION BASS** INCA SILVER	4,728	**3,497**	3,004	2,512
ELGUIT	67	FENDER	**PRECISION BASS** CANDY APPLE RED, SERIAL #187113-303652	1,959	**1,449**	1,245	1,040
ELGUIT	68	FENDER	**PRECISION BASS** SUNBURST	1,195	**883**	759	634
ELGUIT	69	FENDER	**PRECISION BASS** SUNBURST, SERIAL #228425-635656	1,261	**932**	801	670
ELGUIT	69	FENDER	**PRECISION BASS** OLYMPIC WHITE, FIGURED BIRDS EYE NECK, ROSWD FRTBRD	1,441	**1,066**	916	766
ELGUIT	70	FENDER	**PRECISION BASS** SUNBURST, FRETLESS, SERIAL #292195-322961	1,054	**779**	669	559
ELGUIT	70	FENDER	**PRECISION BASS** OLYMPIC WHITE, SERIAL #292195-322961	1,306	**966**	830	694
ELGUIT	71	FENDER	**PRECISION BASS** SUNBURST	964	**713**	613	512
ELGUIT	71	FENDER	**PRECISION BASS** OLYMPIC WHITE	1,232	**911**	783	654
ELGUIT	72	FENDER	**PRECISION BASS** RED, FRETLESS, SERIAL #315451-390396	851	**629**	541	452
ELGUIT	72	FENDER	**PRECISION BASS** SUNBURST, FRETLESS	893	**661**	567	474
ELGUIT	72	FENDER	**PRECISION BASS** BLOND, FRETLESS, ROSEWOOD	929	**687**	590	493
ELGUIT	72	FENDER	**PRECISION BASS** SUNBURST	1,155	**854**	734	614
ELGUIT	72	FENDER	**PRECISION BASS** CANDY APPLE RED	1,198	**886**	761	636
ELGUIT	73	FENDER	**PRECISION BASS** SUNBURST, MAPLE NECK	781	**577**	496	415
ELGUIT	73	FENDER	**PRECISION BASS** SUNBURST, FRETLESS	818	**605**	520	435
ELGUIT	73	FENDER	**PRECISION BASS** BLACK, MAPLE NECK	864	**639**	549	459
ELGUIT	73	FENDER	**PRECISION BASS** CREAM	939	**695**	597	499
ELGUIT	73	FENDER	**PRECISION BASS** OLYMPIC WHITE	954	**705**	606	506
ELGUIT	73	FENDER	**PRECISION BASS** NATURAL, MAPLE NECK	961	**711**	611	511
ELGUIT	74	FENDER	**PRECISION BASS** BROWN	571	**422**	362	303
ELGUIT	74	FENDER	**PRECISION BASS** NATURAL, MAPLE NECK	579	**428**	368	308
ELGUIT	74	FENDER	**PRECISION BASS** NATURAL, LEFT-HANDED	588	**435**	373	312
ELGUIT	74	FENDER	**PRECISION BASS** ROSEWOOD, FRETLESS	601	**445**	382	319
ELGUIT	74	FENDER	**PRECISION BASS** SUNBURST	622	**460**	395	330
ELGUIT	74	FENDER	**PRECISION BASS** BLACK, MAPLE BOARD, SERIAL #402899-7652691	639	**472**	406	339
ELGUIT	74	FENDER	**PRECISION BASS** NATURAL, FRETLESS, SERIAL #402899-7652691	753	**557**	478	400
ELGUIT	74	FENDER	**PRECISION BASS** SUNBURST, FRETLESS, SERIAL #402899-580000	784	**580**	498	416
ELGUIT	74	FENDER	**PRECISION BASS** OLYMPIC WHITE	1,027	**759**	652	545
ELGUIT	74	FENDER	**PRECISION BASS** LAKE PLACID BLUE, ROSEWOOD	1,032	**763**	656	548
ELGUIT	75	FENDER	**PRECISION BASS** BROWN, MAPLE NECK, SERIAL #619243	553	**409**	351	294
ELGUIT	75	FENDER	**PRECISION BASS** SUNBURST, SERIAL #608195-650392	581	**430**	369	309
ELGUIT	75	FENDER	**PRECISION BASS** NATURAL, MAPLE NECK, SERIAL #608195-650392	625	**462**	397	332
ELGUIT	75	FENDER	**PRECISION BASS** NATURAL, MAPLE NECK, LEFT-HANDED	633	**468**	402	336
ELGUIT	75	FENDER	**PRECISION BASS** SUNBURST, LEFT-HANDED	665	**492**	422	353
ELGUIT	75	FENDER	**PRECISION BASS** BLACK, MAPLE NECK	705	**521**	448	374
ELGUIT	75	FENDER	**PRECISION BASS** SUNBURST, FRETLESS, SERIAL #608195-650392	710	**525**	451	377
ELGUIT	75	FENDER	**PRECISION BASS** BLOND, SERIAL #608195-650392	713	**527**	453	378
ELGUIT	76	FENDER	**PRECISION BASS** NATURAL, SERIAL #588481-7651858/S870439	629	**465**	400	334
ELGUIT	76	FENDER	**PRECISION BASS** SUNBURST, MAPLE NECK, SERIAL #588481-7651858	633	**468**	402	336
ELGUIT	76	FENDER	**PRECISION BASS** OLYMPIC WHITE, SERIAL #588481-7651858/S870439	721	**533**	458	383

TYPE	YR	MFG	PRICES--BASED ON 100% ORIGINAL MODEL	SELL EXC	SELL AVG	BUY EXC	BUY AVG
ELGUIT	76	FENDER	**PRECISION BASS** BLACK, MAPLE NECK, SERIAL #588481-7651858/S870439	728	**538**	462	387
ELGUIT	76	FENDER	**PRECISION BASS** CANDY APPLE RED	776	**574**	493	412
ELGUIT	76	FENDER	**PRECISION BASS** BLACK, LEFT-HANDED, SERIAL #588481-7651858/S870439	792	**586**	503	421
ELGUIT	76	FENDER	**PRECISION BASS** FRETLESS MAPLE NECK	796	**589**	506	423
ELGUIT	77	FENDER	**PRECISION BASS** NATURAL, MAPLE NECK, SERIAL #45606	626	**463**	398	333
ELGUIT	77	FENDER	**PRECISION BASS** SUNBURST, MAPLE NECK	650	**481**	413	345
ELGUIT	77	FENDER	**PRECISION BASS** NATURAL, FRETLESS, ROSEWOOD	729	**539**	463	387
ELGUIT	77	FENDER	**PRECISION BASS** BLACK, MAPLE NECK	739	**546**	469	392
ELGUIT	78	FENDER	**PRECISION BASS** SUNBURST, MAPLE NECK, SERIAL #S745231-S868960	629	**465**	400	334
ELGUIT	78	FENDER	**PRECISION BASS** CHERRY TRANSPARENT	633	**468**	402	336
ELGUIT	78	FENDER	**PRECISION BASS** ANTIGUA, MAPLE NECK, SERIAL #S745231-S868960	662	**489**	420	351
ELGUIT	78	FENDER	**PRECISION BASS** NATURAL, SERIAL #S745231-S868960	662	**489**	420	351
ELGUIT	78	FENDER	**PRECISION BASS** SUNBURST, LEFT-HANDED, SERIAL #S745231-S868960	699	**517**	444	371
ELGUIT	78	FENDER	**PRECISION BASS** OLYMPIC WHITE	707	**523**	449	375
ELGUIT	78	FENDER	**PRECISION BASS** BLACK, MAPLE NECK, SERIAL #S745231-S868960	713	**527**	453	378
ELGUIT	78	FENDER	**PRECISION BASS** BLACK, LEFT-HANDED	718	**531**	456	381
ELGUIT	78	FENDER	**PRECISION BASS** NATURAL, FRETLESS	725	**536**	461	385
ELGUIT	79	FENDER	**PRECISION BASS** NATURAL	586	**433**	372	311
ELGUIT	79	FENDER	**PRECISION BASS** SAPPHIRE BLUE	588	**435**	373	312
ELGUIT	79	FENDER	**PRECISION BASS** SUNBURST	668	**494**	424	354
ELGUIT	79	FENDER	**PRECISION BASS** OLYMPIC WHITE, ROSEWOOD, SERIAL #S792565-S904744	830	**614**	527	441
ELGUIT	79	FENDER	**PRECISION BASS** BLACK, MAPLE NECK	907	**670**	576	481
ELGUIT	87	FENDER	**PRECISION BASS '57 REISSUE** SUNBURST	617	**456**	392	327
ELGUIT	83	FENDER	**PRECISION BASS ELITE II** PEWTER METALLIC	518	**383**	329	275
ELGUIT	80	FENDER	**PRECISION BASS SPECIAL**	474	**350**	301	251
ELGUIT	80	FENDER	**PRECISION BASS SPECIAL** BLUE METALLIC	611	**452**	388	324
ELGUIT	81	FENDER	**PRECISION BASS SPECIAL** RED, ACTIVE ELECTRONICS	473	**350**	300	251
ELGUIT	82	FENDER	**PRECISION BASS SPECIAL** CANDY APPLE RED	611	**452**	388	324
ELGUIT	80	FENDER	**SQUIER BULLET** SUNBURST, MAPLE	177	**131**	112	94
ELGUIT	75	FENDER	**STARCASTER** SUNBURST, HOLLOW BODY, 2 PU's	837	**619**	531	444
ELGUIT	76	FENDER	**STARCASTER** SUNBURST, HOLLOW BODY, 2 PU's	785	**580**	498	417
ELGUIT	76	FENDER	**STARCASTER** BLOND, HOLLOW BODY, 2 PU's	871	**644**	553	463
ELGUIT	77	FENDER	**STARCASTER** BLACK, HOLLOW BODY, 2 PU's, SERIAL #S709138	864	**639**	549	459
ELGUIT	77	FENDER	**STARCASTER** NATURAL, HOLLOW BODY, 2 PU's	952	**704**	605	505
ELGUIT	77	FENDER	**STARCASTER** WHITE, HOLLOW BODY, 2 PU's, SERIAL #S709138	960	**710**	610	510
ELGUIT	54	FENDER	**STRATOCASTER** SUNBURST 2-TONE, SERIAL #19-09599	18,667	**13,805**	11,861	9,916
ELGUIT	54	FENDER	**STRATOCASTER** SUNBURST, NON-TREMOLO/TWO-TONE	19,008	**14,058**	12,078	10,098
ELGUIT	54	FENDER	**STRATOCASTER** BLOND, GOLD HARDWARE, SERIAL #19-09599	19,641	**14,526**	12,480	10,434
ELGUIT	54	FENDER	**STRATOCASTER** SHORELINE GOLD	38,513	**28,483**	24,471	20,460
ELGUIT	55	FENDER	**STRATOCASTER** SUNBURST 2-TONE, SERIAL #0962-10910	20,155	**14,906**	12,806	10,707
ELGUIT	55	FENDER	**STRATOCASTER** SUNBURST 2-TONE, SERIAL #0962-10910 LEFT-HANDED	20,343	**15,045**	12,926	10,807
ELGUIT	55	FENDER	**STRATOCASTER** SUNBURST	23,590	**17,446**	14,989	12,532

TYPE	YR	MFG	PRICES--BASED ON 100% ORIGINAL MODEL	SELL EXC	SELL AVG	BUY EXC	BUY AVG
ELGUIT	56	FENDER	**STRATOCASTER** SUNBURST	12,475	**9,226**	7,926	6,627
ELGUIT	56	FENDER	**STRATOCASTER** CANDY APPLE RED	16,816	**12,437**	10,685	8,933
ELGUIT	56	FENDER	**STRATOCASTER** SUNBURST 2-TONE, SERIAL #0999-29629	19,289	**14,266**	12,256	10,247
ELGUIT	57	FENDER	**STRATOCASTER** SUNBURST	11,820	**8,742**	7,510	6,279
ELGUIT	57	FENDER	**STRATOCASTER** SHELL PINK	12,962	**9,587**	8,236	6,886
ELGUIT	57	FENDER	**STRATOCASTER** DAKOTA RED, SERIAL #7019-027770 NON-TREMOLO	18,777	**13,887**	11,931	9,975
ELGUIT	57	FENDER	**STRATOCASTER** SUNBURST 2-TONE, SERIAL #7019-02770/L16720-L25700	21,463	**15,874**	13,638	11,402
ELGUIT	57	FENDER	**STRATOCASTER** SUNBURST 2-TONE, TREMOLO	23,633	**17,478**	15,016	12,555
ELGUIT	57	FENDER	**STRATOCASTER** BLOND, GOLD HARDWARE, "MARY KAYE"	26,875	**19,876**	17,076	14,277
ELGUIT	57	FENDER	**STRATOCASTER** SHORELINE GOLD, SERIAL #7019-027770/L16720-L25700	28,047	**20,743**	17,821	14,900
ELGUIT	58	FENDER	**STRATOCASTER** SUNBURST, NON-TREMOLO	9,384	**6,940**	5,962	4,985
ELGUIT	58	FENDER	**STRATOCASTER** SUNBURST, HARD-TAIL	9,589	**7,092**	6,093	5,094
ELGUIT	58	FENDER	**STRATOCASTER** SUNBURST, LEFT-HANDED	12,967	**9,590**	8,239	6,889
ELGUIT	58	FENDER	**STRATOCASTER** BLACK, SERIAL #7954-028255/-21257- -223972	16,060	**11,878**	10,205	8,532
ELGUIT	58	FENDER	**STRATOCASTER** SUNBURST 2-TONE	17,275	**12,776**	10,976	9,177
ELGUIT	58	FENDER	**STRATOCASTER** SUNBURST 3-TONE, SERIAL #7954-028255/-21257- -223972	17,722	**13,107**	11,261	9,415
ELGUIT	58	FENDER	**STRATOCASTER** BLOND, GOLD HARDWARE, SERIAL #7954-028255/-21257- 223972	23,056	**17,052**	14,650	12,248
ELGUIT	59	FENDER	**STRATOCASTER** SUNBURST 2-TONE, SERIAL #29178-027343/-19655	16,887	**12,489**	10,730	8,971
ELGUIT	59	FENDER	**STRATOCASTER** SUNBURST 3-TONE	17,213	**12,731**	10,937	9,144
ELGUIT	59	FENDER	**STRATOCASTER** BLOND, GOLD HARDWARE, "MARY KAYE"	21,109	**15,612**	13,413	11,214
ELGUIT	60	FENDER	**STRATOCASTER** SUNBURST, 2.5-TONE	10,248	**7,579**	6,511	5,444
ELGUIT	60	FENDER	**STRATOCASTER** BLACK	10,443	**7,724**	6,636	5,548
ELGUIT	60	FENDER	**STRATOCASTER** SUNBURST 2-TONE, SERIAL #44221-64087	10,479	**7,750**	6,658	5,567
ELGUIT	60	FENDER	**STRATOCASTER** LEFT-HANDED, 2.5-TONE	10,497	**7,763**	6,670	5,576
ELGUIT	60	FENDER	**STRATOCASTER** SUNBURST, NON-TREMOLO	12,287	**9,087**	7,807	6,527
ELGUIT	60	FENDER	**STRATOCASTER** SUNBURST, 3-TONE	12,552	**9,283**	7,975	6,668
ELGUIT	60	FENDER	**STRATOCASTER** CANDY APPLE RED METALLIC, SERIAL #44221-64087	13,434	**9,935**	8,536	7,136
ELGUIT	60	FENDER	**STRATOCASTER** OLYMPIC WHITE, SERIAL #44221-64087	13,438	**9,938**	8,538	7,138
ELGUIT	60	FENDER	**STRATOCASTER** BLOND, GOLD HARDWARE	14,073	**10,408**	8,942	7,476
ELGUIT	60	FENDER	**STRATOCASTER** FIESTA RED	14,208	**10,508**	9,028	7,548
ELGUIT	60	FENDER	**STRATOCASTER** SURF GREEN, SERIAL #44221-64087	14,280	**10,561**	9,073	7,586
ELGUIT	60	FENDER	**STRATOCASTER** DAKOTA RED	14,764	**10,919**	9,381	7,843
ELGUIT	60	FENDER	**STRATOCASTER** SHORELINE GOLD, LEFT-HANDED, SERIAL #44221-64087	16,246	**12,015**	10,323	8,630
ELGUIT	60	FENDER	**STRATOCASTER** DAPHNE BLUE, NON-TREMOLO	17,126	**12,666**	10,882	9,098
ELGUIT	60	FENDER	**STRATOCASTER** BURGUNDY MIST, SERIAL #44254-	18,202	**13,462**	11,566	9,670
ELGUIT	61	FENDER	**STRATOCASTER** SUNBURST, SERIAL #52034-92689	10,247	**7,578**	6,511	5,443
ELGUIT	61	FENDER	**STRATOCASTER** SUNBURST, LEFT-HANDED	11,105	**8,213**	7,056	5,899
ELGUIT	61	FENDER	**STRATOCASTER** OLYMPIC WHITE	11,630	**8,601**	7,390	6,178
ELGUIT	61	FENDER	**STRATOCASTER** BLOND SEE-THRU	12,922	**9,557**	8,211	6,865
ELGUIT	61	FENDER	**STRATOCASTER** FIESTA RED	14,566	**10,772**	9,255	7,738
ELGUIT	61	FENDER	**STRATOCASTER** SHERWOOD GREEN METALLIC, SLAB ROSEWOOD BOARD	18,760	**13,874**	11,920	9,966
ELGUIT	62	FENDER	**STRATOCASTER** SUNBURST, SERIAL #55045-97560/L00543-L19427	7,313	**5,408**	4,646	3,885

TYPE	YR	MFG	PRICES--BASED ON 100% ORIGINAL MODEL	SELL EXC	SELL AVG	BUY EXC	BUY AVG
ELGUIT	62	FENDER	STRATOCASTER OLYMPIC WHITE, SERIAL #55045-97560/L00543-L19427	10,211	7,552	6,488	5,424
ELGUIT	62	FENDER	STRATOCASTER SONIC BLUE	10,447	7,726	6,638	5,550
ELGUIT	62	FENDER	STRATOCASTER FIESTA RED	13,454	9,950	8,549	7,147
ELGUIT	62	FENDER	STRATOCASTER LAKE PLACID BLUE	15,038	11,122	9,555	7,989
ELGUIT	62	FENDER	STRATOCASTER BURGUNDY MIST, SERIAL #55045-97560/L00543-L19427	15,774	11,666	10,023	8,380
ELGUIT	62	FENDER	STRATOCASTER SHORELINE GOLD, SERIAL #55045-97560/L00543-L19427	16,008	11,839	10,171	8,504
ELGUIT	63	FENDER	STRATOCASTER SUNBURST 3-TONE	8,608	6,366	5,469	4,573
ELGUIT	63	FENDER	STRATOCASTER SUNBURST,ROSEWD FNGRBRD,SERIAL #29582-007020/L00201-L43141	9,163	6,776	5,822	4,867
ELGUIT	63	FENDER	STRATOCASTER OLYMPIC WHITE, SERIAL #29582-007020/L00201-L43141	9,475	7,007	6,020	5,033
ELGUIT	63	FENDER	STRATOCASTER CANDY APPLE RED, SERIAL #29582-007020/L00201-L43141	9,518	7,039	6,048	5,056
ELGUIT	63	FENDER	STRATOCASTER FIESTA RED, SERIAL #29582-007020/L00201-L43141	10,579	7,824	6,722	5,620
ELGUIT	63	FENDER	STRATOCASTER SEA FOAM GREEN	16,847	12,459	10,704	8,949
ELGUIT	63	FENDER	STRATOCASTER BLOND, GOLD HARDWARE, "MARY KAYE"	16,857	12,467	10,711	8,955
ELGUIT	64	FENDER	STRATOCASTER SUNBURST, SERIAL #27180-190815/L04974-L87120	6,595	4,877	4,190	3,503
ELGUIT	64	FENDER	STRATOCASTER CANDY APPLE RED, SERIAL #27180-190815/L04974-L87120	7,886	5,832	5,011	4,189
ELGUIT	64	FENDER	STRATOCASTER RED, LEFT-HANDED, SERIAL #27180-190815/L04974-L87120	8,365	6,186	5,315	4,444
ELGUIT	64	FENDER	STRATOCASTER OLYMPIC WHITE, SERIAL #27180-190815/L04974-L87120	8,568	6,337	5,444	4,552
ELGUIT	64	FENDER	STRATOCASTER SALMON PINK	8,875	6,563	5,639	4,714
ELGUIT	64	FENDER	STRATOCASTER CANDY APPLE RED, LEFT-HANDED	8,876	6,564	5,640	4,715
ELGUIT	64	FENDER	STRATOCASTER LAKE PLACID BLUE	9,447	6,987	6,003	5,018
ELGUIT	64	FENDER	STRATOCASTER SHORELINE GOLD, SERIAL #27180-190815/L04974-L87120	12,112	8,958	7,696	6,434
ELGUIT	64	FENDER	STRATOCASTER BURGUNDY MIST, SERIAL #27180-190815/L04974-L87120	12,305	9,100	7,818	6,537
ELGUIT	65	FENDER	STRATOCASTER SUNBURST, LEFT-HANDED, SERIAL #26704-139227/L26114-L99809	7,200	5,325	4,575	3,825
ELGUIT	65	FENDER	STRATOCASTER SUNBURST, SERIAL #26704-139227/L26114-L99809	7,348	5,435	4,669	3,904
ELGUIT	65	FENDER	STRATOCASTER CANDY APPLE RED, SERIAL #26704-139227/L26114-L99809	9,035	6,682	5,741	4,800
ELGUIT	65	FENDER	STRATOCASTER LAKE PLACID BLUE, SERIAL #26704-139227/L26114-L99809	9,164	6,777	5,823	4,868
ELGUIT	65	FENDER	STRATOCASTER OLYMPIC WHITE	9,230	6,826	5,865	4,903
ELGUIT	65	FENDER	STRATOCASTER SONIC BLUE, SERIAL #26704-139227/L26114-L99809	9,480	7,011	6,023	5,036
ELGUIT	65	FENDER	STRATOCASTER DAPHNE BLUE	9,503	7,028	6,038	5,048
ELGUIT	65	FENDER	STRATOCASTER CHARCOAL FROST	9,998	7,394	6,353	5,311
ELGUIT	65	FENDER	STRATOCASTER BLACK	10,068	7,446	6,397	5,348
ELGUIT	65	FENDER	STRATOCASTER BURGUNDY/BLUE SPARKLE	10,156	7,511	6,453	5,395
ELGUIT	65	FENDER	STRATOCASTER BLUE ICE METALLIC	12,249	9,059	7,783	6,507
ELGUIT	65	FENDER	STRATOCASTER FIREMIST GOLD	13,076	9,670	8,308	6,946
ELGUIT	65	FENDER	STRATOCASTER SEA FOAM GREEN, SERIAL #26704-139227/L26114-L99809	13,761	10,177	8,744	7,310
ELGUIT	66	FENDER	STRATOCASTER SUNBURST 3-TONE	4,107	3,038	2,610	2,182
ELGUIT	66	FENDER	STRATOCASTER SUNBURST, ROSEWOOD FINGERBOARD	4,737	3,503	3,010	2,516
ELGUIT	66	FENDER	STRATOCASTER BLOND, SERIAL #112115-361639	5,606	4,146	3,562	2,978
ELGUIT	66	FENDER	STRATOCASTER CANDY APPLE RED, SERIAL #112115-361639	6,600	4,881	4,193	3,506
ELGUIT	66	FENDER	STRATOCASTER OLYMPIC WHITE	6,969	5,154	4,428	3,702
ELGUIT	66	FENDER	STRATOCASTER SONIC BLUE	7,512	5,556	4,773	3,991
ELGUIT	66	FENDER	STRATOCASTER BLACK, SERIAL #112115-361639	7,532	5,570	4,786	4,001

TYPE	YR	MFG	PRICES--BASED ON 100% ORIGINAL	SELL EXC	SELL AVG	BUY EXC	BUY AVG
			MODEL				
ELGUIT	66	FENDER	**STRATOCASTER** INCA SILVER	10,134	**7,495**	6,439	5,384
ELGUIT	67	FENDER	**STRATOCASTER** SUNBURST, MAPLE CAP, SERIAL #182354-239316	6,624	**4,899**	4,209	3,519
ELGUIT	67	FENDER	**STRATOCASTER** OLYMPIC WHITE, MAPLE CAP	7,008	**5,183**	4,453	3,723
ELGUIT	67	FENDER	**STRATOCASTER** LAKE PLACID BLUE	9,096	**6,727**	5,780	4,832
ELGUIT	67	FENDER	**STRATOCASTER** INCA SILVER, SERIAL #182354-239316	9,565	**7,074**	6,078	5,081
ELGUIT	68	FENDER	**STRATOCASTER** SUNBURST, NON-TREMOLO	4,761	**3,521**	3,025	2,529
ELGUIT	68	FENDER	**STRATOCASTER** SUNBURST, ROSEWOOD CAP	5,006	**3,702**	3,181	2,659
ELGUIT	68	FENDER	**STRATOCASTER** BLACK, MAPLE CAP ONLY	6,623	**4,898**	4,208	3,518
ELGUIT	68	FENDER	**STRATOCASTER** OLYMPIC WHITE, MAPLE CAP	6,720	**4,970**	4,270	3,570
ELGUIT	69	FENDER	**STRATOCASTER** SUNBURST, ROSEWOOD CAP, SERIAL #167362-356440	3,706	**2,741**	2,355	1,969
ELGUIT	69	FENDER	**STRATOCASTER** SUNBURST, LEFT-HANDED, SERIAL #167362-356440	3,822	**2,827**	2,429	2,030
ELGUIT	69	FENDER	**STRATOCASTER** BLOND	4,752	**3,514**	3,019	2,524
ELGUIT	69	FENDER	**STRATOCASTER** OLYMPIC WHITE, MAPLE CAP	4,879	**3,608**	3,100	2,592
ELGUIT	70	FENDER	**STRATOCASTER** SUNBURST, NON-TREMOLO	1,873	**1,385**	1,190	995
ELGUIT	70	FENDER	**STRATOCASTER** SUNBURST, TREMOLO	2,374	**1,755**	1,508	1,261
ELGUIT	70	FENDER	**STRATOCASTER** CANDY APPLE RED	5,670	**4,193**	3,603	3,012
ELGUIT	70	FENDER	**STRATOCASTER** LAKE PLACID BLUE	5,888	**4,355**	3,741	3,128
ELGUIT	71	FENDER	**STRATOCASTER** OLYMPIC WHITE, SERIAL #66767-581817	2,378	**1,759**	1,511	1,263
ELGUIT	71	FENDER	**STRATOCASTER** SUNBURST	3,000	**2,218**	1,906	1,593
ELGUIT	71	FENDER	**STRATOCASTER** SUNBURST, LEFT-HANDED	3,710	**2,744**	2,357	1,971
ELGUIT	72	FENDER	**STRATOCASTER** NATURAL, TREMOLO	1,635	**1,209**	1,039	869
ELGUIT	72	FENDER	**STRATOCASTER** SUNBURST, NON-TREMOLO	1,802	**1,333**	1,145	957
ELGUIT	72	FENDER	**STRATOCASTER** BLOND	1,872	**1,385**	1,190	995
ELGUIT	72	FENDER	**STRATOCASTER** BLACK, TREMOLO, 4 BOLT, SERIAL #000001-712344	2,135	**1,579**	1,356	1,134
ELGUIT	72	FENDER	**STRATOCASTER** BLACK, LEFT-HANDED	2,229	**1,648**	1,416	1,184
ELGUIT	72	FENDER	**STRATOCASTER** OLYMPIC WHITE	2,961	**2,190**	1,881	1,573
ELGUIT	72	FENDER	**STRATOCASTER** DAKOTA RED	2,995	**2,215**	1,903	1,591
ELGUIT	73	FENDER	**STRATOCASTER** SUNBURST, SERIAL #358820-552416/S777565	1,366	**1,010**	868	725
ELGUIT	73	FENDER	**STRATOCASTER** BLACK, TREMOLO, 3 BOLT	1,370	**1,013**	871	728
ELGUIT	73	FENDER	**STRATOCASTER** NATURAL, SERIAL #358820-552416/S777565	1,377	**1,018**	875	731
ELGUIT	73	FENDER	**STRATOCASTER** BROWN, TREMOLO	1,415	**1,046**	899	751
ELGUIT	73	FENDER	**STRATOCASTER** BLOND	1,417	**1,048**	900	753
ELGUIT	73	FENDER	**STRATOCASTER** OLYMPIC WHITE	1,739	**1,286**	1,105	924
ELGUIT	73	FENDER	**STRATOCASTER** LAKE PLACID BLUE	1,868	**1,381**	1,187	992
ELGUIT	73	FENDER	**STRATOCASTER** WALNUT, LEFT-HANDED	2,189	**1,619**	1,391	1,163
ELGUIT	73	FENDER	**STRATOCASTER** CANDY APPLE RED, SERIAL #358820-552416/S777565	3,371	**2,493**	2,142	1,791
ELGUIT	74	FENDER	**STRATOCASTER** NATURAL, NON-TREMOLO	996	**736**	633	529
ELGUIT	74	FENDER	**STRATOCASTER** SUNBURST	1,027	**759**	652	545
ELGUIT	74	FENDER	**STRATOCASTER** BROWN, HARD-TAIL	1,088	**805**	691	578
ELGUIT	74	FENDER	**STRATOCASTER** BLACK, HARD-TAIL	1,100	**813**	699	584
ELGUIT	74	FENDER	**STRATOCASTER** BLOND	1,291	**954**	820	685
ELGUIT	74	FENDER	**STRATOCASTER** NATURAL, TREMOLO	1,394	**1,031**	886	741

TYPE	YR	MFG	PRICES--BASED ON 100% ORIGINAL MODEL	SELL EXC	SELL AVG	BUY EXC	BUY AVG
ELGUIT	74	FENDER	**STRATOCASTER** SUNBURST, LEFT-HANDED	1,419	**1,050**	902	754
ELGUIT	74	FENDER	**STRATOCASTER** NATURAL, LEFT-HANDED	1,562	**1,155**	993	830
ELGUIT	74	FENDER	**STRATOCASTER** OLYMPIC WHITE	1,582	**1,170**	1,005	840
ELGUIT	74	FENDER	**STRATOCASTER** OLYMPIC WHITE, LEFT-HANDED	1,974	**1,460**	1,254	1,049
ELGUIT	75	FENDER	**STRATOCASTER** SUNBURST, SERIAL #562789-717257	963	**712**	612	512
ELGUIT	75	FENDER	**STRATOCASTER** SUNBURST, NON-TREMOLO, SERIAL #562789-717257	982	**726**	624	521
ELGUIT	75	FENDER	**STRATOCASTER** BLACK, TREMOLO, SERIAL #562789-717257	989	**732**	628	525
ELGUIT	75	FENDER	**STRATOCASTER** SUNBURST, LEFT-HANDED	991	**733**	630	526
ELGUIT	75	FENDER	**STRATOCASTER** BROWN	1,073	**793**	681	570
ELGUIT	75	FENDER	**STRATOCASTER** CREAM	1,090	**806**	692	579
ELGUIT	75	FENDER	**STRATOCASTER** NATURAL	1,108	**820**	704	589
ELGUIT	75	FENDER	**STRATOCASTER** OLYMPIC WHITE	1,431	**1,058**	909	760
ELGUIT	76	FENDER	**STRATOCASTER** SUNBURST, SERIAL #7679077	792	**586**	503	421
ELGUIT	76	FENDER	**STRATOCASTER** BLACK	800	**592**	508	425
ELGUIT	76	FENDER	**STRATOCASTER** NATURAL, SERIAL #554808-7667908/S767274-S769905	846	**626**	538	449
ELGUIT	76	FENDER	**STRATOCASTER** WHITE, LEFT-HANDED, SERIAL #554808-7667908/S767274-S769905	904	**668**	574	480
ELGUIT	76	FENDER	**STRATOCASTER** NATURAL, NON-TREMOLO	920	**680**	584	489
ELGUIT	76	FENDER	**STRATOCASTER** SUNBURST, LEFT-HANDED	982	**726**	624	521
ELGUIT	77	FENDER	**STRATOCASTER** SUNBURST, NON-TREMOLO	722	**534**	459	384
ELGUIT	77	FENDER	**STRATOCASTER** NATURAL, SERIAL #5778859/S770029-S775989	737	**545**	468	391
ELGUIT	77	FENDER	**STRATOCASTER** BROWN, HARDTAIL	796	**589**	506	423
ELGUIT	77	FENDER	**STRATOCASTER** SUNBURST	927	**685**	589	492
ELGUIT	77	FENDER	**STRATOCASTER** BLACK, SERIAL #5778859/S770029-S775989	967	**715**	614	514
ELGUIT	77	FENDER	**STRATOCASTER** BLOND	1,155	**854**	734	614
ELGUIT	77	FENDER	**STRATOCASTER** NATURAL, LEFT-HANDED	1,191	**881**	757	632
ELGUIT	77	FENDER	**STRATOCASTER** OLYMPIC WHITE	1,199	**886**	761	636
ELGUIT	77	FENDER	**STRATOCASTER** BLACK, LEFT-HANDED	1,206	**892**	766	641
ELGUIT	77	FENDER	**STRATOCASTER** SHELL PINK	8,206	**6,069**	5,214	4,359
ELGUIT	78	FENDER	**STRATOCASTER** ANTIGUA, SERIAL #5942888/S766838-S940993	740	**547**	470	393
ELGUIT	78	FENDER	**STRATOCASTER** SUNBURST, NON-TREMOLO	750	**555**	477	398
ELGUIT	78	FENDER	**STRATOCASTER** SUNBURST	767	**567**	487	407
ELGUIT	78	FENDER	**STRATOCASTER** CREAM, SERIAL #5942888/S766838-S940993	808	**597**	513	429
ELGUIT	78	FENDER	**STRATOCASTER** NATURAL	832	**615**	528	442
ELGUIT	78	FENDER	**STRATOCASTER** BROWN	835	**617**	530	443
ELGUIT	78	FENDER	**STRATOCASTER** BLOND	861	**636**	547	457
ELGUIT	78	FENDER	**STRATOCASTER** BLACK	1,067	**789**	678	567
ELGUIT	78	FENDER	**STRATOCASTER** BLOND, LEFT-HANDED	1,113	**823**	707	591
ELGUIT	78	FENDER	**STRATOCASTER** BLACK, LEFT-HANDED, TREMOLO, MAPLE NECK	1,131	**837**	719	601
ELGUIT	79	FENDER	**STRATOCASTER** CREAM, SERIAL #250025-900301/S360837-S938786	609	**450**	387	323
ELGUIT	79	FENDER	**STRATOCASTER** BROWN, SERIAL #250025-900301/S360837-S938786 NON-TREMOLO	660	**488**	419	350
ELGUIT	79	FENDER	**STRATOCASTER** SUNBURST, NON-TREMOLO	660	**488**	419	350
ELGUIT	79	FENDER	**STRATOCASTER** NATURAL, NON-TREMOLO	691	**511**	439	367

TYPE	YR	MFG	PRICES--BASED ON 100% ORIGINAL MODEL	SELL EXC	SELL AVG	BUY EXC	BUY AVG
ELGUIT	79	FENDER	**STRATOCASTER** ORANGE, SERIAL #S980453	700	**518**	445	372
ELGUIT	79	FENDER	**STRATOCASTER** ANTIGUA, NON-TREMOLO, SERIAL #250025-900301/S360837-S938786	702	**519**	446	373
ELGUIT	79	FENDER	**STRATOCASTER** WALNUT, SERIAL #250025-900301/S360837-S938786	705	**521**	448	374
ELGUIT	79	FENDER	**STRATOCASTER** SUNBURST, SERIAL #250025-900301/S360837-S938786	724	**536**	460	385
ELGUIT	79	FENDER	**STRATOCASTER** RED, SERIAL #S938786	756	**559**	480	401
ELGUIT	79	FENDER	**STRATOCASTER** ANTIGUA, SERIAL #250025-900301/S360837-S938786	757	**560**	481	402
ELGUIT	79	FENDER	**STRATOCASTER** NATURAL, HARD-TAIL	758	**560**	481	402
ELGUIT	79	FENDER	**STRATOCASTER** MAUI BLUE, MAPLE NECK	786	**581**	499	417
ELGUIT	79	FENDER	**STRATOCASTER** WHITE, SERIAL #250025-900301/S360837-S938786	791	**585**	502	420
ELGUIT	79	FENDER	**STRATOCASTER** BLACK, NON-TREMOLO, SERIAL #250025-900301/S360837-S938786	817	**604**	519	434
ELGUIT	79	FENDER	**STRATOCASTER** BLOND, SERIAL #250025-900301/S360837-S938786	826	**611**	525	439
ELGUIT	79	FENDER	**STRATOCASTER** BLACK, SERIAL #250025-900301/S360837-S938786	837	**619**	531	444
ELGUIT	79	FENDER	**STRATOCASTER** BLACK, LEFT-HANDED	869	**643**	552	462
ELGUIT	79	FENDER	**STRATOCASTER** CANDY APPLE RED	1,005	**743**	638	533
ELGUIT	79	FENDER	**STRATOCASTER** OLYMPIC WHITE	1,025	**758**	651	544
ELGUIT	80	FENDER	**STRATOCASTER** BLACK, SERIAL #5869789	471	**348**	299	250
ELGUIT	80	FENDER	**STRATOCASTER** CANDY APPLE RED	531	**393**	337	282
ELGUIT	80	FENDER	**STRATOCASTER** BLACK, LEFT-HANDED	537	**397**	341	285
ELGUIT	81	FENDER	**STRATOCASTER** WALNUT	531	**393**	337	282
ELGUIT	81	FENDER	**STRATOCASTER** SHORELINE GOLD, GOLD HARDWARE	1,264	**935**	803	671
ELGUIT	82	FENDER	**STRATOCASTER** BLACK	492	**364**	312	261
ELGUIT	82	FENDER	**STRATOCASTER** RED 2-TONE	494	**365**	314	262
ELGUIT	83	FENDER	**STRATOCASTER** BLACK, LEFT-HANDED	468	**346**	297	248
ELGUIT	83	FENDER	**STRATOCASTER** BLACK	499	**369**	317	265
ELGUIT	84	FENDER	**STRATOCASTER** BOWLING BALL BLUE	1,378	**1,019**	875	732
ELGUIT	88	FENDER	**STRATOCASTER** PAISLEY	657	**486**	417	349
ELGUIT	80	FENDER	**STRATOCASTER "THE STRAT"**	611	**452**	388	324
ELGUIT	82	FENDER	**STRATOCASTER '62 REISSUE** FIESTA RED	590	**436**	375	313
ELGUIT	83	FENDER	**STRATOCASTER '62 REISSUE** SUNBURST	590	**436**	375	313
ELGUIT	86	FENDER	**STRATOCASTER '62 REISSUE** LAKE PLACID BLUE	588	**435**	373	312
ELGUIT	79	FENDER	**STRATOCASTER 25th ANNIVERSARY** SILVER METALLIC, MAPLE 4-BOLT NECK	587	**434**	373	312
ELGUIT	89	FENDER	**STRATOCASTER 35th ANNIVERSARY** SUNBURST	1,394	**1,031**	886	741
ELGUIT	78	FENDER	**STRATOCASTER ANNIVERSARY** WHITE, SERIAL #5942888/S766838-S940993	925	**684**	588	491
ELGUIT	79	FENDER	**STRATOCASTER ANNIVERSARY** SILVER, SERIAL #250025-258078/S51853	811	**599**	515	430
ELGUIT	79	FENDER	**STRATOCASTER ANNIVERSARY IV** IVORY	1,423	**1,052**	904	756
ELGUIT	69	FENDER	**STRATOCASTER CUSTOM VINTAGE** 3-TONE BURST, PEARLOID PICKGUARD, TREMOLO, MAPLE NECK	808	**597**	513	429
ELGUIT	88	FENDER	**STRATOCASTER DELUXE PLUS**	598	**442**	380	317
ELGUIT	83	FENDER	**STRATOCASTER ELITE** NATURAL	738	**545**	469	392
ELGUIT	83	FENDER	**STRATOCASTER GOLD ELITE**	717	**530**	455	380
ELGUIT	81	FENDER	**STRATOCASTER SMITH**	728	**538**	462	387
ELGUIT	88	FENDER	**STRATOCASTER YNGWIE MALMSTEEN**	837	**619**	531	444
ELGUIT	51	FENDER	**TELECASTER** BUTTERSCOTCH	13,532	**10,008**	8,598	7,188
ELGUIT	51	FENDER	**TELECASTER** NO-CASTER, SERIAL #0585-2752	18,778	**13,888**	11,932	9,976
ELGUIT	52	FENDER	**TELECASTER** BLOND, SERIAL #0293-5221	10,286	**7,607**	6,536	5,464

TYPE	YR	MFG	PRICES--BASED ON 100% ORIGINAL MODEL	SELL EXC	SELL AVG	BUY EXC	BUY AVG
ELGUIT	52	FENDER	TELECASTER BUTTERSCOTCH	10,907	8,067	6,930	5,794
ELGUIT	53	FENDER	TELECASTER BLOND	9,604	7,103	6,103	5,102
ELGUIT	53	FENDER	TELECASTER BUTTERSCOTCH	11,376	8,414	7,229	6,044
ELGUIT	54	FENDER	TELECASTER BLOND, WHITE PICKGUARD, SERIAL #0502-11035	9,255	6,845	5,881	4,916
ELGUIT	54	FENDER	TELECASTER BUTTERSCOTCH	9,568	7,076	6,079	5,083
ELGUIT	54	FENDER	TELECASTER WHITE PICKGUARD, SERIAL #0502-11035	9,606	7,104	6,104	5,103
ELGUIT	54	FENDER	TELECASTER BLOND	9,964	7,369	6,331	5,293
ELGUIT	54	FENDER	TELECASTER BLOND, LEFT-HANDED	10,023	7,413	6,369	5,324
ELGUIT	55	FENDER	TELECASTER BLOND, SERIAL #0617-28705	4,200	3,106	2,668	2,231
ELGUIT	55	FENDER	TELECASTER WHITE PICKGUARD, SERIAL #7045-12842/-21616	7,505	5,550	4,768	3,987
ELGUIT	56	FENDER	TELECASTER BLOND	6,000	4,437	3,812	3,187
ELGUIT	56	FENDER	TELECASTER BLOND, REPRO TUNERS	6,416	4,745	4,077	3,408
ELGUIT	56	FENDER	TELECASTER WHITE PICKGUARD, SERIAL #2431-16492/-11406	7,532	5,570	4,786	4,001
ELGUIT	56	FENDER	TELECASTER FLAME MAPLE NECK, SERIAL 2431-16492/-11406	8,443	6,244	5,364	4,485
ELGUIT	57	FENDER	TELECASTER BLOND, SERIAL #18817-023394/-17815- -20077	6,659	4,925	4,231	3,537
ELGUIT	57	FENDER	TELECASTER V-NECK, SERIAL #18817-023394/-17815- -20077	7,025	5,195	4,463	3,732
ELGUIT	57	FENDER	TELECASTER BLOND, MAPLE NECK	7,983	5,904	5,072	4,241
ELGUIT	57	FENDER	TELECASTER NATURAL	8,517	6,299	5,411	4,524
ELGUIT	57	FENDER	TELECASTER FIESTA RED	10,560	7,810	6,710	5,610
ELGUIT	57	FENDER	TELECASTER DAKOTA RED, MAPLE NECK	14,324	10,593	9,101	7,609
ELGUIT	58	FENDER	TELECASTER SUNBURST, SERIAL #28721-027722/-24785	5,802	4,291	3,686	3,082
ELGUIT	58	FENDER	TELECASTER BLOND	6,000	4,437	3,812	3,187
ELGUIT	59	FENDER	TELECASTER MAPLE NECK, SERIAL #37659	5,929	4,385	3,767	3,150
ELGUIT	59	FENDER	TELECASTER BLOND, MAPLE NECK	7,215	5,336	4,584	3,833
ELGUIT	60	FENDER	TELECASTER BLOND	5,769	4,267	3,666	3,065
ELGUIT	60	FENDER	TELECASTER SONIC BLUE	9,323	6,895	5,924	4,953
ELGUIT	61	FENDER	TELECASTER BLOND, SERIAL #59330-72711	7,016	5,189	4,458	3,727
ELGUIT	62	FENDER	TELECASTER BLOND	6,888	5,094	4,377	3,659
ELGUIT	62	FENDER	TELECASTER FIESTA RED	7,857	5,811	4,992	4,174
ELGUIT	63	FENDER	TELECASTER BLOND, SERIAL #83717/L10439-L43106	5,501	4,069	3,495	2,922
ELGUIT	63	FENDER	TELECASTER SONIC BLUE	7,323	5,416	4,653	3,890
ELGUIT	63	FENDER	TELECASTER BLACK, SERIAL #83717/L10439-L43106	7,649	5,657	4,860	4,063
ELGUIT	63	FENDER	TELECASTER FIESTA RED, CURVED ROSEWOOD FRETBOARD	8,640	6,390	5,490	4,590
ELGUIT	64	FENDER	TELECASTER SUNBURST, CLAY DOTS	5,355	3,961	3,403	2,845
ELGUIT	65	FENDER	TELECASTER POST-CBS, SERIAL #103997-158977/L69635-L78135	4,054	2,998	2,576	2,153
ELGUIT	65	FENDER	TELECASTER BLOND	4,813	3,559	3,058	2,557
ELGUIT	65	FENDER	TELECASTER CANDY APPLE RED	6,240	4,615	3,965	3,315
ELGUIT	66	FENDER	TELECASTER BLOND, SERIAL #112172-293692	3,011	2,227	1,913	1,599
ELGUIT	66	FENDER	TELECASTER MAHOGANY, SERIAL #112172-293692	3,022	2,235	1,920	1,605
ELGUIT	66	FENDER	TELECASTER SUNBURST, SERIAL #112172-293692	3,207	2,372	2,038	1,703
ELGUIT	66	FENDER	TELECASTER BUTTERSCOTCH, SERIAL #142069	3,975	2,940	2,526	2,111
ELGUIT	66	FENDER	TELECASTER MAPLE NECK, BIGSBY	4,415	3,265	2,805	2,345

TYPE	YR	MFG	PRICES--BASED ON 100% ORIGINAL MODEL	SELL EXC	SELL AVG	BUY EXC	BUY AVG
ELGUIT	67	FENDER	**TELECASTER** NATURAL	1,948	**1,441**	1,238	1,035
ELGUIT	67	FENDER	**TELECASTER** BLOND, ROSEWOOD BOARD, SERIAL #115560-3156657	2,162	**1,599**	1,374	1,149
ELGUIT	67	FENDER	**TELECASTER** NATURAL, LEFT-HANDED, ROSEWOOD BOARD, SERIAL #115560-315665	2,186	**1,617**	1,389	1,161
ELGUIT	67	FENDER	**TELECASTER** MAPLE NECK, SERIAL #115560-3156657	2,188	**1,618**	1,390	1,162
ELGUIT	67	FENDER	**TELECASTER** CREAM, BIGSBY	2,219	**1,641**	1,410	1,179
ELGUIT	67	FENDER	**TELECASTER** BLOND, SERIAL #115560-3156657	2,314	**1,711**	1,470	1,229
ELGUIT	67	FENDER	**TELECASTER** CANDY APPLE RED	3,273	**2,421**	2,080	1,739
ELGUIT	67	FENDER	**TELECASTER** DAKOTA RED, ROSEWOOD SLAB BOARD	9,816	**7,259**	6,237	5,214
ELGUIT	68	FENDER	**TELECASTER** BLOND, SERIAL #125316-397081	1,975	**1,461**	1,255	1,049
ELGUIT	68	FENDER	**TELECASTER** BLOND, ROSEWOOD BOARD, SERIAL #125316-397081	1,994	**1,475**	1,267	1,059
ELGUIT	68	FENDER	**TELECASTER** BLOND, MAPLE NECK	2,005	**1,483**	1,274	1,065
ELGUIT	68	FENDER	**TELECASTER** WHITE, ROSEWOOD FRETBOARD	2,041	**1,510**	1,297	1,084
ELGUIT	68	FENDER	**TELECASTER** MAPLE FINGERBOARD, SERIAL #125316-397081	2,079	**1,537**	1,321	1,104
ELGUIT	68	FENDER	**TELECASTER** BLACK, SERIAL #125316-397081	2,351	**1,738**	1,493	1,248
ELGUIT	68	FENDER	**TELECASTER** CANDY APPLE RED, MAPLE NECK	3,993	**2,953**	2,537	2,121
ELGUIT	68	FENDER	**TELECASTER** LAKE PLACID BLUE, SERIAL #125316-397081	4,589	**3,394**	2,916	2,438
ELGUIT	68	FENDER	**TELECASTER** PAISLEY, SERIAL #125316-397081	5,193	**3,841**	3,300	2,759
ELGUIT	68	FENDER	**TELECASTER** ROSEWOOD BODY	5,263	**3,892**	3,344	2,796
ELGUIT	68	FENDER	**TELECASTER** FLORAL, SERIAL #125316-397081	5,462	**4,039**	3,470	2,901
ELGUIT	69	FENDER	**TELECASTER** BLOND	1,583	**1,170**	1,005	840
ELGUIT	69	FENDER	**TELECASTER** CREAM, ROSEWOOD BOARD, SERIAL #219796-286616	1,640	**1,213**	1,042	871
ELGUIT	69	FENDER	**TELECASTER** MAPLE NECK, BIGSBY	1,661	**1,229**	1,055	882
ELGUIT	69	FENDER	**TELECASTER** BLOND, ROSEWOOD BOARD, SERIAL #219796-286616	1,684	**1,246**	1,070	895
ELGUIT	69	FENDER	**TELECASTER** SUNBURST	1,976	**1,461**	1,255	1,050
ELGUIT	69	FENDER	**TELECASTER** PAISLEY	4,425	**3,273**	2,812	2,351
ELGUIT	69	FENDER	**TELECASTER** ROSEWOOD BODY	6,158	**4,554**	3,913	3,271
ELGUIT	70	FENDER	**TELECASTER** BLOND, SERIAL #206276-615270	1,394	**1,031**	886	741
ELGUIT	70	FENDER	**TELECASTER** CREAM, SERIAL #206276-615270	1,484	**1,097**	943	788
ELGUIT	70	FENDER	**TELECASTER** BLOND, MAPLE NECK, SERIAL #206276-615270	1,713	**1,267**	1,088	910
ELGUIT	70	FENDER	**TELECASTER** CANDY APPLE RED	3,802	**2,812**	2,416	2,020
ELGUIT	70	FENDER	**TELECASTER** ROSEWOOD	4,588	**3,393**	2,915	2,437
ELGUIT	71	FENDER	**TELECASTER** CREAM	1,071	**792**	680	569
ELGUIT	71	FENDER	**TELECASTER** SUNBURST, MAPLE NECK	1,149	**849**	730	610
ELGUIT	71	FENDER	**TELECASTER** BLACK	1,201	**888**	763	638
ELGUIT	71	FENDER	**TELECASTER** BLOND, MAPLE NECK, SERIAL #32501-509993	1,286	**951**	817	683
ELGUIT	71	FENDER	**TELECASTER** BLOND, ROSEWOOD NECK	1,287	**952**	818	683
ELGUIT	71	FENDER	**TELECASTER** BLOND	1,408	**1,041**	894	748
ELGUIT	71	FENDER	**TELECASTER** LAKE PLACID BLUE, SERIAL #32501-509993	1,835	**1,357**	1,166	975
ELGUIT	71	FENDER	**TELECASTER** CANDY APPLE RED, MAPLE NECK	1,840	**1,361**	1,169	977
ELGUIT	71	FENDER	**TELECASTER** ROSEWOOD BODY, SERIAL #32501-509993	5,376	**3,976**	3,416	2,856
ELGUIT	72	FENDER	**TELECASTER** BROWN	837	**619**	531	444
ELGUIT	72	FENDER	**TELECASTER** NATURAL, SERIAL #56115-539372/S723141	1,116	**825**	709	593

TYPE	YR	MFG	PRICES--BASED ON 100% ORIGINAL MODEL	SELL EXC	SELL AVG	BUY EXC	BUY AVG
ELGUIT	72	FENDER	**TELECASTER** SUNBURST, MAPLE NECK, SERIAL #56115-539372/S723141	1,142	**844**	725	606
ELGUIT	72	FENDER	**TELECASTER** BLACK, SERIAL #56115-539372/S723141	1,159	**857**	736	616
ELGUIT	72	FENDER	**TELECASTER** BLOND, MAPLE NECK	1,275	**943**	810	677
ELGUIT	72	FENDER	**TELECASTER** LAKE PLACID BLUE, SERIAL #56115-539372/S723141	1,962	**1,451**	1,246	1,042
ELGUIT	72	FENDER	**TELECASTER** ROSEWOOD BODY, SERIAL #56115	5,664	**4,189**	3,599	3,009
ELGUIT	73	FENDER	**TELECASTER** BLACK	1,155	**854**	734	614
ELGUIT	73	FENDER	**TELECASTER** BLOND, MAPLE NECK	1,223	**904**	777	649
ELGUIT	73	FENDER	**TELECASTER** BLOND, LEFT-HANDED	1,295	**957**	822	687
ELGUIT	73	FENDER	**TELECASTER** BROWN w/BIGSBY	1,353	**1,001**	860	719
ELGUIT	74	FENDER	**TELECASTER** NATURAL	733	**542**	466	389
ELGUIT	74	FENDER	**TELECASTER** SUNBURST, MAPLE NECK	927	**685**	589	492
ELGUIT	74	FENDER	**TELECASTER** BLOND, MAPLE NECK	988	**731**	628	525
ELGUIT	74	FENDER	**TELECASTER** BLOND, SERIAL #60443-580031/S702161	994	**735**	631	528
ELGUIT	74	FENDER	**TELECASTER** BLACK	1,035	**766**	658	550
ELGUIT	74	FENDER	**TELECASTER** CANDY APPLE RED, MAPLE NECK	1,413	**1,045**	897	750
ELGUIT	75	FENDER	**TELECASTER** SUNBURST, MAPLE NECK	760	**562**	483	403
ELGUIT	75	FENDER	**TELECASTER** BLOND	980	**724**	622	520
ELGUIT	75	FENDER	**TELECASTER** CREAM, MAPLE NECK, SERIAL #606109-655092	984	**727**	625	522
ELGUIT	75	FENDER	**TELECASTER** BLACK	1,006	**744**	639	534
ELGUIT	75	FENDER	**TELECASTER** BLOND, MAPLE NECK	1,212	**896**	770	644
ELGUIT	76	FENDER	**TELECASTER** BLOND, MAPLE NECK	798	**590**	507	424
ELGUIT	76	FENDER	**TELECASTER** CREAM, BLACK PICKGUARD	816	**604**	519	434
ELGUIT	76	FENDER	**TELECASTER** CREAM, MAPLE NECK	825	**610**	524	438
ELGUIT	76	FENDER	**TELECASTER** CREAM, WHITE PICKGUARD	825	**610**	524	438
ELGUIT	77	FENDER	**TELECASTER** BLOND	759	**561**	482	403
ELGUIT	77	FENDER	**TELECASTER** NATURAL, LEFT-HANDED, MAPLE NECK	851	**629**	541	452
ELGUIT	78	FENDER	**TELECASTER** WINE, MAPLE NECK	658	**487**	418	349
ELGUIT	78	FENDER	**TELECASTER** SUNBURST, LEFT-HANDED	673	**498**	428	358
ELGUIT	78	FENDER	**TELECASTER** BLOND, LEFT-HANDED	737	**545**	468	391
ELGUIT	78	FENDER	**TELECASTER** SUNBURST, ROSEWOOD	765	**565**	486	406
ELGUIT	78	FENDER	**TELECASTER** BLACK	776	**574**	493	412
ELGUIT	78	FENDER	**TELECASTER** ANTIGUA	785	**580**	498	417
ELGUIT	78	FENDER	**TELECASTER** NATURAL, ROSEWOOD BOARD	819	**606**	520	435
ELGUIT	78	FENDER	**TELECASTER** BLOND, MAPLE NECK, SERIAL #S806520-S846983	883	**653**	561	469
ELGUIT	78	FENDER	**TELECASTER** OLYMPIC WHITE	890	**658**	566	473
ELGUIT	82	FENDER	**TELECASTER** BLACK AND GOLD	737	**545**	468	391
ELGUIT	84	FENDER	**TELECASTER**	438	**324**	278	233
ELGUIT	88	FENDER	**TELECASTER 40th ANNIVERSARY**	837	**619**	531	444
ELGUIT	68	FENDER	**TELECASTER BASS** BLOND, MAPLE NECK	1,259	**931**	800	669
ELGUIT	68	FENDER	**TELECASTER BASS** PINK PAISLEY, SERIAL #139157-289309	3,162	**2,338**	2,009	1,679
ELGUIT	68	FENDER	**TELECASTER BASS** FLORAL	3,840	**2,840**	2,440	2,040
ELGUIT	69	FENDER	**TELECASTER BASS** BLOND, SERIAL #228951-271946	1,178	**871**	749	626
ELGUIT	69	FENDER	**TELECASTER BASS** FLORAL, SERIAL #228951-271946	2,390	**1,767**	1,518	1,269

TYPE	YR	MFG	PRICES--BASED ON 100% ORIGINAL MODEL	SELL EXC	SELL AVG	BUY EXC	BUY AVG
ELGUIT	69	FENDER	**TELECASTER BASS** PINK PAISLEY, SERIAL #228951-271946	3,053	**2,258**	1,940	1,622
ELGUIT	70	FENDER	**TELECASTER BASS** BLOND, MAPLE NECK	1,051	**777**	667	558
ELGUIT	70	FENDER	**TELECASTER BASS** PINK PAISLEY	3,810	**2,817**	2,421	2,024
ELGUIT	72	FENDER	**TELECASTER BASS** BROWN STAIN, SERIAL #351991	641	**474**	407	340
ELGUIT	72	FENDER	**TELECASTER BASS** NATURAL, SERIAL #351436-402487	698	**516**	444	371
ELGUIT	72	FENDER	**TELECASTER BASS** CREAM, SERIAL #351436-402487	723	**535**	459	384
ELGUIT	72	FENDER	**TELECASTER BASS** BLOND, MAPLE NECK, SERIAL #351436-402487	954	**705**	606	506
ELGUIT	73	FENDER	**TELECASTER BASS** CREAM	696	**514**	442	369
ELGUIT	73	FENDER	**TELECASTER BASS** BLOND, SERIAL #400779-402188	743	**549**	472	394
ELGUIT	73	FENDER	**TELECASTER BASS** NATURAL	897	**663**	570	476
ELGUIT	74	FENDER	**TELECASTER BASS** BLOND	819	**606**	520	435
ELGUIT	75	FENDER	**TELECASTER BASS** BLOND, MAPLE NECK	760	**562**	483	403
ELGUIT	77	FENDER	**TELECASTER BASS** BLACK	656	**485**	417	348
ELGUIT	78	FENDER	**TELECASTER BASS** SUNBURST	637	**471**	405	338
ELGUIT	78	FENDER	**TELECASTER BASS** ANTIGUA, MAPLE BOARD	668	**494**	424	354
ELGUIT	59	FENDER	**TELECASTER CUSTOM** SUNBURST	8,636	**6,387**	5,487	4,587
ELGUIT	60	FENDER	**TELECASTER CUSTOM** SUNBURST, 2-TONE, SERIAL #44282-57746	9,284	**6,866**	5,899	4,932
ELGUIT	60	FENDER	**TELECASTER CUSTOM** SUNBURST	10,478	**7,749**	6,658	5,566
ELGUIT	61	FENDER	**TELECASTER CUSTOM** SUNBURST, SERIAL #63204	10,358	**7,660**	6,581	5,502
ELGUIT	62	FENDER	**TELECASTER CUSTOM** SUNBURST, SERIAL #94745/L01635-L13181	8,412	**6,221**	5,345	4,469
ELGUIT	62	FENDER	**TELECASTER CUSTOM** RED, SERIAL #76816-85944	9,619	**7,114**	6,112	5,110
ELGUIT	63	FENDER	**TELECASTER CUSTOM** SUNBURST, SERIAL #97069-99304/L15823-L63644	6,971	**5,156**	4,429	3,703
ELGUIT	63	FENDER	**TELECASTER CUSTOM** ROSEWOOD, SERIAL #L16550-L42308	7,709	**5,702**	4,898	4,095
ELGUIT	64	FENDER	**TELECASTER CUSTOM** BLACK, SERIAL #L50451-L69740	14,304	**10,579**	9,089	7,599
ELGUIT	66	FENDER	**TELECASTER CUSTOM** SUNBURST, ROSEWOOD BOARD	5,745	**4,249**	3,650	3,052
ELGUIT	67	FENDER	**TELECASTER CUSTOM** SUNBURST, SERIAL #208410	4,139	**3,061**	2,630	2,199
ELGUIT	68	FENDER	**TELECASTER CUSTOM** WHITE, BLACK BINDING	3,050	**2,256**	1,938	1,620
ELGUIT	68	FENDER	**TELECASTER CUSTOM** SUNBURST	4,741	**3,506**	3,012	2,518
ELGUIT	68	FENDER	**TELECASTER CUSTOM** CANDY APPLE RED	8,985	**6,645**	5,709	4,773
ELGUIT	69	FENDER	**TELECASTER CUSTOM** CANDY APPLE RED	3,553	**2,628**	2,258	1,888
ELGUIT	70	FENDER	**TELECASTER CUSTOM** SUNBURST	2,200	**1,627**	1,398	1,168
ELGUIT	71	FENDER	**TELECASTER CUSTOM** SUNBURST, ROSEWOOD	2,952	**2,183**	1,875	1,568
ELGUIT	72	FENDER	**TELECASTER CUSTOM** BLACK, 2nd EDITION	816	**604**	519	434
ELGUIT	72	FENDER	**TELECASTER CUSTOM** SUNBURST	817	**604**	519	434
ELGUIT	72	FENDER	**TELECASTER CUSTOM** WHITE	830	**614**	527	441
ELGUIT	72	FENDER	**TELECASTER CUSTOM** SUNBURST, 2nd EDITION	956	**707**	607	507
ELGUIT	72	FENDER	**TELECASTER CUSTOM** BLACK, WHITE BINDING, SERIAL #356969-419864	3,447	**2,549**	2,190	1,831
ELGUIT	72	FENDER	**TELECASTER CUSTOM** MAPLE NECK, SERIAL #356969-419864	3,629	**2,684**	2,306	1,928
ELGUIT	73	FENDER	**TELECASTER CUSTOM** BLOND, MAPLE NECK, SERIAL #417124-517644	829	**613**	527	440
ELGUIT	73	FENDER	**TELECASTER CUSTOM** SUNBURST	829	**613**	527	440
ELGUIT	73	FENDER	**TELECASTER CUSTOM** BLACK	830	**614**	527	441
ELGUIT	74	FENDER	**TELECASTER CUSTOM** WALNUT	755	**558**	480	401

TYPE	YR	MFG	PRICES--BASED ON 100% ORIGINAL MODEL	SELL EXC	SELL AVG	BUY EXC	BUY AVG
ELGUIT	74	FENDER	TELECASTER CUSTOM SUNBURST, SERIAL #554139	761	563	483	404
ELGUIT	74	FENDER	TELECASTER CUSTOM BROWN	870	643	553	462
ELGUIT	74	FENDER	TELECASTER CUSTOM NATURAL, MAPLE	871	644	553	463
ELGUIT	74	FENDER	TELECASTER CUSTOM BLOND, SERIAL #576865	872	645	554	463
ELGUIT	74	FENDER	TELECASTER CUSTOM BLACK, MAPLE FINGERBOARD	907	670	576	481
ELGUIT	75	FENDER	TELECASTER CUSTOM SUNBURST	674	499	428	358
ELGUIT	75	FENDER	TELECASTER CUSTOM NATURAL, MAPLE NECK	705	521	448	374
ELGUIT	75	FENDER	TELECASTER CUSTOM WALNUT	743	549	472	394
ELGUIT	75	FENDER	TELECASTER CUSTOM BLACK, SERIAL #555119	829	613	527	440
ELGUIT	75	FENDER	TELECASTER CUSTOM BLOND, ROSEWOOD BOARD, SERIAL #555119	1,206	892	766	641
ELGUIT	76	FENDER	TELECASTER CUSTOM BROWN	702	519	446	373
ELGUIT	76	FENDER	TELECASTER CUSTOM SUNBURST, ROSEWOOD	728	538	462	387
ELGUIT	76	FENDER	TELECASTER CUSTOM BLACK	769	569	489	409
ELGUIT	77	FENDER	TELECASTER CUSTOM SUNBURST, SERIAL #S712043	715	528	454	379
ELGUIT	77	FENDER	TELECASTER CUSTOM BLACK	754	558	479	400
ELGUIT	77	FENDER	TELECASTER CUSTOM FIESTA RED	829	613	527	440
ELGUIT	78	FENDER	TELECASTER CUSTOM BROWN	668	494	424	354
ELGUIT	78	FENDER	TELECASTER CUSTOM NATURAL	735	543	467	390
ELGUIT	78	FENDER	TELECASTER CUSTOM WINE	779	576	495	414
ELGUIT	72	FENDER	TELECASTER DELUXE	717	530	455	380
ELGUIT	73	FENDER	TELECASTER DELUXE SUNBURST, SERIAL #516776-672663	704	521	447	374
ELGUIT	73	FENDER	TELECASTER DELUXE NATURAL, 2 HUMBUCKER PU's	761	563	483	404
ELGUIT	74	FENDER	TELECASTER DELUXE BROWN, 2 PU's	670	495	425	355
ELGUIT	74	FENDER	TELECASTER DELUXE BLACK, MAPLE NECK, SERIAL #568350	744	550	473	395
ELGUIT	75	FENDER	TELECASTER DELUXE BROWN, MAPLE NECK, SERIAL #656632	638	472	405	339
ELGUIT	75	FENDER	TELECASTER DELUXE BLACK, SERIAL #656632	653	483	415	347
ELGUIT	75	FENDER	TELECASTER DELUXE NATURAL	663	490	421	352
ELGUIT	76	FENDER	TELECASTER DELUXE BROWN, MAPLE BOARD	728	538	462	387
ELGUIT	76	FENDER	TELECASTER DELUXE BLACK	743	549	472	394
ELGUIT	76	FENDER	TELECASTER DELUXE BLOND, MAPLE NECK	747	553	475	397
ELGUIT	77	FENDER	TELECASTER DELUXE NATURAL	718	531	456	381
ELGUIT	77	FENDER	TELECASTER DELUXE BLACK, MAPLE NECK	743	549	472	394
ELGUIT	77	FENDER	TELECASTER DELUXE BLOND, MAPLE NECK	766	566	486	406
ELGUIT	78	FENDER	TELECASTER DELUXE NATURAL	722	534	459	384
ELGUIT	78	FENDER	TELECASTER DELUXE WHITE	733	542	466	389
ELGUIT	78	FENDER	TELECASTER DELUXE ANTIGUA	779	576	495	414
ELGUIT	79	FENDER	TELECASTER DELUXE	677	501	430	360
ELGUIT	67	FENDER	TELECASTER THINLINE SUNBURST	3,575	2,644	2,271	1,899
ELGUIT	68	FENDER	TELECASTER THINLINE SUNBURST	1,798	1,329	1,142	955
ELGUIT	68	FENDER	TELECASTER THINLINE NATURAL	2,069	1,530	1,315	1,099
ELGUIT	68	FENDER	TELECASTER THINLINE MAHOGANY, MAPLE	2,924	2,162	1,858	1,553
ELGUIT	68	FENDER	TELECASTER THINLINE ASH, TELE PU, SERIAL #125316-397081	3,689	2,728	2,344	1,959
ELGUIT	69	FENDER	TELECASTER THINLINE NATURAL, SERIAL #219796-286616	1,863	1,378	1,184	989

TYPE	YR	MFG	PRICES--BASED ON 100% ORIGINAL MODEL	SELL EXC	SELL AVG	BUY EXC	BUY AVG
ELGUIT	69	FENDER	**TELECASTER THINLINE** SUNBURST, SERIAL #219796-286616	2,327	**1,721**	1,478	1,236
ELGUIT	69	FENDER	**TELECASTER THINLINE** MAHOGANY, SERIAL #219796-286616	2,377	**1,758**	1,510	1,263
ELGUIT	69	FENDER	**TELECASTER THINLINE** CANDY APPLE RED	3,422	**2,531**	2,174	1,818
ELGUIT	69	FENDER	**TELECASTER THINLINE** BLACK PEARL	3,468	**2,565**	2,203	1,842
ELGUIT	69	FENDER	**TELECASTER THINLINE** OCEAN TURQUOISE	3,914	**2,895**	2,487	2,079
ELGUIT	70	FENDER	**TELECASTER THINLINE** SUNBURST, SERIAL #206276-615270	1,038	**768**	660	551
ELGUIT	70	FENDER	**TELECASTER THINLINE** SILVER SPARKLE, SERIAL #206276-615270	1,686	**1,247**	1,071	896
ELGUIT	70	FENDER	**TELECASTER THINLINE** NATURAL	1,814	**1,341**	1,152	963
ELGUIT	71	FENDER	**TELECASTER THINLINE** BLACK, SERIAL #32501-509993	1,037	**767**	659	551
ELGUIT	71	FENDER	**TELECASTER THINLINE** MAHOGANY	1,037	**767**	659	551
ELGUIT	71	FENDER	**TELECASTER THINLINE** NATURAL, HOLLOW BODY	1,037	**767**	659	551
ELGUIT	71	FENDER	**TELECASTER THINLINE** OLYMPIC WHITE, SERIAL #32501-509993	2,111	**1,561**	1,341	1,121
ELGUIT	71	FENDER	**TELECASTER THINLINE** SALMON PINK	3,256	**2,408**	2,069	1,729
ELGUIT	72	FENDER	**TELECASTER THINLINE** BLACK, MAPLE FRET	1,032	**763**	656	548
ELGUIT	72	FENDER	**TELECASTER THINLINE** BLOND	1,037	**767**	659	551
ELGUIT	72	FENDER	**TELECASTER THINLINE** MAHOGANY, SERIAL #56115-539372/S723141	1,037	**767**	659	551
ELGUIT	72	FENDER	**TELECASTER THINLINE** WHITE	1,037	**767**	659	551
ELGUIT	72	FENDER	**TELECASTER THINLINE** SUNBURST, SERIAL #56115-539372/S723141	1,073	**793**	681	570
ELGUIT	72	FENDER	**TELECASTER THINLINE** NATURAL ASH, SERIAL #56115-539372/S723141	1,292	**955**	821	686
ELGUIT	73	FENDER	**TELECASTER THINLINE** NATURAL ASH, SERIAL #316015-527527	1,037	**767**	659	551
ELGUIT	73	FENDER	**TELECASTER THINLINE** SUNBURST	1,037	**767**	659	551
ELGUIT	74	FENDER	**TELECASTER THINLINE** BLACK	1,016	**751**	645	540
ELGUIT	74	FENDER	**TELECASTER THINLINE** ASH	1,037	**767**	659	551
ELGUIT	74	FENDER	**TELECASTER THINLINE** BROWN, SERIAL #60443-580031/S702161	1,037	**767**	659	551
ELGUIT	74	FENDER	**TELECASTER THINLINE** SUNBURST, SERIAL #60443-580031/S702161	1,037	**767**	659	551
ELGUIT	75	FENDER	**TELECASTER THINLINE** BROWN, SERIAL #606109-655092	1,075	**795**	683	571
ELGUIT	75	FENDER	**TELECASTER THINLINE** NATURAL, SERIAL #606109-655092	1,094	**809**	695	581
ELGUIT	76	FENDER	**TELECASTER THINLINE** NATURAL	1,006	**744**	639	534
ELGUIT	77	FENDER	**TELECASTER THINLINE** MOCCA	991	**733**	630	526
ELGUIT	77	FENDER	**TELECASTER THINLINE** BLACK	1,000	**739**	635	531
ELGUIT	78	FENDER	**TELECASTER THINLINE** SUNBURST, LEFT-HANDED, SERIAL #S806520-S846983	1,107	**819**	703	588
GUITAR AMP	54	FENDER	**BANDMASTER** TWEED, 1x15"	3,083	**2,280**	1,959	1,638
GTAMP	56	FENDER	**BANDMASTER** TWEED, 3x10"	2,990	**2,211**	1,900	1,588
GTAMP	58	FENDER	**BANDMASTER** TWEED, NARROW PANEL, 3x10"	2,318	**1,714**	1,473	1,231
GTAMP	59	FENDER	**BANDMASTER** TWEED, 3x10	3,758	**2,779**	2,388	1,996
GTAMP	59	FENDER	**BANDMASTER** TWEED, 3x10"	4,277	**3,163**	2,718	2,272
GTAMP	62	FENDER	**BANDMASTER** WHITE, HEAD ONLY	469	**347**	298	249
GTAMP	62	FENDER	**BANDMASTER** BLOND-WHEAT, 2x12" CAB	621	**459**	394	329
GTAMP	63	FENDER	**BANDMASTER** ROUGH TOLEX, HEAD ONLY	417	**308**	265	221
GTAMP	63	FENDER	**BANDMASTER** WHITE TOLEX, BLACK FACE, 2x12" CABINET	1,114	**824**	708	592
GTAMP	64	FENDER	**BANDMASTER** BLACK FACE, 2x12"	844	**624**	536	448
GTAMP	64	FENDER	**BANDMASTER** WHITE, HEAD AND CABINET	869	**643**	552	462

TYPE	YR	MFG	PRICES--BASED ON 100% ORIGINAL MODEL	SELL EXC	SELL AVG	BUY EXC	BUY AVG
GTAMP	64	FENDER	**BANDMASTER** TAN GRILL, WHITE TOLEX, HEAD AND CABINET	944	**698**	600	501
GTAMP	65	FENDER	**BANDMASTER** BLACK, HEAD ONLY	460	**340**	292	244
GTAMP	65	FENDER	**BANDMASTER** HEAD AND BOTTOM	466	**345**	296	247
GTAMP	65	FENDER	**BANDMASTER** BLACK, PRE-CBS ELECTRIC	617	**456**	392	327
GTAMP	66	FENDER	**BANDMASTER** HEAD ONLY	444	**328**	282	236
GTAMP	67	FENDER	**BANDMASTER** BLACK FACE, HEAD ONLY	425	**314**	270	225
GTAMP	68	FENDER	**BANDMASTER** SILVER FACE, REVERB, HEAD	418	**309**	265	222
GTAMP	68	FENDER	**BANDMASTER** BLACK FACE, 2x12"	442	**327**	281	235
GTAMP	69	FENDER	**BANDMASTER** SILVER FAVE, HEAD ONLY	377	**279**	239	200
GTAMP	71	FENDER	**BANDMASTER** REVERB	351	**259**	223	186
GTAMP	72	FENDER	**BANDMASTER** REVERB, HEAD ONLY	339	**251**	215	180
GTAMP	75	FENDER	**BANDMASTER** REVERB, 2x12"	419	**310**	266	222
GTAMP	79	FENDER	**BANDMASTER** SILVER, REVERB, HEAD ONLY	337	**249**	214	179
GTAMP	80	FENDER	**BANDMASTER** SILVER FACE, REVERB	319	**236**	203	169
GTAMP	52	FENDER	**BASSMAN** TWEED, 1x15"	2,986	**2,208**	1,897	1,586
GTAMP	53	FENDER	**BASSMAN** TWEED, 1x15"	1,431	**1,058**	909	760
GTAMP	54	FENDER	**BASSMAN** TWEED, 1x15"	1,681	**1,243**	1,068	893
GTAMP	55	FENDER	**BASSMAN** TWEED, 4x10"	3,492	**2,582**	2,219	1,855
GTAMP	55	FENDER	**BASSMAN** TWEED, 4x10"	3,715	**2,747**	2,360	1,973
GTAMP	56	FENDER	**BASSMAN** TWEED, 2-INPUT, 4x10"	3,270	**2,418**	2,078	1,737
GTAMP	57	FENDER	**BASSMAN** TWEED	3,364	**2,488**	2,138	1,787
GTAMP	57	FENDER	**BASSMAN** TWEED	3,413	**2,524**	2,169	1,813
GTAMP	58	FENDER	**BASSMAN** TWEED, 4x10"	4,176	**3,088**	2,653	2,218
GTAMP	58	FENDER	**BASSMAN** MID RANGE CONTROL, 4-INPUT, 4x10"	4,339	**3,209**	2,757	2,305
GTAMP	59	FENDER	**BASSMAN** TWEED, MID CONTROL	3,409	**2,521**	2,166	1,811
GTAMP	61	FENDER	**BASSMAN** WHITE TOLEX TOP/BOTTOM, 2x12"	1,112	**822**	706	591
GTAMP	62	FENDER	**BASSMAN** WHITE, HEAD	828	**612**	526	440
GTAMP	62	FENDER	**BASSMAN** TOP/BOTTOM, 2x12"	832	**615**	528	442
GTAMP	63	FENDER	**BASSMAN** BLOND TOP/BOTTOM, 2x12"	885	**654**	562	470
GTAMP	64	FENDER	**BASSMAN** CABINET	480	**355**	305	255
GTAMP	64	FENDER	**BASSMAN** BLACK FACE, HEAD	498	**368**	316	264
GTAMP	64	FENDER	**BASSMAN** WHITE TOLEX, GOLD GRILL CLOTH	738	**545**	469	392
GTAMP	65	FENDER	**BASSMAN** BLACK TOLEX, BLACK FACE, 2x12"	664	**491**	422	352
GTAMP	68	FENDER	**BASSMAN** SILVER FACE, HEAD ONLY	559	**413**	355	297
GTAMP	69	FENDER	**BASSMAN** SILVER, HEAD	637	**471**	405	338
GTAMP	69	FENDER	**BASSMAN** TOP/BOTTOM, 2x15"	796	**589**	506	423
GTAMP	70	FENDER	**BASSMAN** HEAD	480	**355**	305	255
GTAMP	70	FENDER	**BASSMAN** SILVER FACE, 2x15"	526	**389**	334	279
GTAMP	70	FENDER	**BASSMAN** SILVER PANEL, 4x10"	546	**403**	347	290
GTAMP	72	FENDER	**BASSMAN** 2x15"	496	**367**	315	263
GTAMP	73	FENDER	**BASSMAN** SILVER FACE, HEAD	442	**327**	281	235
GTAMP	74	FENDER	**BASSMAN** SILVER FACE, 4x10"	480	**355**	305	255

TYPE	YR	MFG	PRICES--BASED ON 100% ORIGINAL MODEL	SELL EXC	SELL AVG	BUY EXC	BUY AVG
GTAMP	72	FENDER	BASSMAN 10 4x10" SPEAKERS	494	365	314	262
GTAMP	75	FENDER	BASSMAN 10	432	319	274	229
GTAMP	81	FENDER	BASSMAN 10 4x10" SPEAKERS	422	312	268	224
GTAMP	70	FENDER	BASSMAN 50 SILVER FACE, 2x15" SPEAKERS	502	371	319	266
GTAMP	73	FENDER	BASSMAN 50 2x12" SPEAKERS	432	319	274	229
GTAMP	76	FENDER	BASSMAN 50 2x15" SPEAKERS	498	368	316	264
GTAMP	73	FENDER	BASSMAN 100 2x15" CABINET	432	320	275	230
GTAMP	73	FENDER	BASSMAN 100 4x12"	468	346	297	248
GTAMP	77	FENDER	BASSMAN 100	438	324	278	233
GTAMP	78	FENDER	BASSMAN 100 2x15" CABINET	386	286	245	205
GTAMP	80	FENDER	BASSMAN 100 4x10"	384	284	244	204
GTAMP	68	FENDER	BRONCO 8" SPEAKER	192	142	122	102
GTAMP	69	FENDER	BRONCO	192	142	122	102
GTAMP	70	FENDER	BRONCO 8" SPEAKER	192	142	122	102
GTAMP	53	FENDER	CHAMP TWEED	609	450	387	323
GTAMP	55	FENDER	CHAMP TWEED	611	452	388	324
GTAMP	56	FENDER	CHAMP 6" SPEAKER	580	429	369	308
GTAMP	57	FENDER	CHAMP TWEED	641	474	407	340
GTAMP	58	FENDER	CHAMP 8" SPEAKER	620	458	394	329
GTAMP	59	FENDER	CHAMP TWEED	624	462	397	332
GTAMP	59	FENDER	CHAMP 8" SPEAKER	669	494	425	355
GTAMP	61	FENDER	CHAMP 6" SPEAKER	559	426	362	277
GTAMP	62	FENDER	CHAMP TWEED	516	381	328	274
GTAMP	63	FENDER	CHAMP 6" SPEAKER	530	392	337	282
GTAMP	63	FENDER	CHAMP TWEED, BLACK CABINET, 8" SPEAKER	563	416	358	299
GTAMP	63	FENDER	CHAMP TWEED	669	494	425	355
GTAMP	64	FENDER	CHAMP BLACK FACE	448	331	284	238
GTAMP	65	FENDER	CHAMP BLACK FACE, SCRIPT NAME PLATE	408	302	259	217
GTAMP	66	FENDER	CHAMP BLACK FACE, SCRIPT NAME PLATE	323	239	205	171
GTAMP	68	FENDER	CHAMP SILVER FACE, 8" SPEAKER	277	205	176	147
GTAMP	70	FENDER	CHAMP SILVER FACE	259	191	164	137
GTAMP	74	FENDER	CHAMP SILVER FACE	251	186	159	133
GTAMP	75	FENDER	CHAMP SILVER FACE	259	191	164	137
GTAMP	76	FENDER	CHAMP SILVER FACE	288	213	183	153
GTAMP	79	FENDER	CHAMP SILVER FACE	291	215	185	155
GTAMP	49	FENDER	CHAMP 600 LEATHERETTE 2-TONE	1,357	1,003	862	721
GTAMP	50	FENDER	CHAMP 600 BROWN	670	495	425	355
GTAMP	51	FENDER	CHAMP 600	766	566	486	406
GTAMP	52	FENDER	CHAMP 600 BROWN AND WHITE 2-TONE	705	521	448	374
GTAMP	48	FENDER	CHAMP 800 GREY TWEED	929	687	590	493
GTAMP	60	FENDER	CONCERT BROWN, 4x10"	1,297	959	824	689
GTAMP	62	FENDER	CONCERT BROWN, 4x10"	1,180	873	750	627
GTAMP	63	FENDER	CONCERT BROWN, 4x10"	920	680	584	489
GTAMP	64	FENDER	CONCERT BLACK TOLEX, 4x10"	964	713	613	512

TYPE	YR	MFG	PRICES--BASED ON 100% ORIGINAL MODEL	SELL EXC	SELL AVG	BUY EXC	BUY AVG
GTAMP	68	FENDER	D-120 JBL SPEAKER ONLY	144	107	92	77
GTAMP	49	FENDER	DELUXE TWEED, TV FRONT	1,313	971	834	697
GTAMP	51	FENDER	DELUXE	1,274	942	810	677
GTAMP	51	FENDER	DELUXE TV FRONT, 12" SPEAKER	1,297	959	824	689
GTAMP	52	FENDER	DELUXE WIDE BODY, NO TUBES, JENSEN	1,136	840	722	603
GTAMP	52	FENDER	DELUXE TWEED, TV MODEL	1,278	945	812	679
GTAMP	52	FENDER	DELUXE TWEED	1,433	1,060	910	761
GTAMP	53	FENDER	DELUXE WIDE PANEL, NO TUBES, JENSEN	1,085	803	689	576
GTAMP	53	FENDER	DELUXE TWEED	1,164	861	739	618
GTAMP	53	FENDER	DELUXE TWEED, TV FRONT	1,186	877	753	630
GTAMP	54	FENDER	DELUXE TWEED	1,303	964	828	692
GTAMP	55	FENDER	DELUXE TWEED, JENSEN ALNICO	1,113	823	707	591
GTAMP	56	FENDER	DELUXE TWEED	1,206	892	766	641
GTAMP	57	FENDER	DELUXE	1,252	926	796	665
GTAMP	58	FENDER	DELUXE	1,373	1,016	872	729
GTAMP	58	FENDER	DELUXE TWEED	1,550	1,146	985	823
GTAMP	59	FENDER	DELUXE TWEED	1,435	1,061	911	762
GTAMP	60	FENDER	DELUXE TWEED, 12" JENSEN	1,136	840	722	603
GTAMP	61	FENDER	DELUXE BROWN TOLEX	914	676	581	486
GTAMP	62	FENDER	DELUXE BROWN TOLEX	944	698	600	501
GTAMP	63	FENDER	DELUXE BROWN TOLEX	1,403	1,038	891	745
GTAMP	63	FENDER	DELUXE BLACK FACE, REVERB	3,072	2,272	1,952	1,632
GTAMP	64	FENDER	DELUXE OXFORD, REVERB	1,239	916	787	658
GTAMP	64	FENDER	DELUXE BLACK TOLEX	1,269	938	806	674
GTAMP	65	FENDER	DELUXE BLACK TOLEX	1,077	796	684	572
GTAMP	65	FENDER	DELUXE BLACK FACE, REVERB, NAME PLATE	1,228	908	780	652
GTAMP	66	FENDER	DELUXE BLACK FACE, REVERB, NAME PLATE	1,067	789	678	567
GTAMP	67	FENDER	DELUXE BLACK FACE, REVERB, NAME PLATE	1,050	776	667	557
GTAMP	68	FENDER	DELUXE SILVER FACE, REVERB	794	587	505	422
GTAMP	71	FENDER	DELUXE REVERB	677	501	430	360
GTAMP	72	FENDER	DELUXE SILVER FACE, REVERB, 12" JENSEN	853	631	542	453
GTAMP	73	FENDER	DELUXE SILVER FACE, REVERB	620	458	394	329
GTAMP	74	FENDER	DELUXE SILVER FACE, REVERB	618	457	392	328
GTAMP	75	FENDER	DELUXE SILVER FACE	560	414	356	297
GTAMP	75	FENDER	DELUXE REVERB	566	418	359	300
GTAMP	77	FENDER	DELUXE REVERB	524	387	333	278
GTAMP	78	FENDER	DELUXE REVERB	484	358	308	257
GTAMP	68	FENDER	DIMENSION IV VIBRATO ECHO	366	271	233	194
GTAMP	46	FENDER	DUAL PROFESSIONAL 2x10" DUAL 616's	3,640	2,692	2,313	1,933
GTAMP	63	FENDER	DUAL SHOWMAN WHITE, 2x12" JBL's	1,761	1,302	1,119	935
GTAMP	64	FENDER	DUAL SHOWMAN BLACK	1,768	1,307	1,123	939
GTAMP	67	FENDER	DUAL SHOWMAN BLACK FACE, HEAD	856	633	544	454
GTAMP	68	FENDER	DUAL SHOWMAN SILVER FACE, CABINET, FENDER SPEAKERS	677	501	430	360

TYPE	YR	MFG	PRICES--BASED ON 100% ORIGINAL MODEL	SELL EXC	SELL AVG	BUY EXC	BUY AVG
GTAMP	69	FENDER	DUAL SHOWMAN SILVER FACE, HEAD	377	279	239	200
GTAMP	69	FENDER	DUAL SHOWMAN SILVER FACE, 2x15" CABINET	1,085	803	689	576
GTAMP	74	FENDER	DUAL SHOWMAN 2 D-130F SPEAKERS AND CAIBNET	426	315	270	226
GTAMP	56	FENDER	HARVARD 10" SPEAKER	918	679	583	488
GTAMP	56	FENDER	HARVARD TWEED, 1x18", 10 WATTS	953	705	605	506
GTAMP	57	FENDER	HARVARD TWEED, 1x18"	741	548	470	393
GTAMP	58	FENDER	HARVARD TWEED, 1x12"	815	602	517	432
GTAMP	59	FENDER	HARVARD TWEED, 1x10"	743	549	472	394
GTAMP	60	FENDER	HARVARD TWEED, 1x10"	742	548	471	394
GTAMP	79	FENDER	HARVARD SOLID STATE	276	204	175	146
GTAMP	70	FENDER	LIBRA 105 WALL, SOLID STATE	456	337	289	242
GTAMP	47	FENDER	MODEL 26 6" SPEAKER	1,741	1,287	1,106	925
GTAMP	47	FENDER	MODEL 26 15" SPEAKER	1,806	1,336	1,148	959
GTAMP	47	FENDER	MODEL 26 2 6V6 TUBES, 6", 8", 10" SPEAKERS	3,155	2,333	2,005	1,676
GTAMP	76	FENDER	MODEL G-105 2x12" SPEAKERS, SOLID STATE	264	195	167	140
GTAMP	70	FENDER	MUSICMASTER BASS SILVER FACE, 1x12"	250	185	159	133
GTAMP	76	FENDER	MUSICMASTER BASS 1x12", 12 WATTS	239	176	151	126
GTAMP	82	FENDER	MUSICMASTER BASS	233	172	148	123
GTAMP	49	FENDER	PRINCETON TWEED	1,157	856	735	615
GTAMP	49	FENDER	PRINCETON TWEED, TV FRONT	1,208	893	767	642
GTAMP	50	FENDER	PRINCETON TWEED, TV FRONT	1,014	750	644	539
GTAMP	51	FENDER	PRINCETON TWEED, TV FRONT	1,037	767	659	551
GTAMP	52	FENDER	PRINCETON TWEED	964	713	613	512
GTAMP	53	FENDER	PRINCETON TWEED	928	686	589	493
GTAMP	54	FENDER	PRINCETON TWEED, 8" SPEAKER	1,037	767	659	551
GTAMP	56	FENDER	PRINCETON TWEED, 8" SPEAKER	977	722	620	519
GTAMP	57	FENDER	PRINCETON TWEED	945	699	600	502
GTAMP	58	FENDER	PRINCETON TWEED	915	677	581	486
GTAMP	59	FENDER	PRINCETON TWEED	957	707	608	508
GTAMP	59	FENDER	PRINCETON TWEED	977	722	620	519
GTAMP	60	FENDER	PRINCETON TWEED	945	699	600	502
GTAMP	61	FENDER	PRINCETON BROWN TOLEX	689	509	437	366
GTAMP	62	FENDER	PRINCETON BROWN TOLEX	764	565	485	405
GTAMP	63	FENDER	PRINCETON BROWN TOLEX	465	344	295	247
GTAMP	63	FENDER	PRINCETON BLACK	497	367	315	264
GTAMP	64	FENDER	PRINCETON BLACK TOLEX, REVERB	480	355	305	255
GTAMP	64	FENDER	PRINCETON BROWN TOLEX	517	382	328	274
GTAMP	64	FENDER	PRINCETON REVERB	715	528	454	379
GTAMP	65	FENDER	PRINCETON BLACK FACE, REVERB, 1x10"	598	442	380	317
GTAMP	65	FENDER	PRINCETON BLACK TOLEX, REVERB	645	477	409	342
GTAMP	65	FENDER	PRINCETON BLACK TOLEX, REVERB	791	585	502	420
GTAMP	66	FENDER	PRINCETON OXFORD	438	324	278	233
GTAMP	66	FENDER	PRINCETON BLACK FACE	469	347	298	249

TYPE	YR	MFG	PRICES--BASED ON 100% ORIGINAL MODEL	SELL EXC	SELL AVG	BUY EXC	BUY AVG
GTAMP	66	FENDER	**PRINCETON** BLACK TOLEX, REVERB	728	**538**	462	387
GTAMP	66	FENDER	**PRINCETON** BLACK FACE, REVERB	745	**551**	473	396
GTAMP	67	FENDER	**PRINCETON** BLACK FACE, REVERB	589	**435**	374	313
GTAMP	67	FENDER	**PRINCETON** REVERB, SCRIPT NAME PLATE	625	**462**	397	332
GTAMP	68	FENDER	**PRINCETON** SILVER FACE, REVERB	498	**368**	316	264
GTAMP	69	FENDER	**PRINCETON** REVERB	433	**320**	275	230
GTAMP	69	FENDER	**PRINCETON** SILVER FACE, REVERB	486	**359**	309	258
GTAMP	70	FENDER	**PRINCETON** SILVER FACE, REVERB	451	**333**	286	239
GTAMP	70	FENDER	**PRINCETON** REVERB	480	**355**	305	255
GTAMP	71	FENDER	**PRINCETON** REVERB	424	**313**	269	225
GTAMP	74	FENDER	**PRINCETON** SILVER FACE	360	**266**	229	191
GTAMP	74	FENDER	**PRINCETON** REVERB	399	**295**	253	212
GTAMP	76	FENDER	**PRINCETON** REVERB	400	**296**	254	212
GTAMP	77	FENDER	**PRINCETON** REVERB	321	**237**	204	170
GTAMP	48	FENDER	**PRO** TWEED, TV FRONT	1,115	**825**	708	592
GTAMP	49	FENDER	**PRO** TWEED, TV FRONT	1,376	**1,018**	874	731
GTAMP	50	FENDER	**PRO** TWEED, TV FRONT	1,183	**875**	752	628
GTAMP	53	FENDER	**PRO** TWEED, TV FRONT	1,225	**906**	778	651
GTAMP	54	FENDER	**PRO** TWEED, NARROW PANEL	1,595	**1,180**	1,013	847
GTAMP	55	FENDER	**PRO** TWEED, NARROW PANEL	1,362	**1,007**	865	723
GTAMP	60	FENDER	**PRO** BROWN TOLEX	1,040	**769**	661	552
GTAMP	61	FENDER	**PRO** BROWN TOLEX, 1x15" JENSEN	783	**579**	497	416
GTAMP	62	FENDER	**PRO** BROWN TOLEX	823	**609**	523	437
GTAMP	63	FENDER	**PRO** BROWN TOLEX, 1x15" JENSEN	778	**575**	494	413
GTAMP	64	FENDER	**PRO** BLACK TOLEX, 1x15" JENSEN	706	**522**	448	375
GTAMP	65	FENDER	**PRO** BLACK FACE, REVERB	1,183	**875**	752	628
GTAMP	66	FENDER	**PRO** BLACK, REVERB, SCRIPT NAME PLATE, 2x12"	1,139	**842**	724	605
GTAMP	67	FENDER	**PRO** BLACK, REVERB, SCRIPT NAME PLATE, 2x12"	1,041	**770**	661	553
GTAMP	67	FENDER	**PRO** BLACK FACE, REVERB	1,092	**807**	694	580
GTAMP	68	FENDER	**PRO** SILVER FACE, REVERB, 2x12"	875	**647**	556	465
GTAMP	69	FENDER	**PRO** SILVER FACE, REVERB	800	**592**	508	425
GTAMP	70	FENDER	**PRO** REVERB, 10.5" DEEP	703	**520**	447	373
GTAMP	71	FENDER	**PRO** SILVER FACE, REVERB	658	**487**	418	349
GTAMP	72	FENDER	**PRO** SILVER FACE, REVERB	644	**476**	409	342
GTAMP	72	FENDER	**PRO** REVERB, 2x12"	663	**490**	421	352
GTAMP	73	FENDER	**PRO** SILVER FACE, REVERB	583	**431**	370	310
GTAMP	74	FENDER	**PRO** REVERB, 2x12"	620	**458**	394	329
GTAMP	76	FENDER	**PRO** SILVER FACE, REVERB	457	**338**	290	243
GTAMP	82	FENDER	**PRO** BLACK FACE, REVERB	438	**324**	278	233
GTAMP	72	FENDER	**QUAD** REVERB	518	**383**	329	275
GTAMP	79	FENDER	**QUAD** REVERB, 4x12", 100 WATTS	498	**368**	316	264
GTAMP	61	FENDER	**REVERB UNIT** BROWN TOLEX	741	**548**	470	393

TYPE	YR	MFG	PRICES--BASED ON 100% ORIGINAL MODEL	SELL EXC	SELL AVG	BUY EXC	BUY AVG
GTAMP	62	FENDER	**REVERB UNIT** BROWN TOLEX	803	**594**	510	426
GTAMP	62	FENDER	**REVERB UNIT** WHITE TOLEX, MAROON GRILL	815	**602**	517	432
GTAMP	63	FENDER	**REVERB UNIT** WHITE TOLEX	677	**501**	430	360
GTAMP	63	FENDER	**REVERB UNIT** BLOND	778	**575**	494	413
GTAMP	63	FENDER	**REVERB UNIT** BROWN TOLEX	783	**579**	497	416
GTAMP	63	FENDER	**REVERB UNIT** WHITE TOLEX	815	**602**	517	432
GTAMP	64	FENDER	**REVERB UNIT**	677	**501**	430	360
GTAMP	64	FENDER	**REVERB UNIT** BLACK FACE	696	**515**	442	370
GTAMP	64	FENDER	**REVERB UNIT** BROWN TOLEX, TAN GRILL	740	**547**	470	393
GTAMP	65	FENDER	**REVERB UNIT** BLACK FACE, WHITE KNOBS	617	**456**	392	327
GTAMP	65	FENDER	**REVERB UNIT**	629	**465**	400	334
GTAMP	66	FENDER	**REVERB UNIT** BLACK FACE	598	**442**	380	317
GTAMP	70	FENDER	**REVERB UNIT**	446	**330**	283	237
GTAMP	72	FENDER	**REVERB UNIT**	397	**293**	252	211
GTAMP	75	FENDER	**REVERB UNIT** SILVER	384	**284**	244	204
GTAMP	71	FENDER	**SCORPIO** SOLID STATE, 2,x12", 56 WATTS	360	**266**	228	191
GTAMP	61	FENDER	**SHOWMAN** WHITE TOLEX, 12 AMP	1,152	**852**	732	612
GTAMP	61	FENDER	**SHOWMAN** BLOND, 15 AMP	1,440	**1,065**	915	765
GTAMP	62	FENDER	**SHOWMAN** BROWN, WHITE KNOBS/HEAD	1,202	**889**	764	639
GTAMP	64	FENDER	**SHOWMAN** BLOND, 15 AMP	1,164	**861**	739	618
GTAMP	65	FENDER	**SHOWMAN** BLACK FACE, TOP/BOTTOM, JBL	1,104	**816**	701	586
GTAMP	65	FENDER	**SHOWMAN** BLACK, HEAD ONLY, 15 AMP	1,830	**1,353**	1,163	972
GTAMP	66	FENDER	**SHOWMAN** BLACK FACE, HEAD AND CABINET	1,284	**949**	816	682
GTAMP	66	FENDER	**SHOWMAN** BLACK FACE, HEAD	1,414	**1,045**	898	751
GTAMP	68	FENDER	**SHOWMAN SINGLE** BOTTOM, JBL 15" CABINET	685	**506**	435	364
GTAMP	82	FENDER	**SUPER CHAMP** 2x10" SPEAKER	509	**377**	323	270
GTAMP	51	FENDER	**SUPER REVERB** TWEED	3,086	**2,282**	1,961	1,639
GTAMP	55	FENDER	**SUPER REVERB** TWEED	1,450	**1,072**	921	770
GTAMP	60	FENDER	**SUPER REVERB** BLACK TOLEX	956	**707**	607	507
GTAMP	60	FENDER	**SUPER REVERB** TWEED	1,656	**1,224**	1,052	879
GTAMP	62	FENDER	**SUPER REVERB** TOLEX, 2x10" M.L.D.	827	**612**	525	439
GTAMP	63	FENDER	**SUPER REVERB** BLACK FACE	1,166	**862**	741	619
GTAMP	64	FENDER	**SUPER REVERB** BLACK FACE, 24x25" SPEAKER	1,186	**877**	753	630
GTAMP	65	FENDER	**SUPER REVERB** BLACK FACE, 4x10" SPEAKERS	1,362	**1,007**	865	723
GTAMP	66	FENDER	**SUPER REVERB** BLACK FACE	1,176	**869**	747	624
GTAMP	66	FENDER	**SUPER REVERB** 1-TONE NB, TV FRONT	1,436	**1,062**	912	762
GTAMP	67	FENDER	**SUPER REVERB** SILVER FACE	738	**545**	469	392
GTAMP	67	FENDER	**SUPER REVERB** BLACK FACE, VINYL COVER	1,244	**920**	790	660
GTAMP	69	FENDER	**SUPER REVERB** SILVER FACE, 4x10" SPEAKERS	734	**543**	466	390
GTAMP	70	FENDER	**SUPER REVERB** SILVER FACE	708	**523**	450	376
GTAMP	71	FENDER	**SUPER REVERB**	640	**473**	406	340
GTAMP	72	FENDER	**SUPER REVERB**	500	**369**	317	265
GTAMP	75	FENDER	**SUPER REVERB** SILVER FACE	518	**383**	329	275
GTAMP	76	FENDER	**SUPER REVERB** SILVER FACE	500	**369**	317	265

TYPE	YR	MFG	PRICES--BASED ON 100% ORIGINAL MODEL	SELL EXC	SELL AVG	BUY EXC	BUY AVG
GTAMP	78	FENDER	**SUPER REVERB** SILVER FACE	518	**383**	329	275
GTAMP	79	FENDER	**SUPER REVERB** SILVER FACE	513	**379**	326	272
GTAMP	57	FENDER	**TREMOLUX** TWEED, 1x12"	1,300	**962**	826	691
GTAMP	58	FENDER	**TREMOLUX** TWEED	1,320	**976**	839	701
GTAMP	59	FENDER	**TREMOLUX** TWEED, 1x12"	1,347	**996**	856	716
GTAMP	60	FENDER	**TREMOLUX** TWEED	1,332	**985**	846	707
GTAMP	61	FENDER	**TREMOLUX** YELLOWED WHITE, PIGGY BACK, SINGLE 10" CABINET	1,216	**899**	772	646
GTAMP	62	FENDER	**TREMOLUX** BLOND, 1x10" CABINET	1,047	**774**	665	556
GTAMP	64	FENDER	**TREMOLUX** BLACK, HEAD ONLY	347	**257**	220	184
GTAMP	64	FENDER	**TREMOLUX** BLACK FACE, PIGGYBACK	587	**434**	373	312
GTAMP	65	FENDER	**TREMOLUX** BLACK, PIGGYBACK, 2x12"	1,095	**810**	696	581
GTAMP	66	FENDER	**TREMOLUX** HEAD	1,115	**825**	708	592
GTAMP	64	FENDER	**TUBE REVERB** WHITE TOLEX, CREAM GRILL	645	**477**	409	342
GTAMP	70	FENDER	**TUBE REVERB** BLACK	429	**317**	272	227
GTAMP	53	FENDER	**TWIN** TWEED	2,390	**1,767**	1,518	1,269
GTAMP	55	FENDER	**TWIN** TWEED, 1x12"	2,191	**1,620**	1,392	1,164
GTAMP	55	FENDER	**TWIN** TWEED, 100 WATT	8,616	**6,372**	5,474	4,577
GTAMP	57	FENDER	**TWIN** TWEED, 40 WATT, 2x12"	3,360	**2,485**	2,135	1,785
GTAMP	58	FENDER	**TWIN** TWEED, 100 WATT, 2x12"	8,273	**6,118**	5,256	4,395
GTAMP	59	FENDER	**TWIN** TWEED, 100 WATT	2,203	**1,629**	1,399	1,170
GTAMP	62	FENDER	**TWIN** WHITE TOLEX	3,734	**2,761**	2,372	1,983
GTAMP	63	FENDER	**TWIN** BLACK FACE, REVERB	850	**629**	540	451
GTAMP	63	FENDER	**TWIN** WHITE TOLEX	2,125	**1,571**	1,350	1,129
GTAMP	65	FENDER	**TWIN** BLACK FACE, 10" DEEP, REVERB	1,129	**835**	717	600
GTAMP	66	FENDER	**TWIN** BLACK FACE, 10" DEEP, REVERB	931	**688**	591	494
GTAMP	67	FENDER	**TWIN** REVERB	855	**632**	543	454
GTAMP	67	FENDER	**TWIN** BLACK FACE, REVERB	947	**700**	602	503
GTAMP	68	FENDER	**TWIN** SILVER, 9 3/4" DEEP, REVERB	568	**420**	361	301
GTAMP	69	FENDER	**TWIN** SILVER FACE, REVERB	564	**417**	358	299
GTAMP	69	FENDER	**TWIN** 85 RMS, 12" JENSENS, REVERB	733	**542**	466	389
GTAMP	70	FENDER	**TWIN** SILVER FACE, REVERB	552	**408**	351	293
GTAMP	70	FENDER	**TWIN** 100 RMS, REVERB	720	**532**	457	382
GTAMP	70	FENDER	**TWIN** REVERB	798	**590**	507	424
GTAMP	72	FENDER	**TWIN** SILVER FACE, REVERB, NON-MASTER VOLUME	506	**374**	322	269
GTAMP	74	FENDER	**TWIN** SILVER FACE, REVERB	506	**374**	322	269
GTAMP	74	FENDER	**TWIN** CASTERS, MASTER VOLUME, REVERB	632	**467**	401	336
GTAMP	75	FENDER	**TWIN** MASTER VOLUME, REVERB	548	**405**	348	291
GTAMP	75	FENDER	**TWIN** CASTERS, REVERB	632	**467**	401	336
GTAMP	76	FENDER	**TWIN** REVERB	505	**374**	321	268
GTAMP	77	FENDER	**TWIN** REVERB	504	**372**	320	267
GTAMP	77	FENDER	**TWIN** SILVER FACE, SUPER REVERB	606	**448**	385	322
GTAMP	78	FENDER	**TWIN** REVERB	505	**374**	321	268

TYPE	YR	MFG	PRICES--BASED ON 100% ORIGINAL MODEL	SELL EXC	SELL AVG	BUY EXC	BUY AVG
GTAMP	64	FENDER	**VIBRO CHAMP** BLACK FACE	462	**342**	294	245
GTAMP	65	FENDER	**VIBRO CHAMP** BLACK FACE	365	**270**	232	194
GTAMP	66	FENDER	**VIBRO CHAMP** BLACK FACE, SCRIPT NAME PLATE	394	**291**	250	209
GTAMP	67	FENDER	**VIBRO CHAMP** BLACK FACE, SCRIPT NAME PLATE	388	**287**	247	206
GTAMP	68	FENDER	**VIBRO CHAMP** SILVER FACE	385	**285**	245	205
GTAMP	70	FENDER	**VIBRO CHAMP** SILVER FACE	481	**356**	306	256
GTAMP	75	FENDER	**VIBRO CHAMP** SILVER FACE	338	**250**	215	180
GTAMP	78	FENDER	**VIBRO CHAMP** 8" SPEAKER	288	**213**	183	153
GTAMP	57	FENDER	**VIBROLUX** TWEED	1,094	**809**	695	581
GTAMP	58	FENDER	**VIBROLUX** TWEED, 1x10" SPEAKER	958	**708**	608	508
GTAMP	59	FENDER	**VIBROLUX** TWEED, 1x10" BLUE CAP SPEAKER	986	**729**	627	524
GTAMP	60	FENDER	**VIBROLUX** TWEED, 1x12" SPEAKER	960	**710**	610	510
GTAMP	61	FENDER	**VIBROLUX** BROWN, 12"	970	**717**	616	515
GTAMP	62	FENDER	**VIBROLUX** BROWN	1,043	**771**	663	554
GTAMP	63	FENDER	**VIBROLUX** BROWN	1,005	**743**	638	533
GTAMP	64	FENDER	**VIBROLUX** TWEED, 1x10" SPEAKER	913	**675**	580	485
GTAMP	64	FENDER	**VIBROLUX REVERB** BLACK FACE, 2x10"	1,306	**966**	830	694
GTAMP	65	FENDER	**VIBROLUX REVERB** BLACK FACE, 2x10"	1,299	**961**	825	690
GTAMP	66	FENDER	**VIBROLUX REVERB** BLACK FACE	1,296	**958**	823	688
GTAMP	67	FENDER	**VIBROLUX REVERB** BLACK FACE, 2x10"	1,291	**954**	820	685
GTAMP	69	FENDER	**VIBROLUX REVERB** SILVER FACE, 2x10"	598	**442**	380	317
GTAMP	70	FENDER	**VIBROLUX REVERB** 40 RMS	593	**438**	376	315
GTAMP	73	FENDER	**VIBROLUX REVERB**	525	**388**	333	278
GTAMP	75	FENDER	**VIBROLUX REVERB** SILVER FACE	590	**436**	375	313
GTAMP	78	FENDER	**VIBROLUX REVERB**	438	**324**	278	233
GTAMP	60	FENDER	**VIBROSONIC** BROWN TOLEX	1,023	**756**	650	543
GTAMP	62	FENDER	**VIBROSONIC** BROWN TOLEX	1,975	**1,461**	1,255	1,049
GTAMP	63	FENDER	**VIBROSONIC** M.L.D.	826	**611**	525	439
GTAMP	63	FENDER	**VIBROVERB** BROWN, 2x10"	3,356	**2,482**	2,132	1,782
GTAMP	64	FENDER	**VIBROVERB** BROWN or BLACK FACE	3,302	**2,442**	2,098	1,754
GTAMP	65	FENDER	**VIBROVERB** BLACK TOLEX	1,344	**994**	854	714
GUITAR (ACOUSTIC)	64	FENDER	**CONCERT** ROSEWOOD, FLATTOP	508	**376**	323	270
GUITAR	65	FENDER	**CONCERT** MAHOGANY, FLATTOP	448	**341**	290	222
GUITAR	68	FENDER	**CONCERT** ZEBRA BACK/SIDES, FLATTOP	409	**303**	260	217
GUITAR	69	FENDER	**CUSTOM** SUNBURST, SOLID BODY, SERIAL #232438-258071	817	**604**	519	434
GUITAR	84	FENDER	**FLAME ULTRA** ALDER BODY, CARVED MAPLE TOP, INTERNAL TONE	1,307	**996**	846	647
GUITAR	62	FENDER	**KING** NATURAL, FLATTOP	539	**399**	342	286
GUITAR	63	FENDER	**KING** NATURAL, FLATTOP	499	**369**	317	265
GUITAR	64	FENDER	**KING** NATURAL, FLATTOP	491	**363**	312	261
GUITAR	66	FENDER	**KINGMAN** ANTIGUA, FLATTOP	522	**398**	338	258
GUITAR	66	FENDER	**KINGMAN** SUNBURST, FLATTOP	571	**422**	362	303
GUITAR	68	FENDER	**KINGMAN** NATURAL, FLATTOP	442	**327**	281	235
GUITAR	68	FENDER	**KINGMAN** ANTIGUA, FLATTOP	564	**417**	358	299

TYPE	YR	MFG	PRICES--BASED ON 100% ORIGINAL MODEL	SELL EXC	SELL AVG	BUY EXC	BUY AVG
GUITAR	69	FENDER	**LTD** SUNBURST, CURLY MAPLE, GOLD HARDWARE	2,006	**1,483**	1,274	1,065
GUITAR	65	FENDER	**MALIBU** FLATTOP	475	**351**	301	252
GUITAR	66	FENDER	**MALIBU** FLATTOP	441	**326**	280	234
GUITAR	67	FENDER	**MALIBU** FLATTOP	440	**325**	279	234
GUITAR	68	FENDER	**MALIBU** FLATTOP	438	**324**	278	233
GUITAR	70	FENDER	**MALIBU**	432	**319**	274	229
GUITAR	67	FENDER	**NEWPORTER**	384	**284**	244	204
GUITAR	68	FENDER	**NEWPORTER** MAHOGANY, FLATTOP, SERIAL #232576	473	**350**	300	251
GUITAR	66	FENDER	**PALOMINO** NATURAL, FLATTOP	476	**352**	302	252
GUITAR	68	FENDER	**PALOMINO** NATURAL, FLATTOP	456	**337**	289	242
GUITAR	69	FENDER	**PALOMINO** NATURAL, FLATTOP	426	**315**	270	226
GUITAR	66	FENDER	**REDONDO** FLATTOP	441	**326**	280	234
GUITAR	66	FENDER	**SHENANDOAH** NATURAL, 12-STRING	478	**353**	303	253
GUITAR	68	FENDER	**SHENANDOAH** ANTIGUA, 12-STRING	410	**303**	261	218
GUITAR	68	FENDER	**SHENANDOAH** BLACK, 12-STRING	476	**352**	302	252
GUITAR	67	FENDER	**VILLAGER** 12-STRING, FLATTOP	452	**334**	287	240
GUITAR	68	FENDER	**VILLAGER** 12-STRING, FLATTOP	470	**347**	298	249
GUITAR	69	FENDER	**VILLAGER** 12-STRING, FLATTOP	494	**365**	314	262
GUITAR	71	FENDER	**VILLAGER** 12-STRING	384	**284**	244	204
GUITAR	67	FENDER	**WILDWOOD** BLUE, FLATTOP	649	**480**	412	345
GUITAR	68	FENDER	**WILDWOOD** FLATTOP	678	**501**	431	360
GUITAR	67	FENDER	**WILDWOOD II**	895	**662**	569	475
GUITAR	68	FENDER	**WILDWOOD II** NATURAL TOP	576	**426**	366	306
GUITAR	67	FENDER	**WILDWOOD III** ROSEWOOD BACK/SIDES	723	**535**	459	384
GUITAR	68	FENDER	**WILDWOOD V** DREADNOUGHT, FLATTOP	720	**532**	457	382
GUITAR	67	FENDER	**WILDWOOD VI** GREEN, FLATTOP	725	**536**	461	385
GUITAR	68	FENDER	**WILDWOOD C II** HOLLOW BODY, THINLINE	519	**384**	330	275
GUITAR	68	FENDER	**WILDWOOD C XII** HOLLOW BODY, 12-STRING	532	**394**	338	283
MANDOLIN	56	FENDER	**ELECTRIC MANDOLIN** BLOND, TELECASTER, SERIAL #980-00985	1,415	**1,046**	899	751
MANDOL	57	FENDER	**ELECTRIC MANDOLIN** SUNBURST, 4-STRING, SERIAL #01308	1,206	**892**	766	641
MANDOL	58	FENDER	**ELECTRIC MANDOLIN** SUNBURST 3-TONE, SERIAL #00541-00647	1,202	**889**	764	639
MANDOL	59	FENDER	**ELECTRIC MANDOLIN** SUNBURST 2-TONE, SERIAL #01253-027724	1,204	**891**	765	640
MANDOL	60	FENDER	**ELECTRIC MANDOLIN** SUNBURST. SERIAL #01407-03046	1,144	**846**	727	607
MANDOL	61	FENDER	**ELECTRIC MANDOLIN** SUNBURST 3-TONE	1,147	**848**	728	609
MANDOL	62	FENDER	**ELECTRIC MANDOLIN** SUNBURST	1,216	**899**	772	646
MANDOL	64	FENDER	**ELECTRIC MANDOLIN** SUNBURST, ROSEWOOD BOARD, SERIAL #01729-02027	1,125	**832**	714	597
MANDOL	69	FENDER	**ELECTRIC MANDOLIN** SUNBURST	825	**610**	524	438
MANDOL	74	FENDER	**ELECTRIC MANDOLIN** SUNBURST, ROSEWOOD BRIDGE	854	**631**	542	453
MANDOL	59	FENDER	**MANDOCASTER** SUNBURST, ROSEWOOD FRETBOARD, SERIAL #01243	1,115	**825**	708	592
MANDOL	62	FENDER	**MANDOCASTER** SUNBURST, 4-STRING, SERIAL #02217	1,002	**764**	649	496
MANDOL	66	FENDER	**MANDOCASTER** SUNBURST, SOLID BODY	876	**648**	556	465
MANDOL	57	FENDER	**MANDOLIN** BLOND, MAPLE NECK	1,121	**829**	712	595
STEEL GUITAR	58	FENDER	**400** FLAME MAPLE, 8-STRING, PEDAL STEEL	1,315	**972**	835	698

TYPE	YR	MFG	PRICES--BASED ON 100% ORIGINAL MODEL	SELL EXC	SELL AVG	BUY EXC	BUY AVG
STGUIT	60	FENDER	**400** BROWN, 8-STRING, PEDAL STEEL	565	**418**	359	300
STGUIT	61	FENDER	**400** 8-STRING, PEDAL STEEL	478	**353**	303	253
STGUIT	62	FENDER	**400** BLACK, 8-STRING, PEDAL STEEL	478	**353**	303	253
STGUIT	65	FENDER	**400** SUNBURST, 8-STRING, PEDAL STEEL	432	**320**	275	230
STGUIT	64	FENDER	**800** SUNBURST, 10-STRING, PEDAL STEEL	428	**316**	272	227
STGUIT	60	FENDER	**1000** SUNBURST, (2)8-STRING, PEDAL STEEL	619	**457**	393	328
STGUIT	68	FENDER	**1000** SUNBURST, (2)8-STRING, PEDAL STEEL	571	**422**	362	303
STGUIT	65	FENDER	**2000** SUNBURST, (2)10-STRING NECKS	621	**459**	394	329
STGUIT	49	FENDER	**CHAMP LAP STEEL** YELLOW	552	**408**	351	293
STGUIT	50	FENDER	**CHAMP LAP STEEL** YELLOW PEARLOID	529	**391**	336	281
STGUIT	52	FENDER	**CHAMP LAP STEEL** YELLOW PEARLOID	475	**351**	301	252
STGUIT	54	FENDER	**CHAMP LAP STEEL** YELLOW PEARLIOD	456	**337**	290	242
STGUIT	55	FENDER	**CHAMP LAP STEEL** DESERT FAWN	536	**396**	340	285
STGUIT	57	FENDER	**CHAMP LAP STEEL** BLOND	518	**383**	329	275
STGUIT	57	FENDER	**CHAMP LAP STEEL** DESERT FAWN	518	**383**	329	275
STGUIT	58	FENDER	**CHAMP LAP STEEL** DESERT FAWN	488	**361**	310	259
STGUIT	60	FENDER	**CHAMP LAP STEEL** DESERT FAWN	422	**312**	268	224
STGUIT	62	FENDER	**CHAMP LAP STEEL** DESERT FAWN	480	**355**	305	255
STGUIT	46	FENDER	**DELUXE** ELECTRIC STEEL	625	**462**	397	332
STGUIT	55	FENDER	**DELUXE** 8-STRING	480	**355**	305	255
STGUIT	68	FENDER	**DELUXE** 8-STRING	476	**352**	302	252
STGUIT	57	FENDER	**DELUXE 6** BLOND, ELECTRIC STEEL	422	**312**	268	224
STGUIT	65	FENDER	**DELUXE 6** ELECTRIC STEEL	478	**353**	303	253
STGUIT	52	FENDER	**DUAL 6 PROFESSIONAL** BLOND, (2)6-STRING NECKS	598	**442**	380	317
STGUIT	61	FENDER	**DUAL 6 PROFESSIONAL** DOUBLE NECK, TABLE STEEL	590	**436**	375	313
STGUIT	67	FENDER	**DUAL 6 PROFESSIONAL** DOUBLE NECK	504	**372**	320	267
STGUIT	48	FENDER	**DUAL 8 PROFESSIONAL** WALNUT, (2)8-STRING	1,058	**783**	672	562
STGUIT	50	FENDER	**DUAL 8 PROFESSIONAL** BLOND, (2)8-STRING	663	**490**	421	352
STGUIT	50	FENDER	**DUAL 8 PROFESSIONAL** WALNUT, (2)8-STRING	663	**490**	421	352
STGUIT	52	FENDER	**DUAL 8 PROFESSIONAL** WALNUT, (2)8-STRING	616	**455**	391	327
STGUIT	54	FENDER	**DUAL 8 PROFESSIONAL** (2)8-STRING	677	**501**	430	360
STGUIT	58	FENDER	**DUAL 8 PROFESSIONAL** BLOND, (2)8-STRING	663	**490**	421	352
STGUIT	49	FENDER	**LAP STEEL** YELLOW PEARLOID, SN #5211	1,015	**773**	657	502
STGUIT	50	FENDER	**LAP STEEL** WHITE, SINGLE NECK	438	**324**	278	233
STGUIT	54	FENDER	**LAP STEEL** CREAM, 8-STRING, 3 LEGS	713	**527**	453	378
STGUIT	55	FENDER	**LAP STEEL** TAN, 6-STRING	438	**324**	278	233
STGUIT	47	FENDER	**PRINCETON** NATURAL, NON-PEDAL STEEL	426	**315**	270	226
STGUIT	48	FENDER	**PRINCETON** NATURAL, NON-PEDAL STEEL	425	**314**	270	225
STGUIT	55	FENDER	**STRINGMASTER** (2)8-STRING NECKS	696	**514**	442	369
STGUIT	56	FENDER	**STRINGMASTER** (3)8-STRING NECKS	1,281	**947**	814	680
STGUIT	57	FENDER	**STRINGMASTER** (4)8-STRING NECKS	829	**613**	527	440
STGUIT	58	FENDER	**STRINGMASTER** (2)8-STRING NECKS	820	**607**	521	436

TYPE	YR	MFG	PRICES--BASED ON 100% ORIGINAL MODEL	SELL EXC	SELL AVG	BUY EXC	BUY AVG
STGUIT	59	FENDER	**STRINGMASTER** (3)8-STRING NECKS	791	**585**	502	420
STGUIT	60	FENDER	**STRINGMASTER** (2)8-STRING NECKS	663	**490**	421	352
STGUIT	61	FENDER	**STRINGMASTER** (3)8-STRING NECKS	653	**483**	415	347
STGUIT	65	FENDER	**STRINGMASTER** (2)8-STRING NECKS	671	**496**	426	356
STGUIT	68	FENDER	**STRINGMASTER** 4-NECK	657	**486**	417	349
STGUIT	71	FENDER	**STRINGMASTER** (2)8-STRING NECKS	696	**515**	442	370
STGUIT	76	FENDER	**STRINGMASTER** (3)8-STRING NECKS	694	**513**	441	368
STGUIT	80	FENDER	**STRINGMASTER** (3)8-STRING NECKS	537	**397**	341	285
STGUIT	56	FENDER	**STUDIO DELUXE** 3 LEGS	580	**429**	369	308
STGUIT	57	FENDER	**STUDIO DELUXE** 3 LEGS	590	**436**	375	313

FISHER

TYPE	YR	MFG	MODEL	SELL EXC	SELL AVG	BUY EXC	BUY AVG
PRE	73	FISHER	**50C** MONO TUBE	145	**107**	92	77
PRE	73-78	FISHER	**50PR** MONO TUBE	55	**41**	35	29
PRE	59-63	FISHER	**400C** TUBE STEREO	230	**170**	146	122
PRE	61	FISHER	**400CX** TUBE STEREO	293	**217**	186	156
PWR	62-68	FISHER	**20A** MONO TUBE	155	**115**	98	82
PWR	62	FISHER	**30A** MONO TUBE	120	**88**	76	63
PWR	62	FISHER	**50A** TUBE	134	**99**	85	71
PWR	62-68	FISHER	**55A** MONO TUBE	360	**266**	228	191
PWR	55	FISHER	**70-AZ TUBE**	192	**142**	122	102
PWR	68-68	FISHER	**80AZ** MONO TUBE	315	**233**	200	167
PWR	62	FISHER	**90A** MONO TUBE	106	**78**	67	56
PWR	62	FISHER	**125A/AX** MONO TUBE	242	**179**	154	129
PWR	62	FISHER	**200** MONO TUBE	430	**318**	273	228
PWR	64-98	FISHER	**KX-100 INTEGRATED** 12 WATT	148	**110**	94	79
PWR	60-61	FISHER	**SA-100** STEREO TUBE, 20 WATT	233	**172**	148	123
PWR	60-64	FISHER	**SA-300B** STEREO TUBE, 30 WATT	427	**315**	271	226
PWR	64-66	FISHER	**SA-300B** STEREO TUBE, 30 WATT	336	**248**	213	178
PWR	62	FISHER	**SA-1000** STEREO TUBE	419	**310**	266	222
PWR	62-68	FISHER	**SA-1000** STEREO TUBE, 65 WATT	713	**527**	453	378
PWR	61-62	FISHER	**X-100 INTEGRATED** STEREO TUBE, 15 WATT	163	**120**	103	86
TUNER	60	FISHER	**FM-50** TUBE	211	**156**	134	112
TUNER	62	FISHER	**FM-100** TUBE	202	**149**	128	107
TUNER	64	FISHER	**FM-100B** BLACK, TUBE	235	**173**	149	124
TUNER	64-66	FISHER	**FM-1000 CLASSIC** TUBE	672	**497**	427	357
TUNER	64	FISHER	**FMR-1**	914	**676**	581	486

FRAMUS (GERMANY)

TYPE	YR	MFG	MODEL	SELL EXC	SELL AVG	BUY EXC	BUY AVG
ELEC. GUITAR	69	FRAMUS	**ATILLA ZOLLER** ARCHTOP	432	**319**	274	229
ELGUIT	62	FRAMUS	**BASS (WYMAN)**	192	**142**	122	102
ELGUIT	64	FRAMUS	**BASS IV**	400	**296**	254	212
ELGUIT	59	FRAMUS	**BILLY LORENTO**	635	**470**	403	337
ELGUIT	62	FRAMUS	**BILLY LORENTO**	438	**324**	278	233
ELGUIT	69	FRAMUS	**BILLY LORENTO**	489	**362**	311	260
ELGUIT	60	FRAMUS	**CARAVELLE**	360	**266**	228	191
ELGUIT	67	FRAMUS	**CARAVELLE** DOUBLE CUTAWAY, 2 PU's	379	**280**	240	201
ELGUIT	74	FRAMUS	**CARAVELLE** DOUBLE CUTAWAY, 2 PU's	288	**213**	183	153

TYPE	YR	MFG	PRICES--BASED ON 100% ORIGINAL MODEL	SELL EXC	SELL AVG	BUY EXC	BUY AVG
ELGUIT	66	FRAMUS	FRET JET BLACK TO RED BURST, DOUBLE CUTAWAY	200	148	127	106
ELGUIT	64	FRAMUS	GOLDEN TELEVISION	438	324	278	233
ELGUIT	74	FRAMUS	JAN AKKERMAN SINGLE CUTAWAY, 2 PU's	541	400	344	287
ELGUIT	75	FRAMUS	JAN AKKERMAN	480	355	305	255
ELGUIT	63	FRAMUS	KING MODEL 5/98	384	284	244	204
ELGUIT	64	FRAMUS	MISSOURI RED-BLACK SUNBURST, 2 PU's	384	284	244	204
ELGUIT	71	FRAMUS	NASHVILLE	393	291	250	209
ELGUIT	64	FRAMUS	SORELLA BLACK TO RED BURST, ARCHTOP	244	181	155	130
ELGUIT	66	FRAMUS	SPORTSMAN	168	124	106	89
ELGUIT	60	FRAMUS	STAR BASS SUNBURST, THIN BODY, 2 PU's	471	348	299	250
ELGUIT	65	FRAMUS	STAR BASS SUNBURST, THIN BODY, 2 PU's	297	220	189	158
ELGUIT	65	FRAMUS	STRATO DELUXE 12-STRING	378	279	240	200
ELGUIT	65	FRAMUS	STRATO MELODIE 9-STRING	500	369	317	265
GUITAR (ACOUSTIC)	75	FRAMUS	SPORT 39"	206	152	131	109
GUITAR	72	FRAMUS	TEXAN CHERRY SUNBURST, ENGRAVED PICKGUARD	480	355	305	255
GUITAR	75	FRAMUS	TEXAN FLAME CHERRY SUNBURST	336	248	213	178
UPRIG	46	FRAMUS	UPRIGHT BASS CARVED TOP	3,753	2,776	2,385	1,994

FUTTERMAN

TYPE	YR	MFG	MODEL	SELL EXC	SELL AVG	BUY EXC	BUY AVG
PWR	68-69	FUTT	H-1 MONO, PAIR, 12 WATT	227	168	144	120
PWR	62-69	FUTT	H-3 STEREO, 50 WATT	354	261	225	188
PWR	68-73	FUTT	H-3 STEREO, 40 WATT	397	293	252	211
PWR	73-78	FUTT	H-3A STEREO, 60 WATT	408	302	259	217
PWR	78-82	FUTT	H3AA DUAL MONO, 125 WATT, PAIR	566	418	359	300

GALLAGHER

TYPE	YR	MFG	MODEL	SELL EXC	SELL AVG	BUY EXC	BUY AVG
GUITAR (ACOUSTIC)	79	GALLAGHER	71 SPECIAL ROSEWOOD BACK/SIDES	1,225	906	778	651
GUITAR	65	GALLAGHER	CUSTOM MAHOGANY, 12-STRING, 12-FRET	996	736	633	529
GUITAR	81	GALLAGHER	DOC WATSON CUTAWAY	1,992	1,473	1,265	1,058
GUITAR	85	GALLAGHER	DOC WATSON CUTAWAY	1,315	972	835	698
GUITAR	67	GALLAGHER	G-40 MAHOGANY BACK/SIDES, FLATTOP	729	539	463	387
GUITAR	80	GALLAGHER	G-45 MAHOGANY	996	736	633	529
GUITAR	66	GALLAGHER	G-50 MAHOGANY BACK/SIDES, DREADNOUGHT	958	730	620	474
GUITAR	67	GALLAGHER	G-50 MAHOGANY, DREADNOUGHT	1,056	781	671	561
GUITAR	70	GALLAGHER	G-50 MAHOGANY BACK/SIDES	855	632	543	454
GUITAR	66	GALLAGHER	G-60	677	501	430	360
GUITAR	68	GALLAGHER	G-70 SUNBURST, DREADNOUGHT	1,099	812	698	583
GUITAR	73	GALLAGHER	G-70	1,602	1,184	1,018	851
GUITAR	78	GALLAGHER	G-70 INDIAN ROSEWOOD	996	736	633	529
GUITAR	79	GALLAGHER	G-70 HERRINGBONE TRIM	1,195	883	759	634
GUITAR	70	GALLAGHER	G-70M FLATTOP	1,008	745	640	535
GUITAR	75	GALLAGHER	G-70M HERRINGBONE TRIM	1,078	797	685	572
GUITAR	73	GALLAGHER	G-71 SPECIAL INDIAN ROSEWOOD, HERRINGBONE	1,195	883	759	634
GUITAR	68	GALLAGHER	GC-65 ROSEWOOD BACK/SIDES, 12-FRET	1,528	1,130	971	811

GETZEN CO

TYPE	YR	MFG	MODEL	SELL EXC	SELL AVG	BUY EXC	BUY AVG
BANJO	60	GETZEN	SEVERENSEN 900 SEV Bb	517	382	328	274

GIBSON, SEE ALSO EPIPHONE, KALAMAZOO,RECORDING KING,RAMIRE

TYPE	YR	MFG	MODEL	SELL EXC	SELL AVG	BUY EXC	BUY AVG
BANJO	71	GIBSON	ALL AMERICAN	6,457	4,776	4,103	3,430
BANJO	72	GIBSON	ALL AMERICAN	6,545	4,840	4,158	3,477

TYPE	YR	MFG	PRICES--BASED ON 100% ORIGINAL MODEL	SELL EXC	SELL AVG	BUY EXC	BUY AVG
BANJO	78	GIBSON	**ALL AMERICAN**	5,953	**4,403**	3,783	3,163
BANJO	24	GIBSON	**BANJO-MANDOLIN** TRAP DOOR, 8-STRING	691	**511**	439	367
BANJO	27	GIBSON	**BELLA VOCE** WHITE HOLLY, 5-STRING	7,956	**5,884**	5,055	4,226
BANJO	27	GIBSON	**BELLA VOCE** TENOR, ARCHTOP	8,160	**6,035**	5,185	4,335
BANJO	28	GIBSON	**BELLA VOCE** TENOR, WHITE HOLLY	9,022	**6,672**	5,732	4,792
BANJO	35	GIBSON	**BU-2 BANJO-UKE** LARGER HEAD	432	**319**	274	229
BANJO	32	GIBSON	**BU-3 BANJO-UKE** SUNBURST, 8" HEAD, MAPLE	598	**442**	380	317
BANJO	24	GIBSON	**CB-4 CELLO-BANJO**	1,593	**1,178**	1,012	846
BANJO	32	GIBSON	**CUSTOM** TENOR,12" HEAD, DBLECUT TB-4 STYLE PGHD,TBE&PLTE FLNGE	1,093	**808**	694	580
BANJO	38	GIBSON	**ELECTRIC BANJO** SUNBURST	3,360	**2,485**	2,135	1,785
BANJO	39	GIBSON	**ETB ELECTRIC** TENOR, INLAY LIKE TOP TENSION STYLE #7	3,731	**2,759**	2,371	1,982
BANJO	28	GIBSON	**FLORENTINE** TENOR	8,160	**6,035**	5,185	4,335
BANJO	30	GIBSON	**FLORENTINE** TENOR	8,352	**6,177**	5,307	4,437
BANJO	34	GIBSON	**FLORENTINE** RESONATOR	14,374	**10,630**	9,133	7,636
BANJO	72	GIBSON	**FLORENTINE** NATURAL MAPLE	7,713	**5,704**	4,901	4,097
BANJO	78	GIBSON	**FLORENTINE**	5,965	**4,411**	3,790	3,169
BANJO	28	GIBSON	**FLORENTINE CUSTOM** PLECTRUM, WHITE	8,953	**6,622**	5,689	4,756
BANJO	18	GIBSON	**GB-1 GUITAR-BANJO** OPEN BACK, 14" HEAD	760	**562**	483	403
BANJO	19	GIBSON	**GB-1 GUITAR-BANJO**	757	**560**	481	402
BANJO	20	GIBSON	**GB-1 GUITAR-BANJO** OPEN BACK, 14" HEAD, SERIAL #53800-62200	717	**530**	455	380
BANJO	27	GIBSON	**GB-1 GUITAR-BANJO** ROTOMATIC TUNERS	775	**573**	492	412
BANJO	32	GIBSON	**GB-1 GUITAR-BANJO**	761	**563**	483	404
BANJO	29	GIBSON	**GB-3 GUITAR-BANJO MASTERTONE**	1,674	**1,238**	1,063	889
BANJO	22	GIBSON	**GB-4 GUITAR-BANJO** SUNBURST	997	**737**	633	529
BANJO	25	GIBSON	**GRANADA** TENOR, 5-STRING, SERIAL #80300-82700	2,248	**1,662**	1,428	1,194
BANJO	26	GIBSON	**GRANADA** PLECTRUM, SERIAL #-85400	3,776	**2,793**	2,399	2,006
BANJO	28	GIBSON	**GRANADA** PLECTRUM, HEARTS & FLOWERS INLAY,NO-HOLE	4,101	**3,033**	2,605	2,178
BANJO	30	GIBSON	**GRANADA** TENOR, 2 PIECE FLANGE	2,177	**1,610**	1,383	1,156
BANJO	32	GIBSON	**KEL KROYDEN** TENOR, WALNUT, SERIAL #90400-90700	794	**587**	505	422
BANJO	34	GIBSON	**KEL KROYDEN** TENOR	735	**543**	467	390
BANJO	35	GIBSON	**KEL KROYDEN** TENOR, BLUE, SERIAL #92400-93500	788	**582**	500	418
BANJO	25	GIBSON	**MASTERTONE** TENOR, GRANADA, 18-FRET	2,051	**1,517**	1,303	1,089
BANJO	26	GIBSON	**MASTERTONE** TENOR	956	**707**	607	507
BANJO	28	GIBSON	**MASTERTONE** RESONATOR, 5-STRING, SERIAL #89800-90200	1,129	**835**	717	600
BANJO	60	GIBSON	**MASTERTONE** FLATHEAD	955	**706**	606	507
BANJO	36	GIBSON	**MB- 0 MANDOLIN-BANJO**	482	**357**	306	256
BANJO	35	GIBSON	**MB- 00 MANDOLIN-BANJO** 1 PIECE FLANGE	533	**394**	339	283
BANJO	19	GIBSON	**MB- 1 MANDOLIN-BANJO** OPEN BACK	532	**394**	338	283
BANJO	20	GIBSON	**MB- 1 MANDOLIN-BANJO**	515	**381**	327	273
BANJO	22	GIBSON	**MB- 1 MANDOLIN-BANJO** TRAP DOOR RES	444	**328**	282	236
BANJO	28	GIBSON	**MB- 1 MANDOLIN-BANJO** SERIAL #85400-87300	443	**328**	281	235
BANJO	25	GIBSON	**MB- 2 MANDOLIN-BANJO** 10.5" HEAD	456	**337**	290	242
BANJO	24	GIBSON	**MB- 3 MANDOLIN-BANJO** SERIAL #74900-80300	532	**394**	338	283
BANJO	26	GIBSON	**MB- 3 MANDOLIN-BANJO** DIAMOND HOLE, SERIAL #82700-	534	**395**	339	284
BANJO	20	GIBSON	**MB- 4 MANDOLIN-BANJO** OPEN BACK	538	**398**	342	286

TYPE	YR	MFG	PRICES--BASED ON 100% ORIGINAL MODEL	SELL EXC	SELL AVG	BUY EXC	BUY AVG
BANJO	21	GIBSON	MB- 4 MANDOLIN-BANJO TRAP DOOR RESONATOR	537	397	341	285
BANJO	24	GIBSON	MB- 4 MANDOLIN-BANJO	533	394	339	283
BANJO	24	GIBSON	MB-JR MANDOLIN-BANJO	448	331	284	238
BANJO	22	GIBSON	ORIOLE TENOR, OPEN BACK	598	442	380	317
BANJO	26	GIBSON	PB- 3 MASTERTONE PLECTRUM	1,407	1,040	894	747
BANJO	27	GIBSON	PB- 3 MASTERTONE PLECTRUM	1,089	830	705	539
BANJO	34	GIBSON	PB- 3 MASTERTONE FLATHEAD, 5-STRING	9,609	7,107	6,106	5,105
BANJO	31	GIBSON	PB- 6 FLATHEAD, RESONATOR	9,448	6,987	6,003	5,019
BANJO	37	GIBSON	PB- 7 FLATHEAD, ROSEWOOD BOARD, RESONATOR, WALNUT	678	501	431	360
BANJO	40	GIBSON	PB- 7 MASTERTONE	11,520	8,520	7,320	6,120
BANJO	66	GIBSON	PB-100 PLECTRUM	637	471	405	338
BANJO	67	GIBSON	PB-100 PLECTRUM, SUNBURST, RESONATOR	735	543	467	390
BANJO	69	GIBSON	PB-100 PLECTRUM	637	471	405	338
BANJO	72	GIBSON	PB-100 PLECTRUM	639	472	406	339
BANJO	62	GIBSON	PB-250 PLECTRUM	825	610	524	438
BANJO	65	GIBSON	PB-250 PLECTRUM	890	658	566	473
BANJO	66	GIBSON	PB-250 PLECTRUM	811	599	515	430
BANJO	67	GIBSON	PB-250 PLECTRUM	808	597	513	429
BANJO	66	GIBSON	PB-800 PLECTRUM. NATURAL	1,195	883	759	634
BANJO	24	GIBSON	PB-JUNIOR OPEN PACK	428	316	272	227
BANJO	29	GIBSON	PT-6 FLATHEAD, GOLD TRIM, HIGH PROFILE	12,000	8,875	7,625	6,375
BANJO	35	GIBSON	RB- 00 5-STRING	796	589	506	423
BANJO	34	GIBSON	RB- 1 5-STRING, FLATHEAD	2,954	2,185	1,877	1,569
BANJO	35	GIBSON	RB- 1 5-STRING, FLATHEAD	2,188	1,618	1,390	1,162
BANJO	25	GIBSON	RB- 3 5-STRING, RESONATOR	1,884	1,393	1,197	1,001
BANJO	27	GIBSON	RB- 3 5-STRING, RESONATOR	1,989	1,471	1,263	1,056
BANJO	28	GIBSON	RB- 3 5-STRING, RESONATOR	1,952	1,444	1,240	1,037
BANJO	29	GIBSON	RB- 3 5-STRING, RESONATOR	1,892	1,399	1,202	1,005
BANJO	31	GIBSON	RB- 3 5-STRING, RESONATOR	1,808	1,337	1,149	960
BANJO	32	GIBSON	RB- 4	4,224	3,124	2,684	2,244
BANJO	26	GIBSON	RB- 4 MASTERTONE 5-STRING	6,240	4,615	3,965	3,315
BANJO	26	GIBSON	RB- 4BB MASTERTONE 5-STRING, RESONATOR	7,200	5,325	4,575	3,825
BANJO	29	GIBSON	RB- 6 FLATHEAD	10,869	8,038	6,906	5,774
BANJO	32	GIBSON	RB- 6 MASTERTONE	12,475	9,226	7,926	6,627
BANJO	35	GIBSON	RB- 75 5-STRING	5,443	4,025	3,458	2,891
BANJO	39	GIBSON	RB- 75 5-STRING, FLATHEAD, TONE RING	9,695	7,170	6,160	5,150
BANJO	61	GIBSON	RB-100 5-STRING	1,149	849	730	610
BANJO	62	GIBSON	RB-100 5-STRING	1,149	849	730	610
BANJO	64	GIBSON	RB-100 5-STRING	1,150	850	730	610
BANJO	67	GIBSON	RB-100 5-STRING	1,151	851	731	611
BANJO	70	GIBSON	RB-100 5-STRING	970	717	616	515
BANJO	73	GIBSON	RB-100 5-STRING	970	717	616	515
BANJO	50	GIBSON	RB-150 5-STRING	1,306	966	830	694
BANJO	64	GIBSON	RB-170 STANDARD LENGTH NECK, OPEN BACK	1,030	761	654	547

TYPE	YR	MFG	PRICES--BASED ON 100% ORIGINAL MODEL	SELL EXC	SELL AVG	BUY EXC	BUY AVG
BANJO	67	GIBSON	**RB-170** 11" FIBERSKYN HEAD, DOT INLAY	1,027	**759**	652	545
BANJO	63	GIBSON	**RB-175** LONG NECK	1,029	**761**	653	546
BANJO	64	GIBSON	**RB-175** LONG NECK, OPEN BACK	1,002	**741**	636	532
BANJO	65	GIBSON	**RB-175** LONG NECK, OPEN BACK	984	**728**	625	523
BANJO	66	GIBSON	**RB-175** LONG NECK, OPEN BACK	965	**714**	613	513
BANJO	67	GIBSON	**RB-175** LONG NECK, OPEN BACK	986	**729**	627	524
BANJO	65	GIBSON	**RB-180** LONG NECK, OPEN BACK	1,124	**831**	714	597
BANJO	74	GIBSON	**RB-200** CHERRY SUNBURST	1,802	**1,333**	1,145	957
BANJO	55	GIBSON	**RB-250**	1,669	**1,234**	1,060	886
BANJO	60	GIBSON	**RB-250**	1,466	**1,084**	932	779
BANJO	61	GIBSON	**RB-250**	1,353	**1,001**	860	719
BANJO	62	GIBSON	**RB-250**	1,413	**1,045**	897	750
BANJO	63	GIBSON	**RB-250**	1,413	**1,045**	897	750
BANJO	64	GIBSON	**RB-250**	1,394	**1,031**	886	741
BANJO	65	GIBSON	**RB-250**	1,450	**1,072**	921	770
BANJO	68	GIBSON	**RB-250**	1,275	**943**	810	677
BANJO	69	GIBSON	**RB-250** 5-STRING, RESONATOR	1,150	**850**	730	610
BANJO	70	GIBSON	**RB-250**	1,174	**868**	746	623
BANJO	71	GIBSON	**RB-250**	1,126	**832**	715	598
BANJO	72	GIBSON	**RB-250**	1,217	**900**	773	646
BANJO	74	GIBSON	**RB-250**	1,080	**798**	686	573
BANJO	75	GIBSON	**RB-250**	1,035	**766**	658	550
BANJO	75	GIBSON	**RB-250**	1,143	**845**	726	607
BANJO	77	GIBSON	**RB-250**	1,063	**786**	675	565
BANJO	78	GIBSON	**RB-250**	956	**707**	607	507
BANJO	79	GIBSON	**RB-250**	964	**713**	613	512
BANJO	80	GIBSON	**RB-250**	1,310	**969**	832	696
BANJO	62	GIBSON	**RB-250 MASTERTONE**	1,622	**1,199**	1,030	861
BANJO	65	GIBSON	**RB-250 MASTERTONE**	1,366	**1,010**	868	725
BANJO	76	GIBSON	**RB-250 MASTERTONE**	961	**711**	611	511
BANJO	70	GIBSON	**RB-800** CHERRY SUNBURST	1,315	**972**	835	698
BANJO	72	GIBSON	**RB-800** CHERRY SUNBURST	1,320	**976**	838	701
BANJO	77	GIBSON	**RB-800** CHERRY SUNBURST	1,146	**847**	728	608
BANJO	72	GIBSON	**RB-800 ARGENTINE** GRAY SUNBURST	1,315	**972**	835	698
BANJO	75	GIBSON	**RB-800 MASTERTONE** CHERRY SUNBURST, GOLD HARDWARE	1,862	**1,377**	1,183	989
BANJO	72	GIBSON	**RB-800 VICEROY** SUNBURST	1,235	**913**	785	656
BANJO	24	GIBSON	**RB-JUNIOR** BLACK	751	**555**	477	399
BANJO	28	GIBSON	**RECORDING KING** TENOR	1,396	**1,033**	887	742
BANJO	30	GIBSON	**STYLE 6** TENOR/PLECTRUM NECK	5,982	**4,424**	3,801	3,178
BANJO	24	GIBSON	**TB- 0** TENOR	748	**553**	475	397
BANJO	40	GIBSON	**TB- 00** TENOR, 1 PIECE FLANGE	749	**554**	476	398
BANJO	18	GIBSON	**TB- 1** TENOR, 5-STRING, HOLLOW RIM, SERIAL #39500-47900	2,966	**2,193**	1,884	1,575
BANJO	20	GIBSON	**TB- 1** TENOR	750	**555**	477	398
BANJO	23	GIBSON	**TB- 1** TENOR	748	**553**	475	397
BANJO	24	GIBSON	**TB- 1** TENOR	749	**554**	476	398
BANJO	25	GIBSON	**TB- 1** TENOR	748	**553**	475	397
BANJO	26	GIBSON	**TB- 1** TENOR, DIAMOND HOLE FLANGE, SERIAL #82700-	1,309	**968**	832	695
BANJO	27	GIBSON	**TB- 1** TENOR, DIAMOND HOLE FLANGE, SERIAL #-85400	1,308	**967**	831	695
BANJO	29	GIBSON	**TB- 1** TENOR	749	**554**	476	398
BANJO	30	GIBSON	**TB- 1** TENOR, 1 PIECE FLANGE	792	**586**	503	421
BANJO	30	GIBSON	**TB- 1** TENOR, 1-PIECE FLANGE	804	**594**	511	427

TYPE	YR	MFG	PRICES--BASED ON 100% ORIGINAL MODEL	SELL EXC	SELL AVG	BUY EXC	BUY AVG
BANJO	31	GIBSON	**TB- 1** TENOR, HEXAGON HOLE FLANGE	1,309	**968**	832	695
BANJO	32	GIBSON	**TB- 1** TENOR, 5-STRING, SERIAL #90400-90700	1,296	**958**	823	688
BANJO	38	GIBSON	**TB- 1** TENOR	1,416	**1,047**	900	752
BANJO	30	GIBSON	**TB- 1 REPLICA** 5-STRING	1,115	**825**	708	592
BANJO	26	GIBSON	**TB- 2** TENOR	983	**727**	624	522
BANJO	28	GIBSON	**TB- 2** SERIAL #85400-87300	1,498	**1,108**	952	796
BANJO	30	GIBSON	**TB- 2 CONVERSION** 5-STRING, OPEN BACK	1,496	**1,106**	950	795
BANJO	29	GIBSON	**TB- 2 TENOR**	1,382	**1,022**	878	734
BANJO	23	GIBSON	**TB- 3** TENOR, OPEN BACK	934	**690**	593	496
BANJO	24	GIBSON	**TB- 3** TENOR, OPEN BACK, SERIAL #74900-80300	1,573	**1,163**	999	835
BANJO	25	GIBSON	**TB- 3** TENOR, BALL BERING TONE RING	819	**606**	520	435
BANJO	25	GIBSON	**TB- 3** TENOR, SERIAL #80300-82700	913	**675**	580	485
BANJO	26	GIBSON	**TB- 3** 5-STRING, SERIAL #82700-	1,213	**897**	771	644
BANJO	27	GIBSON	**TB- 3** TENOR	2,187	**1,618**	1,390	1,162
BANJO	27	GIBSON	**TB- 3** 5-STRING CONVERSION, DUAL NECK	2,963	**2,191**	1,883	1,574
BANJO	28	GIBSON	**TB- 3** 5-STRING, SERIAL #85400-87300	1,614	**1,194**	1,026	857
BANJO	29	GIBSON	**TB- 3** TENOR	1,413	**1,045**	897	750
BANJO	30	GIBSON	**TB- 3** 5-STRING, SERIAL #89800-90200	1,397	**1,033**	888	742
BANJO	25	GIBSON	**TB- 3 MASTERTONE** TENOR	1,881	**1,391**	1,195	999
BANJO	26	GIBSON	**TB- 3 MASTERTONE** TENOR	1,918	**1,418**	1,218	1,018
BANJO	27	GIBSON	**TB- 3 MASTERTONE** TENOR	1,793	**1,326**	1,139	952
BANJO	28	GIBSON	**TB- 3 MASTERTONE** TENOR, 2 PIECE FLANGE	1,773	**1,311**	1,126	941
BANJO	29	GIBSON	**TB- 3 MASTERTONE** TENOR	1,685	**1,246**	1,071	895
BANJO	30	GIBSON	**TB- 3 MASTERTONE** TENOR	1,244	**920**	790	660
BANJO	18	GIBSON	**TB- 4** TENOR, SERIAL #39500-47900	1,121	**829**	712	595
BANJO	20	GIBSON	**TB- 4** TENOR, 17-FRET, OPEN BACK	1,121	**829**	712	595
BANJO	22	GIBSON	**TB- 4** TENOR	1,122	**829**	713	596
BANJO	23	GIBSON	**TB- 4** TENOR	1,028	**760**	653	546
BANJO	24	GIBSON	**TB- 4** TENOR, OPEN BACK	1,120	**828**	711	595
BANJO	25	GIBSON	**TB- 4** TENOR, MAHOGANY NECK, RESONATOR	1,315	**972**	835	698
BANJO	26	GIBSON	**TB- 4** TENOR, MAHOGANY NECK, RESONATOR, SERIAL #82700-	1,214	**898**	771	645
BANJO	29	GIBSON	**TB- 4** TENOR, MAHOGANY, RESONATOR, SERIAL #87300-89800	1,476	**1,091**	938	784
BANJO	32	GIBSON	**TB- 4** TENOR	1,593	**1,178**	1,012	846
BANJO	32	GIBSON	**TB- 4** TENOR, CURLY WALNUT NECK SERIAL #90400-90700	2,013	**1,488**	1,279	1,069
BANJO	32	GIBSON	**TB- 4** WALNUT, FLYING EAGLE INLAY, 40-HOLE RAISED HEAD TONE RING	4,080	**3,017**	2,592	2,167
BANJO	24	GIBSON	**TB- 4 JUNIOR TRAPDOOR** TENOR	1,029	**761**	653	546
BANJO	25	GIBSON	**TB- 4 MASTERTONE** TENOR, SERIAL #80300-82700	1,408	**1,041**	894	748
BANJO	26	GIBSON	**TB- 4 MASTERTONE** TENOR	1,312	**970**	833	697
BANJO	24	GIBSON	**TB- 4 TRAPDOOR** TENOR, RESONATOR	1,120	**828**	711	595
BANJO	24	GIBSON	**TB- 5** TENOR, SERIAL #74900-80300	2,133	**1,577**	1,355	1,133
BANJO	29	GIBSON	**TB- 5** TENOR	3,360	**2,485**	2,135	1,785
BANJO	28	GIBSON	**TB- 6** TENOR, SERIAL #85400-87300	7,201	**5,326**	4,576	3,826

TYPE	YR	MFG	PRICES--BASED ON 100% ORIGINAL MODEL	SELL EXC	SELL AVG	BUY EXC	BUY AVG
BANJO	29	GIBSON	**TB- 6** TENOR, SERIAL# 9226-34	5,760	**4,260**	3,660	3,060
BANJO	30	GIBSON	**TB- 6** TENOR, 4 HOLE, RAISED HEAD, TONE RING	4,891	**3,617**	3,107	2,598
BANJO	31	GIBSON	**TB- 6** TENOR	4,541	**3,359**	2,885	2,412
BANJO	35	GIBSON	**TB- 11** 5-STRING, SERIAL #92400-93500	1,959	**1,449**	1,245	1,040
BANJO	38	GIBSON	**TB- 12** 5-STRING, SERIAL #95400	7,680	**5,680**	4,880	4,080
BANJO	38	GIBSON	**TB- 18** TENOR	19,200	**14,200**	12,200	10,200
BANJO	29	GIBSON	**TB- 75** ARCHTOP	1,243	**919**	789	660
BANJO	50	GIBSON	**TB-100** TENOR, SUNBURST, CURLY MAPLE	1,201	**888**	763	638
BANJO	62	GIBSON	**TB-100** TENOR	844	**624**	536	448
BANJO	67	GIBSON	**TB-100** TENOR	635	**470**	403	337
BANJO	68	GIBSON	**TB-100** TENOR	582	**430**	370	309
BANJO	54	GIBSON	**TB-250 MASTERTONE** TENOR	1,106	**818**	703	588
BANJO	55	GIBSON	**TB-250 MASTERTONE** TENOR, SERIAL #A19000-A22000	1,098	**812**	697	583
BANJO	56	GIBSON	**TB-250 MASTERTONE** TENOR	1,154	**854**	733	613
BANJO	61	GIBSON	**TB-250 MASTERTONE** TENOR	945	**699**	600	502
BANJO	62	GIBSON	**TB-250 MASTERTONE** TENOR	965	**714**	613	513
BANJO	68	GIBSON	**TB-250 MASTERTONE** TENOR, SERIAL #959115	907	**670**	576	481
BANJO	69	GIBSON	**TB-250 MASTERTONE** TENOR, SERIAL #813724	896	**663**	569	476
BANJO	67	GIBSON	**TB-500 MASTERTONE** TENOR	1,239	**916**	787	658
BANJO	70	GIBSON	**TB-800** TENOR, SUNBURST	1,212	**896**	770	644
BANJO	24	GIBSON	**TB-JUNIOR** TENOR, NATURAL, OPEN BACK	840	**621**	533	446
BANJO	30	GIBSON	**TG- 1** TENOR, SUNBURST, SPRUCE TOP	934	**690**	593	496
BANJO	29	GIBSON	**UB- 1 UKE-BANJO** 8" HEAD	288	**213**	183	153
BANJO	30	GIBSON	**UB- 1 UKE-BANJO** FLAT RESONATOR, SERIAL #89800-90200	264	**195**	167	140
BANJO	28	GIBSON	**UB- 2 UKE-BANJO** 8" HEAD	293	**217**	186	156
BANJO	28	GIBSON	**UB- 3 UKE-BANJO** SUNBURST	796	**589**	506	423
BANJO	29	GIBSON	**UB- 3 UKE-BANJO** SUNBURST	794	**587**	505	422
ELEC. GUITAR	77	GIBSON	**ARTISAN** WALNUT	876	**648**	556	465
ELGUIT	85	GIBSON	**B B KING CUSTOM**	1,035	**766**	658	550
ELGUIT	85	GIBSON	**B B KING STANDARD**	936	**692**	594	497
ELGUIT	61	GIBSON	**BARNEY KESSEL**	2,208	**1,633**	1,403	1,173
ELGUIT	62	GIBSON	**BARNEY KESSEL**	2,053	**1,518**	1,304	1,090
ELGUIT	63	GIBSON	**BARNEY KESSEL**	2,138	**1,581**	1,359	1,136
ELGUIT	64	GIBSON	**BARNEY KESSEL** NICKEL PARTS	2,138	**1,581**	1,359	1,136
ELGUIT	65	GIBSON	**BARNEY KESSEL**	1,779	**1,316**	1,130	945
ELGUIT	66	GIBSON	**BARNEY KESSEL** CHERRY SUNBURST	1,605	**1,187**	1,019	852
ELGUIT	67	GIBSON	**BARNEY KESSEL**	1,992	**1,473**	1,265	1,058
ELGUIT	68	GIBSON	**BARNEY KESSEL**	1,464	**1,083**	930	778
ELGUIT	69	GIBSON	**BARNEY KESSEL**	1,593	**1,178**	1,012	846
ELGUIT	61	GIBSON	**BARNEY KESSEL CUSTOM** SUNBURST	3,669	**2,713**	2,331	1,949
ELGUIT	66	GIBSON	**BARNEY KESSEL CUSTOM**	1,992	**1,473**	1,265	1,058
ELGUIT	66	GIBSON	**BARNEY KESSEL CUSTOM** SUNBURST, WHL MUSIC NOTE	3,028	**2,240**	1,924	1,609
ELGUIT	68	GIBSON	**BARNEY KESSEL CUSTOM** SUNBURST	1,899	**1,405**	1,207	1,009
ELGUIT	69	GIBSON	**BARNEY KESSEL CUSTOM** SUNBURST	2,312	**1,710**	1,469	1,228
ELGUIT	56	GIBSON	**BYRDLAND** SUNBURST	8,640	**6,390**	5,490	4,590
ELGUIT	56	GIBSON	**BYRDLAND** NATURAL	9,228	**6,825**	5,863	4,902

TYPE	YR	MFG	PRICES--BASED ON 100% ORIGINAL MODEL	SELL EXC	SELL AVG	BUY EXC	BUY AVG
ELGUIT	57	GIBSON	**BYRDLAND** SUNBURST	9,004	**6,659**	5,721	4,783
ELGUIT	58	GIBSON	**BYRDLAND** NATURAL	7,598	**5,619**	4,828	4,036
ELGUIT	59	GIBSON	**BYRDLAND** NATURAL	9,151	**6,768**	5,815	4,861
ELGUIT	60	GIBSON	**BYRDLAND** SUNBURST	8,277	**6,121**	5,259	4,397
ELGUIT	60	GIBSON	**BYRDLAND** NATURAL	10,126	**7,489**	6,434	5,379
ELGUIT	61	GIBSON	**BYRDLAND** NATURAL	8,284	**6,127**	5,264	4,401
ELGUIT	63	GIBSON	**BYRDLAND** SUNBURST	6,550	**4,844**	4,162	3,479
ELGUIT	63	GIBSON	**BYRDLAND** NATURAL	6,700	**4,955**	4,257	3,559
ELGUIT	64	GIBSON	**BYRDLAND** SUNBURST	6,547	**4,842**	4,160	3,478
ELGUIT	65	GIBSON	**BYRDLAND** NATURAL	5,986	**4,427**	3,803	3,180
ELGUIT	65	GIBSON	**BYRDLAND** SUNBURST	6,125	**4,530**	3,892	3,254
ELGUIT	66	GIBSON	**BYRDLAND** SUNBURST	4,764	**3,523**	3,027	2,531
ELGUIT	66	GIBSON	**BYRDLAND** NATURAL	4,832	**3,574**	3,070	2,567
ELGUIT	67	GIBSON	**BYRDLAND** SUNBURST	4,506	**3,332**	2,863	2,393
ELGUIT	67	GIBSON	**BYRDLAND** NATURAL	4,779	**3,535**	3,037	2,539
ELGUIT	68	GIBSON	**BYRDLAND** SUNBURST	4,728	**3,496**	3,004	2,511
ELGUIT	68	GIBSON	**BYRDLAND** NATURAL	4,780	**3,535**	3,037	2,539
ELGUIT	69	GIBSON	**BYRDLAND** SUNBURST	3,878	**2,868**	2,464	2,060
ELGUIT	70	GIBSON	**BYRDLAND** SUNBURST	3,744	**2,769**	2,379	1,989
ELGUIT	70	GIBSON	**BYRDLAND** NATURAL	4,154	**3,072**	2,640	2,207
ELGUIT	71	GIBSON	**BYRDLAND** SUNBURST	4,060	**3,003**	2,580	2,157
ELGUIT	72	GIBSON	**BYRDLAND** SUNBURST	3,218	**2,380**	2,045	1,710
ELGUIT	72	GIBSON	**BYRDLAND** WINE RED	3,631	**2,685**	2,307	1,929
ELGUIT	73	GIBSON	**BYRDLAND** SUNBURST	3,912	**2,893**	2,485	2,078
ELGUIT	74	GIBSON	**BYRDLAND** SUNBURST	3,467	**2,564**	2,203	1,842
ELGUIT	74	GIBSON	**BYRDLAND** WINE RED, 2 PU's	3,897	**2,882**	2,476	2,070
ELGUIT	75	GIBSON	**BYRDLAND** SUNBURST	3,865	**2,859**	2,456	2,053
ELGUIT	76	GIBSON	**BYRDLAND** SUNBURST	2,224	**1,645**	1,413	1,181
ELGUIT	77	GIBSON	**BYRDLAND** NATURAL	2,941	**2,175**	1,869	1,562
ELGUIT	77	GIBSON	**BYRDLAND** SUNBURST	3,168	**2,343**	2,013	1,683
ELGUIT	78	GIBSON	**BYRDLAND** SUNBURST	2,224	**1,645**	1,413	1,181
ELGUIT	81	GIBSON	**BYRDLAND** WINE RED	2,965	**2,193**	1,884	1,575
ELGUIT	59	GIBSON	**BYRDLAND CUSTOM** SUNBURST, 24 3/4", 2 PU's	7,859	**5,812**	4,994	4,175
ELGUIT	50	GIBSON	**CF-100 E** SUNBURST, FLATTOP, CUTAWAY, 1 PU	1,896	**1,402**	1,204	1,007
ELGUIT	51	GIBSON	**CF-100 E** SUNBURST, FLATTOP, CUTAWAY, 1 PU	1,624	**1,201**	1,032	862
ELGUIT	53	GIBSON	**CF-100 E** SUNBURST, FLATTOP, CUTAWAY, 1 PU, SERIAL #A13000-A16000	1,075	**795**	683	571
ELGUIT	54	GIBSON	**CF-100 E** SUNBURST, FLATTOP, CUTAWAY, 1 PU, SERIAL #A16000-A19000	1,074	**794**	682	570
ELGUIT	55	GIBSON	**CF-100 E** SUNBURST, FLATTOP, CUTAWAY, 1 PU	1,072	**793**	681	569
ELGUIT	56	GIBSON	**CF-100 E** SUNBURST, FLATTOP, CUTAWAY, 1 PU	1,070	**791**	680	568
ELGUIT	60	GIBSON	**CF-100 E** SUNBURST, FLATTOP, CUTAWAY, 1 PU	907	**670**	576	481
ELGUIT	82	GIBSON	**CHET ATKINS CE** NATURAL	851	**629**	541	452
ELGUIT	84	GIBSON	**CHET ATKINS CE** NATURAL	637	**471**	405	338

TYPE	YR	MFG	PRICES--BASED ON 100% ORIGINAL MODEL	SELL EXC	SELL AVG	BUY EXC	BUY AVG
ELGUIT	84	GIBSON	**CHET ATKINS CE** WHITE	653	**483**	415	347
ELGUIT	85	GIBSON	**CHET ATKINS CEC** NATURAL	637	**471**	405	338
ELGUIT	87	GIBSON	**CHET ATKINS COUNTRY GENTLEMAN** WINE RED	1,593	**1,178**	1,012	846
ELGUIT	89	GIBSON	**CHET ATKINS SST-12** MAHOGANY/SPRUCE BODY, 12-STRING	956	**707**	607	507
ELGUIT	69	GIBSON	**CREST GOLD** BRAZILIAN ROSEWOOD, DOUBLE CUTAWAY	3,145	**2,326**	1,998	1,671
ELGUIT	71	GIBSON	**CREST GOLD** BRAZILIAN ROSEWOOD	3,215	**2,377**	2,042	1,707
ELGUIT	69	GIBSON	**CREST SILVER** BRAZILIAN ROSEWOOD, DOUBLE CUTAWAY	2,280	**1,686**	1,448	1,211
ELGUIT	70	GIBSON	**CREST SILVER** BRAZILIAN ROSEWOOD, DOUBLE CUTAWAY	2,390	**1,767**	1,518	1,269
ELGUIT	59	GIBSON	**EB- 0 BASS** CHERRY, 1 HB, LES PAUL BODY	796	**589**	506	423
ELGUIT	60	GIBSON	**EB- 0 BASS** CHERRY, 1 HB, LES PAUL BODY	794	**587**	505	422
ELGUIT	61	GIBSON	**EB- 0 BASS** CHERRY, 1 HB, LES PAUL BODY	792	**586**	503	421
ELGUIT	62	GIBSON	**EB- 0 BASS** CHERRY, 1 HB, SINGLE BODY	696	**515**	442	370
ELGUIT	63	GIBSON	**EB- 0 BASS** CHERRY, 1 HB, SINGLE BODY	696	**514**	442	369
ELGUIT	64	GIBSON	**EB- 0 BASS** CHERRY, 1 HB, SINGLE BODY	693	**512**	440	368
ELGUIT	65	GIBSON	**EB- 0 BASS** CHERRY, 1 HB, SINGLE BODY	689	**509**	437	366
ELGUIT	65	GIBSON	**EB- 0 BASS** CARDINAL, 1 HB, SINGLE BODY	691	**511**	439	367
ELGUIT	66	GIBSON	**EB- 0 BASS** CHERRY, 1 HB, SINGLE BODY	717	**530**	455	380
ELGUIT	67	GIBSON	**EB- 0 BASS** CHERRY, 1 HB, SINGLE BODY	621	**459**	394	329
ELGUIT	68	GIBSON	**EB- 0 BASS** CHERRY, 1 HB, SINGLE BODY	518	**383**	329	275
ELGUIT	69	GIBSON	**EB- 0 BASS** CHERRY, 1HB, SINGLE BODY	498	**368**	316	264
ELGUIT	69	GIBSON	**EB- 0 BASS** WALNUT, 1 HB, SINGLE BODY	498	**368**	316	264
ELGUIT	70	GIBSON	**EB- 0 BASS** CHERRY, 1 HB, SINGLE BODY	457	**338**	290	243
ELGUIT	70	GIBSON	**EB- 0 BASS** SPARKLING BURGUNDY. SINGLE BODY	457	**338**	290	243
ELGUIT	71	GIBSON	**EB- 0 BASS** WALNUT, 1 HB, SINGLE BODY	470	**347**	298	249
ELGUIT	72	GIBSON	**EB- 0 BASS** CHERRY, 1 HB, SINGLE BODY	476	**352**	302	252
ELGUIT	73	GIBSON	**EB- 0 BASS** CHERRY, 1HB, SINGLE BODY	471	**348**	299	250
ELGUIT	74	GIBSON	**EB- 0 BASS** CHERRY, 1 HB, SINGLE BODY	472	**349**	300	250
ELGUIT	63	GIBSON	**EB- 0F BASS**	916	**678**	582	487
ELGUIT	71	GIBSON	**EB- 0L BASS** CHERRY	489	**362**	311	260
ELGUIT	53	GIBSON	**EB- 1 BASS** NATURAL, 1 PU, VIOLIN SHAPE, SERIAL #A13000-A16000	2,245	**1,660**	1,426	1,192
ELGUIT	55	GIBSON	**EB- 1 BASS** VIOLIN SHAPE, SERIAL #A19000-A22000	1,339	**990**	850	711
ELGUIT	56	GIBSON	**EB- 1 BASS** BLACK, VIOLIN SHAPE, SERIAL #A22000-A24600	1,339	**990**	850	711
ELGUIT	57	GIBSON	**EB- 1 BASS** SOLID BODY	2,245	**1,660**	1,426	1,192
ELGUIT	58	GIBSON	**EB- 1 BASS** NATURAL, 1 PU, SOLID BODY	1,338	**989**	850	710
ELGUIT	69	GIBSON	**EB- 1 BASS** MOUNTAIN TONE, VIOLIN SHAPE	827	**612**	525	439
ELGUIT	70	GIBSON	**EB- 1 BASS** CONVENTIONAL TUNERS	717	**530**	455	380
ELGUIT	58	GIBSON	**EB- 2 BASS** SUNBURST	1,593	**1,178**	1,012	846
ELGUIT	59	GIBSON	**EB- 2 BASS** NATURAL	1,474	**1,090**	936	783
ELGUIT	59	GIBSON	**EB- 2 BASS** SUNBURST	1,593	**1,178**	1,012	846
ELGUIT	60	GIBSON	**EB- 2 BASS** SUNBURST, SEMI-SOLID	1,011	**748**	642	537
ELGUIT	65	GIBSON	**EB- 2 BASS** CHERRY	711	**526**	452	377
ELGUIT	65	GIBSON	**EB- 2 BASS** SUNBURST, SEMI-SOLID	794	**587**	505	422

TYPE	YR	MFG	PRICES--BASED ON 100% ORIGINAL MODEL	SELL EXC	SELL AVG	BUY EXC	BUY AVG
ELGUIT	66	GIBSON	**EB- 2 BASS** CHERRY, 1 PU	712	**526**	452	378
ELGUIT	66	GIBSON	**EB- 2 BASS** SUNBURST, HOLLOW BODY	712	**526**	452	378
ELGUIT	66	GIBSON	**EB- 2 BASS** TOBACCOBURST	775	**573**	492	412
ELGUIT	67	GIBSON	**EB- 2 BASS** WALNUT	711	**526**	452	377
ELGUIT	67	GIBSON	**EB- 2 BASS** CHERRY	712	**526**	452	378
ELGUIT	67	GIBSON	**EB- 2 BASS** SPARKLING BURGUNDY	712	**526**	452	378
ELGUIT	67	GIBSON	**EB- 2 BASS** SUNBURST, DOUBLE CUTAWAY	712	**526**	452	378
ELGUIT	68	GIBSON	**EB- 2 BASS** CHERRY	712	**526**	452	378
ELGUIT	68	GIBSON	**EB- 2 BASS** WALNUT	712	**526**	452	378
ELGUIT	69	GIBSON	**EB- 2 BASS** CHERRY	711	**526**	452	377
ELGUIT	70	GIBSON	**EB- 2 BASS** SUNBURST	711	**526**	452	377
ELGUIT	66	GIBSON	**EB- 2C BASS** CHERRY	1,044	**772**	663	554
ELGUIT	67	GIBSON	**EB- 2D BASS** SUNBURST	796	**589**	506	423
ELGUIT	67	GIBSON	**EB- 2D BASS** CHERRY, 2 PU's	1,106	**818**	703	588
ELGUIT	68	GIBSON	**EB- 2D BASS** WALNUT	876	**648**	556	465
ELGUIT	68	GIBSON	**EB- 2D BASS** SUNBURST, 2 PU's	961	**711**	611	511
ELGUIT	69	GIBSON	**EB- 2D BASS** WALNUT	796	**589**	506	423
ELGUIT	71	GIBSON	**EB- 2D BASS** WALNUT, 2 PU's	736	**544**	467	391
ELGUIT	62	GIBSON	**EB- 3 BASS**	1,178	**871**	749	626
ELGUIT	63	GIBSON	**EB- 3 BASS** CHERRY, SOLID PEGHEAD	1,076	**795**	683	571
ELGUIT	65	GIBSON	**EB- 3 BASS** SUNBURST, MUTE, 2 PU's	712	**526**	452	378
ELGUIT	65	GIBSON	**EB- 3 BASS** CHERRY, OWNED BY JEFFRY BEALS	850	**629**	540	451
ELGUIT	65	GIBSON	**EB- 3 BASS** CHERRY, SINGLE BODY	1,076	**795**	683	571
ELGUIT	67	GIBSON	**EB- 3 BASS** CHERRY	631	**467**	401	335
ELGUIT	68	GIBSON	**EB- 3 BASS** CHERRY	631	**467**	401	335
ELGUIT	69	GIBSON	**EB- 3 BASS** CHERRY	596	**440**	378	316
ELGUIT	70	GIBSON	**EB- 3 BASS** CHERRY	595	**440**	378	316
ELGUIT	71	GIBSON	**EB- 3 BASS** CHERRY	557	**412**	354	296
ELGUIT	71	GIBSON	**EB- 3 BASS** WALNUT	710	**525**	451	377
ELGUIT	72	GIBSON	**EB- 3 BASS** NATURAL MAHOGANY	578	**428**	367	307
ELGUIT	72	GIBSON	**EB- 3 BASS** WALNUT, SINGLE BODY, 2 PU's	622	**460**	395	330
ELGUIT	73	GIBSON	**EB- 3 BASS** WALNUT, SINGLE BODY	621	**459**	394	329
ELGUIT	73	GIBSON	**EB- 3 BASS** CHERRY, SOLID PEGHEAD	637	**471**	405	338
ELGUIT	74	GIBSON	**EB- 3 BASS** CHERRY STAIN, 2 PU's	553	**409**	351	294
ELGUIT	74	GIBSON	**EB- 3 BASS** WALNUT	572	**423**	363	303
ELGUIT	76	GIBSON	**EB- 3 BASS** WALNUT	598	**442**	380	317
ELGUIT	77	GIBSON	**EB- 3 BASS**	489	**362**	311	260
ELGUIT	70	GIBSON	**EB- 3L BASS** CHERRY	595	**440**	378	316
ELGUIT	71	GIBSON	**EB- 3L BASS** CHERRY	593	**438**	376	315
ELGUIT	71	GIBSON	**EB- 3L BASS** NATURAL	656	**485**	417	348
ELGUIT	73	GIBSON	**EB- 3L BASS** CHERRY	569	**421**	361	302
ELGUIT	72	GIBSON	**EB- 4L BASS** WALNUT	537	**397**	341	285
ELGUIT	60	GIBSON	**EB- 6 BASS** SUNBURST, SEMI-HOLLOW	2,073	**1,533**	1,317	1,101

TYPE	YR	MFG	PRICES--BASED ON 100% ORIGINAL MODEL	SELL EXC	SELL AVG	BUY EXC	BUY AVG
ELGUIT	61	GIBSON	**EB- 6 BASS** SUNBURST	3,981	**2,944**	2,529	2,114
ELGUIT	63	GIBSON	**EB- 6 BASS** SINGLE BODY, 6-STRING	1,673	**1,237**	1,063	888
ELGUIT	65	GIBSON	**EB- 6 BASS** SINGLE BODY, 6-STRING	1,456	**1,077**	925	773
ELGUIT	63	GIBSON	**EBS-1250 DOUBLE BASS** CHERRY, 2 PU's	956	**707**	607	507
ELGUIT	65	GIBSON	**EBS-1250 DOUBLE BASS**	2,194	**1,623**	1,394	1,165
ELGUIT	66	GIBSON	**EBS-1250 DOUBLE BASS**	2,009	**1,486**	1,276	1,067
ELGUIT	58	GIBSON	**EDS-1275** BLACK, 6 & 12-STRING, DOUBLE NECK, SERIAL #A26500-A28000	1,044	**772**	663	554
ELGUIT	59	GIBSON	**EDS-1275** WHITE, 6 & 12-STRING, DOUBLE NECK	16,368	**12,105**	10,400	8,695
ELGUIT	62	GIBSON	**EDS-1275** SUNBURST, 6 & 12-STRING, DOUBLE NECK	8,543	**6,318**	5,428	4,538
ELGUIT	64	GIBSON	**EDS-1275** SUNBURST, 6 & 12-STRING, DOUBLE NECK	8,345	**6,172**	5,302	4,433
ELGUIT	65	GIBSON	**EDS-1275** SUNBURST, 6 & 12-STRING, DOUBLE NECK	4,134	**3,057**	2,627	2,196
ELGUIT	67	GIBSON	**EDS-1275** WHITE, 6 & 12-STRING, DOUBLE NECK	4,143	**3,064**	2,632	2,201
ELGUIT	68	GIBSON	**EDS-1275** SUNBURST, 6 & 12-STRING, DOUBLE NECK	3,532	**2,612**	2,244	1,876
ELGUIT	74	GIBSON	**EDS-1275** SUNBURST, 6 & 12-STRING, DOUBLE NECK	1,999	**1,478**	1,270	1,062
ELGUIT	76	GIBSON	**EDS-1275** WALNUT, 6 & 12-STRING, DOUBLE NECK	1,566	**1,158**	995	832
ELGUIT	78	GIBSON	**EDS-1275** SUNBURST, 6 & 12-STRING, DOUBLE NECK	1,567	**1,159**	996	832
ELGUIT	78	GIBSON	**EDS-1275** WALNUT, 6 & 12-STRING, DOUBLE NECK	1,567	**1,159**	996	832
ELGUIT	56	GIBSON	**ELECTRIC BASS** BROWN STAIN, BANJO TUNERS	1,793	**1,326**	1,139	952
ELGUIT	80	GIBSON	**ES ARTIST** SUNBURST, ACTIVE ELECTRONICS	982	**726**	624	521
ELGUIT	49	GIBSON	**ES- 5** SUNBURST, 3 PU's, SERIAL #A2800-A4400	4,453	**3,293**	2,829	2,365
ELGUIT	49	GIBSON	**ES- 5** NATURAL, 3 PU's, SERIAL #A2800-A4400	6,476	**4,789**	4,115	3,440
ELGUIT	50	GIBSON	**ES- 5** SUNBURST, 3 PU's, SERIAL #A4400-A6000	4,796	**3,547**	3,047	2,547
ELGUIT	51	GIBSON	**ES- 5** SUNBURST, 3 PU's, SERIAL #A6000-A9400	4,441	**3,285**	2,822	2,359
ELGUIT	51	GIBSON	**ES- 5** NATURAL, 3 PU's, SERIAL #A6000-A9400	5,496	**4,064**	3,492	2,919
ELGUIT	52	GIBSON	**ES- 5** SUNBURST, 3 PU's, SERIAL #A9400-A13000	5,027	**3,718**	3,194	2,670
ELGUIT	52	GIBSON	**ES- 5** NATURAL, 3 PU's, SERIAL #A9400-A13000	5,280	**3,905**	3,355	2,805
ELGUIT	53	GIBSON	**ES- 5** SUNBURST, 3 PU's, SERIAL #A13000-A16000	4,387	**3,244**	2,787	2,330
ELGUIT	53	GIBSON	**ES- 5** NATURAL, 3 PU's, SERIAL #A13000-A16000	5,373	**3,973**	3,414	2,854
ELGUIT	54	GIBSON	**ES- 5** SUNBURST, 3 PU's, SERIAL #A16000-A19000	4,325	**3,199**	2,748	2,298
ELGUIT	54	GIBSON	**ES- 5** NATURAL, 3 PU's, SERIAL #A16000-A19000	5,373	**3,973**	3,414	2,854
ELGUIT	55	GIBSON	**ES- 5 SWITCHMASTER** SUNBURST, 3 PU's, SERIAL #A19000-A22000	7,368	**5,449**	4,681	3,914
ELGUIT	56	GIBSON	**ES- 5 SWITCHMASTER** SUNBURST, 3 PU's, SERIAL #A22000-A24600	7,508	**5,552**	4,770	3,988
ELGUIT	57	GIBSON	**ES- 5 SWITCHMASTER** SUNBURST, 3 PU's, PAF	8,434	**6,238**	5,359	4,480
ELGUIT	57	GIBSON	**ES- 5 SWITCHMASTER** NATURAL 3 PU's, PAF	9,134	**6,755**	5,804	4,852
ELGUIT	58	GIBSON	**ES- 5 SWITCHMASTER** SUNBURST, 3 PU's, PAF	8,444	**6,245**	5,365	4,485
ELGUIT	59	GIBSON	**ES- 5 SWITCHMASTER** BLOND	7,200	**5,325**	4,575	3,825
ELGUIT	59	GIBSON	**ES- 5 SWITCHMASTER** NATURAL, 3 PU's, PAF	8,678	**6,418**	5,514	4,610
ELGUIT	59	GIBSON	**ES- 5 SWITCHMASTER** SUNBURST, 3 PU's, SERIAL #A28000/PAF	10,085	**7,459**	6,408	5,358
ELGUIT	60	GIBSON	**ES- 5 SWITCHMASTER** SUNBURST, PAF	8,178	**6,048**	5,196	4,344
ELGUIT	60	GIBSON	**ES- 5 SWITCHMASTER** NATURAL, 3 PU's, PAF	9,932	**7,345**	6,311	5,276
ELGUIT	60	GIBSON	**ES- 5 SWITCHMASTER** BLOND	12,288	**9,088**	7,808	6,528
ELGUIT	57	GIBSON	**ES- 5N SWITCHMASTER** SUNBURST, 3 PAF's,	8,563	**6,333**	5,441	4,549
ELGUIT	57	GIBSON	**ES- 5N SWITCHMASTER** NATURAL, 3 PAF's, CURLY MAPLE	12,815	**9,477**	8,142	6,807

TYPE	YR	MFG	PRICES--BASED ON 100% ORIGINAL MODEL	SELL EXC	SELL AVG	BUY EXC	BUY AVG
ELGUIT	38	GIBSON	**ES-100 ELECTRIC ACOUSTIC** SUNBURST, SERIAL #-96000	936	**692**	594	497
ELGUIT	39	GIBSON	**ES-100 ELECTRIC ACOUSTIC** SUNBURST, BAR PU	956	**707**	607	507
ELGUIT	41	GIBSON	**ES-100 ELECTRIC ACOUSTIC** SUNBURST, SERIAL #96000-96600	843	**624**	536	448
ELGUIT	61	GIBSON	**ES-120 T** SUNBURST, NON-CUTAWAY, THINLINE, 1 PU	438	**324**	278	233
ELGUIT	62	GIBSON	**ES-120 T** SUNBURST, NON-CUTAWAY, THINLINE, 1 PU	435	**322**	276	231
ELGUIT	63	GIBSON	**ES-120 T** SUNBURST, NON-CUTAWAY, THINLINE, 1 PU, SERIAL #118802	433	**320**	275	230
ELGUIT	64	GIBSON	**ES-120 T** SUNBURST, NON-CUTAWAY, THINLINE, 1 PU	432	**319**	274	229
ELGUIT	65	GIBSON	**ES-120 T** SUNBURST, NON-CUTAWAY, THINLINE, 1 PU	430	**318**	273	228
ELGUIT	66	GIBSON	**ES-120 T** SUNBURST, NON-CUTAWAY, THINLINE, 1 PU	429	**317**	272	227
ELGUIT	67	GIBSON	**ES-120 T** SUNBURST, NON-CUTAWAY, THINLINE 1 PU	557	**412**	354	296
ELGUIT	68	GIBSON	**ES-120 T** SUNBURST, NON-CUTAWAY, THINLINE 1 PU	426	**315**	270	226
ELGUIT	41	GIBSON	**ES-125** SUNBURST, NON-CUTAWAY, THICK, 1 PU	752	**556**	478	399
ELGUIT	47	GIBSON	**ES-125** MAHOGANY, NON-CUTAWAY, THICK, 1 PU	715	**528**	454	379
ELGUIT	47	GIBSON	**ES-125** SUNBURST, NON-CUTAWAY, THICK, 1 PU	715	**528**	454	379
ELGUIT	48	GIBSON	**ES-125** SUNBURST, NON-CUTAWAY, THICK, 1 PU	711	**526**	452	377
ELGUIT	49	GIBSON	**ES-125** MAHOGANY, NON-CUTAWAY, THICK, 1 PU	708	**523**	450	376
ELGUIT	49	GIBSON	**ES-125** SUNBURST, NON-CUTAWAY, THICK, 1 PU	708	**523**	450	376
ELGUIT	50	GIBSON	**ES-125** SUNBURST, NON-CUTAWAY, THICK, 1 PU	703	**520**	447	373
ELGUIT	51	GIBSON	**ES-125** SUNBURST, NON-CUTAWAY, THICK, 1 PU	700	**518**	445	372
ELGUIT	52	GIBSON	**ES-125** SUNBURST, NON-CUTAWAY, THICK, 1 PU	716	**529**	455	380
ELGUIT	53	GIBSON	**ES-125** SUNBURST, NON-CUTAWAY, THICK, 1 PU, SERIAL #A13000-A16000	693	**512**	440	368
ELGUIT	54	GIBSON	**ES-125** SUNBURST, NON-CUTAWAY, THICK, 1 PU, SERIAL #A16000-A19000	689	**509**	437	366
ELGUIT	55	GIBSON	**ES-125** SUNBURST, NON-CUTAWAY, THICK, 1 PU, SERIAL #A19000-A22000	685	**506**	435	364
ELGUIT	56	GIBSON	**ES-125** SUNBURST, NON-CUTAWAY, THICK, 1 PU	681	**504**	433	362
ELGUIT	57	GIBSON	**ES-125** SUNBURST, NON-CUTAWAY, THICK, 1 PU	673	**498**	428	358
ELGUIT	58	GIBSON	**ES-125** SUNBURST, NON-CUTAWAY, THICK, 1 PU, SERIAL #A26500-A28000	668	**494**	424	354
ELGUIT	59	GIBSON	**ES-125** SUNBURST, NON-CUTAWAY, THICK, 1 PU	795	**588**	505	422
ELGUIT	61	GIBSON	**ES-125** SUNBURST, NON-CUTAWAY, THICK, 1 PU	664	**491**	422	352
ELGUIT	62	GIBSON	**ES-125** SUNBURST, NON-CUTAWAY, THICK, 1 PU	633	**468**	402	336
ELGUIT	63	GIBSON	**ES-125** SUNUBRST, NON-CUTAWAY, THICK, 1 PU	622	**460**	395	330
ELGUIT	64	GIBSON	**ES-125** SUNBURST, NON-CUTAWAY, THICK, 1 PU	611	**452**	388	324
ELGUIT	65	GIBSON	**ES-125** SUNBURST, NON-CUTAWAY, THICK, 1 PU	603	**446**	383	320
ELGUIT	66	GIBSON	**ES-125** SUNBURST, NON-CUTAWAY, THICK, 1 PU	578	**428**	367	307
ELGUIT	67	GIBSON	**ES-125** SUNBURST, NON-CUTAWAY, THICK, 1 PU	588	**435**	373	312
ELGUIT	57	GIBSON	**ES-125 3/4** SUNBURST, NON-CUTAWAY, THIN, 13" WIDE	939	**695**	597	499
ELGUIT	59	GIBSON	**ES-125 3/4** SUNBURST, NON-CUTAWAY, THIN, 13" WIDE	938	**694**	596	498
ELGUIT	61	GIBSON	**ES-125 3/4** SUNBURST, NON-CUTAWAY, THIN, 13" WIDE	936	**692**	594	497
ELGUIT	64	GIBSON	**ES-125 3/4** SUNBURST, NON-CUTAWAY, THIN, 13" WIDE	956	**707**	607	507
ELGUIT	65	GIBSON	**ES-125 3/4** SUNBURST, NON-CUTAWAY, THIN, 13" WIDE	750	**555**	477	398
ELGUIT	67	GIBSON	**ES-125 3/4** SUNBURST, NON-CUTAWAY, THIN, 13" WIDE	747	**553**	475	397
ELGUIT	68	GIBSON	**ES-125C** SUNBURST, CUTAWAY, THICK 1 PU	996	**736**	633	529
ELGUIT	66	GIBSON	**ES-125CD** SUNBURST, THICK CUTAWAY, 2 PU's	1,327	**981**	843	705

TYPE	YR	MFG	PRICES--BASED ON 100% ORIGINAL MODEL	SELL EXC	SELL AVG	BUY EXC	BUY AVG
ELGUIT	69	GIBSON	**ES-125CD**	837	**619**	531	444
ELGUIT	56	GIBSON	**ES-125T** SUNBURST, NON-CUTTAWAY, THIN, 1 PU, SERIAL #A22000-A24600	823	**609**	523	437
ELGUIT	57	GIBSON	**ES-125T** SUNBURST, NON-CUTAWAY, THIN, 1 PU	788	**582**	500	418
ELGUIT	58	GIBSON	**ES-125T** SUNBURST, NON-CUTAWAY, THIN, 1 PU, SERIAL #A24600-A26500	780	**577**	495	414
ELGUIT	59	GIBSON	**ES-125T** SUNBURST, NON-CUTAWAY, THIN, 1 PU	640	**473**	406	340
ELGUIT	60	GIBSON	**ES-125T** SUNBURST, NON-CUTAWAY, THIN, 1 PU	606	**448**	385	322
ELGUIT	61	GIBSON	**ES-125T** SUNBURST, NON-CUTAWAY, THIN, 1 PU	583	**431**	370	310
ELGUIT	63	GIBSON	**ES-125T** SUNBURST, NON-CUTAWAY, THIN, 1 PU	576	**426**	366	306
ELGUIT	64	GIBSON	**ES-125T** SUNBURST, NON-CUTAWAY, THIN, 1 PU	574	**424**	364	304
ELGUIT	65	GIBSON	**ES-125T** SUNBURST, NON-CUTAWAY, THIN, 1 PU	569	**421**	361	302
ELGUIT	66	GIBSON	**ES-125T** SUNBURST, NON-CUTAWAY, THIN, 1 PU	562	**416**	357	298
ELGUIT	67	GIBSON	**ES-125T** SUNBURST, NON-CUTAWAY, THIN, 1 PU	555	**411**	353	295
ELGUIT	68	GIBSON	**ES-125T** SUNBURST, NON-CUTAWAY, THIN, 1 PU	547	**404**	347	290
ELGUIT	69	GIBSON	**ES-125T** SUNBURST, NON-CUTAWAY, THIN, 1 PU	540	**399**	343	287
ELGUIT	60	GIBSON	**ES-125T 3/4**	717	**530**	455	380
ELGUIT	61	GIBSON	**ES-125T 3/4** SUNBURST, 1 P-90 PU	716	**529**	455	380
ELGUIT	60	GIBSON	**ES-125TC** SUNBURST, CUTAWAY, THIN, 1 PU	821	**607**	522	436
ELGUIT	61	GIBSON	**ES-125TC** CHERRY SUNBURST, CUTAWAY, THIN HOLLOW BODY, 1 P-90 PU	677	**501**	430	360
ELGUIT	62	GIBSON	**ES-125TC** SUNBURST, CUTAWAY, THIN, 1 PU	762	**563**	484	404
ELGUIT	63	GIBSON	**ES-125TC** CHERRY SUNBURST, CUTAWAY THIN BODY, 1 P-90 PU	796	**589**	506	423
ELGUIT	64	GIBSON	**ES-125TC** SUNBURST, CUTAWAY, THIN, 1 PU	754	**558**	479	400
ELGUIT	65	GIBSON	**ES-125TC** SUNBURST, CUTAWAY, THIN, 1 PU	749	**554**	476	398
ELGUIT	66	GIBSON	**ES-125TC** SUNBURST, CUTAWAY, THIN, 1 PU	745	**551**	473	396
ELGUIT	67	GIBSON	**ES-125TC** SUNBURST, CUTAWAY, THIN, 1 PU	736	**544**	467	391
ELGUIT	68	GIBSON	**ES-125TC** SUNBURST, CUTAWAY, THIN, 1 PU	723	**535**	459	384
ELGUIT	57	GIBSON	**ES-125TD** SUNBURST, NON-CUTAWAY, THIN, 2 PU's	843	**624**	536	448
ELGUIT	58	GIBSON	**ES-125TD** SUNBURST, NON-CUTAWAY, THIN, 2 PU's, SERIAL #A26500-A28000	696	**514**	442	369
ELGUIT	59	GIBSON	**ES-125TD** SUNBURST, NON-CUTAWAY, THIN, 2 PU's, SERIAL #A28000	687	**508**	436	365
ELGUIT	60	GIBSON	**ES-125TD** SUNBURST, NON-CUTAWAY, THIN, 2 PU's	671	**496**	426	356
ELGUIT	61	GIBSON	**ES-125TD** SUNBURST, NON-CUTAWAY, THIN, 2 PU's	658	**487**	418	349
ELGUIT	62	GIBSON	**ES-125TD** SUNBURST, NON-CUTAWAY, THIN, 2 PU's	796	**589**	506	423
ELGUIT	63	GIBSON	**ES-125TD** SUNBURST, NON-CUTAWAY, THIN, 2 PU's	640	**473**	406	340
ELGUIT	60	GIBSON	**ES-125TDC**	1,035	**766**	658	550
ELGUIT	61	GIBSON	**ES-125TDC** SUNBURST, CUTAWAY, THIN, 2 PU's	677	**501**	430	360
ELGUIT	62	GIBSON	**ES-125TDC** SUNBURST, CUTAWAY, THIN, 2 PU's	651	**482**	414	346
ELGUIT	63	GIBSON	**ES-125TDC** SUNBURST, CUTAWAY, THIN, 2 PU's	655	**484**	416	348
ELGUIT	65	GIBSON	**ES-125TDC** SUNBURST, CUTAWAY, THIN, 2 PU's	624	**461**	396	331
ELGUIT	67	GIBSON	**ES-125TDC** SUNBURST, CUTAWAY, THIN, 2 PU's	633	**468**	402	336
ELGUIT	69	GIBSON	**ES-125TDC** SUNBURST, CUTAWAY, THIN, 2 PU's	625	**462**	397	332
ELGUIT	70	GIBSON	**ES-125TDC**	796	**589**	506	423
ELGUIT	55	GIBSON	**ES-130** SUNBURST, P-90 PU, INLAY, BOUND NECK	956	**707**	607	507
ELGUIT	56	GIBSON	**ES-135**	717	**530**	455	380
ELGUIT	50	GIBSON	**ES-140 3/4** SUNBURST, SINGLE CUT, 1 PU	1,047	**774**	665	556
ELGUIT	51	GIBSON	**ES-140 3/4** SUNBURST, SINGLE CUT, 1 PU, SERIAL #A6000-A9400	1,071	**792**	680	569

TYPE	YR	MFG	PRICES--BASED ON 100% ORIGINAL MODEL	SELL EXC	SELL AVG	BUY EXC	BUY AVG
ELGUIT	52	GIBSON	**ES-140 3/4** SUNBURST, SINGLE CUT, 1 PU. SERIAL #A9400-A13000	1,066	**788**	677	566
ELGUIT	53	GIBSON	**ES-140 3/4** SUNBURST, SIGNLE CUT, 1 PU, SERIAL #A13000-A16000	1,127	**833**	716	598
ELGUIT	54	GIBSON	**ES-140 3/4** SUNBURST, SINGLE CUT, 1 PU, SERIAL #A16000-A19000	1,126	**832**	715	598
ELGUIT	55	GIBSON	**ES-140 3/4** SUNBURST, SINGLE, CUT, 1 PU, SERIAL #A19000-A22000	1,126	**832**	715	598
ELGUIT	56	GIBSON	**ES-140 3/4** SUNBURST, SINGLE, CUT, 1 PU, SERIAL #A22000-A24600	1,126	**832**	715	598
ELGUIT	57	GIBSON	**ES-140 3/4** SUNBURST, SINGLE CUTAWAY, THIN BODY, 1 PU	1,076	**795**	683	571
ELGUIT	57	GIBSON	**ES-140 3/4** NATURAL, SINGLE, CUT, 1 PU, SERIAL #A24600-A26500	1,297	**959**	824	689
ELGUIT	59	GIBSON	**ES-140 3/4T** SUNBURST, LEFT-HANDED	900	**665**	572	478
ELGUIT	59	GIBSON	**ES-140 3/4T** SUNBURST, SINGLE CUT, 1 PU, SERIAL #A28000	938	**694**	596	498
ELGUIT	60	GIBSON	**ES-140 3/4T** SUNBURST	876	**648**	556	465
ELGUIT	62	GIBSON	**ES-140 3/4T** SUNBURST, SINGLE CUT, 1 PU	938	**694**	596	498
ELGUIT	62	GIBSON	**ES-140 3/4T**	1,195	**883**	759	634
ELGUIT	63	GIBSON	**ES-140 3/4T** SUNBURST, SINGLE CUT	867	**641**	551	461
ELGUIT	65	GIBSON	**ES-140 3/4T** SUNBURST, SINGLE CUT, 1 PU	921	**681**	585	489
ELGUIT	66	GIBSON	**ES-140 3/4T** SUNBURST, SINGLE CUT, 1 PU	845	**625**	537	449
ELGUIT	68	GIBSON	**ES-140 3/4T** SUNBURST, 1 PU	845	**625**	537	449
ELGUIT	68	GIBSON	**ES-140 3/4T** SUNBURST, L5-STYLE	1,425	**1,054**	905	757
ELGUIT	61	GIBSON	**ES-140TC** TINY SUNBURST	958	**730**	620	474
ELGUIT	59	GIBSON	**ES-140TD** SUNBURST, 2 PU's	1,992	**1,473**	1,265	1,058
ELGUIT	35	GIBSON	**ES-150** SUNBURST, CHARLIE CHRISTIAN PU	3,936	**2,911**	2,501	2,091
ELGUIT	36	GIBSON	**ES-150** SUNBURST, CHARLIE CHRISTIAN PU	4,198	**3,104**	2,667	2,230
ELGUIT	37	GIBSON	**ES-150** CHARLIE CHRISTIAN PU	3,277	**2,423**	2,082	1,741
ELGUIT	38	GIBSON	**ES-150** SUNBURST, CHARLIE CHRISTIAN PU, SERIAL #95400	3,078	**2,276**	1,956	1,635
ELGUIT	39	GIBSON	**ES-150** SUNBURST, CHARLIE CHRISTIAN PU, SERIAL #-96000	2,287	**1,691**	1,453	1,215
ELGUIT	40	GIBSON	**ES-150** SUNBURST, CHARLIE CHRISTIAN PU, SERIAL #96000-96600	2,288	**1,692**	1,454	1,215
ELGUIT	46	GIBSON	**ES-150** SUNBURST, P-90 PU	2,235	**1,653**	1,420	1,187
ELGUIT	47	GIBSON	**ES-150** SUNBURST, P-90 PU, SERIAL #-A1400	2,064	**1,526**	1,311	1,096
ELGUIT	48	GIBSON	**ES-150** SUNBURST, P-90 PU, SERIAL #A1400-A2800	2,045	**1,513**	1,299	1,086
ELGUIT	49	GIBSON	**ES-150** SUNBURST, P-90 PU, SERIAL #A2800-A4400	2,133	**1,577**	1,355	1,133
ELGUIT	50	GIBSON	**ES-150** SUNBURST, P-90 PU, SERIAL #A4400-A6000	2,050	**1,516**	1,302	1,089
ELGUIT	51	GIBSON	**ES-150** SUNBURST, P-90 PU, SERIAL #A2800-A4400	2,040	**1,509**	1,296	1,084
ELGUIT	52	GIBSON	**ES-150** SUNBURST, P-90 PU	2,066	**1,528**	1,313	1,098
ELGUIT	53	GIBSON	**ES-150** SUNBURST, P-90 PU	1,714	**1,268**	1,089	910
ELGUIT	54	GIBSON	**ES-150** SUNBURST, P-90 PU, SERIAL #A16000-A19000	1,588	**1,175**	1,009	844
ELGUIT	69	GIBSON	**ES-150** WALNUT	1,315	**972**	835	698
ELGUIT	71	GIBSON	**ES-150** WALNUT	1,315	**972**	835	698
ELGUIT	70	GIBSON	**ES-150D** WALNUT	1,195	**883**	759	634
ELGUIT	52	GIBSON	**ES-150DC** SUNBURST, DOUBLE CUT, 1 PU	1,422	**1,052**	904	755
ELGUIT	69	GIBSON	**ES-150DC** WALNUT, DOUBLE CUT, 2 HB	1,237	**915**	786	657
ELGUIT	70	GIBSON	**ES-150DC** NATURAL, DOUBLE CUT, 2 HB	1,035	**766**	658	550
ELGUIT	70	GIBSON	**ES-150DC** WALNUT, DOUBLE CUT, 2 HB	1,063	**786**	675	565
ELGUIT	70	GIBSON	**ES-150DC** CHERRY, DOUBLE CUT, 2 HB	1,208	**893**	767	642

TYPE	YR	MFG	PRICES--BASED ON 100% ORIGINAL MODEL	SELL EXC	SELL AVG	BUY EXC	BUY AVG
ELGUIT	71	GIBSON	**ES-150DC** NATURAL, DOUBLE CUT, 2 HB	1,026	**758**	652	545
ELGUIT	71	GIBSON	**ES-150DC** WALNUT, DOUBLE CUT, 2 HB, SERIAL #727976	1,195	**883**	759	634
ELGUIT	72	GIBSON	**ES-150DC** WALNUT, DOUBLE CUT, 2 HB	979	**724**	622	520
ELGUIT	74	GIBSON	**ES-150DC** NATURAL, DOUBLE CUT, 2 HB	820	**607**	521	436
ELGUIT	70	GIBSON	**ES-150DW** WALNUT	1,055	**780**	670	560
ELGUIT	72	GIBSON	**ES-150DW** WALNUT	996	**736**	633	529
ELGUIT	40	GIBSON	**ES-150T** CHARLIE CHRISTIAN PU	2,162	**1,599**	1,374	1,149
ELGUIT	49	GIBSON	**ES-175** NATURAL, 1 PU, SERIAL #A4400-A6000	3,226	**2,386**	2,050	1,714
ELGUIT	49	GIBSON	**ES-175** SUNBURST, 1 PU, SERIAL #A2800-A4400	3,270	**2,418**	2,078	1,737
ELGUIT	50	GIBSON	**ES-175** SUNBURST, 1 PU, SERIAL #A4400-A6000	2,219	**1,641**	1,410	1,179
ELGUIT	50	GIBSON	**ES-175** NATURAL, 1 PU, SERIAL #A4400-A6000	3,083	**2,280**	1,959	1,638
ELGUIT	51	GIBSON	**ES-175** NATURAL, 1 PU	2,071	**1,532**	1,316	1,100
ELGUIT	51	GIBSON	**ES-175** SUNBURST, 1 PU, SERIAL #A6000-A9400	2,925	**2,163**	1,858	1,553
ELGUIT	52	GIBSON	**ES-175** NATURAL, 1 PU	1,832	**1,355**	1,164	973
ELGUIT	52	GIBSON	**ES-175** SUNBURST, 1 PU, SERIAL #A9400-A13000	2,153	**1,592**	1,368	1,143
ELGUIT	53	GIBSON	**ES-175** SUNBURST, 1 PU, SERIAL #A13000-A16000	1,987	**1,469**	1,262	1,055
ELGUIT	54	GIBSON	**ES-175** SUNBURST, 1 PU	2,331	**1,724**	1,481	1,238
ELGUIT	55	GIBSON	**ES-175** NATURAL, 1 PU	1,774	**1,312**	1,127	942
ELGUIT	55	GIBSON	**ES-175** SUNBURST, 1 PU	1,919	**1,419**	1,219	1,019
ELGUIT	55	GIBSON	**ES-175** SUNBURST, 2 P-90 PU's, BIGSBY, NON-FOLDING ARM	2,390	**1,767**	1,518	1,269
ELGUIT	56	GIBSON	**ES-175** SUNBURST, 1 PU	2,271	**1,679**	1,443	1,206
ELGUIT	57	GIBSON	**ES-175** NATURAL, 1 PU, SERIAL #A24600-A26500	1,834	**1,356**	1,165	974
ELGUIT	57	GIBSON	**ES-175** SUNBURST, 1 PU	2,917	**2,157**	1,853	1,549
ELGUIT	59	GIBSON	**ES-175** SUNBURST, 1 PU	1,809	**1,338**	1,149	961
ELGUIT	60	GIBSON	**ES-175** SUNBURST, 1 PU	1,767	**1,307**	1,123	938
ELGUIT	61	GIBSON	**ES-175** SUNBURST, 1 PU	2,378	**1,759**	1,511	1,263
ELGUIT	62	GIBSON	**ES-175** SUNBURST, 1 PU	1,415	**1,046**	899	751
ELGUIT	62	GIBSON	**ES-175** TOBACCO SUNBURST, 2 PU's, BRAZILIAN RSWD FNGRBRD, PEARL INLAY	3,600	**2,662**	2,287	1,912
ELGUIT	63	GIBSON	**ES-175** SUNBURST, 1 PU	1,468	**1,086**	933	780
ELGUIT	64	GIBSON	**ES-175** SUNBURST, 1 PU	1,396	**1,033**	887	742
ELGUIT	65	GIBSON	**ES-175** SUNBURST, 1 PU	1,395	**1,032**	886	741
ELGUIT	65	GIBSON	**ES-175** NATURAL, 1 PU	1,783	**1,319**	1,133	947
ELGUIT	66	GIBSON	**ES-175** SUNBURST, 1 PU	1,561	**1,155**	992	829
ELGUIT	67	GIBSON	**ES-175** SUNBURST, 1 PU	2,191	**1,620**	1,392	1,164
ELGUIT	68	GIBSON	**ES-175** NATURAL, 1 PU	1,713	**1,267**	1,088	910
ELGUIT	70	GIBSON	**ES-175** SUNBURST, 1 PU	1,352	**1,000**	859	718
ELGUIT	71	GIBSON	**ES-175** SUNBURST, 1 PU	1,611	**1,192**	1,024	856
ELGUIT	75	GIBSON	**ES-175** SUNBURST, 1 PU	1,248	**923**	793	663
ELGUIT	76	GIBSON	**ES-175** SUNBURST, 1 PU	1,120	**828**	711	595
ELGUIT	82	GIBSON	**ES-175** WHITE, 1 PU	1,070	**791**	680	568
ELGUIT	78	GIBSON	**ES-175CC** WALNUT, CHARLIE CHRISTIAN PU	1,704	**1,260**	1,083	905
ELGUIT	79	GIBSON	**ES-175CC** SUNBURST, CHARLIE CHRISTIAN PU	1,855	**1,372**	1,179	985

TYPE	YR	MFG	PRICES--BASED ON 100% ORIGINAL MODEL	SELL EXC	SELL AVG	BUY EXC	BUY AVG
ELGUIT	52	GIBSON	**ES-175D** SUNBURST, 2 PU's	3,551	**2,626**	2,256	1,886
ELGUIT	53	GIBSON	**ES-175D** NATURAL, 2 PU's	3,530	**2,611**	2,243	1,875
ELGUIT	53	GIBSON	**ES-175D** SUNBURST, 2 PU's, LEFT-HANDED, SERIAL #A13000-A16000	4,007	**2,963**	2,546	2,128
ELGUIT	53	GIBSON	**ES-175D** SUNBURST, 2 PU's	4,187	**3,097**	2,660	2,224
ELGUIT	54	GIBSON	**ES-175D** NATURAL, 2 PU's, SERIAL #A16000-A19000	3,467	**2,564**	2,203	1,842
ELGUIT	55	GIBSON	**ES-175D** NATURAL, 2 PU's, SERIAL #A19000-A22000	3,857	**2,852**	2,450	2,049
ELGUIT	55	GIBSON	**ES-175D** SUNBURST, 2 PU's,	3,955	**2,925**	2,513	2,101
ELGUIT	56	GIBSON	**ES-175D** SUNBURST, 2 PU's, SERIAL #A22000-A24600	3,281	**2,426**	2,084	1,743
ELGUIT	56	GIBSON	**ES-175D** NATURAL, 2 PU's, SERIAL #A22000-A24600	3,848	**2,846**	2,445	2,044
ELGUIT	57	GIBSON	**ES-175D** SUNBURST, 2 PU's, LEFT-HANDED	3,698	**2,735**	2,350	1,965
ELGUIT	57	GIBSON	**ES-175D** SUNBURST, 2 PU's, SERIAL #A24600-A26500	3,759	**2,780**	2,388	1,997
ELGUIT	57	GIBSON	**ES-175D** NATURAL, 2 PU's, PAF'S, SERIAL #A24600-A26500	4,655	**3,442**	2,957	2,472
ELGUIT	58	GIBSON	**ES-175D** NATURAL, 2 PU's, SERIAL #A26500-A28000	5,235	**3,872**	3,326	2,781
ELGUIT	59	GIBSON	**ES-175D** SUNBURST, 2 PU's	3,648	**2,698**	2,318	1,938
ELGUIT	60	GIBSON	**ES-175D** SUNBURST, 2 PU's	3,790	**2,803**	2,408	2,013
ELGUIT	61	GIBSON	**ES-175D** SUNBURST, 2 PU's	4,176	**3,088**	2,653	2,218
ELGUIT	62	GIBSON	**ES-175D** SUNBURST	1,908	**1,411**	1,212	1,013
ELGUIT	62	GIBSON	**ES-175D** NATURAL, 2 PU's	1,968	**1,455**	1,250	1,045
ELGUIT	63	GIBSON	**ES-175D** SUNBURST, 2 PU's	2,225	**1,645**	1,413	1,182
ELGUIT	64	GIBSON	**ES-175D** SUNBURST, 2 PU's	2,897	**2,142**	1,840	1,539
ELGUIT	65	GIBSON	**ES-175D** SUNBURST, 2 PU's	3,237	**2,394**	2,056	1,719
ELGUIT	66	GIBSON	**ES-175D** SUNBURST, 2 PU's	2,112	**1,562**	1,342	1,122
ELGUIT	67	GIBSON	**ES-175D** SUNBURST, 2 PU's	2,144	**1,586**	1,362	1,139
ELGUIT	68	GIBSON	**ES-175D** SUNBURST, 2 PU's	2,005	**1,483**	1,274	1,065
ELGUIT	68	GIBSON	**ES-175D** NATURAL, 2 PU's	2,116	**1,565**	1,345	1,124
ELGUIT	69	GIBSON	**ES-175D** SUNBURST, 2 PU's	2,005	**1,483**	1,274	1,065
ELGUIT	70	GIBSON	**ES-175D** SUNBURST, 2 PU's	1,541	**1,140**	979	819
ELGUIT	70	GIBSON	**ES-175D** NATURAL, 2 PU's	1,773	**1,311**	1,126	941
ELGUIT	72	GIBSON	**ES-175D** SUNBURST, 2 PU's	1,202	**889**	764	639
ELGUIT	73	GIBSON	**ES-175D** SUNBURST, 2 PU's	1,202	**889**	764	639
ELGUIT	74	GIBSON	**ES-175D** SUNBURST, 2 PU's	1,198	**886**	761	636
ELGUIT	74	GIBSON	**ES-175D** NATURAL, 2 PU's	1,660	**1,228**	1,055	882
ELGUIT	75	GIBSON	**ES-175D** NATURAL, 2 PU's	1,586	**1,173**	1,008	843
ELGUIT	76	GIBSON	**ES-175D** SUNBURST, 2 PU's	1,120	**828**	711	595
ELGUIT	76	GIBSON	**ES-175D** NATURAL, 2 PU's	1,586	**1,173**	1,008	843
ELGUIT	77	GIBSON	**ES-175D** SUNBURST, 2 PU's	1,120	**828**	711	595
ELGUIT	78	GIBSON	**ES-175D** SUNBURST, 2 PU's	1,120	**828**	711	595
ELGUIT	78	GIBSON	**ES-175D** NATURAL, 2 PU's	1,474	**1,090**	936	783
ELGUIT	79	GIBSON	**ES-175D** NATURAL, 2 PU's	925	**684**	588	491
ELGUIT	80	GIBSON	**ES-175D** SUNBURST, 2 PU's	1,309	**968**	832	695
ELGUIT	85	GIBSON	**ES-175D** BLOND	1,666	**1,232**	1,058	885
ELGUIT	86	GIBSON	**ES-175D** NATURAL	1,443	**1,067**	917	767

TYPE	YR	MFG	PRICES--BASED ON 100% ORIGINAL MODEL	SELL EXC	SELL AVG	BUY EXC	BUY AVG
ELGUIT	54	GIBSON	**ES-175DN** BLOND, 2 PU's	3,262	**2,412**	2,072	1,732
ELGUIT	55	GIBSON	**ES-175DN** NATURAL, 2 PU's	3,462	**2,560**	2,200	1,839
ELGUIT	57	GIBSON	**ES-175DN** PAF's	7,598	**5,619**	4,828	4,036
ELGUIT	59	GIBSON	**ES-175DN** BLOND, 2 PU's	2,318	**1,714**	1,473	1,231
ELGUIT	79	GIBSON	**ES-175DN** BLOND	2,121	**1,569**	1,348	1,127
ELGUIT	63	GIBSON	**ES-175DSPD** WALNUT, 2 PU's	2,325	**1,719**	1,477	1,235
ELGUIT	77	GIBSON	**ES-175T** WINE RED, 2 PU's	1,144	**846**	727	607
ELGUIT	77	GIBSON	**ES-175T** NATURAL, 2 PU's	1,338	**989**	850	710
ELGUIT	78	GIBSON	**ES-175T** NATURAL, 2 PU's	1,068	**790**	678	567
ELGUIT	78	GIBSON	**ES-175T** WINE RED, 2 PU's	1,068	**790**	678	567
ELGUIT	78	GIBSON	**ES-175T** WINE RED	1,354	**1,001**	860	719
ELGUIT	79	GIBSON	**ES-175T** SUNBURST, 2 PU's	1,066	**788**	677	566
ELGUIT	79	GIBSON	**ES-175T** NATURAL, 2 PU's	1,109	**820**	705	589
ELGUIT	58	GIBSON	**ES-225N** BLOND	1,656	**1,224**	1,052	879
ELGUIT	55	GIBSON	**ES-225T** SUNBURST, 1 P-90 PU	1,155	**854**	734	614
ELGUIT	56	GIBSON	**ES-225T** SUNBURST	1,346	**996**	855	715
ELGUIT	57	GIBSON	**ES-225T** SUNBURST	1,331	**984**	846	707
ELGUIT	58	GIBSON	**ES-225T** SUNBURST	1,106	**818**	703	588
ELGUIT	58	GIBSON	**ES-225T** NATURAL	1,274	**942**	810	677
ELGUIT	59	GIBSON	**ES-225T** SUNBURST, SERIAL #S822314	956	**707**	607	507
ELGUIT	56	GIBSON	**ES-225TD** SUNBURST, 2 PU's, SERIAL #A22000-A24600	1,537	**1,137**	977	817
ELGUIT	56	GIBSON	**ES-225TD** NATURAL, 2 PU's, SERIAL #22000-A24600	1,778	**1,315**	1,130	945
ELGUIT	57	GIBSON	**ES-225TD** SUNBURST, 2 PU's, SERIAL #A24600-A26500	1,505	**1,113**	956	799
ELGUIT	57	GIBSON	**ES-225TD** NATURAL, 2 PU's, SERIAL #A24600-A26500	1,804	**1,334**	1,146	958
ELGUIT	58	GIBSON	**ES-225TD** SUNBURST, 2 PU's, SERIAL #A26500-A28000	1,505	**1,113**	956	799
ELGUIT	58	GIBSON	**ES-225TD** NATURAL, 2 PU's, SERIAL #A26500-A28000	1,786	**1,321**	1,135	949
ELGUIT	59	GIBSON	**ES-225TD** SUNBURST, 2 PU's, SERIAL #A28000	1,483	**1,096**	942	787
ELGUIT	59	GIBSON	**ES-225TD** NATURAL, 2 PU's	2,182	**1,613**	1,386	1,159
ELGUIT	62	GIBSON	**ES-225TD** SUNBURST, 2 PU's	1,269	**938**	806	674
ELGUIT	39	GIBSON	**ES-250** SUNBURST	8,252	**6,103**	5,243	4,383
ELGUIT	40	GIBSON	**ES-250** NATURAL, SERIAL #96000-96600	7,516	**5,559**	4,776	3,993
ELGUIT	80	GIBSON	**ES-250T** ANTIQUE SUNBURST	1,076	**795**	683	571
ELGUIT	55	GIBSON	**ES-295** GOLD	4,454	**3,294**	2,830	2,366
ELGUIT	56	GIBSON	**ES-295** P-90 PU's	4,320	**3,195**	2,745	2,295
ELGUIT	58	GIBSON	**ES-295** HUMBUCKER PU's	7,440	**5,502**	4,727	3,952
ELGUIT	52	GIBSON	**ES-295TD** GOLD, SERIAL #A9400-A13000	4,298	**3,179**	2,731	2,283
ELGUIT	53	GIBSON	**ES-295TD** GOLD, SERIAL #A13000-A16000	4,216	**3,118**	2,679	2,239
ELGUIT	54	GIBSON	**ES-295TD** GOLD, SERIAL #A16000-A19000	4,213	**3,116**	2,677	2,238
ELGUIT	55	GIBSON	**ES-295TD** GOLD, SERIAL #A19000-A22000	4,392	**3,248**	2,791	2,333
ELGUIT	56	GIBSON	**ES-295TD** GOLD, SERIAL #A22000-A24600	4,391	**3,247**	2,790	2,332
ELGUIT	57	GIBSON	**ES-295TD** GOLD, SERIAL #A24600-A26500	4,384	**3,242**	2,785	2,329
ELGUIT	58	GIBSON	**ES-295TD** GOLD, PAF, SERIAL #A26500-A28000	5,860	**4,334**	3,724	3,113

TYPE	YR	MFG	PRICES--BASED ON 100% ORIGINAL MODEL	SELL EXC	SELL AVG	BUY EXC	BUY AVG
ELGUIT	40	GIBSON	ES-300 NATURAL, DIAGONAL PU, SERIAL #96000-96600	3,672	2,715	2,333	1,950
ELGUIT	41	GIBSON	ES-300 NATURAL, DIAGONAL PU	2,232	1,650	1,418	1,185
ELGUIT	41	GIBSON	ES-300 SUNBURST, DIAGONAL PU	2,285	1,690	1,452	1,214
ELGUIT	44	GIBSON	ES-300 SUNBURST, P-90 PU	2,025	1,498	1,287	1,076
ELGUIT	45	GIBSON	ES-300 SUNBURST, P-90 PU	2,010	1,486	1,277	1,067
ELGUIT	46	GIBSON	ES-300 NATURAL, P-90 PU	1,621	1,199	1,030	861
ELGUIT	46	GIBSON	ES-300 SUNBURST, P-90 PU, SERIAL #98600-99500	1,668	1,233	1,060	886
ELGUIT	47	GIBSON	ES-300 NATURAL, P-90 PU	1,624	1,201	1,032	862
ELGUIT	47	GIBSON	ES-300 SUNBURST, P-90 PU	1,628	1,204	1,034	864
ELGUIT	48	GIBSON	ES-300 1 P-90 PU	1,474	1,090	936	783
ELGUIT	49	GIBSON	ES-300 2 P-90 PU's	1,474	1,090	936	783
ELGUIT	50	GIBSON	ES-300 SUNBURST, P-90 PU, SERIAL #A4400-A6000	1,728	1,278	1,098	918
ELGUIT	51	GIBSON	ES-300 SUNBURST, P-90 PU, SERIAL #A9400-A13000	1,699	1,256	1,079	902
ELGUIT	52	GIBSON	ES-300 SUNBURST, P-90 PU	1,682	1,244	1,069	894
ELGUIT	48	GIBSON	ES-300N BLOND	2,352	1,739	1,494	1,249
ELGUIT	71	GIBSON	ES-320 CHERRY RED, MELODY MAKER STYLE PU's	677	501	430	360
ELGUIT	71	GIBSON	ES-320TD NATURAL, 2 MELODY MAKER PU's	606	448	385	322
ELGUIT	72	GIBSON	ES-325TD CHERRY, 1 F-HOLE, 2 MINI-HB	552	408	350	293
ELGUIT	72	GIBSON	ES-325TD WALNUT, 1 F-HOLE, 2 MINI-HB	641	474	407	340
ELGUIT	73	GIBSON	ES-325TD WALNUT, 1 F-HOLE, 2 MINI-HB	677	501	430	360
ELGUIT	76	GIBSON	ES-325TD CHERRY, 2 F-HOLE, 2 MINI-HB	598	442	380	317
ELGUIT	66	GIBSON	ES-330 CHERRY RED	1,493	1,104	949	793
ELGUIT	67	GIBSON	ES-330 CHERRY RED	1,593	1,178	1,012	846
ELGUIT	69	GIBSON	ES-330 SUNBURST, ES-335 LENGTH NECK	1,593	1,178	1,012	846
ELGUIT	59	GIBSON	ES-330D SUNBURST	1,502	1,111	954	798
ELGUIT	60	GIBSON	ES-330D SUNBURST	1,673	1,237	1,063	888
ELGUIT	61	GIBSON	ES-330D SUNBURST	1,436	1,062	912	762
ELGUIT	66	GIBSON	ES-330D SUNBURST	1,416	1,047	900	752
ELGUIT	68	GIBSON	ES-330D SUNBURST, LONG NECK	1,406	1,040	893	747
ELGUIT	59	GIBSON	ES-330T NATURAL	1,416	1,047	899	752
ELGUIT	59	GIBSON	ES-330T SUNBURST	1,589	1,175	1,010	844
ELGUIT	60	GIBSON	ES-330T SUNBURST	1,328	982	844	705
ELGUIT	60	GIBSON	ES-330T BLOND	1,751	1,295	1,112	930
ELGUIT	61	GIBSON	ES-330T SUNBURST	1,398	1,034	888	743
ELGUIT	61	GIBSON	ES-330T CHERRY	1,415	1,046	899	751
ELGUIT	62	GIBSON	ES-330T SUNBURST	1,119	827	711	594
ELGUIT	62	GIBSON	ES-330T NATURAL	1,235	913	785	656
ELGUIT	63	GIBSON	ES-330T SUNBURST	1,199	886	761	636
ELGUIT	66	GIBSON	ES-330T CHERRY, LONG NECK, HUMBUCKER	1,089	805	692	578
ELGUIT	60	GIBSON	ES-330TD CHERRY RED	1,450	1,072	921	770
ELGUIT	60	GIBSON	ES-330TD SUNBURST	1,560	1,154	991	829
ELGUIT	60	GIBSON	ES-330TD NATURAL	2,236	1,654	1,421	1,188

TYPE	YR	MFG	PRICES--BASED ON 100% ORIGINAL MODEL	SELL EXC	SELL AVG	BUY EXC	BUY AVG
ELGUIT	61	GIBSON	**ES-330TD** CHERRY RED	1,320	**976**	839	701
ELGUIT	61	GIBSON	**ES-330TD** SUNBURST	1,488	**1,101**	946	791
ELGUIT	62	GIBSON	**ES-330TD** SUNBURST	1,291	**954**	820	685
ELGUIT	62	GIBSON	**ES-330TD** CHERRY RED	1,333	**986**	847	708
ELGUIT	63	GIBSON	**ES-330TD** CHERRY RED	1,245	**920**	791	661
ELGUIT	63	GIBSON	**ES-330TD** SUNBURST	1,249	**924**	794	664
ELGUIT	64	GIBSON	**ES-330TD** CHERRY RED	1,289	**953**	819	684
ELGUIT	64	GIBSON	**ES-330TD** SUNBURST	1,295	**957**	822	687
ELGUIT	65	GIBSON	**ES-330TD** CHERRY RED	1,276	**944**	811	678
ELGUIT	65	GIBSON	**ES-330TD** SUNBURST	1,469	**1,087**	933	780
ELGUIT	66	GIBSON	**ES-330TD** CHERRY RED	1,043	**771**	663	554
ELGUIT	66	GIBSON	**ES-330TD** SUNBURST	1,146	**847**	728	608
ELGUIT	66	GIBSON	**ES-330TD** SPARKLING BURGUNDY	1,276	**944**	811	678
ELGUIT	67	GIBSON	**ES-330TD** CHERRY RED	1,042	**771**	662	553
ELGUIT	67	GIBSON	**ES-330TD** SUNBURST	1,146	**847**	728	608
ELGUIT	67	GIBSON	**ES-330TD** SPARKLING BURGUNDY	1,276	**944**	811	678
ELGUIT	68	GIBSON	**ES-330TD** SUNBURST, NON-TREMOLO	1,127	**833**	716	598
ELGUIT	68	GIBSON	**ES-330TD** CHERRY RED, TRAPEZE TAIL, SERIAL #527101	1,155	**854**	734	614
ELGUIT	68	GIBSON	**ES-330TD** SUNBURST	1,186	**877**	753	630
ELGUIT	69	GIBSON	**ES-330TD** CHERRY RED	996	**736**	633	529
ELGUIT	69	GIBSON	**ES-330TD** SUNBURST	1,066	**788**	677	566
ELGUIT	70	GIBSON	**ES-330TD** WALNUT	944	**698**	600	501
ELGUIT	72	GIBSON	**ES-330TD** SUNBURST	734	**543**	466	390
ELGUIT	73	GIBSON	**ES-330TD** CHERRY RED	817	**604**	519	434
ELGUIT	67	GIBSON	**ES-330TDC**	1,185	**876**	753	629
ELGUIT	60	GIBSON	**ES-335** BLOND, DOT NECK, SLIM NECK	1,003	**741**	637	532
ELGUIT	61	GIBSON	**ES-335** SUNBURST, EXF, DOT INLAY, HB PU's	17,261	**12,766**	10,968	9,170
ELGUIT	67	GIBSON	**ES-335** BURGNADY MIST	2,944	**2,177**	1,870	1,564
ELGUIT	68	GIBSON	**ES-335** NATURAL, 2-TONE BURGUNDY	1,065	**788**	677	566
ELGUIT	74	GIBSON	**ES-335** WALNUT	1,281	**947**	814	680
ELGUIT	79	GIBSON	**ES-335** WINE RED	1,136	**840**	722	603
ELGUIT	81	GIBSON	**ES-335** BLOND, DOT NECK, BIG NECK	677	**501**	430	360
ELGUIT	82	GIBSON	**ES-335** CHERRY, DOT	837	**619**	531	444
ELGUIT	82	GIBSON	**ES-335** BLOND, DOT NECK, BIG NECK	876	**648**	556	465
ELGUIT	79	GIBSON	**ES-335 PRO** ANTIQUE SUNBURST, 2 PU's	864	**639**	549	459
ELGUIT	81	GIBSON	**ES-335 PRO** CHERRY RED	868	**642**	552	461
ELGUIT	82	GIBSON	**ES-335 PRO** SUNBURST	1,035	**766**	658	550
ELGUIT	65	GIBSON	**ES-335-12** SUNBURST, 12-STRING	1,338	**989**	850	710
ELGUIT	66	GIBSON	**ES-335-12** WINE, 12-STRING	1,325	**980**	842	704
ELGUIT	66	GIBSON	**ES-335-12** SUNBURST, 12-STRING	1,427	**1,055**	907	758
ELGUIT	67	GIBSON	**ES-335-12** CHERRY RED, 12-STRING	1,325	**980**	842	704
ELGUIT	67	GIBSON	**ES-335-12** SPARKLING BURGUNDY, 12-STRING	1,325	**980**	842	704

TYPE	YR	MFG	PRICES--BASED ON 100% ORIGINAL MODEL	SELL EXC	SELL AVG	BUY EXC	BUY AVG
ELGUIT	67	GIBSON	**ES-335-12** SUNBURST, 12-STRING	1,352	**1,000**	859	718
ELGUIT	68	GIBSON	**ES-335-12** SPARKLING BURGUNDY, 12-STRING	1,325	**980**	842	704
ELGUIT	68	GIBSON	**ES-335-12** SUNBURST, 12-STRING	1,405	**1,039**	893	746
ELGUIT	69	GIBSON	**ES-335-12** CHERRY RED, 12-STRING	1,206	**892**	766	641
ELGUIT	58	GIBSON	**ES-335N** NATURAL, FIGURED BIGSBY	32,542	**24,067**	20,677	17,287
ELGUIT	59	GIBSON	**ES-335N** BLOND, NATURAL, STOP TAILPIECE	26,314	**19,461**	16,720	13,979
ELGUIT	60	GIBSON	**ES-335N** NATURAL	22,728	**16,809**	14,441	12,074
ELGUIT	80	GIBSON	**ES-335S CUSTOM**	1,195	**883**	759	634
ELGUIT	58	GIBSON	**ES-335TD** CHERRY RED	10,538	**7,794**	6,696	5,598
ELGUIT	58	GIBSON	**ES-335TD** SUNBURST, DOT INLAY, LEFT-HANDED	11,899	**8,800**	7,560	6,321
ELGUIT	58	GIBSON	**ES-335TD** SUNBURST, DOT INLAY, SERIAL #A26500-A28000	13,007	**9,619**	8,264	6,909
ELGUIT	58	GIBSON	**ES-335TD** NATURAL, DOT INLAY, SERIAL #A26500-A28000	27,739	**20,515**	17,625	14,736
ELGUIT	59	GIBSON	**ES-335TD** CHERRY RED	9,559	**7,070**	6,074	5,078
ELGUIT	59	GIBSON	**ES-335TD** SUNBURST, DOT INLAY	12,456	**9,212**	7,915	6,617
ELGUIT	59	GIBSON	**ES-335TD** NATURAL, DOT INLAY	25,325	**18,730**	16,092	13,454
ELGUIT	60	GIBSON	**ES-335TD** CHERRY RED	9,667	**7,149**	6,142	5,135
ELGUIT	60	GIBSON	**ES-335TD** SUNBURST, BIGSBY	11,022	**8,152**	7,004	5,855
ELGUIT	60	GIBSON	**ES-335TD** SUNBURST, DOT INLAY	11,130	**8,231**	7,072	5,912
ELGUIT	60	GIBSON	**ES-335TD** NATURAL, DOT INLAY	22,126	**16,364**	14,059	11,754
ELGUIT	61	GIBSON	**ES-335TD** SUNBURST, DOT INLAY	10,055	**7,436**	6,389	5,341
ELGUIT	61	GIBSON	**ES-335TD** CHERRY RED, DOT INLAY	10,568	**7,816**	6,715	5,614
ELGUIT	62	GIBSON	**ES-335TD** SUNBURST, LEFT-HANDED	5,353	**3,959**	3,401	2,844
ELGUIT	62	GIBSON	**ES-335TD** SUNBURST, BLOCK INLAY	6,023	**4,454**	3,827	3,199
ELGUIT	62	GIBSON	**ES-335TD** CHERRY RED, BLOCK INLAY	7,946	**5,877**	5,049	4,221
ELGUIT	62	GIBSON	**ES-335TD** CHERRY RED, DOT INLAY	8,042	**5,948**	5,110	4,272
ELGUIT	62	GIBSON	**ES-335TD** SUNBURST	8,252	**6,103**	5,243	4,383
ELGUIT	62	GIBSON	**ES-335TD** SUNBURST, DOT INLAY	8,271	**6,117**	5,255	4,394
ELGUIT	63	GIBSON	**ES-335TD** CHERRY RED, BIGSBY VIB	4,114	**3,043**	2,614	2,185
ELGUIT	63	GIBSON	**ES-335TD** CHERRY RED	4,400	**3,254**	2,796	2,337
ELGUIT	63	GIBSON	**ES-335TD** SUNBURST	4,593	**3,397**	2,918	2,440
ELGUIT	64	GIBSON	**ES-335TD** SUNBURST	3,741	**2,766**	2,377	1,987
ELGUIT	64	GIBSON	**ES-335TD** CHERRY RED, NICKEL PARTS	3,883	**2,871**	2,467	2,062
ELGUIT	65	GIBSON	**ES-335TD** SUNBURST, TRAPEZE TAIL	1,959	**1,449**	1,245	1,040
ELGUIT	65	GIBSON	**ES-335TD** CHERRY RED, CHROME PARTS	2,159	**1,596**	1,371	1,146
ELGUIT	65	GIBSON	**ES-335TD** MAHOGANY, BIG NECK	4,077	**3,015**	2,590	2,165
ELGUIT	65	GIBSON	**ES-335TD** WHITE, GOLD-PLATED HARDWARE	5,356	**3,961**	3,403	2,845
ELGUIT	66	GIBSON	**ES-335TD** CHERRY RED	1,911	**1,413**	1,214	1,015
ELGUIT	66	GIBSON	**ES-335TD** SUNBURST	1,959	**1,449**	1,245	1,040
ELGUIT	66	GIBSON	**ES-335TD** CHERRY RED	2,131	**1,576**	1,354	1,132
ELGUIT	66	GIBSON	**ES-335TD** CHERRY RED, LEFT-HANDED	3,268	**2,417**	2,077	1,736
ELGUIT	66	GIBSON	**ES-335TD** SPARKLING BURGUNDY	4,759	**3,520**	3,024	2,528
ELGUIT	66	GIBSON	**ES-335TD** PELHAM BLUE	6,984	**5,165**	4,437	3,710

TYPE	YR	MFG	PRICES--BASED ON 100% ORIGINAL MODEL	SELL EXC	SELL AVG	BUY EXC	BUY AVG
ELGUIT	67	GIBSON	**ES-335TD** CHERRY RED, CHECKING, TRAPEZE	1,612	**1,192**	1,024	856
ELGUIT	67	GIBSON	**ES-335TD** SUNBURST	1,661	**1,229**	1,055	882
ELGUIT	67	GIBSON	**ES-335TD** CHERRY RED	1,866	**1,380**	1,185	991
ELGUIT	67	GIBSON	**ES-335TD** BLACK	2,230	**1,649**	1,417	1,184
ELGUIT	67	GIBSON	**ES-335TD** SPARKLING BURGANDY	4,747	**3,510**	3,016	2,521
ELGUIT	68	GIBSON	**ES-335TD** WALNUT, BIGSBY VIBRATO	1,338	**989**	850	710
ELGUIT	68	GIBSON	**ES-335TD** SUNBURST	1,662	**1,229**	1,056	883
ELGUIT	68	GIBSON	**ES-335TD** CHERRY RED	1,853	**1,371**	1,177	984
ELGUIT	68	GIBSON	**ES-335TD** SPARKLING BURGUNDY	4,689	**3,468**	2,979	2,491
ELGUIT	69	GIBSON	**ES-335TD** WALNUT	1,354	**1,001**	860	719
ELGUIT	69	GIBSON	**ES-335TD** CHERRY RED, 3 PIECE NECK	1,668	**1,233**	1,060	886
ELGUIT	69	GIBSON	**ES-335TD** SUNBURST	1,802	**1,333**	1,145	957
ELGUIT	69	GIBSON	**ES-335TD** SPARKLING BURGUNDY	4,617	**3,415**	2,934	2,453
ELGUIT	70	GIBSON	**ES-335TD** WALNUT	1,159	**857**	736	616
ELGUIT	70	GIBSON	**ES-335TD** CHERRY RED	1,310	**969**	832	696
ELGUIT	70	GIBSON	**ES-335TD** CHERRY RED, VALITE MADE WITH GUITAR AMP	1,356	**1,003**	861	720
ELGUIT	70	GIBSON	**ES-335TD** SUNBURST, LEFT-HANDED	1,613	**1,193**	1,025	857
ELGUIT	70	GIBSON	**ES-335TD** SUNBURST	1,844	**1,363**	1,171	979
ELGUIT	71	GIBSON	**ES-335TD** WINE RED	1,195	**883**	759	634
ELGUIT	71	GIBSON	**ES-335TD** CHERRY RED,MAHOGANY NECK,TRAPEZE TAILPIECE	1,310	**969**	832	696
ELGUIT	71	GIBSON	**ES-335TD** WALNUT	1,374	**1,016**	873	730
ELGUIT	72	GIBSON	**ES-335TD** WALNUT	1,140	**843**	724	605
ELGUIT	72	GIBSON	**ES-335TD** WINE RED	1,159	**857**	736	616
ELGUIT	72	GIBSON	**ES-335TD** CHERRY RED	1,315	**972**	835	698
ELGUIT	72	GIBSON	**ES-335TD** SUNBURST	1,455	**1,076**	924	773
ELGUIT	72	GIBSON	**ES-335TD** SPARKLING BURGANDY	3,726	**2,756**	2,368	1,979
ELGUIT	73	GIBSON	**ES-335TD** WALNUT, SERIAL #055039	1,015	**751**	645	539
ELGUIT	73	GIBSON	**ES-335TD** CHERRY RED, SERIAL #055039	1,316	**973**	836	699
ELGUIT	74	GIBSON	**ES-335TD** WALNUT	1,115	**825**	708	592
ELGUIT	74	GIBSON	**ES-335TD** CHERRY RED	1,314	**971**	835	698
ELGUIT	75	GIBSON	**ES-335TD** WALNUT	916	**678**	582	487
ELGUIT	75	GIBSON	**ES-335TD** SUNBURST	1,163	**860**	739	618
ELGUIT	76	GIBSON	**ES-335TD** WALNUT	817	**604**	519	434
ELGUIT	76	GIBSON	**ES-335TD** SUNBURST	956	**707**	607	507
ELGUIT	76	GIBSON	**ES-335TD** WINE RED	1,035	**766**	658	550
ELGUIT	76	GIBSON	**ES-335TD** NATURAL	1,115	**825**	708	592
ELGUIT	77	GIBSON	**ES-335TD** WALNUT	794	**587**	505	422
ELGUIT	77	GIBSON	**ES-335TD** SUNBURST	1,123	**830**	713	596
ELGUIT	77	GIBSON	**ES-335TD** CHERRY RED	1,253	**927**	796	666
ELGUIT	78	GIBSON	**ES-335TD** WALNUT	920	**680**	584	489
ELGUIT	78	GIBSON	**ES-335TD** WINE RED	1,031	**762**	655	547
ELGUIT	78	GIBSON	**ES-335TD** SUNBURST	1,092	**807**	694	580

TYPE	YR	MFG	PRICES--BASED ON 100% ORIGINAL MODEL	SELL EXC	SELL AVG	BUY EXC	BUY AVG
ELGUIT	79	GIBSON	**ES-335TD** WINE RED	846	**626**	538	449
ELGUIT	79	GIBSON	**ES-335TD** WALNUT	874	**646**	555	464
ELGUIT	79	GIBSON	**ES-335TD** SUNBURST	1,094	**809**	695	581
ELGUIT	79	GIBSON	**ES-335TD** CHERRY RED	1,155	**854**	734	614
ELGUIT	61	GIBSON	**ES-335TDC** CHERRY SUNBURST, 2 PAF's	7,874	**6,000**	5,100	3,899
ELGUIT	64	GIBSON	**ES-335TDC** CHERRY RED	6,240	**4,615**	3,965	3,315
ELGUIT	59	GIBSON	**ES-335TDSV** CHERRY RED, STEREO	5,760	**4,260**	3,660	3,060
ELGUIT	66	GIBSON	**ES-335TDSV** CHERRY RED, TREMOLO	2,113	**1,563**	1,343	1,123
ELGUIT	79	GIBSON	**ES-335TDSV** SUNBURST, STEREO	1,195	**883**	759	634
ELGUIT	69	GIBSON	**ES-340TD** NATURAL, 2 PU's	1,070	**791**	680	568
ELGUIT	69	GIBSON	**ES-340TD** WALNUT, 2 PU's	1,138	**842**	723	604
ELGUIT	70	GIBSON	**ES-340TD** NATURAL, 2 PU's	1,038	**768**	660	551
ELGUIT	70	GIBSON	**ES-340TD** WALNUT	1,195	**883**	759	634
ELGUIT	72	GIBSON	**ES-340TD** NATURAL, 2 PU's	988	**731**	628	525
ELGUIT	61	GIBSON	**ES-345** SUNBURST, LEFT-HANDED, PAF HB PU's.STEREO & VARITONE	9,600	**7,100**	6,100	5,100
ELGUIT	68	GIBSON	**ES-345** WALNUT FINISH, STEREO CORD	1,592	**1,177**	1,011	846
ELGUIT	59	GIBSON	**ES-345TD** SUNBURST, DOUBLE CUTAWAY, STEREO, 2 PU's	5,484	**4,056**	3,484	2,913
ELGUIT	59	GIBSON	**ES-345TD** CHERRY, DOUBLE CUTAWAY, STEREO, 2 PU's	5,603	**4,144**	3,560	2,976
ELGUIT	59	GIBSON	**ES-345TD** NATURAL, DOUBLE CUTAWAY, STEREO, 2 PU's	7,267	**5,374**	4,617	3,860
ELGUIT	60	GIBSON	**ES-345TD** CHERRY, DOUBLE CUTAWAY, STEREO, 2 PU's	5,273	**3,900**	3,350	2,801
ELGUIT	60	GIBSON	**ES-345TD** SUNBURST, DOUBLE CUTAWAY, STEREO, 2 PU's	5,760	**4,260**	3,660	3,060
ELGUIT	61	GIBSON	**ES-345TD** CHERRY, DOUBLE CUTAWAY, STEREO, 2 PU's	5,760	**4,260**	3,660	3,060
ELGUIT	62	GIBSON	**ES-345TD** CHERRY, DOUBLE CUTAWAY, STEREO, 2 PU's	5,568	**4,118**	3,538	2,958
ELGUIT	62	GIBSON	**ES-345TD** CHERRY, DOUBLE CUATAWAY, STEREO, LEFT-HANDED, 2 PU's	5,760	**4,260**	3,660	3,060
ELGUIT	63	GIBSON	**ES-345TD** SUNBURST, DOUBLE CUTAWAY, STEREO, 2 PU's	2,206	**1,631**	1,401	1,171
ELGUIT	63	GIBSON	**ES-345TD** CHERRY, DOUBLE CUTAWAY, STEREO, 2 PU's	2,354	**1,741**	1,496	1,251
ELGUIT	64	GIBSON	**ES-345TD** CHERRY, DOUBLE CUTAWAY, STEREO, 2 PU's	3,073	**2,273**	1,953	1,633
ELGUIT	65	GIBSON	**ES-345TD** CHERRY, DOUBLE CUTAWAY, STEREO, 2 PU's	1,883	**1,393**	1,196	1,000
ELGUIT	66	GIBSON	**ES-345TD** SUNBURST, DOUBLE CUTAWAY, STEREO, 2 PU's	1,736	**1,284**	1,103	922
ELGUIT	66	GIBSON	**ES-345TD** CHERRY, DOUBLE CUTAWAY, STEREO, 2 PU's	2,079	**1,537**	1,321	1,104
ELGUIT	67	GIBSON	**ES-345TD** CHERRY, DOUBLE CUTAWAY, STEREO, 2 PU's	1,587	**1,174**	1,008	843
ELGUIT	68	GIBSON	**ES-345TD** WALNUT, DOUBLE CUTAWAY, STEREO, 2 PU's	1,273	**942**	809	676
ELGUIT	68	GIBSON	**ES-345TD** SUNBURST, DOUBLE CUTAWAY, STEREO, 2 PU's	1,723	**1,274**	1,094	915
ELGUIT	69	GIBSON	**ES-345TD** SUNBURST, DOUBLE CUTAWAY, STEREO, 2 PU's	1,264	**935**	803	671
ELGUIT	69	GIBSON	**ES-345TD** WALNUT, DOUBLE CUTAWAY, STEREO, 2 PU's	1,264	**935**	803	671
ELGUIT	70	GIBSON	**ES-345TD** SUNBURST, DOUBLE CUTAWAY, STEREO, 2 PU's	1,062	**785**	675	564
ELGUIT	70	GIBSON	**ES-345TD** WALNUT, DOUBLE CUTAWAY, STEREO, 2 PU's	1,219	**901**	774	647
ELGUIT	70	GIBSON	**ES-345TD** CHERRY, DOUBLE CUTAWAY, STEREO, 2 PU's	1,367	**1,011**	868	726
ELGUIT	71	GIBSON	**ES-345TD** WALNUT, DOUBLE CUTAWAY, STEREO, 2 PU's	1,206	**892**	766	641
ELGUIT	72	GIBSON	**ES-345TD** WALNUT, DOUBLE CUTAWAY, STEREO, 2 PU's	961	**711**	611	511
ELGUIT	73	GIBSON	**ES-345TD** WALNUT, DOUBLE CUTAWAY, STEREO, 2 PU's	1,146	**847**	728	608
ELGUIT	74	GIBSON	**ES-345TD** CHERRY, DOUBLE CUTAWAY, STEREO, 2 PU's	1,296	**958**	823	688

TYPE	YR	MFG	PRICES--BASED ON 100% ORIGINAL MODEL	SELL EXC	SELL AVG	BUY EXC	BUY AVG
ELGUIT	77	GIBSON	**ES-345TD** WINE RED, DOUBLE CUTAWAY, 2 PU's	1,117	**826**	710	593
ELGUIT	78	GIBSON	**ES-345TD** WALNUT, DOUBLE CUTAWAY, STEREO, 2 PU's	1,042	**771**	662	553
ELGUIT	79	GIBSON	**ES-345TD** NATURAL, DOUBLE CUTAWAY, 2 PU's	1,113	**823**	707	591
ELGUIT	60	GIBSON	**ES-345TDC** CHERRY SUNBURST, BIGSBY	4,114	**3,043**	2,614	2,185
ELGUIT	68	GIBSON	**ES-345TDC** CHERRY, BISBY, VARITONE	1,194	**883**	758	634
ELGUIT	59	GIBSON	**ES-345TDSV** SUNBURST	5,419	**4,007**	3,443	2,878
ELGUIT	67	GIBSON	**ES-345TDSV** CHERRY RED	1,663	**1,230**	1,057	883
ELGUIT	68	GIBSON	**ES-345TDSV** SUNBURST, SERIAL# 519851	1,344	**994**	854	714
ELGUIT	78	GIBSON	**ES-345TDSV** WINE RED	928	**686**	589	493
ELGUIT	72	GIBSON	**ES-345TDVS** CHERRY RED	1,002	**741**	636	532
ELGUIT	84	GIBSON	**ES-347** THIN LINE	1,035	**766**	658	550
ELGUIT	84	GIBSON	**ES-347 THIN LINE**	956	**707**	607	507
ELGUIT	78	GIBSON	**ES-347TD** NATURAL	971	**718**	617	516
ELGUIT	79	GIBSON	**ES-347TD** SUNBURST, DOUBLE CUTAWAY, TP-6, 2 PU's	933	**690**	592	495
ELGUIT	83	GIBSON	**ES-347TD**	1,115	**825**	708	592
ELGUIT	47	GIBSON	**ES-350** NATURAL, ROUNDED CUTAWAY, 1 PU	4,296	**3,177**	2,730	2,282
ELGUIT	47	GIBSON	**ES-350** SUNBURST, ROUNDED CUTAWAY, 1 PU	5,119	**3,786**	3,253	2,719
ELGUIT	48	GIBSON	**ES-350** SUNBURST, 1 P-90	4,080	**3,017**	2,592	2,167
ELGUIT	48	GIBSON	**ES-350** NATURAL, ROUNDED CUTAWAY, 1 PU	4,920	**3,639**	3,126	2,614
ELGUIT	48	GIBSON	**ES-350** SUNBURST, ROUNDED CUTAWAY, 2 PU's	4,920	**3,639**	3,126	2,614
ELGUIT	49	GIBSON	**ES-350** SUNBURST, ROUNDED CUTAWAY, 2 PU's	4,474	**3,309**	2,843	2,377
ELGUIT	49	GIBSON	**ES-350** NATURAL, 2 P-90's	4,656	**3,443**	2,958	2,473
ELGUIT	50	GIBSON	**ES-350** SUNBURST, ROUNDED CUTAWAY, 1 PU	4,221	**3,121**	2,682	2,242
ELGUIT	51	GIBSON	**ES-350** SUNBURST, ROUNDED CUTAWAY, 2 PU's	4,118	**3,045**	2,616	2,187
ELGUIT	52	GIBSON	**ES-350** SUNBURST, ROUNDED CUTAWAY, 2 PU's	4,206	**3,111**	2,673	2,234
ELGUIT	54	GIBSON	**ES-350** SUNBURST, ROUNDED CUTAWAY, 2 PU's	4,029	**2,979**	2,560	2,140
ELGUIT	56	GIBSON	**ES-350** BLOND, 2 P-90 PU's, SINGLE CUT, 1 OF 4 MADE	6,230	**4,607**	3,958	3,309
ELGUIT	56	GIBSON	**ES-350T** SUNBURST, ROUNDED CUTAWAY, 2 PU's, SERIAL #A22000-A24600	4,800	**3,550**	3,050	2,550
ELGUIT	56	GIBSON	**ES-350T** NATURAL, ROUNDED CUTAWAY, 2 PU's, SERIAL #A22000-A24600	5,760	**4,260**	3,660	3,060
ELGUIT	57	GIBSON	**ES-350T** SUNBURST, ROUNDED CUTAWAY, 2 PU's, PAF'S	6,240	**4,615**	3,965	3,315
ELGUIT	58	GIBSON	**ES-350T** SUNBURST, ROUNDED CUTAWAY, 2 PU's, PAF'S	6,240	**4,615**	3,965	3,315
ELGUIT	59	GIBSON	**ES-350T** BROWN, ROUNDED CUTAWAY, 2 PU's, STEREO VARITONE	5,280	**3,905**	3,355	2,805
ELGUIT	59	GIBSON	**ES-350T** SUNBURST, ROUNDED CUTAWAY, 2 PU's	6,240	**4,615**	3,965	3,315
ELGUIT	62	GIBSON	**ES-350T** SUNBURST, ROUNDED CUTAWAY, 2 PU's	4,800	**3,550**	3,050	2,550
ELGUIT	63	GIBSON	**ES-350T** NATURAL	4,800	**3,550**	3,050	2,550
ELGUIT	77	GIBSON	**ES-350T** SUNBURST, ROUNDED CUTAWAY, 2 PU's	1,992	**1,473**	1,265	1,058
ELGUIT	77	GIBSON	**ES-350T** BLACK, ROUNDED CUTAWAY, 2 PU's	2,390	**1,767**	1,518	1,269
ELGUIT	77	GIBSON	**ES-350T** NATURAL, ROUNDED CUTAWAY, 2 PU's	2,390	**1,767**	1,518	1,269
ELGUIT	78	GIBSON	**ES-350T** NATURAL	1,832	**1,355**	1,164	973
ELGUIT	78	GIBSON	**ES-350T** FIREBURST, ROUNDED CUTAWAY, 2 PU's	2,190	**1,620**	1,392	1,163
ELGUIT	58	GIBSON	**ES-350TD** SUNBURST, ROUNDED CUTAWAY, 2 PU's, SERIAL #A26500-A28000	4,297	**3,178**	2,730	2,283
ELGUIT	59	GIBSON	**ES-350TD** NATURAL, ROUNDED CUTAWAY, 2 PU's	4,269	**3,157**	2,712	2,267
ELGUIT	59	GIBSON	**ES-350TD** SUNBURST, ROUNDED CUTAWAY, 2 PU's	5,005	**3,701**	3,180	2,659

TYPE	YR	MFG	PRICES--BASED ON 100% ORIGINAL MODEL	SELL EXC	SELL AVG	BUY EXC	BUY AVG
ELGUIT	60	GIBSON	**ES-350TD** SUNBURST, POINTED CUTAWAY, 2 PU's	4,288	**3,171**	2,724	2,278
ELGUIT	61	GIBSON	**ES-350TD** SUNBURST, POINTED CUTAWAY, 2 PU's	4,290	**3,172**	2,726	2,279
ELGUIT	62	GIBSON	**ES-350TD** NATURAL, POINTED CUTAWAY, 2 PU's	4,291	**3,173**	2,726	2,279
ELGUIT	62	GIBSON	**ES-350TD** SUNBURST, POINTED CUTAWAY, 2 PU's	4,291	**3,173**	2,726	2,279
ELGUIT	58	GIBSON	**ES-355TD** CHERRY RED, MONO, BIGSBY	6,812	**5,038**	4,328	3,618
ELGUIT	59	GIBSON	**ES-355TD** CHERRY RED, BIGSBY, 2 PAF HB PU's, STEREO & VARITONE WIRING	7,200	**5,325**	4,575	3,825
ELGUIT	60	GIBSON	**ES-355TD** CHERRY RED, STEREO, 2 PU's	5,453	**4,033**	3,465	2,897
ELGUIT	61	GIBSON	**ES-355TD** CHERRY RED, MONO	1,329	**983**	844	706
ELGUIT	61	GIBSON	**ES-355TD** MONO, AMERICAN VINTAGE	5,981	**4,424**	3,800	3,177
ELGUIT	64	GIBSON	**ES-355TD** CHERRY RED, MONO	2,206	**1,631**	1,401	1,171
ELGUIT	64	GIBSON	**ES-355TD** CHERRY RED, MONO, BIGSBY	2,354	**1,741**	1,496	1,251
ELGUIT	66	GIBSON	**ES-355TD** CHERRY RED, MONO, BIGSBY	2,120	**1,568**	1,347	1,126
ELGUIT	67	GIBSON	**ES-355TD** CHERRY RED, MONO, VIBRATO	1,949	**1,442**	1,238	1,035
ELGUIT	67	GIBSON	**ES-355TD** SUNBURST, MONO	1,957	**1,447**	1,243	1,039
ELGUIT	69	GIBSON	**ES-355TD** WALNUT, MONO	1,134	**839**	721	602
ELGUIT	72	GIBSON	**ES-355TD** WALNUT, MONO	1,177	**871**	748	625
ELGUIT	74	GIBSON	**ES-355TD** BURGUNDY	1,235	**913**	785	656
ELGUIT	67	GIBSON	**ES-355TDC** BURGUNDY, MONO	1,957	**1,447**	1,243	1,039
ELGUIT	79	GIBSON	**ES-355TDS THIN LINE**	795	**588**	505	422
ELGUIT	59	GIBSON	**ES-355TDSV** FLAMED, STEREO, VARITONE, PAFS	5,136	**3,798**	3,263	2,728
ELGUIT	60	GIBSON	**ES-355TDSV** CHERRY RED, STEREO, BIGSBY	5,280	**3,905**	3,355	2,805
ELGUIT	61	GIBSON	**ES-355TDSV** CHERRY RED, STEREO, BIGSBY, PAF'S	4,153	**3,072**	2,639	2,206
ELGUIT	62	GIBSON	**ES-355TDSV** CHERRY RED, STEREO, BIGSBY	4,342	**3,211**	2,759	2,306
ELGUIT	63	GIBSON	**ES-355TDSV** CHERRY RED, STEREO, BIGSBY	3,740	**2,766**	2,376	1,986
ELGUIT	64	GIBSON	**ES-355TDSV** CHERRY RED, STEREO, VIBRATO	3,157	**2,335**	2,006	1,677
ELGUIT	65	GIBSON	**ES-355TDSV** RED, STEREO	2,290	**1,694**	1,455	1,216
ELGUIT	66	GIBSON	**ES-355TDSV** CHERRY RED, STEREO, VIBRATO	2,150	**1,590**	1,366	1,142
ELGUIT	67	GIBSON	**ES-355TDSV** CHERRY RED, STEREO, VIBRATO	2,042	**1,510**	1,298	1,085
ELGUIT	68	GIBSON	**ES-355TDSV** CHERRY RED, STEREO, VIBRATO	1,832	**1,355**	1,164	973
ELGUIT	69	GIBSON	**ES-355TDSV** CHERRY RED, STEREO, VIBRATO	1,681	**1,243**	1,068	893
ELGUIT	70	GIBSON	**ES-355TDSV** CHERRY RED, STEREO, BIGSBY	944	**698**	600	501
ELGUIT	71	GIBSON	**ES-355TDSV** CHERRY RED, STEREO	958	**708**	608	508
ELGUIT	71	GIBSON	**ES-355TDSV** WALNUT	1,673	**1,237**	1,063	888
ELGUIT	72	GIBSON	**ES-355TDSV** CHERRY RED, STEREO, BIGSBY	930	**687**	591	494
ELGUIT	72	GIBSON	**ES-355TDSV** WALNUT, STEREO, BIGSBY	1,099	**812**	698	583
ELGUIT	74	GIBSON	**ES-355TDSV** CHERRY RED, STEREO, BIGSBY	881	**651**	559	468
ELGUIT	74	GIBSON	**ES-355TDSV** WALNUT, STEREO, BIGSBY	1,024	**757**	650	544
ELGUIT	79	GIBSON	**ES-355TDSV** SUNBURST, STEREO, VIBRATO	813	**601**	516	431
ELGUIT	81	GIBSON	**ES-369** SUNBURST	1,196	**884**	760	635
ELGUIT	82	GIBSON	**ES-369**	1,115	**825**	708	592
ELGUIT	78	GIBSON	**ES-555TDSV** BURGUNDY, STEREO	1,464	**1,083**	930	778
ELGUIT	79	GIBSON	**ES-ARTIST** BLACK, PEARL LOGO	1,684	**1,246**	1,070	895
ELGUIT	80	GIBSON	**ES-ARTIST** BLACK, PEARL LOGO	1,277	**945**	811	678

TYPE	YR	MFG	PRICES--BASED ON 100% ORIGINAL MODEL	SELL EXC	SELL AVG	BUY EXC	BUY AVG
ELGUIT	38	GIBSON	**EST-150** TENOR, 4-STRING	956	**707**	607	507
ELGUIT	40	GIBSON	**ETG-150** TENOR	1,195	**883**	759	634
ELGUIT	52	GIBSON	**ETG-150**	617	**456**	392	327
ELGUIT	55	GIBSON	**ETG-150** TENOR	910	**673**	578	483
ELGUIT	56	GIBSON	**ETG-150** TENOR	961	**711**	611	511
ELGUIT	57	GIBSON	**ETG-150** TENOR	897	**663**	570	476
ELGUIT	58	GIBSON	**ETG-150** TENOR	841	**622**	534	447
ELGUIT	62	GIBSON	**ETG-150**	587	**434**	373	312
ELGUIT	62	GIBSON	**ETG-150** TENOR	648	**479**	412	344
ELGUIT	66	GIBSON	**ETG-150** TENOR	617	**456**	392	327
ELGUIT	58	GIBSON	**EXPLORER** NATURAL, KORINA, SERIAL #A26500-A28000	84,284	**62,335**	53,555	44,775
ELGUIT	59	GIBSON	**EXPLORER** NATURAL, KORINA, SERIAL #A28000- (ONLY 3 SHIPPED IN 1959)	88,800	**65,675**	56,425	47,175
ELGUIT	63	GIBSON	**EXPLORER** NATURAL, KORINA	57,778	**42,732**	36,713	30,694
ELGUIT	76	GIBSON	**EXPLORER** NATURAL, MAHOGANY	830	**614**	527	441
ELGUIT	76	GIBSON	**EXPLORER** WHITE, MAHOGANY	954	**705**	606	506
ELGUIT	76	GIBSON	**EXPLORER** BLACK, MAHOGANY	984	**728**	625	523
ELGUIT	77	GIBSON	**EXPLORER** MAHOGANY	940	**695**	597	499
ELGUIT	78	GIBSON	**EXPLORER** MAHOGANY BODY	1,195	**883**	759	634
ELGUIT	79	GIBSON	**EXPLORER** WHITE, MAHOGANY	878	**649**	558	466
ELGUIT	79	GIBSON	**EXPLORER** NATURAL, MAHOGANY	905	**669**	575	480
ELGUIT	82	GIBSON	**EXPLORER** KORINA	1,958	**1,448**	1,244	1,040
ELGUIT	83	GIBSON	**EXPLORER** KORINA	2,184	**1,615**	1,387	1,160
ELGUIT	84	GIBSON	**EXPLORER** ALDER BODY	518	**383**	329	275
ELGUIT	85	GIBSON	**EXPLORER BASS** WHITE	438	**324**	278	233
ELGUIT	81	GIBSON	**EXPLORER HERITAGE** WHITE	1,584	**1,172**	1,007	842
ELGUIT	81	GIBSON	**EXPLORER HERITAGE** MAHOGANY	1,624	**1,201**	1,032	862
ELGUIT	83	GIBSON	**EXPLORER HERITAGE** WHITE	1,593	**1,178**	1,012	846
ELGUIT	83	GIBSON	**EXPLORER HERITAGE** NATURAL	2,013	**1,488**	1,279	1,069
ELGUIT	81	GIBSON	**EXPLORER II** SUNBURST, EBONY BOARD	569	**421**	361	302
ELGUIT	84	GIBSON	**EXPLORER III**	518	**383**	329	275
ELGUIT	65	GIBSON	**F- 25 FOLKSINGER** NATURAL, 12-FRET NECK	637	**471**	405	338
ELGUIT	76	GIBSON	**FIREBIRD BICENTENNIAL 76** BLACK	963	**712**	612	512
ELGUIT	76	GIBSON	**FIREBIRD BICENTENNIAL 76** NATURAL	1,217	**900**	773	646
ELGUIT	76	GIBSON	**FIREBIRD BICENTENNIAL 76** NATURAL, MAHOGANY	1,254	**927**	797	666
ELGUIT	76	GIBSON	**FIREBIRD BICENTENNIAL 76** SUNBURST	1,422	**1,052**	904	755
ELGUIT	63	GIBSON	**FIREBIRD I** GOLD, REVERSE	4,288	**3,171**	2,724	2,278
ELGUIT	63	GIBSON	**FIREBIRD I** SUNBURST, REVERSE	5,636	**4,168**	3,581	2,994
ELGUIT	64	GIBSON	**FIREBIRD I** SUNBURST, REVERSE	3,210	**2,374**	2,039	1,705
ELGUIT	64	GIBSON	**FIREBIRD I** POLARIS WHITE, REVERSE	4,282	**3,167**	2,721	2,275
ELGUIT	64	GIBSON	**FIREBIRD I** CARDINAL, REVERSE	4,416	**3,266**	2,806	2,346
ELGUIT	65	GIBSON	**FIREBIRD I** CARDINAL, NON-REVERSE	1,992	**1,473**	1,265	1,058
ELGUIT	65	GIBSON	**FIREBIRD I** SUNBURST, REVERSE	3,406	**2,519**	2,164	1,809
ELGUIT	65	GIBSON	**FIREBIRD I** GOLD, REVERSE	4,428	**3,275**	2,813	2,352

TYPE	YR	MFG	PRICES--BASED ON 100% ORIGINAL MODEL	SELL EXC	SELL AVG	BUY EXC	BUY AVG
ELGUIT	66	GIBSON	FIREBIRD I SUNBURST, NON-REVERSE	1,143	845	726	607
ELGUIT	67	GIBSON	FIREBIRD I SUNBURST, NON-REVERSE	1,064	787	676	565
ELGUIT	67	GIBSON	FIREBIRD I POLARIS WHITE, NON-REVERSE	1,071	792	680	569
ELGUIT	68	GIBSON	FIREBIRD I CARDINAL, NON-REVERSE	1,038	768	660	551
ELGUIT	68	GIBSON	FIREBIRD I SUNBURST, NON-REVERSE	1,066	788	677	566
ELGUIT	63	GIBSON	FIREBIRD III CARDINAL RED	6,240	4,615	3,965	3,315
ELGUIT	63	GIBSON	FIREBIRD III GOLD, REVERSE	6,499	4,806	4,129	3,452
ELGUIT	63	GIBSON	FIREBIRD III SUNBURST, REVERSE	7,507	5,552	4,770	3,988
ELGUIT	63	GIBSON	FIREBIRD III POLARIS WHITE, REVERSE	8,016	5,929	5,094	4,259
ELGUIT	63	GIBSON	FIREBIRD III FROST BLUE, REVERSE	8,032	5,940	5,103	4,267
ELGUIT	64	GIBSON	FIREBIRD III POLARIS WHITE, BIG NECK	4,977	3,681	3,162	2,644
ELGUIT	64	GIBSON	FIREBIRD III METALLIC BRONZE, REVERSE	7,501	5,547	4,766	3,985
ELGUIT	64	GIBSON	FIREBIRD III CARDINAL, REVERSE	7,501	5,547	4,766	3,985
ELGUIT	64	GIBSON	FIREBIRD III SUNBURST, REVERSE	7,595	5,617	4,826	4,035
ELGUIT	65	GIBSON	FIREBIRD III SUNBURST, NON-REVERSE	1,157	856	735	615
ELGUIT	65	GIBSON	FIREBIRD III CARDINAL, REVERSE	4,433	3,278	2,816	2,355
ELGUIT	65	GIBSON	FIREBIRD III FROST BLUE, REVERSE	4,560	3,373	2,898	2,423
ELGUIT	65	GIBSON	FIREBIRD III SUNBURST, REVERSE	7,354	5,439	4,673	3,907
ELGUIT	66	GIBSON	FIREBIRD III SUNBURST, NON-REVERSE	1,956	1,446	1,243	1,039
ELGUIT	66	GIBSON	FIREBIRD III POLARIS WHITE, REVERSE	8,282	6,125	5,263	4,400
ELGUIT	67	GIBSON	FIREBIRD III SUNBURST, NON-REVERSE	1,775	1,312	1,127	942
ELGUIT	67	GIBSON	FIREBIRD III PELHAM BLUE, NON-REVERSE	3,103	2,295	1,972	1,648
ELGUIT	68	GIBSON	FIREBIRD III SUNBURST, NON-REVERSE	1,774	1,312	1,127	942
ELGUIT	69	GIBSON	FIREBIRD III CARDINAL, NON-REVERSE	1,774	1,312	1,127	942
ELGUIT	59	GIBSON	FIREBIRD V CARDINAL, REVERSE	5,673	4,196	3,605	3,014
ELGUIT	63	GIBSON	FIREBIRD V SUNBURST, REVERSE	4,944	3,656	3,141	2,626
ELGUIT	63	GIBSON	FIREBIRD V PELHAM BLUE, REVERSE	5,812	4,299	3,693	3,088
ELGUIT	64	GIBSON	FIREBIRD V POLARIS WHITE, REVERSE	5,231	3,868	3,323	2,778
ELGUIT	64	GIBSON	FIREBIRD V CUSTOM ORANGE, REVERSE	6,247	4,620	3,969	3,319
ELGUIT	64	GIBSON	FIREBIRD V FROST BLUE, REVERSE	6,247	4,620	3,969	3,319
ELGUIT	64	GIBSON	FIREBIRD V SUNBURST, REVERSE	6,296	4,656	4,000	3,345
ELGUIT	65	GIBSON	FIREBIRD V SUNBURST, NON-REVERSE	1,474	1,090	936	783
ELGUIT	65	GIBSON	FIREBIRD V KELLY GREEN, REVERSE	5,147	3,807	3,270	2,734
ELGUIT	65	GIBSON	FIREBIRD V CARDNIAL RED, REVERSE	6,240	4,615	3,965	3,315
ELGUIT	66	GIBSON	FIREBIRD V SUNBURST, NON-REVERSE, 12-STRING	1,172	866	744	622
ELGUIT	67	GIBSON	FIREBIRD V SUNBURST, NON-REVERSE	1,774	1,312	1,127	942
ELGUIT	67	GIBSON	FIREBIRD V FROST BLUE, NON-REVERSE	1,777	1,314	1,129	944
ELGUIT	68	GIBSON	FIREBIRD V SUNBURST, NON-REVERSE	1,116	825	709	593
ELGUIT	71	GIBSON	FIREBIRD V MEDALLION SUNBURST, REVERSE	3,216	2,378	2,043	1,708
ELGUIT	72	GIBSON	FIREBIRD V MEDALLION SUNBURST, REVERSE	3,215	2,377	2,042	1,707
ELGUIT	73	GIBSON	FIREBIRD V MEDALLION LE REISSUE	1,763	1,304	1,120	936
ELGUIT	63	GIBSON	FIREBIRD VII SUNBURST, REVERSE	7,210	5,332	4,581	3,830

TYPE	YR	MFG	PRICES--BASED ON 100% ORIGINAL MODEL	SELL EXC	SELL AVG	BUY EXC	BUY AVG
ELGUIT	64	GIBSON	**FIREBIRD VII** SUNBURST, REVERSE	7,155	**5,292**	4,546	3,801
ELGUIT	64	GIBSON	**FIREBIRD VII** CARDINAL, REVERSE	9,055	**6,697**	5,754	4,810
ELGUIT	65	GIBSON	**FIREBIRD VII** SUNBURST, REVERSE	7,071	**5,229**	4,493	3,756
ELGUIT	68	GIBSON	**FIREBIRD VII** PELHAM BLUE, NON-REVERSE	3,899	**2,884**	2,477	2,071
ELGUIT	67	GIBSON	**FJ-N JUMBO FOLK SINGER**	696	**515**	442	370
ELGUIT	58	GIBSON	**FLYING V** NATURAL, KORINA, 2 PU's, SERIAL #A26500-A28000	73,037	**54,017**	46,409	38,801
ELGUIT	58	GIBSON	**FLYING V** KORINA "05"	75,216	**55,628**	47,793	39,958
ELGUIT	59	GIBSON	**FLYING V** NATURAL, KORINA, 2 PU's, SERIAL #A28000	72,488	**53,611**	46,060	38,509
ELGUIT	62	GIBSON	**FLYING V** NATURAL, KORINA, 2 PU's	29,476	**21,800**	18,730	15,659
ELGUIT	63	GIBSON	**FLYING V** NATURAL, KORINA, 2 PU's	27,663	**20,459**	17,577	14,696
ELGUIT	66	GIBSON	**FLYING V** SUNBURST, 2 PU's	4,800	**3,550**	3,050	2,550
ELGUIT	67	GIBSON	**FLYING V** TOBACCO SUNBURST, 2 PU's	3,468	**2,565**	2,203	1,842
ELGUIT	67	GIBSON	**FLYING V** CHERRY, 2 PU's	4,303	**3,182**	2,734	2,286
ELGUIT	71	GIBSON	**FLYING V** SUNBURST, MEDALLION, 2 PU's	1,131	**837**	719	601
ELGUIT	71	GIBSON	**FLYING V** CHERRY, MEDALLION, 2 PU's	2,905	**2,149**	1,846	1,543
ELGUIT	75	GIBSON	**FLYING V** BLACK, 2 PU's	574	**424**	364	304
ELGUIT	75	GIBSON	**FLYING V** NATURAL, MAHOGANY, 2 PU's	873	**646**	555	464
ELGUIT	76	GIBSON	**FLYING V** BLACK, 2 PU's	552	**408**	350	293
ELGUIT	76	GIBSON	**FLYING V** SUNBURST, 2 PU's	806	**596**	512	428
ELGUIT	76	GIBSON	**FLYING V** WHITE, 2 PU's	818	**605**	520	435
ELGUIT	76	GIBSON	**FLYING V** NATURAL, MAHOGANY, 2 PU's	864	**639**	549	459
ELGUIT	78	GIBSON	**FLYING V**	916	**678**	582	487
ELGUIT	79	GIBSON	**FLYING V** NATURAL, MAHOGANY, 2 PU's	868	**642**	552	461
ELGUIT	81	GIBSON	**FLYING V** SUNBURST, EBONY BOARD, 2 PU's	793	**587**	504	421
ELGUIT	82	GIBSON	**FLYING V** BLACK, KORINA BODY	1,394	**1,031**	886	741
ELGUIT	85	GIBSON	**FLYING V** ALDER BODY	537	**397**	341	285
ELGUIT	60	GIBSON	**FLYING V 1957 PROTOTYPE**	72,480	**53,605**	46,055	38,505
ELGUIT	83	GIBSON	**FLYING V HERITAGE** NATURAL	2,138	**1,581**	1,359	1,136
ELGUIT	79	GIBSON	**FLYING V II** NATURAL, V-SHAPED PU's	664	**491**	422	352
ELGUIT	81	GIBSON	**FLYING V II** V-SHAPED PU's	617	**456**	392	327
ELGUIT	82	GIBSON	**FLYING V** MAHOGANY	876	**648**	556	465
ELGUIT	72	GIBSON	**G-3 BASS** NATURAL	529	**391**	336	281
ELGUIT	74	GIBSON	**G-3 BASS** NATURAL	469	**347**	298	249
ELGUIT	76	GIBSON	**G-3 BASS** BLACK, SOLID MAPLE, 3 PU's	468	**346**	297	248
ELGUIT	78	GIBSON	**G-3 BASS** NATURAL, SOLID MAPLE, 3 PU's	468	**346**	297	248
ELGUIT	81	GIBSON	**G-3 BASS** NATURAL	456	**337**	290	242
ELGUIT	19	GIBSON	**GB-1**	1,076	**795**	683	571
ELGUIT	28	GIBSON	**GB-1**	996	**736**	633	529
ELGUIT	74	GIBSON	**GRABBER BASS** NATURAL	498	**368**	316	264
ELGUIT	75	GIBSON	**GRABBER BASS** SOLID MAPLE, 1 PU	466	**345**	296	247
ELGUIT	76	GIBSON	**GRABBER BASS** NATURAL	451	**333**	286	239
ELGUIT	77	GIBSON	**GRABBER BASS** SOLID MAPLE, 1 PU	420	**310**	267	223
ELGUIT	78	GIBSON	**GRABBER BASS** SOLID MAPLE, 1 PU	420	**310**	267	223
ELGUIT	78	GIBSON	**GRABBER BASS** BURGUNDY, MAPLE NECK	429	**317**	272	227

TYPE	YR	MFG	PRICES--BASED ON 100% ORIGINAL MODEL	SELL EXC	SELL AVG	BUY EXC	BUY AVG
ELGUIT	79	GIBSON	**GRABBER BASS** SOLID MAPLE, 1 PU	420	**310**	267	223
ELGUIT	79	GIBSON	**GRABBER BASS** BLACK, MAPLE	476	**352**	302	252
ELGUIT	66	GIBSON	**GRANADA** SUNBURST	469	**347**	298	249
ELGUIT	77	GIBSON	**HOWARD ROBERTS ARTIST** SUNBURST	1,250	**925**	794	664
ELGUIT	78	GIBSON	**HOWARD ROBERTS ARTIST** CHERRY RED	1,250	**925**	794	664
ELGUIT	78	GIBSON	**HOWARD ROBERTS ARTIST** SUNBURST	1,250	**925**	794	664
ELGUIT	79	GIBSON	**HOWARD ROBERTS ARTIST** SUNBURST	1,249	**924**	794	664
ELGUIT	74	GIBSON	**HOWARD ROBERTS CUSTOM** CHERRY RED	1,247	**922**	792	662
ELGUIT	74	GIBSON	**HOWARD ROBERTS CUSTOM** WINE RED	1,247	**922**	792	662
ELGUIT	78	GIBSON	**HOWARD ROBERTS FUSION** SUNBURST	1,244	**920**	790	660
ELGUIT	81	GIBSON	**HOWARD ROBERTS FUSION** SUNBURST	1,218	**900**	774	647
ELGUIT	61	GIBSON	**JOHNNY SMITH** NATURAL, 1 PU	8,787	**6,499**	5,583	4,668
ELGUIT	61	GIBSON	**JOHNNY SMITH** TORTOISE SUNBURST, 1 PU	8,788	**6,500**	5,584	4,669
ELGUIT	62	GIBSON	**JOHNNY SMITH** SUNBURST, 1 PU	8,395	**6,208**	5,334	4,459
ELGUIT	63	GIBSON	**JOHNNY SMITH** SUNBURST, 1 PU	8,295	**6,135**	5,271	4,406
ELGUIT	64	GIBSON	**JOHNNY SMITH** SUNBURST, 1 PU	8,195	**6,061**	5,207	4,353
ELGUIT	65	GIBSON	**JOHNNY SMITH** SUNBURST, 1 PU	6,964	**5,151**	4,425	3,700
ELGUIT	66	GIBSON	**JOHNNY SMITH** SUNBURST, 2 PU's	5,088	**3,763**	3,233	2,703
ELGUIT	67	GIBSON	**JOHNNY SMITH** SUNBURST, 1 PU	6,985	**5,166**	4,438	3,711
ELGUIT	68	GIBSON	**JOHNNY SMITH** SUNBURST, 1 PU	6,216	**4,597**	3,949	3,302
ELGUIT	68	GIBSON	**JOHNNY SMITH** NATURAL, 1 PU	6,744	**4,988**	4,285	3,583
ELGUIT	69	GIBSON	**JOHNNY SMITH** SUNBURST, 1 PU	6,012	**4,446**	3,820	3,194
ELGUIT	69	GIBSON	**JOHNNY SMITH** NATURAL, 1 PU	6,194	**4,581**	3,936	3,291
ELGUIT	72	GIBSON	**JOHNNY SMITH** SUNBURST, 1 PU	5,360	**3,964**	3,406	2,847
ELGUIT	74	GIBSON	**JOHNNY SMITH** SUNBURST, 1 PU	5,827	**4,309**	3,702	3,095
ELGUIT	76	GIBSON	**JOHNNY SMITH** BLOND, 1 PU	4,464	**3,301**	2,836	2,371
ELGUIT	76	GIBSON	**JOHNNY SMITH** SUNBURST, 1 PU	4,828	**3,571**	3,068	2,565
ELGUIT	77	GIBSON	**JOHNNY SMITH** SUNBURST, 1 PU	4,088	**3,023**	2,597	2,172
ELGUIT	78	GIBSON	**JOHNNY SMITH** SUNBURST, 1 PU	4,476	**3,310**	2,844	2,378
ELGUIT	79	GIBSON	**JOHNNY SMITH** SUNBURST, 1 PU	4,829	**3,572**	3,068	2,565
ELGUIT	81	GIBSON	**JOHNNY SMITH** FLAMED SUNBURST, 1 PU	5,016	**3,709**	3,187	2,664
ELGUIT	67	GIBSON	**JOHNNY SMITH D** SUNBURST, 2 PU's	6,319	**4,673**	4,015	3,357
ELGUIT	68	GIBSON	**JOHNNY SMITH D** SUNBURST, 2 PU's	6,961	**5,148**	4,423	3,698
ELGUIT	72	GIBSON	**JOHNNY SMITH D** SUNBURST, 2 PU's	5,361	**3,965**	3,406	2,848
ELGUIT	78	GIBSON	**JOHNNY SMITH D** NATURAL, 2 PU's	4,596	**3,399**	2,920	2,441
ELGUIT	70	GIBSON	**JOHNNY SMITH H** SUNBURST, 1 PU	5,361	**3,965**	3,406	2,848
ELGUIT	78	GIBSON	**JOHNNY SMITH SINGLE** CASE	1,952	**1,444**	1,240	1,037
ELGUIT	78	GIBSON	**KALAMAZOO AWARD MODEL** NATURAL	5,760	**4,260**	3,660	3,060
ELGUIT	51	GIBSON	**L- 5CES** NATURAL	8,170	**6,042**	5,191	4,340
ELGUIT	51	GIBSON	**L- 5CES** SUNBURST, SERIAL #A6000-A9400	9,879	**7,306**	6,277	5,248
ELGUIT	53	GIBSON	**L- 5CES**	9,599	**7,099**	6,099	5,099
ELGUIT	55	GIBSON	**L- 5CES** SUNBURST, SERIAL #A19000-A22000	8,101	**5,991**	5,147	4,303

TYPE	YR	MFG	PRICES--BASED ON 100% ORIGINAL MODEL	SELL EXC	SELL AVG	BUY EXC	BUY AVG
ELGUIT	56	GIBSON	**L- 5CES** NATURAL, P-90 PU	7,910	**5,850**	5,026	4,202
ELGUIT	57	GIBSON	**L- 5CES** SUNBURST	9,485	**7,015**	6,027	5,039
ELGUIT	60	GIBSON	**L- 5CES** SUNBURST, ROUNDED CUTAWAY	8,489	**6,278**	5,394	4,509
ELGUIT	61	GIBSON	**L- 5CES** NATURAL, PAF PU	9,895	**7,318**	6,287	5,257
ELGUIT	62	GIBSON	**L- 5CES** SUNBURST, FLORENTINE CUTAWAY, 2 PU's, INLAY	8,496	**6,283**	5,398	4,513
ELGUIT	63	GIBSON	**L- 5CES** SUNBURST	8,442	**6,243**	5,364	4,484
ELGUIT	64	GIBSON	**L- 5CES** SUNBURST, POINTED CUTAWAY	8,442	**6,243**	5,364	4,484
ELGUIT	65	GIBSON	**L- 5CES** NATURAL	6,426	**4,752**	4,083	3,413
ELGUIT	65	GIBSON	**L- 5CES** SUNBURST	6,685	**4,944**	4,248	3,551
ELGUIT	67	GIBSON	**L- 5CES** SUNBURST	6,406	**4,737**	4,070	3,403
ELGUIT	68	GIBSON	**L- 5CES** NATURAL	5,356	**3,961**	3,403	2,845
ELGUIT	68	GIBSON	**L- 5CES** SUNBURST, SHARP CUTAWAY	5,952	**4,402**	3,782	3,162
ELGUIT	69	GIBSON	**L- 5CES** NATURAL	5,353	**3,959**	3,401	2,844
ELGUIT	69	GIBSON	**L- 5CES** SUNBURST	5,851	**4,327**	3,717	3,108
ELGUIT	69	GIBSON	**L- 5CES** BLOND	7,720	**5,709**	4,905	4,101
ELGUIT	70	GIBSON	**L- 5CES** NATURAL	4,803	**3,552**	3,052	2,552
ELGUIT	70	GIBSON	**L- 5CES** SUNBURST	5,731	**4,238**	3,641	3,044
ELGUIT	71	GIBSON	**L- 5CES** NATURAL	4,424	**3,272**	2,811	2,350
ELGUIT	71	GIBSON	**L- 5CES** SUNBURST	5,508	**4,073**	3,500	2,926
ELGUIT	72	GIBSON	**L- 5CES** SUNBURST	4,997	**3,696**	3,175	2,655
ELGUIT	73	GIBSON	**L- 5CES** SUNBURST	5,032	**3,721**	3,197	2,673
ELGUIT	74	GIBSON	**L- 5CES** NATURAL	3,762	**2,782**	2,390	1,998
ELGUIT	75	GIBSON	**L- 5CES** SUNBURST	5,024	**3,716**	3,192	2,669
ELGUIT	76	GIBSON	**L- 5CES** SUNBURST, ARCHTOP	4,866	**3,598**	3,092	2,585
ELGUIT	77	GIBSON	**L- 5CES** NATURAL	3,762	**2,782**	2,390	1,998
ELGUIT	77	GIBSON	**L- 5CES** BURGUNDY	4,294	**3,175**	2,728	2,281
ELGUIT	77	GIBSON	**L- 5CES** SUNBURST	4,740	**3,505**	3,012	2,518
ELGUIT	78	GIBSON	**L- 5CES** SUNBURST	4,720	**3,491**	2,999	2,507
ELGUIT	79	GIBSON	**L- 5CES** ANTIQUE SUNBURST	3,907	**2,889**	2,482	2,075
ELGUIT	69	GIBSON	**L- 5CESN** BLOND	6,624	**4,899**	4,209	3,519
ELGUIT	77	GIBSON	**L- 5CESN** ARCHTOP	6,680	**4,940**	4,244	3,549
ELGUIT	84	GIBSON	**L- 5CESN 50TH ANNIVERSARY** BLOND	4,880	**3,609**	3,101	2,592
ELGUIT	72	GIBSON	**L- 5S** CHERRY SUNBURST, CUTAWAY	3,094	**2,288**	1,966	1,643
ELGUIT	73	GIBSON	**L- 5S** CHERRY SUNBURST, CUTAWAY	1,670	**1,235**	1,061	887
ELGUIT	74	GIBSON	**L- 5S** CHERRY SUNBURST, CUTAWAY	1,672	**1,236**	1,062	888
ELGUIT	75	GIBSON	**L- 5S** CHERRY SUNBURST, CUTAWAY, HUMBUCKER	1,507	**1,114**	957	800
ELGUIT	76	GIBSON	**L- 5S** CHERRY SUNBURST, CUTAWAY	1,507	**1,114**	957	800
ELGUIT	76	GIBSON	**L- 5S** NATURAL	1,793	**1,326**	1,139	952
ELGUIT	76	GIBSON	**L- 5S** NATURAL, CUTAWAY	1,819	**1,345**	1,155	966
ELGUIT	77	GIBSON	**L- 5S** CHERRY SUNBURST, CUTAWAY	1,508	**1,115**	958	801
ELGUIT	77	GIBSON	**L- 5S** NATURAL, CUTAWAY	1,789	**1,323**	1,137	950
ELGUIT	78	GIBSON	**L- 5S** CHERRY SUNBURST, CUTAWAY	1,507	**1,114**	957	800

TYPE	YR	MFG	PRICES--BASED ON 100% ORIGINAL MODEL	SELL EXC	SELL AVG	BUY EXC	BUY AVG
ELGUIT	78	GIBSON	**L- 5S** NATURAL, CUTAWAY	1,861	**1,376**	1,182	988
ELGUIT	79	GIBSON	**L- 5S** NATURAL, CUTAWAY	1,830	**1,353**	1,163	972
ELGUIT	70	GIBSON	**L- 6S** BLACK	469	**347**	298	249
ELGUIT	72	GIBSON	**L- 6S** NATURAL	464	**343**	295	246
ELGUIT	72	GIBSON	**L- 6S** BLACK	469	**347**	298	249
ELGUIT	73	GIBSON	**L- 6S** BLACK	421	**311**	267	223
ELGUIT	75	GIBSON	**L- 6S** NATURAL	435	**322**	276	231
ELGUIT	75	GIBSON	**L- 6S** BLACK	469	**347**	298	249
ELGUIT	75	GIBSON	**L- 6S**	478	**353**	303	253
ELGUIT	78	GIBSON	**L- 6S** NATURAL	480	**355**	305	255
ELGUIT	80	GIBSON	**L- 6S** SUNBURST	477	**352**	303	253
ELGUIT	75	GIBSON	**L- 6S CUSTOM** BLACK	478	**353**	303	253
ELGUIT	77	GIBSON	**L- 6S CUSTOM** NATURAL	468	**346**	297	248
ELGUIT	78	GIBSON	**L- 6S CUSTOM** SUNBURST	431	**318**	273	228
ELGUIT	78	GIBSON	**L- 6S CUSTOM** BLACK	470	**347**	298	249
ELGUIT	78	GIBSON	**L- 6S CUSTOM** NATURAL	553	**409**	351	294
ELGUIT	79	GIBSON	**L- 6S CUSTOM**	557	**412**	354	296
ELGUIT	74	GIBSON	**L- 6S DELUXE** NATURAL	495	**366**	314	263
ELGUIT	75	GIBSON	**L- 6S DELUXE** NATURAL	495	**366**	314	263
ELGUIT	76	GIBSON	**L- 6S DELUXE** BLACK	438	**324**	278	233
ELGUIT	80	GIBSON	**L- 6S DELUXE**	518	**383**	329	275
ELGUIT	36	GIBSON	**L-C/CENTURY**	2,390	**1,767**	1,518	1,269
ELGUIT	55	GIBSON	**LES PAUL** TV MAHOGANY, SINGLE CUTAWAY	3,588	**2,653**	2,280	1,906
ELGUIT	56	GIBSON	**LES PAUL** TV MAHOGANY, SINGLE CUTAWAY	3,611	**2,671**	2,294	1,918
ELGUIT	57	GIBSON	**LES PAUL** TV MAHOGANY, SINGLE CUTAWAY	3,788	**2,801**	2,407	2,012
ELGUIT	58	GIBSON	**LES PAUL** TV MAHOGANY, DOUBLE CUTAWAY	4,032	**2,982**	2,562	2,142
ELGUIT	59	GIBSON	**LES PAUL** TV MAHOGANY, DOUBLE CUTAWAY	4,118	**3,045**	2,616	2,187
ELGUIT	60	GIBSON	**LES PAUL** TV MAHOGANY, DOUBLE CUTAWAY	3,383	**2,502**	2,149	1,797
ELGUIT	77	GIBSON	**LES PAUL 25 50th ANNIVERSARY** SUNBURST	1,405	**1,039**	893	746
ELGUIT	77	GIBSON	**LES PAUL 25 50th ANNIVERSARY** NATURAL	1,410	**1,042**	896	749
ELGUIT	78	GIBSON	**LES PAUL 25 50th ANNIVERSARY** WINE RED	1,160	**858**	737	616
ELGUIT	78	GIBSON	**LES PAUL 25 50th ANNIVERSARY** NATURAL	1,386	**1,025**	880	736
ELGUIT	78	GIBSON	**LES PAUL 25 50th ANNIVERSARY** TOBACCO SUNBURST	1,541	**1,140**	979	819
ELGUIT	78	GIBSON	**LES PAUL 25 50th ANNIVERSARY** CHERRY SUNBURST	1,554	**1,149**	987	825
ELGUIT	79	GIBSON	**LES PAUL 25 50th ANNIVERSARY** ANTIQUE	1,313	**971**	834	697
ELGUIT	79	GIBSON	**LES PAUL 25 50th ANNIVERSARY** SUNBURST	1,347	**996**	856	716
ELGUIT	79	GIBSON	**LES PAUL 25 50th ANNIVERSARY** NATURAL	1,489	**1,101**	946	791
ELGUIT	79	GIBSON	**LES PAUL 25 50th ANNIVERSARY** WINE RED	1,542	**1,140**	980	819
ELGUIT	76	GIBSON	**LES PAUL ARTISAN** WALNUT, 3 PU's	1,427	**1,055**	907	758
ELGUIT	77	GIBSON	**LES PAUL ARTISAN** WALNUT, 3 PU's, GOLD HARDWARE	1,202	**889**	764	639
ELGUIT	78	GIBSON	**LES PAUL ARTISAN** BLACK, 3 PU's	1,423	**1,052**	904	756
ELGUIT	78	GIBSON	**LES PAUL ARTISAN** WALNUT	1,469	**1,087**	933	780
ELGUIT	78	GIBSON	**LES PAUL ARTISAN** TOBACCO SUNBURST	1,541	**1,140**	979	819
ELGUIT	79	GIBSON	**LES PAUL ARTISAN** TOBACCO SUNBURST, 3 PU's	1,504	**1,112**	955	799

TYPE	YR	MFG	PRICES--BASED ON 100% ORIGINAL MODEL	SELL EXC	SELL AVG	BUY EXC	BUY AVG
ELGUIT	79	GIBSON	LES PAUL ARTISAN BLACK, 3 PU's	1,509	**1,116**	958	801
ELGUIT	80	GIBSON	LES PAUL ARTISAN SUNBURST, 2 PU's	1,272	**940**	808	675
ELGUIT	80	GIBSON	LES PAUL ARTISAN BLACK	1,383	**1,023**	879	734
ELGUIT	81	GIBSON	LES PAUL ARTISAN TOBACCO SUNBURST	1,356	**1,003**	861	720
ELGUIT	69	GIBSON	LES PAUL BASS NATURAL, TRIUMPH BASS	960	**710**	610	510
ELGUIT	70	GIBSON	LES PAUL BASS WALNUT, SOLID MAHOGANY	844	**624**	536	448
ELGUIT	72	GIBSON	LES PAUL BASS WALNUT	808	**597**	513	429
ELGUIT	73	GIBSON	LES PAUL BASS NATURAL, WALNUT	813	**601**	516	431
ELGUIT	54	GIBSON	LES PAUL CUSTOM EBONY, GOLD HARDWARE, 2 PU's	7,561	**5,592**	4,804	4,017
ELGUIT	55	GIBSON	LES PAUL CUSTOM EBONY, GOLD HARDWARE, 2 PU's	6,969	**5,154**	4,428	3,702
ELGUIT	55	GIBSON	LES PAUL CUSTOM BLACK	7,003	**5,179**	4,449	3,720
ELGUIT	55	GIBSON	LES PAUL CUSTOM EBONY, LEFT-HANDED	7,918	**5,856**	5,031	4,206
ELGUIT	56	GIBSON	LES PAUL CUSTOM EBONY, GOLD HARDWARE, 2 PU's	6,746	**4,989**	4,287	3,584
ELGUIT	56	GIBSON	LES PAUL CUSTOM BLACK, BIGSBY, 2 PU's	6,988	**5,168**	4,440	3,712
ELGUIT	56	GIBSON	LES PAUL CUSTOM NATURAL	9,408	**6,958**	5,978	4,998
ELGUIT	57	GIBSON	LES PAUL CUSTOM EBONY, GOLD HARDWARE, 2 PU's	6,720	**4,970**	4,270	3,570
ELGUIT	57	GIBSON	LES PAUL CUSTOM EBONY, GOLD HARDWARE, 3 PU's	9,574	**7,080**	6,083	5,086
ELGUIT	58	GIBSON	LES PAUL CUSTOM EBONY, GOLD HARDWARE, 3 PU's	9,357	**6,920**	5,945	4,970
ELGUIT	58	GIBSON	LES PAUL CUSTOM BLACK	9,403	**6,954**	5,974	4,995
ELGUIT	59	GIBSON	LES PAUL CUSTOM EBONY, GOLD HARDWARE, 3 PU's	9,574	**7,080**	6,083	5,086
ELGUIT	59	GIBSON	LES PAUL CUSTOM BLACK	9,823	**7,265**	6,242	5,218
ELGUIT	60	GIBSON	LES PAUL CUSTOM EBONY, GOLD HARDWARE, 3 PU's	9,520	**7,041**	6,049	5,057
ELGUIT	61	GIBSON	LES PAUL CUSTOM WHITE, 3 PU's, VIB, 3 PAF'S	4,661	**3,447**	2,962	2,476
ELGUIT	62	GIBSON	LES PAUL CUSTOM WHITE, 3 PU's, VIB	5,182	**3,832**	3,292	2,752
ELGUIT	68	GIBSON	LES PAUL CUSTOM BLACK, GOLD HARDWARE, 2 PU's	4,128	**3,053**	2,623	2,193
ELGUIT	69	GIBSON	LES PAUL CUSTOM BLACK, GOLD HARDWARE, 2 PU's, 3 PIECE NECK	2,928	**2,165**	1,860	1,555
ELGUIT	70	GIBSON	LES PAUL CUSTOM BLACK, GOLD HARDWARE, 2 PU's, VALITE NECK MADE IN USA	1,418	**1,049**	901	753
ELGUIT	71	GIBSON	LES PAUL CUSTOM BLACK, GOLD HARDWARE, 2 PU's	1,463	**1,082**	929	777
ELGUIT	71	GIBSON	LES PAUL CUSTOM CHERRY SUNBURST, 2 PU's	1,545	**1,143**	982	821
ELGUIT	71	GIBSON	LES PAUL CUSTOM BLACK, LEFT-HANDED	1,891	**1,398**	1,201	1,004
ELGUIT	72	GIBSON	LES PAUL CUSTOM TOBACCO SUNBURST	1,316	**973**	836	699
ELGUIT	72	GIBSON	LES PAUL CUSTOM BLACK, GOLD HARDWARE, 2 PU's	1,332	**985**	846	707
ELGUIT	72	GIBSON	LES PAUL CUSTOM CHERRY SUNBURST, 2 PU's	1,759	**1,301**	1,118	934
ELGUIT	73	GIBSON	LES PAUL CUSTOM CHERRY SUNBURST	1,375	**1,017**	874	730
ELGUIT	73	GIBSON	LES PAUL CUSTOM BLACK, 2 PU's	1,434	**1,060**	911	761
ELGUIT	74	GIBSON	LES PAUL CUSTOM CHERRY SUNBURST, 2 PU's	1,104	**816**	701	586
ELGUIT	75	GIBSON	LES PAUL CUSTOM BLACK, GOLD HARDWARE, 2 PU's	1,090	**806**	692	579
ELGUIT	75	GIBSON	LES PAUL CUSTOM CHERRY SUNBURST, 2 PU's	1,104	**817**	702	587
ELGUIT	75	GIBSON	LES PAUL CUSTOM WINE RED	1,110	**821**	705	590
ELGUIT	75	GIBSON	LES PAUL CUSTOM WHITE, GOLD HARDWARE, 2 PU's	1,299	**961**	825	690
ELGUIT	75	GIBSON	LES PAUL CUSTOM SUNBURST	1,354	**1,001**	860	719
ELGUIT	76	GIBSON	LES PAUL CUSTOM NATURAL, 2 PU's	1,007	**744**	639	534

TYPE	YR	MFG	PRICES--BASED ON 100% ORIGINAL MODEL	SELL EXC	SELL AVG	BUY EXC	BUY AVG
ELGUIT	76	GIBSON	**LES PAUL CUSTOM** WINE RED	1,083	**801**	688	575
ELGUIT	76	GIBSON	**LES PAUL CUSTOM** CHERRY SUNBURST, 2 PU's	1,094	**809**	695	581
ELGUIT	76	GIBSON	**LES PAUL CUSTOM** TOBACCO SUNBURST	1,098	**812**	697	583
ELGUIT	76	GIBSON	**LES PAUL CUSTOM** BLACK, GOLD HARDWARE, 2 PU's	1,103	**815**	700	585
ELGUIT	77	GIBSON	**LES PAUL CUSTOM** CHERRY SUNBURST, 2 PU's	1,064	**787**	676	565
ELGUIT	77	GIBSON	**LES PAUL CUSTOM** BLACK, GOLD HARDWARE, 2 PU's	1,103	**815**	700	585
ELGUIT	78	GIBSON	**LES PAUL CUSTOM** CHROME HARDWARE	956	**707**	607	507
ELGUIT	78	GIBSON	**LES PAUL CUSTOM** NATURAL, 2 PU's	992	**734**	630	527
ELGUIT	78	GIBSON	**LES PAUL CUSTOM** WINE RED, 2 PU's	1,084	**802**	689	576
ELGUIT	78	GIBSON	**LES PAUL CUSTOM** BLACK, GOLD HARDWARE, 2 PU's	1,085	**803**	689	576
ELGUIT	78	GIBSON	**LES PAUL CUSTOM** CHERRY SUNBURST, 2 PU's	1,089	**805**	692	578
ELGUIT	78	GIBSON	**LES PAUL CUSTOM** TOBACCO SUNBURST	1,089	**805**	692	578
ELGUIT	78	GIBSON	**LES PAUL CUSTOM** WHITE, GOLD HARDWARE, 2 PU's	1,253	**927**	796	666
ELGUIT	78	GIBSON	**LES PAUL CUSTOM** BLACK, LEFT-HANDED	1,281	**947**	814	680
ELGUIT	79	GIBSON	**LES PAUL CUSTOM** NATURAL, 2 PU's	1,001	**740**	636	531
ELGUIT	79	GIBSON	**LES PAUL CUSTOM** WINE RED	1,050	**776**	667	557
ELGUIT	79	GIBSON	**LES PAUL CUSTOM** CHERRY SUNBURST, 2 PU's	1,090	**806**	692	579
ELGUIT	79	GIBSON	**LES PAUL CUSTOM** CREAM, GOLD HARDWARE, 2 PU's	1,098	**812**	697	583
ELGUIT	79	GIBSON	**LES PAUL CUSTOM** BLACK, GOLD HARDWARE, 2 PU's	1,244	**920**	790	660
ELGUIT	79	GIBSON	**LES PAUL CUSTOM** SILVERBURST	1,292	**955**	821	686
ELGUIT	80	GIBSON	**LES PAUL CUSTOM** NATURAL, GOLD HARDWARE	1,002	**741**	636	532
ELGUIT	80	GIBSON	**LES PAUL CUSTOM** WINE RED	1,085	**803**	689	576
ELGUIT	80	GIBSON	**LES PAUL CUSTOM** WHITE, GOLD HARDWARE	1,088	**805**	691	578
ELGUIT	81	GIBSON	**LES PAUL CUSTOM** WINE RED	1,080	**798**	686	573
ELGUIT	81	GIBSON	**LES PAUL CUSTOM** BURGUNDY	1,082	**800**	688	575
ELGUIT	81	GIBSON	**LES PAUL CUSTOM** WINE RED, LEFT-HANDED	1,167	**863**	741	620
ELGUIT	82	GIBSON	**LES PAUL CUSTOM** TOBACCO SUNBURST	980	**724**	622	520
ELGUIT	86	GIBSON	**LES PAUL CUSTOM** SUNBURST	1,290	**954**	819	685
ELGUIT	86	GIBSON	**LES PAUL CUSTOM** BLACK	1,310	**969**	832	696
ELGUIT	72	GIBSON	**LES PAUL CUSTOM '54** 1954 REISSUE	1,793	**1,326**	1,139	952
ELGUIT	73	GIBSON	**LES PAUL CUSTOM '54** 1954 REISSUE	1,778	**1,315**	1,130	945
ELGUIT	74	GIBSON	**LES PAUL CUSTOM 20th ANNIVERSARY** WINE RED	1,347	**996**	856	716
ELGUIT	74	GIBSON	**LES PAUL CUSTOM 20th ANNIVERSARY** SUNBURST	1,550	**1,146**	985	823
ELGUIT	74	GIBSON	**LES PAUL CUSTOM 20th ANNIVERSARY** BLACK	1,753	**1,297**	1,114	931
ELGUIT	74	GIBSON	**LES PAUL CUSTOM 20th ANNIVERSARY** WHITE, RANDY RHONDEL STYLE	1,915	**1,416**	1,216	1,017
ELGUIT	68	GIBSON	**LES PAUL DELUXE** GOLD TOP	3,552	**2,627**	2,257	1,887
ELGUIT	69	GIBSON	**LES PAUL DELUXE** CHERRY SUNBURST	1,908	**1,411**	1,212	1,013
ELGUIT	69	GIBSON	**LES PAUL DELUXE** CHERRY SUNBURST, LEFT-HANDED	1,976	**1,461**	1,255	1,050
ELGUIT	69	GIBSON	**LES PAUL DELUXE** GOLD TOP	2,222	**1,643**	1,412	1,180
ELGUIT	70	GIBSON	**LES PAUL DELUXE** CHERRY SUNBURST	1,078	**797**	685	572
ELGUIT	70	GIBSON	**LES PAUL DELUXE** GOLD TOP	1,593	**1,178**	1,012	846
ELGUIT	70	GIBSON	**LES PAUL DELUXE** CHERRY SUNBURST, LEFT-HANDED	1,772	**1,310**	1,126	941

TYPE	YR	MFG	PRICES--BASED ON 100% ORIGINAL MODEL	SELL EXC	SELL AVG	BUY EXC	BUY AVG
ELGUIT	71	GIBSON	LES PAUL DELUXE GOLD TOP	1,244	920	790	660
ELGUIT	71	GIBSON	LES PAUL DELUXE WINE RED	1,260	932	800	669
ELGUIT	71	GIBSON	LES PAUL DELUXE NATURAL, SERIAL # 678381	1,352	1,000	859	718
ELGUIT	71	GIBSON	LES PAUL DELUXE TOBACCO SUNBURST	1,528	1,130	971	811
ELGUIT	72	GIBSON	LES PAUL DELUXE GOLD TOP	1,173	867	745	623
ELGUIT	72	GIBSON	LES PAUL DELUXE CHERRY SUNBURST	1,196	884	760	635
ELGUIT	72	GIBSON	LES PAUL DELUXE SUNBURST	1,291	954	820	685
ELGUIT	72	GIBSON	LES PAUL DELUXE GOLD TOP, LEFT-HANDED	1,400	1,035	889	744
ELGUIT	73	GIBSON	LES PAUL DELUXE SUNBURST	1,131	837	719	601
ELGUIT	73	GIBSON	LES PAUL DELUXE NATURAL	1,305	965	829	693
ELGUIT	73	GIBSON	LES PAUL DELUXE GOLD TOP	1,363	1,008	866	724
ELGUIT	73	GIBSON	LES PAUL DELUXE CHERRY SUNBURST	1,642	1,214	1,043	872
ELGUIT	74	GIBSON	LES PAUL DELUXE GOLD TOP	1,442	1,067	916	766
ELGUIT	74	GIBSON	LES PAUL DELUXE CHERRY SUNBURST	1,490	1,102	947	792
ELGUIT	74	GIBSON	LES PAUL DELUXE RED SPARKLE	2,897	2,142	1,840	1,539
ELGUIT	74	GIBSON	LES PAUL DELUXE BLUE SPARKLE	3,349	2,477	2,128	1,779
ELGUIT	75	GIBSON	LES PAUL DELUXE WINE RED	1,011	748	642	537
ELGUIT	75	GIBSON	LES PAUL DELUXE GOLD TOP	1,256	929	798	667
ELGUIT	75	GIBSON	LES PAUL DELUXE NATURAL	1,314	971	835	698
ELGUIT	75	GIBSON	LES PAUL DELUXE BLUE SPARKLE	3,360	2,485	2,135	1,785
ELGUIT	76	GIBSON	LES PAUL DELUXE SUNBURST	871	644	553	463
ELGUIT	76	GIBSON	LES PAUL DELUXE WINE RED	1,002	741	636	532
ELGUIT	76	GIBSON	LES PAUL DELUXE TOBACCO SUNBURST	1,008	745	640	535
ELGUIT	76	GIBSON	LES PAUL DELUXE BURGUNDY	1,084	802	689	576
ELGUIT	76	GIBSON	LES PAUL DELUXE NATURAL	1,141	844	725	606
ELGUIT	76	GIBSON	LES PAUL DELUXE GOLD TOP	1,176	870	747	625
ELGUIT	77	GIBSON	LES PAUL DELUXE SUNBURST, 2 MINI PU's	892	660	567	474
ELGUIT	77	GIBSON	LES PAUL DELUXE WINE RED	912	674	579	484
ELGUIT	77	GIBSON	LES PAUL DELUXE BLACK	1,078	797	685	572
ELGUIT	77	GIBSON	LES PAUL DELUXE NATURAL, BLOND	1,254	927	797	666
ELGUIT	78	GIBSON	LES PAUL DELUXE SUNBURST	862	637	547	457
ELGUIT	78	GIBSON	LES PAUL DELUXE WINE RED	864	639	549	459
ELGUIT	78	GIBSON	LES PAUL DELUXE CHERRY SUNBURST	929	687	590	493
ELGUIT	78	GIBSON	LES PAUL DELUXE LEFT-HANDED	956	707	607	507
ELGUIT	78	GIBSON	LES PAUL DELUXE GOLD TOP	1,388	1,026	882	737
ELGUIT	79	GIBSON	LES PAUL DELUXE SUNBURST	855	632	543	454
ELGUIT	79	GIBSON	LES PAUL DELUXE GOLD TOP	880	651	559	467
ELGUIT	79	GIBSON	LES PAUL DELUXE BLACK, CREAM TRIM	1,031	762	655	547
ELGUIT	79	GIBSON	LES PAUL DELUXE WINE RED	1,115	825	708	592
ELGUIT	80	GIBSON	LES PAUL DELUXE SUNBURST	752	556	478	399
ELGUIT	52	GIBSON	LES PAUL GOLD TOP TRAPEZE BRIDGE	5,280	3,905	3,355	2,805
ELGUIT	53	GIBSON	LES PAUL GOLD TOP TRAPEZE BRIDGE	4,560	3,372	2,897	2,422

TYPE	YR	MFG	PRICES--BASED ON 100% ORIGINAL MODEL	SELL EXC	SELL AVG	BUY EXC	BUY AVG
ELGUIT	53	GIBSON	**LES PAUL GOLD TOP** STUD BRIDGE	8,880	**6,567**	5,642	4,717
ELGUIT	54	GIBSON	**LES PAUL GOLD TOP** STUD BRIDGE	8,173	**6,044**	5,193	4,342
ELGUIT	55	GIBSON	**LES PAUL GOLD TOP** TUNE-O-MATIC	8,771	**6,487**	5,573	4,659
ELGUIT	55	GIBSON	**LES PAUL GOLD TOP** STUD BRIDGE	8,978	**6,640**	5,705	4,770
ELGUIT	56	GIBSON	**LES PAUL GOLD TOP** TUNE-O-MATIC	8,921	**6,598**	5,668	4,739
ELGUIT	57	GIBSON	**LES PAUL GOLD TOP** 2 HB PU's	15,600	**11,538**	9,913	8,288
ELGUIT	58	GIBSON	**LES PAUL GOLD TOP** 2 HB PU's	22,964	**16,983**	14,591	12,199
ELGUIT	68	GIBSON	**LES PAUL GOLD TOP** 2 P-90's	5,087	**3,762**	3,232	2,702
ELGUIT	71	GIBSON	**LES PAUL GOLD TOP** CREAM	3,372	**2,494**	2,142	1,791
ELGUIT	81	GIBSON	**LES PAUL HERITAGE 80** BLACK	1,834	**1,356**	1,165	974
ELGUIT	81	GIBSON	**LES PAUL HERITAGE 80** CHERRY SUNBURST	2,921	**2,160**	1,856	1,551
ELGUIT	81	GIBSON	**LES PAUL HERITAGE 80 ELITE** SUNBURST	2,352	**1,739**	1,494	1,249
ELGUIT	82	GIBSON	**LES PAUL HERITAGE 80 ELITE**	1,793	**1,326**	1,139	952
ELGUIT	82	GIBSON	**LES PAUL HERITAGE AWARD** CHERRY SUNBURST, GOLD HARDWARE	2,191	**1,620**	1,392	1,164
ELGUIT	69	GIBSON	**LES PAUL JUMBO** CUTAWAY	1,077	**796**	684	572
ELGUIT	70	GIBSON	**LES PAUL JUMBO** CUTAWAY	1,256	**929**	798	667
ELGUIT	54	GIBSON	**LES PAUL JUNIOR** SUNBURST, SINGLE CUTAWAY	1,957	**1,447**	1,243	1,039
ELGUIT	55	GIBSON	**LES PAUL JUNIOR** SUNBURST, SINGLE CUTAWAY	1,722	**1,273**	1,094	914
ELGUIT	56	GIBSON	**LES PAUL JUNIOR** SUNBURST, SINGLE CUTAWAY	2,036	**1,505**	1,293	1,081
ELGUIT	57	GIBSON	**LES PAUL JUNIOR** CHERRY RED, SINGLE CUTAWAY	1,752	**1,296**	1,113	931
ELGUIT	57	GIBSON	**LES PAUL JUNIOR** SUNBURST, SINGLE CUTAWAY	2,038	**1,507**	1,295	1,082
ELGUIT	57	GIBSON	**LES PAUL JUNIOR** TV	4,408	**3,260**	2,801	2,341
ELGUIT	58	GIBSON	**LES PAUL JUNIOR** CHERRY RED, DOUBLE CUTAWAY	1,709	**1,264**	1,086	908
ELGUIT	58	GIBSON	**LES PAUL JUNIOR** SUNBURST, SINGLE CUTAWAY	1,963	**1,451**	1,247	1,042
ELGUIT	59	GIBSON	**LES PAUL JUNIOR** SUNBURST, SINGLE CUTAWAY	1,744	**1,290**	1,108	926
ELGUIT	59	GIBSON	**LES PAUL JUNIOR** CHERRY RED, DOUBLE CUTAWAY	1,801	**1,332**	1,144	957
ELGUIT	59	GIBSON	**LES PAUL JUNIOR** TV MAHOGANY, DOUBLE CUTAWAY	4,019	**2,972**	2,554	2,135
ELGUIT	60	GIBSON	**LES PAUL JUNIOR** CHERRY RED, DOUBLE CUTAWAY	1,608	**1,189**	1,021	854
ELGUIT	60	GIBSON	**LES PAUL JUNIOR** TV YELLOW, SLIM NECK	4,478	**3,312**	2,845	2,379
ELGUIT	61	GIBSON	**LES PAUL JUNIOR** CHERRY RED, SINGLE CUTAWAY	1,212	**896**	770	644
ELGUIT	62	GIBSON	**LES PAUL JUNIOR** CHERRY, 1 BLACK P-90 PU, SG BODY STYLE	1,195	**883**	759	634
ELGUIT	86	GIBSON	**LES PAUL JUNIOR** DOUBLE CUTAWAY	557	**412**	354	296
ELGUIT	56	GIBSON	**LES PAUL JUNIOR 3/4** SUNBURST	1,386	**1,025**	880	736
ELGUIT	57	GIBSON	**LES PAUL JUNIOR 3/4** SUNBURST	1,743	**1,289**	1,107	926
ELGUIT	58	GIBSON	**LES PAUL JUNIOR 3/4** SUNBURST	1,394	**1,031**	886	741
ELGUIT	58	GIBSON	**LES PAUL JUNIOR 3/4** CHERRY RED	1,719	**1,271**	1,092	913
ELGUIT	59	GIBSON	**LES PAUL JUNIOR 3/4** CHERRY RED	1,375	**1,017**	874	730
ELGUIT	60	GIBSON	**LES PAUL JUNIOR 3/4** CHERRY RED	1,225	**906**	778	651
ELGUIT	61	GIBSON	**LES PAUL JUNIOR 3/4** CHERRY RED	1,076	**795**	683	571
ELGUIT	79	GIBSON	**LES PAUL KALAMAZOO** CHERRY SUNBURST	1,244	**920**	790	660
ELGUIT	69	GIBSON	**LES PAUL PERSONAL** WALNUT	1,356	**1,003**	861	720
ELGUIT	69	GIBSON	**LES PAUL PROFESSIONAL**	896	**663**	569	476
ELGUIT	69	GIBSON	**LES PAUL PROFESSIONAL** WALNUT	1,089	**805**	692	578

TYPE	YR	MFG	PRICES--BASED ON 100% ORIGINAL MODEL	SELL EXC	SELL AVG	BUY EXC	BUY AVG
ELGUIT	69	GIBSON	**LES PAUL PROFESSIONAL** TERRY KATH STYLE	1,136	**840**	722	603
ELGUIT	70	GIBSON	**LES PAUL PROFESSIONAL**	956	**707**	607	507
ELGUIT	71	GIBSON	**LES PAUL PROFESSIONAL** WALNUT	1,082	**800**	688	575
ELGUIT	77	GIBSON	**LES PAUL PROFESSIONAL DELUXE** SUNBURST	1,121	**829**	712	595
ELGUIT	77	GIBSON	**LES PAUL PROFESSIONAL DELUXE** BLACK	1,209	**894**	768	642
ELGUIT	82	GIBSON	**LES PAUL PROFESSIONAL DELUXE**	916	**678**	582	487
ELGUIT	70	GIBSON	**LES PAUL RECORDING** WALNUT	869	**643**	552	462
ELGUIT	71	GIBSON	**LES PAUL RECORDING** WALNUT	856	**633**	544	454
ELGUIT	72	GIBSON	**LES PAUL RECORDING** WALNUT	845	**625**	537	449
ELGUIT	72	GIBSON	**LES PAUL RECORDING** MAHOGANY	884	**653**	561	469
ELGUIT	73	GIBSON	**LES PAUL RECORDING**	737	**545**	468	391
ELGUIT	73	GIBSON	**LES PAUL RECORDING** WALNUT	845	**625**	537	449
ELGUIT	74	GIBSON	**LES PAUL RECORDING** WALNUT	845	**625**	537	449
ELGUIT	75	GIBSON	**LES PAUL RECORDING** WALNUT	845	**625**	537	449
ELGUIT	75	GIBSON	**LES PAUL RECORDING** WHITE	940	**695**	597	499
ELGUIT	76	GIBSON	**LES PAUL RECORDING** WHITE	977	**722**	620	519
ELGUIT	76	GIBSON	**LES PAUL RECORDING** WALNUT	1,066	**788**	677	566
ELGUIT	78	GIBSON	**LES PAUL RECORDING** WHITE	969	**717**	616	515
ELGUIT	78	GIBSON	**LES PAUL RECORDING** SUNBURST	978	**723**	621	519
ELGUIT	78	GIBSON	**LES PAUL RECORDING** WALNUT	1,004	**742**	638	533
ELGUIT	61	GIBSON	**LES PAUL SG** TV YELLOW, SINGLE CUTAWAY	4,667	**3,452**	2,965	2,479
ELGUIT	62	GIBSON	**LES PAUL SG** CHERRY RED, TREMOLO	3,031	**2,242**	1,926	1,610
ELGUIT	62	GIBSON	**LES PAUL SG** BROWN	3,183	**2,354**	2,022	1,691
ELGUIT	62	GIBSON	**LES PAUL SG** RED, VIBROLA	3,599	**2,661**	2,286	1,911
ELGUIT	63	GIBSON	**LES PAUL SG CUSTOM** WHITE	3,685	**2,725**	2,341	1,957
ELGUIT	63	GIBSON	**LES PAUL SG CUSTOM** BLACK, 2 PAG's	4,428	**3,275**	2,813	2,352
ELGUIT	61	GIBSON	**LES PAUL SG SPECIAL** CHERRY RED, 2 PU's	2,102	**1,554**	1,335	1,116
ELGUIT	60	GIBSON	**LES PAUL SG STANDARD** CHERRY RED	5,075	**3,753**	3,225	2,696
ELGUIT	61	GIBSON	**LES PAUL SG STANDARD** CHERRY RED	3,780	**2,795**	2,402	2,008
ELGUIT	62	GIBSON	**LES PAUL SG STANDARD** CHERRY RED, EBONY BLACK	4,336	**3,207**	2,755	2,303
ELGUIT	62	GIBSON	**LES PAUL SG STANDARD** CHERRY RED	5,199	**3,845**	3,303	2,762
ELGUIT	63	GIBSON	**LES PAUL SG STANDARD** CHERRY RED	3,028	**2,240**	1,924	1,609
ELGUIT	73	GIBSON	**LES PAUL SIGNATURE** GOLD TOP	1,718	**1,270**	1,091	912
ELGUIT	77	GIBSON	**LES PAUL SIGNATURE** GOLD	1,155	**854**	734	614
ELGUIT	71	GIBSON	**LES PAUL SIGNATURE GOLD TOP**	1,962	**1,451**	1,246	1,042
ELGUIT	72	GIBSON	**LES PAUL SIGNATURE GOLD TOP**	1,831	**1,354**	1,163	973
ELGUIT	74	GIBSON	**LES PAUL SIGNATURE GOLD TOP** w/LOW IMP PICKUPS	1,433	**1,060**	910	761
ELGUIT	74	GIBSON	**LES PAUL SIGNATURE BASS GOLD TOP**	1,377	**1,018**	875	731
ELGUIT	55	GIBSON	**LES PAUL SPECIAL** TV MAHOGANY, SINGLE CUTAWAY	4,290	**3,172**	2,726	2,279
ELGUIT	56	GIBSON	**LES PAUL SPECIAL** TV MAHOGANY, SINGLE CUTAWAY	3,814	**2,820**	2,423	2,026
ELGUIT	56	GIBSON	**LES PAUL SPECIAL** NATURAL	4,629	**3,423**	2,941	2,459
ELGUIT	57	GIBSON	**LES PAUL SPECIAL** TV YELLOW, SINGLE CUTAWAY	3,483	**2,576**	2,213	1,850
ELGUIT	57	GIBSON	**LES PAUL SPECIAL** TV MAHOGANY, SINGLE CUTAWAY	3,829	**2,832**	2,433	2,034
ELGUIT	58	GIBSON	**LES PAUL SPECIAL** TV MAHOGANY, SINGLE CUTAWAY	3,781	**2,796**	2,402	2,008

TYPE	YR	MFG	PRICES--BASED ON 100% ORIGINAL MODEL	SELL EXC	SELL AVG	BUY EXC	BUY AVG
ELGUIT	59	GIBSON	**LES PAUL SPECIAL** CHERRY RED, DOUBLE CUTAWAY	2,970	**2,196**	1,887	1,577
ELGUIT	60	GIBSON	**LES PAUL SPECIAL** CHERRY RED, DOUBLE CUTAWAY	3,314	**2,451**	2,106	1,761
ELGUIT	60	GIBSON	**LES PAUL SPECIAL** TV MAHOGANY, DOUBLE CUTAWAY	3,480	**2,573**	2,211	1,848
ELGUIT	61	GIBSON	**LES PAUL SPECIAL** CHERRY SUNBURST, DOUBLE CUTAWAY	2,195	**1,623**	1,395	1,166
ELGUIT	76	GIBSON	**LES PAUL SPECIAL** DOUBLE CUTAWAY	657	**486**	417	349
ELGUIT	78	GIBSON	**LES PAUL SPECIAL** TOBACCO SUNBURST, DOUBLE CUTAWAY	643	**475**	408	341
ELGUIT	79	GIBSON	**LES PAUL SPECIAL** SUNBURST, DOUBLE CUTAWAY	669	**494**	425	355
ELGUIT	59	GIBSON	**LES PAUL SPECIAL 3/4** CHERRY RED	1,940	**1,434**	1,232	1,030
ELGUIT	60	GIBSON	**LES PAUL SPECIAL 3/4** CHERRY RED	1,081	**800**	687	574
ELGUIT	58	GIBSON	**LES PAUL STANDARD** FLAME SUNBURST	53,829	**39,811**	34,203	28,596
ELGUIT	59	GIBSON	**LES PAUL STANDARD** SUNBURST, NO FLAME	33,600	**24,850**	21,350	17,850
ELGUIT	59	GIBSON	**LES PAUL STANDARD** CHERRY SUNBURST, PAF/TUNE-O-MATIC BRIDGE/2 PU/JUMBO FRETS	36,488	**26,986**	23,185	19,384
ELGUIT	59	GIBSON	**LES PAUL STANDARD** FLAME SUNBURST, LEFT-HANDED, ONLY 3 MADE	48,116	**35,585**	30,573	25,561
ELGUIT	59	GIBSON	**LES PAUL STANDARD** CURLY MAPLE	53,373	**39,473**	33,914	28,354
ELGUIT	59	GIBSON	**LES PAUL STANDARD** FLAME SUNBURST, HIGH FLAME	53,710	**39,723**	34,128	28,533
ELGUIT	60	GIBSON	**LES PAUL STANDARD** CHERRY SUNBURST, NO FLAME/THIN NECK	43,080	**31,861**	27,374	22,886
ELGUIT	60	GIBSON	**LES PAUL STANDARD** CHERRY, LEFT-HANDED	48,672	**35,997**	30,927	25,857
ELGUIT	60	GIBSON	**LES PAUL STANDARD** FLAME SUNBURST	54,018	**39,950**	34,324	28,697
ELGUIT	61	GIBSON	**LES PAUL STANDARD** CHERRY SUNBURST, SG STYLE	3,750	**2,773**	2,383	1,992
ELGUIT	70	GIBSON	**LES PAUL STANDARD**	1,832	**1,355**	1,164	973
ELGUIT	72	GIBSON	**LES PAUL STANDARD** TOBACCO SUNBURST	1,713	**1,267**	1,088	910
ELGUIT	73	GIBSON	**LES PAUL STANDARD** TOBACCO SUNBURST	1,633	**1,208**	1,038	868
ELGUIT	74	GIBSON	**LES PAUL STANDARD** TOBACCO SUNBURST	1,513	**1,119**	961	804
ELGUIT	75	GIBSON	**LES PAUL STANDARD** NATURAL	976	**722**	620	518
ELGUIT	75	GIBSON	**LES PAUL STANDARD** TOBACCO SUNBURST	1,115	**825**	708	592
ELGUIT	75	GIBSON	**LES PAUL STANDARD** BLACK	1,235	**913**	785	656
ELGUIT	76	GIBSON	**LES PAUL STANDARD** NATURAL	916	**678**	582	487
ELGUIT	76	GIBSON	**LES PAUL STANDARD** CHERRY SUNBURST	947	**700**	602	503
ELGUIT	76	GIBSON	**LES PAUL STANDARD** WINE RED	956	**707**	607	507
ELGUIT	76	GIBSON	**LES PAUL STANDARD** TOBACCO SUNBURST	1,076	**795**	683	571
ELGUIT	77	GIBSON	**LES PAUL STANDARD** NATURAL	902	**667**	573	479
ELGUIT	77	GIBSON	**LES PAUL STANDARD** WINE RED	928	**686**	589	493
ELGUIT	78	GIBSON	**LES PAUL STANDARD** BLACK	908	**671**	577	482
ELGUIT	78	GIBSON	**LES PAUL STANDARD** CHERRY SUNBURST	913	**675**	580	485
ELGUIT	78	GIBSON	**LES PAUL STANDARD** BURGUNDY	927	**685**	589	492
ELGUIT	78	GIBSON	**LES PAUL STANDARD** NATURAL	1,027	**759**	652	545
ELGUIT	78	GIBSON	**LES PAUL STANDARD** TOBACCO SUNBURST	1,027	**759**	652	545
ELGUIT	78	GIBSON	**LES PAUL STANDARD** WINE RED	1,159	**857**	736	616
ELGUIT	79	GIBSON	**LES PAUL STANDARD** CHERRY SUNBURST	925	**684**	588	491
ELGUIT	79	GIBSON	**LES PAUL STANDARD** TOBACCO SUNBURST	925	**684**	588	491
ELGUIT	81	GIBSON	**LES PAUL STANDARD** WINE RED	886	**655**	563	470
ELGUIT	81	GIBSON	**LES PAUL STANDARD** TOBACOC SUNBURST	892	**660**	567	474

TYPE	YR	MFG	PRICES--BASED ON 100% ORIGINAL MODEL	SELL EXC	SELL AVG	BUY EXC	BUY AVG
ELGUIT	83	GIBSON	**LES PAUL STANDARD** BLACK	775	**573**	492	412
ELGUIT	83	GIBSON	**LES PAUL STANDARD** CHERRY SUNBURST	859	**635**	545	456
ELGUIT	71	GIBSON	**LES PAUL STANDARD '54 REISSUE**	1,776	**1,314**	1,129	944
ELGUIT	71	GIBSON	**LES PAUL STANDARD '58 REISSUE**	1,593	**1,178**	1,012	846
ELGUIT	72	GIBSON	**LES PAUL STANDARD '58 REISSUE**	1,752	**1,296**	1,113	931
ELGUIT	58	GIBSON	**LES PAUL STANDARD GOLD TOP** PAF's	19,712	**14,579**	12,525	10,472
ELGUIT	68	GIBSON	**LES PAUL STANDARD GOLD TOP**	4,155	**3,073**	2,640	2,207
ELGUIT	69	GIBSON	**LES PAUL STANDARD GOLD TOP**	2,276	**1,683**	1,446	1,209
ELGUIT	71	GIBSON	**LES PAUL STANDARD GOLD TOP**	1,380	**1,020**	877	733
ELGUIT	87	GIBSON	**LES PAUL STUDIO LITE**	657	**486**	417	349
ELGUIT	75	GIBSON	**LES PAUL TRIUMPH BASS** BROWN	617	**456**	392	327
ELGUIT	55	GIBSON	**LES PAUL TV**	3,120	**2,307**	1,982	1,657
ELGUIT	56	GIBSON	**LES PAUL TV**	4,560	**3,372**	2,897	2,422
ELGUIT	81	GIBSON	**LES PAUL XR-1**	426	**315**	270	226
ELGUIT	82	GIBSON	**LES PAUL XR-2**	414	**306**	263	220
ELGUIT	76	GIBSON	**MARAUDER FINGERBOARD** ROSEWOOD	492	**364**	312	261
ELGUIT	78	GIBSON	**MARAUDER FINGERBOARD** MAPLE	382	**282**	242	202
ELGUIT	79	GIBSON	**MARAUDER FINGERBOARD** MAPLE	397	**293**	252	211
ELGUIT	59	GIBSON	**MELODY MAKER** SUNBURST, SINGLE CUTAWAY	677	**501**	430	360
ELGUIT	60	GIBSON	**MELODY MAKER** SUNBURST, SINGLE CUTAWAY, 1 PU	657	**486**	417	349
ELGUIT	61	GIBSON	**MELODY MAKER** SUNBURST, SINGLE CUTAWAY	609	**450**	387	323
ELGUIT	62	GIBSON	**MELODY MAKER** SUNBURST, DOUBLE CUTAWAY, 1 PU	625	**462**	397	332
ELGUIT	63	GIBSON	**MELODY MAKER** SUNBURST, DOUBLE CUTAWAY, 1 PU	616	**455**	391	327
ELGUIT	64	GIBSON	**MELODY MAKER** SUNBURST, 1 PU	625	**462**	397	332
ELGUIT	64	GIBSON	**MELODY MAKER** CHERRY RED, 1 PU	796	**589**	506	423
ELGUIT	65	GIBSON	**MELODY MAKER** SUNBURST, 1 PU	625	**462**	397	332
ELGUIT	65	GIBSON	**MELODY MAKER** CARDINAL RED, 1 PU	717	**530**	455	380
ELGUIT	65	GIBSON	**MELODY MAKER** CHERRY RED, 1 PU	717	**530**	455	380
ELGUIT	65	GIBSON	**MELODY MAKER** CHERRY RED, DOUBLE CUTAWAY	717	**530**	455	380
ELGUIT	65	GIBSON	**MELODY MAKER** PELHAM BLUE, 12-STRNG	806	**596**	512	428
ELGUIT	66	GIBSON	**MELODY MAKER** OPAQUE RED, 1 PU, DOUBLE CUTAWAY	438	**324**	278	233
ELGUIT	66	GIBSON	**MELODY MAKER** PELHAM BLUE, 2 PU's	637	**471**	405	338
ELGUIT	67	GIBSON	**MELODY MAKER** CARDINAL RED, 1 PU	495	**366**	314	263
ELGUIT	67	GIBSON	**MELODY MAKER** PELHAM BLUE, 12-STRING	808	**597**	513	429
ELGUIT	67	GIBSON	**MELODY MAKER** PELHAM BLUE, 1 PU	810	**599**	514	430
ELGUIT	68	GIBSON	**MELODY MAKER** CARDINAL RED, 1 PU	487	**360**	309	259
ELGUIT	68	GIBSON	**MELODY MAKER** WALNUT	625	**462**	397	332
ELGUIT	68	GIBSON	**MELODY MAKER** PELHAM BLUE, 1 PU	751	**555**	477	399
ELGUIT	68	GIBSON	**MELODY MAKER** BURGUNDY, 12-STRING	804	**594**	511	427
ELGUIT	68	GIBSON	**MELODY MAKER** PELHAM BLUE, 12-STRING	808	**597**	513	429
ELGUIT	70	GIBSON	**MELODY MAKER** WALNUT, 2 PU's	591	**437**	375	314
ELGUIT	59	GIBSON	**MELODY MAKER 3/4** SUNBURST	540	**399**	343	287
ELGUIT	60	GIBSON	**MELODY MAKER 3/4** SINGLE CUTAWAY	438	**324**	278	233
ELGUIT	60	GIBSON	**MELODY MAKER 3/4** SUNBURST	539	**399**	342	286
ELGUIT	62	GIBSON	**MELODY MAKER 3/4** DOUBLE CUTAWAY	426	**315**	270	226
ELGUIT	62	GIBSON	**MELODY MAKER 3/4** SUNBURST	537	**397**	341	285
ELGUIT	63	GIBSON	**MELODY MAKER 3/4** SUNBURST	536	**396**	340	285

TYPE	YR	MFG	PRICES--BASED ON 100% ORIGINAL MODEL	SELL EXC	SELL AVG	BUY EXC	BUY AVG
ELGUIT	64	GIBSON	**MELODY MAKER 3/4** SUNBURST	536	**396**	340	285
ELGUIT	65	GIBSON	**MELODY MAKER 3/4** SUNBURST	534	**395**	339	284
ELGUIT	68	GIBSON	**MELODY MAKER 3/4** PELHAM BLUE	525	**388**	333	278
ELGUIT	60	GIBSON	**MELODY MAKER D** SUNBURST, SINGLE CUTAWAY	599	**443**	380	318
ELGUIT	61	GIBSON	**MELODY MAKER D** SUNBURST, SINGLE CUTAWAY, 2 PU's	580	**429**	369	308
ELGUIT	62	GIBSON	**MELODY MAKER D** SUNBURST, DOUBLE CUTAWAY	573	**423**	364	304
ELGUIT	64	GIBSON	**MELODY MAKER D** SUNBURST, 2 PU's	616	**455**	391	327
ELGUIT	65	GIBSON	**MELODY MAKER D** CHERRY RED, 2 PU's	430	**318**	273	228
ELGUIT	65	GIBSON	**MELODY MAKER D** RED, 2 PU's	488	**361**	310	259
ELGUIT	65	GIBSON	**MELODY MAKER D** PELHAM BLUE, 2 PU's	497	**367**	315	264
ELGUIT	67	GIBSON	**MELODY MAKER D** RED, 2 PU's	477	**352**	303	253
ELGUIT	67	GIBSON	**MELODY MAKER D** PELHAM BLUE, 2 PU's	480	**355**	305	255
ELGUIT	68	GIBSON	**MELODY MAKER D** BURGUNDY, 2 PU's	477	**352**	303	253
ELGUIT	70	GIBSON	**MELODY MAKER D** WALNUT	490	**362**	311	260
ELGUIT	76	GIBSON	**MELODY MAKER D** CHERRY RED, 2 PU's	493	**364**	313	262
ELGUIT	77	GIBSON	**MELODY MAKER DOUBLE REISSUE**	480	**355**	305	255
ELGUIT	66	GIBSON	**MELODY MAKER III** SPARKLING BURGUNDY, 3 PU's	591	**437**	375	314
ELGUIT	68	GIBSON	**MELODY MAKER III** PELHAM BLUE, 3 PU's	426	**315**	270	226
ELGUIT	68	GIBSON	**MELODY MAKER III** SPARKLING BURGUNDY, 3 PU'S	647	**478**	411	343
ELGUIT	69	GIBSON	**MELODY MAKER III** PELHAM BLUE	581	**430**	369	309
ELGUIT	82	GIBSON	**MODERNE** BLACK, KORINA	1,917	**1,460**	1,241	949
ELGUIT	82	GIBSON	**MODERNE** NATURAL, KORINA	2,205	**1,630**	1,401	1,171
ELGUIT	83	GIBSON	**MODERNE** WHITE, KORINA	1,374	**1,016**	873	730
ELGUIT	83	GIBSON	**MODERNE** NATURAL, KORINA	1,908	**1,411**	1,212	1,013
ELGUIT	82	GIBSON	**MODERNE HERITAGE** BLACK, KORINA WOOD	1,354	**1,001**	860	719
ELGUIT	83	GIBSON	**MODERNE HERITAGE** BLACK	1,492	**1,104**	948	793
ELGUIT	83	GIBSON	**MODERNE HERITAGE** WHITE	1,492	**1,104**	948	793
ELGUIT	83	GIBSON	**MODERNE HERITAGE** NATURAL, KORINA WOOD	2,191	**1,620**	1,392	1,164
ELGUIT	87	GIBSON	**Q-80 BASS**	432	**319**	274	229
ELGUIT	77	GIBSON	**RD ARTIST** NATURAL	504	**372**	320	267
ELGUIT	78	GIBSON	**RD ARTIST** NATURAL	412	**305**	262	219
ELGUIT	78	GIBSON	**RD ARTIST** SUNBURST	432	**319**	274	229
ELGUIT	79	GIBSON	**RD ARTIST** SUNBURST	393	**291**	250	209
ELGUIT	77	GIBSON	**RD ARTIST BASS** SUNBURST	566	**418**	359	300
ELGUIT	77	GIBSON	**RD ARTIST BASS** NATURAL	648	**479**	412	344
ELGUIT	78	GIBSON	**RD ARTIST BASS** SUNBURST	478	**353**	303	253
ELGUIT	78	GIBSON	**RD ARTIST BASS** BLACK	569	**421**	361	302
ELGUIT	79	GIBSON	**RD ARTIST BASS** SUNBURST	565	**418**	359	300
ELGUIT	81	GIBSON	**RD ARTIST BASS** FIREBURST	569	**421**	361	302
ELGUIT	78	GIBSON	**RD CUSTOM**	537	**397**	341	285
ELGUIT	78	GIBSON	**RD CUSTOM** NATURAL	540	**399**	343	287
ELGUIT	78	GIBSON	**RD STANDARD** BLACK	530	**392**	337	282
ELGUIT	78	GIBSON	**RD STANDARD** BROWN SUNBURST	557	**412**	354	296

TYPE	YR	MFG	**PRICES--BASED ON 100% ORIGINAL** MODEL	SELL EXC	SELL AVG	BUY EXC	BUY AVG
ELGUIT	78	GIBSON	**RD STANDARD** WALNUT	566	**418**	359	300
ELGUIT	79	GIBSON	**RD STANDARD BASS** NATURAL	559	**413**	355	297
ELGUIT	73	GIBSON	**RIPPER BASS** NATURAL	564	**417**	358	299
ELGUIT	74	GIBSON	**RIPPER BASS** NATURAL	419	**310**	266	222
ELGUIT	75	GIBSON	**RIPPER BASS** NATURAL	458	**339**	291	243
ELGUIT	75	GIBSON	**RIPPER BASS** BLACK, FRETLESS	498	**368**	316	264
ELGUIT	76	GIBSON	**RIPPER BASS** SUNBURST, EBONY FINGERBOARD	423	**313**	269	224
ELGUIT	76	GIBSON	**RIPPER BASS** BLACK	563	**416**	358	299
ELGUIT	78	GIBSON	**RIPPER BASS** NATURAL	423	**313**	269	224
ELGUIT	78	GIBSON	**RIPPER BASS** BLACK	443	**328**	281	235
ELGUIT	79	GIBSON	**RIPPER BASS** NATURAL	423	**313**	269	224
ELGUIT	79	GIBSON	**RIPPER BASS** SUNBURST	423	**313**	269	224
ELGUIT	81	GIBSON	**RIPPER BASS** NATURAL	424	**313**	269	225
ELGUIT	53	GIBSON	**ROYALTONE**	371	**274**	236	197
ELGUIT	76	GIBSON	**S-1** NATURAL, 3 PU's	436	**323**	277	232
ELGUIT	77	GIBSON	**S-1** SUNBURST, 3 PU's	436	**323**	277	232
ELGUIT	78	GIBSON	**S-1** BLACK, 3 PU's	441	**326**	280	234
ELGUIT	40	GIBSON	**SB-350 BASS** WALNUT, SG BODY SHAPE	487	**360**	309	259
ELGUIT	72	GIBSON	**SB-450 BASS** CHERRY RED, SG BODY SHAPE	486	**359**	309	258
ELGUIT	59	GIBSON	**SG** TV, DOUBLE CUT	3,360	**2,485**	2,135	1,785
ELGUIT	60	GIBSON	**SG** TV YELLOW, DOUBLE CUTAWAY	2,231	**1,650**	1,417	1,185
ELGUIT	61	GIBSON	**SG** TV MAHOGANY, 1 PU	860	**636**	546	456
ELGUIT	62	GIBSON	**SG** TV WHITE, 1 PU	842	**623**	535	447
ELGUIT	63	GIBSON	**SG** TV WHITE, 1 PU	842	**623**	535	447
ELGUIT	72	GIBSON	**SG** WINE RED, BIGSBY	870	**643**	553	462
ELGUIT	74	GIBSON	**SG** WALNUT, 3 PU's	842	**623**	535	447
ELGUIT	87	GIBSON	**SG '62 REISSUE**	796	**589**	506	423
ELGUIT	89	GIBSON	**SG 90** DOUBLE	478	**353**	303	253
ELGUIT	73	GIBSON	**SG 100** WALNUT	498	**368**	316	264
ELGUIT	79	GIBSON	**SG 100** WALNUT	497	**367**	315	264
ELGUIT	70	GIBSON	**SG 200** WALNUT	491	**363**	312	261
ELGUIT	71	GIBSON	**SG 250** CHERRY RED	435	**322**	276	231
ELGUIT	61	GIBSON	**SG CUSTOM** WHITE	4,760	**3,520**	3,024	2,529
ELGUIT	62	GIBSON	**SG CUSTOM** WHITE	2,220	**1,642**	1,410	1,179
ELGUIT	63	GIBSON	**SG CUSTOM** WHITE	3,069	**2,269**	1,950	1,630
ELGUIT	64	GIBSON	**SG CUSTOM** WHITE	3,007	**2,224**	1,911	1,597
ELGUIT	65	GIBSON	**SG CUSTOM** WHITE, GOLD HARDWARE	2,306	**1,706**	1,465	1,225
ELGUIT	66	GIBSON	**SG CUSTOM** WHITE	1,783	**1,319**	1,133	947
ELGUIT	67	GIBSON	**SG CUSTOM** WHITE	1,943	**1,437**	1,234	1,032
ELGUIT	68	GIBSON	**SG CUSTOM** WHITE	1,067	**789**	678	567
ELGUIT	68	GIBSON	**SG CUSTOM** WALNUT	1,225	**906**	778	651
ELGUIT	69	GIBSON	**SG CUSTOM** WALNUT	1,225	**906**	778	651
ELGUIT	70	GIBSON	**SG CUSTOM** WHITE	1,069	**790**	679	568

TYPE	YR	MFG	PRICES--BASED ON 100% ORIGINAL MODEL	SELL EXC	SELL AVG	BUY EXC	BUY AVG
ELGUIT	71	GIBSON	**SG CUSTOM** WHITE	1,065	**788**	677	566
ELGUIT	72	GIBSON	**SG CUSTOM** METALLIC GREEN	1,195	**883**	759	634
ELGUIT	72	GIBSON	**SG CUSTOM** WALNUT	1,232	**911**	783	654
ELGUIT	73	GIBSON	**SG CUSTOM** WALNUT, 3 PU's, TREMOLO	1,123	**830**	713	596
ELGUIT	74	GIBSON	**SG CUSTOM** WALNUT	1,003	**741**	637	532
ELGUIT	75	GIBSON	**SG CUSTOM** WALNUT	988	**731**	628	525
ELGUIT	76	GIBSON	**SG CUSTOM** WHITE	859	**635**	545	456
ELGUIT	76	GIBSON	**SG CUSTOM** WALNUT	922	**682**	586	490
ELGUIT	77	GIBSON	**SG CUSTOM** CHERRY RED	1,072	**793**	681	569
ELGUIT	78	GIBSON	**SG CUSTOM** WALNUT	798	**590**	507	424
ELGUIT	78	GIBSON	**SG CUSTOM** CHERRY RED	1,064	**787**	676	565
ELGUIT	71	GIBSON	**SG DELUXE** WALNUT	755	**558**	480	401
ELGUIT	71	GIBSON	**SG DELUXE** CHERRY RED	911	**673**	578	483
ELGUIT	72	GIBSON	**SG DELUXE**	518	**383**	329	275
ELGUIT	78	GIBSON	**SG EXCLUSIVE** BLACK, CREAM PARTS	739	**546**	469	392
ELGUIT	73	GIBSON	**SG I** CHERRY RED	657	**486**	417	349
ELGUIT	75	GIBSON	**SG I**	384	**284**	244	204
ELGUIT	72	GIBSON	**SG II** WALNUT	478	**353**	303	253
ELGUIT	73	GIBSON	**SG II** WALNUT	599	**443**	380	318
ELGUIT	74	GIBSON	**SG II** CHERRY, 2 MINI HB PU's, SOLID BODY	479	**354**	304	254
ELGUIT	61	GIBSON	**SG JUNIOR** CHERRY RED	1,243	**919**	789	660
ELGUIT	61	GIBSON	**SG JUNIOR** TV	3,897	**2,882**	2,476	2,070
ELGUIT	62	GIBSON	**SG JUNIOR** CHERRY RED	1,002	**741**	636	532
ELGUIT	62	GIBSON	**SG JUNIOR** WHITE, 1 PU	1,104	**816**	701	586
ELGUIT	63	GIBSON	**SG JUNIOR** CHERRY RED	920	**680**	584	489
ELGUIT	64	GIBSON	**SG JUNIOR** CHERRY RED	947	**700**	602	503
ELGUIT	64	GIBSON	**SG JUNIOR** WHITE	1,338	**989**	850	710
ELGUIT	65	GIBSON	**SG JUNIOR** CHERRY RED	819	**606**	520	435
ELGUIT	65	GIBSON	**SG JUNIOR** WHITE	954	**705**	606	506
ELGUIT	66	GIBSON	**SG JUNIOR** CHERRY RED	696	**515**	442	370
ELGUIT	66	GIBSON	**SG JUNIOR** PELHAM BLUE	1,568	**1,160**	996	833
ELGUIT	67	GIBSON	**SG JUNIOR** CHERRY RED	633	**468**	402	336
ELGUIT	68	GIBSON	**SG JUNIOR** CHERRY RED, LARGE GUARD, MAESTRO VIBROLA	723	**535**	459	384
ELGUIT	69	GIBSON	**SG JUNIOR** CHERRY RED	621	**459**	394	329
ELGUIT	71	GIBSON	**SG JUNIOR** WALNUT	480	**355**	305	255
ELGUIT	71	GIBSON	**SG PRO** WALNUT	643	**475**	408	341
ELGUIT	72	GIBSON	**SG PRO** WALNUT, SERIAL #685131	641	**474**	407	340
ELGUIT	73	GIBSON	**SG PRO**	518	**383**	329	275
ELGUIT	74	GIBSON	**SG PRO** WALNUT	556	**411**	353	295
ELGUIT	60	GIBSON	**SG SPECIAL** CHERRY RED	1,615	**1,194**	1,026	858
ELGUIT	61	GIBSON	**SG SPECIAL** CHERRY RED	1,330	**984**	845	706
ELGUIT	62	GIBSON	**SG SPECIAL** WHITE	1,254	**927**	797	666
ELGUIT	62	GIBSON	**SG SPECIAL** CHERRY RED	1,357	**1,003**	862	721

TYPE	YR	MFG	PRICES--BASED ON 100% ORIGINAL MODEL	SELL EXC	SELL AVG	BUY EXC	BUY AVG
ELGUIT	63	GIBSON	**SG SPECIAL** CHERRY RED	1,216	**899**	772	646
ELGUIT	63	GIBSON	**SG SPECIAL** WHITE	1,619	**1,197**	1,029	860
ELGUIT	64	GIBSON	**SG SPECIAL** WHITE	972	**719**	617	516
ELGUIT	64	GIBSON	**SG SPECIAL** CHERRY RED	1,155	**854**	734	614
ELGUIT	64	GIBSON	**SG SPECIAL** LIMED MAHOGANY	2,944	**2,177**	1,870	1,564
ELGUIT	65	GIBSON	**SG SPECIAL** WHITE	1,071	**792**	680	569
ELGUIT	65	GIBSON	**SG SPECIAL** CHERRY RED, CHROME HARDWARE	1,216	**899**	772	646
ELGUIT	65	GIBSON	**SG SPECIAL** LIMED MAHOGANY	2,073	**1,533**	1,317	1,101
ELGUIT	66	GIBSON	**SG SPECIAL** WHITE	832	**615**	528	442
ELGUIT	66	GIBSON	**SG SPECIAL** CHERRY RED	1,214	**898**	771	645
ELGUIT	67	GIBSON	**SG SPECIAL** CHERRY RED	832	**615**	528	442
ELGUIT	67	GIBSON	**SG SPECIAL** WHITE	832	**615**	528	442
ELGUIT	68	GIBSON	**SG SPECIAL** CHERRY RED	826	**611**	525	439
ELGUIT	68	GIBSON	**SG SPECIAL** WINE RED	967	**715**	614	514
ELGUIT	69	GIBSON	**SG SPECIAL** CHERRY RED	826	**611**	525	439
ELGUIT	69	GIBSON	**SG SPECIAL** WALNUT	877	**648**	557	466
ELGUIT	70	GIBSON	**SG SPECIAL** WALNUT	748	**553**	475	397
ELGUIT	70	GIBSON	**SG SPECIAL** CHERRY RED	785	**580**	498	417
ELGUIT	71	GIBSON	**SG SPECIAL** WALNUT	733	**542**	466	389
ELGUIT	72	GIBSON	**SG SPECIAL** CHERRY RED	687	**508**	436	365
ELGUIT	72	GIBSON	**SG SPECIAL** WALNUT	721	**533**	458	383
ELGUIT	73	GIBSON	**SG SPECIAL** WALNUT	598	**442**	380	317
ELGUIT	76	GIBSON	**SG SPECIAL** CHERRY RED	578	**428**	367	307
ELGUIT	63	GIBSON	**SG STANDARD** CHERRY RED	2,940	**2,174**	1,868	1,562
ELGUIT	64	GIBSON	**SG STANDARD** CHERRY RED	2,131	**1,576**	1,354	1,132
ELGUIT	65	GIBSON	**SG STANDARD** CHERRY RED	2,100	**1,553**	1,334	1,115
ELGUIT	66	GIBSON	**SG STANDARD** CHERRY RED	1,675	**1,238**	1,064	889
ELGUIT	67	GIBSON	**SG STANDARD** CHERRY RED	1,594	**1,179**	1,013	847
ELGUIT	68	GIBSON	**SG STANDARD** CHERRY RED	1,752	**1,296**	1,113	931
ELGUIT	69	GIBSON	**SG STANDARD** WALNUT, LEFT-HANDED	1,224	**905**	778	650
ELGUIT	69	GIBSON	**SG STANDARD** CHERRY RED	1,764	**1,304**	1,121	937
ELGUIT	70	GIBSON	**SG STANDARD** SUNBURST	918	**679**	583	488
ELGUIT	70	GIBSON	**SG STANDARD** CHERRY RED	1,120	**828**	711	595
ELGUIT	70	GIBSON	**SG STANDARD** WALNUT	1,146	**847**	728	608
ELGUIT	71	GIBSON	**SG STANDARD**	856	**633**	544	454
ELGUIT	71	GIBSON	**SG STANDARD** CHERRY RED	875	**647**	556	465
ELGUIT	71	GIBSON	**SG STANDARD** CHERRY RED, LEFT-HANDED	901	**666**	572	478
ELGUIT	71	GIBSON	**SG STANDARD** SUNBURST	937	**693**	595	498
ELGUIT	71	GIBSON	**SG STANDARD** WALNUT	960	**710**	610	510
ELGUIT	72	GIBSON	**SG STANDARD** CHERRY RED	672	**497**	427	357
ELGUIT	72	GIBSON	**SG STANDARD** WALNUT	813	**601**	516	431
ELGUIT	73	GIBSON	**SG STANDARD** CHERRY RED	672	**497**	427	357

TYPE	YR	MFG	PRICES--BASED ON 100% ORIGINAL MODEL	SELL EXC	SELL AVG	BUY EXC	BUY AVG
ELGUIT	73	GIBSON	**SG STANDARD** WHITE	677	**501**	430	360
ELGUIT	73	GIBSON	**SG STANDARD** NATURAL	747	**553**	475	397
ELGUIT	74	GIBSON	**SG STANDARD** CHERRY RED	630	**466**	400	335
ELGUIT	74	GIBSON	**SG STANDARD** WALNUT, PRO-INSTALLED KAHLER, BIG FRETS	675	**499**	429	359
ELGUIT	75	GIBSON	**SG STANDARD** MAHOGANY BODY/NECK, 2# PAH HB's	716	**529**	455	380
ELGUIT	76	GIBSON	**SG STANDARD** WHITE	676	**500**	430	359
ELGUIT	77	GIBSON	**SG STANDARD** SUNBURST, LEFT-HANDED	766	**566**	486	406
ELGUIT	78	GIBSON	**SG STANDARD** WALNUT	548	**405**	348	291
ELGUIT	78	GIBSON	**SG STANDARD** CHERRY RED	598	**442**	380	317
ELGUIT	78	GIBSON	**SG STANDARD** NATURAL	615	**455**	391	326
ELGUIT	78	GIBSON	**SG STANDARD** BLACK	789	**583**	501	419
ELGUIT	79	GIBSON	**SG STANDARD** WALNUT	539	**399**	342	286
ELGUIT	79	GIBSON	**SG STANDARD** CHERRY RED	684	**506**	434	363
ELGUIT	80	GIBSON	**SG STANDARD** WALNUT	622	**460**	395	330
ELGUIT	81	GIBSON	**SG STANDARD**	529	**391**	336	281
ELGUIT	81	GIBSON	**SONEX-180 CUSTOM**	360	**266**	228	191
ELGUIT	81	GIBSON	**SONEX-180 DELUXE**	330	**244**	209	175
ELGUIT	83	GIBSON	**SONEX-180 DELUXE**	312	**230**	198	165
ELGUIT	83	GIBSON	**SONEX-180 STANDARD**	384	**284**	244	204
ELGUIT	39	GIBSON	**SUPER 100 JUMBO** MOUSTACHE BRIDTE, STAIRSTEP PEGHEAD	13,440	**9,940**	8,540	7,140
ELGUIT	51	GIBSON	**SUPER 400 CES** SUNBURST, ROUNDED CUTAWAY	10,962	**8,107**	6,965	5,823
ELGUIT	52	GIBSON	**SUPER 400 CES** NATURAL, ROUNDED CUTAWAY, SERIAL #A9400-A13000	11,110	**8,216**	7,059	5,902
ELGUIT	53	GIBSON	**SUPER 400 CES** SUNBURST, ROUNDED CUTAWAY, SERIAL #A13000-A16000	11,811	**8,735**	7,505	6,275
ELGUIT	53	GIBSON	**SUPER 400 CES** NATURAL, ROUNDED CUTAWAY, SERIAL #A13000-A16000	12,148	**8,985**	7,719	6,454
ELGUIT	54	GIBSON	**SUPER 400 CES** SUNBURST, ROUNDED CUATWAY, ALNICO V PU's	11,520	**8,520**	7,320	6,120
ELGUIT	55	GIBSON	**SUPER 400 CES** SUNBURST, ROUNDED CUTAWAY, SERIAL #A19000-A22000	11,820	**8,742**	7,510	6,279
ELGUIT	56	GIBSON	**SUPER 400 CES** SUNBURST, ROUNDED CUTAWAY, SERIAL #A22000-A24600	11,809	**8,734**	7,504	6,274
ELGUIT	57	GIBSON	**SUPER 400 CES** HUMBUCKERS	14,400	**10,650**	9,150	7,650
ELGUIT	58	GIBSON	**SUPER 400 CES** SUNBURST, HB	12,793	**9,462**	8,129	6,796
ELGUIT	58	GIBSON	**SUPER 400 CES** NATURAL, ROUNDED CUTAWAY	13,135	**9,714**	8,346	6,978
ELGUIT	60	GIBSON	**SUPER 400 CES** SUNBURST, VENETIAN CUTAWAY	10,865	**8,035**	6,903	5,772
ELGUIT	60	GIBSON	**SUPER 400 CES** NATURAL, ROUNDED CUTAWAY	11,244	**8,316**	7,144	5,973
ELGUIT	61	GIBSON	**SUPER 400 CES** SUNBURST, POINTED CUTAWAY	10,792	**7,981**	6,857	5,733
ELGUIT	62	GIBSON	**SUPER 400 CES** SUNBURST, POINTED CUTAWAY	10,938	**8,089**	6,950	5,810
ELGUIT	63	GIBSON	**SUPER 400 CES** NATURAL, POINTED CUTAWAY	9,676	**7,156**	6,148	5,140
ELGUIT	63	GIBSON	**SUPER 400 CES** SUNBURST	11,904	**8,804**	7,564	6,324
ELGUIT	64	GIBSON	**SUPER 400 CES** NATURAL, POINTED CUTAWAY	9,673	**7,154**	6,146	5,139
ELGUIT	64	GIBSON	**SUPER 400 CES** SUNBURST, POINTED CUTAWAY	10,617	**7,852**	6,746	5,640
ELGUIT	65	GIBSON	**SUPER 400 CES** NATURAL, POINTED CUTAWAY	9,613	**7,109**	6,108	5,107
ELGUIT	66	GIBSON	**SUPER 400 CES**	8,640	**6,390**	5,490	4,590
ELGUIT	68	GIBSON	**SUPER 400 CES** SUNBURST, LEFT-HANDED	7,466	**5,522**	4,744	3,966
ELGUIT	68	GIBSON	**SUPER 400 CES** SUNBURST, POINTED CUTAWAY	8,635	**6,386**	5,486	4,587
ELGUIT	68	GIBSON	**SUPER 400 CES** NATURAL, POINTED CUTAWAY, SERIAL #523714	8,903	**6,584**	5,657	4,729
ELGUIT	69	GIBSON	**SUPER 400 CES** SUNBURST, POINTED CUTAWAY	8,684	**6,422**	5,518	4,613

TYPE	YR	MFG	PRICES--BASED ON 100% ORIGINAL MODEL	SELL EXC	SELL AVG	BUY EXC	BUY AVG
ELGUIT	70	GIBSON	**SUPER 400 CES** NATURAL, ROUNDED CUTAWAY	6,264	**4,633**	3,980	3,328
ELGUIT	71	GIBSON	**SUPER 400 CES** SUNBURST, ROUNDED CUTAWAY	6,594	**4,876**	4,190	3,503
ELGUIT	72	GIBSON	**SUPER 400 CES** SUNBURST, ROUNDED CUTAWAY	6,511	**4,815**	4,137	3,459
ELGUIT	73	GIBSON	**SUPER 400 CES** SUNBURST, ROUNDED CUTAWAY	6,476	**4,789**	4,115	3,440
ELGUIT	74	GIBSON	**SUPER 400 CES** NATURAL, ROUNDED CUTAWAY	5,249	**3,882**	3,335	2,788
ELGUIT	76	GIBSON	**SUPER 400 CES** SUNBURST, ROUNDED CUTAWAY	6,240	**4,615**	3,965	3,315
ELGUIT .	77	GIBSON	**SUPER 400 CES** SUNBURST, ROUNDED CUTAWAY	6,468	**4,783**	4,110	3,436
ELGUIT	79	GIBSON	**SUPER 400 CES** SUNBURST, ROUNDED CUTAWAY	5,710	**4,223**	3,628	3,033
ELGUIT	80	GIBSON	**SUPER 400 CES** SUNBURST	5,777	**4,272**	3,670	3,069
ELGUIT	87	GIBSON	**SUPER 400 CES**	4,800	**3,550**	3,050	2,550
ELGUIT	61	GIBSON	**SUPER 400 CES SPECIAL** SUNBURST, PAF's	9,159	**6,774**	5,820	4,865
ELGUIT	52	GIBSON	**SUPER 400 CESN** NATURAL, P-90's	13,440	**9,940**	8,540	7,140
ELGUIT	54	GIBSON	**SUPER 400 CESN** ALNICO V PU's	12,960	**9,585**	8,235	6,885
ELGUIT	62	GIBSON	**SUPER 400 CESN** NATURAL, ROUNDED CUTAWAY	13,291	**9,829**	8,445	7,060
ELGUIT	63	GIBSON	**SUPER 400 CESN** NATURAL, POINTED CUTAWAY	12,793	**9,462**	8,129	6,796
ELGUIT	66	GIBSON	**SUPER 400 CESN**	9,840	**7,277**	6,252	5,227
ELGUIT	69	GIBSON	**SUPER 400 CESN** NATURAL, 2 HB's	11,904	**8,804**	7,564	6,324
ELGUIT	70	GIBSON	**SUPER 400 CESN** NATURAL	6,499	**4,806**	4,129	3,452
ELGUIT	74	GIBSON	**SUPER 400 CESN** NATURAL	6,490	**4,800**	4,124	3,448
ELGUIT	80	GIBSON	**SUPER 400 CESN**	6,720	**4,970**	4,270	3,570
ELGUIT	48	GIBSON	**SUPER 400 N**	8,640	**6,390**	5,490	4,590
ELGUIT	83	GIBSON	**SUPER V** NATURAL	6,750	**4,992**	4,289	3,586
ELGUIT	78	GIBSON	**SUPER V CES** ANTIQUE SUNBURST	4,852	**3,589**	3,083	2,578
ELGUIT	79	GIBSON	**SUPER V CES** ANTIQUE SUNBURST, HOLLOW BODY	4,534	**3,353**	2,881	2,408
ELGUIT	80	GIBSON	**SUPER V CES** SUNBURST	4,800	**3,550**	3,050	2,550
ELGUIT	62	GIBSON	**TAL FARLOW** HOLLOW BODY	7,612	**5,630**	4,837	4,044
ELGUIT	64	GIBSON	**TAL FARLOW** HOLLOW BODY	6,615	**4,892**	4,203	3,514
ELGUIT	65	GIBSON	**TAL FARLOW** HOLLOW BODY	6,657	**4,923**	4,230	3,536
ELGUIT	66	GIBSON	**TAL FARLOW** HOLLOW BODY	6,508	**4,813**	4,135	3,457
ELGUIT	63	GIBSON	**TAL FARROW** FLAMEY	9,719	**7,188**	6,175	5,163
ELGUIT	63	GIBSON	**THUNDERBIRD II BASS** SUNBURST, 1 PU	2,162	**1,599**	1,374	1,149
ELGUIT	64	GIBSON	**THUNDERBIRD II BASS** SUNBURST, 1 PU	1,905	**1,409**	1,210	1,012
ELGUIT	65	GIBSON	**THUNDERBIRD II BASS** SUNBURST, 1 PU	2,293	**1,696**	1,457	1,218
ELGUIT	66	GIBSON	**THUNDERBIRD II BASS** SUNBURST, 1 PU	1,019	**754**	647	541
ELGUIT	67	GIBSON	**THUNDERBIRD II BASS** SUNBURST, 1 PU	1,066	**788**	677	566
ELGUIT	68	GIBSON	**THUNDERBIRD II BASS** CARDINAL RED, 1 PU	1,067	**789**	678	567
ELGUIT	63	GIBSON	**THUNDERBIRD IV BASS** SUNBURST, 2 PU's	3,244	**2,399**	2,061	1,723
ELGUIT	64	GIBSON	**THUNDERBIRD IV BASS** SUNBURST, 2 PU's	3,212	**2,375**	2,041	1,706
ELGUIT	64	GIBSON	**THUNDERBIRD IV BASS** PELHAM BLUE METALLIC, REVERSE BODY	3,984	**2,946**	2,531	2,116
ELGUIT	65	GIBSON	**THUNDERBIRD IV BASS** INVERNESS GREEN, NON-REVERSE BODY	2,191	**1,620**	1,392	1,164
ELGUIT	67	GIBSON	**THUNDERBIRD IV BASS** SUNBURST, 2 PU's	1,069	**790**	679	568
ELGUIT	68	GIBSON	**THUNDERBIRD IV BASS** SUNBURST, 2 PU's	1,064	**787**	676	565
ELGUIT	68	GIBSON	**THUNDERBIRD IV BASS** CUSTOM BLUE, 2 PU's	1,073	**793**	681	570
ELGUIT	89	GIBSON	**THUNDERBIRD IV BASS REISSUE** SUNBURST	737	**545**	468	391

TYPE	YR	MFG	PRICES--BASED ON 100% ORIGINAL MODEL	SELL EXC	SELL AVG	BUY EXC	BUY AVG
ELGUIT	76	GIBSON	**THUNDERBIRD 76 BASS** SUNBURST	916	**678**	582	487
ELGUIT	76	GIBSON	**THUNDERBIRD 76 BASS** BLACK, 2 PU's	1,003	**741**	637	532
ELGUIT	76	GIBSON	**THUNDERBIRD 76 BASS** NATURAL, MAHOGANY, 2 PU's	1,015	**751**	645	539
ELGUIT	76	GIBSON	**THUNDERBIRD 76 BASS** WHITE, 2 PU's	1,029	**761**	653	546
ELGUIT	79	GIBSON	**THUNDERBIRD 79 BASS** SUNBURST	1,104	**816**	701	586
ELGUIT	65	GIBSON	**TRINI LOPEZ CUSTOM** CHERRY RED	3,312	**2,449**	2,104	1,759
ELGUIT	68	GIBSON	**TRINI LOPEZ CUSTOM** SUNBURST	2,229	**1,648**	1,416	1,184
ELGUIT	66	GIBSON	**TRINI LOPEZ DELUXE** CHERRY SUNBURST	2,891	**2,138**	1,837	1,536
ELGUIT	67	GIBSON	**TRINI LOPEZ DELUXE** CHERRY SUNBURST	1,970	**1,457**	1,252	1,047
ELGUIT	68	GIBSON	**TRINI LOPEZ DELUXE** CHERRY SUNBURST	1,913	**1,415**	1,215	1,016
ELGUIT	69	GIBSON	**TRINI LOPEZ DELUXE**	1,721	**1,273**	1,093	914
ELGUIT	65	GIBSON	**TRINI LOPEZ STANDARD** CHERRY RED	1,426	**1,055**	906	757
ELGUIT	66	GIBSON	**TRINI LOPEZ STANDARD** CHERRY RED	1,593	**1,178**	1,012	846
ELGUIT	67	GIBSON	**TRINI LOPEZ STANDARD** PELHAM BLUE	1,638	**1,211**	1,041	870
ELGUIT	67	GIBSON	**TRINI LOPEZ STANDARD** CHERRY RED	1,645	**1,216**	1,045	874
ELGUIT	68	GIBSON	**TRINI LOPEZ STANDARD** CHERRY RED	1,494	**1,105**	949	794
ELGUIT	69	GIBSON	**TRINI LOPEZ STANDARD** CHERRY RED	1,440	**1,065**	915	765
ELGUIT	81	GIBSON	**VICTORY** SILVER	457	**338**	290	243
ELGUIT	81	GIBSON	**VICTORY** SUNBURST	564	**417**	358	299
ELGUIT	82	GIBSON	**VICTORY** PELHAM BLUE	408	**301**	259	216
ELGUIT	81	GIBSON	**VICTORY ARTIST BASS** FIREBURST	438	**324**	278	233
ELGUIT	82	GIBSON	**VICTORY CUSTOM BASS**	504	**372**	320	267
ELGUIT	81	GIBSON	**VICTORY MV X** 3 PU's	518	**383**	329	275
ELGUIT	85	GIBSON	**XPL CUSTOM**	557	**412**	354	296
GUITAR AMP	45	GIBSON	**BR- 1** BROWN TOLEX, 10" SPEAKER	329	**243**	209	174
GTAMP	47	GIBSON	**BR- 6** BROWN, WHITE GRILL, 10" SPEAKER	330	**244**	209	175
GTAMP	49	GIBSON	**BR- 6** 10" SPEAKER	337	**249**	214	179
GTAMP	52	GIBSON	**BR- 6** 10" SPEAKER	325	**240**	206	172
GTAMP	48	GIBSON	**BR- 9** BROWN	489	**362**	311	260
GTAMP	50	GIBSON	**BR- 9**	384	**284**	244	204
GTAMP	52	GIBSON	**BR- 9** BROWN	288	**213**	183	153
GTAMP	53	GIBSON	**BR- 9**	280	**207**	178	148
GTAMP	54	GIBSON	**BR- 9** TAN	375	**277**	238	199
GTAMP	55	GIBSON	**BR- 9** 1x8" JENSEN, TV FRONT	476	**352**	302	252
GTAMP	40	GIBSON	**EH-125**	301	**222**	191	160
GTAMP	41	GIBSON	**EH-125**	384	**284**	244	204
GTAMP	38	GIBSON	**EH-150** TWEED, 12" SPEAKER	494	**365**	314	262
GTAMP	54	GIBSON	**EXPLORER** TWEED, 1x10" SPEAKERS	497	**367**	315	264
GTAMP	60	GIBSON	**FALCON** BROWN TOLEX, 1x12" SPEAKER	337	**249**	214	179
GTAMP	63	GIBSON	**FALCON** BROWN TOLEX, 12" JENSEN, REVERB	266	**197**	169	141
GTAMP	64	GIBSON	**FALCON** BLACK TOLEX, 12" REV, TREMOLO	284	**210**	180	150
GTAMP	62	GIBSON	**FALCON GA- 19RVT** TWEED	486	**359**	309	258
GTAMP	64	GIBSON	**FALCON GA- 19RVT** BROWN	319	**236**	203	169
GTAMP	65	GIBSON	**FALCON GA- 19RVT** 12" SPEAKER	302	**223**	192	160
GTAMP	66	GIBSON	**G-100** 100 WATTS, 2 SPEAKER BOTTOMS,2x10" SPEAKERS IN EACH BOTTOM	290	**215**	184	154

TYPE	YR	MFG	PRICES--BASED ON 100% ORIGINAL MODEL	SELL EXC	SELL AVG	BUY EXC	BUY AVG
GTAMP	62	GIBSON	GA- 3RV TUBE REVERB	366	**271**	233	194
GTAMP	72	GIBSON	GA- 3RV TUBE REVERB II, SOLID STATE	283	**209**	179	150
GTAMP	55	GIBSON	GA- 5 LES PAUL JR.	489	**362**	311	260
GTAMP	56	GIBSON	GA- 5 LES PAUL JR.	442	**327**	281	235
GTAMP	57	GIBSON	GA- 5 LES PAUL JR.	497	**367**	315	264
GTAMP	58	GIBSON	GA- 5 SKYLARK	471	**348**	299	250
GTAMP	60	GIBSON	GA- 5 SKYLARK 10" SPEAKER	144	**106**	91	76
GTAMP	62	GIBSON	GA- 5 SKYLARK	142	**105**	90	75
GTAMP	63	GIBSON	GA- 5 SKYLARK 1x10" SPEAKER	141	**104**	89	74
GTAMP	65	GIBSON	GA- 5 SKYLARK	139	**102**	88	73
GTAMP	66	GIBSON	GA- 5 SKYLARK BLACK	192	**142**	122	102
GTAMP	64	GIBSON	GA- 5T SKYLARK BLOND	225	**166**	143	119
GTAMP	65	GIBSON	GA- 5T SKYLARK 10" JENSEN SPEAKER	168	**124**	106	89
GTAMP	66	GIBSON	GA- 5T SKYLARK	160	**118**	101	85
GTAMP	75	GIBSON	GA- 5T SKYLARK 10" SPEAKER	143	**105**	90	75
GTAMP	58	GIBSON	GA- 6 12" SPEAKER	461	**341**	293	245
GTAMP	60	GIBSON	GA- 8 DISCOVERER	223	**165**	142	118
GTAMP	64	GIBSON	GA- 8 DISCOVERER TREMOLO	149	**110**	95	79
GTAMP	52	GIBSON	GA- 8 GIBSONETTE 1x10" SPEAKER	283	**209**	179	150
GTAMP	55	GIBSON	GA- 9	288	**213**	183	153
GTAMP	67	GIBSON	GA- 15RT BLACK TOLEX, 10" SPEAKER	144	**106**	91	76
GTAMP	64	GIBSON	GA- 15RVT	238	**176**	151	126
GTAMP	66	GIBSON	GA- 15RVT EXPLORER	192	**142**	122	102
GTAMP	59	GIBSON	GA- 18 1x10" SPEAKER, 14 WATTS	404	**298**	256	214
GTAMP	62	GIBSON	GA- 18T EXPLORER	376	**278**	239	199
GTAMP	50	GIBSON	GA- 20 TWEED, RANGER, 1x12" SPEAKER	486	**359**	309	258
GTAMP	52	GIBSON	GA- 20 BROWN, P12-R JENSEN	498	**368**	316	264
GTAMP	55	GIBSON	GA- 20 BROWN, P12-R JENSEN	437	**323**	278	232
GTAMP	57	GIBSON	GA- 20	152	**112**	96	81
GTAMP	60	GIBSON	GA- 20 WHITE, CABINET ONLY	78	**58**	50	41
GTAMP	60	GIBSON	GA- 20 TWEED	398	**294**	253	211
GTAMP	66	GIBSON	GA- 20 RANTER, TREMOLO	166	**122**	105	88
GTAMP	70	GIBSON	GA- 20 BLACK, REVERB, SOLID STATE	140	**103**	89	74
GTAMP	65	GIBSON	GA- 20RVT MINUTEMAN REVERB	309	**228**	196	164
GTAMP	67	GIBSON	GA- 20RVT MINUTEMAN 1x12" SPEAKER	408	**302**	259	217
GTAMP	55	GIBSON	GA- 20T 12" SPEAKER	463	**342**	294	246
GTAMP	59	GIBSON	GA- 20T TWEED, RANGER, 12" SPEAKER	490	**362**	311	260
GTAMP	60	GIBSON	GA- 20T TWEED, RANTER, 12" SPEAKER	444	**328**	282	236
GTAMP	61	GIBSON	GA- 20T TWEED	415	**307**	264	220
GTAMP	64	GIBSON	GA- 20TVT MINUTEMAN BLACK, REVERB, TREMOLO	192	**142**	122	102
GTAMP	50	GIBSON	GA- 25 HAWK 1x12", 1x8" JENSEN	265	**196**	168	141
GTAMP	49	GIBSON	GA- 30 JENSEN SPEAKERS	480	**355**	305	255
GTAMP	51	GIBSON	GA- 30 BROWN COVERED CAB, 8", 12" JENSEN SPEAKERS	433	**320**	275	230
GTAMP	52	GIBSON	GA- 30	480	**355**	305	255
GTAMP	54	GIBSON	GA- 30 TWEED, 12" JENSEN SPEAKERS	451	**333**	286	239
GTAMP	59	GIBSON	GA- 30	408	**301**	259	216
GTAMP	63	GIBSON	GA- 30 10" AND 12" SPEAKERS	505	**374**	321	268
GTAMP	61	GIBSON	GA- 30RV INVADER 1x12" JENSEN SPEAKERS	192	**142**	122	102

TYPE	YR	MFG	PRICES--BASED ON 100% ORIGINAL MODEL	SELL EXC	SELL AVG	BUY EXC	BUY AVG
GTAMP	61	GIBSON	**GA- 35 LANCER** 2x12" SPEAKERS, REVERB, TREMOLO	192	**142**	122	102
GTAMP	65	GIBSON	**GA- 35RVT** GREY	192	**142**	122	102
GTAMP	53	GIBSON	**GA- 40 LES PAUL**	1,003	**741**	637	532
GTAMP	54	GIBSON	**GA- 40 LES PAUL**	693	**512**	440	368
GTAMP	55	GIBSON	**GA- 40 LES PAUL** TWEED, 2 CHANNEL, 20 WATTS	637	**471**	405	338
GTAMP	60	GIBSON	**GA- 40 LES PAUL**	767	**567**	487	407
GTAMP	50	GIBSON	**GA- 50** 8" AND 12" SPEAKERS, 25 WATTS	457	**338**	290	243
GTAMP	63	GIBSON	**GA- 50T** 8" AND 12" BLUE JENSENS	563	**416**	358	299
GTAMP	65	GIBSON	**GA- 55 RVT RANGER** 4x10" COMBO	501	**370**	318	266
GTAMP	66	GIBSON	**GA- 55 RVT RANGER**	448	**331**	284	238
GTAMP	52	GIBSON	**GA- 75** 15" JENSEN	727	**538**	462	386
GTAMP	61	GIBSON	**GA- 77 VANGUARD**	973	**719**	618	517
GTAMP	61	GIBSON	**GA- 79 RV** TREMOLO	1,017	**752**	646	540
GTAMP	61	GIBSON	**GA- 79 RVT** TWEED, STEREO	862	**637**	547	457
GTAMP	64	GIBSON	**GA- 79 RVT** STEREO	1,610	**1,191**	1,023	855
GTAMP	56	GIBSON	**GA- 90**	419	**310**	266	
GTAMP	62	GIBSON	**GA-100 BASS** TWEED	463	**342**	294	246
GTAMP	66	GIBSON	**GSS-100** GREY, 2x12" SPEAKERS	451	**333**	286	239
GTAMP	60	GIBSON	**GT- 8T DISCOVERER** 1x12" SPEAKER	340	**252**	216	181
GTAMP	62	GIBSON	**GT- 8T DISCOVERER** TREMOLO 1x12", 15 WATTS	412	**305**	262	219
GTAMP	62	GIBSON	**HAWK** 15" SPEAKER, REVERB	249	**184**	158	132
GTAMP	60	GIBSON	**MINUTEMAN** BLACK, REVERB	192	**142**	122	102
GTAMP	66	GIBSON	**REVERB III** SOLID STATE	240	**177**	152	127
GTAMP	64	GIBSON	**VANGUARD** 1x15" SPEAKER, 2 CHANNEL	241	**178**	153	128
GUITAR (ACOUSTIC)	36	GIBSON	**ADVANCED JUMBO** SUNBURST, BRAZILIAN ROSEWOOD	26,880	**19,880**	17,080	14,280
GUITAR	38	GIBSON	**ADVANCED JUMBO** ROSEWOOD BACK/SIDES/ FLATTOP, SERIAL #95400-	20,519	**15,175**	13,038	10,900
GUITAR	39	GIBSON	**ADVANCED JUMBO** ROSEWOOD BACK/SIDES, FLATTOP	15,749	**12,000**	10,200	7,799
GUITAR	68	GIBSON	**B- 15** NATURAL, FLATTOP	478	**353**	303	253
GUITAR	69	GIBSON	**B- 15 STUDENT MODEL**	456	**337**	289	242
GUITAR	62	GIBSON	**B- 25** CHERRY SUNBURST, FLATTOP	647	**478**	411	343
GUITAR	63	GIBSON	**B- 25** CHERRY SUNBURST, FLATTOP	642	**474**	408	341
GUITAR	64	GIBSON	**B- 25** CHERRY SUNBURST, FLATTOP	635	**470**	403	337
GUITAR	65	GIBSON	**B- 25** CHERRY SUNBURST, FLATTOP	620	**458**	394	329
GUITAR	66	GIBSON	**B- 25** CHERRY SUNBURST, FLATTOP	612	**452**	389	325
GUITAR	66	GIBSON	**B- 25** CHERRY BACK/SIDES, BLOND TOP, FLATTOP	656	**485**	417	348
GUITAR	67	GIBSON	**B- 25** CHERRY SUNBURST, FLATTOP	604	**447**	384	321
GUITAR	68	GIBSON	**B- 25** CHERRY SUNBURST, FLATTOP	590	**436**	375	313
GUITAR	69	GIBSON	**B- 25** CHERRY SUNBURST, FLATTOP	583	**431**	370	310
GUITAR	70	GIBSON	**B- 25** CHERRY SUNBURST, FLATTOP	581	**430**	369	309
GUITAR	61	GIBSON	**B- 25 3/4** SUNBURST, FLATTOP	621	**459**	394	329
GUITAR	63	GIBSON	**B- 25 3/4** SUNBURST, FLATTOP	600	**443**	381	318
GUITAR	64	GIBSON	**B- 25 3/4** SUNBURST, FLATTOP	563	**416**	358	299
GUITAR	68	GIBSON	**B- 25 3/4** NATURAL, FLATTOP	496	**367**	315	263
GUITAR	63	GIBSON	**B- 25-12** SUNBURST, 12-STRING	478	**353**	303	253
GUITAR	65	GIBSON	**B- 25-12** SUNBURST, 12-STRING	454	**335**	288	241

TYPE	YR	MFG	PRICES--BASED ON 100% ORIGINAL MODEL	SELL EXC	SELL AVG	BUY EXC	BUY AVG
GUITAR	67	GIBSON	**B- 25-12** SUNBURST, 12-STRING	438	**324**	278	233
GUITAR	68	GIBSON	**B- 25-12** SUNBURST, 12-STRING	430	**318**	273	228
GUITAR	69	GIBSON	**B- 25-12** SUNBURST, 12-STRING	422	**312**	268	224
GUITAR	62	GIBSON	**B- 25-12N**	478	**353**	303	253
GUITAR	63	GIBSON	**B- 25-12N** NATURAL, 12-STRING	470	**347**	298	249
GUITAR	65	GIBSON	**B- 25-12N** NATURAL, 12-STRING	454	**335**	288	241
GUITAR	66	GIBSON	**B- 25-12N** NATURAL, 12-STRING	446	**330**	283	237
GUITAR	67	GIBSON	**B- 25-12N** NATURAL, 12-STRING	438	**324**	278	233
GUITAR	68	GIBSON	**B- 25-12N** NATURAL, 12-STRING	430	**318**	273	228
GUITAR	69	GIBSON	**B- 25-12N** NATURAL, 12-STRING	422	**312**	268	224
GUITAR	72	GIBSON	**B- 25-12N** NATURAL, 12-STRING	499	**369**	317	265
GUITAR	75	GIBSON	**B- 25-12N** NATURAL, 12-STRING	480	**355**	305	255
GUITAR	63	GIBSON	**B- 25N** NATURAL, FLATTOP	969	**717**	616	515
GUITAR	64	GIBSON	**B- 25N** NATAURAL, FLATTOP	948	**701**	602	503
GUITAR	65	GIBSON	**B- 25N** NATURAL, FLATTOP	762	**563**	484	404
GUITAR	67	GIBSON	**B- 25N** NATURAL, FLATTOP	759	**561**	482	403
GUITAR	68	GIBSON	**B- 25N** NATURAL, FLATTOP	749	**554**	476	398
GUITAR	69	GIBSON	**B- 25N** NATURAL, FLATTOP	858	**634**	545	455
GUITAR	71	GIBSON	**B- 25N** NATURAL, FLATTOP	644	**476**	409	342
GUITAR	74	GIBSON	**B- 25N**	504	**372**	320	267
GUITAR	66	GIBSON	**B- 25N 3/4**	438	**324**	278	233
GUITAR	61	GIBSON	**B- 45-12** CHERRY SUNBURST, FLATTOP, 12-STRING	956	**707**	607	507
GUITAR	63	GIBSON	**B- 45-12** SQUARE SHOULDERS	677	**501**	430	360
GUITAR	64	GIBSON	**B- 45-12** CHERRY SUNBURST, FLATTOP, 12-STRING	760	**562**	483	403
GUITAR	66	GIBSON	**B- 45-12** SUNBURST, 12-STRING	1,067	**789**	678	567
GUITAR	67	GIBSON	**B- 45-12** CHERRY SUNBURST, FLATTOP, 12-STRING	672	**497**	427	357
GUITAR	68	GIBSON	**B- 45-12** CHERRY SUNBURST, FLATTOP, 12-STRING	668	**494**	424	354
GUITAR	69	GIBSON	**B- 45-12** CHERRY SUNBURST, FLATTOP, 12-STRING	634	**469**	403	337
GUITAR	73	GIBSON	**B- 45-12** CHERRY SUNBURST, FLATTOP, 12-STRING	637	**471**	405	338
GUITAR	75	GIBSON	**B- 45-12**	518	**383**	329	275
GUITAR	63	GIBSON	**B- 45-12N** NATURAL, FLATTOP, 12-STRING	717	**530**	455	380
GUITAR	67	GIBSON	**B- 45-12N** NATURAL, FLATTOP, 12-STRING	672	**497**	427	357
GUITAR	68	GIBSON	**B- 45-12N** NATURAL, FLATTOP, 12-STRING	668	**494**	424	354
GUITAR	69	GIBSON	**B- 45-12N** NATURAL, FLATTOP, 12-STRING	634	**469**	403	337
GUITAR	70	GIBSON	**B- 45-12N** NATURAL, FLATTOP, 12-STRING	567	**419**	360	301
GUITAR	73	GIBSON	**B- 45-12N** NATURAL, FLATTOP, 12-STRING	550	**406**	349	292
GUITAR	74	GIBSON	**B- 45-12N**	637	**471**	405	338
GUITAR	76	GIBSON	**B- 45-12N** NATURAL, FLATTOP, 12-STRING	557	**412**	354	296
GUITAR	68	GIBSON	**BLUE RIDGE** ROSEWOOD BACK/SIDES, FLATTOP	864	**639**	549	459
GUITAR	69	GIBSON	**BLUE RIDGE** ROSEWOOD BACK/SIDES, FLATTOP	840	**621**	533	446
GUITAR	70	GIBSON	**BLUE RIDGE** ROSEWOOD BACK/SIDES, FLATTOP	916	**678**	582	487
GUITAR	72	GIBSON	**BLUE RIDGE** ROSEWOOD BACK/SIDES, FLATTOP	745	**551**	473	396
GUITAR	73	GIBSON	**BLUE RIDGE** ROSEWOOD BACK/SIDES, FLATTOP	796	**589**	506	423
GUITAR	74	GIBSON	**BLUE RIDGE** ROSEWOOD BACK/SIDES, FLATTOP	687	**508**	436	365

TYPE	YR	MFG	PRICES--BASED ON 100% ORIGINAL MODEL	SELL EXC	SELL AVG	BUY EXC	BUY AVG
GUITAR	75	GIBSON	**BLUE RIDGE** ROSEWOOD BACK/SIDES, FLATTOP	672	**497**	427	357
GUITAR	73	GIBSON	**BLUE RIDGE CUSTOM** INDIAN ROSEWOOD	800	**592**	508	425
GUITAR	52	GIBSON	**BURL IVES 6004** NATURAL, FLATTOP	621	**459**	394	329
GUITAR	62	GIBSON	**C-0 CLASSICAL** MAHOGANY BACK/SIDES	480	**355**	305	255
GUITAR	64	GIBSON	**C-0 CLASSICAL** MAHOGANY BACK/SIDES	478	**353**	303	253
GUITAR	65	GIBSON	**C-0 CLASSICAL** MAHOGANY BACK/SIDES	456	**337**	290	242
GUITAR	66	GIBSON	**C-0 CLASSICAL** MAHOGANY BACK/SIDES	436	**323**	277	232
GUITAR	59	GIBSON	**C-1 CLASSICAL** MAHOGANY BACK/SIDES	539	**399**	342	286
GUITAR	60	GIBSON	**C-1 CLASSICAL** MAHOGANY BACK/SIDES	498	**368**	316	264
GUITAR	64	GIBSON	**C-1 CLASSICAL** MAHOGANY BACK/SIDES. 3/4 SIZE	384	**284**	244	204
GUITAR	66	GIBSON	**C-1 CLASSICAL** MAHOGANY BACK/SIDES	497	**367**	315	264
GUITAR	69	GIBSON	**C-1 CLASSICAL** MAHOGANY BACK/SIDES	469	**347**	298	249
GUITAR	67	GIBSON	**C-2 CLASSICAL**	480	**355**	305	255
GUITAR	63	GIBSON	**C-4 CLASSICAL** MAPLE BACK/SIDES	518	**383**	329	275
GUITAR	65	GIBSON	**C-6 CLASSICAL** BRAZILIAN ROSEWOOD	935	**691**	594	496
GUITAR	58	GIBSON	**C-6 CLASSICAL CUSTOM** BRAZILIAN ROSEWOOD BACK/SIDES	892	**660**	567	474
GUITAR	60	GIBSON	**C-6 CLASSICAL CUSTOM** BRAZILIAN ROSEWOOD BACK/SIDES	889	**658**	565	472
GUITAR	64	GIBSON	**C-6 CLASSICAL CUSTOM** BRAZILIAN ROSEWOOD BACK/SIDES	688	**509**	437	365
GUITAR	66	GIBSON	**C-8 CLASSICAL**	577	**427**	367	307
GUITAR	68	GIBSON	**C-8 CLASSICAL** ROSEWOOD BACK/SIDES	888	**657**	564	472
GUITAR	33	GIBSON	**CENTURY OF PROGRESS**	1,146	**847**	728	608
GUITAR	49	GIBSON	**CF-100** SUNBURST, CUTAWAY, INLAY	1,778	**1,315**	1,130	945
GUITAR	50	GIBSON	**CF-100** SUNBURST, CUTAWAY, INLAY, SERIAL #A4400-A6000	1,635	**1,209**	1,039	869
GUITAR	51	GIBSON	**CF-100** SUNBURST, CUTAWAY, INLAY	1,626	**1,202**	1,033	863
GUITAR	55	GIBSON	**CF-100** SUNBURST, CUTAWAY, INLAY, SERIAL #A19000-A22000	1,624	**1,201**	1,032	862
GUITAR	56	GIBSON	**CF-100** SUNBURST, CUTAWAY, INLAY, SERIAL #A22000-A24600	1,624	**1,201**	1,032	862
GUITAR	58	GIBSON	**CF-100** SUNBURST, CUTAWAY, INLAY	1,624	**1,201**	1,032	862
GUITAR	53	GIBSON	**CF-100E**	1,474	**1,090**	936	783
GUITAR	58	GIBSON	**CF-100E** CUATWAY, GOLD KNOBS	2,091	**1,547**	1,329	1,111
GUITAR	67	GIBSON	**CHALLENGER I**	384	**284**	244	204
GUITAR	83	GIBSON	**CHALLENGER II**	336	**248**	213	178
GUITAR	69	GIBSON	**CITATION** BLOND	14,409	**10,657**	9,156	7,655
GUITAR	69	GIBSON	**CITATION** SUNBURST	14,410	**10,657**	9,156	7,655
GUITAR	55	GIBSON	**COUNTRY WESTERN** NATURAL	1,637	**1,211**	1,040	870
GUITAR	56	GIBSON	**COUNTRY WESTERN** NATURAL	1,655	**1,224**	1,051	879
GUITAR	57	GIBSON	**COUNTRY WESTERN** NATURAL, SERIAL #A24600-A26500	1,663	**1,230**	1,057	883
GUITAR	59	GIBSON	**COUNTRY WESTERN** NATURAL, SERIAL #A28000-	1,672	**1,236**	1,062	888
GUITAR	62	GIBSON	**COUNTRY WESTERN** NATURAL	1,523	**1,126**	968	809
GUITAR	63	GIBSON	**COUNTRY WESTERN** NATURAL	1,474	**1,090**	936	783
GUITAR	64	GIBSON	**COUNTRY WESTERN** NATURAL	1,328	**982**	844	705
GUITAR	65	GIBSON	**COUNTRY WESTERN** NATURAL	1,328	**982**	844	705
GUITAR	66	GIBSON	**COUNTRY WESTERN** NATURAL, SERIAL #403787	1,350	**998**	858	717
GUITAR	67	GIBSON	**COUNTRY WESTERN** NATURAL	1,010	**747**	642	537
GUITAR	68	GIBSON	**COUNTRY WESTERN** NATURAL	1,107	**819**	703	588

TYPE	YR	MFG	MODEL	SELL EXC	SELL AVG	BUY EXC	BUY AVG
GUITAR	69	GIBSON	**COUNTRY WESTERN** NATURAL	978	**723**	621	519
GUITAR	70	GIBSON	**D-12-20** LEFT-HANDED, 12-STRING	1,111	**822**	706	590
GUITAR	62	GIBSON	**DOVE** CHERRY SUNBURST	1,746	**1,291**	1,109	927
GUITAR	63	GIBSON	**DOVE** NATURAL	1,745	**1,290**	1,108	927
GUITAR	64	GIBSON	**DOVE** CHERRY SUNBURST	1,694	**1,253**	1,076	900
GUITAR	65	GIBSON	**DOVE** NATURAL	1,707	**1,263**	1,085	907
GUITAR	65	GIBSON	**DOVE** CHERRY SUNBURST	1,757	**1,300**	1,116	933
GUITAR	66	GIBSON	**DOVE** CHERRY SUNBURST	1,689	**1,249**	1,073	897
GUITAR	66	GIBSON	**DOVE** NATURAL	1,707	**1,263**	1,085	907
GUITAR	67	GIBSON	**DOVE** CHERRY SUNBURST	1,721	**1,273**	1,093	914
GUITAR	68	GIBSON	**DOVE** CHERRY SUNBURST	1,671	**1,236**	1,062	887
GUITAR	68	GIBSON	**DOVE** NATURAL	1,707	**1,263**	1,085	907
GUITAR	69	GIBSON	**DOVE** CHERRY SUNBURST	1,671	**1,236**	1,062	887
GUITAR	69	GIBSON	**DOVE** NATURAL	1,689	**1,249**	1,073	897
GUITAR	70	GIBSON	**DOVE** CHERRY SUNBURST	1,390	**1,028**	883	738
GUITAR	70	GIBSON	**DOVE** NATURAL	1,430	**1,057**	908	759
GUITAR	72	GIBSON	**DOVE** CHERRY SUNBURST	1,632	**1,207**	1,037	867
GUITAR	73	GIBSON	**DOVE** CHERRY SUNBURST	1,632	**1,207**	1,037	867
GUITAR	74	GIBSON	**DOVE** NATURAL	1,411	**1,043**	896	749
GUITAR	76	GIBSON	**DOVE** CHERRY SUNBURST	1,151	**851**	731	611
GUITAR	76	GIBSON	**DOVE** NATURAL	1,373	**1,016**	872	729
GUITAR	77	GIBSON	**DOVE** NATURAL	1,228	**908**	780	652
GUITAR	62	GIBSON	**EVERLY BROTHERS** BLACK, FLATTOP	8,513	**6,296**	5,409	4,522
GUITAR	63	GIBSON	**EVERLY BROTHERS** BLACK, FLATTOP	7,497	**5,545**	4,764	3,983
GUITAR	63	GIBSON	**EVERLY BROTHERS** NATURAL, FLATTOP, CHERRY RED BACK/SIDES	11,030	**8,157**	7,008	5,859
GUITAR	64	GIBSON	**EVERLY BROTHERS** BLACK, FLATTOP	8,567	**6,336**	5,443	4,551
GUITAR	65	GIBSON	**EVERLY BROTHERS** BLACK, FLATTOP	8,280	**6,123**	5,261	4,398
GUITAR	66	GIBSON	**EVERLY BROTHERS** BLACK, FLATTOP	8,200	**6,064**	5,210	4,356
GUITAR	68	GIBSON	**EVERLY BROTHERS** NATURAL, FLATTOP	7,702	**5,696**	4,894	4,091
GUITAR	68	GIBSON	**EVERLY BROTHERS** BLACK, FLATTOP	7,896	**5,839**	5,017	4,194
GUITAR	69	GIBSON	**EVERLY BROTHERS** NATURAL, FLATTOP	7,569	**5,598**	4,809	4,021
GUITAR	70	GIBSON	**EVERLY BROTHERS** BLACK, FLATTOP	7,536	**5,573**	4,788	4,003
GUITAR	71	GIBSON	**EVERLY BROTHERS** NATURAL, FLATTOP	7,467	**5,523**	4,745	3,967
GUITAR	41	GIBSON	**EXPERIMENTAL MODEL** 17" WIDE	1,992	**1,473**	1,265	1,058
GUITAR	63	GIBSON	**F-25 FOLKSINGER**	720	**533**	458	383
GUITAR	64	GIBSON	**F-25 FOLKSINGER**	781	**577**	496	415
GUITAR	65	GIBSON	**F-25 FOLKSINGER**	750	**555**	477	398
GUITAR	68	GIBSON	**F-25 FOLKSINGER**	730	**540**	464	388
GUITAR	55	GIBSON	**GF-100E** SUNBURST, 1 PU	1,713	**1,267**	1,088	910
GUITAR	73	GIBSON	**GOSPEL** NATURAL	648	**479**	412	344
GUITAR	74	GIBSON	**GOSPEL** NATURAL	943	**697**	599	501
GUITAR	76	GIBSON	**GOSPEL** NATURAL	1,026	**758**	652	545
GUITAR	73	GIBSON	**GOSPEL DREADNOUGHT** BLOND, MAPLE BACK/SIDES, SPRUCE TOP	1,115	**825**	708	592
GUITAR	55	GIBSON	**GS-1 CLASSICAL** MAHOGANY BACK/SIDES	324	**239**	206	172

TYPE	YR	MFG	PRICES--BASED ON 100% ORIGINAL MODEL	SELL EXC	SELL AVG	BUY EXC	BUY AVG
GUITAR	39	GIBSON	**GS-35 CLASSICAL** SPRUCE TOP, MAHOGANY BACK/SIDES	796	**589**	506	423
GUITAR	18	GIBSON	**GY ARMY-NAVY** FLAT TOP	1,115	**825**	708	592
GUITAR	18	GIBSON	**GY ARMY-NAVY SPECIAL** MAHOGANY	1,232	**911**	783	654
GUITAR	66	GIBSON	**HERITAGE** ROSEWOOD BACK/SIDES, FLATTOP	1,447	**1,070**	919	769
GUITAR	68	GIBSON	**HERITAGE** ROSEWOOD BACK/SIDES, FLATTOP	1,473	**1,089**	936	782
GUITAR	68	GIBSON	**HERITAGE** NATURAL, FLATTOP	1,474	**1,090**	936	783
GUITAR	69	GIBSON	**HERITAGE** ROSEWOOD BACK/SIDES, FLATTOP	1,464	**1,082**	930	777
GUITAR	70	GIBSON	**HERITAGE** NATURAL, FLATTOP	1,513	**1,119**	961	804
GUITAR	73	GIBSON	**HERITAGE** ROSEWOOD BACK/SIDES, FLATTOP	1,082	**800**	688	575
GUITAR	74	GIBSON	**HERITAGE** ROSEWOOD BACK/SIDES, FLATTOP	1,086	**803**	690	577
GUITAR	75	GIBSON	**HERITAGE** ROSEWOOD BACK/SIDES, FLATTOP	1,039	**768**	660	552
GUITAR	76	GIBSON	**HERITAGE** NATURAL, FLATTOP	1,000	**739**	635	531
GUITAR	76	GIBSON	**HERITAGE**	1,274	**942**	810	677
GUITAR	80	GIBSON	**HERITAGE** NATURAL, FLATTOP	729	**539**	463	387
GUITAR	69	GIBSON	**HERITAGE-12** NATURAL, 12-STRING	717	**530**	455	380
GUITAR	37	GIBSON	**HG-00**	1,095	**810**	696	581
GUITAR	39	GIBSON	**HG-00** SUNBURST, SERIAL #-96000	892	**660**	567	474
GUITAR	32	GIBSON	**HG-20 HAWAIIAN** BLACK	1,195	**883**	759	634
GUITAR	37	GIBSON	**HG-CENTURY** ROSEWOOD AND PEARL INLAYS	2,112	**1,562**	1,342	1,122
GUITAR	39	GIBSON	**HG-CENTURY** ROSEWOOD AND PEARL INLAYS	1,992	**1,473**	1,265	1,058
GUITAR	78	GIBSON	**HOWARD ROBERTS ARTIST** 1 PU	1,274	**942**	810	677
GUITAR	74	GIBSON	**HOWARD ROBERTS CUSTOM** SUNBURST	1,345	**995**	855	715
GUITAR	76	GIBSON	**HOWARD ROBERTS CUSTOM**	1,195	**883**	759	634
GUITAR	60	GIBSON	**HUMMINGBIRD** CHERRY SUNBURST	2,217	**1,640**	1,409	1,178
GUITAR	61	GIBSON	**HUMMINGBIRD** CHERRY SUNBURST	2,102	**1,554**	1,335	1,116
GUITAR	62	GIBSON	**HUMMINGBIRD** CHERRY SUNBURST	2,102	**1,554**	1,335	1,116
GUITAR	63	GIBSON	**HUMMINGBIRD** CHERRY SUNBURST	2,063	**1,525**	1,310	1,095
GUITAR	64	GIBSON	**HUMMINGBIRD** NATURAL	2,040	**1,508**	1,296	1,083
GUITAR	64	GIBSON	**HUMMINGBIRD** CHERRY SUNBURST	2,083	**1,540**	1,323	1,106
GUITAR	65	GIBSON	**HUMMINGBIRD** CHERRY SUNBURST	2,988	**2,210**	1,898	1,587
GUITAR	66	GIBSON	**HUMMINGBIRD** CHERRY SUNBURST	2,083	**1,540**	1,323	1,106
GUITAR	67	GIBSON	**HUMMINGBIRD** CHERRY SUNBURST	1,416	**1,047**	899	752
GUITAR	67	GIBSON	**HUMMINGBIRD** NATURAL	1,930	**1,427**	1,226	1,025
GUITAR	68	GIBSON	**HUMMINGBIRD** CHERRY SUNBURST	1,416	**1,047**	899	752
GUITAR	68	GIBSON	**HUMMINGBIRD** NATURAL BLOND	1,894	**1,400**	1,203	1,006
GUITAR	69	GIBSON	**HUMMINGBIRD** CHERRY SUNBURST	1,270	**939**	807	674
GUITAR	70	GIBSON	**HUMMINGBIRD** CHERRY SUNBURST	2,122	**1,569**	1,348	1,127
GUITAR	72	GIBSON	**HUMMINGBIRD** CHERRY SUNBURST	2,021	**1,495**	1,284	1,074
GUITAR	73	GIBSON	**HUMMINGBIRD** CHERRY SUNBURST	1,961	**1,450**	1,246	1,041
GUITAR	74	GIBSON	**HUMMINGBIRD** CHERRY SUNBURST	1,874	**1,386**	1,191	996
GUITAR	75	GIBSON	**HUMMINGBIRD** NATURAL	1,503	**1,111**	955	798
GUITAR	75	GIBSON	**HUMMINGBIRD** CHERRY SUNBURST	1,852	**1,370**	1,177	984
GUITAR	76	GIBSON	**HUMMINGBIRD** CHERRY SUNBURST	1,792	**1,325**	1,138	952

TYPE	YR	MFG	PRICES--BASED ON 100% ORIGINAL MODEL	SELL EXC	SELL AVG	BUY EXC	BUY AVG
GUITAR	77	GIBSON	**HUMMINGBIRD** WINE RED	1,572	**1,162**	999	835
GUITAR	79	GIBSON	**HUMMINGBIRD** BURGUNDY	1,424	**1,053**	905	756
GUITAR	87	GIBSON	**J- 25**	456	**337**	289	242
GUITAR	84	GIBSON	**J- 30**	637	**471**	405	338
GUITAR	37	GIBSON	**J- 35** SUNBURST, SERIAL #-95400	3,776	**2,793**	2,399	2,006
GUITAR	38	GIBSON	**J- 35** NATURAL, SERIAL #95400-	7,059	**5,221**	4,485	3,750
GUITAR	39	GIBSON	**J- 35** SUNBURST, SERIAL #-96000	3,624	**2,680**	2,303	1,925
GUITAR	39	GIBSON	**J- 35** NATURAL	7,051	**5,214**	4,480	3,745
GUITAR	40	GIBSON	**J- 35** NATURAL, SERIAL #96000-96600	3,136	**2,319**	1,992	1,666
GUITAR	40	GIBSON	**J- 35** SUNBURST	3,811	**2,818**	2,421	2,024
GUITAR	41	GIBSON	**J- 35** NATURAL, SERIAL #96600-97400	4,800	**3,550**	3,050	2,550
GUITAR	71	GIBSON	**J- 40** NATURAL	682	**504**	433	362
GUITAR	72	GIBSON	**J- 40** NATURAL	581	**430**	369	309
GUITAR	74	GIBSON	**J- 40** NATURAL	781	**577**	496	415
GUITAR	75	GIBSON	**J- 40** NATURAL	780	**577**	495	414
GUITAR	78	GIBSON	**J- 40** NATURAL	637	**471**	405	338
GUITAR	42	GIBSON	**J- 45** SUNBURST, BANNER PEGHEAD LOGO	2,999	**2,218**	1,905	1,593
GUITAR	43	GIBSON	**J- 45** SUNBURST	3,391	**2,508**	2,155	1,801
GUITAR	43	GIBSON	**J- 45** MAHOGANY	6,986	**5,167**	4,439	3,711
GUITAR	44	GIBSON	**J- 45** SUNBURST	3,158	**2,335**	2,006	1,677
GUITAR	45	GIBSON	**J- 45** SUNBURST	3,218	**2,380**	2,045	1,710
GUITAR	45	GIBSON	**J- 45** MAPLE	7,185	**5,314**	4,565	3,817
GUITAR	46	GIBSON	**J- 45** SUNBURST, BANNER LOGO	3,081	**2,279**	1,958	1,637
GUITAR	47	GIBSON	**J- 45** STANDARD LOGO	2,151	**1,591**	1,367	1,142
GUITAR	47	GIBSON	**J- 45** SUNBURST	3,264	**2,414**	2,074	1,734
GUITAR	47	GIBSON	**J- 45** MAPLE	6,762	**5,001**	4,296	3,592
GUITAR	48	GIBSON	**J- 45** SUNBURST	2,976	**2,201**	1,891	1,581
GUITAR	49	GIBSON	**J- 45** SUNBURST	2,042	**1,510**	1,298	1,085
GUITAR	50	GIBSON	**J- 45** SUNBURST	2,073	**1,533**	1,317	1,101
GUITAR	51	GIBSON	**J- 45** SUNBURST	2,034	**1,504**	1,292	1,080
GUITAR	52	GIBSON	**J- 45** SUNBURST	3,297	**2,438**	2,095	1,751
GUITAR	53	GIBSON	**J- 45** SUNBURST	1,926	**1,424**	1,224	1,023
GUITAR	55	GIBSON	**J- 45** SUNBURST	1,895	**1,401**	1,204	1,006
GUITAR	57	GIBSON	**J- 45** SUNBURST	1,822	**1,347**	1,157	967
GUITAR	58	GIBSON	**J- 45** SUNBURST	1,684	**1,246**	1,070	895
GUITAR	59	GIBSON	**J- 45** SUNBURST	1,713	**1,267**	1,088	910
GUITAR	60	GIBSON	**J- 45** SUNBURST	1,475	**1,091**	937	783
GUITAR	61	GIBSON	**J- 45** SUNBURST	1,475	**1,091**	937	783
GUITAR	62	GIBSON	**J- 45** SUNBURST	1,423	**1,052**	904	756
GUITAR	63	GIBSON	**J- 45** SUNBURST	1,401	**1,036**	890	744
GUITAR	64	GIBSON	**J- 45** SUNBURST	1,398	**1,034**	888	743
GUITAR	65	GIBSON	**J- 45** SUNBURST	1,331	**984**	846	707
GUITAR	66	GIBSON	**J- 45** SUNBURST	1,248	**923**	793	663

TYPE	YR	MFG	PRICES--BASED ON 100% ORIGINAL MODEL	SELL EXC	SELL AVG	BUY EXC	BUY AVG
GUITAR	67	GIBSON	J- 45 SUNBURST	1,081	800	687	574
GUITAR	68	GIBSON	J- 45 SUNBURST	1,069	790	679	568
GUITAR	69	GIBSON	J- 45 SUNBURST	950	702	603	504
GUITAR	70	GIBSON	J- 45 SUNBURST	796	589	506	423
GUITAR	71	GIBSON	J- 45 SUNBURST	806	596	512	428
GUITAR	72	GIBSON	J- 45 SUNBURST	796	589	506	423
GUITAR	73	GIBSON	J- 45 SUNBURST	794	587	505	422
GUITAR	74	GIBSON	J- 45 SUNBURST	798	590	507	424
GUITAR	75	GIBSON	J- 45 SUNBURST	801	592	509	425
GUITAR	76	GIBSON	J- 45 SUNBURST	770	570	489	409
GUITAR	77	GIBSON	J- 45 SUNBURST	758	560	481	402
GUITAR	78	GIBSON	J- 45 SUNBURST	749	554	476	398
GUITAR	79	GIBSON	J- 45 SUNBURST	722	534	459	384
GUITAR	85	GIBSON	**J- 45 CELEBRITY**	1,354	1,001	860	719
GUITAR	49	GIBSON	J- 50 NATURAL	1,908	1,411	1,212	1,013
GUITAR	50	GIBSON	J- 50 NATURAL	1,775	1,312	1,127	942
GUITAR	51	GIBSON	J- 50 NATURAL	1,850	1,368	1,176	983
GUITAR	52	GIBSON	J- 50 NATURAL	1,908	1,411	1,212	1,013
GUITAR	53	GIBSON	J- 50 NATURAL	1,778	1,315	1,130	945
GUITAR	54	GIBSON	J- 50 NATURAL	1,777	1,314	1,129	944
GUITAR	56	GIBSON	J- 50 NATURAL	1,872	1,385	1,190	995
GUITAR	57	GIBSON	J- 50 NATURAL	1,673	1,237	1,063	888
GUITAR	58	GIBSON	J- 50 NATURAL	1,746	1,291	1,109	927
GUITAR	59	GIBSON	J- 50 NATURAL	1,672	1,236	1,062	888
GUITAR	60	GIBSON	J- 50 NATURAL	1,561	1,155	992	829
GUITAR	61	GIBSON	J- 50 NATURAL	1,512	1,118	961	803
GUITAR	62	GIBSON	J- 50 NATURAL	1,475	1,091	937	783
GUITAR	63	GIBSON	J- 50 NATURAL	1,402	1,037	891	745
GUITAR	63	GIBSON	J- 50 SUNBURST	1,440	1,065	915	765
GUITAR	64	GIBSON	J- 50 NATURAL	1,319	975	838	700
GUITAR	65	GIBSON	J- 50 NATURAL	1,268	937	805	673
GUITAR	66	GIBSON	J- 50 NATURAL	1,211	896	769	643
GUITAR	67	GIBSON	J- 50 NATURAL	1,147	848	728	609
GUITAR	68	GIBSON	J- 50 NATURAL	1,099	812	698	583
GUITAR	68	GIBSON	J- 50 NATURAL, LEFT-HANDED	1,102	815	700	585
GUITAR	69	GIBSON	J- 50 NATURAL	1,019	754	647	541
GUITAR	70	GIBSON	J- 50 NATURAL	975	721	619	518
GUITAR	71	GIBSON	J- 50 NATURAL	927	685	589	492
GUITAR	72	GIBSON	J- 50 NATURAL	912	675	580	485
GUITAR	73	GIBSON	J- 50 NATURAL	858	634	545	455
GUITAR	74	GIBSON	J- 50 NATURAL	826	611	525	439
GUITAR	74	GIBSON	J- 50 NATURAL, LEFT-HANDED	832	615	528	442

TYPE	YR	MFG	PRICES--BASED ON 100% ORIGINAL MODEL	SELL EXC	SELL AVG	BUY EXC	BUY AVG
GUITAR	76	GIBSON	J- 50 NATURAL	730	**540**	464	388
GUITAR	39	GIBSON	J- 55 SUNBURST	6,720	**4,970**	4,270	3,570
GUITAR	40	GIBSON	J- 55 SUNBURST	3,043	**2,250**	1,933	1,616
GUITAR	41	GIBSON	J- 55 SUNBURST	3,043	**2,250**	1,933	1,616
GUITAR	66	GIBSON	J- 55 BLOND	1,063	**786**	675	565
GUITAR	70	GIBSON	J- 55 NATURAL	1,209	**894**	768	642
GUITAR	74	GIBSON	J- 55 SUNBURST	1,032	**763**	655	548
GUITAR	74	GIBSON	J- 55 NATURAL	1,124	**831**	714	597
GUITAR	76	GIBSON	J- 55 NATURAL	1,124	**831**	714	597
GUITAR	79	GIBSON	J- 55	796	**589**	506	423
GUITAR	40	GIBSON	J- 55R SITKA SPRUCE, INDIAN ROSEWOOD	4,508	**3,334**	2,864	2,394
GUITAR	40	GIBSON	J-100 NATURAL	8,156	**6,032**	5,182	4,332
GUITAR	72	GIBSON	J-100 SUNBURST	1,224	**905**	777	650
GUITAR	74	GIBSON	J-100 NATURAL	996	**736**	633	529
GUITAR	89	GIBSON	J-100 MAPLE BACK/SIDES	757	**560**	481	402
GUITAR	54	GIBSON	J-160E SUNBURST, ADJUSTABLE BRIDGE, SERIAL #A16000-A19000	2,950	**2,181**	1,874	1,567
GUITAR	55	GIBSON	J-160E SUNBURST, SERIAL #A19000-A22000	2,106	**1,557**	1,338	1,118
GUITAR	56	GIBSON	J-160E SUNBURST	2,085	**1,542**	1,324	1,107
GUITAR	57	GIBSON	J-160E SUNBURST	2,083	**1,540**	1,323	1,106
GUITAR	58	GIBSON	J-160E SUNBURST	2,081	**1,539**	1,322	1,105
GUITAR	59	GIBSON	J-160E SUNBURST	2,955	**2,186**	1,878	1,570
GUITAR	60	GIBSON	J-160E SUNBURST	1,876	**1,388**	1,192	997
GUITAR	62	GIBSON	J-160E SUNBURST	1,799	**1,330**	1,143	955
GUITAR	63	GIBSON	J-160E SUNBURST	2,232	**1,650**	1,418	1,185
GUITAR	64	GIBSON	J-160E SUNBURST	1,870	**1,383**	1,188	993
GUITAR	65	GIBSON	J-160E SUNBURST	1,736	**1,284**	1,103	922
GUITAR	66	GIBSON	J-160E SUNBURST	1,783	**1,319**	1,133	947
GUITAR	67	GIBSON	J-160E SUNBURST	1,364	**1,008**	866	724
GUITAR	68	GIBSON	J-160E SUNBURST	1,632	**1,207**	1,037	867
GUITAR	69	GIBSON	J-160E SUNBURST	1,499	**1,109**	952	796
GUITAR	70	GIBSON	J-160E SUNBURST	1,351	**999**	858	718
GUITAR	72	GIBSON	J-160E SUNBURSI	1,305	**965**	829	693
GUITAR	73	GIBSON	J-160E SUNBURST	1,305	**965**	829	693
GUITAR	75	GIBSON	J-160E SUNBURST	1,124	**831**	714	597
GUITAR	51	GIBSON	J-185 SUNBURST, FLATTOP	8,993	**6,651**	5,714	4,777
GUITAR	52	GIBSON	J-185 SUNBURST, FLATTOP	8,058	**5,959**	5,120	4,280
GUITAR	53	GIBSON	J-185 SUNBURST, FLATTOP, SERIAL #A13000-A16000	6,631	**4,904**	4,213	3,523
GUITAR	55	GIBSON	J-185 NATURAL, FLATTOP	8,494	**6,282**	5,397	4,512
GUITAR	58	GIBSON	J-185 SUNBURST, FLATTOP	7,494	**5,542**	4,762	3,981
GUITAR	58	GIBSON	J-185 NATURAL, FLATTOP	8,493	**6,281**	5,396	4,511
GUITAR	40	GIBSON	J-200 SUNBURST	10,849	**8,024**	6,894	5,764
GUITAR	50	GIBSON	J-200 SUNBURST, SERIAL #A4400-A6000	9,598	**7,098**	6,098	5,098

TYPE	YR	MFG	PRICES--BASED ON 100% ORIGINAL MODEL	SELL EXC	SELL AVG	BUY EXC	BUY AVG
GUITAR	50	GIBSON	**J-200** NATURAL	10,671	**7,892**	6,780	5,669
GUITAR	51	GIBSON	**J-200** SUNBURST, SERIAL #A28000-	8,566	**6,335**	5,443	4,550
GUITAR	51	GIBSON	**J-200** NATURAL	10,672	**7,893**	6,781	5,669
GUITAR	52	GIBSON	**J-200** SUNBURST	8,566	**6,335**	5,443	4,550
GUITAR	53	GIBSON	**J-200** SUNBURST	7,616	**5,633**	4,839	4,046
GUITAR	53	GIBSON	**J-200** NATURAL	10,097	**7,467**	6,415	5,364
GUITAR	54	GIBSON	**J-200** NATURAL	7,342	**5,430**	4,665	3,900
GUITAR	55	GIBSON	**J-200** SUNBURST, SERIAL #A19000-A22000	8,032	**5,940**	5,103	4,267
GUITAR	55	GIBSON	**J-200** NATURAL	9,402	**6,953**	5,974	4,994
GUITAR	56	GIBSON	**J-200** SUNBURST	8,234	**6,090**	5,232	4,374
GUITAR	56	GIBSON	**J-200** NATURAL	9,133	**6,754**	5,803	4,852
GUITAR	57	GIBSON	**J-200** SUNBURST	7,381	**5,459**	4,690	3,921
GUITAR	57	GIBSON	**J-200** NATURAL, SERIAL #A24600-A26500	8,058	**5,959**	5,120	4,280
GUITAR	58	GIBSON	**J-200** SUNBURST, SERIAL #A26500-A28000	7,202	**5,327**	4,576	3,826
GUITAR	58	GIBSON	**J-200** BROWN SUNBURST	9,133	**6,754**	5,803	4,852
GUITAR	59	GIBSON	**J-200** SUNBURST	6,521	**4,823**	4,143	3,464
GUITAR	59	GIBSON	**J-200** NATURAL	7,958	**5,885**	5,056	4,227
GUITAR	60	GIBSON	**J-200** SUNBURST	6,427	**4,753**	4,083	3,414
GUITAR	61	GIBSON	**J-200** SUNBURST	4,293	**3,175**	2,727	2,280
GUITAR	61	GIBSON	**J-200** NATURAL	6,447	**4,768**	4,096	3,425
GUITAR	62	GIBSON	**J-200** SUNBURST	4,625	**3,420**	2,938	2,457
GUITAR	63	GIBSON	**J-200** SUNBURST	4,356	**3,221**	2,768	2,314
GUITAR	63	GIBSON	**J-200** NATURAL	5,374	**3,974**	3,414	2,854
GUITAR	64	GIBSON	**J-200** SUNBURST	3,408	**2,520**	2,165	1,810
GUITAR	64	GIBSON	**J-200** NATURAL	3,733	**2,761**	2,372	1,983
GUITAR	65	GIBSON	**J-200** SUNBURST	3,761	**2,781**	2,389	1,998
GUITAR	65	GIBSON	**J-200** NATURAL	3,935	**2,910**	2,500	2,090
GUITAR	66	GIBSON	**J-200** SUNBURST	2,341	**1,731**	1,487	1,243
GUITAR	66	GIBSON	**J-200** NATURAL	3,168	**2,343**	2,013	1,683
GUITAR	67	GIBSON	**J-200** NATURAL	2,222	**1,643**	1,412	1,180
GUITAR	67	GIBSON	**J-200** SUNBURST	3,412	**2,524**	2,168	1,813
GUITAR	68	GIBSON	**J-200** NATURAL	2,221	**1,642**	1,411	1,180
GUITAR	68	GIBSON	**J-200** SUNBURST	3,165	**2,340**	2,011	1,681
GUITAR	69	GIBSON	**J-200** NATURAL	2,219	**1,641**	1,410	1,179
GUITAR	69	GIBSON	**J-200** SUNBURST	2,351	**1,738**	1,493	1,248
GUITAR	70	GIBSON	**J-200** NATURAL	1,425	**1,054**	905	757
GUITAR	72	GIBSON	**J-200** NATURAL	1,377	**1,018**	875	731
GUITAR	73	GIBSON	**J-200** NATURAL	1,336	**988**	849	709
GUITAR	74	GIBSON	**J-200** SUNBURST	1,881	**1,391**	1,195	999
GUITAR	70	GIBSON	**J-200 ARTIST** CHERRY SUNBURST	1,315	**972**	835	698
GUITAR	85	GIBSON	**J-200 CELEBRITY**	2,223	**1,644**	1,412	1,181
GUITAR	54	GIBSON	**J-200N**	4,128	**3,053**	2,623	2,193
GUITAR	72	GIBSON	**J-250R**	1,593	**1,178**	1,012	846

TYPE	YR	MFG	PRICES--BASED ON 100% ORIGINAL MODEL	SELL EXC	SELL AVG	BUY EXC	BUY AVG
GUITAR	77	GIBSON	**J-250R**	1,717	**1,270**	1,091	912
GUITAR	62	GIBSON	**JOHNNY SMITH** SUNBURST ICE TEA	6,632	**4,905**	4,214	3,523
GUITAR	62	GIBSON	**JOHNNY SMITH** NATURAL	6,632	**4,905**	4,214	3,523
GUITAR	63	GIBSON	**JOHNNY SMITH** NATURAL	6,253	**4,624**	3,973	3,322
GUITAR	63	GIBSON	**JOHNNY SMITH** SUNBURST	6,994	**5,173**	4,444	3,715
GUITAR	67	GIBSON	**JOHNNY SMITH** NATURAL	5,760	**4,260**	3,660	3,060
GUITAR	67	GIBSON	**JOHNNY SMITH** SUNBURST	6,495	**4,803**	4,127	3,450
GUITAR	75	GIBSON	**JOHNNY SMITH** NATURAL	5,040	**3,727**	3,202	2,677
GUITAR	77	GIBSON	**JOHNNY SMITH** WINE RED	4,818	**3,563**	3,061	2,559
GUITAR	81	GIBSON	**JOHNNY SMITH** SUNBURST	4,320	**3,195**	2,745	2,295
GUITAR	88	GIBSON	**JOHNNY SMITH** SUNBURST, DOUBLE PU	4,603	**3,404**	2,924	2,445
GUITAR	69	GIBSON	**JUBILEE** NATURAL	883	**653**	561	469
GUITAR	69	GIBSON	**JUBILEE** MAHOGANY BACK/SIDES	890	**658**	566	473
GUITAR	71	GIBSON	**JUBILEE** NATURAL, 12-STRING	619	**457**	393	328
GUITAR	70	GIBSON	**JUBILEE DELUXE** ROSEWOOD BACK/SIDES	619	**457**	393	328
GUITAR	34	GIBSON	**JUMBO** SUNBURST, MAHOGANY BACK/SIDES, SERIAL #91500-92400	9,600	**7,100**	6,100	5,100
GUITAR	35	GIBSON	**JUMBO** SUNBURST	11,175	**8,265**	7,101	5,936
GUITAR	36	GIBSON	**JUMBO** SUNBURST	7,988	**5,907**	5,075	4,243
GUITAR	37	GIBSON	**JUMBO** SUNBURST	9,892	**7,316**	6,286	5,255
GUITAR	36	GIBSON	**JUMBO 35** SUNBURST	7,296	**5,396**	4,636	3,876
GUITAR	38	GIBSON	**JUMBO 35** SUNBURST	7,490	**5,540**	4,759	3,979
GUITAR	40	GIBSON	**JUMBO 35** NATURAL	4,320	**3,195**	2,745	2,295
GUITAR	39	GIBSON	**JUMBO 55** SUNBURST	8,640	**6,390**	5,490	4,590
GUITAR	78	GIBSON	**KALAMAZOO AWARD MODEL** NATURAL	10,080	**7,455**	6,405	5,355
GUITAR	80	GIBSON	**KALAMAZOO AWARD MODEL** SUNBURST	12,118	**8,962**	7,700	6,437
GUITAR	81	GIBSON	**KALAMAZOO AWARD MODEL** NATURAL	12,960	**9,585**	8,235	6,885
GUITAR	85	GIBSON	**KENNY BURRELL PROTYPE** DARK BLUE, WOODEN PICKGUARD, 17 7/8" BODY	33,600	**24,850**	21,350	17,850
GUITAR	26	GIBSON	**L- 0** AMBER, FLATTOP, EBONY FRETBOARD & BRIDGE/DIAGONAL LOGO	776	**574**	493	412
GUITAR	27	GIBSON	**L- 0** AMBER, FLATTOP	887	**656**	563	471
GUITAR	28	GIBSON	**L- 0** AMBER, FLATTOP	867	**641**	551	461
GUITAR	29	GIBSON	**L- 0** AMBER, FLATTOP, SERIAL #87300-89800	858	**634**	545	455
GUITAR	30	GIBSON	**L- 0** AMBER, FLATTOP, SERIAL #89800-90200	819	**606**	520	435
GUITAR	31	GIBSON	**L- 0** AMBER, FLATTOP	686	**507**	436	364
GUITAR	35	GIBSON	**L- 0** SUNBURST, FLATTOP	681	**504**	433	362
GUITAR	36	GIBSON	**L- 0** SUNBURST, FLATTOP, SERIAL #93500	680	**503**	432	361
GUITAR	37	GIBSON	**L- 0** BLACK, FLATTOP	668	**494**	424	354
GUITAR	37	GIBSON	**L- 0** SUNBURST, FLATTOP, SERIAL #-95400	670	**495**	425	355
GUITAR	38	GIBSON	**L- 0** BLACK, FLATTOP, SERIAL #95400	790	**584**	502	419
GUITAR	41	GIBSON	**L- 0** BLACK, FLATTOP, SERIAL #96600-97400	672	**497**	427	357
GUITAR	42	GIBSON	**L- 0** BLACK, FLATTOP	780	**577**	495	414
GUITAR	30	GIBSON	**L- 00** BLACK, FLATTOP, SERIAL #89800-90200	926	**685**	588	492
GUITAR	31	GIBSON	**L- 00** BLACK, FLATTOP	892	**660**	567	474

TYPE	YR	MFG	MODEL	SELL EXC	SELL AVG	BUY EXC	BUY AVG
GUITAR	32	GIBSON	L- 00 BLACK, FLATTOP	926	685	588	492
GUITAR	33	GIBSON	L- 00 BLACK, FLATTOP	926	685	588	492
GUITAR	34	GIBSON	L- 00 SUNBURST, FLATTOP	1,380	1,020	877	733
GUITAR	34	GIBSON	L- 00 MAPLE, FLATTOP	1,992	1,473	1,265	1,058
GUITAR	35	GIBSON	L- 00 BLACK, FLATTOP, SERIAL #92400-93500	1,093	808	694	580
GUITAR	35	GIBSON	L- 00 SUNBURST, FLATTOP, SERIAL #92400-93500	1,281	947	814	680
GUITAR	36	GIBSON	L- 00 SUNBURST, FLATTOP	1,206	892	766	641
GUITAR	37	GIBSON	L- 00 SUNBURST, FLATTOP, SERIAL #-95400	1,640	1,213	1,042	871
GUITAR	38	GIBSON	L- 00 SUNBURST, FLATTOP, SERIAL #95400-	1,164	861	739	618
GUITAR	39	GIBSON	L- 00 SUNBURST, FLATTOP	1,117	826	710	593
GUITAR	41	GIBSON	L- 00 BLACK, FLATTOP SERIAL #96600-97400	912	675	580	485
GUITAR	05	GIBSON	L- 1 BLACK, ARCHTOP, SERIAL #1850-2550	972	719	617	516
GUITAR	07	GIBSON	L- 1 BLACK, ARCHTOP	974	720	619	517
GUITAR	14	GIBSON	L- 1 ORANGE, ARCHTOP, SERIAL #16100-20150	974	720	619	517
GUITAR	15	GIBSON	L- 1 NATURAL, ARCHTOP, SERIAL #20150-25150	896	663	569	476
GUITAR	15	GIBSON	L- 1 BLACK, ARCHTOP	956	707	607	507
GUITAR	16	GIBSON	L- 1 NATURAL, ARCHTOP	869	643	552	462
GUITAR	16	GIBSON	L- 1 ORANGE, ARCHTOP	1,197	885	760	635
GUITAR	17	GIBSON	L- 1 NATURAL, ARCHTOP	1,005	743	638	533
GUITAR	17	GIBSON	L- 1 NATURAL, CARVED TOP	1,331	984	846	707
GUITAR	18	GIBSON	L- 1 NATURAL, ARCHTOP, SERIAL #32000-39500	974	720	619	517
GUITAR	19	GIBSON	L- 1 BROWN, ARCHTOP, SERIAL #47900-53800	986	729	627	524
GUITAR	20	GIBSON	L- 1 BROWN, ARCHTOP, SERIAL #53800-62200	972	719	617	516
GUITAR	21	GIBSON	L- 1 BROWN, ARCHTOP, SERIAL #62200-69300	1,536	1,136	976	816
GUITAR	21	GIBSON	L- 1 NATURAL TOP	1,638	1,211	1,041	870
GUITAR	26	GIBSON	L- 1 FLATTOP	1,334	986	847	708
GUITAR	27	GIBSON	L- 1 AMBER, FLATTOP	1,333	986	847	708
GUITAR	29	GIBSON	L- 1 FLATTOP, CONCERT SIZE, SERIAL #87300-89800	1,152	852	732	612
GUITAR	29	GIBSON	L- 1 SUNBURST, FLATTOP	1,430	1,057	908	759
GUITAR	29	GIBSON	L- 1 SUNBURST, 12-FRET	1,970	1,457	1,252	1,047
GUITAR	30	GIBSON	L- 1 SUNBURST, 12-FRET	1,982	1,466	1,259	1,053
GUITAR	31	GIBSON	L- 1 SUNBURST, 12-FRET	1,875	1,387	1,191	996
GUITAR	35	GIBSON	L- 1 SUNBURST, FLATTOP, SERIAL #9240-93500	1,152	852	732	612
GUITAR	37	GIBSON	L- 1	1,274	942	810	677
GUITAR	42	GIBSON	L- 1 NATURAL, FLATTOP	1,332	985	846	707
GUITAR	62	GIBSON	L- 1 NATURAL, WALNUT STAINED BACK	1,333	986	847	708
GUITAR	05	GIBSON	L- 2 ORANGE, ARCHTOP, SERIAL #1850-2550	798	590	507	424
GUITAR	24	GIBSON	L- 2 AMBER, ARCHTOP	804	594	511	427
GUITAR	25	GIBSON	L- 2 SNAKEHEAD BROWN, ARCHTOP	2,051	1,517	1,303	1,089
GUITAR	30	GIBSON	L- 2 NATURAL, FLATTOP, SERIAL #89800-90200	1,699	1,256	1,079	902
GUITAR	31	GIBSON	L- 2 SUNBURST, FLATTOP, SERIAL #90200-90400	1,624	1,201	1,032	862
GUITAR	32	GIBSON	L- 2 SUNBURST, FLATTOP	1,624	1,201	1,032	862

TYPE	YR	MFG	PRICES--BASED ON 100% ORIGINAL MODEL	SELL EXC	SELL AVG	BUY EXC	BUY AVG
GUITAR	15	GIBSON	**L- 3** ARCHTOP, SERIAL #20150-25150	1,699	**1,256**	1,079	902
GUITAR	16	GIBSON	**L- 3** RED MAHOGANY, ARCHTOP, SERIAL #25150-32000	1,281	**947**	814	680
GUITAR	17	GIBSON	**L- 3** RED SUNBURST, ARCHTOP, SERIAL #32000-39500	1,253	**927**	796	666
GUITAR	18	GIBSON	**L- 3** RED SUNBURST, ARCHTOP	1,253	**927**	796	666
GUITAR	19	GIBSON	**L- 3** RED SUNBURST, ARCHTOP, SERIAL #47900-53800	1,253	**927**	796	666
GUITAR	20	GIBSON	**L- 3** RED SUNBURST, ARCHTOP, SERIAL #53800-62200	1,253	**927**	796	666
GUITAR	21	GIBSON	**L- 3** RED SUNBURST, ARCHTOP	1,318	**974**	837	700
GUITAR	24	GIBSON	**L- 3** RED SUNBURST, ARCHTOP	1,178	**871**	749	626
GUITAR	25	GIBSON	**L- 3** RED SUNBURST, SNAKE HEAD	1,300	**962**	826	691
GUITAR	26	GIBSON	**L- 3** RED SUNBURST, ARCHTOP, SERIAL #82700	1,178	**871**	749	626
GUITAR	27	GIBSON	**L- 3** RED SUNBURST, ARCHTOP, SERIAL #85400	1,180	**873**	750	627
GUITAR	28	GIBSON	**L- 3** IVORY, ARCHTOP, SERIAL #85400-87300	1,332	**985**	846	707
GUITAR	29	GIBSON	**L- 3** RED SUNBURST, ARCHTOP, SERIAL #87300-89800	1,105	**817**	702	587
GUITAR	29	GIBSON	**L- 3** IVORY, ARCHTOP	1,331	**984**	846	707
GUITAR	12	GIBSON	**L- 4** BLACK, ARCHTOP	4,166	**3,081**	2,647	2,213
GUITAR	13	GIBSON	**L- 4** BLACK	1,394	**1,031**	886	741
GUITAR	14	GIBSON	**L- 4** SUNBURST, ARCHTOP, SERIAL #16100-20150	1,446	**1,069**	919	768
GUITAR	15	GIBSON	**L- 4** SUNBURST, ARCHTOP, SERIAL #20150-25150	1,447	**1,070**	919	769
GUITAR	17	GIBSON	**L- 4** SUNBURST, ARCHTOP	1,695	**1,253**	1,077	900
GUITAR	18	GIBSON	**L- 4** SUNBURST, ARCHTOP	1,066	**788**	677	566
GUITAR	19	GIBSON	**L- 4** SUNBURST, ARCHTOP	1,075	**795**	683	571
GUITAR	20	GIBSON	**L- 4** SUNBURST, ARCHTOP	1,067	**789**	678	567
GUITAR	24	GIBSON	**L- 4** SUNBURST, ARCHTOP	1,073	**793**	681	570
GUITAR	24	GIBSON	**L- 4** RED SUNBURST	1,513	**1,119**	961	804
GUITAR	25	GIBSON	**L- 4** SUNBURST, ARCHTOP	1,069	**790**	679	568
GUITAR	27	GIBSON	**L- 4** SUNBURST, ARCHTOP	1,063	**786**	675	565
GUITAR	28	GIBSON	**L- 4** SUNBURST, ARCHTOP, SERIAL #85400-87300	1,065	**788**	677	566
GUITAR	29	GIBSON	**L- 4** SUNBURST, ARCHTOP, SERIAL #87300-89800	1,066	**788**	677	566
GUITAR	31	GIBSON	**L- 4** SUNBURST, ARCHTOP	1,063	**786**	675	565
GUITAR	32	GIBSON	**L- 4** SUNBURST, ARCHTOP	1,067	**789**	678	567
GUITAR	33	GIBSON	**L- 4** SUNBURST, ARCHTOP	1,066	**788**	677	566
GUITAR	34	GIBSON	**L- 4** SUNBURST, ARCHTOP, SERIAL #91500-92400	1,068	**790**	678	567
GUITAR	35	GIBSON	**L- 4** SUNBURST, F-HOLES	1,454	**1,075**	924	772
GUITAR	36	GIBSON	**L- 4** SUNBURST, ARCHTOP, SERIAL #93500	1,066	**788**	677	566
GUITAR	37	GIBSON	**L- 4** SUNBURST, ARCHTOP, SERIAL #93500-95400	1,115	**825**	708	592
GUITAR	38	GIBSON	**L- 4** SUNBURST, ARCHTOP	1,068	**790**	678	567
GUITAR	39	GIBSON	**L- 4** SUNBURST, ARCHTOP	1,362	**1,007**	865	723
GUITAR	40	GIBSON	**L- 4** BLOND, ARCHTOP, NON-CUTAWAY	1,227	**908**	780	652
GUITAR	46	GIBSON	**L- 4** SUNBURST, SUNBURST	1,066	**788**	677	566
GUITAR	47	GIBSON	**L- 4** NATURAL, ARCHTOP, TRIPLE BOUND	1,793	**1,326**	1,139	952
GUITAR	48	GIBSON	**L- 4** SUNBURST, ARCHTOP, SERIAL #A1400-A2800	1,038	**768**	660	551
GUITAR	48	GIBSON	**L- 4** BLOND, SOLID CARVED TOP, NON-CUTAWAY, ARCHTOP	1,802	**1,333**	1,145	957

TYPE	YR	MFG	PRICES--BASED ON 100% ORIGINAL MODEL	SELL EXC	SELL AVG	BUY EXC	BUY AVG
GUITAR	49	GIBSON	L- 4 SUNBURST, ARCHTOP	956	**707**	607	507
GUITAR	49	GIBSON	L- 4 NATURAL, ARCHTOP, SERIAL #A2801-A4400	1,502	**1,111**	954	798
GUITAR	51	GIBSON	L- 4 SUNBURST, ARCHTOP, SERIAL #A6000-A9400	1,003	**741**	637	532
GUITAR	54	GIBSON	L- 4 SUNBURST, ARCHTOP	887	**656**	563	471
GUITAR	49	GIBSON	L- 4C SUNBURST, CUTAWAY	3,390	**2,507**	2,154	1,801
GUITAR	50	GIBSON	L- 4C SUNBURST, CUTAWAY, SERIAL #A4400-A6000	1,783	**1,319**	1,133	947
GUITAR	51	GIBSON	L- 4C SUNBURST, CUTAWAY, SERIAL #A6000-A9400	1,788	**1,322**	1,136	950
GUITAR	51	GIBSON	L- 4C NATURAL, CUTAWAY	2,240	**1,657**	1,423	1,190
GUITAR	52	GIBSON	L- 4C SUNBURST, CUTAWAY, SERIAL #A9400-A13000	1,777	**1,314**	1,129	944
GUITAR	53	GIBSON	L- 4C SUNBURST, CUTAWAY, SERIAL #A13000-A16000	1,775	**1,312**	1,127	942
GUITAR	53	GIBSON	L- 4C NATURAL, CUTAWAY, SERIAL #A13000-A16000	2,225	**1,645**	1,413	1,182
GUITAR	54	GIBSON	L- 4C SUNBURST, CUTAWAY	1,777	**1,314**	1,129	944
GUITAR	55	GIBSON	L- 4C NATURAL, CUTAWAY	1,872	**1,385**	1,190	995
GUITAR	55	GIBSON	L- 4C SUNBURST, CUTAWAY	1,924	**1,423**	1,223	1,022
GUITAR	56	GIBSON	L- 4C NATURAL, CUTAWAY, SERIAL #A22000-A24600	1,832	**1,355**	1,164	973
GUITAR	58	GIBSON	L- 4C SUNBURST, CUTAWAY, SERIAL #A26500-A28000	1,783	**1,319**	1,133	947
GUITAR	60	GIBSON	L- 4C SUNBURST, CUTAWAY	1,737	**1,285**	1,104	923
GUITAR	63	GIBSON	L- 4C NATURAL, CUTAWAY	1,912	**1,414**	1,215	1,015
GUITAR	65	GIBSON	L- 4C SUNBURST, CUTAWAY	1,744	**1,290**	1,108	926
GUITAR	66	GIBSON	L- 4C SUNBURST, CUTAWAY	1,752	**1,296**	1,113	931
GUITAR	68	GIBSON	L- 4C SUNBURST, CUTAWAY	1,377	**1,018**	875	731
GUITAR	69	GIBSON	L- 4CES SPRUCE, ROSEWOOD, ARCHTOP	4,009	**2,965**	2,547	2,130
GUITAR	87	GIBSON	L- 4CES NATURAL	2,071	**1,532**	1,316	1,100
GUITAR	22	GIBSON	L- 5 SUNBURST, LLOYD LOAR	29,760	**22,010**	18,910	15,810
GUITAR	23	GIBSON	L- 5 SUNBURST, NON-CUTAWAY, SERIAL #53800-62200	8,597	**6,358**	5,463	4,567
GUITAR	24	GIBSON	L- 5 SUNBURST, NON-CUTAWAY, SERIAL #74900-80300	8,597	**6,358**	5,463	4,567
GUITAR	24	GIBSON	L- 5 SUNBURST, SIGNED BY LLOYD LOAR	42,065	**31,110**	26,728	22,347
GUITAR	25	GIBSON	L- 5 SUNBURST, NON-CUTAWAY, SERIAL #80300-82700	11,712	**8,662**	7,442	6,222
GUITAR	27	GIBSON	L- 5 SUNBURST	6,720	**4,970**	4,270	3,570
GUITAR	27	GIBSON	L- 5 SUNBURST, NON-CUTAWAY	11,712	**8,662**	7,442	6,222
GUITAR	28	GIBSON	L- 5 SUNBURST, NON-CUTAWAY, SERIAL #85400-87300	7,200	**5,325**	4,575	3,825
GUITAR	29	GIBSON	L- 5 DOT INLAY	7,920	**5,857**	5,032	4,207
GUITAR	29	GIBSON	L- 5 SUNBURST, NON-CUTAWAY	8,160	**6,035**	5,185	4,335
GUITAR	30	GIBSON	L- 5 SUNBURST, NON-CUTAWAY	6,240	**4,615**	3,965	3,315
GUITAR	31	GIBSON	L- 5 BLOCK INLAY, GOLD HARDWARE	5,824	**4,307**	3,700	3,094
GUITAR	33	GIBSON	L- 5 SUNBURST, NON-CUTAWAY	6,240	**4,615**	3,965	3,315
GUITAR	34	GIBSON	L- 5 BLOCK INLAY, NON-CUTAWAY	4,284	**3,168**	2,722	2,276
GUITAR	34	GIBSON	L- 5 SUNBURST, NON-CUTAWAY, SERIAL #91500-92400	7,180	**5,310**	4,562	3,814
GUITAR	35	GIBSON	L- 5 SUNBURST, NON-CUTAWAY SERIAL #92400-93500	6,641	**4,911**	4,219	3,528
GUITAR	36	GIBSON	L- 5 SUNBURST, NON-CUTAWAY, SERIAL #93500	6,226	**4,605**	3,956	3,307
GUITAR	37	GIBSON	L- 5 SUNBURST, NON-CUTAWAY	5,040	**3,727**	3,202	2,677
GUITAR	38	GIBSON	L- 5 SUNBURST, NON-CUTAWAY	5,760	**4,260**	3,660	3,060

TYPE	YR	MFG	**PRICES--BASED ON 100% ORIGINAL** MODEL	SELL EXC	SELL AVG	BUY EXC	BUY AVG
GUITAR	38	GIBSON	L- 5 NATURAL, NON-CUTAWAY, SERIAL #95400	6,772	**5,009**	4,303	3,598
GUITAR	39	GIBSON	L- 5 SUNBURST, NON-CUTAWAY	5,290	**3,912**	3,361	2,810
GUITAR	39	GIBSON	L- 5 NATURAL, NON-CUTAWAY	6,767	**5,004**	4,299	3,594
GUITAR	40	GIBSON	L- 5 SUNBURST, NON-CUTAWAY, SERIAL #96000	4,997	**3,696**	3,175	2,655
GUITAR	40	GIBSON	L- 5 NATURAL, NON-CUTAWAY	6,240	**4,615**	3,965	3,315
GUITAR	41	GIBSON	L- 5 SUNBURST, NON-CUTAWAY	5,114	**3,782**	3,250	2,717
GUITAR	43	GIBSON	L- 5 SUNBURST, NON-CUTAWAY	4,820	**3,564**	3,062	2,560
GUITAR	45	GIBSON	L- 5 SUNBURST, NON-CUTAWAY	4,752	**3,514**	3,019	2,524
GUITAR	46	GIBSON	L- 5 SUNBURST, NON-CUTAWAY	4,711	**3,484**	2,993	2,503
GUITAR	46	GIBSON	L- 5 NATURAL, NON-CUTAWAY, SERIAL #95400	5,832	**4,313**	3,705	3,098
GUITAR	47	GIBSON	L- 5 SUNBURST, NON-CUTAWAY, SERIAL #99500-A1400	4,533	**3,352**	2,880	2,408
GUITAR	47	GIBSON	L- 5 NATURAL, NON-CUTAWAY	5,520	**4,082**	3,507	2,932
GUITAR	48	GIBSON	L- 5 SUNBURST, NON-CUTAWAY, SERIAL #A1400-A2800	4,443	**3,286**	2,823	2,360
GUITAR	49	GIBSON	L- 5 SUNBURST, NON-CUTAWAY	4,444	**3,287**	2,824	2,361
GUITAR	49	GIBSON	L- 5 NATURAL, NON-CUTAWAY, SERIAL #A2800-A4400	4,823	**3,567**	3,064	2,562
GUITAR	51	GIBSON	L- 5 NATURAL, NON-CUTAWAY, SERIAL #A6000-A9400	5,520	**4,082**	3,507	2,932
GUITAR	52	GIBSON	L- 5 SUNBURST, NON-CUTAWAY	5,760	**4,260**	3,660	3,060
GUITAR	53	GIBSON	L- 5 SUNBURST, NON-CUTAWAY, SERIAL #A13000-A16000	4,171	**3,084**	2,650	2,215
GUITAR	55	GIBSON	L- 5 NATURAL, NON-CUTAWAY	4,819	**3,564**	3,062	2,560
GUITAR	56	GIBSON	L- 5 SUNBURST	6,096	**4,508**	3,873	3,238
GUITAR	71	GIBSON	L- 5 SUNBURST, NON-CUTAWAY	3,898	**2,883**	2,477	2,071
GUITAR	77	GIBSON	L- 5 SUNBURST, NON-CUTAWAY	3,614	**2,673**	2,296	1,920
GUITAR	78	GIBSON	L- 5 SUNBURST, NON-CUTAWAY	3,558	**2,631**	2,261	1,890
GUITAR	34	GIBSON	**L- 5 CUSTOM** MAHOGANY	4,909	**3,630**	3,119	2,608
GUITAR	28	GIBSON	**L- 5 SPECIAL** 16" SNAKE HEAD	6,240	**4,615**	3,965	3,315
GUITAR	28	GIBSON	**L- 5C** CURLY MAPLE FIGURED, CUTAWAY	14,400	**10,650**	9,150	7,650
GUITAR	39	GIBSON	**L- 5C** NATURAL, CUTAWAY, PREMIER	12,134	**8,974**	7,710	6,446
GUITAR	40	GIBSON	**L- 5C** BLOND, CUTAWAY	11,156	**8,250**	7,088	5,926
GUITAR	48	GIBSON	**L- 5C** SUNBURST	11,040	**8,164**	7,015	5,865
GUITAR	49	GIBSON	**L- 5C** NATURAL, CUTAWAY, SERIAL #A2800-A4400	11,626	**8,598**	7,387	6,176
GUITAR	50	GIBSON	**L- 5C** SUNBURST, CUTAWAY, SERIAL #A4400-A6000	8,596	**6,358**	5,462	4,567
GUITAR	51	GIBSON	**L- 5C** SUNBURST, CUTAWAY	8,160	**6,035**	5,185	4,335
GUITAR	54	GIBSON	**L- 5C** SUNBURST, CUTAWAY	8,948	**6,617**	5,685	4,753
GUITAR	55	GIBSON	**L- 5C** NATURAL, CUTAWAY, SERIAL #A19000-A22000	11,624	**8,597**	7,386	6,175
GUITAR	57	GIBSON	**L- 5C** NATURAL, CUTAWAY, PAF's	9,185	**6,793**	5,836	4,879
GUITAR	58	GIBSON	**L- 5C** SUNBURST, CUTAWAY	8,512	**6,295**	5,408	4,522
GUITAR	58	GIBSON	**L- 5C** SUNBURST	9,648	**7,135**	6,130	5,125
GUITAR	58	GIBSON	**L- 5C** NATURAL, CUTAWAY, SERIAL #A26500-A28000	13,409	**9,917**	8,520	7,123
GUITAR	59	GIBSON	**L- 5C** SUNBURST, CUTAWAY	6,694	**4,950**	4,253	3,556
GUITAR	60	GIBSON	**L- 5C** NATURAL, CUTAWAY	8,951	**6,620**	5,687	4,755
GUITAR	62	GIBSON	**L- 5C** SUNBURST, CUTAWAY	6,457	**4,776**	4,103	3,430
GUITAR	64	GIBSON	**L- 5C** FLAMEY SUNBURST, 1 PU	5,760	**4,260**	3,660	3,060

TYPE	YR	MFG	**PRICES--BASED ON 100% ORIGINAL** MODEL	SELL EXC	SELL AVG	BUY EXC	BUY AVG
GUITAR	64	GIBSON	**L- 5C** SUNBURST, CUTAWAY	6,433	**4,758**	4,088	3,418
GUITAR	67	GIBSON	**L- 5C** SUNBURST, CUTAWAY	6,433	**4,758**	4,088	3,418
GUITAR	68	GIBSON	**L- 5C** NATURAL, CUTAWAY	6,720	**4,970**	4,270	3,570
GUITAR	68	GIBSON	**L- 5C** SUNBURST, CUTAWAY	7,298	**5,398**	4,637	3,877
GUITAR	69	GIBSON	**L- 5C** SUNBURST, CUTAWAY	7,087	**5,241**	4,503	3,765
GUITAR	70	GIBSON	**L- 5C** SUNBURST, CUTAWAY	6,884	**5,091**	4,374	3,657
GUITAR	72	GIBSON	**L- 5C** SUNBURST, CUTAWAY	6,704	**4,958**	4,260	3,561
GUITAR	74	GIBSON	**L- 5C** SUNBURST, CUTAWAY	6,048	**4,473**	3,843	3,213
GUITAR	75	GIBSON	**L- 5C** SUNBURST, CUTAWAY	5,683	**4,203**	3,611	3,019
GUITAR	76	GIBSON	**L- 5C** SUNBURST, CUTAWAY	5,327	**3,939**	3,384	2,829
GUITAR	77	GIBSON	**L- 5C** SUNBURST, CUTAWAY	5,281	**3,906**	3,356	2,806
GUITAR	78	GIBSON	**L- 5C** SUNBURST, CUTAWAY	5,253	**3,885**	3,337	2,790
GUITAR	54	GIBSON	**L- 5CN** ARCHTOP	12,862	**9,512**	8,172	6,832
GUITAR	76	GIBSON	**L- 5CN** SUNBURST, TUNE-O-MATIC	3,378	**2,498**	2,146	1,794
GUITAR	59	GIBSON	**L- 5CT GEORGE GOBEL** CHERRY RED	19,200	**14,200**	12,200	10,200
GUITAR	60	GIBSON	**L- 5CT GEORGE GOBEL** CHERRY RED	14,974	**11,074**	9,514	7,954
GUITAR	61	GIBSON	**L- 5CT GEORGE GOBEL** CHERRY RED	19,200	**14,200**	12,200	10,200
GUITAR	38	GIBSON	**L- 5P PREMIER** BLOND	14,846	**10,980**	9,433	7,887
GUITAR	39	GIBSON	**L- 5P PREMIER** NATURAL BLOND, SERIAL #-96000	16,486	**12,192**	10,475	8,758
GUITAR	40	GIBSON	**L- 5P PREMIER** SUNBURST, SERIAL #96000-96600	11,597	**8,577**	7,369	6,161
GUITAR	40	GIBSON	**L- 5P PREMIER** NATURAL BLOND, SERIAL #96000-96600	13,582	**10,045**	8,630	7,215
GUITAR	41	GIBSON	**L- 5P PREMIER** NATURAL BLOND, SERIAL #96600-97400	9,341	**6,909**	5,935	4,962
GUITAR	47	GIBSON	**L- 5P PREMIER** SUNBURST	6,208	**4,591**	3,944	3,298
GUITAR	33	GIBSON	**L- 7** SUNBURST, NON-CUTAWAY, SERIAL #90700-91500	1,931	**1,428**	1,227	1,026
GUITAR	34	GIBSON	**L- 7** SUNBURST, NON-CUTAWAY, SERIAL #91500-92400	1,656	**1,225**	1,052	880
GUITAR	35	GIBSON	**L- 7** SUNBURST, NON-CUTAWAY, SERIAL #92400-93500	1,783	**1,319**	1,133	947
GUITAR	36	GIBSON	**L- 7** SUNBURST, NON-CUTAWAY, SERIAL #93500	1,651	**1,221**	1,049	877
GUITAR	37	GIBSON	**L- 7** NATURAL, NON-CUTAWAY, SERIAL #-95400	1,488	**1,100**	945	790
GUITAR	37	GIBSON	**L- 7** SUNBURST, NON-CUTAWAY, SERIAL #-95400	1,735	**1,283**	1,102	922
GUITAR	38	GIBSON	**L- 7** SUNBURST, NON-CUTAWAY, SERIAL #95400	1,857	**1,373**	1,180	986
GUITAR	39	GIBSON	**L- 7** NATURAL, NON-CUTAWAY	1,785	**1,320**	1,134	948
GUITAR	39	GIBSON	**L- 7** SUNBURST, NON-CUTAWAY, SERIAL #-96000	1,868	**1,381**	1,187	992
GUITAR	40	GIBSON	**L- 7** NATURAL, NON-CUTAWAY	1,778	**1,315**	1,130	945
GUITAR	42	GIBSON	**L- 7** SUNBURST, NON-CUTAWAY, SERIAL #97400-97600	1,834	**1,356**	1,165	974
GUITAR	43	GIBSON	**L- 7** SUNBURST, NON-CUTAWAY	1,866	**1,380**	1,185	991
GUITAR	44	GIBSON	**L- 7** SUNBURST, NON-CUTAWAY, SERIAL #97800-98300	1,782	**1,318**	1,132	947
GUITAR	45	GIBSON	**L- 7** NATURAL, NON-CUTAWAY, SERIAL #98300-98600	1,779	**1,316**	1,130	945
GUITAR	46	GIBSON	**L- 7** SUNBURST, NON-CUTAWAY	1,713	**1,267**	1,088	910
GUITAR	46	GIBSON	**L- 7** NATURAL, NON-CUTAWAY, SERIAL #98600-99500	1,779	**1,316**	1,130	945
GUITAR	47	GIBSON	**L- 7** SUNBURST, NON-CUTAWAY, SERIAL #99500-A1400	1,726	**1,276**	1,096	916
GUITAR	48	GIBSON	**L- 7** SUNBURST, NON-CUTAWAY, SERIAL #A1400-A2800	1,122	**829**	713	596
GUITAR	48	GIBSON	**L- 7** NATURAL, NON-CUTAWAY, SERIAL #A1400-A2800	1,778	**1,315**	1,130	945

TYPE	YR	MFG	PRICES--BASED ON 100% ORIGINAL MODEL	SELL EXC	SELL AVG	BUY EXC	BUY AVG
GUITAR	49	GIBSON	**L- 7** BLACK, NON-CUTAWAY, SERIAL #A2800-A4400	1,122	**829**	713	596
GUITAR	49	GIBSON	**L- 7** SUNBURST, NON-CUTAWAY, SERIAL #A2800-A4400	1,122	**829**	713	596
GUITAR	50	GIBSON	**L- 7** SUNBURST, NON-CUTAWAY, SERIAL #A4400-A6000	1,104	**817**	702	587
GUITAR	50	GIBSON	**L- 7** NATURAL, NON-CUTAWAY, SERIAL #A4400-A6000	2,062	**1,525**	1,310	1,095
GUITAR	51	GIBSON	**L- 7** SUNBURST, NON-CUTAWAY, SERIAL #A6000-A9400	1,096	**810**	696	582
GUITAR	52	GIBSON	**L- 7** SUNBURST, NON-CUTAWAY, SERIAL #A9400-A13000	1,094	**809**	695	581
GUITAR	54	GIBSON	**L- 7** SUNBURST, NON-CUTAWAY	1,752	**1,296**	1,113	931
GUITAR	55	GIBSON	**L- 7** SUNBURST, NON-CUTAWAY	1,455	**1,076**	924	773
GUITAR	48	GIBSON	**L- 7C** SUNBURST	3,120	**2,307**	1,982	1,657
GUITAR	48	GIBSON	**L- 7C** NATURAL, CUTAWAY	4,080	**3,017**	2,592	2,167
GUITAR	50	GIBSON	**L- 7C** SUNBURST, CUTAWAY	5,350	**3,956**	3,399	2,842
GUITAR	51	GIBSON	**L- 7C** SUNBURST, CUTAWAY, SERIAL #A6000-A9400	4,290	**3,172**	2,726	2,279
GUITAR	52	GIBSON	**L- 7C** NATURAL, CUTAWAY, SERIAL #A9400-A13000	2,002	**1,481**	1,272	1,063
GUITAR	52	GIBSON	**L- 7C** SUNBURST, CUTAWAY, SERIAL #A9400-A13000	3,959	**2,928**	2,515	2,103
GUITAR	53	GIBSON	**L- 7C** SUNBURST, CUTAWAY	4,512	**3,337**	2,867	2,397
GUITAR	54	GIBSON	**L- 7C** NATURAL, CUTAWAY, SERIAL #16000-A19000	3,744	**2,769**	2,379	1,989
GUITAR	56	GIBSON	**L- 7C** NATURAL, CUTAWAY, SERIAL #A22000-A24600	3,739	**2,765**	2,375	1,986
GUITAR	58	GIBSON	**L- 7C** SUNBURST, CUTAWAY	3,360	**2,485**	2,135	1,785
GUITAR	60	GIBSON	**L- 7C** SUNBURST	2,191	**1,620**	1,392	1,164
GUITAR	60	GIBSON	**L- 7C** SUNBURST, CUTAWAY	3,741	**2,766**	2,377	1,987
GUITAR	61	GIBSON	**L- 7C** SUNBURST, CUTAWAY	3,741	**2,766**	2,377	1,987
GUITAR	63	GIBSON	**L- 7C** VINTAGE SUNBURST, DeARMOND	3,216	**2,378**	2,043	1,708
GUITAR	67	GIBSON	**L- 7C** NATURAL, CUTAWAY	1,572	**1,162**	999	835
GUITAR	67	GIBSON	**L- 7C** SUNBURST, CUTAWAY	2,976	**2,201**	1,891	1,581
GUITAR	69	GIBSON	**L- 7C** SUNBURST, CUTAWAY	3,168	**2,343**	2,013	1,683
GUITAR	49	GIBSON	**L- 7CE** NATURAL, CUTAWAY, SERIAL #A2800-A4400	4,285	**3,169**	2,723	2,276
GUITAR	51	GIBSON	**L- 7CED** SUNBURST, CUTAWAY, SERIAL #A6000-A9400	4,171	**3,084**	2,650	2,215
GUITAR	50	GIBSON	**L- 7CN** BROWN, 1 PU	4,224	**3,124**	2,684	2,244
GUITAR	51	GIBSON	**L- 7CN** CARMEL, 2 PU's	3,600	**2,662**	2,287	1,912
GUITAR	56	GIBSON	**L- 7CN** BLONDE	4,405	**3,258**	2,799	2,340
GUITAR	52	GIBSON	**L- 7CT** TENOR, SUNBURST, CUTAWAY	3,157	**2,335**	2,006	1,677
GUITAR	52	GIBSON	**L- 7E** SUNBURST, NO-CUTAWAY	1,781	**1,317**	1,132	946
GUITAR	49	GIBSON	**L- 7ED** SUNBURST, NON-CUTAWAY, SERIAL #A2800-A4400	3,160	**2,337**	2,008	1,678
GUITAR	50	GIBSON	**L- 7ED** SUNBURST, CUTAWAY, SERIAL #A4400-A6000	2,213	**1,637**	1,406	1,176
GUITAR	41	GIBSON	**L- 7N** NATURAL	1,912	**1,414**	1,215	1,015
GUITAR	31	GIBSON	**L- 10**	1,195	**883**	759	634
GUITAR	31	GIBSON	**L- 10** BLACK, ARCHTOP, SERIAL #90200-90400	1,469	**1,087**	933	780
GUITAR	32	GIBSON	**L- 10** BLACK, ARCHTOP	2,064	**1,527**	1,312	1,097
GUITAR	33	GIBSON	**L- 10** BLACK, ARCHTOP	2,390	**1,767**	1,518	1,269
GUITAR	34	GIBSON	**L- 10** BLACK, ARCHTOP	1,670	**1,235**	1,061	887
GUITAR	34	GIBSON	**L- 10** SUNBURST, ARCHTOP	1,816	**1,343**	1,154	964
GUITAR	35	GIBSON	**L- 10** BLACK, ARCHTOP, SERIAL #92400-93500	1,632	**1,207**	1,037	867

TYPE	YR	MFG	PRICES--BASED ON 100% ORIGINAL MODEL	SELL EXC	SELL AVG	BUY EXC	BUY AVG
GUITAR	35	GIBSON	**L- 10** SUNBURST, ARCHTOP	1,724	**1,275**	1,095	915
GUITAR	36	GIBSON	**L- 10** SUNBURST, ARCHTOP, SERIAL #93500	1,559	**1,153**	990	828
GUITAR	37	GIBSON	**L- 10** ARCHTOP, CHECKER BINDING	1,643	**1,215**	1,044	873
GUITAR	39	GIBSON	**L- 10** SUNBURST, ARCHTOP, SERIAL #96000	1,484	**1,097**	943	788
GUITAR	32	GIBSON	**L- 12** SUNBURST, ARCHTOP, SERIAL #90400-90700	2,340	**1,730**	1,487	1,243
GUITAR	33	GIBSON	**L- 12** SUNBURST, ARCHTOP	2,390	**1,767**	1,518	1,269
GUITAR	34	GIBSON	**L- 12** SUNBURST, ARCHTOP, SERIAL #91500-92400	2,340	**1,730**	1,487	1,243
GUITAR	35	GIBSON	**L- 12** SUNBURST, ARCHTOP	2,040	**1,509**	1,296	1,084
GUITAR	36	GIBSON	**L- 12** SUNBURST, ARCHTOP	2,346	**1,735**	1,490	1,246
GUITAR	37	GIBSON	**L- 12** SUNBURST, ARCHTOP, NON-CUTAWAY	1,988	**1,470**	1,263	1,056
GUITAR	37	GIBSON	**L- 12** SUNBURST, ARCHTOP, SERIAL #95400	2,341	**1,731**	1,487	1,243
GUITAR	39	GIBSON	**L- 12** SUNBURST, ARCHTOP	1,648	**1,219**	1,047	875
GUITAR	40	GIBSON	**L- 12** SUNBURST, ARCHTOP, SERIAL #96000	2,340	**1,730**	1,487	1,243
GUITAR	41	GIBSON	**L- 12** SUNBURST, ARCHTOP, SERIAL #97400	2,340	**1,730**	1,487	1,243
GUITAR	46	GIBSON	**L- 12**	3,072	**2,272**	1,952	1,632
GUITAR	47	GIBSON	**L- 12** SUNBURST, CUTAWAY, SERIAL #99500-A1400	1,874	**1,386**	1,191	996
GUITAR	48	GIBSON	**L- 12** SUNBURST, ARCHTOP, SERIAL #A1400-A2800	2,345	**1,734**	1,490	1,245
GUITAR	52	GIBSON	**L- 12** SUNBURST, ARCHTOP	1,874	**1,386**	1,191	996
GUITAR	49	GIBSON	**L- 12C** SUNBURST	5,280	**3,905**	3,355	2,805
GUITAR	48	GIBSON	**L- 12P PREMIER** SUNBURST, ARCHTOP, SERIAL #A1400-A2800	1,876	**1,388**	1,192	997
GUITAR	48	GIBSON	**L- 12P PREMIER** BROWN	2,003	**1,481**	1,273	1,064
GUITAR	49	GIBSON	**L- 12P PREMIER** SUNBURST, ARCHTOP, SERIAL #A2800-A4400	2,111	**1,561**	1,341	1,121
GUITAR	35	GIBSON	**L- 30** BLACK, ARCHTOP, SERIAL #92400-93500	1,114	**824**	708	592
GUITAR	37	GIBSON	**L- 30** BLACK, ARACHTOP	929	**687**	590	493
GUITAR	37	GIBSON	**L- 30** SUNBURST, ARCHTOP, SERIAL #95400	929	**687**	590	493
GUITAR	38	GIBSON	**L- 30** BLACK, ARCHTOP, SERIAL #95400	925	**684**	588	491
GUITAR	38	GIBSON	**L- 30** SUNBURST, ARCHTOP	935	**691**	594	496
GUITAR	39	GIBSON	**L- 30** SUNBURST, ARCHTOP	916	**678**	582	487
GUITAR	40	GIBSON	**L- 30** SUNBURST, ARCHTOP, SERIAL #96000-96600	788	**582**	500	418
GUITAR	41	GIBSON	**L- 30** SUNBURST, ARCHTOP	788	**582**	500	418
GUITAR	42	GIBSON	**L- 30** SUNBURST, ARCHTOP	750	**555**	477	398
GUITAR	37	GIBSON	**L- 37** BROWN SUNBURST, SERIAL #95400	1,126	**832**	715	598
GUITAR	39	GIBSON	**L- 37** BROWN SUNBURST	1,123	**830**	713	596
GUITAR	41	GIBSON	**L- 47** NATURAL BLOND, SERIAL #97400	939	**695**	597	499
GUITAR	46	GIBSON	**L- 48**	657	**486**	417	349
GUITAR	47	GIBSON	**L- 48** SUNBURST	638	**472**	405	339
GUITAR	48	GIBSON	**L- 48** SUNBURST	598	**442**	380	317
GUITAR	49	GIBSON	**L- 48** SUNBURST	619	**457**	393	328
GUITAR	50	GIBSON	**L- 48** SUNBURST	610	**451**	387	324
GUITAR	51	GIBSON	**L- 48** SUNBURST	593	**438**	376	315
GUITAR	52	GIBSON	**L- 48** SUNBURST	600	**443**	381	318
GUITAR	53	GIBSON	**L- 48** SUNBURST	592	**438**	376	314
GUITAR	54	GIBSON	**L- 48** SUNBURST	581	**430**	369	309

TYPE	YR	MFG	PRICES--BASED ON 100% ORIGINAL MODEL	SELL EXC	SELL AVG	BUY EXC	BUY AVG
GUITAR	55	GIBSON	L- 48 SUNBURST	573	423	364	304
GUITAR	56	GIBSON	L- 48 SUNBURST	561	415	356	298
GUITAR	57	GIBSON	L- 48 SUNBURST	552	408	350	293
GUITAR	58	GIBSON	L- 48 SUNBURST	544	402	345	289
GUITAR	59	GIBSON	L- 48 SUNBURST	598	442	380	317
GUITAR	61	GIBSON	L- 48 SUNBURST	535	396	340	284
GUITAR	62	GIBSON	L- 48 SUNBURST	541	400	344	287
GUITAR	63	GIBSON	L- 48 SUNBURST	517	382	328	274
GUITAR	65	GIBSON	L- 48 SUNBURST	651	482	414	346
GUITAR	67	GIBSON	L- 48 SUNBURST	498	368	316	264
GUITAR	70	GIBSON	L- 48 SUNBURST	518	383	329	275
GUITAR	56	GIBSON	L- 4C SUNBURST	1,793	1,326	1,139	952
GUITAR	32	GIBSON	L- 50 SUNBURST, ARCHTOP	785	580	498	417
GUITAR	33	GIBSON	L- 50 SUNBURST, ARCHTOP	715	528	454	379
GUITAR	34	GIBSON	L- 50 SUNBURST, ARCHTOP	711	526	452	377
GUITAR	35	GIBSON	L- 50 SUNBURST, ARCHTOP	742	548	471	394
GUITAR	36	GIBSON	L- 50 SUNBURST, ARCHTOP	703	520	447	373
GUITAR	37	GIBSON	L- 50 SUNBURST, ARCHTOP	700	518	445	372
GUITAR	39	GIBSON	L- 50 SUNBURST, ARCHTOP	696	515	442	370
GUITAR	40	GIBSON	L- 50 SUNBURST, ARCHTOP	693	512	440	368
GUITAR	41	GIBSON	L- 50 SUNBURST, ARCHTOP	690	510	438	366
GUITAR	42	GIBSON	L- 50 SUNBURST, ARCHTOP	685	506	435	364
GUITAR	43	GIBSON	L- 50 SUNBURST, ARCHTOP	681	504	433	362
GUITAR	46	GIBSON	L- 50 SUNBURST, ARCHTOP	774	572	492	411
GUITAR	47	GIBSON	L- 50 SUNBURST, ARCHTOP	819	606	520	435
GUITAR	48	GIBSON	L- 50 SUNBURST, ARCHTOP	671	496	426	356
GUITAR	49	GIBSON	L- 50 SUNBURST, ARCHTOP	666	492	423	353
GUITAR	50	GIBSON	L- 50 SUNBURST, ARCHTOP	663	490	421	352
GUITAR	51	GIBSON	L- 50 SUNBURST, ARCHTOP	661	489	420	351
GUITAR	52	GIBSON	L- 50 SUNBURST, ARCHTOP	658	487	418	349
GUITAR	54	GIBSON	L- 50 SUNBURST, ARCHTOP	655	484	416	348
GUITAR	55	GIBSON	L- 50 SUNBURST, ARCHTOP	649	480	412	345
GUITAR	56	GIBSON	L- 50 SUNBURST, ARCHTOP	644	476	409	342
GUITAR	57	GIBSON	L- 50 SUNBURST, ARCHTOP	663	490	421	352
GUITAR	58	GIBSON	L- 50 SUNBURST, ARCHTOP	636	470	404	338
GUITAR	59	GIBSON	L- 50 SUNBURST, ARCHTOP	633	468	402	336
GUITAR	60	GIBSON	L- 50 SUNBURST, DeARMOND FLOATING PU	898	664	570	477
GUITAR	62	GIBSON	L- 50 SUNBURST, ARCHTOP	777	575	494	413
GUITAR	66	GIBSON	L- 50 SUNBURST, ARCHTOP	621	459	394	329
GUITAR	34	GIBSON	L- 75 SUNBURST, SERIAL #91500-92400	1,824	1,349	1,159	969
GUITAR	35	GIBSON	L- 75 SUNBURST	1,483	1,096	942	787
GUITAR	35	GIBSON	L- 75 SUNBURST, SERIAL #144A-10	1,492	1,104	948	793

TYPE	YR	MFG	PRICES--BASED ON 100% ORIGINAL MODEL	SELL EXC	SELL AVG	BUY EXC	BUY AVG
GUITAR	36	GIBSON	L- 75 SUNBURST, SERIAL #93500	1,383	1,023	879	734
GUITAR	30	GIBSON	L-C CENTURY MAPLE BACK/SIDES, SERIAL #89800-90200	3,744	2,769	2,379	1,989
GUITAR	33	GIBSON	L-C CENTURY SUNBURST	2,226	1,646	1,414	1,182
GUITAR	34	GIBSON	L-C CENTURY SUNBURST, SERIAL #91500-92400	2,219	1,641	1,410	1,179
GUITAR	36	GIBSON	L-C CENTURY SUNBURST	2,991	2,212	1,900	1,589
GUITAR	37	GIBSON	L-C CENTURY SUNBURST, SERIAL #95400	2,238	1,655	1,422	1,189
GUITAR	38	GIBSON	L-C CENTURY CURLY MAPLE	3,617	2,675	2,298	1,921
GUITAR	22	GIBSON	L-JR BROWN, ARCHTOP, ROUND HOLE, SERIAL #69300-71400	1,061	785	674	564
GUITAR	23	GIBSON	L-JR BLOND, ARCHTOP	748	553	475	397
GUITAR	24	GIBSON	L-JR BROWN, ARCHTOP, ROUND HOLE	748	553	475	397
GUITAR	58	GIBSON	LG- 0 SERIAL #A26500-A28000	445	329	283	236
GUITAR	59	GIBSON	LG- 0 SERIAL #A28000	463	342	294	246
GUITAR	60	GIBSON	LG- 0	455	336	289	241
GUITAR	61	GIBSON	LG- 0	429	317	272	227
GUITAR	62	GIBSON	LG- 0	379	280	240	201
GUITAR	63	GIBSON	LG- 0	409	303	260	217
GUITAR	64	GIBSON	LG- 0 NATURAL, FLAT TOP	636	470	404	338
GUITAR	65	GIBSON	LG- 0	397	293	252	211
GUITAR	66	GIBSON	LG- 0	392	290	249	208
GUITAR	67	GIBSON	LG- 0	375	277	238	199
GUITAR	68	GIBSON	LG- 0	377	279	239	200
GUITAR	69	GIBSON	LG- 0	364	269	231	193
GUITAR	70	GIBSON	LG- 0	358	264	227	190
GUITAR	47	GIBSON	LG- 1 SUNBURST	838	619	532	445
GUITAR	48	GIBSON	LG- 1	598	442	380	317
GUITAR	49	GIBSON	LG- 1 SUNBURST	648	479	412	344
GUITAR	50	GIBSON	LG- 1 SUNBURST	648	479	412	344
GUITAR	51	GIBSON	LG- 1 SUNBURST	646	477	410	343
GUITAR	52	GIBSON	LG- 1 SUNBURST, SERIAL #A9400-A13000	623	460	395	330
GUITAR	53	GIBSON	LG- 1 SUNBURST	837	619	531	444
GUITAR	54	GIBSON	LG- 1 SUNBURST, SERIAL #A16000-A19000	621	459	394	329
GUITAR	55	GIBSON	LG- 1 SUNBURST	618	457	392	328
GUITAR	56	GIBSON	LG- 1 SUNBURST, SERIAL #A22000-A24600	613	453	389	325
GUITAR	57	GIBSON	LG- 1 SUNBURST, SERIAL #A24600-A26500	610	451	387	324
GUITAR	58	GIBSON	LG- 1 SUNBURST	605	448	384	321
GUITAR	59	GIBSON	LG- 1 SUNBURST	604	447	384	321
GUITAR	60	GIBSON	LG- 1 SUNBURST	580	429	369	308
GUITAR	62	GIBSON	LG- 1 SUNBURST	577	427	367	307
GUITAR	63	GIBSON	LG- 1 SUNBURST	559	413	355	297
GUITAR	64	GIBSON	LG- 1 SUNBURST	559	413	355	297
GUITAR	65	GIBSON	LG- 1 SUNBURST	557	412	354	296
GUITAR	66	GIBSON	LG- 1 SUNBURST	539	399	342	286
GUITAR	67	GIBSON	LG- 1 SUNBURST	537	397	341	285
GUITAR	68	GIBSON	LG- 1	457	338	290	243
GUITAR	42	GIBSON	LG- 2 FIRESTRIPE GUARD	1,313	971	834	697
GUITAR	43	GIBSON	LG- 2 SUNBURST	1,560	1,154	991	829
GUITAR	43	GIBSON	LG- 2 MAHOGANY	1,661	1,229	1,055	882

TYPE	YR	MFG	PRICES--BASED ON 100% ORIGINAL MODEL	SELL EXC	SELL AVG	BUY EXC	BUY AVG
GUITAR	44	GIBSON	LG- 2 SUNBURST	1,560	**1,154**	991	829
GUITAR	45	GIBSON	LG- 2 SUNBURST	1,558	**1,152**	990	827
GUITAR	46	GIBSON	LG- 2 SUNBURST	1,557	**1,151**	989	827
GUITAR	49	GIBSON	LG- 2 SUNBURST	1,670	**1,235**	1,061	887
GUITAR	50	GIBSON	LG- 2 SUNBURST	1,486	**1,099**	944	789
GUITAR	52	GIBSON	LG- 2 SUNBURST	1,412	**1,044**	897	750
GUITAR	53	GIBSON	LG- 2 SUNBURST	1,338	**989**	850	710
GUITAR	54	GIBSON	LG- 2 SUNBURST	1,426	**1,055**	906	757
GUITAR	56	GIBSON	LG- 2 SUNBURST	1,184	**876**	752	629
GUITAR	57	GIBSON	LG- 2 SUNBURST	1,112	**822**	706	591
GUITAR	59	GIBSON	LG- 2 SUNBURST	1,069	**790**	679	568
GUITAR	66	GIBSON	LG- 2 SUNBURST	1,023	**756**	650	543
GUITAR	50	GIBSON	LG- 2 3/4 SUNBURST	1,038	**768**	660	551
GUITAR	52	GIBSON	LG- 2 3/4	637	**471**	405	338
GUITAR	58	GIBSON	LG- 2 3/4 SUNBURST	906	**670**	575	481
GUITAR	60	GIBSON	LG- 2 3/4 SUNBURST	710	**525**	451	377
GUITAR	61	GIBSON	LG- 2 3/4 SUNBURST	868	**642**	552	461
GUITAR	62	GIBSON	LG- 2 3/4 CHERRY SUNBURST	816	**604**	519	434
GUITAR	49	GIBSON	LG- 3 NATURAL	1,103	**815**	700	585
GUITAR	50	GIBSON	LG- 3 NATURAL	1,061	**785**	674	564
GUITAR	51	GIBSON	LG- 3 NATURAL	717	**530**	455	380
GUITAR	53	GIBSON	LG- 3 NATURAL	711	**526**	452	377
GUITAR	54	GIBSON	LG- 3 NATURAL	710	**525**	451	377
GUITAR	55	GIBSON	LG- 3	757	**560**	481	402
GUITAR	58	GIBSON	LG- 3 NATURAL	713	**527**	453	378
GUITAR	68	GIBSON	LG- 12 NATURAL, 12-STRING	710	**525**	451	377
GUITAR	61	GIBSON	LG-2 CHERRY SUNBURST	1,063	**786**	675	565
GUITAR	36	GIBSON	LOAR ARCHTOP	2,178	**1,660**	1,411	1,079
GUITAR	75	GIBSON	MARK 35 MAHOGANY BACK/SIDES	510	**377**	324	271
GUITAR	76	GIBSON	MARK 35	379	**280**	240	201
GUITAR	77	GIBSON	MARK 35 NATURAL	375	**277**	238	199
GUITAR	77	GIBSON	MARK 35 SUNBURST	502	**371**	319	266
GUITAR	75	GIBSON	MARK 53	537	**397**	341	285
GUITAR	77	GIBSON	MARK 53 NATURAL, MAPLE BACK/SIDES	557	**412**	354	296
GUITAR	75	GIBSON	MARK 72	677	**501**	430	360
GUITAR	76	GIBSON	MARK 72 ROSEWOOD BACK/SIDES	711	**526**	452	377
GUITAR	77	GIBSON	MARK 72 ROSEWOOD BACK/SIDES	705	**521**	448	374
GUITAR	75	GIBSON	MARK 81	743	**549**	472	394
GUITAR	76	GIBSON	MARK 81	728	**538**	462	387
GUITAR	77	GIBSON	MARK 81 ROSEWOOD BACK/SIDES	845	**625**	537	449
GUITAR	78	GIBSON	MARK 81	685	**506**	435	364
GUITAR	26	GIBSON	NICK LUCAS SUNBURST, FLATTOP	3,652	**2,701**	2,321	1,940
GUITAR	27	GIBSON	NICK LUCAS SUNBURST, FLATTOP, SERIAL #-85400	3,649	**2,699**	2,319	1,939
GUITAR	28	GIBSON	NICK LUCAS SUNBURST, FLATTOP	3,552	**2,627**	2,257	1,887
GUITAR	29	GIBSON	NICK LUCAS SUNBURST, FLATTOP, SERIAL #87300-89800	3,651	**2,700**	2,320	1,940

TYPE	YR	MFG	PRICES--BASED ON 100% ORIGINAL MODEL	SELL EXC	SELL AVG	BUY EXC	BUY AVG
GUITAR	30	GIBSON	**NICK LUCAS** SUNBURST, FLATTOP, SERIAL #89800-90200	3,473	**2,568**	2,206	1,845
GUITAR	32	GIBSON	**NICK LUCAS** SUNBURST, BRAZILIAN ROSEWOOD BACK/SIDES	3,984	**2,946**	2,531	2,116
GUITAR	33	GIBSON	**NICK LUCAS** SUNBURST, FLATTOP, SERIAL #90700-91500	3,473	**2,568**	2,206	1,845
GUITAR	34	GIBSON	**NICK LUCAS** SUNBURST, FLATTOP, SERIAL #91500-92400	3,470	**2,566**	2,205	1,843
GUITAR	35	GIBSON	**NICK LUCAS** SUNBURST, FLATTOP, SERIAL #92400-93500	3,468	**2,565**	2,203	1,842
GUITAR	36	GIBSON	**NICK LUCAS** SUNBURST, FLATTOP	3,465	**2,563**	2,202	1,841
GUITAR	28	GIBSON	**PG- 1** PLECTRUM, SUNBURST, FLATTOP, SERIAL #85400-87300	654	**484**	416	347
GUITAR	34	GIBSON	**ROY SMECK RADIO GRANDE** NATURAL	3,467	**2,564**	2,203	1,842
GUITAR	35	GIBSON	**ROY SMECK RADIO GRANDE** NATURAL	3,216	**2,379**	2,044	1,709
GUITAR	34	GIBSON	**ROY SMECK STAGE DELUXE**	1,872	**1,385**	1,190	995
GUITAR	34	GIBSON	**ROY SMECK STAGE DELUXE** SUNBURST	3,932	**2,908**	2,498	2,088
GUITAR	35	GIBSON	**ROY SMECK STAGE DELUXE** SERIAL #92400-93500	3,868	**2,861**	2,458	2,055
GUITAR	37	GIBSON	**ROY SMECK STAGE DELUXE** SERIAL #95400	4,704	**3,479**	2,989	2,499
GUITAR	42	GIBSON	**SJ** SUNBURST	5,081	**3,758**	3,228	2,699
GUITAR	43	GIBSON	**SJ** SUNBURST, SERIAL #97600-97800	4,273	**3,160**	2,715	2,270
GUITAR	44	GIBSON	**SJ** SUNBURST, SERIAL #97800-98300	4,277	**3,163**	2,718	2,272
GUITAR	45	GIBSON	**SJ** SUNBURST, SERIAL #98300-98600	4,267	**3,155**	2,711	2,266
GUITAR	46	GIBSON	**SJ** SUNBURST, SERIAL #98600-99500	4,267	**3,155**	2,711	2,266
GUITAR	47	GIBSON	**SJ** SUNBURST	3,360	**2,485**	2,135	1,785
GUITAR	48	GIBSON	**SJ** SUNBURST	3,674	**2,800**	2,380	1,819
GUITAR	49	GIBSON	**SJ** SUNBURST	4,373	**3,234**	2,779	2,323
GUITAR	50	GIBSON	**SJ** SUNBURST	2,237	**1,655**	1,421	1,188
GUITAR	51	GIBSON	**SJ** SUNBURST	2,234	**1,652**	1,420	1,187
GUITAR	52	GIBSON	**SJ** SUNBURST	2,230	**1,649**	1,417	1,184
GUITAR	53	GIBSON	**SJ** SUNBURST, SERIAL #A13000-A16000	2,222	**1,643**	1,412	1,180
GUITAR	54	GIBSON	**SJ** SUNBURST	2,231	**1,650**	1,417	1,185
GUITAR	55	GIBSON	**SJ** SUNBURST, SERIAL #A19000-A22000	2,217	**1,640**	1,409	1,178
GUITAR	56	GIBSON	**SJ** SUNBURST	2,214	**1,637**	1,407	1,176
GUITAR	58	GIBSON	**SJ** SUNBURST, SERIAL #A26500-A28000	2,214	**1,637**	1,407	1,176
GUITAR	59	GIBSON	**SJ** SUNBURST	2,249	**1,663**	1,429	1,194
GUITAR	61	GIBSON	**SJ** SUNBURST	1,066	**788**	677	566
GUITAR	62	GIBSON	**SJ** SUNBURST	1,064	**787**	676	565
GUITAR	63	GIBSON	**SJ** SUNBURST	1,070	**791**	680	568
GUITAR	65	GIBSON	**SJ** SUNBURST	1,076	**795**	683	571
GUITAR	66	GIBSON	**SJ** SUNBURST	1,071	**792**	680	569
GUITAR	67	GIBSON	**SJ** SUNBURST	1,066	**788**	677	566
GUITAR	67	GIBSON	**SJ** SUNBURST, FLATTOP	1,408	**1,041**	894	748
GUITAR	68	GIBSON	**SJ** SUNBURST	1,065	**788**	677	566
GUITAR	68	GIBSON	**SJ** SUNBURST, FLATTOP	1,408	**1,041**	894	748
GUITAR	70	GIBSON	**SJ** SUNBURST	1,031	**762**	655	547
GUITAR	72	GIBSON	**SJ** SUNBURST	1,031	**762**	655	547
GUITAR	73	GIBSON	**SJ** SUNBURST	1,031	**762**	655	547

TYPE	YR	MFG	PRICES--BASED ON 100% ORIGINAL MODEL	SELL EXC	SELL AVG	BUY EXC	BUY AVG
GUITAR	74	GIBSON	**SJ** SUNBURST	1,031	**762**	655	547
GUITAR	72	GIBSON	**SJ DELUXE**	677	**501**	430	360
GUITAR	73	GIBSON	**SJ DELUXE** NATURAL	598	**442**	380	317
GUITAR	73	GIBSON	**SJ DELUXE** FLATTOP	796	**589**	506	423
GUITAR	50	GIBSON	**SJ NATURAL**	3,648	**2,698**	2,318	1,938
GUITAR	60	GIBSON	**SJ SOUTHERN JUMBO** SUNBURST	1,535	**1,135**	975	815
GUITAR	68	GIBSON	**SJ SOUTHERN JUMBO DELUXE** SUNBURST	1,210	**895**	769	643
GUITAR	34	GIBSON	**SJ- 40** SERIAL #94400-94957	6,240	**4,615**	3,965	3,315
GUITAR	39	GIBSON	**SJ- 44**	1,673	**1,237**	1,063	888
GUITAR	41	GIBSON	**SJ- 45** SERIAL #96600-97400	3,498	**2,587**	2,222	1,858
GUITAR	46	GIBSON	**SJ- 45 BANNER** MAHOGANY BACK/SIDES	4,032	**2,982**	2,562	2,142
GUITAR	40	GIBSON	**SJ-100** MAHOGANY BACK/SIDES, FLATTOP, SERIAL #96000	8,986	**6,646**	5,710	4,774
GUITAR	41	GIBSON	**SJ-100** SUNBURST	6,335	**4,685**	4,025	3,365
GUITAR	39	GIBSON	**SJ-100 CENTENNIAL** ONLY 100 MADE/STAIRSTEP HEAD STACK/MOUSTACHE BRIDGE	12,299	**9,096**	7,815	6,534
GUITAR	38	GIBSON	**SJ-200** SUNBURST, ROSEWOOD BACK/SIDES	31,630	**23,393**	20,098	16,803
GUITAR	38	GIBSON	**SJ-200** ROSEWOOD, FLATTOP	33,600	**24,850**	21,350	17,850
GUITAR	39	GIBSON	**SJ-200** SUNBURST, ROSEWOOD BACK/SIDES	29,760	**22,010**	18,910	15,810
GUITAR	40	GIBSON	**SJ-200** SUNBURST	31,449	**23,259**	19,983	16,707
GUITAR	41	GIBSON	**SJ-200** SUNBURST	31,364	**23,196**	19,929	16,662
GUITAR	48	GIBSON	**SJ-200** SUNBURST, SERIAL #A1400-A2800	8,503	**6,289**	5,403	4,517
GUITAR	49	GIBSON	**SJ-200** SUNBURST, SERIAL #A2800-A4400	7,059	**5,221**	4,485	3,750
GUITAR	49	GIBSON	**SJ-200** BLOND, SERIAL #A2800-A4400	13,885	**10,269**	8,823	7,376
GUITAR	50	GIBSON	**SJ-200** SUNBURST	7,587	**5,611**	4,821	4,031
GUITAR	51	GIBSON	**SJ-200** SUNBURST, SERIAL #A6000-A9400	6,672	**4,934**	4,239	3,544
GUITAR	51	GIBSON	**SJ-200** NATURAL, SERIAL #A9400-A13000	7,560	**5,591**	4,804	4,016
GUITAR	52	GIBSON	**SJ-200** SUNBURST	7,467	**5,523**	4,745	3,967
GUITAR	53	GIBSON	**SJ-200** NATURAL	5,240	**3,875**	3,329	2,784
GUITAR	53	GIBSON	**SJ-200** SUNBURST	7,967	**5,892**	5,062	4,232
GUITAR	54	GIBSON	**SJ-200** SUNBURST	7,101	**5,251**	4,512	3,772
GUITAR	41	GIBSON	**SP-TG4 CUSTOM** TENOR, NATURAL, 6-STRING	1,155	**854**	734	614
GUITAR	83	GIBSON	**SPIRIT I** CHERRY, BOUND BODY	384	**284**	244	204
GUITAR	08	GIBSON	**STYLE O ARTIST** BLACK, OVAL HOLE	3,694	**2,732**	2,347	1,962
GUITAR	12	GIBSON	**STYLE O ARTIST** BLACK, OVAL HOLE, SERIAL #10850-13350	3,339	**2,470**	2,122	1,774
GUITAR	13	GIBSON	**STYLE O ARTIST** BLACK, OVAL HOLE	3,972	**2,937**	2,524	2,110
GUITAR	14	GIBSON	**STYLE O ARTIST** BLACK, OVAL HOLE	3,969	**2,935**	2,522	2,108
GUITAR	15	GIBSON	**STYLE O ARTIST** BLACK, OVAL HOLE	3,876	**2,866**	2,463	2,059
GUITAR	16	GIBSON	**STYLE O ARTIST** BLACK, OVAL HOLE	3,799	**2,810**	2,414	2,018
GUITAR	18	GIBSON	**STYLE O ARTIST** BLACK, OVAL HOLE, SERIAL #39500-47900	4,655	**3,442**	2,957	2,472
GUITAR	19	GIBSON	**STYLE O ARTIST**	1,422	**1,052**	904	755
GUITAR	20	GIBSON	**STYLE O ARTIST** SUNBURST, OVAL HOLE, RED MAHOGANY, SERIAL #53800-62200	3,763	**2,783**	2,391	1,999
GUITAR	21	GIBSON	**STYLE O ARTIST** SUNBURST, OVAL HOLE, RED MAHOGANY	3,762	**2,782**	2,390	1,998
GUITAR	22	GIBSON	**STYLE O ARTIST** SUNBURST, OVAL HOLE, RED MAHOGANY, SERIAL #69300-71400	3,760	**2,781**	2,389	1,997
GUITAR	23	GIBSON	**STYLE O ARTIST** SUNBURST, OVAL HOLE, RED MAHOGANY	4,392	**3,248**	2,790	2,333
GUITAR	07	GIBSON	**STYLE O-1** BLACK TOP, SERIAL #3350-4250	3,728	**2,757**	2,369	1,980

TYPE	YR	MFG	PRICES--BASED ON 100% ORIGINAL MODEL	SELL EXC	SELL AVG	BUY EXC	BUY AVG
GUITAR	04	GIBSON	STYLE O-2 BLACK TOP, SERIAL #1150-1850	3,731	2,759	2,371	1,982
GUITAR	06	GIBSON	STYLE O-2 BLACK TOP, SERIAL #2550-3350	3,731	2,759	2,371	1,982
GUITAR	05	GIBSON	STYLE O-3 BLACK TOP, SERIAL #1850-2550	3,743	2,768	2,378	1,988
GUITAR	02	GIBSON	STYLE R HARP GUITAR ORANGE, SERIAL #1850-2550	3,467	2,564	2,203	1,842
GUITAR	02	GIBSON	STYLE R-1 HARP GUITAR BLACK, SERIAL #2550-3350	3,467	2,564	2,203	1,842
GUITAR	09	GIBSON	STYLE U HARP GUITAR BLACK TOP, SERIAL #5450-6950	3,472	2,568	2,206	1,844
GUITAR	10	GIBSON	STYLE U HARP GUITAR BLACK TOP, SERIAL #6950-8750	3,232	2,390	2,053	1,717
GUITAR	12	GIBSON	STYLE U HARP GUITAR BLACK TOP, SERIAL #10850-13350	3,231	2,389	2,053	1,716
GUITAR	13	GIBSON	STYLE U HARP GUITAR BLACK TOP, SERIAL #13350-16100	3,792	2,805	2,410	2,015
GUITAR	15	GIBSON	STYLE U HARP GUITAR ORANGE	2,969	2,196	1,886	1,577
GUITAR	15	GIBSON	STYLE U HARP GUITAR BLACK TOP	3,229	2,388	2,052	1,715
GUITAR	15	GIBSON	STYLE U HARP GUITAR SUNBURST, RED MAHOGANY, SERIAL #20150-25150	3,762	2,782	2,390	1,998
GUITAR	16	GIBSON	STYLE U HARP GUITAR BLACK TOP	3,226	2,386	2,050	1,714
GUITAR	16	GIBSON	STYLE U HARP GUITAR SUNBURST, RED MAHOGANY	3,233	2,391	2,054	1,717
GUITAR	17	GIBSON	STYLE U HARP GUITAR SUNBURST, RED MAHOGANY, SERIAL #32000-39500	5,908	4,370	3,754	3,139
GUITAR	18	GIBSON	STYLE U HARP GUITAR SUNBURST, RED MAHOGANY	5,907	4,369	3,753	3,138
GUITAR	19	GIBSON	STYLE U HARP GUITAR SUNBURST, RED MAHOGANY	5,910	4,371	3,755	3,140
GUITAR	20	GIBSON	STYLE U HARP GUITAR SUNBURST, RED MAHOGANY	5,909	4,370	3,755	3,139
GUITAR	06	GIBSON	STYLE U-1 HARP GUITAR BLACK TOP, SERIAL #2550-3350	3,469	2,565	2,204	1,843
GUITAR	50	GIBSON	SUPER 300 SUNBURST, ARCHTOP, SERIAL #A4400-A6000	3,747	2,771	2,381	1,991
GUITAR	51	GIBSON	SUPER 300 SUNBURST, ARCHTOP	3,697	2,734	2,349	1,964
GUITAR	52	GIBSON	SUPER 300 SUNBURST, ARCHTOP, SERIAL #A9400-A13000	3,659	2,706	2,325	1,944
GUITAR	54	GIBSON	SUPER 300 SUNBURST, ARCHTOP, SERIAL #A16000-A19000	3,659	2,706	2,325	1,944
GUITAR	57	GIBSON	SUPER 300 SUNBURST, CUTAWAY	6,240	4,615	3,965	3,315
GUITAR	58	GIBSON	SUPER 300C SUNBURST	5,280	3,905	3,355	2,805
GUITAR	34	GIBSON	SUPER 400 SUNBURST, NON-CUTAWAY	9,016	6,668	5,729	4,789
GUITAR	35	GIBSON	SUPER 400 SUNBURST, NON-CUTAWAY, SERIAL #92400-93500	8,905	6,586	5,658	4,731
GUITAR	36	GIBSON	SUPER 400 SUNBURST, NON-CUTAWAY, SERIAL #95400	9,405	6,955	5,976	4,996
GUITAR	37	GIBSON	SUPER 400 SUNBURST, NON-CUTAWAY, SERIAL #95400	9,300	6,878	5,909	4,940
GUITAR	38	GIBSON	SUPER 400 SUNBURST, NON-CUTAWAY, SERIAL #96000	11,520	8,520	7,320	6,120
GUITAR	40	GIBSON	SUPER 400 SUNBURST, NON-CUTAWAY	7,585	5,610	4,820	4,030
GUITAR	41	GIBSON	SUPER 400 NATURAL, NON-CUTAWAY	8,662	6,406	5,504	4,601
GUITAR	46	GIBSON	SUPER 400 SUNBURST, NON-CUTAWAY	8,060	5,961	5,121	4,281
GUITAR	47	GIBSON	SUPER 400 SUNBURST, NON-CUTAWAY	8,116	6,003	5,157	4,312
GUITAR	48	GIBSON	SUPER 400 SUNBURST, NON-CUTAWAY	7,944	5,875	5,048	4,220
GUITAR	48	GIBSON	SUPER 400 NATURAL, NON-CUTAWAY	8,042	5,948	5,110	4,272
GUITAR	49	GIBSON	SUPER 400 SUNBURST, NON-CUTAWAY, SERIAL #A2800-A4400	7,944	5,875	5,047	4,220
GUITAR	50	GIBSON	SUPER 400 NATURAL, NON-CUTAWAY	9,031	6,679	5,738	4,798
GUITAR	51	GIBSON	SUPER 400 SUNBURST, NON-CUTAWAY	7,829	5,790	4,975	4,159
GUITAR	51	GIBSON	SUPER 400 NATURAL, NON-CUTAWAY	7,831	5,792	4,976	4,160
GUITAR	77	GIBSON	SUPER 400 BLOND	5,443	4,025	3,458	2,891
GUITAR	39	GIBSON	SUPER 400C NATURAL, CUTAWAY	13,951	10,318	8,865	7,411

TYPE	YR	MFG	PRICES--BASED ON 100% ORIGINAL MODEL	SELL EXC	SELL AVG	BUY EXC	BUY AVG
GUITAR	41	GIBSON	**SUPER 400C** PREMIER	14,880	**11,005**	9,455	7,905
GUITAR	46	GIBSON	**SUPER 400C** SUNBURST, CUTAWAY	10,222	**7,560**	6,495	5,430
GUITAR	49	GIBSON	**SUPER 400C** NATURAL, CUTAWAY	9,832	**7,271**	6,247	5,223
GUITAR	50	GIBSON	**SUPER 400C** SUNBURST, CUTAWAY	9,905	**7,325**	6,293	5,262
GUITAR	52	GIBSON	**SUPER 400C** SUNBURST, CUTAWAY	10,560	**7,810**	6,710	5,610
GUITAR	54	GIBSON	**SUPER 400C** SUNBURST, CUTAWAY	9,117	**6,742**	5,793	4,843
GUITAR	56	GIBSON	**SUPER 400C** SUNBURST, CUTAWAY	9,104	**6,733**	5,785	4,836
GUITAR	58	GIBSON	**SUPER 400C** SUNBURST, CUTAWAY	9,103	**6,732**	5,784	4,836
GUITAR	59	GIBSON	**SUPER 400C** SUNBURST, CUTAWAY	9,475	**7,007**	6,020	5,033
GUITAR	61	GIBSON	**SUPER 400C** NATURAL, CUTAWAY	8,946	**6,616**	5,684	4,752
GUITAR	62	GIBSON	**SUPER 400C** SUNBURST, CUTAWAY	9,120	**6,745**	5,795	4,845
GUITAR	63	GIBSON	**SUPER 400C** NATURAL, CUTAWAY	8,940	**6,612**	5,680	4,749
GUITAR	64	GIBSON	**SUPER 400C** CHARLIE CHRISTIAN PU	7,095	**5,247**	4,508	3,769
GUITAR	64	GIBSON	**SUPER 400C** SUNBURST, CUTAWAY, FLOATING PU	8,965	**6,630**	5,696	4,762
GUITAR	66	GIBSON	**SUPER 400C** SUNBURST, CUTAWAY	6,966	**5,152**	4,426	3,701
GUITAR	67	GIBSON	**SUPER 400C** SUNBURST	7,718	**5,708**	4,904	4,100
GUITAR	68	GIBSON	**SUPER 400C** NATURAL, CUTAWAY	7,380	**5,458**	4,689	3,920
GUITAR	69	GIBSON	**SUPER 400C** SUNBURST, CUTAWAY	6,888	**5,094**	4,377	3,659
GUITAR	70	GIBSON	**SUPER 400C** SUNBURST, CUTAWAY	5,880	**4,349**	3,736	3,124
GUITAR	72	GIBSON	**SUPER 400C** SUNBURST, CUTAWAY	5,727	**4,235**	3,639	3,042
GUITAR	73	GIBSON	**SUPER 400C** SUNBURST, CUTAWAY	7,200	**5,325**	4,575	3,825
GUITAR	74	GIBSON	**SUPER 400C** SUNBURST, CUTAWAY	6,720	**4,970**	4,270	3,570
GUITAR	76	GIBSON	**SUPER 400C** NATURAL, CUTAWAY	3,657	**2,705**	2,324	1,943
GUITAR	77	GIBSON	**SUPER 400C** SUNBURST, CUTAWAY	4,514	**3,339**	2,868	2,398
GUITAR	41	GIBSON	**SUPER 400CN**	14,830	**10,968**	9,423	7,878
GUITAR	50	GIBSON	**SUPER 400CN** BLOND	12,939	**9,570**	8,222	6,874
GUITAR	57	GIBSON	**SUPER 400CN** BLOND	10,945	**8,095**	6,955	5,815
GUITAR	59	GIBSON	**SUPER 400CN** BLOND	11,086	**8,199**	7,044	5,889
GUITAR	61	GIBSON	**SUPER 400CN** FLAMEY BACK/SIDES	33,600	**24,850**	21,350	17,850
GUITAR	69	GIBSON	**SUPER 400CN** NATURAL, CUTAWAY	8,526	**6,306**	5,418	4,529
GUITAR	49	GIBSON	**SUPER 400N** QUILTED MAPLE BACK, NON-CUTAWAY	9,054	**6,696**	5,753	4,810
GUITAR	36	GIBSON	**SUPER 400P PREMIER** SUNBURST, CUTAWAY, SERIAL #93500	14,949	**11,056**	9,498	7,941
GUITAR	39	GIBSON	**SUPER 400P PREMIER** SUNBURST, CUTAWAY, SERIAL #96000	12,264	**9,070**	7,793	6,515
GUITAR	41	GIBSON	**SUPER 400P PREMIER** SUNBURST, CUTAWAYSERIAL #96600-97400	13,057	**9,657**	8,297	6,937
GUITAR	75	GIBSON	**SUPER V CES** SUNBURST	8,160	**6,035**	5,185	4,335
GUITAR	27	GIBSON	**TG- 0** TENOR, MAHOGANY, FLATTOP	319	**236**	203	169
GUITAR	28	GIBSON	**TG- 0** TENOR, MAHOGANY, FLATTOP, SERIAL #85400-87300	598	**442**	380	317
GUITAR	30	GIBSON	**TG- 0** TENOR, MAHOGANY, FLATTOP, SERIAL #89800-90200	456	**337**	289	242
GUITAR	60	GIBSON	**TG- 0** TENOR, MAHOGANY, FLATTOP	478	**353**	303	253
GUITAR	61	GIBSON	**TG- 0** TENOR, MAHOGANY, FLATTOP	457	**338**	290	243
GUITAR	63	GIBSON	**TG- 0** TENOR, MAHOGANY, FLATTOP	422	**312**	268	224
GUITAR	64	GIBSON	**TG- 0** TENOR, MAHOGANY, FLATTOP	451	**333**	286	239

TYPE	YR	MFG	PRICES--BASED ON 100% ORIGINAL MODEL	SELL EXC	SELL AVG	BUY EXC	BUY AVG
GUITAR	65	GIBSON	**TG- 0** TENOR, MAHOGANY, FLATTOP	450	**332**	286	239
GUITAR	70	GIBSON	**TG- 0** TENOR	480	**355**	305	255
GUITAR	30	GIBSON	**TG- 00** TENOR, BLACK, FLATTOLP, SERIAL #89800-90200	409	**303**	260	217
GUITAR	30	GIBSON	**TG- 00** TENOR, SUNBURST, FLATTOP, SERIAL #89800-90200	475	**351**	301	252
GUITAR	32	GIBSON	**TG- 00** TENOR, BLACK, FLATTOP, SERIAL #90400-90700	384	**284**	244	204
GUITAR	34	GIBSON	**TG- 00** TENOR, SUNBURST, FLATTOP, SERIAL #91500-92400	453	**335**	287	240
GUITAR	35	GIBSON	**TG- 00** TENOR, SUNBURST, FLATTOP	456	**337**	289	242
GUITAR	37	GIBSON	**TG- 00** TENOR, SUNBURST, FLATTOP, SERIAL #95400	408	**301**	259	216
GUITAR	40	GIBSON	**TG- 00** TENOR, SUNBURST, FLATTOP, SERIAL #96000-96600	385	**285**	245	205
GUITAR	27	GIBSON	**TG- 1** TENOR, SUNBURST, FLATTOP, SERIAL #85400	469	**347**	298	249
GUITAR	28	GIBSON	**TG- 1** TENOR, SUNBURST, FLATTOP, SERIAL #85400-87300	480	**355**	305	255
GUITAR	30	GIBSON	**TG- 1** TENOR, SUNBURST, FLATTOP	480	**355**	305	255
GUITAR	31	GIBSON	**TG- 1** TENOR, SUNBURST, FLATTOP	475	**351**	301	252
GUITAR	36	GIBSON	**TG- 1** TENOR	518	**383**	329	275
GUITAR	33	GIBSON	**TG- 7** TENOR, SUNBURST, FLATTOP	1,370	**1,013**	871	728
GUITAR	35	GIBSON	**TG- 7** TENOR, SUNBURST, FLATTOP, SERIAL #92400-93500	1,403	**1,038**	891	745
GUITAR	38	GIBSON	**TG- 7** TENOR, SUNBURST, FLATTOP	1,315	**972**	835	698
GUITAR	39	GIBSON	**TG- 7** TENOR	1,195	**883**	759	634
GUITAR	65	GIBSON	**TG- 25** TENOR, SUNBURST, FLATTOP	419	**310**	266	222
GUITAR	66	GIBSON	**TG- 25** TENOR, SUNBURST, FLATTOP	480	**355**	305	255
GUITAR	64	GIBSON	**TG- 25N** TENOR, NATURAL, FLATTOP	446	**340**	289	220
GUITAR	65	GIBSON	**TG- 25N** TENOR, NATURAL, FLATTOP	438	**324**	278	233
GUITAR	36	GIBSON	**TG- 50** TENOR, SUNBURST, ARCHTOP, SERIAL #93500	796	**589**	506	423
GUITAR	40	GIBSON	**TG- 50** TENOR, SUNBURST, ARCHTOP, SERIAL #96000	626	**463**	398	333
GUITAR	46	GIBSON	**TG- 50** TENOR, SUNBURS, ARCHTOP, SERIAL #98600-99500	593	**438**	376	315
GUITAR	47	GIBSON	**TG- 50** TENOR, SUNBURST, ARCHTOP, SERIAL #A1400	583	**431**	370	310
GUITAR	48	GIBSON	**TG- 50** TENOR, SUNBURST, ARCHTOP	575	**425**	365	305
GUITAR	50	GIBSON	**TG- 50** TENOR, SUNBURST, ARCHTOP	518	**383**	329	275
GUITAR	52	GIBSON	**TG- 50** TENOR, SUNBURST, ARCHTOP	529	**391**	336	281
GUITAR	54	GIBSON	**TG- 50** TENOR, SUNBURST, ARCHTOP, SERIAL #A16000-A19000	513	**379**	326	272
GUITAR	57	GIBSON	**TG- 50** TENOR, SUNBURST, ARCHTOP	677	**501**	430	360
GUITAR	64	GIBSON	**TG- 50** TENOR, SUNBURST	697	**516**	443	370
MANDOLA	36	GIBSON	**H-0** SUNBURST, F-HOLES, FLAT BACK	633	**468**	402	336
MANDLA	06	GIBSON	**H-1** NATURAL	1,243	**919**	789	660
MANDLA	07	GIBSON	**H-1** BLOND TOP, INLAID PICKGUARD	1,234	**913**	784	655
MANDLA	09	GIBSON	**H-1** BLACK TOP, SERIAL #5450-6950	1,196	**884**	760	635
MANDLA	12	GIBSON	**H-1** BLOND TOP	1,157	**856**	735	615
MANDLA	14	GIBSON	**H-1** SHERIDAN BROWN, SERIAL #16100-20150	738	**545**	469	392
MANDLA	14	GIBSON	**H-1** BLOND TOP	1,191	**881**	757	632
MANDLA	16	GIBSON	**H-1** NATURAL	1,244	**920**	790	660
MANDLA	16	GIBSON	**H-1** PUMPKIN, SERIAL #25485	1,522	**1,160**	986	754
MANDLA	18	GIBSON	**H-1** NATURAL	1,531	**1,132**	972	813

TYPE	YR	MFG	PRICES--BASED ON 100% ORIGINAL MODEL	SELL EXC	SELL AVG	BUY EXC	BUY AVG
MANDLA	20	GIBSON	H-1 BROWN	13,846	**10,240**	8,798	7,355
MANDLA	22	GIBSON	H-1 BROWN, SERIAL #69300-71400	9,904	**7,325**	6,293	5,261
MANDLA	26	GIBSON	H-1 BLACK TOP	1,593	**1,178**	1,012	846
MANDLA	29	GIBSON	H-1 BLACK TOP, SERIAL #87300-89800	816	**604**	519	434
MANDLA	13	GIBSON	H-2 BLACK TOP, SERIAL #13350-16100	1,239	**916**	787	658
MANDLA	15	GIBSON	H-2 RED SUNBURST	1,147	**848**	728	609
MANDLA	17	GIBSON	H-2 BLACK TOP	1,191	**881**	757	632
MANDLA	18	GIBSON	H-2 RED SUNBURST	1,211	**896**	769	643
MANDLA	20	GIBSON	H-2 RED SUNBURST	1,244	**920**	790	660
MANDLA	21	GIBSON	H-2 RED SUNBURST	1,131	**837**	719	601
MANDLA	14	GIBSON	H-4 RED SUNBURST	5,040	**3,727**	3,202	2,677
MANDLA	15	GIBSON	H-4 RED SUNBURST	5,479	**4,052**	3,481	2,911
MANDLA	18	GIBSON	H-4 RED MAHOGANY	3,840	**2,840**	2,440	2,040
MANDLA	19	GIBSON	H-4 RED SUNBURST	4,800	**3,550**	3,050	2,550
MANDLA	20	GIBSON	H-4 RED SUNBURST	4,800	**3,550**	3,050	2,550
MANDLA	21	GIBSON	H-4 RED SUNBURST	6,332	**4,683**	4,023	3,363
MANDLA	23	GIBSON	H-4 RED SUNBURST	6,432	**4,757**	4,087	3,417
MANDLA	24	GIBSON	H-4 RED SUNBURST	5,520	**4,082**	3,507	2,932
MANDLA	24	GIBSON	H-4 NATURAL, VIRZI TONE	5,755	**4,256**	3,656	3,057
MANDLA	25	GIBSON	H-4 RED SUNBURST	5,473	**4,048**	3,478	2,908
MANDLA	27	GIBSON	H-4 RED SUNBURST	5,116	**3,784**	3,251	2,718
MANDOLIN 06		GIBSON	A GOLDEN ORANGE	1,402	**1,037**	891	745
MANDOL	11	GIBSON	A NATURAL TOP	1,063	**786**	675	565
MANDOL	12	GIBSON	A NATURAL TOP	936	**692**	594	497
MANDOL	13	GIBSON	A NATURAL TOP	817	**604**	519	434
MANDOL	13	GIBSON	A BLACK TOP	935	**691**	594	496
MANDOL	13	GIBSON	A PUMPKIN TOP, SERIAL #14841	935	**691**	594	496
MANDOL	13	GIBSON	A BLOND TOP, SERIAL #13350-16100	1,122	**829**	713	596
MANDOL	14	GIBSON	A NATURAL TOP, SERIAL #16100-20150	936	**692**	594	497
MANDOL	14	GIBSON	A PUMPKIN TOP	936	**692**	594	497
MANDOL	14	GIBSON	A BROWN	938	**694**	596	498
MANDOL	15	GIBSON	A NATURAL TOP, SERIAL #20150-25150	934	**690**	593	496
MANDOL	15	GIBSON	A BLOND TOP, SERIAL #20150-25150	936	**692**	594	497
MANDOL	15	GIBSON	A AMBER TOP	1,076	**795**	683	571
MANDOL	16	GIBSON	A PUMPKIN TOP	803	**594**	510	426
MANDOL	16	GIBSON	A AMBER TOP	937	**693**	595	498
MANDOL	16	GIBSON	A BLOND TOP	939	**695**	597	499
MANDOL	16	GIBSON	A BLACK TOP	1,009	**746**	641	536
MANDOL	17	GIBSON	A PUMPKIN TOP, SERIAL #32000-39500	803	**594**	510	426
MANDOL	17	GIBSON	A BROWN	937	**693**	595	498
MANDOL	17	GIBSON	A NATURAL TOP, SERIAL #32000-39500	937	**693**	595	498
MANDOL	18	GIBSON	A BROWN, SERIAL #39500-47900	936	**692**	594	497

TYPE	YR	MFG	MODEL	SELL EXC	SELL AVG	BUY EXC	BUY AVG
			PRICES--BASED ON 100% ORIGINAL				
MANDOL	18	GIBSON	**A** NATURAL TOP, SERIAL #39500-47900	982	**726**	624	521
MANDOL	19	GIBSON	**A** BLOND TOP	935	**691**	594	496
MANDOL	20	GIBSON	**A** PUMPKIN	717	**530**	455	380
MANDOL	20	GIBSON	**A** BLACK TOP	817	**604**	519	434
MANDOL	20	GIBSON	**A** WALNUT	916	**678**	582	487
MANDOL	20	GIBSON	**A** BROWN	935	**691**	594	496
MANDOL	21	GIBSON	**A** BROWN	939	**695**	597	499
MANDOL	21	GIBSON	**A** WALNUT	996	**736**	633	529
MANDOL	22	GIBSON	**A** BROWN, SERIAL #69300-71400	969	**717**	616	515
MANDOL	22	GIBSON	**A** BROWN, SNAKEHEAD	1,223	**904**	777	649
MANDOL	23	GIBSON	**A** GOLDEN ORANGE	876	**648**	556	465
MANDOL	23	GIBSON	**A** BROWN, SNAKEHEAD	1,269	**938**	806	674
MANDOL	23	GIBSON	**A** BROWN, LEFT-HANDED, SERIAL #71400-74900	1,557	**1,151**	989	827
MANDOL	24	GIBSON	**A** BROWN, SNAKEHEAD	1,264	**935**	803	671
MANDOL	24	GIBSON	**A** BLACK TOP, SNAKEHEAD PEGHEAD	1,274	**942**	810	677
MANDOL	26	GIBSON	**A** BLACK TOP, SNAKEHEAD PEGHEAD, SERIAL #82700	1,331	**984**	846	707
MANDOL	27	GIBSON	**A** BLACK TOP	876	**648**	556	465
MANDOL	28	GIBSON	**A** BLACK TOP	939	**695**	597	499
MANDOL	n/a	GIBSON	**A (1899)** BLACK, HANDMADE BY ORVILLE GIBSON, PRE GIBSON COMPANY	24,744	**18,300**	15,722	13,145
MANDOL	20	GIBSON	**A JUNIOR** BROWN	1,035	**766**	658	550
MANDOL	21	GIBSON	**A JUNIOR** BROWN	817	**604**	519	434
MANDOL	22	GIBSON	**A JUNIOR** BROWN	1,035	**766**	658	550
MANDOL	24	GIBSON	**A JUNIOR** BROWN	803	**594**	510	426
MANDOL	25	GIBSON	**A JUNIOR** BROWN	912	**674**	579	484
MANDOL	26	GIBSON	**A JUNIOR** BROWN	826	**611**	525	439
MANDOL	26	GIBSON	**A JUNIOR** BROWN, SNAKEHEAD	826	**611**	525	439
MANDOL	32	GIBSON	**A JUNIOR** BROWN	757	**560**	481	402
MANDOL	29	GIBSON	**A- 0** BROWN	717	**530**	455	380
MANDOL	35	GIBSON	**A- 00** SUNBURST	557	**412**	354	296
MANDOL	36	GIBSON	**A- 00** SUNBURST, FLAT BACK, SERIAL #93500	935	**691**	594	496
MANDOL	41	GIBSON	**A- 00** SUNBURST	687	**508**	436	365
MANDOL	05	GIBSON	**A- 1** BLOND	1,992	**1,473**	1,265	1,058
MANDOL	07	GIBSON	**A- 1** BLOND	1,647	**1,218**	1,046	875
MANDOL	08	GIBSON	**A- 1** SERIAL #4250-5450	1,433	**1,060**	910	761
MANDOL	10	GIBSON	**A- 1**	792	**586**	503	421
MANDOL	13	GIBSON	**A- 1** BLOND	1,010	**747**	642	537
MANDOL	13	GIBSON	**A- 1** NATURAL	1,123	**830**	713	596
MANDOL	14	GIBSON	**A- 1** BLOND	938	**694**	596	498
MANDOL	14	GIBSON	**A- 1** NATURAL	1,123	**830**	713	596
MANDOL	15	GIBSON	**A- 1** PUMPKIN TOP	863	**638**	548	458
MANDOL	15	GIBSON	**A- 1** BLOND	924	**683**	587	491
MANDOL	15	GIBSON	**A- 1** NATURAL, SERIAL #20150-25150	1,125	**832**	714	597

TYPE	YR	MFG	PRICES--BASED ON 100% ORIGINAL MODEL	SELL EXC	SELL AVG	BUY EXC	BUY AVG
MANDOL	16	GIBSON	A- 1 BLOND	941	**696**	598	500
MANDOL	17	GIBSON	A- 1 NATURAL, SERIAL #32000-39500	1,125	**832**	714	597
MANDOL	18	GIBSON	A- 1 NATURAL, SERIAL #39500-47900	796	**589**	506	423
MANDOL	23	GIBSON	A- 1 BLACK, SNAKEHEAD, SERIAL #71400-74900	1,402	**1,037**	891	745
MANDOL	24	GIBSON	A- 1 BLACK, SNAKEHEAD, SERIAL #74900-80300	1,365	**1,009**	867	725
MANDOL	25	GIBSON	A- 1 BLACK, SNAKEHEAD	1,392	**1,030**	885	740
MANDOL	35	GIBSON	A- 1 SUNBURST, F-HOLES, SERIAL #93500	1,124	**831**	714	597
MANDOL	37	GIBSON	A- 1 SUNBURST, F-HOLES, CURLY MAPLE	959	**709**	609	509
MANDOL	38	GIBSON	A- 1 SUNBURST, F-HOLES	952	**704**	605	505
MANDOL	39	GIBSON	A- 1	942	**697**	599	500
MANDOL	40	GIBSON	A- 1 SUNBURST	934	**690**	593	496
MANDOL	41	GIBSON	A- 1 SUNBURST	926	**685**	588	492
MANDOL	42	GIBSON	A- 1 SUNBURST	916	**678**	582	487
MANDOL	51	GIBSON	A- 1 PUMPKIN	720	**533**	458	383
MANDOL	18	GIBSON	A- 2 BROWN, SERIAL #39500-47900	1,124	**831**	714	597
MANDOL	19	GIBSON	A- 2 BROWN, SERIAL #47900-53800	1,126	**832**	715	598
MANDOL	20	GIBSON	A- 2 BROWN, SERIAL #53800-62200	1,049	**776**	666	557
MANDOL	21	GIBSON	A- 2 BROWN	974	**720**	619	517
MANDOL	22	GIBSON	A- 2 BROWN	1,474	**1,090**	936	783
MANDOL	23	GIBSON	A- 2Z BROWN	1,127	**833**	716	598
MANDOL	24	GIBSON	A- 2Z BLOND, SNAKEHEAD	3,552	**2,627**	2,257	1,887
MANDOL	05	GIBSON	A- 3 BLACK, FANCY INLAY	2,280	**1,686**	1,449	1,211
MANDOL	07	GIBSON	A- 3 NATURAL	1,338	**989**	850	710
MANDOL	07	GIBSON	A- 3 BLOND	1,535	**1,135**	975	815
MANDOL	14	GIBSON	A- 3 NATURAL, SERIAL #16100-20150	1,403	**1,038**	891	745
MANDOL	15	GIBSON	A- 3 BLOND	1,408	**1,041**	894	748
MANDOL	16	GIBSON	A- 3 BLOND	1,409	**1,042**	895	748
MANDOL	16	GIBSON	A- 3 GOLDEN ORANGE	1,492	**1,104**	948	793
MANDOL	17	GIBSON	A- 3 NATURAL, SERIAL #32000-39500	1,402	**1,037**	891	745
MANDOL	18	GIBSON	A- 3 WHITE FACE	1,408	**1,041**	894	748
MANDOL	19	GIBSON	A- 3 WHITE FACE, SERIAL #47900-53800	1,408	**1,041**	894	748
MANDOL	20	GIBSON	A- 3 WHITE FACE, SERIAL #53800-62200	1,315	**972**	835	698
MANDOL	21	GIBSON	A- 3 WHITE FACE	1,408	**1,041**	894	748
MANDOL	22	GIBSON	A- 3 WHITE FACE, IVROID PICKGUARD	1,407	**1,040**	894	747
MANDOL	22	GIBSON	A- 3 IVORY, WHITE IVROID PICKGUARD	1,534	**1,134**	974	814
MANDOL	06	GIBSON	A- 4 BLACK TOP	1,593	**1,178**	1,012	846
MANDOL	07	GIBSON	A- 4 BLACK TOP	1,651	**1,221**	1,049	877
MANDOL	08	GIBSON	A- 4 BLACK TOP	1,830	**1,353**	1,163	972
MANDOL	09	GIBSON	A- 4 BLACK TOP, INLAID TUNERS, SERIAL #5450-6950	1,872	**1,385**	1,190	995
MANDOL	12	GIBSON	A- 4 BLACK TOP, INLAID TUNERS, MAROON BACK/SIDES	1,806	**1,336**	1,148	959
MANDOL	13	GIBSON	A- 4 BLACK TOP	1,662	**1,229**	1,056	883
MANDOL	13	GIBSON	A- 4 BLACK TOP	1,682	**1,244**	1,069	894

TYPE	YR	MFG	PRICES--BASED ON 100% ORIGINAL MODEL	SELL EXC	SELL AVG	BUY EXC	BUY AVG
MANDOL	14	GIBSON	**A- 4** BLACK TOP, INLAID TUNERS	1,766	**1,306**	1,122	938
MANDOL	15	GIBSON	**A- 4** BLACK TOP, INLAID TUNERS, SERIAL #20150-25150	1,703	**1,259**	1,082	904
MANDOL	16	GIBSON	**A- 4** BLACK TOP, SERIAL #25308	1,590	**1,176**	1,010	845
MANDOL	16	GIBSON	**A- 4** RED SUNBURST	1,709	**1,264**	1,086	908
MANDOL	17	GIBSON	**A- 4** RED SUNBURST, INLAID TUNER BUTTONS, SERIAL #32000-39500	1,461	**1,080**	928	776
MANDOL	18	GIBSON	**A- 4** RED MAHOGANY	1,554	**1,149**	987	825
MANDOL	19	GIBSON	**A- 4** RED SUNBURST, SERIAL #47900-53800	1,658	**1,226**	1,054	881
MANDOL	20	GIBSON	**A- 4** RED MAHOGANY	1,461	**1,080**	928	776
MANDOL	20	GIBSON	**A- 4** RED SUNBURST	1,505	**1,113**	956	799
MANDOL	20	GIBSON	**A- 4** RED SUNBURST	1,525	**1,128**	969	810
MANDOL	20	GIBSON	**A- 4** MAROON SUNBURST	1,966	**1,454**	1,249	1,044
MANDOL	21	GIBSON	**A- 4** RED SUNBURST, SERIAL #62200-69300	1,272	**941**	808	676
MANDOL	21	GIBSON	**A- 4** MAROON SUNBURST, SERIAL #62200-69300	1,571	**1,162**	998	834
MANDOL	22	GIBSON	**A- 4** BLACK TOP	1,348	**997**	857	716
MANDOL	22	GIBSON	**A- 4** RED SUNBURST	1,369	**1,013**	870	727
MANDOL	23	GIBSON	**A- 4** RED SUNBURST, SERIAL #71400-74900	1,315	**972**	835	698
MANDOL	23	GIBSON	**A- 4** RED MAHOGANY, SNAKEHEAD	2,954	**2,185**	1,877	1,569
MANDOL	24	GIBSON	**A- 4** RED MAHOGANY, SNAKEHEAD, SERIAL #74900-80300	2,308	**1,707**	1,467	1,226
MANDOL	27	GIBSON	**A- 4** RED MAHOGANY	1,593	**1,178**	1,012	846
MANDOL	28	GIBSON	**A- 4** RED SUNBURST, SERIAL #85400-87300	1,089	**805**	692	578
MANDOL	34	GIBSON	**A- 5** SUNBURST, SERIAL #91500-92400	1,867	**1,380**	1,186	991
MANDOL	51	GIBSON	**A- 5** SUNBURST	1,603	**1,185**	1,018	851
MANDOL	60	GIBSON	**A- 5** CHERRY SUNBURST	1,245	**920**	791	661
MANDOL	63	GIBSON	**A- 5** CHERRY SUNBURST	1,608	**1,189**	1,022	854
MANDOL	64	GIBSON	**A- 5** CHERRY SUNBURST	1,408	**1,041**	894	748
MANDOL	71	GIBSON	**A- 5** CHERRY SUNBURST	1,195	**883**	759	634
MANDOL	72	GIBSON	**A- 5** SUNBURST, LUMP SCROLL	1,405	**1,039**	893	746
MANDOL	73	GIBSON	**A- 5** SUNBURST, LUMP SCROLL	1,404	**1,038**	892	746
MANDOL	74	GIBSON	**A- 5** SUNBURST	896	**663**	569	476
MANDOL	79	GIBSON	**A- 5** GOLDEN SUNBURST, LUMP SCROLL	1,408	**1,041**	894	748
MANDOL	71	GIBSON	**A-12** LUMP SCROLL	996	**736**	633	529
MANDOL	72	GIBSON	**A-12** LUMP SCROLL	1,125	**832**	714	597
MANDOL	73	GIBSON	**A-12** SUNBURST, SOLID SCROLLS	1,035	**766**	658	550
MANDOL	74	GIBSON	**A-12** LUMP SCROLL	1,244	**920**	790	660
MANDOL	75	GIBSON	**A-12** LUMP SCROLL	1,045	**796**	677	517
MANDOL	78	GIBSON	**A-12** LUMP SCROLL	1,127	**833**	716	598
MANDOL	35	GIBSON	**A-40** NATURAL	938	**694**	596	498
MANDOL	48	GIBSON	**A-40** SUNBURST	816	**604**	519	434
MANDOL	49	GIBSON	**A-40** NATURAL, SERIAL #A2800-A4400	780	**577**	495	414
MANDOL	50	GIBSON	**A-40** NATURAL, SERIAL #A4400-A6000	795	**588**	505	422
MANDOL	52	GIBSON	**A-40** NATURAL	788	**582**	500	418
MANDOL	54	GIBSON	**A-40** NATURAL	767	**567**	487	407

TYPE	YR	MFG	PRICES--BASED ON 100% ORIGINAL MODEL	SELL EXC	SELL AVG	BUY EXC	BUY AVG
MANDOL	59	GIBSON	**A-40** NATURAL	730	**540**	464	388
MANDOL	60	GIBSON	**A-40** NATURAL	730	**540**	464	388
MANDOL	63	GIBSON	**A-40** SUNBURST	693	**512**	440	368
MANDOL	64	GIBSON	**A-40** SUNBURST	693	**512**	440	368
MANDOL	65	GIBSON	**A-40** SUNBURST	688	**509**	437	365
MANDOL	66	GIBSON	**A-40** SUNBURST	693	**512**	440	368
MANDOL	68	GIBSON	**A-40** SUNBURST	438	**324**	278	233
MANDOL	68	GIBSON	**A-40** NATURAL	598	**442**	380	317
MANDOL	69	GIBSON	**A-40** SUNBURST	617	**456**	392	327
MANDOL	32	GIBSON	**A-50** SUNBURST	1,403	**1,038**	891	745
MANDOL	33	GIBSON	**A-50** SUNBURST	1,405	**1,039**	893	746
MANDOL	34	GIBSON	**A-50** SUNBURST, SERIAL #91500-92400	1,400	**1,035**	889	744
MANDOL	35	GIBSON	**A-50** SUNBURST	1,400	**1,035**	889	744
MANDOL	38	GIBSON	**A-50** SUNBURST, SERIAL #95400	1,870	**1,383**	1,188	993
MANDOL	39	GIBSON	**A-50** SUNBURST, SERIAL #96000	1,853	**1,371**	1,177	984
MANDOL	40	GIBSON	**A-50** SUNBURST, WIDE BODY	1,156	**855**	735	614
MANDOL	41	GIBSON	**A-50** SUNBURST	1,183	**875**	752	628
MANDOL	43	GIBSON	**A-50** SUNBURST	1,062	**785**	675	564
MANDOL	45	GIBSON	**A-50** SUNBURST	1,125	**832**	714	597
MANDOL	47	GIBSON	**A-50** SUNBURST	1,123	**830**	713	596
MANDOL	48	GIBSON	**A-50** SUNBURST	989	**732**	628	525
MANDOL	49	GIBSON	**A-50** SUNBURST	980	**732**	628	525
MANDOL	50	GIBSON	**A-50** SUNBURST	934	**690**	593	496
MANDOL	51	GIBSON	**A-50** SUNBURST	816	**604**	519	434
MANDOL	53	GIBSON	**A-50** SUNBURST	856	**633**	544	454
MANDOL	60	GIBSON	**A-50** SUNBURST	982	**726**	624	521
MANDOL	61	GIBSON	**A-50** SUNBURST	982	**726**	624	521
MANDOL	63	GIBSON	**A-50** SUNBURST	966	**714**	614	513
MANDOL	64	GIBSON	**A-50** SUNBURST	965	**714**	613	513
MANDOL	66	GIBSON	**A-50** SUNBURST	824	**609**	523	438
MANDOL	67	GIBSON	**A-50** SUNBURST	637	**471**	405	338
MANDOL	68	GIBSON	**A-50** SUNBURST	823	**609**	523	437
MANDOL	35	GIBSON	**A-C CENTURY** SUNBURST, PEARLOID INLAY	2,073	**1,533**	1,317	1,101
MANDOL	36	GIBSON	**A-C CENTURY** SUNBURST, PEARLOID	1,752	**1,296**	1,113	931
MANDOL	17	GIBSON	**ALRITE STYLE D** ORANGE, FLATTOP	750	**555**	477	398
MANDOL	18	GIBSON	**ALRITE STYLE D** ORANGE, FLATTOP AND BACK	749	**554**	476	398
MANDOL	12	GIBSON	**ARMY-NAVY MODEL** DARK BROWN, SERIAL #10850-13350	747	**553**	475	397
MANDOL	30	GIBSON	**ARMY-NAVY MODEL** BROWN	749	**554**	476	398
MANDOL	07	GIBSON	**ARTIST MODEL** 3-POINT BODY, SERIAL #3350-4250	4,824	**3,567**	3,065	2,562
MANDOL	32	GIBSON	**C- 1** FLATTOP	796	**589**	506	423
MANDOL	58	GIBSON	**DOUBLE MANDOLIN** SUNBURST, 2-NECK	1,235	**913**	785	656
MANDOL	62	GIBSON	**DOUBLE MANDOLIN** SUNBURST, 2-NECK	5,351	**3,957**	3,400	2,842

TYPE	YR	MFG	PRICES--BASED ON 100% ORIGINAL MODEL	SELL EXC	SELL AVG	BUY EXC	BUY AVG
MANDOL	65	GIBSON	**ELECTRIC FLORETINE**	1,609	**1,190**	1,022	855
MANDOL	39	GIBSON	**EM-150 ELECTRIC**	1,278	**945**	812	679
MANDOL	52	GIBSON	**EM-150 ELECTRIC**	800	**592**	508	425
MANDOL	54	GIBSON	**EM-150 ELECTRIC**	719	**531**	456	381
MANDOL	55	GIBSON	**EM-150 ELECTRIC**	797	**590**	506	423
MANDOL	56	GIBSON	**EM-150 ELECTRIC**	680	**503**	432	361
MANDOL	57	GIBSON	**EM-150 ELECTRIC**	678	**501**	431	360
MANDOL	63	GIBSON	**EM-150 ELECTRIC**	864	**639**	549	459
MANDOL	66	GIBSON	**EM-150 ELECTRIC**	788	**582**	500	418
MANDOL	68	GIBSON	**EM-150 ELECTRIC**	790	**584**	502	419
MANDOL	69	GIBSON	**EM-150 ELECTRIC**	781	**577**	496	415
MANDOL	50	GIBSON	**EM-250 ELECTRIC** SERIAL #A4400-A6000	1,330	**984**	845	706
MANDOL	58	GIBSON	**EMS-1235 DOUBLE** WHITE	1,064	**787**	676	565
MANDOL	66	GIBSON	**EMS-1235 DOUBLE**	3,168	**2,343**	2,013	1,683
MANDOL	05	GIBSON	**F- 2** BLACK TOP	3,024	**2,236**	1,921	1,606
MANDOL	06	GIBSON	**F- 2** BLACK TOP	2,230	**1,649**	1,417	1,184
MANDOL	08	GIBSON	**F- 2** BLACK TOP, SERIAL #4250-5450	2,342	**1,732**	1,488	1,244
MANDOL	09	GIBSON	**F- 2** BLACK TOP	2,345	**1,734**	1,490	1,245
MANDOL	11	GIBSON	**F- 2** BLACK TOP, TORTOISE PICKGUARD, SERIAL #10762	2,251	**1,664**	1,430	1,195
MANDOL	12	GIBSON	**F- 2** BLACK TOP, SERIAL #10850-13350	2,202	**1,628**	1,399	1,169
MANDOL	13	GIBSON	**F- 2** BLACK TOP, SERIAL #13350-16100	2,169	**1,604**	1,378	1,152
MANDOL	13	GIBSON	**F- 2** RED SUNBURST, SERIAL #53800-62200	2,205	**1,630**	1,401	1,171
MANDOL	14	GIBSON	**F- 2** BLACK TOP, INLAID TUNERS	2,053	**1,518**	1,304	1,090
MANDOL	15	GIBSON	**F- 2** BLACK TOP, INLAID TUNERS, SERIAL #20150-25150	2,195	**1,623**	1,395	1,166
MANDOL	16	GIBSON	**F- 2** BLACK TOP	2,071	**1,532**	1,316	1,100
MANDOL	17	GIBSON	**F- 2** BLACK TOP	2,213	**1,637**	1,406	1,176
MANDOL	18	GIBSON	**F- 2** RED SUNBURST	3,388	**2,506**	2,153	1,800
MANDOL	19	GIBSON	**F- 2** RED SUNBURST	1,975	**1,461**	1,255	1,049
MANDOL	20	GIBSON	**F- 2** SUNBURST	1,525	**1,128**	969	810
MANDOL	21	GIBSON	**F- 2** RED SUNBURST	1,972	**1,459**	1,253	1,048
MANDOL	23	GIBSON	**F- 2** RED SUNBURST	1,836	**1,358**	1,166	975
MANDOL	24	GIBSON	**F- 2** RED SUNBURST	1,760	**1,302**	1,118	935
MANDOL	26	GIBSON	**F- 2** RED SUNBURST, SERIAL #82700	1,727	**1,277**	1,097	917
MANDOL	07	GIBSON	**F- 4** BLACK TOP, ORNATE INLAY	3,600	**2,662**	2,287	1,912
MANDOL	10	GIBSON	**F- 4** BLACK TOP, SERIAL #6950-8750	2,013	**1,488**	1,279	1,069
MANDOL	10	GIBSON	**F- 4** ORANGE, 3-POINT SHALLOW BODY, ELABORATE PEGHEAD INLAY	3,360	**2,485**	2,135	1,785
MANDOL	12	GIBSON	**F- 4** ORANGE, FLOWERPOT INLAY	3,917	**2,897**	2,489	2,081
MANDOL	14	GIBSON	**F- 4** BLACK TOP	2,982	**2,205**	1,895	1,584
MANDOL	14	GIBSON	**F- 4** ORANGE, 1-PIECE HIGHLY FIGURED MAPLE BACK	3,211	**2,374**	2,040	1,705
MANDOL	14	GIBSON	**F- 4** RED MAHOGANY, SERIAL #16100-20150	3,381	**2,500**	2,148	1,796
MANDOL	15	GIBSON	**F- 4** RED MAHOGANY SUNBURST, SERIAL #20150-25150	2,338	**1,729**	1,485	1,242
MANDOL	16	GIBSON	**F- 4** BLACK TOP	1,992	**1,473**	1,265	1,058
MANDOL	16	GIBSON	**F- 4** RED MAHOGANY SUNBURST, INLAID TUNERS	2,329	**1,723**	1,480	1,237
MANDOL	17	GIBSON	**F- 4** RED SUNBURST, FLOWER INLAY, SERIAL #35590	3,342	**2,472**	2,124	1,775
MANDOL	17	GIBSON	**F- 4** RED MAHOGANY	3,747	**2,771**	2,381	1,991
MANDOL	18	GIBSON	**F- 4** RED SUNBURST	3,672	**2,716**	2,333	1,951
MANDOL	19	GIBSON	**F- 4** RED SUNBURST	3,212	**2,375**	2,041	1,706

TYPE	YR	MFG	PRICES--BASED ON 100% ORIGINAL MODEL	SELL EXC	SELL AVG	BUY EXC	BUY AVG
MANDOL	20	GIBSON	**F- 4** RED SUNBURST, CURLY MAPLE	1,874	**1,428**	1,213	928
MANDOL	20	GIBSON	**F- 4** RED MAHOGANY	2,390	**1,767**	1,518	1,269
MANDOL	20	GIBSON	**F- 4** RED SUNBURST, FLAMEY, FLORAL, SERIAL #53800-62200	3,819	**2,825**	2,427	2,029
MANDOL	21	GIBSON	**F- 4** RED SUNBURST, DOUBLE FLOWER-POT PEGHEAD INLAY	2,136	**1,580**	1,357	1,135
MANDOL	22	GIBSON	**F- 4** RED SUNBURST, 2-PC CURLY MAPLE, SERIAL #69300-71400	3,497	**2,586**	2,222	1,857
MANDOL	23	GIBSON	**F- 4** RED SUNBURST, SERIAL #71400-74900	2,905	**2,149**	1,846	1,543
MANDOL	24	GIBSON	**F- 4** RED SUNBURST	3,210	**2,374**	2,039	1,705
MANDOL	26	GIBSON	**F- 4** RED SUNBURST	4,205	**3,110**	2,672	2,234
MANDOL	28	GIBSON	**F- 4** RED SUNBURST	2,112	**1,562**	1,342	1,122
MANDOL	29	GIBSON	**F- 4** RED SUNBURST	2,242	**1,658**	1,424	1,191
MANDOL	37	GIBSON	**F- 4** RED SUNBURST	1,959	**1,449**	1,245	1,040
MANDOL	42	GIBSON	**F- 4** RED SUNBURST	1,938	**1,433**	1,231	1,029
MANDOL	23	GIBSON	**F- 5** FLAMED MAPLE, FLOWERPOT INLAY	40,929	**30,270**	26,007	21,743
MANDOL	24	GIBSON	**F- 5** FLOWERPOT INLAY	41,260	**30,515**	26,217	21,919
MANDOL	26	GIBSON	**F- 5** FERN PEGHEAD INLAY	26,400	**19,525**	16,775	14,025
MANDOL	27	GIBSON	**F- 5** SUNBURST, SERIAL #85400	13,441	**9,941**	8,541	7,141
MANDOL	29	GIBSON	**F- 5** FERN PEGHEAD INLAY, SERIAL #87300-89800	23,465	**17,354**	14,910	12,465
MANDOL	34	GIBSON	**F- 5** FERN SUNBURST	25,611	**18,942**	16,274	13,606
MANDOL	41	GIBSON	**F- 5** SUNBURST	13,893	**10,275**	8,827	7,380
MANDOL	41	GIBSON	**F- 5** SUNBURST, FLOWERPOT INLAY	14,992	**11,088**	9,526	7,964
MANDOL	42	GIBSON	**F- 5** FLEUR-DE-LIS PEGHEAD INLAY	12,000	**8,875**	7,625	6,375
MANDOL	42	GIBSON	**F- 5** SUNBURST, SERIAL #97418	15,280	**11,300**	9,715	8,122
MANDOL	65	GIBSON	**F- 5** 3-PC MAPLE NECK	3,669	**2,713**	2,331	1,949
MANDOL	67	GIBSON	**F- 5** SUNBURST	3,456	**2,556**	2,196	1,836
MANDOL	71	GIBSON	**F- 5** 2-PC CURLY MAPLE BACK	1,487	**1,099**	944	789
MANDOL	71	GIBSON	**F- 5** TOBACCO SUNBURST, FLAMED BACK/NECK	3,362	**2,487**	2,136	1,786
MANDOL	74	GIBSON	**F- 5** CURLY MAPLE	2,346	**1,735**	1,490	1,246
MANDOL	75	GIBSON	**F- 5** SUNBURST	2,047	**1,514**	1,301	1,087
MANDOL	76	GIBSON	**F- 5** 2-PC QUILTED MAPLE BACK	1,663	**1,230**	1,057	883
MANDOL	77	GIBSON	**F- 5** 2-PC FLAMED MAPLE BACK	1,474	**1,090**	936	783
MANDOL	77	GIBSON	**F- 5** CURLY MAPLE	1,485	**1,098**	943	788
MANDOL	64	GIBSON	**F- 5 CUSTOM** FIGURED MAPLE BACK/SIDES	3,954	**2,924**	2,512	2,100
MANDOL	67	GIBSON	**F- 5 CUSTOM**	2,904	**2,147**	1,845	1,542
MANDOL	79	GIBSON	**F- 5 L** MAPLE SUNBURST	2,894	**2,140**	1,839	1,537
MANDOL	22	GIBSON	**F- 5 LLOYD LOAR**	44,751	**33,097**	28,435	23,774
MANDOL	23	GIBSON	**F- 5 LLOYD LOAR**	44,374	**32,818**	28,196	23,573
MANDOL	24	GIBSON	**F- 5 LLOYD LOAR**	38,400	**28,400**	24,400	20,400
MANDOL	25	GIBSON	**F- 5 LLOYD LOAR**	24,173	**17,878**	15,360	12,842
MANDOL	35	GIBSON	**F- 7** FLEUR-DE-LIS PEGHEAD INLAY, "F" HOLES (RARE)	4,496	**3,325**	2,857	2,388
MANDOL	37	GIBSON	**F- 7** SERIAL #95400	4,995	**3,694**	3,174	2,654
MANDOL	89	GIBSON	**F- 7** SUNBURST	4,852	**3,589**	3,083	2,578
MANDOL	36	GIBSON	**F- 10** BLACK, SERIAL #93500	3,852	**2,849**	2,447	2,046
MANDOL	35	GIBSON	**F- 12** SUNBURST, SERIAL #92400-93500	4,331	**3,203**	2,752	2,301
MANDOL	49	GIBSON	**F- 12** SERIAL #A2800-A4400	3,177	**2,350**	2,019	1,688

TYPE	YR	MFG	MODEL	SELL EXC	SELL AVG	BUY EXC	BUY AVG
MANDOL	50	GIBSON	**F-12** SUNBURST	2,123	**1,570**	1,349	1,128
MANDOL	52	GIBSON	**F-12** SUNBURST	3,386	**2,504**	2,152	1,799
MANDOL	54	GIBSON	**F-12** SUNBURST	2,112	**1,562**	1,342	1,122
MANDOL	65	GIBSON	**F-12** SUNBURST	1,991	**1,472**	1,265	1,057
MANDOL	67	GIBSON	**F-12** SUNBURST	1,752	**1,296**	1,113	931
MANDOL	71	GIBSON	**F-12** SUNBURST	1,783	**1,319**	1,133	947
MANDOL	03	GIBSON	**F-MODEL ORVILLE** OVAL SOUNDHOLE, SERIAL #1150	11,722	**8,669**	7,448	6,227
MANDOL	00	GIBSON	**F-MODEL ORVILLE (1900)** OVAL SOUNDHOLE	14,172	**10,481**	9,005	7,529
MANDOL	59	GIBSON	**FLORENTINE ELECTRIC**	1,589	**1,175**	1,010	844
MANDOL	62	GIBSON	**FLORENTINE ELECTRIC**	1,446	**1,069**	919	768
MANDOL	63	GIBSON	**FLORENTINE ELECTRIC**	1,477	**1,092**	938	784
MANDOL	64	GIBSON	**FLORENTINE ELECTRIC**	1,848	**1,367**	1,174	982
MANDOL	65	GIBSON	**FLORENTINE ELECTRIC**	1,578	**1,167**	1,002	838
MANDOL	66	GIBSON	**FLORENTINE ELECTRIC**	1,500	**1,109**	953	797
MANDOL	68	GIBSON	**FLORENTINE ELECTRIC**	1,461	**1,080**	928	776
MANDOL	69	GIBSON	**FLORENTINE ELECTRIC**	1,232	**911**	783	654
MANDOL	16	GIBSON	**H-1** PUMPKIN TOP	1,366	**1,010**	868	725
MANDOL	18	GIBSON	**J MANDO-BASS** RED SUNBURST, SERIAL #39500-47900	1,452	**1,074**	922	771
MANDOL	20	GIBSON	**J MANDO-BASS**	1,992	**1,473**	1,265	1,058
MANDOL	27	GIBSON	**J MANDO-BASS** BLACK TOP, SERIAL #85400	993	**734**	631	527
MANDOL	14	GIBSON	**K- 1 MANDOCELLO** ORANGE TOP	2,345	**1,734**	1,490	1,245
MANDOL	15	GIBSON	**K- 1 MANDOCELLO**	2,339	**1,730**	1,486	1,242
MANDOL	16	GIBSON	**K- 1 MANDOCELLO** PUMPKIN	1,556	**1,150**	988	826
MANDOL	17	GIBSON	**K- 1 MANDOCELLO** PUMPKIN	1,593	**1,178**	1,012	846
MANDOL	17	GIBSON	**K- 1 MANDOCELLO** ORANGE TOP	2,935	**2,171**	1,865	1,559
MANDOL	18	GIBSON	**K- 1 MANDOCELLO** BROWN, SERIAL #39500-47900	3,006	**2,223**	1,910	1,597
MANDOL	27	GIBSON	**K- 1 MANDOCELLO** BLACK TOP	2,346	**1,735**	1,490	1,246
MANDOL	14	GIBSON	**K- 2 MANDOCELLO** BLACK, SERIAL #19359	2,354	**1,741**	1,496	1,251
MANDOL	16	GIBSON	**K- 2 MANDOCELLO** RED SUNBURST	1,776	**1,314**	1,129	944
MANDOL	18	GIBSON	**K- 2 MANDOCELLO** RED SUNBURST, SERIAL #39500-47900	1,619	**1,197**	1,029	860
MANDOL	19	GIBSON	**K- 2 MANDOCELLO** RED SUNBURST, SERIAL #47900-53800	2,349	**1,737**	1,492	1,247
MANDOL	15	GIBSON	**K- 4 MANDOCELLO** BLACK, SERIAL #20150-25150	5,351	**3,957**	3,400	2,842
MANDOL	16	GIBSON	**K- 4 MANDOCELLO** SUNBURST, FLAME MAPLE BACK/SIDES	6,230	**4,607**	3,958	3,309
MANDOL	17	GIBSON	**K- 4 MANDOCELLO** RED SUNBURST	5,760	**4,260**	3,660	3,060
MANDOL	20	GIBSON	**K- 4 MANDOCELLO** RED SUNBURST, SERIAL #53800-62200	5,030	**3,720**	3,196	2,672
MANDOL	21	GIBSON	**K- 4 MANDOCELLO** RED SUNBURST	2,914	**2,155**	1,851	1,548
MANDOL	24	GIBSON	**K- 4 MANDOCELLO** RED SUNBURST, SERIAL #74900-80300	2,195	**1,623**	1,395	1,166
MANDOL	37	GIBSON	**KALAMAZOO** SUNBURST, SERIAL #95400	654	**484**	416	347
MANDOL	38	GIBSON	**KALAMAZOO** SUNBURST, F-HOLES, SERIAL #95400	654	**484**	416	347
MANDOL	39	GIBSON	**KALAMAZOO C** SUNBURST	655	**484**	416	348
MANDOL	10	GIBSON	**MANDO BASS**	2,191	**1,620**	1,392	1,164
MANDOL	24	GIBSON	**MB-JUNIOR** BLACK	452	**334**	287	240
MANDOL	38	GIBSON	**RECORDING KING** SUNBURST, SERIAL #95400	747	**553**	475	397
MANDOL	24	GIBSON	**TL-1 TENOR LUTE-MANDOLIN** 4-STRING	1,274	**942**	810	677
STEEL GUITAR	46	GIBSON	**BR-4 LAP STEEL** SUNBURST, MAHOGANY	421	**311**	267	223
STGUIT	46	GIBSON	**BR-6 LAP STEEL** BLACK	533	**394**	339	283
STGUIT	47	GIBSON	**BR-6 LAP STEEL** BLACK	533	**394**	339	283

TYPE	YR	MFG	PRICES--BASED ON 100% ORIGINAL MODEL	SELL EXC	SELL AVG	BUY EXC	BUY AVG
STGUIT	48	GIBSON	**BR-6 LAP STEEL** BLACK	495	366	314	263
STGUIT	49	GIBSON	**BR-6 LAP STEEL**	432	319	274	229
STGUIT	50	GIBSON	**BR-6 LAP STEEL** SUNBURST	381	281	242	202
STGUIT	52	GIBSON	**BR-6 LAP STEEL** SUNBURST, SERIAL #A9400-A13000	400	296	254	212
STGUIT	55	GIBSON	**BR-6 LAP STEEL** MAHOGANY	312	230	198	165
STGUIT	58	GIBSON	**BR-6 LAP STEEL** SUNBURST	360	266	228	191
STGUIT	50	GIBSON	**BR-9 LAP STEEL** BEIGE, SERIAL #A4400-A6000	406	300	258	215
STGUIT	51	GIBSON	**BR-9 LAP STEEL** SUNBURST	391	289	248	208
STGUIT	52	GIBSON	**BR-9 LAP STEEL** BEIGE	489	362	311	260
STGUIT	53	GIBSON	**BR-9 LAP STEEL** SUNBURST	471	348	299	250
STGUIT	54	GIBSON	**BR-9 LAP STEEL** SUNBURST	478	353	303	253
STGUIT	56	GIBSON	**BR-9 LAP STEEL** BEIGE	480	355	305	255
STGUIT	57	GIBSON	**BR-9 LAP STEEL** BEIGE	480	355	305	255
STGUIT	58	GIBSON	**BR-9 LAP STEEL**	360	266	228	191
STGUIT	54	GIBSON	**CENTURY** SALMON	480	355	305	255
STGUIT	56	GIBSON	**CENTURY 6 LAP STEEL** 6-STRING	518	383	329	275
STGUIT	57	GIBSON	**CENTURY 6 LAP STEEL** 6-STRING, SERIAL #A24600-A26500	494	365	314	262
STGUIT	61	GIBSON	**CENTURY 6 LAP STEEL** 6-STRING	497	367	315	264
STGUIT	48	GIBSON	**CENTURY 10 LAP STEEL** BLACK, 10-STRING, 1 PU	480	355	305	255
STGUIT	55	GIBSON	**CENTURY 10 LAP STEEL** 10-STRING	438	324	278	233
STGUIT	56	GIBSON	**CENTURY 10 LAP STEEL** 10-STRING, SERIAL #A22000-A24600	562	416	357	298
STGUIT	56	GIBSON	**CG 520 DOUBLE NECK STEEL** NATURAL, 8-STRING	750	555	477	398
STGUIT	64	GIBSON	**CG 520 DOUBLE NECK STEEL** NATURAL, 8-STRING	1,252	926	796	665
STGUIT	59	GIBSON	**CG 523 STEEL** NATURAL, 8-STRING, TRIPLE NECK	938	694	596	498
STGUIT	35	GIBSON	**CONSOLE GRANDE** SUNBURST, 2 PU, (1)7-STRING, (1)8-STRING	705	521	448	374
STGUIT	39	GIBSON	**CONSOLE GRANDE 2** NATURAL, 8-STRING, SERIAL #95400-96000	601	445	382	319
STGUIT	46	GIBSON	**CONSOLE GRANDE 2** SUNBURST, 8-STRING	564	417	358	299
STGUIT	49	GIBSON	**CONSOLE GRANDE 2** SUNBURST, 8-STRING, SERIAL #A2800-A4400	499	369	317	265
STGUIT	50	GIBSON	**CONSOLE GRANDE 2** MAPLE, 8-STRING	478	353	303	253
STGUIT	51	GIBSON	**CONSOLE GRANDE 2** SUNBURST, 8-STRING	499	369	317	265
STGUIT	52	GIBSON	**CONSOLE GRANDE 2** SUNBURST, 8-STRING, SERIAL #A9400-A13000	456	337	290	242
STGUIT	53	GIBSON	**CONSOLE GRANDE 2** SUNBURST, 8-STRING	454	335	288	241
STGUIT	52	GIBSON	**CONSOLETTE 2** KORINA WOOD, 8-STRING, SERIAL #A9400-13000	707	523	449	375
STGUIT	53	GIBSON	**CONSOLETTE 2** KORINA WOOD, 8-STRING	668	494	424	354
STGUIT	54	GIBSON	**CONSOLETTE 2** KORINA WOOD, 8-STRING	663	490	421	352
STGUIT	55	GIBSON	**CONSOLETTE 2** KORINA WOOD, 8-STRING	585	433	372	311
STGUIT	36	GIBSON	**EH-100 LAP STEEL** BLACK	561	415	356	298
STGUIT	36	GIBSON	**EH-100 LAP STEEL** SUNBURST	618	457	392	328
STGUIT	38	GIBSON	**EH-100 LAP STEEL** BLACK, BAR PU	518	383	329	275
STGUIT	39	GIBSON	**EH-100 LAP STEEL** SUNBURST	423	313	269	224
STGUIT	40	GIBSON	**EH-100 LAP STEEL** SUNBURST	480	355	305	255
STGUIT	38	GIBSON	**EH-125 LAP STEEL** BLACK	533	394	339	283
STGUIT	39	GIBSON	**EH-125 LAP STEEL** SUNBURST	478	353	303	253

TYPE	YR	MFG	PRICES--BASED ON 100% ORIGINAL MODEL	SELL EXC	SELL AVG	BUY EXC	BUY AVG
STGUIT	40	GIBSON	**EH-125 LAP STEEL** SUNBURST	421	**311**	267	223
STGUIT	35	GIBSON	**EH-150 CHARLIE** SUNBURST, CHRISTIAN PU	617	**456**	392	327
STGUIT	36	GIBSON	**EH-150 CHARLIE** SUNBURST, CHRISTIAN PU	637	**471**	405	338
STGUIT	37	GIBSON	**EH-150 CHARLIE** SUNBURST, CHRISTIAN PU, SERIAL #95400	629	**465**	400	334
STGUIT	38	GIBSON	**EH-150 CHARLIE** SUNBURST, CHRISTIAN PU	518	**383**	329	275
STGUIT	39	GIBSON	**EH-150 CHARLIE** SUNBURST, CHRISTIAN PU	508	**376**	323	270
STGUIT	40	GIBSON	**EH-150 CHARLIE** ORANGE, CHRISTIAN PU	518	**383**	329	275
STGUIT	40	GIBSON	**EH-150 CHARLIE** SUNBURST, CHRISTIAN PU	525	**388**	333	278
STGUIT	39	GIBSON	**EH-185 LAP STEEL** SUNBURST	679	**502**	431	361
STGUIT	40	GIBSON	**EH-185 LAP STEEL** SUNBURST	633	**468**	402	336
STGUIT	40	GIBSON	**EH-185 LAP STEEL** SUNBURST	693	**512**	440	368
STGUIT	41	GIBSON	**EH-185 LAP STEEL** SUNBURST	656	**485**	417	348
STGUIT	42	GIBSON	**EH-185 LAP STEEL** SUNBURST	648	**479**	412	344
STGUIT	60	GIBSON	**EH-820 LAP STEEL**	577	**427**	367	307
STGUIT	39	GIBSON	**ELECTRAHARP** 8-STRING	981	**725**	623	521
STGUIT	41	GIBSON	**ELECTRAHARP** 8-STRING	957	**707**	608	508
STGUIT	49	GIBSON	**ELECTRAHARP** MAPLE, 8-STRING	831	**614**	528	441
STGUIT	53	GIBSON	**ELECTRAHARP** 8-STRING	598	**442**	380	317
STGUIT	60	GIBSON	**ELECTRAHARP** SUNBURST, 8-STRING	535	**396**	340	284
STGUIT	63	GIBSON	**ELECTRAHARP** 8-STRING	535	**396**	340	284
STGUIT	37	GIBSON	**HG-CENTURY HAWAIIAN** SUNBURST	1,593	**1,178**	1,012	846
STGUIT	39	GIBSON	**KALAMAZOO** BAR PU	336	**248**	213	178
STGUIT	68	GIBSON	**MODEL 400 PEDAL STEEL** SUNBURST	842	**623**	535	447
STGUIT	49	GIBSON	**PEDAL HARP** MAPLE, 8-STRING, 4-PEDAL	1,035	**766**	658	550
STGUIT	56	GIBSON	**SKYHAWK LAP STEEL** NATURAL, KORINA	513	**379**	326	272
STGUIT	56	GIBSON	**SKYHAWK LAP STEEL** NATURAL, KORINA	525	**388**	333	278
STGUIT	56	GIBSON	**SKYLARK LAP STEEL** NATURAL, KORINA	498	**368**	316	264
STGUIT	57	GIBSON	**SKYLARK LAP STEEL** NATURAL, KORINA	477	**352**	303	253
STGUIT	58	GIBSON	**SKYLARK LAP STEEL** NATURAL, KORINA	437	**323**	278	232
STGUIT	59	GIBSON	**SKYLARK LAP STEEL** NATURAL, KORINA	424	**313**	269	225
STGUIT	60	GIBSON	**SKYLARK LAP STEEL** NATURAL, KORINA	467	**345**	297	248
STGUIT	61	GIBSON	**SKYLARK LAP STEEL** NATURAL, KORINA	441	**326**	280	234
STGUIT	62	GIBSON	**SKYLARK LAP STEEL** NATURAL, KORINA	408	**302**	259	217
STGUIT	64	GIBSON	**SKYLARK LAP STEEL** NATURAL, KORINA	374	**276**	237	198
STGUIT	66	GIBSON	**SKYLARK LAP STEEL** NATURAL, KORINA	302	**223**	192	160
STGUIT	48	GIBSON	**ULTRATONE 6 LAP STEEL** WHITE, 6-STRING	477	**352**	303	253
STGUIT	50	GIBSON	**ULTRATONE 6 LAP STEEL** BLACK, 6-STRING	438	**324**	278	233
STGUIT	53	GIBSON	**ULTRATONE 6 LAP STEEL** BLUE GREEN, 6-STRING	483	**357**	307	257
UKULELE	29	GIBSON	**TU** TENOR	717	**530**	455	380
UKE	30	GIBSON	**TU** TENOR	564	**417**	358	299
UKE	39	GIBSON	**TU** TENOR	456	**337**	290	242
UKE	50	GIBSON	**TU-1** TENOR	464	**343**	295	246

TYPE	YR	MFG	MODEL	SELL EXC	SELL AVG	BUY EXC	BUY AVG
UKE	53	GIBSON	TU-1 TENOR	464	343	295	246
UKE	55	GIBSON	TU-1 TENOR	399	295	253	212
UKE	56	GIBSON	TU-1 TENOR	399	295	253	212
UKE	58	GIBSON	TU-1 TENOR	423	313	269	224
UKE	25	GIBSON	UKE-1 PLAIN, NO BINDING	432	319	274	229
UKE	30	GIBSON	UKE-1 MAHOGANY	451	333	286	239
UKE	34	GIBSON	UKE-1 SUNBURST	430	318	273	228
UKE	27	GIBSON	UKE-2 MAHOGANY	422	312	268	224
UKE	30	GIBSON	UKE-2 TRIPLE BOUND	336	248	213	178
UKE	28	GIBSON	UKE-3 MAHOGANY	423	313	269	224

GLEEMAN

| SYNTHESIZER | 82 | GLEE | PENTAPHONIC BLACK, CLEAR | 1,434 | 1,060 | 911 | 761 |

GOWER

GUITAR (ACOUSTIC)	65	GOWER	DREADNOUGHT NATURAL	264	195	167	140
GUITAR	60	GOWER	G-55-2 3-PIECE MAHOGANY BACK	384	284	244	204
GUITAR	65	GOWER	G-55-2 SUNBURST, BRAZILIAN ROSEWOOD BACK/SIDES	312	230	198	165
GUITAR	60	GOWER	G-65 NATURAL, MAHOGANY BACK/SIDES	336	248	213	178

GOYA by MARTIN GUITAR CO

ELEC. GUITAR	69	GOYA	JAGUAR 2 PU's, CHERRY SUNBURST	147	109	93	78
ELGUIT	69	GOYA	JAGUAR BASS 2 PU's, RED TO BLACK SUNBURST	142	105	90	75
ELGUIT	65	GOYA	P-26 4-PRESETS, 2 PU's	216	159	137	114
ELGUIT	62	GOYA	P-46 6-PRESETS, 4 PU's	288	213	183	153
ELGUIT	60	GOYA	PANTHER WHITE, VIBRATO, 3 PU's	99	73	63	53
ELGUIT	68	GOYA	PANTHER 2 PU's	117	86	74	62
ELGUIT	68	GOYA	PANTHER BASS	99	73	63	53
ELGUIT	60	GOYA	RANGEMASTER LIME GREEN	99	73	63	53
ELGUIT	64	GOYA	RANGEMASTER SUNBURST	99	73	63	53
ELGUIT	65	GOYA	RANGEMASTER	144	106	91	76
ELGUIT	67	GOYA	RANGEMASTER RED TO BLACK SUNBURST, 2 PU's	99	73	63	53
ELGUIT	67	GOYA	RANGEMASTER RED TO BLACK SUNBURST	105	78	67	56
ELGUIT	67	GOYA	RANGEMASTER 2 PU's, SEMI-HOLLOW, CUTAWAY	115	85	73	61
ELGUIT	68	GOYA	RANGEMASTER CHERRY SUNBURST	99	73	63	53
ELGUIT	69	GOYA	RANGEMASTER 2 PU's	99	73	63	53
ELGUIT	62	GOYA	SPARKLE SOLID BODY, INLAY, 2 PU's	470	347	298	249
GUITAR (ACOUSTIC)	60	GOYA	F-11 WHITE, DOUBLE PICKGUARD	336	248	213	178
GUITAR	65	GOYA	GG-10 CLASSICAL	110	81	70	58
GUITAR	72	GOYA	N-26 SUNBURST, DREADNOUGHT	384	284	244	204

GRAMMER

GUITAR (ACOUSTIC)	67	GRAMMER	DREADNOUGHT BRAZILIAN ROSEWOOD BACK/SIDES	1,195	883	759	634
GUITAR	67	GRAMMER	G-10 NATURAL	621	459	394	329
GUITAR	68	GRAMMER	G-10 SUNBURST, BRAZILIAN ROSEWOOD BACK/SIDES	457	338	290	243
GUITAR	68	GRAMMER	G-10 ROSEWOOD BODY, FLATTOP	796	589	506	423
GUITAR	69	GRAMMER	G-10 SUNBURST, FLATTOP	431	328	279	213
GUITAR	69	GRAMMER	G-10 NATURAL	577	427	367	307

TYPE	YR	MFG	PRICES--BASED ON 100% ORIGINAL MODEL	SELL EXC	SELL AVG	BUY EXC	BUY AVG
GUITAR	70	GRAMMER	G-10 NATURAL, ROSEWOOD BACK/SIDES	475	351	301	252
GUITAR	66	GRAMMER	G-20 MAPLE BODY, FLATTOP	419	310	266	222
GUITAR	67	GRAMMER	G-20 NATURAL, FLATTOP	451	333	286	239
GUITAR	68	GRAMMER	G-20 NATURAL, FLATTOP	360	266	228	191
GUITAR	66	GRAMMER	G-30 MAHOGANY, FLATTOP	385	285	245	205
GUITAR	67	GRAMMER	G-30 MAHOGANY, FLATTOP	459	340	292	244
GUITAR	68	GRAMMER	G-58 FLATTOP	499	369	317	265
GUITAR	70	GRAMMER	G-S	2,062	1,525	1,310	1,095
GUITAR	68	GRAMMER	H-10 MERLE HAGGARD MODEL FLATTOP	590	449	382	292
GUITAR	70	GRAMMER	PROTOTYPE BRAZILIAN ROSEWOOD, FLATTOP	871	664	564	431
GUITAR	68	GRAMMER	S-20 NATURAL, MAPLE BACK/SIDES	367	280	238	182
GUITAR	65	GRAMMER	S-30 MAHOGANY BACK/SIDES, FLATTOP	396	293	251	210
GUITAR	67	GRAMMER	S-40 NATURAL, AFRICAN WALNUT BACK/SIDES, FLATTOP	432	319	274	229

GRETSCH

TYPE	YR	MFG	MODEL	SELL EXC	SELL AVG	BUY EXC	BUY AVG
BANJO	61	GRETSCH	APPALACHIA MOUNTAIN BOWL 5-STRING TENOR, RESONATOR, WALNUT NECK	670	495	425	355
BANJO	52	GRETSCH	B&D SENORITA PEARLOID PEGHEAD VENEER, FINGERBOARD, RIM, RESONATOR	682	504	433	362
BANJO	66	GRETSCH	BACON LONG NECK, OPEN BACK	757	560	481	402
BANJO	55	GRETSCH	BACON BELMONT ORIGINAL 5-STRING	796	589	506	423
BANJO	60	GRETSCH	BACON FOLK MODEL 5-STRING, OPEN BACK	777	575	494	413
BANJO	61	GRETSCH	KENTUCKY MOUNTAIN BOWL 5-STRING, RESONATOR, WALNUT NECK	630	466	400	335
BANJO	50	GRETSCH	NEW YORKER TENOR	540	399	343	287
BANJO	51	GRETSCH	NEW YORKER	273	202	173	145
BANJO	79	GRETSCH	ODE STYLE D	533	394	339	283
BANJO	25	GRETSCH	ORCHESTRELLA TENOR, PEGHEAD INLAY	560	414	356	297
BANJO	29	GRETSCH	PRESIDENT TENOR, WALNUT NECK, ORNAMENTAL ENGRVNG, PEARLOID PEGHEAD	616	455	391	327
BANJO	56	GRETSCH	TENNESSEE MOUNTAIN BOWL 5-STRING, RESONATOR	598	442	380	317
BANJO	69	GRETSCH	TENOR 5-STRING	439	325	279	233
ELEC. GUITAR	60	GRETSCH	12-STRING SUNBURST	596	440	378	316
ELGUIT	36	GRETSCH	65 AMBER	536	396	340	285
ELGUIT	69	GRETSCH	6009 JUMBO SUNBURST	501	370	318	266
ELGUIT	64	GRETSCH	6070 BASS SUNBURST, HOLLOW, DOUBLE CUTAWAY, 1 U	386	294	250	191
ELGUIT	64	GRETSCH	6070 BASS COUNTRY GENTLEMAN 1 PU	718	531	456	381
ELGUIT	68	GRETSCH	6070 BASS COUNTRY GENTLEMAN 1 PU	598	442	380	317
ELGUIT	72	GRETSCH	6070 BASS COUNTRY GENTLEMAN 1 PU	406	300	258	215
ELGUIT	67	GRETSCH	6071 BASS MAHOGANY, HOLLOW, SINGLE CUTAWAY 1 PU	796	589	506	423
ELGUIT	68	GRETSCH	6071 BASS MAHOGANY, HOLLOW, SINGLE CUTAWAY, 1 PU	452	334	287	240
ELGUIT	68	GRETSCH	6072 BASS SUNBURST, HOLLOW, DOUBLE CUTAWAY, 2 PU's	835	617	530	443
ELGUIT	69	GRETSCH	6072 BASS SUNBURST, HOLLOW, DOUBLE CUTAWAY, 2 PU's	475	351	301	252
ELGUIT	69	GRETSCH	6072 BASS SUNBURST, LONG SCALE, 34" LENGTH, 17" WIDE BODY	708	523	450	376
ELGUIT	68	GRETSCH	6073 BASS MAHOGANY, HOLLOW, SINGLE CUTAWAY, 2 PU's	480	355	305	255
ELGUIT	66	GRETSCH	6075 SUNBURST, 12-STRING	483	357	307	257
ELGUIT	67	GRETSCH	6075 SUNBURST, 12-STRING	458	339	291	243
ELGUIT	68	GRETSCH	6075 SUNBURST, 12-STRING	604	447	384	321

TYPE	YR	MFG	PRICES--BASED ON 100% ORIGINAL MODEL	SELL EXC	SELL AVG	BUY EXC	BUY AVG
ELGUIT	69	GRETSCH	**6076** NATURAL, 12-STRING	433	**320**	275	230
ELGUIT	55	GRETSCH	**6120**	2,997	**2,216**	1,904	1,592
ELGUIT	63	GRETSCH	**6162**	238	**176**	151	126
ELGUIT	57	GRETSCH	**6187** METALLIC GREY BACK/SIDES, CUTAWAY	646	**477**	410	343
ELGUIT	58	GRETSCH	**ANNIVERSARY 6124** SUNBURST	516	**381**	328	274
ELGUIT	59	GRETSCH	**ANNIVERSARY 6124** SUNBURST	466	**345**	296	247
ELGUIT	60	GRETSCH	**ANNIVERSARY 6124** SUNBURST	433	**320**	275	230
ELGUIT	61	GRETSCH	**ANNIVERSARY 6124** SUNBURST	428	**316**	272	227
ELGUIT	62	GRETSCH	**ANNIVERSARY 6124** SUNBURST	486	**359**	309	258
ELGUIT	64	GRETSCH	**ANNIVERSARY 6124** SUNBURST	452	**334**	287	240
ELGUIT	65	GRETSCH	**ANNIVERSARY 6124** SUNBURST	430	**318**	273	228
ELGUIT	67	GRETSCH	**ANNIVERSARY 6124** SUNBURST	423	**313**	269	224
ELGUIT	67	GRETSCH	**ANNIVERSARY 6124** SUNBURST, LEFT-HANDED	442	**327**	281	235
ELGUIT	71	GRETSCH	**ANNIVERSARY 6124** SUNBURST	480	**355**	305	255
ELGUIT	58	GRETSCH	**ANNIVERSARY 6125** SMOKE GREEN 2-TONE	829	**613**	527	440
ELGUIT	59	GRETSCH	**ANNIVERSARY 6125** SMOKE GREEN 2-TONE	510	**377**	324	271
ELGUIT	62	GRETSCH	**ANNIVERSARY 6125** SMOKE GREEN 2-TONE	522	**386**	331	277
ELGUIT	63	GRETSCH	**ANNIVERSARY 6125** SMOKE GREEN 2-TONE	492	**364**	312	261
ELGUIT	64	GRETSCH	**ANNIVERSARY 6125** SMOKE GREEN 2-TONE	536	**396**	340	285
ELGUIT	67	GRETSCH	**ANNIVERSARY 6125** SMOKE GREEN 2-TONE	466	**345**	296	247
ELGUIT	68	GRETSCH	**ANNIVERSARY 6125** SMOKE GREEN 2-TONE	439	**325**	279	233
ELGUIT	70	GRETSCH	**ANNIVERSARY 6125** SMOKE GREEN 2-TONE	433	**320**	275	230
ELGUIT	65	GRETSCH	**ASTRO JET 6126** RED, BLACK BACK/SIDES	415	**307**	264	220
ELGUIT	66	GRETSCH	**ASTRO JET 6126** RED, BLACK BACK/SIDES	411	**304**	261	218
ELGUIT	67	GRETSCH	**ASTRO JET 6126** RED, BLACK BACK/SIDES	433	**320**	275	230
ELGUIT	61	GRETSCH	**BIKINI 6023** BLACK	241	**178**	153	128
ELGUIT	62	GRETSCH	**BIKINI 6023** BLACK	198	**146**	126	105
ELGUIT	62	GRETSCH	**BIKINI 6024 BASS** BLACK	266	**197**	169	141
ELGUIT	61	GRETSCH	**BIKINI 6025** BLACK, DOUBLE NECK	705	**521**	448	374
ELGUIT	69	GRETSCH	**BLACKHAWK 6101** BLACK, FLOATING BRIDGE	408	**302**	259	217
ELGUIT	69	GRETSCH	**BOSSA NOVA CLASSICAL ELECTRIC**	454	**335**	288	241
ELGUIT	75	GRETSCH	**BROADKASTER** SOLID BODY	419	**310**	266	222
ELGUIT	75	GRETSCH	**BROADKASTER** HOLLOW BODY	596	**440**	378	316
ELGUIT	78	GRETSCH	**BROADKASTER** SOLID BODY	454	**335**	288	241
ELGUIT	79	GRETSCH	**BROADKASTER** HOLLOWBODY	554	**410**	352	294
ELGUIT	79	GRETSCH	**BST-1000**	283	**209**	179	150
ELGUIT	80	GRETSCH	**BST-1000**	273	**202**	173	145
ELGUIT	79	GRETSCH	**BST-2000**	256	**189**	162	136
ELGUIT	80	GRETSCH	**BST-2000** WALNUT BROWN	261	**193**	165	138
ELGUIT	78	GRETSCH	**BST-5000** NATURAL	252	**186**	160	134
ELGUIT	79	GRETSCH	**BST-5000** NATURAL	241	**178**	153	128
ELGUIT	80	GRETSCH	**BST-5000** NATURAL	223	**165**	142	118
ELGUIT	76	GRETSCH	**CHET ATKINS AXE** ROSEWOOD	652	**482**	414	346
ELGUIT	79	GRETSCH	**CHET ATKINS AXE**	746	**552**	474	396
ELGUIT	70	GRETSCH	**CHET ATKINS JUNIOR** ORANGE	569	**421**	361	302

TYPE	YR	MFG	PRICES--BASED ON 100% ORIGINAL MODEL	SELL EXC	SELL AVG	BUY EXC	BUY AVG
ELGUIT	77	GRETSCH	CHET ATKINS SUPER AXE BLACK	522	386	331	277
ELGUIT	80	GRETSCH	CHET ATKINS SUPER AXE	613	513	427	356
ELGUIT	58	GRETSCH	CHET ATKINS 6119 TENNESSEAN	1,082	800	688	575
ELGUIT	59	GRETSCH	CHET ATKINS 6119 TENNESSEAN	1,074	794	682	570
ELGUIT	60	GRETSCH	CHET ATKINS 6119 TENNESSEAN	1,071	792	680	569
ELGUIT	61	GRETSCH	CHET ATKINS 6119 TENNESSEAN	1,186	877	753	630
ELGUIT	62	GRETSCH	CHET ATKINS 6119 TENNESSEAN	1,171	866	744	622
ELGUIT	63	GRETSCH	CHET ATKINS 6119 TENNESSEAN	1,167	863	741	620
ELGUIT	64	GRETSCH	CHET ATKINS 6119 TENNESSEAN	1,139	842	724	605
ELGUIT	65	GRETSCH	CHET ATKINS 6119 TENNESSEAN	1,114	824	708	592
ELGUIT	66	GRETSCH	CHET ATKINS 6119 TENNESSEAN	979	724	622	520
ELGUIT	67	GRETSCH	CHET ATKINS 6119 TENNESSEAN	967	715	614	514
ELGUIT	68	GRETSCH	CHET ATKINS 6119 TENNESSEAN	955	706	606	507
ELGUIT	69	GRETSCH	CHET ATKINS 6119 TENNESSEAN	941	696	598	500
ELGUIT	71	GRETSCH	CHET ATKINS 6119 TENNESSEAN	930	687	591	494
ELGUIT	72	GRETSCH	CHET ATKINS 6119 TENNESSEAN	921	681	585	489
ELGUIT	75	GRETSCH	CHET ATKINS 6119 TENNESSEAN	917	678	583	487
ELGUIT	54	GRETSCH	CHET ATKINS 6120 NASHVILLE	4,547	3,363	2,889	2,415
ELGUIT	55	GRETSCH	CHET ATKINS 6120 NASHVILLE WHITE CASS COWBOY STRAP, COW & CACTUS INLAYS	4,679	3,460	2,973	2,485
ELGUIT	56	GRETSCH	CHET ATKINS 6120 NASHVILLE HOLLOW BODY	4,374	3,235	2,779	2,324
ELGUIT	57	GRETSCH	CHET ATKINS 6120 NASHVILLE	4,121	3,048	2,618	2,189
ELGUIT	58	GRETSCH	CHET ATKINS 6120 NASHVILLE HOLLOW BODY	3,864	2,858	2,455	2,053
ELGUIT	59	GRETSCH	CHET ATKINS 6120 NASHVILLE HOLLOW BODY	3,856	2,852	2,450	2,048
ELGUIT	60	GRETSCH	CHET ATKINS 6120 NASHVILLE ORANGE, HOLLOW BODY	3,373	2,494	2,143	1,792
ELGUIT	61	GRETSCH	CHET ATKINS 6120 NASHVILLE THINBODY	1,052	778	668	558
ELGUIT	62	GRETSCH	CHET ATKINS 6120 NASHVILLE	1,050	776	667	557
ELGUIT	63	GRETSCH	CHET ATKINS 6120 NASHVILLE	1,040	769	661	552
ELGUIT	64	GRETSCH	CHET ATKINS 6120 NASHVILLE	1,036	766	658	550
ELGUIT	65	GRETSCH	CHET ATKINS 6120 NASHVILLE	1,023	756	650	543
ELGUIT	66	GRETSCH	CHET ATKINS 6120 NASHVILLE	1,011	748	642	537
ELGUIT	67	GRETSCH	CHET ATKINS 6120 NASHVILLE	985	729	626	523
ELGUIT	68	GRETSCH	CHET ATKINS 6120 NASHVILLE	980	724	622	520
ELGUIT	69	GRETSCH	CHET ATKINS 6120 NASHVILLE	962	712	611	511
ELGUIT	72	GRETSCH	CHET ATKINS 6120 NASHVILLE	561	415	356	298
ELGUIT	73	GRETSCH	CHET ATKINS 6120 NASHVILLE	550	406	349	292
ELGUIT	79	GRETSCH	CHET ATKINS 6120 NASHVILLE	548	405	348	291
ELGUIT	55	GRETSCH	CHET ATKINS 6121 SOLID BODY	3,480	2,574	2,211	1,849
ELGUIT	56	GRETSCH	CHET ATKINS 6121 SOLID BODY	3,470	2,566	2,205	1,843
ELGUIT	57	GRETSCH	CHET ATKINS 6121 SOLID BODY	3,168	2,343	2,013	1,683
ELGUIT	58	GRETSCH	CHET ATKINS 6121 SOLID BODY	3,352	2,479	2,130	1,780
ELGUIT	58	GRETSCH	CHET ATKINS 6121 SOLID BODY, LEFT-HANDED	3,437	2,542	2,184	1,826
ELGUIT	59	GRETSCH	CHET ATKINS 6121 SOLID BODY	3,412	2,524	2,168	1,813
ELGUIT	60	GRETSCH	CHET ATKINS 6121 SOLID BODY	3,381	2,500	2,148	1,796
ELGUIT	62	GRETSCH	CHET ATKINS 6121 SOLID BOLDY	3,338	2,469	2,121	1,773
ELGUIT	57	GRETSCH	CHET ATKINS 6122 COUNTRY GENT	3,281	2,426	2,084	1,743
ELGUIT	58	GRETSCH	CHET ATKINS 6122 COUNTRY GENT	3,200	2,367	2,033	1,700
ELGUIT	59	GRETSCH	CHET ATKINS 6122 COUNTRY GENT	1,994	1,475	1,267	1,059
ELGUIT	60	GRETSCH	CHET ATKINS 6122 COUNTRY GENT LEFT-HANDED	2,027	1,499	1,288	1,077
ELGUIT	61	GRETSCH	CHET ATKINS 6122 COUNTRY GENT	1,602	1,184	1,018	851
ELGUIT	62	GRETSCH	CHET ATKINS 6122 COUNTRY GENT	1,664	1,231	1,057	884
ELGUIT	63	GRETSCH	CHET ATKINS 6122 COUNTRY GENT	1,652	1,221	1,049	877
ELGUIT	64	GRETSCH	CHET ATKINS 6122 COUNTRY GENT	1,632	1,207	1,037	867
ELGUIT	65	GRETSCH	CHET ATKINS 6122 COUNTRY GENT	1,609	1,190	1,022	855
ELGUIT	66	GRETSCH	CHET ATKINS 6122 COUNTRY GENT	1,591	1,177	1,011	845
ELGUIT	67	GRETSCH	CHET ATKINS 6122 COUNTRY GENT WALNUT	1,576	1,165	1,001	837
ELGUIT	69	GRETSCH	CHET ATKINS 6122 COUNTRY GENT	1,558	1,152	990	827
ELGUIT	70	GRETSCH	CHET ATKINS 6122 COUNTRY GENT	1,354	1,001	860	719
ELGUIT	71	GRETSCH	CHET ATKINS 6122 COUNTRY GENT	1,344	994	854	714
ELGUIT	72	GRETSCH	CHET ATKINS 6122 COUNTRY GENT	1,326	981	843	704
ELGUIT	73	GRETSCH	CHET ATKINS 6122 COUNTRY GENT	1,304	964	828	693
ELGUIT	74	GRETSCH	CHET ATKINS 6122 COUNTRY GENT	1,195	883	759	634

TYPE	YR	MFG	PRICES--BASED ON 100% ORIGINAL MODEL	SELL EXC	SELL AVG	BUY EXC	BUY AVG
ELGUIT	75	GRETSCH	**CHET ATKINS 6122 COUNTRY GENT**	1,177	**871**	748	625
ELGUIT	76	GRETSCH	**CHET ATKINS 6122 COUNTRY GENT**	1,158	**856**	736	615
ELGUIT	79	GRETSCH	**CHET ATKINS 6122 COUNTRY GENT**	476	**352**	302	252
ELGUIT	71	GRETSCH	**CLIPPER** 1 PU	384	**284**	244	204
ELGUIT	56	GRETSCH	**CLIPPER 6186** SUNBURST	380	**281**	241	201
ELGUIT	57	GRETSCH	**CLIPPER 6186** SUNBURST	384	**284**	244	204
ELGUIT	58	GRETSCH	**CLIPPER 6186** SUNBURST	471	**348**	299	250
ELGUIT	59	GRETSCH	**CLIPPER 6186** SUNBURST	444	**328**	282	236
ELGUIT	60	GRETSCH	**CLIPPER 6186** SUNBURST	423	**313**	269	224
ELGUIT	61	GRETSCH	**CLIPPER 6186** SUNBURST	415	**307**	264	220
ELGUIT	62	GRETSCH	**CLIPPER 6186** SUNBURST	392	**290**	249	208
ELGUIT	63	GRETSCH	**CLIPPER 6186** SUNBURST	365	**270**	232	194
ELGUIT	64	GRETSCH	**CLIPPER 6186** SUNBURST	415	**307**	264	220
ELGUIT	67	GRETSCH	**CLIPPER 6186** SUNBURST	309	**228**	196	164
ELGUIT	69	GRETSCH	**CLIPPER 6186** SUNBURST	328	**242**	208	174
ELGUIT	59	GRETSCH	**CLIPPER 6187** NATURAL	469	**347**	298	249
ELGUIT	72	GRETSCH	**CLIPPER 6187** NATURAL	411	**304**	261	218
ELGUIT	77	GRETSCH	**COMMITTEE 7628** NATURAL	288	**213**	183	153
ELGUIT	77	GRETSCH	**COMMITTEE 7628** ROSEWOOD, DOUBLE HB	311	**230**	197	165
ELGUIT	78	GRETSCH	**COMMITTEE 7628** NATURAL	287	**212**	182	152
ELGUIT	79	GRETSCH	**COMMITTEE 7628** NATURAL	270	**200**	172	143
ELGUIT	55	GRETSCH	**CONVERTIBLE 6199** LOTUS IVORY TOP	921	**681**	585	489
ELGUIT	56	GRETSCH	**CONVERTIBLE 6199** LOTUS IVORY TOP	920	**680**	584	489
ELGUIT	57	GRETSCH	**CONVERTIBLE 6199** LOTUS IVORY TOP	904	**668**	574	480
ELGUIT	56	GRETSCH	**CORSAIR** NATURAL	469	**347**	298	249
ELGUIT	60	GRETSCH	**CORSAIR**	522	**386**	331	277
ELGUIT	57	GRETSCH	**CORVETTE** HOLLOWBODY, ELECTROMATIC	513	**379**	326	272
ELGUIT	76	GRETSCH	**CORVETTE** SOLID BODY	319	**236**	203	169
ELGUIT	61	GRETSCH	**CORVETTE 6132** MAHOGANY, SOLID BODY, 1 PU	490	**362**	311	260
ELGUIT	62	GRETSCH	**CORVETTE 6132** CHERRY RED, 1 PU	518	**383**	329	275
ELGUIT	63	GRETSCH	**CORVETTE 6132** CHERRY RED, 1 PU	401	**296**	254	213
ELGUIT	64	GRETSCH	**CORVETTE 6132** CHERRY RED, 1 PU	362	**268**	230	192
ELGUIT	65	GRETSCH	**CORVETTE 6132** CHERRY RED, 1 PU	396	**293**	251	210
ELGUIT	66	GRETSCH	**CORVETTE 6132** CHERRY RED, 1 PU	408	**302**	259	217
ELGUIT	62	GRETSCH	**CORVETTE 6134** CHERRY RED, VIBRATO, 1 PU	352	**260**	223	187
ELGUIT	66	GRETSCH	**CORVETTE 6134** CHERRY RED, VIBRATO, 1 PU	379	**280**	240	201
ELGUIT	62	GRETSCH	**CORVETTE 6135** CHERRY RED, 2 PU's	458	**339**	291	243
ELGUIT	64	GRETSCH	**CORVETTE 6135** CHERRY RED, 2 PU's	311	**230**	197	165
ELGUIT	65	GRETSCH	**CORVETTE 6135** CHERRY RED, 2 PU's	389	**288**	247	207
ELGUIT	66	GRETSCH	**CORVETTE 6135** CHERRY RED, 2 PU's	380	**281**	241	201
ELGUIT	68	GRETSCH	**CORVETTE 6135** CHERRY RED, 2 PU's	389	**288**	247	207
ELGUIT	55	GRETSCH	**CORVETTE 6182** SUNBURST, HOLLOW BODY	528	**391**	336	281
ELGUIT	55	GRETSCH	**CORVETTE 6183** NATURAL, HOLLOW BODY	543	**401**	345	288
ELGUIT	56	GRETSCH	**CORVETTE 6183** NATURAL, HOLLOW BODY	531	**393**	337	282

TYPE	YR	MFG	MODEL	SELL EXC	SELL AVG	BUY EXC	BUY AVG
			PRICES--BASED ON 100% ORIGINAL				
ELGUIT	57	GRETSCH	**CORVETTE 6183** NATURAL, HOLLOW BODY	546	**403**	347	290
ELGUIT	71	GRETSCH	**CORVETTE 6183** SOLID BODY, BIGSBY	369	**273**	234	196
ELGUIT	53	GRETSCH	**COUNTRY CLUB** NATURAL	1,838	**1,359**	1,168	976
ELGUIT	53	GRETSCH	**COUNTRY CLUB** CADILLAC GREEN	3,409	**2,521**	2,166	1,811
ELGUIT	54	GRETSCH	**COUNTRY CLUB** NATURAL	1,826	**1,351**	1,160	970
ELGUIT	54	GRETSCH	**COUNTRY CLUB** CADILLAC GREEN	1,847	**1,366**	1,173	981
ELGUIT	55	GRETSCH	**COUNTRY CLUB** SUNBURST	1,533	**1,133**	974	814
ELGUIT	55	GRETSCH	**COUNTRY CLUB** NATURAL	1,624	**1,201**	1,032	862
ELGUIT	55	GRETSCH	**COUNTRY CLUB** CADILLAC GREEN	3,144	**2,325**	1,997	1,670
ELGUIT	56	GRETSCH	**COUNTRY CLUB** NATURAL	1,378	**1,050**	892	682
ELGUIT	56	GRETSCH	**COUNTRY CLUB** SUNBURST	1,360	**1,006**	864	722
ELGUIT	56	GRETSCH	**COUNTRY CLUB** CADILLAC GREEN	2,075	**1,535**	1,318	1,102
ELGUIT	57	GRETSCH	**COUNTRY CLUB** SUNBURST	1,248	**923**	793	663
ELGUIT	57	GRETSCH	**COUNTRY CLUB** NATURAL	1,453	**1,074**	923	772
ELGUIT	57	GRETSCH	**COUNTRY CLUB** CADILLAC GREEN	3,068	**2,269**	1,949	1,629
ELGUIT	58	GRETSCH	**COUNTRY CLUB** SUNBURST, PROJECT-O-SONIC	1,690	**1,250**	1,074	898
ELGUIT	58	GRETSCH	**COUNTRY CLUB** NATURAL	1,834	**1,356**	1,165	974
ELGUIT	58	GRETSCH	**COUNTRY CLUB** CADILLAC GREEN	2,252	**1,665**	1,431	1,196
ELGUIT	59	GRETSCH	**COUNTRY CLUB** SUNBURST	1,236	**914**	785	656
ELGUIT	59	GRETSCH	**COUNTRY CLUB** NATURAL	1,410	**1,042**	896	749
ELGUIT	59	GRETSCH	**COUNTRY CLUB** CADILLAC GREEN	1,893	**1,400**	1,202	1,005
ELGUIT	60	GRETSCH	**COUNTRY CLUB** SUNBURST	1,242	**918**	789	659
ELGUIT	61	GRETSCH	**COUNTRY CLUB** BLOND	1,337	**989**	849	710
ELGUIT	61	GRETSCH	**COUNTRY CLUB** SUNBURST	1,431	**1,058**	909	760
ELGUIT	61	GRETSCH	**COUNTRY CLUB** CADILLAC GREEN	1,806	**1,336**	1,148	959
ELGUIT	62	GRETSCH	**COUNTRY CLUB** SUNBURST	1,167	**863**	741	620
ELGUIT	62	GRETSCH	**COUNTRY CLUB** CADILLAC GREEN	1,296	**959**	824	689
ELGUIT	62	GRETSCH	**COUNTRY CLUB** BLOND	1,363	**1,008**	866	724
ELGUIT	64	GRETSCH	**COUNTRY CLUB** SUNBURST	1,086	**803**	690	577
ELGUIT	64	GRETSCH	**COUNTRY CLUB** CADILLAC GREEN	1,296	**959**	824	689
ELGUIT	65	GRETSCH	**COUNTRY CLUB** SUNBURST, TRON PU	1,000	**739**	635	531
ELGUIT	66	GRETSCH	**COUNTRY CLUB** SUNBURST	1,000	**739**	635	531
ELGUIT	67	GRETSCH	**COUNTRY CLUB** NATURAL	802	**611**	519	397
ELGUIT	67	GRETSCH	**COUNTRY CLUB** SUNBURST	999	**739**	635	530
ELGUIT	71	GRETSCH	**COUNTRY CLUB** SUNBURST	687	**508**	436	365
ELGUIT	72	GRETSCH	**COUNTRY CLUB** NATURAL	898	**664**	570	477
ELGUIT	74	GRETSCH	**COUNTRY CLUB** NATURAL	956	**707**	607	507
ELGUIT	75	GRETSCH	**COUNTRY CLUB** NATURAL	773	**572**	491	411
ELGUIT	76	GRETSCH	**COUNTRY CLUB** SUNBURST	1,012	**749**	643	538
ELGUIT	77	GRETSCH	**COUNTRY CLUB** NATURAL	876	**648**	556	465
ELGUIT	78	GRETSCH	**COUNTRY CLUB** NATURAL	865	**640**	550	460
ELGUIT	79	GRETSCH	**COUNTRY CLUB** NATURAL	855	**632**	543	454

TYPE	YR	MFG	PRICES--BASED ON 100% ORIGINAL MODEL	SELL EXC	SELL AVG	BUY EXC	BUY AVG
ELGUIT	79	GRETSCH	COUNTRY CLUB BLOND, GOLD HARDWARE	950	**702**	603	504
ELGUIT	80	GRETSCH	COUNTRY CLUB NATURAL	841	**622**	534	447
ELGUIT	74	GRETSCH	COUNTRY ROC	971	**718**	617	516
ELGUIT	78	GRETSCH	COUNTRY ROC G-BRAND	828	**612**	526	440
ELGUIT	71	GRETSCH	DOUBLE ANNIVERSARY	1,394	**1,031**	886	741
ELGUIT	58	GRETSCH	DOUBLE ANNIVERSARY 6117 SUNBURST	648	**479**	412	344
ELGUIT	59	GRETSCH	DOUBLE ANNIVERSARY 6117 SUNBURST	1,011	**748**	642	537
ELGUIT	60	GRETSCH	DOUBLE ANNIVERSARY 6117 SUNBURST	583	**431**	370	310
ELGUIT	61	GRETSCH	DOUBLE ANNIVERSARY 6117 SUNBURST	591	**437**	375	314
ELGUIT	62	GRETSCH	DOUBLE ANNIVERSARY 6117 SUNBURST	587	**434**	373	312
ELGUIT	64	GRETSCH	DOUBLE ANNIVERSARY 6117 SUNBURST	546	**403**	347	290
ELGUIT	65	GRETSCH	DOUBLE ANNIVERSARY 6117 SUNBURST	700	**518**	445	372
ELGUIT	66	GRETSCH	DOUBLE ANNIVERSARY 6117 SUNBURST	700	**518**	445	372
ELGUIT	67	GRETSCH	DOUBLE ANNIVERSARY 6117 SUNBURST	700	**518**	445	372
ELGUIT	68	GRETSCH	DOUBLE ANNIVERSARY 6117 SUNBURST	699	**517**	444	371
ELGUIT	73	GRETSCH	DOUBLE ANNIVERSARY 6117 SUNBURST	728	**538**	462	387
ELGUIT	58	GRETSCH	DOUBLE ANNIVERSARY 6118 SMOKE GREEN 2-TONE	822	**608**	522	437
ELGUIT	59	GRETSCH	DOUBLE ANNIVERSARY 6118 SMOKE GREEN 2-TONE	687	**508**	436	365
ELGUIT	61	GRETSCH	DOUBLE ANNIVERSARY 6118 SMOKE GREEN 2-TONE	533	**394**	339	283
ELGUIT	62	GRETSCH	DOUBLE ANNIVERSARY 6118 SMOKE GREEN 2-TONE	616	**455**	391	327
ELGUIT	63	GRETSCH	DOUBLE ANNIVERSARY 6118 SMOKE GREEN 2-TONE	625	**462**	397	332
ELGUIT	64	GRETSCH	DOUBLE ANNIVERSARY 6118 SMOKE GREEN 2-TONE	624	**462**	397	332
ELGUIT	67	GRETSCH	DOUBLE ANNIVERSARY 6118 SMOKE GREEN 2-TONE	540	**399**	343	287
ELGUIT	69	GRETSCH	DOUBLE ANNIVERSARY 6118 SMOKE GREEN 2-TONE	575	**425**	365	305
ELGUIT	58	GRETSCH	DOUBLE ANNIVERSARY 7560 SUNBURST	912	**674**	579	484
ELGUIT	73	GRETSCH	DOUBLE ANNIVERSARY 7560 SUNBURST	475	**351**	301	252
ELGUIT	59	GRETSCH	DUO JET 6127 TENOR, 4-STRING	1,065	**788**	677	566
ELGUIT	54	GRETSCH	DUO JET 6128 BLACK, 2 PU's	1,501	**1,110**	954	797
ELGUIT	55	GRETSCH	DUO JET 6128 BLACK, 2 PU's	1,011	**748**	642	537
ELGUIT	56	GRETSCH	DUO JET 6128 BLACK, 2 PU's, BLACK INLAY	1,731	**1,280**	1,100	920
ELGUIT	56	GRETSCH	DUO JET 6128 CADILLAC GREEN, 2 PU's	4,199	**3,105**	2,668	2,230
ELGUIT	57	GRETSCH	DUO JET 6128 BLACK, 2 PU's	1,832	**1,355**	1,164	973
ELGUIT	57	GRETSCH	DUO JET 6128 CADILLAC GREEN, 2 PU's	3,566	**2,637**	2,266	1,894
ELGUIT	58	GRETSCH	DUO JET 6128 BLACK, 2 PU's	1,606	**1,187**	1,020	853
ELGUIT	59	GRETSCH	DUO JET 6128 BLACK, 2 PU's	1,011	**748**	642	537
ELGUIT	60	GRETSCH	DUO JET 6128 BLACK, 2 PU's	1,163	**860**	739	618
ELGUIT	61	GRETSCH	DUO JET 6128 BLACK, DOUBLE CUTAWAY	869	**643**	552	462
ELGUIT	62	GRETSCH	DUO JET 6128 BLACK, DOUBLE CUTAWAY, 2 PU's	906	**670**	575	481
ELGUIT	63	GRETSCH	DUO JET 6128 BLACK, DOUBLE CUTAWAY, 2 PU's	1,006	**744**	639	534
ELGUIT	65	GRETSCH	DUO JET 6128 BLACK, DOUBLE CUTAWAY, 2 PU's	788	**582**	500	418
ELGUIT	69	GRETSCH	DUO JET 6128 BLACK, DOUBLE CUTAWAY, 2 PU's	1,057	**782**	672	562
ELGUIT	53	GRETSCH	DUO-JET 6128 BLACK, 2 PU's	2,390	**1,767**	1,518	1,269
ELGUIT	52	GRETSCH	ELECTRO II 6193 SUNBURST, CUTAWAY	1,614	**1,194**	1,026	857

TYPE	YR	MFG	PRICES--BASED ON 100% ORIGINAL MODEL	SELL EXC	SELL AVG	BUY EXC	BUY AVG
ELGUIT	53	GRETSCH	**ELECTRO II 6193** SUNBURST, CUTAWAY	1,082	**800**	688	575
ELGUIT	56	GRETSCH	**ELECTROMATIC** SUNBURST	796	**589**	506	423
ELGUIT	48	GRETSCH	**ELECTROMATIC 6185** SUNBURST, NON-CUTAWAY	637	**471**	405	338
ELGUIT	51	GRETSCH	**ELECTROMATIC 6185** SUNBURST, CUTAWAY	499	**369**	317	265
ELGUIT	51	GRETSCH	**ELECTROMATIC 6185** NATURAL, NON-CUTAWAY	637	**471**	405	338
ELGUIT	51	GRETSCH	**ELECTROMATIC 6185** CUTAWAY, 2 PU's	699	**517**	444	371
ELGUIT	52	GRETSCH	**ELECTROMATIC 6185** SUNBURST, NON-CUTAWAY	637	**471**	405	338
ELGUIT	52	GRETSCH	**ELECTROMATIC 6185** NATURAL, CUTAWAY	717	**530**	455	380
ELGUIT	53	GRETSCH	**ELECTROMATIC 6185** NATURAL, CUTAWAY	705	**521**	448	374
ELGUIT	54	GRETSCH	**ELECTROMATIC 6185** TENOR, SUNBURST	557	**412**	354	296
ELGUIT	54	GRETSCH	**ELECTROMATIC 6185** PLECTRUM, BLOND	803	**594**	510	426
ELGUIT	56	GRETSCH	**ELECTROMATIC 6185** TENOR, NATURAL	845	**625**	537	449
ELGUIT	54	GRETSCH	**ELECTROMATIC 6190-1** SUNBURST	1,195	**883**	759	634
ELGUIT	66	GRETSCH	**GOLD DUKE** GOLD SPARKLE	2,390	**1,767**	1,518	1,269
ELGUIT	56	GRETSCH	**JET FIREBIRD 6131** RED	3,409	**2,521**	2,166	1,811
ELGUIT	57	GRETSCH	**JET FIREBIRD 6131** RED	4,148	**3,067**	2,635	2,203
ELGUIT	58	GRETSCH	**JET FIREBIRD 6131** RED	2,347	**1,735**	1,491	1,246
ELGUIT	60	GRETSCH	**JET FIREBIRD 6131** RED	2,075	**1,535**	1,318	1,102
ELGUIT	61	GRETSCH	**JET FIREBIRD 6131** SINGLE CUTAWAY	1,793	**1,326**	1,139	952
ELGUIT	62	GRETSCH	**JET FIREBIRD 6131** RED	1,623	**1,200**	1,031	862
ELGUIT	63	GRETSCH	**JET FIREBIRD 6131** RED	2,065	**1,527**	1,312	1,097
ELGUIT	64	CRETSCH	**JET FIREBIRD 6131** RED	2,028	**1,500**	1,288	1,077
ELGUIT	65	GRETSCH	**JET FIREBIRD 6131** RED	1,875	**1,387**	1,191	996
ELGUIT	68	GRETSCH	**JET FIREBIRD 6131** RED	1,874	**1,386**	1,191	996
ELGUIT	69	GRETSCH	**JET FIREBIRD 6131** RED	1,873	**1,385**	1,190	995
ELGUIT	66	GRETSCH	**MONKEES** RED	1,244	**920**	790	660
ELGUIT	67	GRETSCH	**MONKEES** RED	1,593	**1,178**	1,012	846
ELGUIT	68	GRETSCH	**MONKEES** RED	1,141	**844**	725	606
ELGUIT	60	GRETSCH	**NIGHTHAWK** BLACK	1,554	**1,149**	987	825
ELGUIT	63	GRETSCH	**PRINCESS 6106** PINK	1,404	**1,038**	892	746
ELGUIT	63	GRETSCH	**PRINCESS 6106** WHITE	1,418	**1,049**	901	753
ELGUIT	69	GRETSCH	**RALLY 6104** CADILLAC GREEN	1,123	**830**	713	596
ELGUIT	67	GRETSCH	**RALLY 6105** BAMBOO YELLOW	1,129	**835**	717	600
ELGUIT	68	GRETSCH	**RALLY 6105** BAMBOO YELLOW	874	**646**	555	464
ELGUIT	57	GRETSCH	**RAMBLER 6115** IVORY TOP	917	**678**	583	487
ELGUIT	58	GRETSCH	**RAMBLER 6115** IVORY TOP	876	**648**	556	465
ELGUIT	59	GRETSCH	**RAMBLER 6115** IVORY TOP	826	**611**	525	439
ELGUIT	76	GRETSCH	**ROC I**	682	**504**	433	362
ELGUIT	77	GRETSCH	**ROC II** MAHOGANY	683	**505**	434	363
ELGUIT	73	GRETSCH	**ROC JET**	676	**500**	430	359
ELGUIT	70	GRETSCH	**ROC JET 6127** PUMPKIN	758	**560**	481	402
ELGUIT	70	GRETSCH	**ROC JET 6130** BLACK	760	**562**	483	403
ELGUIT	71	GRETSCH	**ROC JET 7610** BLACK	895	**662**	569	475

TYPE	YR	MFG	PRICES--BASED ON 100% ORIGINAL MODEL	SELL EXC	SELL AVG	BUY EXC	BUY AVG
ELGUIT	72	GRETSCH	**ROC JET 7610** BLACK	812	**600**	516	431
ELGUIT	71	GRETSCH	**ROC JET 7611** PUMPKIN	817	**604**	519	434
ELGUIT	54	GRETSCH	**ROUND UP 6130** ORANGE, WESTERN INLAY G BRAND	6,432	**4,757**	4,087	3,417
ELGUIT	55	GRETSCH	**ROUND UP 6130** ORANGE, WESTERN INLAY G BRAND	5,895	**4,360**	3,746	3,131
ELGUIT	57	GRETSCH	**ROUND UP 6130** ORANGE	6,007	**4,443**	3,817	3,191
ELGUIT	59	GRETSCH	**ROUND UP 6130** ORANGE	3,385	**2,504**	2,151	1,798
ELGUIT	58	GRETSCH	**SAL SALVADOR 6199** SUNBURST	1,673	**1,237**	1,063	888
ELGUIT	60	GRETSCH	**SAL SALVADOR 6199** SUNBURST	1,666	**1,232**	1,058	885
ELGUIT	61	GRETSCH	**SAL SALVADOR 6199** SUNBURST	1,496	**1,106**	950	795
ELGUIT	62	GRETSCH	**SAL SALVADOR 6199** SUNBURST	1,251	**925**	795	665
ELGUIT	65	GRETSCH	**SAL SALVADOR 6199** SUNBURST, ARCHTOP	1,167	**863**	741	620
ELGUIT	78	GRETSCH	**SHO-BUD III**	637	**471**	405	338
ELGUIT	70	GRETSCH	**SHO-BUD PRO II**	721	**533**	458	383
ELGUIT	66	GRETSCH	**SILVER DUKE** SILVER SPARKLE	2,191	**1,620**	1,392	1,164
ELGUIT	54	GRETSCH	**SILVER JET 6129** SILVER SPARKLE	4,907	**3,629**	3,118	2,607
ELGUIT	55	GRETSCH	**SILVER JET 6129** SILVER SPARKLE	4,802	**3,552**	3,051	2,551
ELGUIT	56	GRETSCH	**SILVER JET 6129** SILVER SPARKLE	4,704	**3,479**	2,989	2,499
ELGUIT	57	GRETSCH	**SILVER JET 6129** SILVER SPARKLE	5,334	**3,945**	3,389	2,834
ELGUIT	58	GRETSCH	**SILVER JET 6129** SILVER SPARKLE	4,672	**3,455**	2,968	2,482
ELGUIT	60	GRETSCH	**SILVER JET 6129** SILVER SPARKLE, SINGLE CUTAWAY	3,648	**2,698**	2,318	1,938
ELGUIT	61	GRETSCH	**SILVER JET 6129** SILVER SPARKLE, DOUBLE CUTAWAY	3,539	**2,617**	2,249	1,880
ELGUIT	62	GRETSCH	**SILVER JET 6129** SILVER SPARKLE	3,431	**2,537**	2,180	1,822
ELGUIT	63	GRETSCH	**SILVER JET 6129** SILVER SPARKLE	3,333	**2,465**	2,117	1,770
ELGUIT	64	GRETSCH	**SILVER JET 6129** SILVER SPARKLE	3,837	**2,837**	2,438	2,038
ELGUIT	83	GRETSCH	**SOUTHERN BELL 7177** WALNUT	876	**648**	556	465
ELGUIT	69	GRETSCH	**STREAMLINER 6102** SUNBURST, DOUBLE CUTAWAY	666	**492**	423	353
ELGUIT	70	GRETSCH	**STREAMLINER 6102** SUNBURST, DOUBLE CUTAWAY	666	**492**	423	353
ELGUIT	71	GRETSCH	**STREAMLINER 6102** SUNBURST, DOUBLE CUTAWAY	668	**494**	424	354
ELGUIT	72	GRETSCH	**STREAMLINER 6102** SUNBURST, DOUBLE CUTAWAY	625	**462**	397	332
ELGUIT	66	GRETSCH	**STREAMLINER 6103** SUNBURST, DOUBLE CUTAWAY	709	**524**	450	376
ELGUIT	68	GRETSCH	**STREAMLINER 6103** CHERRY, DOUBLE CUTAWAY	708	**523**	450	376
ELGUIT	69	GRETSCH	**STREAMLINER 6103** CHERRY, DOUBLE CUTAWAY	708	**523**	450	376
ELGUIT	71	GRETSCH	**STREAMLINER 6103** CHERRY, DOUBLE CUTAWAY	625	**462**	397	332
ELGUIT	55	GRETSCH	**STREAMLINER 6189** BAMBOO YELLOW	991	**733**	630	526
ELGUIT	55	GRETSCH	**STREAMLINER 6189** JAGUAR TAN	1,082	**800**	688	575
ELGUIT	56	GRETSCH	**STREAMLINER 6189** BAMBOO YELLOW	1,080	**799**	686	574
ELGUIT	57	GRETSCH	**STREAMLINER 6189** BAMBOO YELLOW	1,080	**798**	686	573
ELGUIT	58	GRETSCH	**STREAMLINER 6189** BAMBOO YELLOW, DOUBLE CUTAWAY	1,254	**927**	797	666
ELGUIT	56	GRETSCH	**STREAMLINER 6190** SUNBURST	1,080	**799**	686	574
ELGUIT	57	GRETSCH	**STREAMLINER 6190** SUNBURST	1,143	**845**	726	607
ELGUIT	58	GRETSCH	**STREAMLINER 6190** SUNBURST	1,061	**785**	674	564
ELGUIT	71	GRETSCH	**STREAMLINER 6190** SUNBURST	708	**523**	450	376
ELGUIT	56	GRETSCH	**STREAMLINER 6191** NATURAL	1,099	**812**	698	583

TYPE	YR	MFG	MODEL	SELL EXC	SELL AVG	BUY EXC	BUY AVG
			PRICES--BASED ON 100% ORIGINAL				
ELGUIT	57	GRETSCH	STREAMLINER 6191 NATURAL	1,070	**791**	680	568
ELGUIT	77	GRETSCH	SUPER AXE 7680 RED	878	**649**	558	466
ELGUIT	79	GRETSCH	SUPER AXE 7680 RED	801	**592**	509	425
ELGUIT	76	GRETSCH	SUPER AXE 7681 EBONY	796	**589**	506	423
ELGUIT	78	GRETSCH	SUPER AXE 7681 EBONY	767	**567**	487	407
ELGUIT	79	GRETSCH	SUPER AXE 7681 EBONY	837	**619**	531	444
ELGUIT	72	GRETSCH	SUPER CHET 7690 CHERRY RED	1,474	**1,090**	936	783
ELGUIT	72	GRETSCH	SUPER CHET 7690 AUTUMN RED, LEFT-HANDED	1,992	**1,473**	1,265	1,058
ELGUIT	73	GRETSCH	SUPER CHET 7690 CHERRY RED	1,502	**1,111**	954	798
ELGUIT	74	GRETSCH	SUPER CHET 7690 CHERRY RED	1,474	**1,090**	936	783
ELGUIT	75	GRETSCH	SUPER CHET 7690 CHERRY RED	1,452	**1,074**	922	771
ELGUIT	76	GRETSCH	SUPER CHET 7690 CHERRY RED	1,454	**1,075**	924	772
ELGUIT	77	GRETSCH	SUPER CHET 7690 CHERRY RED	1,269	**938**	806	674
ELGUIT	79	GRETSCH	SUPER CHET 7690 CHERRY RED	1,492	**1,104**	948	793
ELGUIT	73	GRETSCH	SUPER CHET 7691 WALNUT	1,413	**1,045**	897	750
ELGUIT	76	GRETSCH	SUPER CHET 7691 WALNUT	1,394	**1,031**	886	741
ELGUIT	77	GRETSCH	SUPER CHET 7691 WALNUT	1,390	**1,028**	883	738
ELGUIT	49	GRETSCH	SYNCHROMATIC ARCHTOP SUNBURST	1,350	**998**	858	717
ELGUIT	76	GRETSCH	TK 300 7625 NATURAL	498	**368**	316	264
ELGUIT	80	GRETSCH	TK 300 7625 NATURAL	360	**266**	228	191
ELGUIT	68	GRETSCH	VAN EPPS 6079 SUNBURST, 7-STRING	2,281	**1,687**	1,449	1,212
ELGUIT	69	GRETSCH	VAN EPPS 6079 SUNBURST, 7-STRING	1,798	**1,329**	1,142	955
ELGUIT	70	GRETSCH	VAN EPPS 6080 WALNUT, 7-STRING	1,176	**870**	747	625
ELGUIT	70	GRETSCH	VAN EPPS 6081 SUNBURST, 6-STRING	698	**516**	444	371
ELGUIT	69	GRETSCH	VAN EPPS 6082 WALNUT, 6-STRING	807	**615**	522	399
ELGUIT	75	GRETSCH	VAN EPPS 7580 SUNBURST, 7-STRING	2,363	**1,748**	1,501	1,255
ELGUIT	79	GRETSCH	VAN EPPS 7580 SUNBURST, 7-STRING	1,513	**1,119**	961	804
ELGUIT	67	GRETSCH	VIKING 6187 SUNBURST	1,353	**1,001**	860	719
ELGUIT	68	GRETSCH	VIKING 6187 SUNBURST	1,060	**784**	674	563
ELGUIT	69	GRETSCH	VIKING 6187 SUNBURST	1,035	**766**	658	550
ELGUIT	65	GRETSCH	VIKING 6188 NATURAL BLOND	1,135	**839**	721	603
ELGUIT	66	GRETSCH	VIKING 6189 CADILLAC GREEN	2,013	**1,488**	1,279	1,069
ELGUIT	54	GRETSCH	WHITE FALCON SINGLE CUTAWAY	1,746	**1,291**	1,109	927
ELGUIT	55	GRETSCH	WHITE FALCON SINGLE CUTAWAY	18,825	**13,923**	11,962	10,001
ELGUIT	56	GRETSCH	WHITE FALCON SINGLE CUTAWAY	16,800	**12,425**	10,675	8,925
ELGUIT	57	GRETSCH	WHITE FALCON SINGLE CUTAWAY	17,824	**13,182**	11,325	9,469
ELGUIT	58	GRETSCH	WHITE FALCON SINGLE CUTAWAY	16,823	**12,442**	10,689	8,937
ELGUIT	59	GRETSCH	WHITE FALCON SINGLE CUTAWAY	17,760	**13,135**	11,285	9,435
ELGUIT	60	GRETSCH	WHITE FALCON SINGLE CUTAWAY	15,823	**11,702**	10,054	8,406
ELGUIT	61	GRETSCH	WHITE FALCON SINGLE CUTAWAY	10,832	**8,011**	6,883	5,754
ELGUIT	62	GRETSCH	WHITE FALCON DOUBLE CUTAWAY	4,879	**3,608**	3,100	2,592
ELGUIT	63	GRETSCH	WHITE FALCON DOUBLE CUTAWAY, STEREO	1,993	**1,474**	1,266	1,059

TYPE	YR	MFG	PRICES--BASED ON 100% ORIGINAL MODEL	SELL EXC	SELL AVG	BUY EXC	BUY AVG
ELGUIT	63	GRETSCH	**WHITE FALCON** DOUBLE CUTAWAY, MONO WIRING	2,078	**1,537**	1,320	1,104
ELGUIT	64	GRETSCH	**WHITE FALCON** DOUBLE CUTAWAY	1,661	**1,229**	1,055	882
ELGUIT	65	GRETSCH	**WHITE FALCON** DOUBLE CUTAWAY, STEREO	1,661	**1,229**	1,055	882
ELGUIT	66	GRETSCH	**WHITE FALCON** DOUBLE CUTAWAY	1,575	**1,165**	1,001	836
ELGUIT	67	GRETSCH	**WHITE FALCON** DOUBLE CUTAWAY, STEREO	1,212	**896**	770	644
ELGUIT	67	GRETSCH	**WHITE FALCON** DOUBLE CUTAWAY	1,495	**1,106**	950	794
ELGUIT	68	GRETSCH	**WHITE FALCON** DOUBLE CUTAWAY	1,495	**1,106**	950	794
ELGUIT	69	GRETSCH	**WHITE FALCON** DOUBLE CUTAWAY, STEREO	1,493	**1,104**	949	793
ELGUIT	70	GRETSCH	**WHITE FALCON** DOUBLE CUTAWAY	1,274	**942**	810	677
ELGUIT	71	GRETSCH	**WHITE FALCON** DOUBLE CUTAWAY	1,257	**930**	799	668
ELGUIT	72	GRETSCH	**WHITE FALCON** DOUBLE CUTAWAY	1,237	**915**	786	657
ELGUIT	74	GRETSCH	**WHITE FALCON** DOUBLE CUTAWAY, STEREO	1,208	**893**	767	642
ELGUIT	75	GRETSCH	**WHITE FALCON** SINGLE CUTAWAY	1,169	**864**	742	621
ELGUIT	75	GRETSCH	**WHITE FALCON** DOUBLE CUTAWAY, STEREO	1,195	**883**	759	634
ELGUIT	75	GRETSCH	**WHITE FALCON** DOUBLE CUTAWAY	1,197	**885**	760	635
ELGUIT	76	GRETSCH	**WHITE FALCON** DOUBLE CUTAWAY, STEREO	1,158	**856**	736	615
ELGUIT	77	GRETSCH	**WHITE FALCON** SINGLE CUTAWAY	1,131	**837**	719	601
ELGUIT	77	GRETSCH	**WHITE FALCON** DOUBLE CUTAWAY, STEREO	1,143	**845**	726	607
ELGUIT	79	GRETSCH	**WHITE FALCON** DOUBLE CUTAWAY	1,093	**808**	694	580
ELGUIT	79	GRETSCH	**WHITE FALCON** DOUBLE CUTAWAY, STEREO	1,119	**827**	711	594
ELGUIT	80	GRETSCH	**WHITE FALCON** DOUBLE CUTAWAY	1,078	**797**	685	572
ELGUIT	55	GRETSCH	**WHITE PENGUIN 6134**	65,364	**48,342**	41,533	34,724
ELGUIT	56	GRETSCH	**WHITE PENGUIN 6134**	54,891	**40,597**	34,879	29,161
ELGUIT	57	GRETSCH	**WHITE PENGUIN 6134**	79,393	**58,718**	50,448	42,178
ELGUIT	58	GRETSCH	**WHITE PENGUIN 6134**	72,000	**53,250**	45,750	38,250
ELGUIT	59	GRETSCH	**WHITE PENGUIN 6134**	71,829	**53,123**	45,641	38,159
ELGUIT	60	GRETSCH	**WHITE PENGUIN 6134**	50,643	**37,455**	32,179	26,904
GUITAR AMP	68	GRETSCH	**6144** REVERB UNIT	120	**89**	76	64
GTAMP	63	GRETSCH	**6149** POWER REVERB UNIT	205	**151**	130	109
GTAMP	59	GRETSCH	**6150** 1x8" ROLA SPEAKER	250	**185**	159	133
GTAMP	60	GRETSCH	**6150** 1x9" JENSEN SPEAKER	240	**177**	152	127
GTAMP	60	GRETSCH	**6156** 1x10" JENSEN SPEAKER	192	**142**	122	102
GTAMP	65	GRETSCH	**6159** GREY, 2x12" JENSENS	323	**239**	205	171
GTAMP	62	GRETSCH	**6159 DUAL BASS** GREY, TOLEX, 2x12" SPEAKERS	336	**248**	213	178
GTAMP	63	GRETSCH	**6159 DUAL BASS**	315	**233**	200	167
GTAMP	56	GRETSCH	**6161** 3 SPEAKERS, TUBE, TREMOLO	327	**242**	208	173
GTAMP	59	GRETSCH	**6161 DUAL TWIN** 2 OVAL, 1 ROUND SPEAKER	384	**284**	244	204
GTAMP	57	GRETSCH	**6161 ELECTROMATIC** TWIN AMP, WRAP AROUND GRILL	284	**210**	180	150
GTAMP	58	GRETSCH	**6169 FURY MODEL** PIGGYBACK, 2x12" SPEAKERS	373	**276**	237	198
GTAMP	67	GRETSCH	**6169 FURY MODEL** PIGGYBACK, 2x12" SPEAKERS	371	**274**	236	197
GTAMP	60	GRETSCH	**CAROSEL** 10" SPEAKER, TWEETER	193	**143**	123	103
GTAMP	65	GRETSCH	**COMPACT** 8" SPEAKER	150	**111**	95	80
GTAMP	50	GRETSCH	**ELECTROMAT** WESTERN FINISH	395	**292**	251	210
GTAMP	54	GRETSCH	**ELECTROMAT** (2)6x9" AND 1x5" SPEAKERS	318	**235**	202	169
GTAMP	55	GRETSCH	**ELECTROMAT** 10" SPEAKER	349	**258**	222	185

TYPE	YR	MFG	PRICES--BASED ON 100% ORIGINAL MODEL	SELL EXC	SELL AVG	BUY EXC	BUY AVG
GTAMP	68	GRETSCH	**TWIN REVERB** GREY, 2 CHANNEL, 2x10" SPEAKERS	302	**223**	192	160
GUITAR (ACOUSTIC)	40	GRETSCH	**20** SPRUCE TOP, FLATTOP	468	**346**	297	248
GUITAR	30	GRETSCH	**30** SUNBURST, ARCHTOP	562	**416**	357	298
GUITAR	38	GRETSCH	**35** SUNBURST, ARCHTOP	495	**366**	314	263
GUITAR	40	GRETSCH	**35** SUNBURST, ARCHTOP	474	**350**	301	251
GUITAR	41	GRETSCH	**35** SUNBURST, ARCHTOP	564	**417**	358	299
GUITAR	39	GRETSCH	**40** HAWAIIAN, FLATTOP	290	**221**	188	144
GUITAR	40	GRETSCH	**40** HAWAIIAN, FLATTOP	347	**257**	220	184
GUITAR	40	GRETSCH	**50** SUNBURST, ARCHTOP	317	**241**	205	157
GUITAR	53	GRETSCH	**50** SUNBURST, ARCHTOP, NON-CUTAWAY	553	**409**	351	294
GUITAR	36	GRETSCH	**65** PEARL DOTS, ARCHTOP	1,024	**757**	650	544
GUITAR	38	GRETSCH	**75F** SUNBURST, FLATTOP	409	**303**	260	217
GUITAR	41	GRETSCH	**80S** FLATTOP	621	**459**	394	329
GUITAR	69	GRETSCH	**6020** FLATTOP, 12-STRING	422	**312**	268	224
GUITAR	49	GRETSCH	**BURL IVES 6004** NATURAL, FLATTOP	1,593	**1,178**	1,012	846
GUITAR	52	GRETSCH	**BURL IVES 6004**	1,576	**1,165**	1,001	837
GUITAR	53	GRETSCH	**BURL IVES 6004** NATURAL, FLATTOP	1,434	**1,060**	911	761
GUITAR	54	GRETSCH	**BURL IVES 6004** NATURAL, FLATTOP	1,423	**1,052**	904	756
GUITAR	55	GRETSCH	**BURL IVES 6004** NATURAL, FLATTOP	1,354	**1,001**	860	719
GUITAR	64	GRETSCH	**CLIPPER 6186** SUNBURST	430	**318**	273	228
GUITAR	59	GRETSCH	**CONSTELLATION**	1,593	**1,178**	1,012	846
GUITAR	56	GRETSCH	**CONSTELLATION 603** NATURAL, ARCHTOP	2,953	**2,184**	1,876	1,569
GUITAR	55	GRETSCH	**CORSAIR 6014** SUNBURST, ARCHTOP	936	**692**	594	497
GUITAR	56	GRETSCH	**CORSAIR 6014** SUNBURST, ARCHTOP	937	**693**	595	498
GUITAR	62	GRETSCH	**CORSAIR 6014** SUNBURST, ARCHTOP, CUTAWAY	796	**589**	506	423
GUITAR	56	GRETSCH	**CORSAIR 6015** NATURAL, ARCHTOP	932	**689**	592	495
GUITAR	55	GRETSCH	**CORSAIR 6016** BURGUNDY, ARCHTOP	937	**693**	595	498
GUITAR	55	GRETSCH	**ELDORADO 6040** SUNBURST, NON-CUTAWAY	1,434	**1,060**	911	761
GUITAR	57	GRETSCH	**ELDORADO 6040** SUNBURST, ARCHTOP	1,614	**1,194**	1,026	857
GUITAR	58	GRETSCH	**ELDORADO 6040** SUNBURST	3,840	**2,840**	2,440	2,040
GUITAR	59	GRETSCH	**ELDORADO 6040** SUNBURST, ARCHTOP	3,075	**2,274**	1,954	1,634
GUITAR	66	GRETSCH	**ELDORADO 6040** SUNBURST	1,434	**1,060**	911	761
GUITAR	68	GRETSCH	**ELDORADO 6040** SUNBURST, ARCHTOP	1,535	**1,135**	975	815
GUITAR	69	GRETSCH	**ELDORADO 6040** SUNBURST	1,593	**1,178**	1,012	846
GUITAR	55	GRETSCH	**ELDORADO 6041** NATURAL, ARCHTOP	2,036	**1,505**	1,293	1,081
GUITAR	60	GRETSCH	**ELDORADO 6041** NATURAL, ARCHTOP	1,894	**1,400**	1,203	1,006
GUITAR	51	GRETSCH	**ELECTRO II SYNCHROMATIC 6192** SUNBURST, CUTAWAY	1,046	**773**	664	555
GUITAR	52	GRETSCH	**ELECTRO II SYNCHROMATIC 6193** NATURAL, CUTAWAY	1,136	**840**	722	603
GUITAR	56	GRETSCH	**FLEETWOOD 6038** SUNBURST, ARCHTOP	817	**604**	519	434
GUITAR	54	GRETSCH	**FLEETWOOD 6039** NATURAL, ARCHTOP	895	**662**	569	475
GUITAR	69	GRETSCH	**FOLK 6002** SUNBURST, FLATTOP	468	**346**	297	248
GUITAR	60	GRETSCH	**FOLK 6003** NATURAL, FLATTOP	579	**428**	368	308
GUITAR	67	GRETSCH	**FOLK 6003** NATURAL, FLATTOP	579	**428**	368	308

TYPE	YR	MFG	PRICES--BASED ON 100% ORIGINAL MODEL	SELL EXC	SELL AVG	BUY EXC	BUY AVG
GUITAR	69	GRETSCH	**FOLK 6004** MAHOGANY, FLATTOP	498	**368**	316	264
GUITAR	58	GRETSCH	**J-200** NATURAL	561	**415**	356	298
GUITAR	47	GRETSCH	**JUMBO SYNCHROMATIC 6021-125F** NATURAL SUNBURST	1,593	**1,178**	1,012	846
GUITAR	48	GRETSCH	**JUMBO SYNCHROMATIC 6021-125F** NATURAL SUNBURST	1,575	**1,165**	1,001	836
GUITAR	49	GRETSCH	**JUMBO SYNCHROMATIC 6021-125F** NATURAL SUNBURST	1,545	**1,143**	982	821
GUITAR	51	GRETSCH	**JUMBO SYNCHROMATIC 6021-125F** NATURAL SUNBURST	1,510	**1,116**	959	802
GUITAR	49	GRETSCH	**NEW YORKER 6050** SUNBURST, ARCHTOP	693	**512**	440	368
GUITAR	50	GRETSCH	**NEW YORKER 6050** SUNBURST, ARCHTOP	688	**509**	437	365
GUITAR	51	GRETSCH	**NEW YORKER 6050** SUNBURST, ARCHTOP	685	**506**	435	364
GUITAR	54	GRETSCH	**NEW YORKER 6050** SUNBURST, ARCHTOP	678	**501**	431	360
GUITAR	55	GRETSCH	**NEW YORKER 6050** SUNBURST, ARCHTOP	675	**499**	429	359
GUITAR	56	GRETSCH	**NEW YORKER 6050** SUNBURST, ARCHTOP	671	**496**	426	356
GUITAR	62	GRETSCH	**NEW YORKER 6050** SUNBURST, ARCHTOP	667	**493**	423	354
GUITAR	63	GRETSCH	**NEW YORKER 6050** SUNBURST, ARCHTOP	664	**491**	422	352
GUITAR	69	GRETSCH	**NEW YORKER 6050** SUNBURST, ARCHTOP	661	**489**	420	351
GUITAR	55	GRETSCH	**RANCHER 6022** ORANGE, HUMP TOP 17" JUMBO	2,978	**2,203**	1,892	1,582
GUITAR	56	GRETSCH	**RANCHER 6022** ORANGE	2,045	**1,513**	1,299	1,086
GUITAR	57	GRETSCH	**RANCHER 6022** ORANGE, 'G' BRAND	1,990	**1,471**	1,264	1,057
GUITAR	61	GRETSCH	**RANCHER 6022** ORANGE	1,930	**1,427**	1,226	1,025
GUITAR	62	GRETSCH	**RANCHER 6022** ORANGE	1,632	**1,207**	1,037	867
GUITAR	63	GRETSCH	**RANCHER 6022** ORANGE	1,695	**1,253**	1,077	900
GUITAR	67	GRETSCH	**RANCHER 6022** ORANGE	1,460	**1,079**	927	775
GUITAR	68	GRETSCH	**RANCHER 6022** ORANGE	1,629	**1,204**	1,035	865
GUITAR	69	GRETSCH	**RANCHER 6022** ORANGE	1,568	**1,195**	1,015	776
GUITAR	75	GRETSCH	**RANCHER 6022** ORANGE	1,558	**1,152**	990	827
GUITAR	67	GRETSCH	**SAM GOODY** GREEN SUNBURST, "G" F-HOLES	1,720	**1,272**	1,093	913
GUITAR	67	GRETSCH	**SHO BRO 6030** SPANISH, FLATTOP	698	**516**	444	371
GUITAR	69	GRETSCH	**SHO BRO 6030** SPANISH, FLATTOP	717	**530**	455	380
GUITAR	69	GRETSCH	**SHO BRO 6031** HAWAIIAN, FLATTOP	546	**416**	353	270
GUITAR	70	GRETSCH	**SHO BRO 6031** HAWAIIAN, FLATTOP	617	**456**	392	327
GUITAR	71	GRETSCH	**SHO BRO 7715** NATURAL TOP, 6-STRING	872	**645**	554	463
GUITAR	75	GRETSCH	**SHO BRO 7715** NATURAL TOP, 6-STRING	658	**487**	418	349
GUITAR	78	GRETSCH	**SHO BRO DIAMOND** ROSEWOOD	478	**353**	303	253
GUITAR	78	GRETSCH	**SHO BRO GRAND SLAM** MAHOGANY	480	**355**	305	255
GUITAR	72	GRETSCH	**SHO BRO HAWAIIAN**	796	**589**	506	423
GUITAR	78	GRETSCH	**SHO BRO SPADE** ROSEWOOD	478	**353**	303	253
GUITAR	75	GRETSCH	**SHO BRO SPANISH** NATURAL, RESONATOR, ROUND NECK	637	**471**	405	338
GUITAR	78	GRETSCH	**SHO-BUD PRO I**	537	**397**	341	285
GUITAR	78	GRETSCH	**SHO-BUD SUPER PRO** DOUBLE NECK, 10-STRING	956	**707**	607	507
GUITAR	47	GRETSCH	**SIERRA 6007** SUNBURST, FLATTOP	1,375	**1,017**	874	730
GUITAR	58	GRETSCH	**STREAMLINER 1689** CREAM & COPPER	1,310	**969**	832	696
GUITAR	59	GRETSCH	**SUN VALLEY** NATURAL	503	**372**	319	267
GUITAR	65	GRETSCH	**SUN VALLEY**	450	**332**	286	239

TYPE	YR	MFG	PRICES--BASED ON 100% ORIGINAL MODEL	SELL EXC	SELL AVG	BUY EXC	BUY AVG
GUITAR	75	GRETSCH	**SUN VALLEY**	432	**319**	274	229
GUITAR	61	GRETSCH	**SUN VALLEY 6010** NATURAL, FLATTOP	984	**727**	625	522
GUITAR	67	GRETSCH	**SUN VALLEY 6010** NATURAL, FLATTOP	796	**589**	506	423
GUITAR	68	GRETSCH	**SUN VALLEY 6010** NATURAL, FLATTOP	751	**555**	477	399
GUITAR	70	GRETSCH	**SUN VALLEY 6010** NATURAL, FLATTOP	749	**554**	476	398
GUITAR	39	GRETSCH	**SYNCHROMATIC 75** CAT'S EYE SUNBURST	890	**658**	566	473
GUITAR	40	GRETSCH	**SYNCHROMATIC 75** CAT'S EYE SUNBURST	1,403	**1,038**	891	745
GUITAR	47	GRETSCH	**SYNCHROMATIC 75** CAT'S EYE SUNBURST	797	**590**	506	423
GUITAR	48	GRETSCH	**SYNCHROMATIC 75** CAT'S EYE SUNBURST	1,032	**763**	656	548
GUITAR	49	GRETSCH	**SYNCHROMATIC 75XF** BLACK	900	**665**	572	478
GUITAR	46	GRETSCH	**SYNCHROMATIC 100**	717	**530**	455	380
GUITAR	39	GRETSCH	**SYNCHROMATIC 100 6014** SUNBURST, ARCHTOP	893	**661**	567	474
GUITAR	47	GRETSCH	**SYNCHROMATIC 100 6014** SUNBURST, ARCHTOP	939	**695**	597	499
GUITAR	51	GRETSCH	**SYNCHROMATIC 100 6014** SUNBURST, ARCHTOP	891	**659**	566	473
GUITAR	52	GRETSCH	**SYNCHROMATIC 100 6014** SUNBURST, ARCHTOP	938	**694**	596	498
GUITAR	53	GRETSCH	**SYNCHROMATIC 100 6014** SUNBURST, ARCHTOP	884	**653**	561	469
GUITAR	54	GRETSCH	**SYNCHROMATIC 100 6014** SUNBURST, ARCHTOP	937	**693**	595	498
GUITAR	51	GRETSCH	**SYNCHROMATIC 100 6015** NATURAL, ARCHTOP	944	**698**	600	501
GUITAR	53	GRETSCH	**SYNCHROMATIC 100 6015** NATURAL, ARCHTOP	939	**695**	597	499
GUITAR	54	GRETSCH	**SYNCHROMATIC 100 6015** NATURAL, ARCHTOP	932	**689**	592	495
GUITAR	46	GRETSCH	**SYNCHROMATIC 115** TRANSPARENT BLOND, ARCHTOP	1,129	**835**	717	600
GUITAR	51	GRETSCH	**SYNCHROMATIC 125F** SUNBURST	1,394	**1,031**	886	741
GUITAR	39	GRETSCH	**SYNCHROMATIC 160** CAT'S EYE SUNBURST	956	**707**	607	507
GUITAR	48	GRETSCH	**SYNCHROMATIC 160** CAT'S EYE SUNBURST	1,017	**752**	646	540
GUITAR	49	GRETSCH	**SYNCHROMATIC 160** CAT'S EYE SUNBURST	1,878	**1,389**	1,193	998
GUITAR	51	GRETSCH	**SYNCHROMATIC 160**	1,992	**1,473**	1,265	1,058
GUITAR	55	GRETSCH	**SYNCHROMATIC 160** SUNBURST, NON-CUTAWAY	3,340	**2,470**	2,122	1,774
GUITAR	55	GRETSCH	**SYNCHROMATIC 160** CAT'S EYE SUNBURST	3,360	**2,485**	2,135	1,785
GUITAR	39	GRETSCH	**SYNCHROMATIC 200** CAT'S EYE SUNBURST	1,394	**1,031**	886	741
GUITAR	41	GRETSCH	**SYNCHROMATIC 200** CAT'S EYE NATURAL	1,752	**1,296**	1,113	931
GUITAR	47	GRETSCH	**SYNCHROMATIC 200** CAT'S EYE SUNBURST	1,740	**1,287**	1,105	924
GUITAR	48	GRETSCH	**SYNCHROMATIC 200** CAT'S EYE NATURAL	1,593	**1,178**	1,012	846
GUITAR	46	GRETSCH	**SYNCHROMATIC 250** ARCHTOP	1,550	**1,146**	985	823
GUITAR	39	GRETSCH	**SYNCHROMATIC 300** CAT'S EYE SUNBURST	2,245	**1,660**	1,426	1,192
GUITAR	40	GRETSCH	**SYNCHROMATIC 300** CAT'S EYE SUNBURST	3,209	**2,373**	2,039	1,704
GUITAR	40	GRETSCH	**SYNCHROMATIC 400** CAT'S EYE SUNBURST	6,014	**4,448**	3,821	3,195
GUITAR	50	GRETSCH	**SYNCHROMATIC 400** CAT'S EYE NATURAL	6,506	**4,812**	4,134	3,456
GUITAR	51	GRETSCH	**SYNCHROMATIC 6029-160** CAT'S EYE NATURAL	1,872	**1,385**	1,190	995
GUITAR	53	GRETSCH	**SYNCHROMATIC 6030 CONSTELLATION** SUNBURST	1,872	**1,384**	1,189	994
GUITAR	55	GRETSCH	**SYNCHROMATIC 6031** SUNBURST, CUTAWAY	1,591	**1,177**	1,011	845
GUITAR	49	GRETSCH	**SYNCHROMATIC 6036-300** CAT'S EYE SUNBURST	2,982	**2,205**	1,895	1,584
GUITAR	52	GRETSCH	**SYNCHROMATIC 6036-300** CAT'S EYE SUNBURST	2,982	**2,205**	1,895	1,584
GUITAR	54	GRETSCH	**SYNCHROMATIC 6036-300** CAT'S EYE SUNBURST	2,374	**1,755**	1,508	1,261

TYPE	YR	MFG	PRICES--BASED ON 100% ORIGINAL MODEL	SELL EXC	SELL AVG	BUY EXC	BUY AVG
GUITAR	47	GRETSCH	**SYNCHROMATIC 6037-300** CAT'S EYE NATURAL	3,184	**2,355**	2,023	1,691
GUITAR	51	GRETSCH	**SYNCHROMATIC 6037-300** CAT'S EYE NATURAL	2,036	**1,505**	1,293	1,081
GUITAR	53	GRETSCH	**SYNCHROMATIC 6038** SUNBURST, CUTAWAY	2,071	**1,532**	1,316	1,100
GUITAR	48	GRETSCH	**SYNCHROMATIC 6040-400** CAT'S EYE SUNBURST	4,955	**3,665**	3,148	2,632
GUITAR	52	GRETSCH	**SYNCHROMATIC 6040-400** CAT'S EYE SUNBURST	4,780	**3,535**	3,037	2,539
GUITAR	53	GRETSCH	**SYNCHROMATIC 6040-400** CAT'S EYE SUNBURST	4,672	**3,455**	2,968	2,482
GUITAR	49	GRETSCH	**SYNCHROMATIC 6041-400** CAT'S EYE NATURAL	5,817	**4,302**	3,696	3,090
GUITAR	51	GRETSCH	**SYNCHROMATIC 6041-400** CAT'S EYE NATURAL	5,788	**4,281**	3,678	3,075
GUITAR	50	GRETSCH	**SYNCHROMATIC 6042-400F** NATURAL, FLATTOP	738	**545**	469	392
GUITAR	54	GRETSCH	**SYNCHROMATIC FLEETWOOD** SUNBURST, CUTAWAY	3,696	**2,733**	2,348	1,963
GUITAR	48	GRETSCH	**SYNCHROMATIC X75F**	637	**471**	405	338
GUITAR	53	GRETSCH	**TOWN & COUNTRY 6021** SUNBURST	1,873	**1,385**	1,190	995
GUITAR	53	GRETSCH	**TOWN & COUNTRY 6021** NATURAL	1,874	**1,386**	1,191	996
GUITAR	54	GRETSCH	**TOWN & COUNTRY 6021** NATURAL	1,876	**1,388**	1,192	997
GUITAR	56	GRETSCH	**TOWN & COUNTRY 6021** NATURAL	1,867	**1,380**	1,186	991
GUITAR	57	GRETSCH	**TOWN & COUNTRY 6021** NATURAL	1,873	**1,385**	1,190	995
GUITAR	69	GRETSCH	**WAYFARER 6008** NATURAL, CHERRY BACK/SIDES, FLATTOP	592	**438**	376	314
GUITAR	70	GRETSCH	**WAYFARER 6008** NATURAL, CHERRY BACK/SIDES, FLATTOP	543	**401**	345	288
STEEL GUITAR	49	GRETSCH	**ELECTROMATIC CONSOLE 6158** DOUBLE 6	677	**501**	430	360
UKULELE	55	GRETSCH	**MAHOGANY** NO BINDING	384	**284**	244	204

GUILD MUSIC CORP.

TYPE	YR	MFG	MODEL	SELL EXC	SELL AVG	BUY EXC	BUY AVG
EFFECTS	69	GUILD	**FOXEY LADY FUZZ** 2 KNOBS	259	**191**	164	137
EFFECTS	77	GUILD	**FOXEY LADY FUZZ** 3 KNOBS IN ROW	168	**124**	106	89
EFFECTS	76	GUILD	**HH ECHO UNIT**	240	**177**	152	127
ELEC. GUITAR	79	GUILD	**B-300** BLACK, LEFT-HANDED, 1 PU	710	**525**	451	377
ELGUIT	78	GUILD	**B-301** BLACK	336	**248**	213	178
ELGUIT	77	GUILD	**B-301 BASS** WALNUT	352	**260**	223	187
ELGUIT	79	GUILD	**B-301 BASS** BLACK	333	**246**	211	176
ELGUIT	61	GUILD	**BLACKFIRE** BLACK-GREEN TRANSPARENT, SERIAL #14713-18419	636	**470**	404	338
ELGUIT	94	GUILD	**BRIAN MAY STANDARD** SOLID MAHOG, NO VIBRATO SYSTEM, BLACK/WHITE/GREEN	757	**560**	481	402
ELGUIT	94	GUILD	**BRIAN MAY STANDARD** STOP TAILPIECE, 3 SINGLE COIL PU's or 2 HB's	764	**565**	485	405
ELGUIT	61	GUILD	**CE-100** SUNBURST, BIGBSY VIBRATO, SERIAL #14714-18419	438	**324**	278	233
ELGUIT	65	GUILD	**CE-100** SUNBURST, SINGLE CUTAWAY, SERIAL #EF101-211	306	**226**	194	162
ELGUIT	67	GUILD	**CE-100** SUNBURST, CUTAWAY, SERIAL #EF397-549	300	**222**	190	159
ELGUIT	68	GUILD	**CE-100** SUNBURST	504	**372**	320	267
ELGUIT	79	GUILD	**CE-100** SUNBURST	374	**276**	237	198
ELGUIT	79	GUILD	**CE-100** SUNBURST, 2 PU's, LEFT-HANDED	624	**461**	396	331
ELGUIT	57	GUILD	**CE-100 CAPRI** HOLLOW BODY, SERIAL #12035	935	**691**	594	496
ELGUIT	58	GUILD	**CE-100 CAPRI** BLOND, HOLLOW BODY, SERIAL #12035	709	**524**	450	376
ELGUIT	58	GUILD	**CE-100D**	496	**367**	315	263
ELGUIT	66	GUILD	**CE-100D** SUNBURST	495	**366**	314	263
ELGUIT	73	GUILD	**CE-100D** SUNBURST	398	**294**	253	211
ELGUIT	68	GUILD	**CE-100D CAPRI** SUNBURST, HOLLOW BODY, SERIAL #EF650-719	275	**203**	175	146

TYPE	YR	MFG	PRICES--BASED ON 100% ORIGINAL MODEL	SELL EXC	SELL AVG	BUY EXC	BUY AVG
ELGUIT	65	GUILD	**DE-400 DUANE EDDY** SUNBURST, SERIAL #EH101-126	1,475	**1,091**	937	783
ELGUIT	66	GUILD	**DE-400 DUANE EDDY** SERIAL #EH127-233	1,473	**1,089**	936	782
ELGUIT	64	GUILD	**DE-500 DUANE EDDY**	456	**337**	290	242
ELGUIT	66	GUILD	**DE-500 DUANE EDDY** SERIAL #EI108-116	1,770	**1,309**	1,124	940
ELGUIT	78	GUILD	**DE-500 DUANE EDDY** SERIAL #169867-195067	886	**655**	563	470
ELGUIT	63	GUILD	**DE-500 DUANE EDDY DELUXE**	2,065	**1,527**	1,312	1,097
ELGUIT	64	GUILD	**DE-500 DUANE EDDY SPECIAL** BLACK	1,770	**1,309**	1,124	940
ELGUIT	67	GUILD	**GEORGE BARNES** HOLLOW BODY, SERIAL #46609-46637	1,912	**1,414**	1,215	1,015
ELGUIT	64	GUILD	**GEORGE BARNES H** HOLLOW BODY, SERIAL #28944-38636	2,231	**1,650**	1,417	1,185
ELGUIT	77	GUILD	**HOWARD ROBERTS** CHERRY SUNBURST	937	**693**	595	498
ELGUIT	70	GUILD	**J.S. BASS II** NATURAL, MAHOGANY, 2 PU's	560	**414**	356	297
ELGUIT	77	GUILD	**JOHNNY SMITH** BLOND	1,593	**1,178**	1,012	846
ELGUIT	78	GUILD	**JOHNNY SMITH** SUNBURST	1,593	**1,178**	1,012	846
ELGUIT	57	GUILD	**M- 65** SUNBURST, 1 PU, SERIAL #-12035	963	**712**	612	512
ELGUIT	58	GUILD	**M- 65** NATURAL, 1 PU	996	**736**	633	529
ELGUIT	72	GUILD	**M- 65** SUNBURST, THINLINE, SINGLE CUTAWAY, HARP STYLE TAILPIECE	533	**394**	339	283
ELGUIT	73	GUILD	**M- 65 BLUESBIRD** NATURAL, SOLID MAHOGANY	545	**403**	346	289
ELGUIT	60	GUILD	**M- 65 FRESHMAN** HOLLOW BODY, F-HOLE, SERIAL #12036-14713	622	**460**	395	330
ELGUIT	60	GUILD	**M- 65 3/4** SUNBURST	612	**452**	389	325
ELGUIT	64	GUILD	**M- 65 3/4** CHERRY RED, SINGLE CUTAWAY, SERIAL #28944-38636	701	**519**	445	372
ELGUIT	65	GUILD	**M- 65 3/4** WINE RED, SINGLE CUTAWAY	492	**364**	312	261
ELGUIT	59	GUILD	**M- 65 3/4 FRESHMAN**	598	**442**	380	317
ELGUIT	73	GUILD	**M- 65 3/4 FRESHMAN** ARCHTOP, SERIAL #75603-95496	700	**518**	445	372
ELGUIT	70	GUILD	**M- 70** HOLLOW BODY, 2 HB's	749	**554**	476	398
ELGUIT	56	GUILD	**M- 75 ARISTOCRAT** SUNBURST, SERIAL #12035	406	**300**	258	215
ELGUIT	57	GUILD	**M- 75 ARISTOCRAT** SUNBURST, SERIAL #12035	404	**298**	256	214
ELGUIT	58	GUILD	**M- 75 ARISTOCRAT** SUNBURST, SERIAL #12035	403	**298**	256	214
ELGUIT	59	GUILD	**M- 75 ARISTOCRAT** SUNBURST	402	**297**	255	213
ELGUIT	60	GUILD	**M- 75 ARISTOCRAT** BLOND, SERIAL#12325	400	**296**	254	212
ELGUIT	60	GUILD	**M- 75 ARISTOCRAT** SUNBURST	400	**296**	254	212
ELGUIT	71	GUILD	**M- 75 BLUESBIRD**	1,061	**785**	674	564
ELGUIT	75	GUILD	**M- 80 CS** DOUBLE CUTAWAY, SERIAL #112804-130304	498	**368**	316	264
ELGUIT	54	GUILD	**M- 85 BLUESBIRD**	499	**369**	317	265
ELGUIT	66	GUILD	**M- 85 BLUESBIRD** BLACK, SERIAL #46607-46608	275	**203**	175	146
ELGUIT	68	GUILD	**M- 85 BLUESBIRD** SERIAL #DD139-237	300	**222**	190	159
ELGUIT	68	GUILD	**M- 85 BLUESBIRD** CHERRY RED	423	**313**	269	224
ELGUIT	69	GUILD	**M- 85 BLUESBIRD** SUNBURST	275	**203**	175	146
ELGUIT	71	GUILD	**M- 85 BLUESBIRD** 2 HUMBUCKER PU's, SERIAL #50978-61463	250	**185**	159	133
ELGUIT	71	GUILD	**M- 85 BLUESBIRD** SUNBURST, SERIAL #50979-61463	296	**219**	188	157
ELGUIT	75	GUILD	**M- 85 BLUESBIRD** BLACK, GOLD HARDWARE	259	**191**	164	137
ELGUIT	73	GUILD	**M- 85 BLUESBIRD II BASS** WALNUT, SERIAL #75603-95496	448	**331**	284	238
ELGUIT	79	GUILD	**MUSICIAN BASS** NATURAL	563	**416**	358	299
ELGUIT	79	GUILD	**MUSICIAN MC-500** NATURAL	564	**417**	358	299
ELGUIT	64	GUILD	**S- 50 JET STAR BASS**	566	**418**	359	300

TYPE	YR	MFG	PRICES--BASED ON 100% ORIGINAL MODEL	SELL EXC	SELL AVG	BUY EXC	BUY AVG
ELGUIT	65	GUILD	**S- 50 JET STAR BASS** SERIAL #38637-46606	565	**418**	359	300
ELGUIT	66	GUILD	**S- 50 JET STAR BASS**	563	**416**	358	299
ELGUIT	67	GUILD	**S- 50 JET STAR BASS** SERIAL #46609-46637	561	**415**	356	298
ELGUIT	68	GUILD	**S- 50 JET STAR BASS**	558	**413**	355	296
ELGUIT	78	GUILD	**S- 60**	384	**284**	244	204
ELGUIT	79	GUILD	**S- 60** NATURAL, MAHOGANY, 1 PU	336	**248**	213	178
ELGUIT	75	GUILD	**S- 60D** WALNUT	468	**346**	297	248
ELGUIT	78	GUILD	**S- 60D** MAHOGANY	469	**347**	298	249
ELGUIT	76	GUILD	**S- 60DD** WALNUT, 2 PU's	432	**319**	274	229
ELGUIT	78	GUILD	**S- 70** SERIAL #169868-195067	451	**333**	286	239
ELGUIT	65	GUILD	**S-100 POLARA** LEFT-HANDED	200	**148**	127	106
ELGUIT	65	GUILD	**S-100 POLARA** SERIAL #SB101-169	609	**450**	387	323
ELGUIT	66	GUILD	**S-100 POLARA** SUNBURST	536	**396**	340	285
ELGUIT	67	GUILD	**S-100 POLARA** VIBRATO	538	**398**	342	286
ELGUIT	68	GUILD	**S-100 POLARA**	461	**341**	293	245
ELGUIT	69	GUILD	**S-100 POLARA** SERIAL #46657-46695	424	**313**	269	225
ELGUIT	70	GUILD	**S-100 POLARA**	518	**383**	329	275
ELGUIT	72	GUILD	**S-100 POLARA**	465	**344**	295	247
ELGUIT	64	GUILD	**S-200 THUNDERBIRD** SERIAL #28944-38636	250	**185**	159	133
ELGUIT	77	GUILD	**S-300** SUNBURST, 2 HB's	360	**266**	228	191
ELGUIT	77	GUILD	**S-300D** NATURAL	432	**319**	274	229
ELGUIT	65	GUILD	**STARFIRE** SERIAL #38637-46606	458	**339**	291	243
ELGUIT	62	GUILD	**STARFIRE II**	557	**412**	354	296
ELGUIT	63	GUILD	**STARFIRE II**	598	**442**	380	317
ELGUIT	65	GUILD	**STARFIRE II** HOLLOW BODY, SERIAL #EK101-387	549	**406**	348	291
ELGUIT	66	GUILD	**STARFIRE II** CHERRY RED, SERIAL #EK388-2098	593	**438**	376	315
ELGUIT	61	GUILD	**STARFIRE III** SINGLE CUT	403	**298**	256	214
ELGUIT	62	GUILD	**STARFIRE III** CHERRY RED	480	**355**	305	255
ELGUIT	66	GUILD	**STARFIRE III** SERIAL #EK388-2098	369	**273**	234	196
ELGUIT	67	GUILD	**STARFIRE III**	557	**412**	354	296
ELGUIT	72	GUILD	**STARFIRE III** RED, MAHOGANY, SINGLE CUT, 2 PU's	375	**277**	238	199
ELGUIT	70	GUILD	**STARFIRE III SPECIAL** CHERRY RED, CUTAWAY	373	**276**	237	198
ELGUIT	62	GUILD	**STARFIRE IV** SERIAL #18419-22722	470	**347**	298	249
ELGUIT	67	GUILD	**STARFIRE IV** SERIAL #EL1168-1840	459	**340**	292	244
ELGUIT	67	GUILD	**STARFIRE IV** SUNBURST, LEFT-HANDED	467	**345**	297	248
ELGUIT	69	GUILD	**STARFIRE IV** SUNBURST, SERIAL #EL2224-2272	466	**345**	296	247
ELGUIT	70	GUILD	**STARFIRE IV** SUNBURST	457	**338**	290	243
ELGUIT	74	GUILD	**STARFIRE IV** SUNBURST	484	**358**	308	257
ELGUIT	76	GUILD	**STARFIRE IV** SUNBURST	478	**353**	303	253
ELGUIT	79	GUILD	**STARFIRE IV** SUNBURST, SERIAL #195067	476	**352**	302	252
ELGUIT	64	GUILD	**STARFIRE V** CHERRY RED, SERIAL #28944-38636	574	**424**	364	304
ELGUIT	65	GUILD	**STARFIRE V** SERIAL #EN101-194	557	**412**	354	296
ELGUIT	66	GUILD	**STARFIRE V** LEFT-HANDED, SERIAL #EN195-927	482	**357**	306	256
ELGUIT	66	GUILD	**STARFIRE V** SERIAL #EN195-927	554	**410**	352	294
ELGUIT	68	GUILD	**STARFIRE V** CHERRY RED	555	**411**	353	295
ELGUIT	70	GUILD	**STARFIRE V**	837	**619**	531	444

TYPE	YR	MFG	PRICES--BASED ON 100% ORIGINAL MODEL	SELL EXC	SELL AVG	BUY EXC	BUY AVG
ELGUIT	68	GUILD	**STARFIRE VI** SERIAL #DB 275-329	539	**399**	342	286
ELGUIT	75	GUILD	**STARFIRE VI** CHERRY RED, SERIAL #112803-130304	522	**386**	331	277
ELGUIT	66	GUILD	**STARFIRE XII** CHERRY RED, 12-STRING, SERIAL #DC101-586	689	**509**	437	366
ELGUIT	67	GUILD	**STARFIRE XII** CHERRY RED, 12-STRING, SERIAL #DC587-896	601	**445**	382	319
ELGUIT	68	GUILD	**STARFIRE XII** 12-STRING, SERIAL #DC897	587	**434**	373	312
ELGUIT	70	GUILD	**STARFIRE XII**	637	**471**	405	338
ELGUIT	65	GUILD	**STARFIRE BASS** WINE RED, SEMI-HOLLOW	470	**347**	298	249
ELGUIT	66	GUILD	**STARFIRE BASS** CHERRY RED	398	**294**	253	211
ELGUIT	67	GUILD	**STARFIRE BASS** CHERRY RED, 2 PU's, SERIAL #BA655-1696	396	**293**	251	210
ELGUIT	67	GUILD	**STARFIRE BASS** SUNBURST, 1 PU, SERIAL #BA655-1696	470	**347**	298	249
ELGUIT	73	GUILD	**STARFIRE BASS** CHERRY RED, 1 PU	284	**210**	180	150
ELGUIT	67	GUILD	**STARFIRE BASS II** SUNBURST	494	**365**	314	262
ELGUIT	69	GUILD	**STARFIRE BASS II** SERIAL #BA1947-2043	513	**379**	326	272
ELGUIT	71	GUILD	**STARFIRE BASS II** CHERRY RED, 2 PU's, SERIAL #50978-61463	344	**254**	218	183
ELGUIT	75	GUILD	**STARFIRE BASS II** SUNBURST, SERIAL #112804-130304	511	**378**	325	271
ELGUIT	61	GUILD	**STARSONG**	857	**634**	544	455
ELGUIT	65	GUILD	**T- 50 CORDOBA SLIM** SERIAL #EB101-196	559	**413**	355	297
ELGUIT	67	GUILD	**T- 50 CORDOBA SLIM** SUNBURST, SERIAL #EB392-558	452	**334**	287	240
ELGUIT	74	GUILD	**T- 50 CORDOBA SLIM** CHERRY RED	451	**333**	286	239
ELGUIT	58	GUILD	**T-100 SLIM JIM** SUNBURST, SINGLE CUTAWAY	758	**560**	481	402
ELGUIT	59	GUILD	**T-100 SLIM JIM** SUNBURST, 1 PU	696	**515**	442	370
ELGUIT	61	GUILD	**T-100 SLIM JIM**	518	**383**	329	275
ELGUIT	64	GUILD	**T-100 SLIM JIM** SUNBURST, CUTAWAY	478	**353**	303	253
ELGUIT	69	GUILD	**T-100 SLIM JIM** SUNBURST, ARCHTOP, SERIAL #EE3004-3109	561	**415**	356	298
ELGUIT	70	GUILD	**T-100 SLIM JIM** CHERRY RED, 2 PU's, SINGLE CUTAWAY	521	**397**	337	258
ELGUIT	60	GUILD	**T-100D SLIM JIM** SUNBURST	713	**527**	453	378
ELGUIT	61	GUILD	**T-100D SLIM JIM** SUNBURST	518	**383**	329	275
ELGUIT	61	GUILD	**T-100D SLIM JIM** SUNBURST, SERIAL #14713-18419	599	**443**	380	318
ELGUIT	66	GUILD	**T-100D SLIM JIM** HOLLOW BODY, SERIAL #EE602-1939	444	**328**	282	236
ELGUIT	69	GUILD	**T-100D SLIM JIM** SINGLE CUT, SERIAL #95496-112803	459	**340**	292	244
ELGUIT	68	GUILD	**THUNDERBIRD BASS** BUILT-IN STAND	785	**580**	498	417
ELGUIT	55	GUILD	**X- 50** SUNBURST, ARCHTOP	633	**468**	402	336
ELGUIT	57	GUILD	**X- 50** SUNBURST, 1 PU, THICK BODY	747	**553**	475	397
ELGUIT	62	GUILD	**X- 50** SUNBURST, 1 PU, NON-CUTAWAY, SERIAL #18420-22722	465	**344**	295	247
ELGUIT	65	GUILD	**X- 50** SUNBURST, 1 PU	494	**365**	314	262
ELGUIT	67	GUILD	**X- 50** HOLLOW BODY	553	**409**	351	294
ELGUIT	64	GUILD	**X- 50 CORDOBA**	717	**530**	455	380
ELGUIT	67	GUILD	**X- 50 CORDOBA** HOLLOW BODY, SERIAL #EA327-491	562	**416**	357	298
ELGUIT	58	GUILD	**X- 50 GRANADA** HOLLOW BODY, SERIAL #12035	747	**553**	475	397
ELGUIT	53	GUILD	**X-150 JAZZ** SUNBURST, ARCHTOP, SERIAL #12035	792	**586**	503	421
ELGUIT	57	GUILD	**X-150 SAVOY** HOLLOW BODY, SERIAL #12035	749	**554**	476	398
ELGUIT	61	GUILD	**X-150 SAVOY**	1,195	**883**	759	634
ELGUIT	57	GUILD	**X-150B** NATURAL, SINGLE CUTAWAY, 17" WIDE	749	**554**	476	398
ELGUIT	59	GUILD	**X-150LH** SUNBURST, SINGLE CUTAWAY, LEFT-HANDED	936	**692**	594	497

TYPE	YR	MFG	PRICES--BASED ON 100% ORIGINAL MODEL	SELL EXC	SELL AVG	BUY EXC	BUY AVG
ELGUIT	54	GUILD	**X-175** SUNBURST	1,179	**872**	749	626
ELGUIT	55	GUILD	**X-175** SUNBURST, SERIAL #12035	1,173	**867**	745	623
ELGUIT	59	GUILD	**X-175** SUNBURST	1,416	**1,047**	900	752
ELGUIT	62	GUILD	**X-175** BLOND, SINGLE CUTAWAY, 2 PU's, SERIAL #18419-22722	1,167	**863**	741	620
ELGUIT	63	GUILD	**X-175** SUNBURST	1,239	**916**	787	658
ELGUIT	67	GUILD	**X-175** NATURAL	1,232	**911**	783	654
ELGUIT	75	GUILD	**X-175** NATURAL, SERIAL #112803-130304	590	**436**	375	313
ELGUIT	77	GUILD	**X-175** NATURAL	588	**435**	373	312
ELGUIT	79	GUILD	**X-175** SUNBURST, 2 PU's, CUTAWAY	472	**349**	300	250
ELGUIT	55	GUILD	**X-175 MANHATTAN** HOLLOW BODY, SERIAL #12035	485	**359**	308	258
ELGUIT	58	GUILD	**X-175 MANHATTAN**	1,474	**1,090**	936	783
ELGUIT	69	GUILD	**X-175 MANHATTAN** HOLLOW BODY, SERIAL #EG323-346	504	**372**	320	267
ELGUIT	78	GUILD	**X-175 MANHATTAN**	996	**736**	633	529
ELGUIT	54	GUILD	**X-350 STRATFORD** SUNBURST, 3 BLACK PU's	1,876	**1,388**	1,192	997
ELGUIT	55	GUILD	**X-350 STRATFORD** SUNBURST, WHITE, 3 SINGLE COIL PU's	1,878	**1,389**	1,193	998
ELGUIT	56	GUILD	**X-350 STRATFORD** HOLLOW BODY, SERIAL #12035	1,778	**1,315**	1,130	945
ELGUIT	57	GUILD	**X-350 STRATFORD** BLOND, ARCHTOP, SERIAL #12035	1,871	**1,383**	1,188	993
ELGUIT	58	GUILD	**X-350 STRATFORD** SUNBURST, 3 WHITE PU's	1,876	**1,388**	1,192	997
ELGUIT	61	GUILD	**X-350 STRATFORD** SUNBURST	1,354	**1,001**	860	719
ELGUIT	62	GUILD	**X-350B** BLOND, PUSH BUTTONS	2,963	**2,191**	1,883	1,574
ELGUIT	55	GUILD	**X-375** SUNBURST, 3 PU's	1,513	**1,119**	961	804
ELGUIT	58	GUILD	**X-375** NATURL, 3 PU's	1,307	**996**	846	647
ELGUIT	60	GUILD	**X-375 STRATFORD**	1,593	**1,178**	1,012	846
ELGUIT	55	GUILD	**X-440** HOLLOW BODY, SERIAL #12035	1,403	**1,038**	891	745
ELGUIT	57	GUILD	**X-500 STUART** NATURAL, SERIAL #12035	1,953	**1,444**	1,241	1,037
ELGUIT	61	GUILD	**X-500 STUART**	1,513	**1,119**	961	804
ELGUIT	62	GUILD	**X-500 STUART** SUNBURST, WHITE DEARMOND	796	**589**	506	423
ELGUIT	65	GUILD	**X-500 STUART** NATURAL	876	**648**	556	465
ELGUIT	68	GUILD	**X-500 STUART** NATURAL, CURLY MAPLE BACK/SIDE, SERIAL #DA231	866	**641**	550	460
ELGUIT	70	GUILD	**X-500 STUART**	776	**574**	493	412
ELGUIT	73	GUILD	**X-500 STUART** NATURAL	738	**545**	469	392
ELGUIT	74	GUILD	**X-500 STUART** NATURAL, SERIAL #95496-112803	717	**530**	455	380
ELGUIT	75	GUILD	**X-500 STUART** SUNBURST	677	**501**	430	360
ELGUIT	77	GUILD	**X-500 STUART** NATURAL, CURLY MAPLE	676	**500**	430	359
ELGUIT	79	GUILD	**X-500 STUART** NATURAL, SERIAL #195067-	635	**470**	403	337
ELGUIT	79	GUILD	**X-500 STUART** SUNBURST	635	**470**	403	337
ELGUIT	79	GUILD	**X-500 STUART** NATURAL, GOLD TAILPIECE	681	**504**	433	362
ELGUIT	55	GUILD	**X-550 STUART** NATURAL	2,366	**1,750**	1,503	1,257
GUITAR AMP	69	GUILD	**FOXY LADY** 2 KNOBS	240	**177**	152	127
GTAMP	58	GUILD	**MASTER AMP** 12" SPEAKER	335	**247**	212	177
GTAMP	71	GUILD	**STARFIRE V** WALNUT, MAHOGANY	717	**530**	455	380
GTAMP	76	GUILD	**STARFIRE VI** NATURAL, MAHOGANY	796	**589**	506	423
GTAMP	64	GUILD	**THUNDER 1-12** 12" SPEAKER	192	**142**	122	102
GTAMP	67	GUILD	**THUNDER 1-12** 12" SPEAKER	191	**141**	121	101

TYPE	YR	MFG	PRICES--BASED ON 100% ORIGINAL MODEL	SELL EXC	SELL AVG	BUY EXC	BUY AVG
GUITAR (ACOUSTIC)	55	GUILD	**A- 50 GRANADA**	518	**383**	329	275
GUITAR	57	GUILD	**A- 50 GRANADA** SUNBURST	844	**624**	536	448
GUITAR	59	GUILD	**A- 50 GRANADA** SUNBURST	890	**658**	566	473
GUITAR	62	GUILD	**A- 50 GRANADA** BLOND	656	**485**	417	348
GUITAR	65	GUILD	**A- 50 GRANADA** SUNBURST, SERIAL #AB101-136	842	**623**	535	447
GUITAR	51	GUILD	**A- 50 STUART** SUNBURST	937	**693**	595	498
GUITAR	60	GUILD	**A-150 SAVOY** SUNBURST	1,445	**1,069**	918	768
GUITAR	62	GUILD	**A-150 SAVOY** SUNBURST, SERIAL #18420-22722	1,225	**906**	778	651
GUITAR	55	GUILD	**A-350 STRATFORD** ARCHTOP, SERIAL #12035	940	**695**	597	499
GUITAR	61	GUILD	**A-350 STRATFORD** NATURAL	1,155	**854**	734	614
GUITAR	60	GUILD	**A-500 STUART** SUNBURST, ARCHTOP, SERIAL #12035	683	**520**	442	338
GUITAR	61	GUILD	**A-500 STUART** SUNBURST, ARCHTOP	1,512	**1,118**	961	803
GUITAR	62	GUILD	**A-500 STUART** BLOND, ARCHTOP, SERIAL #18420-22722	817	**604**	519	434
GUITAR	63	GUILD	**A-500 STUART** SUNBURST, ARCHTOP, SERIAL #22723-28943	1,141	**844**	725	606
GUITAR	63	GUILD	**ARTIST AWARD** SUNBURST, ARCHTOP	3,554	**2,629**	2,258	1,888
GUITAR	65	GUILD	**ARTIST AWARD** BLOND, ARCHTOP, SERIAL #AA101	3,553	**2,628**	2,258	1,888
GUITAR	69	GUILD	**ARTIST AWARD** SUNBURST, ARCHTOP	3,194	**2,362**	2,030	1,697
GUITAR	69	GUILD	**ARTIST AWARD** NATURAL, ARCHTOP	3,199	**2,366**	2,033	1,699
GUITAR	70	GUILD	**ARTIST AWARD** BLOND, ARCHTOP, SERIAL #46695-50978	2,063	**1,525**	1,310	1,095
GUITAR	70	GUILD	**ARTIST AWARD** SUNBURST, ARCHTOP, SERIAL #46696-50978	2,065	**1,527**	1,312	1,097
GUITAR	72	GUILD	**ARTIST AWARD** ARCHTOP, SERIAL #61464-75602	1,770	**1,309**	1,124	940
GUITAR	76	GUILD	**ARTIST AWARD** SUNBURST, ARCHTOP	1,179	**872**	749	626
GUITAR	77	GUILD	**ARTIST AWARD** SUNBURST, ARCHTOP, MAPLE, ORIGINAL DeARMOND FLOATING PICKUP	1,176	**870**	747	625
GUITAR	77	GUILD	**ARTIST AWARD** NATURAL, ARCHTOP, SERIAL #149626-169867	1,179	**872**	749	626
GUITAR	80	GUILD	**ARTIST AWARD** NATURAL, ARCHTOP	1,450	**1,072**	921	770
GUITAR	76	GUILD	**B-50 BASS** MAHOGANY	956	**707**	607	507
GUITAR	60	GUILD	**CA-100 CAPRI**	856	**633**	544	454
GUITAR	64	GUILD	**CA-100 CAPRI** SUNBURST, CUTAWAY	804	**594**	511	427
GUITAR	66	GUILD	**CA-100 CAPRI** ARCHTOP, SERIAL #46607-46608	799	**591**	508	424
GUITAR	61	GUILD	**CE-100 CAPRI**	717	**530**	455	380
GUITAR	77	GUILD	**CLASSICAL MK2**	466	**345**	296	247
GUITAR	70	GUILD	**D- 25** CHERRY RED	364	**269**	231	193
GUITAR	70	GUILD	**D- 25** MAHOGANY	374	**276**	237	198
GUITAR	71	GUILD	**D- 25** CHERRY RED, SERIAL #50979-61463	360	**266**	228	191
GUITAR	71	GUILD	**D- 25** MAHOGANY	480	**355**	305	255
GUITAR	72	GUILD	**D- 25** NATURAL	359	**265**	228	190
GUITAR	72	GUILD	**D- 25** CHERRY RED	374	**276**	237	198
GUITAR	73	GUILD	**D- 25** CHERRY RED, SERIAL #75603-95496	353	**261**	224	187
GUITAR	74	GUILD	**D- 25** SUNBURST	357	**264**	226	189
GUITAR	75	GUILD	**D- 25** NATURAL	355	**262**	225	188
GUITAR	75	GUILD	**D- 25** SUNBURST	388	**296**	251	192
GUITAR	75	GUILD	**D- 25** MAHOGANY	369	**273**	234	196
GUITAR	76	GUILD	**D- 25** MAHOGANY	364	**269**	231	193
GUITAR	77	GUILD	**D- 25** BROWN	340	**252**	216	181

TYPE	YR	MFG	PRICES--BASED ON 100% ORIGINAL MODEL	SELL EXC	SELL AVG	BUY EXC	BUY AVG
GUITAR	78	GUILD	**D- 25** BLACK	340	**252**	216	181
GUITAR	78	GUILD	**D- 25** CHERRY RED, SERIAL #169867-195067	340	**252**	216	181
GUITAR	78	GUILD	**D- 25** MAHOGANY	355	**262**	225	188
GUITAR	79	GUILD	**D- 25** MAHOGANY, SERIAL #195068	345	**255**	219	183
GUITAR	72	GUILD	**D- 25 BLUEGRASS**	478	**353**	303	253
GUITAR	78	GUILD	**D- 25-12**	340	**252**	216	181
GUITAR	76	GUILD	**D- 25M**	478	**353**	303	253
GUITAR	73	GUILD	**D- 30** MAHOGANY	557	**412**	354	296
GUITAR	70	GUILD	**D- 35** NATURAL, SERIAL #46696-50978	1,244	**920**	790	660
GUITAR	74	GUILD	**D- 35** NATURAL	956	**707**	607	507
GUITAR	76	GUILD	**D- 35** NATURAL LEFT-HANDED	719	**531**	456	381
GUITAR	76	GUILD	**D- 35** NATURAL	728	**538**	462	387
GUITAR	77	GUILD	**D- 35** NATURAL	588	**435**	373	312
GUITAR	78	GUILD	**D- 35** NATURAL, LEFT-HANDED	438	**324**	278	233
GUITAR	78	GUILD	**D- 35** NATURAL, SERIAL #169867-195067	652	**482**	414	346
GUITAR	79	GUILD	**D- 35** NATURAL	569	**421**	361	302
GUITAR	67	GUILD	**D- 35 BLUEGRASS** SERIAL #46609-46637	856	**633**	544	454
GUITAR	68	GUILD	**D- 35 BLUEGRASS** SERIAL #OJ101-1003	837	**619**	531	444
GUITAR	71	GUILD	**D- 35 BLUEGRASS** SERIAL #50979-61463	690	**510**	438	366
GUITAR	72	GUILD	**D- 35 BLUEGRASS** SERIAL #61463-75602	681	**504**	433	362
GUITAR	73	GUILD	**D- 35 BLUEGRASS**	637	**471**	405	338
GUITAR	72	GUILD	**D- 35NT**	481	**356**	306	256
GUITAR	66	GUILD	**D- 40** SERIAL #AJ334-1136	937	**693**	595	498
GUITAR	71	GUILD	**D- 40**	920	**680**	584	489
GUITAR	72	GUILD	**D- 40**	820	**607**	521	436
GUITAR	75	GUILD	**D- 40**	724	**536**	460	385
GUITAR	78	GUILD	**D- 40**	633	**468**	402	336
GUITAR	79	GUILD	**D- 40**	579	**428**	368	308
GUITAR	79	GUILD	**D- 40** LEFT-HANDED	736	**544**	467	391
GUITAR	79	GUILD	**D- 40CNT**	598	**442**	380	317
GUITAR	70	GUILD	**D- 40NT** SERIAL #46696-50978	629	**465**	400	334
GUITAR	75	GUILD	**D- 40NT**	651	**482**	414	346
GUITAR	78	GUILD	**D- 40NT** SERIAL #169868-195067	579	**428**	368	308
GUITAR	79	GUILD	**D- 40NT**	578	**428**	367	307
GUITAR	68	GUILD	**D- 44**	1,026	**758**	652	545
GUITAR	76	GUILD	**D- 44 BLUEGRASS JUBILEE**	677	**501**	430	360
GUITAR	74	GUILD	**D- 44M**	630	**466**	400	335
GUITAR	76	GUILD	**D- 44M**	717	**530**	455	380
GUITAR	73	GUILD	**D- 44NT**	617	**456**	392	327
GUITAR	84	GUILD	**D- 46**	637	**471**	405	338
GUITAR	70	GUILD	**D- 50** NATURAL, SERIAL #46696-50978	872	**645**	554	463
GUITAR	72	GUILD	**D- 50** NATURAL	744	**550**	473	395
GUITAR	73	GUILD	**D- 50** NATURAL	956	**707**	607	507
GUITAR	74	GUILD	**D- 50** NATURAL	708	**523**	450	376
GUITAR	75	GUILD	**D- 50** NATURAL	677	**501**	430	360
GUITAR	76	GUILD	**D- 50** NATURAL, SERIAL #130304-149625	645	**477**	409	342
GUITAR	78	GUILD	**D- 50** NATURAL	605	**448**	384	321
GUITAR	78	GUILD	**D- 50** NATURAL, LEFT-HANDED, SERIAL #181399	628	**465**	399	334
GUITAR	79	GUILD	**D- 50** NATURAL, LEFT-HANDED	598	**442**	380	317
GUITAR	79	GUILD	**D- 50** SUNBURST	598	**442**	380	317

TYPE	YR	MFG	PRICES--BASED ON 100% ORIGINAL MODEL	SELL EXC	SELL AVG	BUY EXC	BUY AVG
GUITAR	68	GUILD	**D- 55**	817	**604**	519	434
GUITAR	73	GUILD	**D- 55** ROSEWOOD, SERIAL #75603-95496	1,092	**807**	694	580
GUITAR	78	GUILD	**D- 55**	1,035	**766**	658	550
GUITAR	66	GUILD	**DE-500 DUANE EDDY DELUXE**	1,474	**1,090**	936	783
GUITAR	75	GUILD	**F- 4-12 JUMBO** MAHOGANY BACK/SIDES, 12-STRING, SERIAL #112803-130304	656	**485**	417	348
GUITAR	55	GUILD	**F- 20 TROUBADOR** SUNBURST, SERIAL #12035	592	**438**	376	314
GUITAR	56	GUILD	**F- 20 TROUBADOR** MAPLE	629	**465**	400	334
GUITAR	58	GUILD	**F- 20 TROUBADOR** NATURAL, SERIAL #12035	628	**465**	399	334
GUITAR	58	GUILD	**F- 20 TROUBADOR** SUNBURST, SERIAL #12035	635	**470**	403	337
GUITAR	59	GUILD	**F- 20 TROUBADOR** MAPLE	625	**462**	397	332
GUITAR	62	GUILD	**F- 20 TROUBADOR** NATURAL	610	**451**	387	324
GUITAR	67	GUILD	**F- 20 TROUBADOR** NATURAL, SERIAL #AG1535-2499	465	**344**	295	247
GUITAR	68	GUILD	**F- 20 TROUBADOR** SUNBURST, SERIAL #AG2500-2793	511	**378**	325	271
GUITAR	73	GUILD	**F- 20 TROUBADOR**	537	**397**	341	285
GUITAR	75	GUILD	**F- 20 TROUBADOR** SUNBURST, LEFT-HANDED, SERIAL #112804-130304	426	**315**	270	226
GUITAR	75	GUILD	**F- 20 TROUBADOR** SUNBURST	438	**324**	278	233
GUITAR	78	GUILD	**F- 20 TROUBADOR** NATURAL	456	**337**	290	242
GUITAR	79	GUILD	**F- 20 TROUBADOR** SUNBURST	419	**310**	266	222
GUITAR	79	GUILD	**F- 20 TROUBADOR** NATURAL	461	**341**	293	245
GUITAR	80	GUILD	**F- 20 TROUBADOR** NATURAL	480	**355**	305	255
GUITAR	82	GUILD	**F- 20 TROUBADOR**	518	**383**	329	275
GUITAR	65	GUILD	**F- 30 ARAGON** SUNBURST, SERIAL #AI101-351	677	**501**	430	360
GUITAR	67	GUILD	**F- 30 ARAGON** NATURAL, SERIAL #AI1143-1855	656	**485**	417	348
GUITAR	68	GUILD	**F- 30 ARAGON** MAHOGANY, SERIAL #AI1856-2270	598	**442**	380	317
GUITAR	78	GUILD	**F- 30 ARAGON** SUNBURST	474	**350**	301	251
GUITAR	79	GUILD	**F- 30 ARAGON**	478	**353**	303	253
GUITAR	74	GUILD	**F- 30R ARAGON** SERIAL #95497-112803	553	**409**	351	294
GUITAR	54	GUILD	**F- 40 VALENCIA** MAPLE BACK/SIDES	956	**707**	607	507
GUITAR	57	GUILD	**F- 40 VALENCIA** MAPLE BACK/SIDES, SERIAL #12035	654	**484**	416	347
GUITAR	59	GUILD	**F- 40 VALENCIA** MAPLE BACK/SIDES, SERIAL #12035	558	**413**	355	296
GUITAR	65	GUILD	**F- 47 BLUEGRASS** NATURAL, SERIAL #AK101-128	1,009	**746**	641	536
GUITAR	72	GUILD	**F- 47 BLUEGRASS** NATURAL	757	**560**	481	402
GUITAR	57	GUILD	**F- 50 NAVARRE** NATURAL, SERIAL #12035	929	**687**	590	493
GUITAR	58	GUILD	**F- 50 NAVARRE** SUNBURST, SERIAL #12035	1,045	**796**	677	517
GUITAR	65	GUILD	**F- 50 NAVARRE** SUNBURST	876	**648**	556	465
GUITAR	67	GUILD	**F- 50 NAVARRE**	1,195	**883**	759	634
GUITAR	71	GUILD	**F- 50 NAVARRE** NATURAL, SERIAL #50979-61463	796	**589**	506	423
GUITAR	72	GUILD	**F- 50 NAVARRE** SUNBURST	864	**639**	549	459
GUITAR	74	GUILD	**F- 50 NAVARRE** NATURAL	675	**514**	437	334
GUITAR	75	GUILD	**F- 50 NAVARRE** NATURAL	757	**560**	481	402
GUITAR	77	GUILD	**F- 50 NAVARRE**	956	**707**	607	507
GUITAR	67	GUILD	**F- 50R NAVARRE** ROSEWOOD, SERIAL #AD191-291	778	**575**	494	413
GUITAR	70	GUILD	**F- 50R NAVARRE** ROSEWOOD	956	**707**	607	507
GUITAR	73	GUILD	**F- 50R NAVARRE** ROSEWOOD	958	**708**	608	508
GUITAR	74	GUILD	**F- 50R NAVARRE** ROSEWOOD	916	**678**	582	487

TYPE	YR	MFG	PRICES--BASED ON 100% ORIGINAL MODEL	SELL EXC	SELL AVG	BUY EXC	BUY AVG
GUITAR	75	GUILD	F- 50R NAVARRE ROSEWOOD	847	626	538	450
GUITAR	77	GUILD	F- 50R NAVARRE ROSEWOOD, SERIAL #149625-169867	776	574	493	412
GUITAR	79	GUILD	F- 50R NAVARRE ROSEWOOD, SERIAL #195067	757	560	481	402
GUITAR	78	GUILD	F- 50RNT NATURAL, FLATTOP	751	555	477	399
GUITAR	68	GUILD	F-112 NATURAL, 12-STRING	737	545	468	391
GUITAR	71	GUILD	F-112 NATURAL, 12-STRING	657	486	417	349
GUITAR	73	GUILD	F-112 NATURAL, 12-STRING	639	472	406	339
GUITAR	76	GUILD	F-112 NATURAL, 12-STRING	637	471	405	338
GUITAR	69	GUILD	F-212 12-STRING, SERIAL #AN2010-2271	569	421	361	302
GUITAR	75	GUILD	F-212 12-STRING	876	648	556	465
GUITAR	77	GUILD	F-212 12-STRING	557	412	354	296
GUITAR	78	GUILD	F-212 12-STRING	562	416	357	298
GUITAR	77	GUILD	F-212C NATURAL, CUTAWAY, 12-STRING, SERIAL #149625-169867	845	625	537	449
GUITAR	65	GUILD	F-212XL 12-STRING, SERIAL #AN101-228	654	484	416	347
GUITAR	67	GUILD	F-212XL 12-STRING	657	486	417	349
GUITAR	75	GUILD	F-212XL 12-STRING	544	402	345	289
GUITAR	79	GUILD	F-212XL 12-STRING	557	412	354	296
GUITAR	82	GUILD	F-212XL 12-STRING	980	724	622	520
GUITAR	65	GUILD	F-312 12-STRING, SERIAL #AS101-141	938	694	596	498
GUITAR	67	GUILD	F-312 12-STRING	825	610	524	438
GUITAR	73	GUILD	F-412 NATURAL, 12-STRING	931	688	591	494
GUITAR	75	GUILD	F-412 NATURAL, 12-STRING	799	591	508	424
GUITAR	76	GUILD	F-412 NATURAL, 12-STRING	757	560	481	402
GUITAR	76	GUILD	F-412 CUSTOM 12-STRING	1,076	795	683	571
GUITAR	72	GUILD	F-512 ROSEWOOD BACK/SIDES, 12-STRING, SERIAL #61463-75602	964	713	613	512
GUITAR	73	GUILD	F-512 ROSEWOOD BACK/SIDES, 12-STRING	972	719	617	516
GUITAR	74	GUILD	F-512 ROSEWOOD BACK/SIDES, 12-STRING	916	678	582	487
GUITAR	77	GUILD	F-512 ROSEWOOD BACK/SIDES, 12-STRING	911	673	578	483
GUITAR	79	GUILD	F-512 ROSEWOOD BACK/SIDES, 12-STRING	796	589	506	423
GUITAR	70	GUILD	F-512 CUSTOM 12-STRING	956	707	607	507
GUITAR	74	GUILD	G- 37 NATURAL	433	320	275	230
GUITAR	76	GUILD	G- 37 NATURAL	478	353	303	253
GUITAR	79	GUILD	G- 37	557	412	354	296
GUITAR	75	GUILD	G- 41	588	435	373	312
GUITAR	74	GUILD	G- 75 NATURAL	823	609	523	437
GUITAR	77	GUILD	G- 75 NATURAL	677	501	430	360
GUITAR	80	GUILD	G- 75 NATURAL	639	472	406	339
GUITAR	75	GUILD	G-212 12-STRING, SERIAL #112803-130304	668	494	424	354
GUITAR	78	GUILD	G-212 12-STRING	598	442	380	317
GUITAR	80	GUILD	G-212 12-STRING	850	629	540	451
GUITAR	76	GUILD	G-312NT ROSEWOOD, 12-STRING	749	554	476	398
GUITAR	77	GUILD	G-312NT ROSEWOOD, 12-STRING	876	648	556	465
GUITAR	76	GUILD	GT-312 NATURAL	565	418	359	300

TYPE	YR	MFG	PRICES--BASED ON 100% ORIGINAL MODEL	SELL EXC	SELL AVG	BUY EXC	BUY AVG
GUITAR	63	GUILD	**JF-65-12 JUMBO** NATURAL	956	**707**	607	507
GUITAR	87	GUILD	**JF-65R**	1,035	**766**	658	550
GUITAR	59	GUILD	**JOHNNY SMITH ARTIST** ARCHTOP, SERIAL #12035	2,087	**1,543**	1,326	1,108
GUITAR	62	GUILD	**M- 20 ECONOMY**	478	**353**	303	253
GUITAR	66	GUILD	**M- 20 ECONOMY** MAHOGANY, SERIAL #46607-46608	563	**416**	358	299
GUITAR	67	GUILD	**M- 20 ECONOMY** MAHOGANY	598	**442**	380	317
GUITAR	77	GUILD	**M- 20 ECONOMY** MAHOGANY	470	**347**	298	249
GUITAR	66	GUILD	**MARK I**	480	**355**	305	255
GUITAR	65	GUILD	**MARK I CLASSICAL** MAHOGANY	475	**351**	301	252
GUITAR	65	GUILD	**MARK III CLASSICAL** MAHOGANY	468	**346**	297	248
GUITAR	69	GUILD	**MARK III CLASSICAL** MAHOGANY, SERIAL #46657-46695	452	**334**	287	240
GUITAR	72	GUILD	**MARK III CLASSICAL** MAHOGANY	427	**315**	271	226
GUITAR	74	GUILD	**MARK III CLASSICAL** MAHOGANY, SERIAL #111926	393	**300**	255	195
GUITAR	78	GUILD	**MARK IV**	438	**324**	278	233
GUITAR	60	GUILD	**S-200 THUNDERBIRD** SERIAL #12036-14713	1,017	**752**	646	540
GUITAR	67	GUILD	**S-200 THUNDERBIRD** SERIAL #46609-46637	595	**440**	378	316
GUITAR	68	GUILD	**S-200 THUNDERBIRD** SERIAL #46638-46656	539	**399**	342	286
GUITAR	24	GUILD	**STUDIO 24** DOUBLE CUTAWAY, FLATTOP	1,350	**998**	858	717
UKULELE	60	GUILD	**B-11 BARITONE**	240	**177**	152	127
UKE	65	GUILD	**BARITONE**	342	**253**	217	182

DAWSON HADLEY

TYPE	YR	MFG	MODEL	SELL EXC	SELL AVG	BUY EXC	BUY AVG
PWR	70	HADLEY	**H-601**	677	**501**	430	360

HAGSTROM

TYPE	YR	MFG	MODEL	SELL EXC	SELL AVG	BUY EXC	BUY AVG
ELEC. GUITAR	65	HAGSTROM	**135** HOLLOW BODY, 2 PU's	336	**248**	213	178
ELGUIT	66	HAGSTROM	**BASS** SUNBURST, 8-STRING	442	**327**	281	235
ELGUIT	67	HAGSTROM	**BASS** RED, 8-STRING	543	**401**	345	288
ELGUIT	68	HAGSTROM	**BASS** SUNBURST, 8-STRING	436	**323**	277	232
ELGUIT	72	HAGSTROM	**BASS** SUNBURST, 8-STRING	475	**351**	301	252
ELGUIT	62	HAGSTROM	**BASS I** RED, PLASTIC TOP, RAISED LABEL	356	**263**	226	189
ELGUIT	65	HAGSTROM	**BASS I** BLACK	293	**217**	186	156
ELGUIT	66	HAGSTROM	**BASS I** RED, 2 PU's	290	**215**	184	154
ELGUIT	71	HAGSTROM	**BASS I** SUNBURST	297	**220**	189	158
ELGUIT	61	HAGSTROM	**BASS II** RED, SOLID BODY, 2 PU's	336	**248**	213	178
ELGUIT	67	HAGSTROM	**BASS II** HOLLOW BODY, 2 PU's	333	**246**	211	176
ELGUIT	62	HAGSTROM	**H- 22** SINGLE CUTAWAY, THINLINE, 1 PU	211	**156**	134	112
ELGUIT	60	HAGSTROM	**HAGSTROM II** RED	198	**146**	126	105
ELGUIT	70	HAGSTROM	**HAGSTROM II** SUNBURST	225	**166**	143	119
ELGUIT	66	HAGSTROM	**KING BASS** 2 PU's	240	**177**	152	127
ELGUIT	66	HAGSTROM	**MODEL I**	285	**210**	181	151
ELGUIT	71	HAGSTROM	**MODEL I**	312	**231**	198	166
ELGUIT	75	HAGSTROM	**MODEL II**	328	**242**	208	174
ELGUIT	65	HAGSTROM	**MODEL III**	245	**181**	156	130
ELGUIT	76	HAGSTROM	**NORWAY** NATURAL, CHERRY	423	**313**	269	224
ELGUIT	71	HAGSTROM	**NORWAY BASS**	405	**299**	257	215
ELGUIT	65	HAGSTROM	**SUPER III** WOOD BACK, PLASTIC TOP	333	**246**	211	176
ELGUIT	78	HAGSTROM	**SUPER SWEDE**	336	**248**	213	178
ELGUIT	76	HAGSTROM	**SWEDE** NATURAL	432	**319**	274	229
ELGUIT	71	HAGSTROM	**SWEDE BASS**	417	**308**	265	221

	TYPE	YR	MFG	PRICES--BASED ON 100% ORIGINAL MODEL	SELL EXC	SELL AVG	BUY EXC	BUY AVG
	ELGUIT	67	HAGSTROM	V-I SUNBURST	432	**319**	274	229
	ELGUIT	74	HAGSTROM	VIKING	384	**284**	244	204

HAMMOND SUZUKI USA, INC.

	TYPE	YR	MFG	MODEL	SELL EXC	SELL AVG	BUY EXC	BUY AVG
ORGAN		35	HAMMOND	A (2)61-KEY MANUALS, 25-PEDS, 18-PRESET KEYS, 4-SETS DRAWBARS	282	**208**	179	149
	ORGAN	59-65	HAMMOND	A-100 (2)61-KEY MANUALS, 25-PEDS, SPLIT/CHORUS VIB, STEREO REVERB	614	**454**	390	326
	ORGAN	61	HAMMOND	A-105 LOCKING TOP (2)61-KEY MANUALS, 25-PEDS, SPLIT VIB, VIB/STEREO CHORUS	716	**529**	455	380
	ORGAN	38	HAMMOND	AB (2)61-KEY MANUALS, 25-PEDS, 18-PRESET KEYS, 4-SETS DRAWBARS	267	**198**	170	142
	ORGAN	49-54	HAMMOND	B-2 CHORUS, 2-TONE GENERATORS (2)61-KEY MANUALS, 25-PEDS, MANUAL SPLIT VIB, STEREO REVERB	739	**546**	469	392
	ORGAN	55	HAMMOND	B-3 TONE CABINET (2)61-KEY MANUALS, 25-PEDS, SPLIT/CHORUS VIB, TOUCH PERC.	1,572	**1,162**	999	835
	ORGAN	36-42	HAMMOND	BC CHORUS, 2-TONE GENERATORS (2)61-KEY MANUALS, 25-PEDS, SPLIT VIB, VIB/STEREO CHORUS	590	**436**	375	313
	ORGAN	46-49	HAMMOND	BV CHORUS, 2-TONE GENERATORS (2)61-KEY MANUALS, 25-PEDS, VARIABLE/CHORUS VIB, STEREO REV	1,122	**829**	713	596
	ORGAN	39-42	HAMMOND	C LOWER CABINET ENCLOSED (2)61-KEY MANUALS, 25-PEDS, 18-PRESET KEYS, 4-SETS DRAWBARS	1,122	**829**	713	596
	ORGAN	49-54	HAMMOND	C-2 LOWER CABINET ENCLOSED (2)61-KEY MANUALS, 25-PEDS, MAN. SPLIT VIBRATO, STEREO REV.	595	**440**	378	316
	ORGAN	55	HAMMOND	C-3 LOWER CABINET ENCLOSED (2)61-KEY MANUALS, 25-PEDS, SPLIT/CHORUS VIB, TOUCH PERC.	803	**594**	510	426
	ORGAN	45-49	HAMMOND	CV LOWER CABINET ENCLOSED (2)61-KEY MANUALS, 25-PEDS, VARIABLE/CHORUS VIB, STEREO REV	230	**170**	146	122

HARMAN/KARDON

	TYPE	YR	MFG	MODEL	SELL EXC	SELL AVG	BUY EXC	BUY AVG
PRE		60-63	HARM	CITATION 1 KIT STEREO TUBE	343	**254**	218	182
	PRE	60	HARM	CITATION 2 STEREO TUBE	436	**323**	277	232
	PRE	60-63	HARM	CITATION 4 KIT STEREO TUBE	229	**169**	145	121
	PRE	60	HARM	CITATION 5 KIT STEREO TUBE	335	**247**	212	177
PWR		60-64	HARM	CITATION 2 STEREO TUBE, 60 WATT	575	**425**	365	305
	PWR	60-64	HARM	CITATION 5 KIT STEREO TUBE	478	**353**	303	253
	PWR	60	HARM	HK-20 MONO TUBE	72	**53**	46	38
	PWR	73	HARM	HK-250	122	**90**	78	65
TUNER		59	HARM	T-220 TUBE	122	**90**	78	65
	TUNER	59	HARM	T-230 TUBE	122	**90**	78	65

HARMONY, SEE ALSO STELLA

	TYPE	YR	MFG	MODEL	SELL EXC	SELL AVG	BUY EXC	BUY AVG
ELEC. GUITAR		56	HARMONY	AIRLINE BLACK w/WHITE, SEMI-HOLLOW	184	**136**	117	97
	ELGUIT	65	HARMONY	H-14	240	**177**	152	127
	ELGUIT	66	HARMONY	H-27 TOBACCO SUNBURST	170	**126**	108	90
	ELGUIT	60	HARMONY	H-61 SUNBURST	160	**118**	101	85
	ELGUIT	57	HARMONY	H-62 BLOND	301	**222**	191	160
	ELGUIT	58	HARMONY	H-62 BLOND	153	**113**	97	81
	ELGUIT	58	HARMONY	H-62 SUNBURST	185	**137**	117	98
	ELGUIT	60	HARMONY	H-62 BLOND, SINGLE CUTAWAY, ROSEWOOD	256	**189**	162	136
	ELGUIT	63	HARMONY	H-62 BLOND, CUTAWAY, ARCHTOP, INLAID BOARD	237	**175**	150	125
	ELGUIT	67	HARMONY	H-71	148	**110**	94	79
	ELGUIT	60	HARMONY	H-72 RED	200	**148**	127	106
	ELGUIT	69	HARMONY	H-72 RED	193	**143**	123	103
	ELGUIT	70	HARMONY	H-72 RED, DOUBLE CUTAWAY, SEMI-HOLLOW, 2 PU's	189	**139**	120	100
	ELGUIT	63	HARMONY	H-73 SUNBURST, SINGLE CUTAWAY, 2 PU's	300	**222**	190	159
	ELGUIT	66	HARMONY	H-73 SUNBURST, DOUBLE CUTAWAY, 2 PU's	300	**222**	190	159
	ELGUIT	58	HARMONY	H-75 RED, SINGLE CUTAWAY, SEMI-HOLLOW, 3 PU's	399	**295**	253	212
	ELGUIT	67	HARMONY	H-75 SUNBURST, 3 PU's	312	**230**	198	165

TYPE	YR	MFG	MODEL	SELL EXC	SELL AVG	BUY EXC	BUY AVG
ELGUIT	60	HARMONY	**H- 77** SUNBURST	432	**319**	274	229
ELGUIT	65	HARMONY	**H- 77** SUNBURST, DOUBLE CUTAWAY, THIN	399	**295**	253	212
ELGUIT	64	HARMONY	**H-116**	443	**328**	281	235
ELGUIT	60	HARMONY	**HOLIDAY** SUNBURST, 1 PU	240	**177**	152	127
ELGUIT	60	HARMONY	**HOLLYWOOD** SUNBURST, NON-CUT, 1 PU	191	**141**	121	101
ELGUIT	58	HARMONY	**METEOR** SUNBURST, SINGLE CUTAWAY, SEMI-HOLLOW	190	**140**	120	100
ELGUIT	65	HARMONY	**METEOR** SUNBURST, 2 PU's	240	**177**	152	127
ELGUIT	63	HARMONY	**METEOR S-60**	234	**173**	148	124
ELGUIT	63	HARMONY	**MONTEREY**	246	**182**	156	131
ELGUIT	65	HARMONY	**R-70** CHERRY RED, 12-STRING	283	**209**	179	150
ELGUIT	65	HARMONY	**R-79** CHERRY RED, 12-STRING	313	**232**	199	166
ELGUIT	60	HARMONY	**ROCKET** RED SUNBURST	177	**131**	112	94
ELGUIT	62	HARMONY	**ROCKET** RED SUNBURST	176	**130**	112	93
ELGUIT	63	HARMONY	**ROCKET** RED SUNBURST	216	**160**	137	115
ELGUIT	64	HARMONY	**ROCKET** RED SUNBURST	182	**134**	115	96
ELGUIT	65	HARMONY	**ROCKET** RED SUNBURST	176	**130**	112	93
ELGUIT	66	HARMONY	**ROCKET** RED SUNBURST	178	**132**	113	94
ELGUIT	68	HARMONY	**ROCKET** RED SUNBURST	195	**144**	124	104
ELGUIT	62	HARMONY	**ROCKET F-65**	169	**125**	107	90
ELGUIT	62	HARMONY	**ROCKET F-70**	168	**124**	107	89
ELGUIT	60	HARMONY	**ROCKET III**	219	**162**	139	116
ELGUIT	50	HARMONY	**ROY SMECK** MIDNIGHT BLUE	424	**313**	269	225
ELGUIT	71	HARMONY	**ROY SMECK** BLACK & WHITE	429	**317**	272	227
ELGUIT	60	HARMONY	**SILVERTONE** BLACK, SEMI-HOLLOW	148	**110**	94	79
ELGUIT	62	HARMONY	**SILVERTONE** BLACK, SEMI-HOLLOW	144	**106**	91	76
ELGUIT	64	HARMONY	**SILVERTONE** BLACK, SEMI-HOLLOW	139	**102**	88	73
ELGUIT	53	HARMONY	**STRAT-O-TONE**	249	**184**	158	132
ELGUIT	55	HARMONY	**STRAT-O-TONE** COPPER MIST	240	**177**	152	127
ELGUIT	56	HARMONY	**STRAT-O-TONE**	350	**259**	222	186
ELGUIT	59	HARMONY	**STRAT-O-TONE**	237	**175**	150	125
ELGUIT	60	HARMONY	**STRAT-O-TONE** MARS SUNBURST	258	**190**	164	137
ELGUIT	60	HARMONY	**STRAT-O-TONE** JUPITER BLACK	293	**217**	186	156
ELGUIT	61	HARMONY	**STRAT-O-TONE** JUPITER SPRUCE	265	**196**	168	141
ELGUIT	62	HARMONY	**STRAT-O-TONE** MERCURY BLOND	264	**195**	167	140
ELGUIT	63	HARMONY	**STRAT-O-TONE**	225	**166**	143	119
GUITAR AMP	67	HARMONY	**H-420** 115" SPEAKER, 20 WATTS, TUBE, COMBO	240	**177**	152	127
GUITAR (ACOUSTIC)	54	HARMONY	**BRILLIANT**	265	**196**	168	141
GUITAR	57	HARMONY	**BRILLIANT** SERIAL #631	375	**277**	238	199
GUITAR	69	HARMONY	**BUCK OWENS** RED, WHITE & BLUE	280	**207**	178	148
GUITAR	44	HARMONY	**CREMONA** ARCHTOP	336	**248**	213	178
GUITAR	50	HARMONY	**CREMONA VI** SUNBURST, MAPLE BACK/SIDES, PEARL INLAY	406	**300**	258	215
GUITAR	60	HARMONY	**ESPANADA**	241	**178**	153	128
GUITAR	59	HARMONY	**F-66GM** SPRUCE TOP	191	**141**	121	101
GUITAR	20	HARMONY	**FLATTOP** PEARL ROSETTE	296	**219**	188	157
GUITAR	62	HARMONY	**FLATTOP** NATURAL	157	**120**	102	78
GUITAR	58	HARMONY	**JAMBOREE**	190	**140**	120	100
GUITAR	50	HARMONY	**K-11** SUNBURST, CUTAWAY, ARCHTOP, 17", SOLID SPRUCE TOP	479	**354**	304	254

TYPE	YR	MFG	PRICES--BASED ON 100% ORIGINAL MODEL	SELL EXC	SELL AVG	BUY EXC	BUY AVG
GUITAR	60	HARMONY	MONTCLAIR BLACK, ARCHTOP	240	177	152	127
GUITAR	30	HARMONY	PATRICIAN ARCHTOP	438	324	278	233
GUITAR	38	HARMONY	PATRICIAN NATURAL, MAHOGANY, ARCHTOP	432	320	275	230
GUITAR	40	HARMONY	PATRICIAN	487	360	309	259
GUITAR	50	HARMONY	PATRICIAN NATURAL, MAHOGANY, ARCHTOP	518	383	329	275
GUITAR	54	HARMONY	PATRICIAN ARCHTOP, F-HOLES	489	362	311	260
GUITAR	55	HARMONY	PATRICIAN NATURAL, SPRUCE, ARCHTOP	441	326	280	234
GUITAR	63	HARMONY	PATRICIAN NATURAL, MAHOGANY, ARCHTOP	419	310	266	222
GUITAR	50	HARMONY	REGAL SUNBURST, ARCHTOP	241	178	153	128
GUITAR	60	HARMONY	SILVERTONE NATURAL, ARCHTOP	190	140	120	100
GUITAR	60	HARMONY	SILVERTONE SUNBURST, FLATTOP	190	140	120	100
GUITAR	57	HARMONY	SINGING COWBOY	168	124	106	89
GUITAR	59	HARMONY	SOVEREIGN FLATTOP	192	142	122	102
GUITAR	60	HARMONY	SOVEREIGN FLATTOP	172	127	109	91
GUITAR	62	HARMONY	SOVEREIGN FLATTOP	131	97	83	69
GUITAR	62	HARMONY	SOVEREIGN FLATTOP	170	126	108	90
GUITAR	63	HARMONY	SOVEREIGN FLATTOP	168	124	106	89
GUITAR	65	HARMONY	SOVEREIGN FLATTOP	142	105	90	75
GUITAR	68	HARMONY	SOVEREIGN FLATTOP	153	113	97	81
GUITAR	70	HARMONY	SOVEREIGN	216	159	137	114
MANDOLIN	50	HARMONY	410	216	159	137	114
MANDOL	40	HARMONY	F-47 SUNBURST, A STYLE F-HOLES	240	177	152	127
MANDOL	76	HARMONY	MODEL A F-HOLES	192	142	122	102
MANDOL	30	HARMONY	MONTEREY SUNBURST, TEARDROP SHAPE	203	150	129	108
MANDOL	60	HARMONY	MONTEREY SUNBURST, A STYLE F-HOLES	205	151	130	109
STEEL GUITAR	53	HARMONY	LAP STEEL GREY PEARLOID	201	149	128	107
UKULELE	54	HARMONY	BARITONE	126	93	80	67
UKE	55	HARMONY	BARITONE	172	127	109	91
UKE	25	HARMONY	JOHNNY MARVIN TENOR	235	173	149	124
UKE	35	HARMONY	ROY SMECK CONCERT	148	110	94	79
UKE	25	HARMONY	ROY SMECK VITA-UKE TEARDROP SHAPE	323	239	205	171
UKE	26	HARMONY	ROY SMECK VITA-UKE PEAR SHAPED, SEAL SHAPED F-HOLES	194	144	123	103
UKE	33	HARMONY	ROY SMECK VITA-UKE TEARDROP SHAPE	250	191	162	124

HAYNES OF BOSTON

GUITAR (ACOUSTIC)	10	HAYNES	BAY STATE BRAZILIAN ROSEWOOD BACK/SIDES	361	267	229	192
GUITAR	01	HAYNES	STYLE 6 BRAZILIAN ROSEWOOD BACK/SIDES	384	284	244	204
GUITAR	01	HAYNES	WURLITZER SPRUCE TOP, OAK BACK/SIDES	192	142	122	102

HEATHKIT

PRE	72	HEATH	WAP-2 MONO TUBE	80	59	51	42
PWR	51	HEATH	W-1 MONO TUBE	81	60	51	43
PWR	54	HEATH	W-2 MONO TUBE	88	65	56	46
PWR	54	HEATH	W-3 MONO TUBE	733	542	466	389
PWR	72	HEATH	W-4AM MONO TUBE	191	141	121	101
PWR	58-62	HEATH	W-4M MONO TUBE, 20 WATT	218	161	139	116
PWR	8	HEATH	W-5 KIT MONO TUBE	420	310	267	223

TYPE	YR	MFG	PRICES--BASED ON 100% ORIGINAL MODEL	SELL EXC	SELL AVG	BUY EXC	BUY AVG
PWR	72	HEATH	**W-5AM** TUBE	191	**141**	121	101
PWR	58-62	HEATH	**W-5M** MONO TUBE, 25 WATT	96	**71**	61	51
PWR	72	HEATH	**W-5M** MONO TUBE, 25 WATTS	192	**142**	122	102
PWR	58-62	HEATH	**W-6 KIT** MONO TUBE, 70 WATT	250	**185**	159	133
PWR	73	HEATH	**W-6M** MONO 70, PAIR	637	**471**	405	338
PWR	58-62	HEATH	**W-7 KIT** MONO TUBE, 55 WATT	180	**133**	114	95

HIEL

TYPE	YR	MFG	MODEL	SELL EXC	SELL AVG	BUY EXC	BUY AVG
EFFECTS	74	HIEL	**SQUAWKBOX "ORANGE"**	493	**364**	313	262
EFFECTS	74	HIEL	**TALKBOX "PURPLE"**	504	**372**	320	267

HIWATT AMPLIFICATION

TYPE	YR	MFG	MODEL	SELL EXC	SELL AVG	BUY EXC	BUY AVG
GUITAR AMP	71	HIWATT	**4x12" CAB FANE SPEAKERS**	598	**442**	380	317
GTAMP	72	HIWATT	**50 WATT HEAD**	556	**411**	353	295
GTAMP	72	HIWATT	**100 WATT HEAD**	685	**506**	435	364
GTAMP	70	HIWATT	**100 WATT PA HEAD**	569	**421**	361	302
GTAMP	75	HIWATT	**DR-504** AMP HEAD	438	**324**	278	233

HOFNER

TYPE	YR	MFG	MODEL	SELL EXC	SELL AVG	BUY EXC	BUY AVG
ELEC. GUITAR	58	HOFNER	**125** HOLLOW BODY, SINGLE CUTAWAY, 1 PU	625	**462**	397	332
ELGUIT	60	HOFNER	**126** HOLLOW BODY, SINGLE CUTAWAY, 2 PU's	644	**476**	409	342
ELGUIT	56	HOFNER	**160** NATURAL, SOLID BODY, 1 PU	456	**337**	290	242
ELGUIT	57	HOFNER	**162** BLACK, SOLID BODY, 2 PU's	472	**349**	300	250
ELGUIT	65	HOFNER	**164** DOUBLE CUTAWAY, 2 PU's	451	**333**	286	239
ELGUIT	60	HOFNER	**175** VINYL COVER	449	**332**	285	238
ELGUIT	67	HOFNER	**176** RED, SOLID BODY	401	**296**	254	213
ELGUIT	65	HOFNER	**185 BASS**	539	**399**	342	286
ELGUIT	64	HOFNER	**335** SUNBURST	499	**369**	317	265
ELGUIT	67	HOFNER	**427** SUNBURST, DOUBLE NECK 4/6	1,593	**1,178**	1,012	846
ELGUIT	74	HOFNER	**448 ELECTRIC UPRIGHT** NATURAL, SPRUCE	621	**459**	394	329
ELGUIT	65	HOFNER	**470 SE2** NATURAL, CUTAWAY, 2 PU's	384	**284**	244	204
ELGUIT	62	HOFNER	**500 1** CLOSE DIAMOND PU, SERIAL #317-349	7,216	**5,337**	4,585	3,833
ELGUIT	57	HOFNER	**500 1 BASS** PRE-BEATLE SPRUCE	4,320	**3,195**	2,745	2,295
ELGUIT	62	HOFNER	**500 1 BEATLE BASS** LEFT-HANDED, SERIAL #191-292	5,723	**4,233**	3,636	3,040
ELGUIT	63	HOFNER	**500 1 BEATLE BASS**	3,360	**2,485**	2,135	1,785
ELGUIT	64	HOFNER	**500 1 BEATLE BASS**	2,915	**2,156**	1,852	1,548
ELGUIT	64	HOFNER	**500 1 BEATLE BASS** LEFT-HANDED	4,122	**3,048**	2,619	2,189
ELGUIT	65	HOFNER	**500 1 BEATLE BASS** SERIAL #402-500	1,606	**1,187**	1,020	853
ELGUIT	65	HOFNER	**500 1 BEATLE BASS** LEFT-HANDED	4,111	**3,040**	2,612	2,184
ELGUIT	66	HOFNER	**500 1 BEATLE BASS**	1,540	**1,139**	979	818
ELGUIT	67	HOFNER	**500 1 BEATLE BASS**	1,502	**1,111**	954	798
ELGUIT	68	HOFNER	**500 1 BEATLE BASS**	1,626	**1,202**	1,033	863
ELGUIT	69	HOFNER	**500 1 BEATLE BASS**	1,264	**935**	803	671
ELGUIT	70	HOFNER	**500 1 BEATLE BASS** ICED TEA SUNBURST	1,271	**940**	807	675
ELGUIT	71	HOFNER	**500 1 BEATLE BASS** LEFT-HANDED	1,088	**805**	691	578
ELGUIT	71	HOFNER	**500 1 BEATLE BASS**	1,135	**839**	721	603
ELGUIT	73	HOFNER	**500 1 BEATLE BASS**	1,102	**815**	700	585
ELGUIT	74	HOFNER	**500 1 BEATLE BASS**	1,100	**813**	699	584
ELGUIT	75	HOFNER	**500 1 BEATLE BASS**	1,101	**814**	699	584
ELGUIT	78	HOFNER	**500 1 BEATLE BASS**	988	**731**	628	525
ELGUIT	79	HOFNER	**500 1 BEATLE BASS**	984	**727**	625	522
ELGUIT	56	HOFNER	**500 1 VIOLIN BASS**	7,680	**5,680**	4,880	4,080
ELGUIT	59	HOFNER	**500 1 VIOLIN BASS** SERIAL #107-191	5,081	**3,758**	3,228	2,699
ELGUIT	60	HOFNER	**500 1 VIOLIN BASS**	5,091	**3,765**	3,235	2,705
ELGUIT	61	HOFNER	**500 1 VIOLIN BASS**	5,081	**3,758**	3,228	2,699

TYPE	YR	MFG	PRICES--BASED ON 100% ORIGINAL MODEL	SELL EXC	SELL AVG	BUY EXC	BUY AVG
ELGUIT	62	HOFNER	**500 1 VIOLIN BASS**	4,800	**3,550**	3,050	2,550
ELGUIT	63	HOFNER	**500 1 VIOLIN BASS** SERIAL #293-401	5,760	**4,260**	3,660	3,060
ELGUIT	57	HOFNER	**500 2 CLUB BASS** SUNBURST, SINGLE CUT, 2 PU's, STARTING SERIAL #29900	1,832	**1,355**	1,164	973
ELGUIT	58	HOFNER	**500 2 CLUB BASS** SUNBURST, SINGLE CUT, 2 PU's	2,346	**1,735**	1,490	1,246
ELGUIT	60	HOFNER	**500 2 CLUB BASS** SUNBURST, SINGLE CUT, 2 PU's, STARTING SERIAL #30290	1,872	**1,385**	1,190	995
ELGUIT	60	HOFNER	**500 3 BEATLE BASS** SUNBURST, SEMI-HOLLOW BODY, 2 PU's	1,422	**1,052**	904	755
ELGUIT	62	HOFNER	**500 3 BEATLE BASS** SEMI-HOLLOW BODY	1,117	**826**	710	593
ELGUIT	62	HOFNER	**500 6 BEATLE BASS** SUNBURST, DOUBLE CUTAWAY, 2 PU's	1,369	**1,013**	870	727
ELGUIT	67	HOFNER	**500 6 BEATLE BASS** SUNBURST, DOUBLE CUTAWAY	977	**722**	620	519
ELGUIT	67	HOFNER	**527** 6/4 DOUBLE NECK, SOLID BODY	1,211	**896**	769	643
ELGUIT	69	HOFNER	**BEATLE BASS**	1,271	**940**	807	675
ELGUIT	58	HOFNER	**CLUB 40** ONE PU	1,115	**825**	708	592
ELGUIT	59	HOFNER	**CLUB 50** BLOND	869	**643**	552	462
ELGUIT	61	HOFNER	**CLUB 50** SUNBURST	790	**584**	502	419
ELGUIT	58-62	HOFNER	**CLUB 60** FLAME MAPLE BACK	1,593	**1,178**	1,012	846
ELGUIT	58	HOFNER	**CLUB 60 BASS** BLACK or NATURAL, 2 PU's, SERIAL #101-147	4,526	**3,347**	2,876	2,404
ELGUIT	59	HOFNER	**CLUB 60 BASS** NATURAL, 2 PU's	2,390	**1,767**	1,518	1,269
ELGUIT	59	HOFNER	**CLUB 60 BASS** BLACK, VERTICAL LOGO, 2 PU's, SERIAL #147-165	3,840	**2,840**	2,440	2,040
ELGUIT	60	HOFNER	**CLUB 60 BASS** VERTICAL LOGO, 2 PU's	3,360	**2,485**	2,135	1,785
ELGUIT	59	HOFNER	**COMMITTEE** F-HOLE, 2 PU's	959	**709**	609	509
ELGUIT	63	HOFNER	**COMMITTEE BASS** NATURAL	1,513	**1,119**	961	804
ELGUIT	61	HOFNER	**GOLDEN HOFNER**	783	**579**	497	416
ELGUIT	59	HOFNER	**PRESIDENT** F-HOLES, 2 PU's	2,145	**1,586**	1,363	1,139
ELGUIT	60	HOFNER	**PRESIDENT** NATURAL	1,677	**1,240**	1,065	890
ELGUIT	66	HOFNER	**PRESIDENT**	796	**589**	506	423
ELGUIT	63	HOFNER	**PRESIDENT BASS** NATURAL	1,000	**739**	635	531
ELGUIT	65	HOFNER	**PRESIDENT BASS** SUNBURST	796	**589**	506	423
ELGUIT	68	HOFNER	**PRESIDENT BASS** SUNBURST, SINGLE CUTAWAY	1,243	**919**	789	660
ELGUIT	65	HOFNER	**RANGER** RAISED LOGO, SINGLE CUTAWAY, TINA WEYMOUTH TALKING HEADS	840	**621**	533	446
ELGUIT	67	HOFNER	**VERI-THIN** RUST	483	**357**	307	257
ELGUIT	67	HOFNER	**VIOLIN GUITAR** FUZZ TONE	480	**355**	305	255
GUITAR AMP	70	HOFNER	**KV-40**	200	**148**	127	106
GUITAR (ACOUSTIC)	51	HOFNER	**463-S** SPRUCE, ARCHTOP, CUTAWAY	2,191	**1,620**	1,392	1,164
GUITAR	72	HOFNER	**974** SPRUCE TOP, MAHOGANY BACK/SIDES	1,007	**744**	639	534
GUITAR	70	HOFNER	**SLAP-BASS STANDARD**	336	**248**	213	178
UPRIG	71	HOFNER	**UPRIGHT BASS** SPRUCE TOP, MAPLE BACK/SIDES	3,840	**2,840**	2,440	2,040

HOHNER

TYPE	YR	MFG	MODEL	SELL EXC	SELL AVG	BUY EXC	BUY AVG
EFFECTS	78	HOHNER	**DIRTY WAH WAH'ER**	96	**71**	61	51
GUITAR AMP	65	HOHNER	**6149 DELUXE REVERB UNIT**	240	**177**	152	127
SYNTHESIZER	72	HOHNER	**C-86 63 KEY**	177	**131**	112	94
SYNTH	70	HOHNER	**C-88 63 KEY**	182	**134**	115	96

TOM HOLMES

TYPE	YR	MFG	MODEL	SELL EXC	SELL AVG	BUY EXC	BUY AVG
ELEC. GUITAR	72	HOLMES	**THC** BLACK	216	**159**	137	114

HOYER

TYPE	YR	MFG	MODEL	SELL EXC	SELL AVG	BUY EXC	BUY AVG
ELEC. GUITAR	67	HOYER	**150** SUNBURST, SEMI-HOLLOW BODY, 2 PU's	288	**213**	183	153
ELGUIT	62	HOYER	**SOLOIST** BLOND, CUTAWAY	654	**498**	423	323
ELGUIT	65	HOYER	**VIOLIN BASS** 1 PU	470	**347**	298	249

TYPE	YR	MFG	PRICES--BASED ON 100% ORIGINAL MODEL	SELL EXC	SELL AVG	BUY EXC	BUY AVG
ELGUIT	66	HOYER	**VIOLIN BASS** 2 PU's	554	**410**	352	294
GUITAR AMP	64	HOYER	**J-45**	288	**213**	183	153

IBANEZ

TYPE	YR	MFG	MODEL	SELL EXC	SELL AVG	BUY EXC	BUY AVG
EFFECTS	80	IBANEZ	**AD-80** MAGENTA, ANALOG DELAY	168	**124**	106	89
EFFECTS	79	IBANEZ	**MUSICIAN EQUALIZER BASS**	456	**337**	289	242
EFFECTS	79	IBANEZ	**PT-909**	120	**88**	76	63
EFFECTS	80	IBANEZ	**PT-909** PHASE TONE	155	**115**	98	82
EFFECTS	75	IBANEZ	**PT-999** PHASE TONE, SLANT TOP	144	**106**	91	76
EFFECTS	79	IBANEZ	**TS- 9**	150	**111**	95	80
EFFECTS	78	IBANEZ	**TS-808** TUBE SCREAMER	438	**324**	278	233
EFFECTS	78	IBANEZ	**UE-300** MULTI-EFFECTS	240	**177**	152	127
ELEC. GUITAR	74	IBANEZ	**175 COPY** SUNBURST or BLOND	480	**355**	305	255
ELGUIT	73	IBANEZ	**2355**	577	**427**	367	307
ELGUIT	74	IBANEZ	**2402**	637	**471**	405	338
ELGUIT	75	IBANEZ	**2404**	557	**412**	354	296
ELGUIT	76	IBANEZ	**2460**	956	**707**	607	507
ELGUIT	78	IBANEZ	**2680 BOB WEIR STANDARD** CARVED SOLID ASH BODY,6-STRING,MAPLE NECK,EBONY FRTBRD	408	**301**	259	216
ELGUIT	79	IBANEZ	**2681 BOB WEIR** CARVED SOLID ASH BODY,6-STRING,MAPLE NECK,EBONY FRTBRD	877	**648**	557	466
ELGUIT	80	IBANEZ	**AM-205**	628	**465**	399	334
ELGUIT	78	IBANEZ	**AR- 50 ARTIST** MAHOG BODY,CARVED MAPLE TOP,BIRCH NECK,CHROME HDWR	464	**343**	295	246
ELGUIT	79	IBANEZ	**AR-200 ARTIST**	778	**575**	494	413
ELGUIT	76	IBANEZ	**ARTIST** SCROLL VINE INLAYS	598	**442**	380	317
ELGUIT	79	IBANEZ	**ARTIST** SEMI HOLLOWBODY	557	**412**	354	296
ELGUIT	80	IBANEZ	**AS- 50 ARTIST SEMI-ACOUSTIC**	477	**352**	303	253
ELGUIT	80	IBANEZ	**AS- 80**	501	**370**	318	266
ELGUIT	78	IBANEZ	**CN-250 CONCERT** VINE INLAY ON BOARD	478	**353**	303	253
ELGUIT	80	IBANEZ	**CUSTOM AGENT LES PAUL STYLE**	580	**429**	369	308
ELGUIT	76	IBANEZ	**DESTROYER** KORINA	764	**565**	485	405
ELGUIT	77	IBANEZ	**DESTROYER** KORINA, NATURAL, MADE IN JAPAN	691	**511**	439	367
ELGUIT	82	IBANEZ	**DESTROYER II**	469	**347**	298	249
ELGUIT	69	IBANEZ	**DOUBLE NECK** SG STYLE, 6+4-STRING	304	**232**	197	150
ELGUIT	76	IBANEZ	**FIREBIRD COPY** NON-REVERSE	342	**253**	217	182
ELGUIT	77	IBANEZ	**GB-10 GEORGE BENSON**	881	**651**	559	468
ELGUIT	78	IBANEZ	**GB-10 GEORGE BENSON** SUNBURST	873	**646**	555	464
ELGUIT	79	IBANEZ	**GB-10 GEORGE BENSON** NATURAL	961	**711**	611	511
ELGUIT	80	IBANEZ	**GB-10 GEORGE BENSON** SUNBURST	867	**641**	551	461
ELGUIT	76	IBANEZ	**ICEMAN** RICK NELSON, KORINA	1,191	**881**	757	632
ELGUIT	77	IBANEZ	**ICEMAN** PAUL STANLEY	955	**706**	606	507
ELGUIT	78	IBANEZ	**ICEMAN** BOLT-ON NECK	384	**284**	244	204
ELGUIT	77	IBANEZ	**JAZZ BASS SILVER SERIES** BROWN	480	**355**	305	255
ELGUIT	76	IBANEZ	**JOHNNY SMITH** BLOND	1,276	**944**	811	678
ELGUIT	82	IBANEZ	**JP-20 JOE PASS**	1,136	**840**	722	603
ELGUIT	76	IBANEZ	**KORINA V**	768	**568**	488	408
ELGUIT	79	IBANEZ	**KORINA V**	761	**563**	483	404
ELGUIT	80	IBANEZ	**LES PAUL DELUXE** 2 PU's	206	**152**	131	109
ELGUIT	78	IBANEZ	**LES PAUL PERFORMER COPY** 3 PU's	220	**163**	140	117
ELGUIT	79	IBANEZ	**LES PAUL TV JUNIOR COPY** GLUED-IN	237	**175**	150	125
ELGUIT	80	IBANEZ	**LES PAUL TV SPECIAL COPY** GLUED-IN	266	**197**	169	141
ELGUIT	76	IBANEZ	**MODERNERE** NATURAL, MADE IN JAPAN	921	**681**	585	489
ELGUIT	80	IBANEZ	**MODERNERE** MAHOGANY	747	**553**	475	397

TYPE		YR	MFG	PRICES--BASED ON 100% ORIGINAL MODEL	SELL EXC	SELL AVG	BUY EXC	BUY AVG
ELGUIT		78	IBANEZ	**PF-100** WALNUT	278	**205**	176	147
ELGUIT		70	IBANEZ	**PF-200** SUNBURST	288	**213**	183	153
ELGUIT		78	IBANEZ	**PF-200** BOLT-ON	288	**213**	183	153
ELGUIT		78	IBANEZ	**PF-300** SET NECK	557	**412**	354	296
ELGUIT		78	IBANEZ	**PROFESSIONAL BOB WEIR**	1,001	**740**	636	531
ELGUIT		78	IBANEZ	**PS-10 PAUL STANLEY SIGNATURE**	699	**517**	444	371
ELGUIT		76	IBANEZ	**SCRUGGS** NATURAL	1,018	**753**	647	541
ELGUIT		78	IBANEZ	**ST-300NT STUDIO** NATURAL	480	**355**	305	255
ELGUIT		62	IBANEZ	**TULIO** RED	537	**397**	341	285
SIGNAL PROCESSOR		82	IBANEZ	**TS- 9 TUBE SCREAMER**	113	**83**	71	60
	SGNPRO	80	IBANEZ	**TS-808 TUBE SCREAMER**	154	**114**	98	82
UPRIG		76	IBANEZ	**CONCORD** NATURAL, CURLY MAPLE, MADE IN JAPAN, COPY OF GUILD F-50	422	**312**	268	224

JBL LOUDSPEAKERS

TYPE		YR	MFG	MODEL	SELL EXC	SELL AVG	BUY EXC	BUY AVG
RAW		76	JBL	**002 SYSTEM** NO CABINET	219	**162**	139	116
	RAW	64	JBL	**075 HORN TWEETER** RING RADIATOR	173	**128**	110	92
	RAW	71	JBL	**077 TWEETER SLOT HORN**	181	**134**	115	96
	RAW	64	JBL	**130A** 15"	267	**198**	170	142
	RAW	64-72	JBL	**130B**	254	**188**	161	135
	RAW	60	JBL	**150-4C** 15" WOOFER	292	**216**	186	155
	RAW	60-72	JBL	**150-4C** 15" WOOFER	300	**222**	190	159
	RAW	75	JBL	**2202** 12" WOOFER	158	**117**	100	84
	RAW	62	JBL	**D-123** 12"	118	**87**	75	62
	RAW	68-82	JBL	**D-130** 15"	196	**145**	125	104
	RAW	60	JBL	**D-216** 8" PAIR	157	**116**	100	83
	RAW	60	JBL	**LE- 8** 8" PAIR	157	**116**	100	83
	RAW	68	JBL	**LE-15A** 15" WOOFER	214	**158**	136	113
SPKR		64-68	JBL	**D-30085 HARTSFIELD**	4,971	**3,677**	3,159	2,641
XOVER		77	JBL	**N-1200 FREQUENCY NETWORK**	85	**63**	54	45

JENSEN

TYPE		YR	MFG	MODEL	SELL EXC	SELL AVG	BUY EXC	BUY AVG
RAW		60	JENSEN	**C-12NF 12" PAIR**	117	**86**	74	62
	RAW	60	JENSEN	**DX-120 12" PAIR**	117	**86**	74	62
	RAW	73	JENSEN	**G-610B**	404	**298**	256	214
	RAW	60	JENSEN	**K-210 12" PAIR**	115	**85**	73	61
	RAW	60	JENSEN	**RP-302A TWEETER PAIR**	115	**85**	73	61

JUZEK

TYPE		YR	MFG	MODEL	SELL EXC	SELL AVG	BUY EXC	BUY AVG
UPRIG		47	JUZEK	**UPRIGHT STRING BASS** FULLY CARVE, SPRUCE TOP, FLAMED MAPLE BACK/SIDES	4,582	**3,388**	2,911	2,434
	UPRIGHT	50	JUZEK	**UPRIGHT STRING BASS** FULLY CARVED, VIOLIN CORNERS	6,111	**4,519**	3,883	3,246

KALAMAZOO

TYPE		YR	MFG	MODEL	SELL EXC	SELL AVG	BUY EXC	BUY AVG
BANJO		37	KALAMAZOO	**KALAMAZOO** 5-STRING	1,056	**781**	671	561
ELEC. GUITAR		67	KALAMAZOO	**KB BASS** RED, 1 PU	432	**320**	275	230
	ELGUIT	68	KALAMAZOO	**KB BASS** RED, 1 PU	400	**296**	254	212
	ELGUIT	66	KALAMAZOO	**KG-1A** BLUE, 1 PU	425	**314**	270	225
	ELGUIT	68	KALAMAZOO	**SG SOLID BODY** RED, 1 PU, ROSEWOOD FRETBOARD	287	**212**	182	152
GUITAR AMP		67	KALAMAZOO	**REVERB 12**	192	**142**	122	102
GUITAR (ACOUSTIC)		40	KALAMAZOO	**HG-00** SUNBURST	371	**274**	236	197
	GUITAR	38	KALAMAZOO	**K-14** SUNBURST	466	**345**	296	247
	GUITAR	36	KALAMAZOO	**KG- 3/4** SUNBURST, FLATTOP	343	**254**	218	182
	GUITAR	35	KALAMAZOO	**KG- 1**	450	**332**	286	239
	GUITAR	39	KALAMAZOO	**KG-10** SUNBURST, ARCHTOP	478	**353**	303	253

	TYPE	YR	MFG	PRICES--BASED ON 100% ORIGINAL MODEL	SELL EXC	SELL AVG	BUY EXC	BUY AVG
	GUITAR	37	KALAMAZOO	**KG-11** SUNBURST, FLATTOP	424	**313**	269	225
	GUITAR	37	KALAMAZOO	**KG-14** SUNBURST, FLATTOP	424	**313**	269	225
	GUITAR	39	KALAMAZOO	**KG-16** SUNBURST, ARCHTOP	415	**307**	264	220
	GUITAR	37	KALAMAZOO	**KG-31** SUNBURST, ARCHTOP	496	**367**	315	263
	GUITAR	41	KALAMAZOO	**KGN-12** NATURAL, FLATTOP	369	**273**	234	196
	GUITAR	40	KALAMAZOO	**KGN-32** BLOND, ORIOLE ARCHTOP	480	**355**	305	255
	GUITAR	41	KALAMAZOO	**KGN-32** NATURAL	280	**207**	178	148
	GUITAR	36	KALAMAZOO	**KHG-11** SUNBURST, HAWAIIAN	349	**258**	222	185
	GUITAR	38	KALAMAZOO	**KTG-14 SENIOR L-0 SIZE TENOR** SUNBURST	384	**284**	244	204
	GUITAR	35	KALAMAZOO	**ORIOLE ARCHTOP**	349	**258**	222	185
	GUITAR	37	KALAMAZOO	**SPORT MODEL**	379	**280**	240	201
	GUITAR	30	KALAMAZOO	**TENOR** SUNBURST, FLATTOP, MAHOGANY BACK/SIDES	309	**228**	196	164
	GUITAR	31	KALAMAZOO	**TENOR** SUNBURST, FLATTOP	312	**231**	198	166
MANDOLIN		37	KALAMAZOO	**KM- 2** SUNBURST, A STYLE F-HOLES, MAPLE BACK/SIDES	389	**288**	247	207
	MANDOL	36	KALAMAZOO	**KM-21** SUNBURST, F-HOLES	466	**345**	296	247
STEEL GUITAR		39	KALAMAZOO	**KEH LAP STEEL** BROWN	261	**193**	165	138
	STGUIT	40	KALAMAZOO	**KEH LAP STEEL** WALNUT, SERIAL #FKE731	334	**247**	212	177

KAMAKA

	TYPE	YR	MFG	MODEL	SELL EXC	SELL AVG	BUY EXC	BUY AVG
UKULELE		70	KAMAKA	**PINEAPPLE**	384	**284**	244	204
	UKE	30	KAMAKA	**PLAIN KOA**	307	**227**	195	163
	UKE	65	KAMAKA	**PLAIN STANDARD SHAPE**	249	**184**	158	132
	UKE	50	KAMAKA	**PLAIN TENOR**	312	**230**	198	165

KAY GUITAR COMPANY

	TYPE	YR	MFG	MODEL	SELL EXC	SELL AVG	BUY EXC	BUY AVG
BANJO		30	KAY	**KRAFT** KEY-CHORD	480	**355**	305	255
	BANJO	35	KAY	**KRAFT** SUNBURST, WOOD BODY, RESONATOR	457	**338**	290	243
	BANJO	36	KAY	**KRAFT TENOR**	184	**136**	117	97
	BANJO	15	KAY	**ORPHEUM #1 TENOR** OPEN BACK	313	**232**	199	166
	BANJO	60	KAY	**SILVERTONE** 5-STRING	192	**142**	122	102
	BANJO	50	KAY	**SILVERTONE TENOR**	102	**75**	65	54
	BANJO	40	KAY	**TENOR** MAHOGANY NECK	152	**112**	96	81
	BANJO	50	KAY	**TENOR** DEEP RESONATOR	125	**93**	79	66
	BANJO	60	KAY	**TENOR** 19-FRET, RESONATOR, SERIAL #2847-28	102	**75**	65	54
ELEC. GUITAR		58	KAY	**BARNEY KESSEL STYLE** MAPLE, ARCHTOP	271	**200**	172	144
	ELGUIT	58	KAY	**BARNEY KESSEL STYLE** BLACK	306	**226**	194	162
	ELGUIT	61	KAY	**CATALINA** SUNBURST	304	**225**	193	161
	ELGUIT	60	KAY	**JAZZ SPECIAL**	311	**230**	197	165
	ELGUIT	58	KAY	**JUMBO** SUNBURST, CUATWAY, ARCHTOP, 2 PU's	261	**193**	165	138
	ELGUIT	52	KAY	**K- 161 THIN TWIN**	185	**137**	117	98
	ELGUIT	53	KAY	**K- 161 THIN TWIN** LES PAUL SHAPE, 2 PU's	162	**119**	103	86
	ELGUIT	58	KAY	**K- 161 THIN TWIN** LES PAUL SHAPE	148	**110**	94	79
	ELGUIT	58	KAY	**K- 161 THIN TWIN** JIMM REED, NATURAL	153	**113**	97	81
	ELGUIT	58	KAY	**K- 161 THIN TWIN** BLOND, CURLY MAPLE	156	**115**	99	83
	ELGUIT	59	KAY	**K- 161 THIN TWIN** SEMI-ACOUSTIC	158	**117**	100	84
	ELGUIT	54	KAY	**K- 21S SPEED DEMON** SOLID BODY	336	**248**	213	178
	ELGUIT	67	KAY	**K- 405** WHITE, BIGSBY VIBRATO	147	**109**	93	78
	ELGUIT	60	KAY	**K- 535** DOUBLE CUTAWAY, VIBRATO, 2 PU's	220	**163**	140	117

	YR	MFG	PRICES--BASED ON 100% ORIGINAL MODEL	SELL EXC	SELL AVG	BUY EXC	BUY AVG
ELGUIT	62	KAY	**K- 671 OLD KRAFTSMAN** FLAME MAPLE	172	**127**	109	91
ELGUIT	63	KAY	**K- 671 OLD KRAFTSMAN** SUNBURST	152	**112**	96	81
ELGUIT	66	KAY	**K-5935** BROWN SUNBURST, STRAT, 1 PU	127	**94**	81	67
ELGUIT	64	KAY	**K-5953 BASS** SOLIDBODY	217	**161**	138	115
ELGUIT	59	KAY	**K-6000**	186	**137**	118	98
ELGUIT	60	KAY	**K-8900 JAZZ SPECIAL**	263	**194**	167	139
ELGUIT	52	KAY	**K-8901** SUNBURST, CUTAWAY, ARCHTOP	269	**199**	171	143
ELGUIT	62	KAY	**KAY** RED, SEMI-HOLLOW, CUTAWAY, 2 PU's	169	**125**	107	90
ELGUIT	55	KAY	**KAY SB** SEMI-SOLLOW, CUTAWAY, 3 PU's	262	**200**	170	130
ELGUIT	30	KAY	**KRAFT RECORDING KING**	345	**255**	219	183
ELGUIT	40	KAY	**O-100 SWING BASS**	690	**510**	438	366
ELGUIT	62	KAY	**SEMI HOLLOW** TRANSPARENT RED, CUTAWAY, 2 PU's	240	**178**	153	128
ELGUIT	58	KAY	**SEMI-HOLLOW** SUNBURST, CUTAWAY, NP F-HOLES	283	**209**	179	150
ELGUIT	62	KAY	**SEMI-HOLLOW** WALNUT, BIGSBY, MAPLE NECK, 3 PU's	280	**207**	178	148
ELGUIT	52	KAY	**SHERWOOD DELUXE** SUNBURST, 16", SINGLE PU	287	**212**	182	152
ELGUIT	55	KAY	**SILVERTONE** SUNBURST, JIMMY REED MODEL	333	**246**	211	176
ELGUIT	60	KAY	**SILVERTONE** NATURAL	192	**142**	122	102
ELGUIT	62	KAY	**SILVERTONE** NATURAL, ARCHED TOP/BACK	143	**105**	90	75
ELGUIT	62	KAY	**SILVERTONE** NATURAL, HOLLOW, CUTAWAY	143	**105**	90	75
ELGUIT	50	KAY	**SOLID BODY** BOLT-ON NECK, 2 MIRROW PU's	168	**124**	106	89
ELGUIT	62	KAY	**SWINGMASTER**	312	**230**	198	165
ELGUIT	50	KAY	**THIN** HOLLOW BODY, ELEC, F-HOLE, 1 PU	215	**159**	136	114
ELGUIT	62	KAY	**THIN** BROWN SUNBURST, HOLLOW BODY, SINGLE CUTAWAY	188	**139**	119	99
ELGUIT	65	KAY	**THIN** HOLLOW BODY, DOUBLE CUTAWAY	243	**180**	154	129
ELGUIT	52	KAY	**TRUETONE** SUNBURST	190	**140**	120	100
ELGUIT	55	KAY	**UPBEAT** SUNBURST, 2 PU's	308	**227**	195	163
GUITAR AMP	60	KAY	**K-503A** BLACK-WHITE, 1x8" SPEAKER	77	**57**	49	41
GTAMP	60	KAY	**MODEL 703** 1x8" SPEAKER, 6 WATTS	105	**78**	67	56
GUITAR (ACOUSTIC)	60	KAY	**CLASSICAL STRING BASS**	717	**530**	455	380
GUITAR	30	KAY	**DELUXE** SUNBURST, ROUND SOUND HOLE	480	**355**	305	255
GUITAR	29	KAY	**GABRIEL** FLATTOP	403	**298**	256	214
GUITAR	62	KAY	**JAZZ II**	234	**173**	148	124
GUITAR	55	KAY	**JUMBO** SPRUCE, ARCHTOP, NON-CUTAWAY, 1 PU	191	**141**	121	101
GUITAR	56	KAY	**JUMBO** SPRUCE TOP, MAHOGANY, FLATTOP	248	**183**	157	132
GUITAR	57	KAY	**K- 18**	240	**177**	152	127
GUITAR	48	KAY	**K- 21** SILVERTONE BLOND, SPRUCE TOP	379	**280**	240	201
GUITAR	50	KAY	**K- 21** BLOND	361	**267**	229	192
GUITAR	52	KAY	**K- 21** CHERRY SUNBURST	357	**264**	226	189
GUITAR	53	KAY	**K- 21** BLOND	358	**264**	227	190
GUITAR	60	KAY	**K- 21S SPEED DEMON**	241	**178**	153	128
GUITAR	50	KAY	**K- 24**	240	**177**	152	127
GUITAR	53	KAY	**K- 27**	241	**178**	153	128
GUITAR	38	KAY	**K- 40** SUNBURST, ARCHTOP	433	**320**	275	230
GUITAR	25	KAY	**KAYKRAFT** SUNBURST, FLATTOP	265	**196**	168	141
GUITAR	32	KAY	**KAYKRAFT** ARCHTOP	240	**178**	153	128
GUITAR	36	KAY	**KAYKRAFT "A"**	265	**196**	168	141
GUITAR	38	KAY	**KAYKRAFT "B"**	313	**232**	199	166
GUITAR	38	KAY	**KAYKRAFT "C"**	369	**281**	239	183

TYPE	YR	MFG	PRICES--BASED ON 100% ORIGINAL MODEL	SELL EXC	SELL AVG	BUY EXC	BUY AVG
GUITAR	59	KAY	**KESSEL ARTIST**	300	**222**	190	159
GUITAR	57	KAY	**KESSEL JAZZ SP**	263	**194**	167	139
GUITAR	58	KAY	**KESSEL JAZZ SP**	286	**211**	181	151
GUITAR	59	KAY	**KESSEL JAZZ SP**	269	**199**	171	143
GUITAR	58	KAY	**KESSEL PRO**	101	**77**	65	50
GUITAR	42	KAY	**LOUISE MASSEY** FLATTOP	408	**301**	259	216
GUITAR	70	KAY	**M-1 MAESTRO STRING BASS**	796	**589**	506	423
GUITAR	70	KAY	**M-5 STRING BASS**	1,434	**1,060**	911	761
GUITAR	30	KAY	**MODEL A**	384	**284**	244	204
GUITAR	58	KAY	**N-1 CUT FLATTOP JUMBO**	288	**213**	183	153
GUITAR	60	KAY	**N-1 CUT FLATTOP JUMBO** SOLID SPRUCE	281	**208**	178	149
GUITAR	36	KAY	**O SUNBURST**	191	**141**	121	101
GUITAR	40	KAY	**ORPHEUM** SUNBURST, ARCHTOP	225	**166**	143	119
GUITAR	62	KAY	**P-3 JUMBO** ORANGE	313	**232**	199	166
GUITAR	50	KAY	**PLECTRUM** 1 PU	158	**117**	100	84
GUITAR	30	KAY	**RECORDING KING** FLATTOP, ASYMMETRICAL	363	**269**	231	193
GUITAR	34	KAY	**RECORDING KING** 2 POINT ARCHTOP	358	**264**	227	190
GUITAR	55	KAY	**RESONATOR** MAHOGANY BODY, 14-FRET	314	**232**	200	167
GUITAR	55	KAY	**SIERRA** SUNBURST, SOLID SPRUCE, CUTAWAY, FLAME MAPLE BACK/SIDES	287	**212**	182	152
GUITAR	50	KAY	**SILVERTONE** SUNBURST, ARCHTOP	213	**157**	135	113
GUITAR	55	KAY	**SILVERTONE** SUNBURST, FLATTOP	230	**170**	146	122
GUITAR	60	KAY	**SILVERTONE** SUNBURST, SINGLE CUTAWAY	427	**315**	271	226
GUITAR	49	KAY	**SPECIAL 40**	313	**232**	199	166
MANDOLIN	30	KAY	**KRAFT** SUNBURST	283	**209**	179	150
STEEL GUITAR	58	KAY	**K- 24**	250	**185**	159	133
STGUIT	61	KAY	**K- 24**	240	**177**	152	127
UPRIG	60	KAY	**BASS FIDDLE** ROSEWOOD FINGERBOARD	816	**604**	519	434
UPRIGHT	45	KAY	**MODEL C-1**	865	**640**	550	460
UPRIGHT	45	KAY	**UPRIGHT BASS** SN-10711	1,058	**783**	672	562
UPRIGHT	55	KAY	**UPRIGHT BASS**	738	**545**	469	392

KENTUCKY

MANDOLIN	88	KENTUCKY	**KM-JR A-MODEL** CARVED, TOP-MATCHED SOLID SPRUCE, SOLID MAPLE BACK/SIDES	171	**127**	109	91

KOLSTEIN

STEEL GUITAR	79	KOLSTEIN	**PANORMO STRING BASS COPY** HARD MAPLE	20,973	**15,511**	13,326	11,141
UPRIG	80	KOLSTEIN	**MAGANTAL** 5-STRING	27,360	**20,235**	17,385	14,535

KRAMER

ELEC. GUITAR	77	KRAMER	**250-B SPECIAL BASS**	438	**324**	278	233
ELGUIT	77	KRAMER	**ARTIST 650-G** ALUMINUM NECK, DOUBLE CUTAWAY	432	**319**	274	229
ELGUIT	78	KRAMER	**DMZ 1000**	480	**355**	305	255
ELGUIT	78	KRAMER	**DMZ 3000** ALUMINUM NECK, SOLID BODY	522	**386**	331	277
ELGUIT	78	KRAMER	**DMZ 4000 BASS**	480	**355**	305	255
ELGUIT	80	KRAMER	**XL-8 BASS** 8-STRING, SOLID BODY, 2 PU's	733	**542**	466	389

KUSTOM

GUITAR AMP	68	KUSTOM	**100 COMBO** BLUE SPARKLE, 50 WATTS	183	**135**	116	97
GTAMP	70	KUSTOM	**200 AMP** 2x15" or 3x12" CABINET	222	**164**	141	118
GTAMP	73	KUSTOM	**220 AMP** 3x12"	195	**144**	124	104
GTAMP	67	KUSTOM	**CHALLENGER** BLUE, SINGLE 12" COMBO	125	**93**	79	66
GTAMP	68	KUSTOM	**ENDEAVOR** GREEN, SINGLE 12" COMBO	116	**85**	73	61
GTAMP	68	KUSTOM	**ENDEAVOR GOLD** GOLD, 2X12" COMBO	144	**107**	92	77

TYPE	YR	MFG	PRICES--BASED ON 100% ORIGINAL MODEL	SELL EXC	SELL AVG	BUY EXC	BUY AVG

LAB SERIES AMPLIFIERS

TYPE	YR	MFG	MODEL	SELL EXC	SELL AVG	BUY EXC	BUY AVG
GUITAR AMP	77	LAB	**L-3** 60 WATT COMBO	192	**142**	122	102
GTAMP	77	LAB	**L-5**	216	**159**	137	114
GTAMP	77	LAB	**L-7** 100 WATT, 20" SPEAKERS	273	**202**	173	145

LAFAYETTE

TYPE	YR	MFG	MODEL	SELL EXC	SELL AVG	BUY EXC	BUY AVG
PWR	69	LAF	**KT-550 KIT**	240	**177**	152	127
PWR	73	LAF	**KT-600A KIT**	79	**58**	50	42

LARSON BROTHERS

TYPE	YR	MFG	MODEL	SELL EXC	SELL AVG	BUY EXC	BUY AVG
GUITAR (ACOUSTIC)	10	LARSON	**DYER**	1,216	**899**	772	646
GUITAR	17	LARSON	**DYER**	1,416	**1,047**	899	752
GUITAR	34	LARSON	**EUPHONON** MAHOGANY BODY, 14"	395	**301**	256	196
GUITAR	37	LARSON	**EUPHONON** ROSEWOOD BACK/SIDES, 18"	15,840	**11,715**	10,065	8,415
GUITAR	38	LARSON	**EUPHONON** DREADNOUGHT, MOP NECK	8,364	**6,186**	5,314	4,443
GUITAR	38	LARSON	**EUPHONON** ROSEWOOD, DREADNOUGHT	9,120	**6,745**	5,795	4,845
GUITAR	39	LARSON	**EUPHONON** ROSEWOOD BODY, 16" JUMBO	963	**734**	624	477
GUITAR	40	LARSON	**EUPHONON** TONE BAR	5,760	**4,260**	3,660	3,060
GUITAR	41	LARSON	**EUPHONON**	2,013	**1,488**	1,279	1,069
GUITAR	42	LARSON	**EUPHONON** CARL FISHER LABEL	3,072	**2,272**	1,952	1,632
GUITAR	44	LARSON	**EUPHONON** KIMBALL HALL LABEL	3,072	**2,272**	1,952	1,632
GUITAR	10	LARSON	**HARP GUITAR** KNUTSON STYLE CONSTRUCTION, 7 SUB-BASS STRINGS	5,609	**4,148**	3,564	2,979
GUITAR	22	LARSON	**J.F. STETSON** ROSEWOOD	3,840	**2,840**	2,440	2,040
GUITAR	14	LARSON	**MAURER** FLATTOP	717	**530**	455	380
GUITAR	15	LARSON	**MAURER**	3,816	**2,822**	2,425	2,027
GUITAR	16	LARSON	**MAURER**	1,721	**1,273**	1,093	914
GUITAR	19	LARSON	**MAURER**	3,817	**2,823**	2,425	2,028
GUITAR	20	LARSON	**MAURER** BRAZILIAN ROSEWOOD BACK/SIDES	3,360	**2,485**	2,135	1,785
GUITAR	32	LARSON	**MAURER** ROSEWOOD	3,072	**2,272**	1,952	1,632
GUITAR	33	LARSON	**MAURER**	1,655	**1,261**	1,072	820
GUITAR	30	LARSON	**MAURER 000** ROSEWOOD, ABALONE TRIM	876	**648**	556	465
GUITAR	10	LARSON	**MAURER 531** SPRUCE TOP, ROSEWOOD BACK/SIDES	1,274	**942**	810	677
GUITAR	20	LARSON	**PRAIRIE STATE** ROSEWOOD BACK/SIDES	4,800	**3,550**	3,050	2,550
GUITAR	32	LARSON	**PRAIRIE STATE**	4,511	**3,336**	2,866	2,396
GUITAR	33	LARSON	**PRAIRIE STATE**	4,513	**3,338**	2,868	2,398
GUITAR	35	LARSON	**PRAIRIE STATE**	3,674	**2,800**	2,380	1,819
GUITAR	38	LARSON	**PRAIRIE STATE**	3,360	**2,485**	2,135	1,785
GUITAR	40	LARSON	**PRAIRIE STATE** MAPLE BACK/SIDES, F-HOLE, 17"	12,393	**9,166**	7,875	6,584
GUITAR	20	LARSON	**STAHL** BRAZILIAN ROSEWOOD BACK/SIDES, FLATTOP	951	**703**	604	505
GUITAR	22	LARSON	**STAHL** ROSEWOOD	1,394	**1,062**	903	690
GUITAR	32	LARSON	**STAHL** ROSEWOOD	4,320	**3,195**	2,745	2,295
GUITAR	30	LARSON	**STAHL 0 SIZE** ROSEWOOD, PEARL TRIM	1,017	**752**	646	540
MANDOLIN	38	LARSON	**EUPHONON** ROSEWOOD	3,648	**2,698**	2,318	1,938
MANDOL	15	LARSON	**MAURER BOWL-BACK** ROSEWOOD RIBS	451	**333**	286	239
MANDOL	10	LARSON	**STAHL BOWL-BACK**	956	**707**	607	507
MANDOL	15	LARSON	**STAHL BOWL-BACK**	1,035	**766**	658	550
MANDOL	20	LARSON	**STAHL BOWL-BACK** ROSEWOOD	1,000	**739**	635	531
MANDOL	25	LARSON	**STAHL BOWL-BACK** ROSEWOOD	757	**560**	481	402
MANDOL	30	LARSON	**STAHL MANDO-CELLO** MAPLE	4,608	**3,408**	2,928	2,448

TYPE		YR	MFG	PRICES--BASED ON 100% ORIGINAL MODEL	SELL EXC	SELL AVG	BUY EXC	BUY AVG
				LEAK by ERCONA CORPORATION				
PRE		58	LEAK	**POINT 1** STEREO TUBE	209	**154**	132	111
PWR		59	LEAK	**STEREO 20** TUBE, 25 WATT	324	**239**	206	172
	PWR	59	LEAK	**STEREO 50** 25 WATTS	318	**235**	202	169
	PWR	64	LEAK	**STEREO 60** TUBE, 30 WATT	360	**266**	229	191
	PWR	55	LEAK	**TL-50 MONO** TUBE, 45 WATT	182	**134**	115	96
				LEVIN (MADE IN SWEDEN)				
GUITAR (ACOUSTIC)		49	LEVIN	**DELUXE** NATURAL, CUTAWAY, 18 1/4" WIDE	4,593	**3,500**	2,975	2,275
	GUITAR	52	LEVIN	**SOLOIST** NATURAL, CUTAWAY, 17 1/8" WIDE	2,178	**1,660**	1,411	1,079
				LINN ELECTRONICS				
PRE		64	LINN	**NAJIK LINE ONLY**	2,364	**1,748**	1,502	1,256
				LUXMAN				
XOVER		73	LUX	**A-2003** 3-WAY ACTIVE, STEREO, TUBE	479	**354**	304	254
				LYON & HEALY				
BANJO		00	LYON	**1900 L&H STAR**	485	**359**	308	258
	BANJO	15	LYON	**STYLE A** 5-STRING	598	**442**	380	317
	BANJO	10	LYON	**TENOR** OPEN BACK	343	**261**	222	170
	BANJO	20	LYON	**TENOR LUTE** MAHOGANY BACK/SIDES, PEAR SHAPED BODY, ATTRACTIVE INLAY	279	**206**	177	148
	BANJO	20	LYON	**VAN EPS RECORDING** 5-STRING	637	**471**	405	338
	BANJO	20	LYON	**VAN EPS RECORDING PLECTRUM**	622	**460**	395	330
	BANJO	22	LYON	**VAN EPS RECORDING PLECTRUM**	624	**461**	396	331
GUITAR (ACOUSTIC)		10	LYON	**AMERICAN CONSERVATORY** BRAZILIAN ROSEWD BACK/SIDES,12" WIDE,12-FRET SLOT HEAD NECK	637	**471**	405	338
	GUITAR	20	LYON	**AMERICAN CONSERVATORY TENOR**	240	**177**	152	127
	GUITAR	05	LYON	**PARLOR GUITAR** SPRUCE TOP, OAK BACK/SIDES	468	**346**	297	248
MANDOLIN		20	LYON	**2-POINT BODY** OVAL SOUND HOLE	518	**383**	329	275
	MANDOL	01	LYON	**AMERICAN CONSERVATORY BOWL-BACK**	412	**305**	262	219
	MANDOL	20	LYON	**DITSON STYLE A**	1,614	**1,194**	1,026	857
	MANDOL	20	LYON	**DITSON STYLE B** SYMETRICAL 2-POINT BODY SHAPE, OVAL SOUND HOLE	677	**501**	430	360
	MANDOL	01	LYON	**HOMER WARREN BOWL-BACK** ROSEWOOD RIBS	747	**553**	475	397
	MANDOL	12	LYON	**STYLE A MANDOCELLO**	5,280	**3,905**	3,355	2,805
	MANDOL	20	LYON	**STYLE A MANDOCELLO** SCROLL PEGHEAD	7,179	**5,310**	4,562	3,814
	MANDOL	18	LYON	**STYLE A PROFESSIONAL** SCROLL PEGHEAD	3,360	**2,485**	2,135	1,785
	MANDOL	12	LYON	**STYLE B** SERIAL #39	1,808	**1,337**	1,149	960
	MANDOL	20	LYON	**STYLE B** MAPLE BACK/SIDES	1,195	**883**	759	634
	MANDOL	20	LYON	**STYLE C** A BODY STYLE	936	**692**	594	497
	MANDOL	20	LYON	**STYLE C** OVAL SOUND HOLE	992	**734**	630	527
UKULELE		25	LYON	**CAMP** SMALL BODY	192	**142**	122	102
	UKE	30	LYON	**TENOR** BOUND TOP	120	**88**	76	63
	UKE	30	LYON	**TENOR**	184	**136**	117	97
				MacCAFERRI/SELMER				
ELEC. GUITAR		52	MAC/SEL	**MAESTRO** PLASTIC, ROUND SOUND HOLE, 1 PU	168	**124**	106	89
GUITAR (ACOUSTIC)		53	MAC/SEL	**G-40** ARCHTOP	217	**161**	138	115
	GUITAR	56	MAC/SEL	**ISLANDER** PLASTIC BODY	144	**106**	91	76
	GUITAR	54	MAC/SEL	**MACCAFERRI** PLASTIC BODY	144	**106**	91	76
	GUITAR	56	MAC/SEL	**MACCAFERRI** PLASTIC BODY, ARCHTOP	153	**113**	97	81
	GUITAR	31	MAC/SEL	**MODELE CONCERT** D SHAPED SOUND HOLE	34,972	**25,865**	22,222	18,579

	TYPE	YR	MFG	PRICES--BASED ON 100% ORIGINAL MODEL	SELL EXC	SELL AVG	BUY EXC	BUY AVG
	GUITAR	32	MAC/SEL	**MODELE CONCERT** D SHAPED SOUND HOLE	33,556	**24,818**	21,322	17,827
	GUITAR	53	MAC/SEL	**PLASTIC** FLATTOP	96	**71**	61	51
	GUITAR	35	MAC/SEL	**SELMER**	8,640	**6,390**	5,490	4,590
	GUITAR	38	MAC/SEL	**SELMER**	9,450	**7,200**	6,120	4,680
	GUITAR	40	MAC/SEL	**SELMER** MADE IN FRANCE,ROSEWOOD B/S,12-FRET,CUTWY, ROUND SOUND HOLE	24,000	**17,750**	15,250	12,750
	GUITAR	47	MAC/SEL	**SELMER** MADE IN FRANCE, CUTAWAY, SMALL OVAL SOUND HOLE	19,200	**14,200**	12,200	10,200
	GUITAR	59	MAC/SEL	**SHOWTIME CLASSICAL**	216	**159**	137	114
UKULELE		50	MAC/SEL	**ISLANDER** PLASTIC	78	**58**	50	41
	UKE	55	MAC/SEL	**PLAYTUNE SENIOR** WHITE STYRENE	144	**106**	91	76
				## MAESTRO				
EFFECTS		72	MAESTRO	**BG-2 BOOMER 2 WAH**	156	**115**	99	83
	EFFECTS	70	MAESTRO	**BOOMERANG WAH**	150	**111**	95	80
	EFFECTS	73	MAESTRO	**ECHOPLEX EP-3 SOLID STATE**	503	**372**	319	267
	EFFECTS	62	MAESTRO	**ECHOPLEX TUBE**	735	**543**	467	390
	EFFECTS	67	MAESTRO	**FG-1A FUZZ TONE**	192	**142**	122	102
	EFFECTS	76	MAESTRO	**FP-1 FUZZ PHASER**	181	**134**	115	96
	EFFECTS	70	MAESTRO	**FZ-1B FUZZ TONE**	126	**93**	80	67
	EFFECTS	70	MAESTRO	**G-2 RHYTHM AND SOUND**	216	**159**	137	114
	EFFECTS	71	MAESTRO	**G-2 RHYTHM AND SOUND**	240	**177**	152	127
	EFFECTS	72	MAESTRO	**ME-1 ENVELOPE MODIFIER**	144	**106**	91	76
	EFFECTS	75	MAESTRO	**MINI PHASE**	113	**83**	71	60
	EFFECTS	78	MAESTRO	**MPP-1 STAGE PHASER**	107	**79**	68	57
GUITAR AMP		65	MAESTRO	**FZ-1A**	240	**177**	152	127
	GTAMP	66	MAESTRO	**FZ-1A**	240	**177**	152	127
	GTAMP	68	MAESTRO	**FZ-1A**	276	**204**	175	146
	GTAMP	69	MAESTRO	**FZ-1A**	276	**204**	175	146
				## MARANTZ AMERICA, INC				
PRE		54	MARANTZ	**1-C**	817	**604**	519	434
	PRE	53-59	MARANTZ	**1-C CONSOLE** MONO TUBE, #4 POWER SUPPLY	1,486	**1,099**	944	789
	PRE	59-66	MARANTZ	**7-C** STEREO TUBE	2,348	**1,736**	1,492	1,247
	PRE	60	MARANTZ	**7-C** TUBE	1,673	**1,237**	1,063	888
	PRE	67	MARANTZ	**7-T CLASSIC U.S. VERSION**	696	**515**	442	370
	PRE	78	MARANTZ	**3650**	821	**607**	522	436
PWR		56-62	MARANTZ	**2** MONO TUBE, 40 WATT	1,507	**1,114**	957	800
	PWR	55-62	MARANTZ	**5** MONO TUBE, 30 WATT	1,315	**972**	835	698
	PWR	59	MARANTZ	**5** MONO, 30 WATTS	757	**560**	481	402
	PWR	60-62	MARANTZ	**8** STEREO TUBE, 30 WATT	1,454	**1,075**	924	772
	PWR	61	MARANTZ	**8** 30 WATTS	962	**712**	611	511
	PWR	60-67	MARANTZ	**8B** STEREO TUBE, 35 WATT	1,304	**964**	828	693
	PWR	64	MARANTZ	**8B** 35 WATTS	1,593	**1,178**	1,012	846
	PWR	61-67	MARANTZ	**9** MONO TUBE, PAIR, 70 WATT, RACK MOUNT PANEL OPTIONAL	7,392	**5,467**	4,697	3,927
	PWR	64	MARANTZ	**9A** MONO	6,595	**4,877**	4,190	3,503
	PWR	68	MARANTZ	**15** DUAL MONO, 60 WATT	277	**205**	176	147
	PWR	73	MARANTZ	**32 VARIABLE OVERLAP DRIVE**	351	**259**	223	186
	PWR	92	MARANTZ	**MA-500BL MONO/THX CERTIFIED**	350	**259**	222	186
	PWR	79	MARANTZ	**SM-7 ESOTEC**	900	**665**	572	478
RCV		68	MARANTZ	**18 CLASSIC U.S. VERSION**	384	**284**	244	204
	RCV	73	MARANTZ	**19**	480	**355**	305	255
	RCV	77	MARANTZ	**2500**	1,387	**1,025**	881	736
	RCV	78	MARANTZ	**2600** SCOPE,TOROIDAL DUAL PWR SUPPLY,DOLBY CAPABLE,QTZ LOCK FM	1,593	**1,178**	1,012	846
SIGNAL PROCESSOR		76	MARANTZ	**SQA-2B DECODER**	105	**78**	67	56
SPKR		77	MARANTZ	**HD-440**	122	**90**	78	65
	SPKR	73	MARANTZ	**IMPERIAL 4G**	126	**93**	80	67
	SPKR	77	MARANTZ	**MODEL 4 MKII**	121	**90**	77	64
	SPKR	77	MARANTZ	**MODEL 6 MKII**	160	**118**	101	85
TUNER		62-63	MARANTZ	**10** STEREO TUBE, SCOPE	1,952	**1,444**	1,240	1,037

TYPE	YR	MFG	PRICES--BASED ON 100% ORIGINAL MODEL	SELL EXC	SELL AVG	BUY EXC	BUY AVG
TUNER	64	MARANTZ	**10** SCOPE	1,436	**1,062**	912	762
TUNER	63-67	MARANTZ	**10B** STEREO TUBE, SCOPE	2,289	**1,693**	1,454	1,216
TUNER	64	MARANTZ	**10B** SCOPE	1,593	**1,178**	1,012	846
TUNER	73	MARANTZ	**112**	160	**118**	101	85
TUNER	76	MARANTZ	**150** SCOPE	674	**499**	428	358
TUNER	78-80	MARANTZ	**2130 QUARTZ LOCK** SCOPE, MULTIPLEX DEMODULATOR	630	**466**	400	335
TUNER	79	MARANTZ	**ST-7 ESOTEC** SCOPE	1,089	**805**	692	578
TUNER	79	MARANTZ	**ST-8 ESOTEC** SCOPE	1,172	**866**	744	622
XOVER		55	MARANTZ	**3 MONO TUBE**	1,483	**1,096**	942	787

MARSHALL AMPS

TYPE	YR	MFG	MODEL	SELL EXC	SELL AVG	BUY EXC	BUY AVG
GUITAR AMP	68	MARSHALL	**JMP- 50 WATT** RED, SMALL BOX, PLEXI 4x12" CABINET	1,151	**851**	731	611
GTAMP	72	MARSHALL	**JMP- 50 WATT**	581	**430**	369	309
GTAMP	74	MARSHALL	**JMP- 50 WATT** MK II LEAD HEAD	495	**366**	314	263
GTAMP	74	MARSHALL	**JMP- 50 WATT**	504	**372**	320	267
GTAMP	75	MARSHALL	**JMP- 50 WATT**	442	**327**	281	235
GTAMP	77	MARSHALL	**JMP- 50 WATT**	486	**359**	309	258
GTAMP	78	MARSHALL	**JMP- 50 WATT**	501	**370**	318	266
GTAMP	79	MARSHALL	**JMP- 50 WATT**	438	**324**	278	233
GTAMP	79	MARSHALL	**JMP- 50 WATT** BEIGE, COMBO	463	**342**	294	246
GTAMP	59	MARSHALL	**JMP-100 WATT**	475	**351**	301	252
GTAMP	75	MARSHALL	**JMP-100 WATT** BLACK	445	**329**	283	236
GTAMP	79	MARSHALL	**JMP-100 WATT**	469	**347**	298	249
GTAMP	80	MARSHALL	**JMP-100 WATT** MK II LEAD	480	**355**	305	255
GTAMP	81	MARSHALL	**JMP-100 WATT**	462	**342**	294	245
GTAMP	63	MARSHALL	**JTM- 45** WHITE PANEL/BACK	1,296	**958**	823	688
GTAMP	63	MARSHALL	**JTM- 45** BLACK AND WHITE FACE, HEAD	1,445	**1,069**	918	768
GTAMP	64	MARSHALL	**JTM- 45** GOLD PLEXIGLASS, LARGE LETTERS, NAME PLATE	1,177	**871**	748	625
GTAMP	64	MARSHALL	**JTM- 45** HALF STACK, G12-15's	1,705	**1,261**	1,083	906
GTAMP	65	MARSHALL	**JTM- 45** WHITE BACK, PLEXI, 4x12" CABINET	988	**731**	628	525
GTAMP	65	MARSHALL	**JTM- 45** HEAD	1,720	**1,272**	1,093	913
GTAMP	66	MARSHALL	**JTM- 45** WHITE BACK, PLEXI	1,272	**940**	808	675
GTAMP	66	MARSHALL	**JTM- 45** HALF STACK, STRIPE FRONT	3,413	**2,524**	2,169	1,813
GTAMP	73	MARSHALL	**JTM- 45** HEAD	796	**589**	506	423
GTAMP	66	MARSHALL	**JTM-100**	604	**447**	384	321
GTAMP	77	MARSHALL	**MASTER MARK II** 50 WATT COMBO	560	**414**	356	297
GTAMP	69	MARSHALL	**MODEL 1930** 10 WATT, 2x10", COMBO	648	**479**	412	344
GTAMP	72	MARSHALL	**MODEL 1960** BLACK, 4x12" SLANT SPEAKER	486	**359**	309	258
GTAMP	68	MARSHALL	**MODEL 1967** MAJOR AMP HEAD	782	**578**	497	415
GTAMP	67	MARSHALL	**MODEL 1987** 50 WATT, HEAD, PLEXI	1,171	**866**	744	622
GTAMP	77	MARSHALL	**MODEL 1987** 50 WATT, HEAD	451	**333**	286	239
GTAMP	67	MARSHALL	**MODEL 1992** SUPER BASS HEAD, PLEXI	1,027	**759**	652	545
GTAMP	72	MARSHALL	**MODEL 1992** 100 WATT, SUPER BASS HEAD	693	**512**	440	368
GTAMP	73	MARSHALL	**MODEL 1992** 100 WATT, SUPER BASS HEAD	646	**477**	410	343
GTAMP	75	MARSHALL	**MODEL 1992** BLACK, SUPER BASS HEAD	428	**316**	272	227
GTAMP	75	MARSHALL	**MODEL 1992** 100 WATT, SUPER BASS HEAD	501	**370**	318	266
GTAMP	80	MARSHALL	**MODEL 2203** LEAD HEAD	452	**334**	287	240
GTAMP	72	MARSHALL	**SLANT "PURPLE TOLEX"** 100 WATT SPEAKERS	663	**490**	421	352

			PRICES--BASED ON 100% ORIGINAL	SELL	SELL	BUY	BUY
TYPE	YR	MFG	MODEL	EXC	AVG	EXC	AVG
GTAMP	72	MARSHALL	**SPECIALIST 2046** 15" SPEAKER	344	**254**	218	183
GTAMP	72	MARSHALL	**STRAIGHT & SLANT** 4x12" 25 WATT GREEN CELESTIONS	454	**335**	288	241
GTAMP	68	MARSHALL	**SUPER BASS 100 WATT** PLEXI, LAY DOWN TRANSFORMER	859	**635**	545	456
GTAMP	70	MARSHALL	**SUPER BASS 100 WATT** PLEXI, LAY DOWN TRANSFORMER	668	**494**	424	354
GTAMP	73	MARSHALL	**SUPER BASS 100 WATT**	455	**336**	289	241
GTAMP	75	MARSHALL	**SUPER BASS 100 WATT**	472	**349**	300	250
GTAMP	69	MARSHALL	**SUPER LEAD 100 WATT** HEAD, PLEXI, LAY DOWN TRANSFORMER	1,236	**914**	785	656
GTAMP	70	MARSHALL	**SUPER LEAD 100 WATT** HEAD, LAY DOWN TRANSFORMER	717	**530**	455	380
GTAMP	71	MARSHALL	**SUPER LEAD 100 WATT** HEAD, LAY DOWN TRANSFORMER	604	**447**	384	321
GTAMP	72	MARSHALL	**SUPER LEAD 100 WATT**	658	**487**	418	349
GTAMP	73	MARSHALL	**SUPER LEAD 100 WATT**	569	**421**	361	302
GTAMP	75	MARSHALL	**SUPER LEAD 100 WATT**	440	**325**	279	234
GTAMP	79	MARSHALL	**SUPER LEAD 100 WATT**	480	**355**	305	255
GTAMP	79	MARSHALL	**SUPER LEAD 100 WATT CUSTOM** WHITE	469	**347**	298	249

MARTIN GUITAR COMPANY

BANJO	70	MARTIN	**VEGA** LONG NECK, 5-STRING, SERIAL #256003-271633	703	**520**	447	373
BANJO	70	MARTIN	**VEGA VIP** SERIAL #256004-271633	598	**442**	380	317
BANJO	72	MARTIN	**VEGA VIP** SERIAL #294271-313302	578	**428**	367	307
ELEC. GUITAR	73	MARTIN	**D- 12-18**	837	**619**	531	444
ELGUIT	59	MARTIN	**D- 18E** FLATTOP, 2 PU's, SERIAL #165577-171047	1,253	**927**	796	666
ELGUIT	59	MARTIN	**D- 28E** FLATTOP, 2 PU's, SERIAL #165577-171047	3,222	**2,383**	2,047	1,712
ELGUIT	69	MARTIN	**D- 41** INDIAN ROSEWOOD	2,390	**1,767**	1,518	1,269
ELGUIT	69	MARTIN	**D- 41** BRAZILIAN ROSEWOOD	9,600	**7,100**	6,100	5,100
ELGUIT	68	MARTIN	**D-1235** BRAZILIAN ROSEWOOD	2,306	**1,706**	1,465	1,225
ELGUIT	79	MARTIN	**E-18** NATURAL,MAPLE/ROSEWOOD BODY,2 DIMARZIO PU's	509	**377**	323	270
ELGUIT	61	MARTIN	**F-50** SUNBURST, ARCHTOP, CUTAWAY, 1 PU, SERIAL #175690-181297	559	**413**	355	297
ELGUIT	64	MARTIN	**F-50** SUNBURST, ARCHTOP, CUTAWAY, 1 PU, SERIAL #193328-199626	555	**411**	353	295
ELGUIT	62	MARTIN	**F-55** SUNBURST, ARCHTOP, CUTAWAY, 1 PU, SERIAL #181298-187384	419	**310**	266	222
ELGUIT	62	MARTIN	**F-65**	617	**456**	392	327
ELGUIT	64	MARTIN	**F-65** SUNBURST,ARCHTOP, 2 PU's,DBL CUTAWAY,SERIAL #193328-199626	749	**554**	476	398
ELGUIT	65	MARTIN	**GT-70** BURGUNDY, ARCHTOP, 2 PU's, CUTAWAY, SERIAL #199627-207030	773	**572**	491	411
ELGUIT	66	MARTIN	**GT-70** BLACK, ARCHTOP, 2 PU's, CUTAWAY, SERIAL #207031-217215	744	**550**	473	395
ELGUIT	66	MARTIN	**GT-70** BURGUNDY, ARCHTOP, 2 PU's, CUTAWAY, SERIAL #207031-217215	749	**554**	476	398
ELGUIT	67	MARTIN	**GT-70** BURGUNDY, ARCHTOP, 2 PU's, CUTAWAY, SERIAL #217216-230095	578	**428**	367	307
ELGUIT	65	MARTIN	**GT-75** BURGUNDY, ARCHTOP, 2 PU's,DBL CUTAWAY,SERIAL #199627-207030	612	**452**	389	325
ELGUIT	66	MARTIN	**GT-75** BURGUNDY,ARCHTOP, 2 PU's,DBL CUTAWAY,SERIAL #207031-217215	626	**463**	398	333
ELGUIT	67	MARTIN	**GT-75** BURGUNDY, ARCHTOP, 2 PU's,DBL CUTAWAY,SERIAL #217216-230095	606	**448**	385	322
GUITAR (ACOUSTIC)	40	MARTIN	**0-15** SERIAL #74062-76734	1,015	**751**	645	539
GUITAR	41	MARTIN	**0-15** SERIAL #76735-80013	1,011	**748**	642	537
GUITAR	42	MARTIN	**0-15** SERIAL #80014-83107	1,009	**746**	641	536
GUITAR	43	MARTIN	**0-15** SERIAL #83108-86724	1,005	**743**	638	533
GUITAR	48	MARTIN	**0-15** SERIAL #103469-108269	1,001	**740**	636	531
GUITAR	50	MARTIN	**0-15** SERIAL #112962-117961	997	**737**	633	529
GUITAR	53	MARTIN	**0-15** SERIAL #128437-134501	1,066	**788**	677	566
GUITAR	55	MARTIN	**0-15** SERIAL #141346-147328	1,062	**785**	675	564

TYPE	YR	MFG	MODEL	SELL EXC	SELL AVG	BUY EXC	BUY AVG
GUITAR	56	MARTIN	0-15 SERIAL #147329-152775	1,057	782	672	562
GUITAR	57	MARTIN	0-15 SERIAL #152776-159061	1,052	778	668	558
GUITAR	59	MARTIN	0-15 MAHOGANY	816	604	519	434
GUITAR	60	MARTIN	0-15 SERIAL #171048-175689	1,047	774	665	556
GUITAR	61	MARTIN	0-15 SERIAL #175690-181297	1,042	771	662	553
GUITAR	40	MARTIN	0-15H HAWAIIAN SERIAL #74062-76734	533	394	339	283
GUITAR	60	MARTIN	0-15T TENOR, SERIAL #171048-175689	788	582	500	418
GUITAR	62	MARTIN	0-16NY	998	738	634	530
GUITAR	63	MARTIN	0-16NY SERIAL #187385-193327	994	735	631	528
GUITAR	64	MARTIN	0-16NY SERIAL #193328-199626	988	731	628	525
GUITAR	65	MARTIN	0-16NY LEFT-HANDED	828	631	536	410
GUITAR	66	MARTIN	0-16NY 12-FRET NECK, SERIAL #207031-217215	996	736	633	529
GUITAR	67	MARTIN	0-16NY SERIAL #217216-230095	917	678	583	487
GUITAR	68	MARTIN	0-16NY SERIAL #230096-241925	912	674	579	484
GUITAR	69	MARTIN	0-16NY SERIAL #241926-256003	908	671	577	482
GUITAR	70	MARTIN	0-16NY SERIAL #256004-271633	829	613	527	440
GUITAR	71	MARTIN	0-16NY SERIAL #271634-294270	794	587	505	422
GUITAR	74	MARTIN	0-16NY 12-FRET NECK, SERIAL #25340-25679	788	582	500	418
GUITAR	75	MARTIN	0-16NY SERIAL #353388-371828	747	553	475	397
GUITAR	10	MARTIN	0-17 SERIAL #11019-11203	1,244	920	790	660
GUITAR	28	MARTIN	0-17 SERIAL #34436-37568	918	679	583	488
GUITAR	33	MARTIN	0-17 SERIAL #52591-55084	854	631	542	453
GUITAR	34	MARTIN	0-17 SERIAL #55085-58679	965	714	613	513
GUITAR	35	MARTIN	0-17 SERIAL #58680-61947	928	686	589	493
GUITAR	36	MARTIN	0-17 SERIAL #61948-65176	982	726	624	521
GUITAR	37	MARTIN	0-17 SERIAL #65177-68865	855	632	543	454
GUITAR	42	MARTIN	0-17 SERIAL#80014-83107	846	626	538	449
GUITAR	43	MARTIN	0-17 SERIAL #83108-86724	832	615	528	442
GUITAR	44	MARTIN	0-17 SERIAL #86725-90149	827	612	525	439
GUITAR	47	MARTIN	0-17 SERIAL #98159-103468	816	604	519	434
GUITAR	36	MARTIN	0-17H HAWAIIAN SERIAL #61948-65176	720	533	458	383
GUITAR	37	MARTIN	0-17H HAWAIIAN SERIAL#67033	805	595	511	427
GUITAR	38	MARTIN	0-17H HAWAIIAN SERIAL #68866-71866	712	526	452	378
GUITAR	28	MARTIN	0-17T TENOR	733	542	466	389
GUITAR	33	MARTIN	0-17T TENOR, SERIAL #52591-55084	726	537	461	386
GUITAR	48	MARTIN	0-17T TENOR, SERIAL #103469-108269	721	533	458	383
GUITAR	49	MARTIN	0-17T TENOR	719	531	456	381
GUITAR	52	MARTIN	0-17T TENOR, SERIAL #122800-128436	714	528	453	379
GUITAR	53	MARTIN	0-17T TENOR, SERIAL #128437-134501	710	525	451	377
GUITAR	59	MARTIN	0-17T TENOR, SERIAL #165577-171047	696	515	442	370
GUITAR	06	MARTIN	0-18 FLATTOP/SMALL BODY	1,669	1,234	1,060	886
GUITAR	18	MARTIN	0-18 SERIAL #12989-13450	1,227	908	780	652
GUITAR	19	MARTIN	0-18	3,315	2,452	2,106	1,761

TYPE	YR	MFG	PRICES--BASED ON 100% ORIGINAL MODEL	SELL EXC	SELL AVG	BUY EXC	BUY AVG
GUITAR	20	MARTIN	**0-18** SERIAL #14513-15848	1,781	**1,317**	1,132	946
GUITAR	23	MARTIN	**0-18**	2,171	**1,606**	1,379	1,153
GUITAR	25	MARTIN	**0-18** SERIAL #22009-24116	2,043	**1,511**	1,298	1,085
GUITAR	26	MARTIN	**0-18** SERIAL #24117-28689	1,819	**1,345**	1,155	966
GUITAR	27	MARTIN	**0-18** SERIAL #28690-34435	1,649	**1,219**	1,047	876
GUITAR	28	MARTIN	**0-18** SERIAL #34436-37568	1,643	**1,215**	1,044	873
GUITAR	29	MARTIN	**0-18** SERIAL #37569-40843	1,637	**1,211**	1,040	870
GUITAR	32	MARTIN	**0-18** SERIAL #49590-52590	1,625	**1,202**	1,032	863
GUITAR	33	MARTIN	**0-18** SERIAL #52591-55084	1,462	**1,081**	929	776
GUITAR	34	MARTIN	**0-18** SHADED TOP, SERIAL #52324	3,408	**2,520**	2,165	1,810
GUITAR	34	MARTIN	**0-18** SUNBURST	3,617	**2,675**	2,298	1,921
GUITAR	35	MARTIN	**0-18** SERIAL #58680-61947	1,463	**1,082**	929	777
GUITAR	36	MARTIN	**0-18** SERIAL #61948-65176	1,457	**1,077**	925	774
GUITAR	37	MARTIN	**0-18** SERIAL #65177-68865	1,455	**1,076**	924	773
GUITAR	38	MARTIN	**0-18** SERIAL #68866-71866	1,452	**1,074**	922	771
GUITAR	39	MARTIN	**0-18** SERIAL #71867-74061	1,447	**1,070**	919	769
GUITAR	40	MARTIN	**0-18** SERIAL #74062-76734	1,273	**942**	809	676
GUITAR	42	MARTIN	**0-18** SERIAL #80014-83107	1,272	**940**	808	675
GUITAR	43	MARTIN	**0-18** SERIAL #83108-86724	1,280	**947**	813	680
GUITAR	44	MARTIN	**0-18**	1,394	**1,031**	886	741
GUITAR	45	MARTIN	**0-18** SERIAL #90150-93623	1,267	**937**	805	673
GUITAR	46	MARTIN	**0-18** SERIAL #93624-98158	1,263	**934**	802	671
GUITAR	47	MARTIN	**0-18** SERIAL #98159-103468	1,261	**932**	801	670
GUITAR	48	MARTIN	**0-18** SERIAL #103469-108269	1,258	**930**	799	668
GUITAR	49	MARTIN	**0-18** SERIAL #108270-112961	1,254	**927**	797	666
GUITAR	50	MARTIN	**0-18** LEFT-HANDED, SERIAL #112962-117961	1,304	**964**	828	693
GUITAR	51	MARTIN	**0-18** SERIAL #117962-122799	1,111	**822**	706	590
GUITAR	52	MARTIN	**0-18** SERIAL #122800-128436	1,091	**807**	693	579
GUITAR	53	MARTIN	**0-18** SERIAL #128437-134501	1,084	**802**	689	576
GUITAR	54	MARTIN	**0-18** SERIAL #134502-141345	1,081	**800**	687	574
GUITAR	55	MARTIN	**0-18** SERIAL #141346-147328	1,079	**798**	685	573
GUITAR	56	MARTIN	**0-18** SERIAL #147329-152775	1,076	**795**	683	571
GUITAR	57	MARTIN	**0-18** SERIAL # 156856	956	**707**	607	507
GUITAR	58	MARTIN	**0-18** SERIAL #159062-165576	1,061	**785**	674	564
GUITAR	59	MARTIN	**0-18** SERIAL #165577-171047	1,063	**786**	675	565
GUITAR	60	MARTIN	**0-18** SERIAL #171048-175689	1,151	**851**	731	611
GUITAR	61	MARTIN	**0-18** SERIAL #175690-181297	1,146	**847**	728	608
GUITAR	62	MARTIN	**0-18** SERIAL #181298-187384	1,141	**844**	725	606
GUITAR	63	MARTIN	**0-18** SERIAL #187385-193327	1,136	**840**	722	603
GUITAR	64	MARTIN	**0-18** SERIAL #193328-199626	1,133	**838**	720	602
GUITAR	65	MARTIN	**0-18** SERIAL #199627-207030	1,128	**834**	717	599
GUITAR	66	MARTIN	**0-18** SERIAL #207031-217215	984	**727**	625	522
GUITAR	67	MARTIN	**0-18** SERIAL #217216-230095	1,021	**755**	649	542

TYPE	YR	MFG	PRICES--BASED ON 100% ORIGINAL MODEL	SELL EXC	SELL AVG	BUY EXC	BUY AVG
GUITAR	68	MARTIN	**0-18** SERIAL #960224T2-106	965	**714**	613	513
GUITAR	69	MARTIN	**0-18** SERIAL #241926-256003	981	**725**	623	521
GUITAR	70	MARTIN	**0-18** SERIAL #256004-271633	805	**595**	511	427
GUITAR	71	MARTIN	**0-18** SERIAL #271634-294270	766	**566**	486	406
GUITAR	72	MARTIN	**0-18** SERIAL #294271-313302	743	**549**	472	394
GUITAR	73	MARTIN	**0-18** SERIAL #313303-333873	738	**545**	469	392
GUITAR	75	MARTIN	**0-18**	733	**542**	466	389
GUITAR	20	MARTIN	**0-18K HAWAIIAN** KOA WOOD, SERIAL #14513-15848	2,169	**1,604**	1,378	1,152
GUITAR	21	MARTIN	**0-18K HAWAIIAN** KOA WOOD, SERIAL #15849-16758	2,165	**1,601**	1,376	1,150
GUITAR	24	MARTIN	**0-18K HAWAIIAN** KOA WOOD, SERIAL #19892-22008	2,123	**1,570**	1,349	1,128
GUITAR	26	MARTIN	**0-18K HAWAIIAN** KOA WOOD, SERIAL #24117-28689	2,118	**1,566**	1,346	1,125
GUITAR	27	MARTIN	**0-18K HAWAIIAN** KOA WOOD, SERIAL #28690-34435	2,128	**1,574**	1,352	1,130
GUITAR	28	MARTIN	**0-18K HAWAIIAN** KOA WOOD, SERIAL #34436-37568	2,114	**1,564**	1,343	1,123
GUITAR	29	MARTIN	**0-18K HAWAIIAN** KOA WOOD, SERIAL #37569-40843	2,112	**1,562**	1,342	1,122
GUITAR	30	MARTIN	**0-18K HAWAIIAN** KOA WOOD, SERIAL #40844-45317	2,117	**1,566**	1,345	1,125
GUITAR	30	MARTIN	**0-18K HAWAIIAN** KOA WOOD, SERIAL 340844-45317	2,121	**1,569**	1,348	1,127
GUITAR	31	MARTIN	**0-18K HAWAIIAN** KOA WOOD, SERIAL #45318-49589	2,135	**1,579**	1,356	1,134
GUITAR	34	MARTIN	**0-18K HAWAIIAN** KOA WOOD, SERIAL #55085-58679	2,115	**1,564**	1,344	1,124
GUITAR	35	MARTIN	**0-18K HAWAIIAN** KOA WOOD	2,134	**1,578**	1,356	1,133
GUITAR	29	MARTIN	**0-18T** TENOR	1,247	**922**	792	662
GUITAR	30	MARTIN	**0-18T** TENOR, SERIAL #40844-45317	1,330	**984**	845	706
GUITAR	36	MARTIN	**0-18T** TENOR	900	**665**	572	478
GUITAR	40	MARTIN	**0-18T** TENOR, SERIAL #74062-76734	863	**638**	548	458
GUITAR	42	MARTIN	**0-18T** TENOR, SERIAL #80014-83107	634	**469**	403	337
GUITAR	44	MARTIN	**0-18T** TENOR, SERIAL #86725-90149	624	**461**	396	331
GUITAR	49	MARTIN	**0-18T** TENOR, SERIAL #108270-112961	620	**458**	394	329
GUITAR	52	MARTIN	**0-18T** TENOR, SERIAL #122800-128436	614	**454**	390	326
GUITAR	64	MARTIN	**0-18T** TENOR, SERIAL #198923	603	**446**	383	320
GUITAR	68	MARTIN	**0-18T** TENOR, SERIAL #199627-207030	585	**433**	372	311
GUITAR	11	MARTIN	**0-21** SERIAL #11204-11413	2,103	**1,555**	1,336	1,117
GUITAR	18	MARTIN	**0-21** SERIAL #12989-13450	2,074	**1,534**	1,318	1,102
GUITAR	19	MARTIN	**0-21** SERIAL #13451-14512	2,071	**1,532**	1,316	1,100
GUITAR	21	MARTIN	**0-21**	2,310	**1,708**	1,468	1,227
GUITAR	23	MARTIN	**0-21** SERIAL #17840-19891	2,088	**1,544**	1,326	1,109
GUITAR	24	MARTIN	**0-21** SERIAL #19892-22008	2,084	**1,541**	1,324	1,107
GUITAR	25	MARTIN	**0-21** SERIAL #22009-24116	2,081	**1,539**	1,322	1,105
GUITAR	26	MARTIN	**0-21** SERIAL #24117-28689	2,076	**1,535**	1,319	1,103
GUITAR	27	MARTIN	**0-21** SERIAL #28690-34435	2,071	**1,532**	1,316	1,100
GUITAR	28	MARTIN	**0-21** SERIAL #34436-37568	3,504	**2,591**	2,226	1,861
GUITAR	29	MARTIN	**0-21** SERIAL #37569-40843	3,499	**2,587**	2,223	1,858
GUITAR	30	MARTIN	**0-21** SERIAL #40844-45317	3,747	**2,771**	2,381	1,991
GUITAR	31	MARTIN	**0-21**	3,360	**2,485**	2,135	1,785
GUITAR	37	MARTIN	**0-21** SERIAL #65177-68865	3,743	**2,768**	2,378	1,988

TYPE	YR	MFG	PRICES--BASED ON 100% ORIGINAL MODEL	SELL EXC	SELL AVG	BUY EXC	BUY AVG
GUITAR	40	MARTIN	**0-21** SERIAL #74062-76734	3,712	**2,745**	2,358	1,972
GUITAR	46	MARTIN	**0-21** SERIAL #94526	3,696	**2,733**	2,348	1,963
GUITAR	47	MARTIN	**0-21** SERIAL #98159-103468	3,692	**2,730**	2,346	1,961
GUITAR	n/a	MARTIN	**0-21 (1899)**	2,151	**1,591**	1,367	1,142
GUITAR	01	MARTIN	**0-28** SERIAL #9129-9310	3,768	**2,786**	2,394	2,001
GUITAR	13	MARTIN	**0-28**	3,749	**2,773**	2,382	1,992
GUITAR	26	MARTIN	**0-28** SERIAL #24117-28689	4,997	**3,696**	3,175	2,655
GUITAR	27	MARTIN	**0-28** SERIAL #28690-34435	4,992	**3,692**	3,172	2,652
GUITAR	30	MARTIN	**0-28** SERIAL #40844-45317	5,496	**4,065**	3,492	2,920
GUITAR	31	MARTIN	**0-28** SERIAL #45318-49589	5,745	**4,249**	3,650	3,052
GUITAR	04	MARTIN	**0-28 HERRINGBONE** SERIAL #9811-9988	3,756	**2,778**	2,386	1,995
GUITAR	13	MARTIN	**0-28 HERRINGBONE** SERIAL #11566-11821	3,750	**2,773**	2,383	1,992
GUITAR	18	MARTIN	**0-28 HERRINGBONE**	3,743	**2,768**	2,378	1,988
GUITAR	20	MARTIN	**0-28 HERRINGBONE** SERIAL #14513-15848	3,734	**2,761**	2,372	1,983
GUITAR	25	MARTIN	**0-28 HERRINGBONE** SERIAL #22009-24116	6,534	**4,832**	4,152	3,471
GUITAR	82	MARTIN	**0-28 HERRINGBONE (1882)**	3,779	**2,795**	2,401	2,007
GUITAR	89	MARTIN	**0-28 HERRINGBONE (1889)** SERIAL #8350-8716	3,775	**2,792**	2,399	2,005
GUITAR	90	MARTIN	**0-28 HERRINGBONE (1890)**	3,770	**2,788**	2,396	2,003
GUITAR	91	MARTIN	**0-28 HERRINGBONE (1891)**	3,767	**2,786**	2,393	2,001
GUITAR	93	MARTIN	**0-28 HERRINGBONE (1893)**	3,763	**2,783**	2,391	1,999
GUITAR	94	MARTIN	**0-28 HERRINGBONE (1894)**	3,760	**2,781**	2,389	1,997
GUITAR	98	MARTIN	**0-28 HERRINGBONE (1898)**	3,752	**2,775**	2,384	1,993
GUITAR	n/a	MARTIN	**0-28 HERRINGBONE (1899)**	3,749	**2,773**	2,382	1,992
GUITAR	20	MARTIN	**0-28K HAWAIIAN** KOA WOOD	4,740	**3,505**	3,012	2,518
GUITAR	21	MARTIN	**0-28K HAWAIIAN** KOA WOOD, SERIAL #15849-16758	2,375	**1,756**	1,509	1,261
GUITAR	26	MARTIN	**0-28K HAWAIIAN** KOA WOOD, SERIAL #24117-28689	4,672	**3,455**	2,968	2,482
GUITAR	29	MARTIN	**0-28K HAWAIIAN** KOA WOOD, SERIAL #37569-40843	4,738	**3,504**	3,010	2,517
GUITAR	31	MARTIN	**0-28K HAWAIIAN** KOA WOOD	3,817	**2,823**	2,425	2,028
GUITAR	39	MARTIN	**0-28K HAWAIIAN** KOA WOOD, SERIAL #71867-74061	3,046	**2,252**	1,935	1,618
GUITAR	31	MARTIN	**0-28T** TENOR, SERIAL #45318-49589	1,627	**1,203**	1,033	864
GUITAR	17	MARTIN	**0-30**	3,840	**2,840**	2,440	2,040
GUITAR	04	MARTIN	**0-42** SERIAL #9811-9988	7,518	**5,560**	4,777	3,994
GUITAR	19	MARTIN	**0-42** SERIAL #13451-14512	7,512	**5,555**	4,773	3,990
GUITAR	24	MARTIN	**0-42** SERIAL #19892-22008	9,600	**7,100**	6,100	5,100
GUITAR	26	MARTIN	**0-42** SERIAL #24117-28689	7,505	**5,550**	4,768	3,987
GUITAR	28	MARTIN	**0-42** SERIAL #34436-37568	7,498	**5,545**	4,764	3,983
GUITAR	30	MARTIN	**0-42** SERIAL #40844-45317	7,488	**5,538**	4,758	3,978
GUITAR	35	MARTIN	**0-42** SERIAL #58680-61947	9,600	**7,100**	6,100	5,100
GUITAR	41	MARTIN	**0-42** SERIAL #76735-80013	9,496	**7,023**	6,034	5,044
GUITAR	42	MARTIN	**0-42** SERIAL #80014-83107	9,493	**7,021**	6,032	5,043
GUITAR	44	MARTIN	**0-42** SERIAL #86725-90149	9,486	**7,016**	6,028	5,039
GUITAR	86	MARTIN	**0-42 (1886)**	7,619	**5,635**	4,841	4,047
GUITAR	96	MARTIN	**0-42 (1896)**	7,472	**5,526**	4,748	3,969
GUITAR	43	MARTIN	**0-44 SOLOIST** SERIAL #83108-86724	4,269	**3,157**	2,712	2,267
GUITAR	06	MARTIN	**0-45**	19,200	**14,200**	12,200	10,200
GUITAR	26	MARTIN	**0-45** SERIAL #24117-28689	11,748	**8,688**	7,465	6,241
GUITAR	26	MARTIN	**0-45** SERIAL #29856	19,680	**14,555**	12,505	10,455
GUITAR	27	MARTIN	**0-45**	11,852	**8,765**	7,531	6,296

TYPE	YR	MFG	PRICES--BASED ON 100% ORIGINAL MODEL	SELL EXC	SELL AVG	BUY EXC	BUY AVG
GUITAR	29	MARTIN	**0-45** SERIAL #37569-40843	11,742	**8,684**	7,461	6,238
GUITAR	38	MARTIN	**0-45** SERIAL #68866-71866	11,736	**8,680**	7,457	6,235
GUITAR	40	MARTIN	**0-45** SERIAL #74062-76734	11,731	**8,676**	7,454	6,232
GUITAR	62	MARTIN	**00-16C CLASSICAL** SERIAL #181298-187384	560	**414**	356	297
GUITAR	65	MARTIN	**00-16C CLASSICAL**	642	**474**	408	341
GUITAR	66	MARTIN	**00-16C CLASSICAL** SERIAL #207031-217215	717	**530**	455	380
GUITAR	68	MARTIN	**00-16C CLASSICAL** SERIAL #230096-241925	715	**528**	454	379
GUITAR	71	MARTIN	**00-16C CLASSICAL** SERIAL #271634-294270	639	**472**	406	339
GUITAR	15	MARTIN	**00-17** SERIAL #12048-12209	1,380	**1,020**	877	733
GUITAR	31	MARTIN	**00-17** SERIAL #45318-49589	1,333	**986**	847	708
GUITAR	41	MARTIN	**00-17** SERIAL #76735-80013	1,442	**1,067**	916	766
GUITAR	45	MARTIN	**00-17** SERIAL #90150-93623	1,176	**869**	747	624
GUITAR	46	MARTIN	**00-17** SERIAL #93624-98158	1,127	**833**	716	598
GUITAR	47	MARTIN	**00-17** SERIAL #98159-103468	1,021	**755**	649	542
GUITAR	49	MARTIN	**00-17** SERIAL #108270-112961	998	**738**	634	530
GUITAR	50	MARTIN	**00-17** SERIAL #112962-117961	993	**734**	631	527
GUITAR	52	MARTIN	**00-17** SERIAL #122800-128436	925	**684**	588	491
GUITAR	53	MARTIN	**00-17** SERIAL #128437-134501	924	**683**	587	491
GUITAR	55	MARTIN	**00-17** SERIAL #141346-147328	887	**656**	563	471
GUITAR	56	MARTIN	**00-17**	1,005	**743**	638	533
GUITAR	57	MARTIN	**00-17** SERIAL #157809	861	**636**	547	457
GUITAR	58	MARTIN	**00-17** SERIAL #159062-165576	841	**622**	534	447
GUITAR	22	MARTIN	**00-18** SERIAL #16759-17839	2,090	**1,546**	1,328	1,110
GUITAR	24	MARTIN	**00-18**	2,160	**1,597**	1,372	1,147
GUITAR	26	MARTIN	**00-18** SERIAL #24117-28689	2,101	**1,554**	1,335	1,116
GUITAR	27	MARTIN	**00-18** SERIAL #28690-34435	2,091	**1,547**	1,329	1,111
GUITAR	29	MARTIN	**00-18** SERIAL #37569-40843	2,090	**1,546**	1,328	1,110
GUITAR	30	MARTIN	**00-18**	2,390	**1,767**	1,518	1,269
GUITAR	34	MARTIN	**00-18** SERIAL #55085-58679	2,088	**1,544**	1,326	1,109
GUITAR	35	MARTIN	**00-18** SERIAL #58680-61947	2,084	**1,541**	1,324	1,107
GUITAR	36	MARTIN	**00-18** SERIAL #61948-65176	2,099	**1,552**	1,334	1,115
GUITAR	37	MARTIN	**00-18** SERIAL #65177-68865 SUNBURST	2,107	**1,558**	1,338	1,119
GUITAR	38	MARTIN	**00-18**	2,033	**1,503**	1,291	1,080
GUITAR	39	MARTIN	**00-18** SERIAL #71867-74061	2,090	**1,546**	1,328	1,110
GUITAR	42	MARTIN	**00-18**	2,390	**1,767**	1,518	1,269
GUITAR	43	MARTIN	**00-18** SERIAL #83108-86724	2,081	**1,539**	1,322	1,105
GUITAR	44	MARTIN	**00-18** SERIAL #86725-90149	2,052	**1,517**	1,304	1,090
GUITAR	46	MARTIN	**00-18** SERIAL #93624-98158	1,786	**1,321**	1,135	949
GUITAR	47	MARTIN	**00-18** SERIAL #98159-103468	1,923	**1,422**	1,222	1,022
GUITAR	48	MARTIN	**00-18**	1,923	**1,422**	1,222	1,022
GUITAR	49	MARTIN	**00-18** SERIAL #108270-112961	1,942	**1,436**	1,234	1,031
GUITAR	52	MARTIN	**00-18**	1,593	**1,178**	1,012	846
GUITAR	53	MARTIN	**00-18** SERIAL #128437-134501	1,799	**1,330**	1,143	955
GUITAR	54	MARTIN	**00-18** SERIAL #134502-141345	1,787	**1,322**	1,135	949
GUITAR	55	MARTIN	**00-18** SERIAL #141346-147328	1,783	**1,319**	1,133	947

TYPE	YR	MFG	PRICES--BASED ON 100% ORIGINAL MODEL	SELL EXC	SELL AVG	BUY EXC	BUY AVG
GUITAR	56	MARTIN	**00-18** SERIAL #147329-152775	1,778	**1,315**	1,130	945
GUITAR	57	MARTIN	**00-18** SERIAL #152776-159061	1,775	**1,312**	1,127	942
GUITAR	58	MARTIN	**00-18** SERIAL #159062-165576	1,769	**1,308**	1,124	939
GUITAR	59	MARTIN	**00-18** SERIAL #165577-171047	1,767	**1,307**	1,123	938
GUITAR	60	MARTIN	**00-18** SERIAL #175537	1,334	**986**	847	708
GUITAR	61	MARTIN	**00-18** SERIAL #175690-181297	1,591	**1,177**	1,011	845
GUITAR	62	MARTIN	**00-18** SERIAL #181298-187384	1,587	**1,174**	1,008	843
GUITAR	64	MARTIN	**00-18** SERIAL #193328-199626	1,407	**1,040**	894	747
GUITAR	65	MARTIN	**00-18** SERIAL #199627-207030	1,404	**1,038**	892	746
GUITAR	66	MARTIN	**00-18** SERIAL #207031-217215	1,400	**1,035**	889	744
GUITAR	67	MARTIN	**00-18** SERIAL #217216-230095	1,394	**1,031**	886	741
GUITAR	68	MARTIN	**00-18** SERIAL #230096-241925	1,237	**915**	786	657
GUITAR	69	MARTIN	**00-18** SERIAL #241926-256003	1,234	**913**	784	655
GUITAR	70	MARTIN	**00-18** SERIAL #256004-271633	1,229	**909**	781	653
GUITAR	71	MARTIN	**00-18** SERIAL #271634-294270	1,186	**877**	753	630
GUITAR	72	MARTIN	**00-18** SERIAL #294271-313302	1,180	**873**	750	627
GUITAR	74	MARTIN	**00-18**	1,200	**888**	763	638
GUITAR	75	MARTIN	**00-18** SERIAL #353388-371828	991	**733**	630	526
GUITAR	63	MARTIN	**00-18C CLASSICAL** SERIAL #187385-193327	582	**430**	370	309
GUITAR	64	MARTIN	**00-18C CLASSICAL** SERIAL #193328-199626	717	**530**	455	380
GUITAR	67	MARTIN	**00-18C CLASSICAL** SERIAL #217216-230095	527	**389**	334	279
GUITAR	68	MARTIN	**00-18C CLASSICAL** SERIAL #230096-241925	526	**389**	334	279
GUITAR	69	MARTIN	**00-18C CLASSICAL** SERIAL #241926-256003	523	**386**	332	277
GUITAR	70	MARTIN	**00-18C CLASSICAL** SERIAL #256004-271633	576	**426**	366	306
GUITAR	72	MARTIN	**00-18C CLASSICAL** SERIAL #294271-313302	489	**362**	311	260
GUITAR	59	MARTIN	**00-18E** FLATTOP, 1 PU, SERIAL #165577-171047	474	**350**	301	251
GUITAR	64	MARTIN	**00-18E** FLATTOP, 1 PU, SERIAL #193328-199626	471	**348**	299	250
GUITAR	38	MARTIN	**00-18G CLASSICAL**	916	**678**	582	487
GUITAR	39	MARTIN	**00-18G CLASSICAL** SERIAL #71867-74061	880	**651**	559	467
GUITAR	40	MARTIN	**00-18G CLASSICAL** SERIAL #74062-76734	864	**639**	549	459
GUITAR	54	MARTIN	**00-18G CLASSICAL** SERIAL #134502-141345	786	**581**	499	417
GUITAR	55	MARTIN	**00-18G CLASSICAL**	1,410	**1,042**	896	749
GUITAR	56	MARTIN	**00-18G CLASSICAL**	749	**554**	476	398
GUITAR	57	MARTIN	**00-18G CLASSICAL** SERIAL #152776-159061	941	**696**	598	500
GUITAR	58	MARTIN	**00-18G CLASSICAL** SERIAL #159062-165576	712	**526**	452	378
GUITAR	60	MARTIN	**00-18G CLASSICAL** SERIAL #171048-175689	675	**499**	429	359
GUITAR	61	MARTIN	**00-18G CLASSICAL** SERIAL #175690-181297	672	**497**	427	357
GUITAR	24	MARTIN	**00-18H HAWAIIAN** SERIAL #19892-22008	1,506	**1,113**	957	800
GUITAR	34	MARTIN	**00-18H HAWAIIAN** SERIAL #55085-58679	1,504	**1,112**	955	799
GUITAR	37	MARTIN	**00-18H HAWAIIAN** SERIAL #65177-68865	1,501	**1,110**	954	797
GUITAR	41	MARTIN	**00-18H HAWAIIAN**	1,473	**1,089**	936	782
GUITAR	26	MARTIN	**00-21** SERIAL #24117-28689	3,761	**2,781**	2,389	1,998
GUITAR	27	MARTIN	**00-21** SERIAL #28690-34435	3,750	**2,773**	2,383	1,992
GUITAR	29	MARTIN	**00-21** SERIAL #37569-40843	3,744	**2,769**	2,379	1,989

TYPE	YR	MFG	PRICES--BASED ON 100% ORIGINAL MODEL	SELL EXC	SELL AVG	BUY EXC	BUY AVG
GUITAR	30	MARTIN	**00-21** SERIAL #40844-45317	3,741	**2,766**	2,377	1,987
GUITAR	31	MARTIN	**00-21** SERIAL #45318-49589	4,250	**3,143**	2,701	2,258
GUITAR	32	MARTIN	**00-21**	3,735	**2,762**	2,373	1,984
GUITAR	34	MARTIN	**00-21** SERIAL #55085-58679	3,732	**2,760**	2,371	1,982
GUITAR	37	MARTIN	**00-21** SERIAL #65177-68865	3,724	**2,754**	2,366	1,978
GUITAR	40	MARTIN	**00-21** SERIAL #74062-76734	4,209	**3,113**	2,674	2,236
GUITAR	50	MARTIN	**00-21**	1,557	**1,151**	989	827
GUITAR	53	MARTIN	**00-21** SERIAL #128437-134501	2,215	**1,638**	1,407	1,177
GUITAR	60	MARTIN	**00-21**	2,073	**1,533**	1,317	1,101
GUITAR	63	MARTIN	**00-21** SERIAL #187385-193327	2,280	**1,686**	1,448	1,211
GUITAR	65	MARTIN	**00-21** SERIAL #199627-207030	2,277	**1,684**	1,446	1,209
GUITAR	66	MARTIN	**00-21** BRAZILIAN ROSEWOOD	2,271	**1,679**	1,443	1,206
GUITAR	67	MARTIN	**00-21** SERIAL #217216-230095	2,265	**1,675**	1,439	1,203
GUITAR	69	MARTIN	**00-21** SERIAL #241926-256003	1,867	**1,380**	1,186	991
GUITAR	71	MARTIN	**00-21** SERIAL #241926-256003	1,450	**1,072**	921	770
GUITAR	72	MARTIN	**00-21** SERIAL # 297575	1,244	**920**	790	660
GUITAR	73	MARTIN	**00-21** SERIAL #313303-333873	1,241	**918**	788	659
GUITAR	75	MARTIN	**00-21**	1,061	**785**	674	564
GUITAR	63	MARTIN	**00-21NY** SERIAL #187385-193327	2,283	**1,689**	1,451	1,213
GUITAR	64	MARTIN	**00-21NY** SERIAL #193328-199626	2,280	**1,686**	1,448	1,211
GUITAR	12	MARTIN	**00-28** SERIAL #11414-11565	4,748	**3,511**	3,017	2,522
GUITAR	13	MARTIN	**00-28**	4,080	**3,017**	2,592	2,167
GUITAR	20	MARTIN	**00-28** SERIAL #14513-15848	3,856	**2,852**	2,450	2,048
GUITAR	24	MARTIN	**00-28** SERIAL #21260	5,319	**3,934**	3,380	2,825
GUITAR	27	MARTIN	**00-28** SERIAL #28690-34435	5,325	**3,938**	3,383	2,828
GUITAR	31	MARTIN	**00-28** SERIAL #45318-49589	8,000	**5,917**	5,083	4,250
GUITAR	32	MARTIN	**00-28** SERIAL #49590-52590	7,996	**5,914**	5,081	4,248
GUITAR	39	MARTIN	**00-28** SERIAL #71867-74061	6,659	**4,925**	4,231	3,537
GUITAR	40	MARTIN	**00-28** SERIAL #74062-76734	6,408	**4,739**	4,071	3,404
GUITAR	44	MARTIN	**00-28** SERIAL #86725-90149	4,946	**3,658**	3,143	2,628
GUITAR	47	MARTIN	**00-28** SERIAL #98159-103468	3,912	**2,893**	2,486	2,078
GUITAR	51	MARTIN	**00-28**	3,624	**2,680**	2,303	1,925
GUITAR	77	MARTIN	**00-28**	1,076	**795**	683	571
GUITAR	n/a	MARTIN	**00-28 (1899)**	4,080	**3,017**	2,592	2,167
GUITAR	66	MARTIN	**00-28C CLASSICAL** SERIAL #207031-217215	1,113	**823**	707	591
GUITAR	68	MARTIN	**00-28C CLASSICAL** SERIAL #230096-241925	1,046	**773**	664	555
GUITAR	69	MARTIN	**00-28C CLASSICAL** SERIAL #241926-256003	1,039	**768**	660	552
GUITAR	71	MARTIN	**00-28C CLASSICAL** SERIAL #271634-294270	983	**727**	624	522
GUITAR	38	MARTIN	**00-28G CLASSICAL** SERIAL #68866-71866	1,550	**1,146**	985	823
GUITAR	40	MARTIN	**00-28G CLASSICAL** SERIAL #74062-76734	1,499	**1,109**	952	796
GUITAR	42	MARTIN	**00-28G CLASSICAL** SERIAL#81588	1,495	**1,106**	950	794
GUITAR	45	MARTIN	**00-28G CLASSICAL**	1,455	**1,076**	924	773
GUITAR	46	MARTIN	**00-28G CLASSICAL** SERIAL #93624-98158	1,402	**1,037**	891	745
GUITAR	47	MARTIN	**00-28G CLASSICAL** SERIAL #98159-103468	1,397	**1,033**	888	742
GUITAR	49	MARTIN	**00-28G CLASSICAL** SERIAL #108270-112961	1,354	**1,001**	860	719
GUITAR	50	MARTIN	**00-28G CLASSICAL** SERIAL #112962-117961	1,350	**998**	858	717

TYPE	YR	MFG	PRICES--BASED ON 100% ORIGINAL MODEL	SELL EXC	SELL AVG	BUY EXC	BUY AVG
GUITAR	51	MARTIN	**00-28G CLASSICAL**	1,355	**1,002**	861	720
GUITAR	55	MARTIN	**00-28G CLASSICAL**	1,336	**988**	849	709
GUITAR	56	MARTIN	**00-28G CLASSICAL** SERIAL #147329-152775	1,276	**944**	811	678
GUITAR	59	MARTIN	**00-28G CLASSICAL** BRAZILIAN ROSEWOOD	2,049	**1,515**	1,302	1,088
GUITAR	60	MARTIN	**00-28G CLASSICAL** SERIAL #171048-175689	981	**725**	623	521
GUITAR	62	MARTIN	**00-28G CLASSICAL** SERIAL#181934	923	**683**	586	490
GUITAR	07	MARTIN	**00-30** SERIAL #10330-10727	1,124	**831**	714	597
GUITAR	29	MARTIN	**00-40H HAWAIIAN** SERIAL #37569-40843	3,658	**2,705**	2,324	1,943
GUITAR	30	MARTIN	**00-40H HAWAIIAN** SERIAL #40844-45317	1,179	**872**	749	626
GUITAR	32	MARTIN	**00-40H HAWAIIAN** SERIAL #49590-52590	4,536	**3,354**	2,882	2,409
GUITAR	34	MARTIN	**00-40H HAWAIIAN** SERIAL #55085-58679	4,430	**3,276**	2,815	2,353
GUITAR	35	MARTIN	**00-40H HAWAIIAN** SERIAL #58680-61947	4,424	**3,272**	2,811	2,350
GUITAR	37	MARTIN	**00-40H HAWAIIAN**	4,492	**3,322**	2,854	2,386
GUITAR	32	MARTIN	**00-40H HAWAIIAN CUSTOM**	12,528	**9,265**	7,960	6,655
GUITAR	04	MARTIN	**00-42** SERIAL #9811-9988	9,690	**7,166**	6,157	5,147
GUITAR	23	MARTIN	**00-42** SERIAL #17840-19891	9,675	**7,156**	6,148	5,140
GUITAR	29	MARTIN	**00-42** SERIAL #37569-40843	14,958	**11,063**	9,505	7,946
GUITAR	30	MARTIN	**00-42**	12,480	**9,230**	7,930	6,630
GUITAR	36	MARTIN	**00-42** SERIAL #61948-65176	18,414	**13,619**	11,701	9,782
GUITAR	37	MARTIN	**00-42** SERIAL #65177-68865	18,411	**13,617**	11,699	9,781
GUITAR	38	MARTIN	**00-42** SERIAL #68866-71866	18,404	**13,611**	11,694	9,777
GUITAR	43	MARTIN	**00-42** SERIAL #83108-86724	16,169	**11,958**	10,274	8,589
GUITAR	00	MARTIN	**00-42 (1900)**	6,192	**4,579**	3,934	3,289
GUITAR	22	MARTIN	**00-42 (WURLITZER MODEL)**	12,000	**8,875**	7,625	6,375
GUITAR	05	MARTIN	**00-45** SERIAL #9989-10120	22,300	**16,493**	14,170	11,847
GUITAR	11	MARTIN	**00-45** SERIAL #11204-11413	22,294	**16,488**	14,166	11,843
GUITAR	19	MARTIN	**00-45** SERIAL #13451-14512	22,295	**16,489**	14,166	11,844
GUITAR	20	MARTIN	**00-45** SERIAL #14513-15848	22,290	**16,485**	14,163	11,841
GUITAR	24	MARTIN	**00-45** SERIAL #19892-22008	22,281	**16,479**	14,158	11,837
GUITAR	25	MARTIN	**00-45** SERIAL #22009-24116	22,871	**16,915**	14,532	12,150
GUITAR	29	MARTIN	**00-45** SERIAL #37569-40843	28,767	**21,275**	18,279	15,282
GUITAR	38	MARTIN	**00-45** SERIAL #68866-71866	31,584	**23,359**	20,069	16,779
GUITAR	26	MARTIN	**000-18** SERIAL #24117-28689	4,966	**3,672**	3,155	2,638
GUITAR	27	MARTIN	**000-18** SERIAL #28690-34435	4,961	**3,669**	3,152	2,635
GUITAR	29	MARTIN	**000-18** SERIAL #37569-40843	4,875	**3,606**	3,098	2,590
GUITAR	31	MARTIN	**000-18** SERIAL #45318-49589	4,743	**3,508**	3,014	2,519
GUITAR	34	MARTIN	**000-18** SERIAL #55085-58679	4,604	**3,405**	2,925	2,445
GUITAR	35	MARTIN	**000-18** SERIAL #58680-61947	5,832	**4,313**	3,705	3,098
GUITAR	36	MARTIN	**000-18** SERIAL #61948-65176	4,428	**3,275**	2,813	2,352
GUITAR	37	MARTIN	**000-18** SERIAL #65177-68865	4,424	**3,272**	2,811	2,350
GUITAR	39	MARTIN	**000-18** SUNBURST	4,800	**3,550**	3,050	2,550
GUITAR	40	MARTIN	**000-18**	4,204	**3,109**	2,671	2,233
GUITAR	41	MARTIN	**000-18** SERIAL #76735-80013	4,197	**3,104**	2,666	2,229
GUITAR	42	MARTIN	**000-18** SERIAL #80014-83107	3,888	**2,876**	2,471	2,066
GUITAR	43	MARTIN	**000-18** SERIAL #83108-86724	3,801	**2,811**	2,415	2,019

TYPE	YR	MFG	PRICES--BASED ON 100% ORIGINAL MODEL	SELL EXC	SELL AVG	BUY EXC	BUY AVG
GUITAR	44	MARTIN	000-18 SERIAL #86725-90149	3,707	2,742	2,355	1,969
GUITAR	45	MARTIN	000-18 SERIAL #90150-93623	3,622	2,678	2,301	1,924
GUITAR	46	MARTIN	000-18 SERIAL #93624-98158	3,486	2,578	2,215	1,852
GUITAR	47	MARTIN	000-18 SERIAL #98159-103468	3,350	2,477	2,128	1,779
GUITAR	48	MARTIN	000-18 SERIAL #103469-108269	3,251	2,404	2,066	1,727
GUITAR	49	MARTIN	000-18 SERIAL #108270-112961	3,241	2,397	2,059	1,722
GUITAR	50	MARTIN	000-18 SERIAL #112962-117961	2,383	1,762	1,514	1,266
GUITAR	51	MARTIN	000-18 SERIAL #117962-122799	2,261	1,672	1,437	1,201
GUITAR	52	MARTIN	000-18 SERIAL #122800-128436	2,186	1,617	1,389	1,161
GUITAR	54	MARTIN	000-18 SERIAL #134502-141345	2,000	1,479	1,271	1,062
GUITAR	55	MARTIN	000-18 SERIAL #141346-147328	1,943	1,437	1,234	1,032
GUITAR	56	MARTIN	000-18 SERIAL #147329-152775	1,887	1,395	1,199	1,002
GUITAR	57	MARTIN	000-18 SERIAL #152776-159061	1,886	1,395	1,198	1,002
GUITAR	58	MARTIN	000-18 SERIAL #159062-165576	1,882	1,392	1,196	1,000
GUITAR	59	MARTIN	000-18 SERIAL #165577-171047	1,765	1,305	1,121	937
GUITAR	61	MARTIN	000-18 SERIAL #175690-181297	1,731	1,280	1,100	920
GUITAR	62	MARTIN	000-18 SERIAL #181298-187384	1,616	1,195	1,027	858
GUITAR	63	MARTIN	000-18 SERIAL #187385-193327	1,524	1,127	968	809
GUITAR	64	MARTIN	000-18	1,461	1,080	928	776
GUITAR	65	MARTIN	000-18 SERIAL #199627-207030	1,504	1,112	955	799
GUITAR	66	MARTIN	000-18 SERIAL #207031-217215	1,393	1,030	885	740
GUITAR	67	MARTIN	000-18 SERIAL #217216-230095	1,380	1,020	877	733
GUITAR	68	MARTIN	000-18 SERIAL #230096-241925	1,483	1,096	942	787
GUITAR	69	MARTIN	000-18	1,217	900	773	646
GUITAR	70	MARTIN	000-18	1,256	929	798	667
GUITAR	71	MARTIN	000-18	1,201	888	763	638
GUITAR	72	MARTIN	000-18 SERIAL #294271-313302	1,194	883	758	634
GUITAR	74	MARTIN	000-18	1,143	845	726	607
GUITAR	30	MARTIN	000-18P SERIAL #40844-45317 PLECTRUM	897	663	570	476
GUITAR	38	MARTIN	000-18T TENOR, SERIAL #68866-71866	893	661	567	474
GUITAR	68	MARTIN	000-18T TENOR	677	501	430	360
GUITAR	38	MARTIN	000-21 SERIAL #68866-71866	9,781	7,234	6,215	5,196
GUITAR	39	MARTIN	000-21 SERIAL #71867-74061	6,421	4,749	4,080	3,411
GUITAR	40	MARTIN	000-21 SERIAL #74062-76734	6,302	4,661	4,004	3,348
GUITAR	43	MARTIN	000-21 SERIAL #83108-86724	5,394	3,989	3,427	2,865
GUITAR	44	MARTIN	000-21 SERIAL #86725-90149	5,348	3,955	3,398	2,841
GUITAR	45	MARTIN	000-21	4,984	3,686	3,167	2,647
GUITAR	46	MARTIN	000-21 SERIAL #93624-98158	4,445	3,288	2,824	2,361
GUITAR	47	MARTIN	000-21 SERIAL #98159-103468	4,492	3,322	2,854	2,386
GUITAR	48	MARTIN	000-21 SERIAL #103469-108269	4,030	2,980	2,560	2,140
GUITAR	49	MARTIN	000-21 SERIAL #108270-112961	3,690	2,729	2,344	1,960
GUITAR	50	MARTIN	000-21 SERIAL #112962-117961	3,450	2,551	2,192	1,832
GUITAR	54	MARTIN	000-21 SERIAL #134502-141345	3,167	2,342	2,012	1,682
GUITAR	58	MARTIN	000-21 SERIAL #159062-165576	2,084	1,541	1,324	1,107

TYPE	YR	MFG	PRICES--BASED ON 100% ORIGINAL MODEL	SELL EXC	SELL AVG	BUY EXC	BUY AVG
GUITAR	59	MARTIN	**000-21** SERIAL #165577-171047	2,235	**1,653**	1,420	1,187
GUITAR	26	MARTIN	**000-28** SERIAL #24117-28689	15,817	**11,698**	10,050	8,403
GUITAR	28	MARTIN	**000-28** SERIAL #34436-37568	14,497	**10,722**	9,212	7,702
GUITAR	29	MARTIN	**000-28**	14,402	**10,652**	9,151	7,651
GUITAR	32	MARTIN	**000-28**	11,270	**8,335**	7,161	5,987
GUITAR	34	MARTIN	**000-28** SERIAL #55085-58679	12,658	**9,362**	8,043	6,724
GUITAR	35	MARTIN	**000-28** SERIAL #58680-61947	11,299	**8,356**	7,179	6,002
GUITAR	37	MARTIN	**000-28** SERIAL #66437	16,381	**12,115**	10,409	8,702
GUITAR	37	MARTIN	**000-28** SERIAL #68449-68865	17,280	**12,780**	10,980	9,180
GUITAR	38	MARTIN	**000-28** SERIAL #68866-71866	17,280	**12,780**	10,980	9,180
GUITAR	40	MARTIN	**000-28** SERIAL #74062-76734	11,750	**8,690**	7,466	6,242
GUITAR	41	MARTIN	**000-28** SERIAL #76735-80013	11,740	**8,683**	7,460	6,237
GUITAR	42	MARTIN	**000-28** SERIAL #80014-83107	11,832	**8,750**	7,518	6,285
GUITAR	43	MARTIN	**000-28** SERIAL #84460	9,241	**6,835**	5,872	4,909
GUITAR	44	MARTIN	**000-28** SCALLOPED BRACES, SERIAL #86725-90149	11,737	**8,681**	7,458	6,235
GUITAR	45	MARTIN	**000-28** SERIAL #90150-93623	8,603	**6,363**	5,466	4,570
GUITAR	46	MARTIN	**000-28** SERIAL #93624-98158	11,520	**8,520**	7,320	6,120
GUITAR	47	MARTIN	**000-28** SERIAL #98159-103468	8,566	**6,335**	5,443	4,550
GUITAR	48	MARTIN	**000-28** SERIAL #103469-108269	8,547	**6,321**	5,431	4,541
GUITAR	49	MARTIN	**000-28** SERIAL #108270-112961	8,555	**6,327**	5,436	4,545
GUITAR	50	MARTIN	**000-28** SERIAL #112962-117961	5,899	**4,362**	3,748	3,133
GUITAR	51	MARTIN	**000-28** SERIAL #117962-122799	5,895	**4,360**	3,746	3,131
GUITAR	52	MARTIN	**000-28** SERIAL #122800-128436	5,891	**4,357**	3,743	3,129
GUITAR	53	MARTIN	**000-28** SERIAL #128437-134501	5,909	**4,370**	3,755	3,139
GUITAR	54	MARTIN	**000-28**	3,547	**2,623**	2,253	1,884
GUITAR	55	MARTIN	**000-28** SERIAL #142772	4,619	**3,416**	2,935	2,454
GUITAR	56	MARTIN	**000-28** SERIAL #147329-152775	4,549	**3,364**	2,890	2,416
GUITAR	57	MARTIN	**000-28** SERIAL #152776-159061	4,626	**3,421**	2,939	2,457
GUITAR	58	MARTIN	**000-28**	3,744	**2,769**	2,379	1,989
GUITAR	60	MARTIN	**000-28**	3,733	**2,761**	2,372	1,983
GUITAR	65	MARTIN	**000-28** BRAZILIAN ROSEWOOD	4,176	**3,088**	2,653	2,218
GUITAR	66	MARTIN	**000-28** SERIAL #207031-217215	4,247	**3,141**	2,698	2,256
GUITAR	67	MARTIN	**000-28** SERIAL #217216-230095	2,186	**1,617**	1,389	1,161
GUITAR	68	MARTIN	**000-28**	2,090	**1,546**	1,328	1,110
GUITAR	70	MARTIN	**000-28** INDIAN ROSEWOOD, SERIAL #256004-271633	1,451	**1,073**	922	771
GUITAR	73	MARTIN	**000-28** SERIAL #313303-333873	1,316	**973**	836	699
GUITAR	74	MARTIN	**000-28** SERIAL #333874-353387	1,191	**881**	757	632
GUITAR	62	MARTIN	**000-28C CLASSICAL** SERIAL #181298-187384	2,073	**1,533**	1,317	1,101
GUITAR	63	MARTIN	**000-28C CLASSICAL** SERIAL #187385-193327	2,068	**1,530**	1,314	1,099
GUITAR	21	MARTIN	**000-42** SERIAL #15849-16758	30,955	**22,893**	19,669	16,444
GUITAR	38	MARTIN	**000-42**	51,499	**38,087**	32,723	27,358
GUITAR	39	MARTIN	**000-42** SERIAL #71867-74061	51,504	**38,091**	32,726	27,361
GUITAR	40	MARTIN	**000-42**	51,499	**38,087**	32,723	27,358
GUITAR	41	MARTIN	**000-42** SERIAL #76735-80013	44,851	**33,171**	28,499	23,827
GUITAR	42	MARTIN	**000-42**	44,850	**33,170**	28,498	23,826
GUITAR	11	MARTIN	**000-45** 12-FRET SLOTHEAD	24,353	**18,011**	15,474	12,937

TYPE	YR	MFG	PRICES--BASED ON 100% ORIGINAL MODEL	SELL EXC	SELL AVG	BUY EXC	BUY AVG
GUITAR	13	MARTIN	**000-45** SERIAL #11566-11821	13,757	**10,175**	8,741	7,308
GUITAR	23	MARTIN	**000-45** SERIAL #17840-19891	22,591	**16,708**	14,355	12,001
GUITAR	24	MARTIN	**000-45** SERIAL #19892-22008	22,560	**16,685**	14,335	11,985
GUITAR	27	MARTIN	**000-45** SERIAL #28690-34435	31,491	**23,290**	20,010	16,730
GUITAR	28	MARTIN	**000-45**	37,963	**28,076**	24,122	20,167
GUITAR	30	MARTIN	**000-45** SERIAL #40844-45317	49,671	**36,736**	31,562	26,387
GUITAR	34	MARTIN	**000-45** SERIAL #55085-58679	66,971	**49,531**	42,554	35,578
GUITAR	35	MARTIN	**000-45** SERIAL #58680-61947	66,968	**49,528**	42,552	35,577
GUITAR	36	MARTIN	**000-45** SERIAL #61948-65176	66,961	**49,523**	42,548	35,573
GUITAR	37	MARTIN	**000-45** 14-FRET NECK, SERIAL #65177-68865	66,975	**49,533**	42,557	35,580
GUITAR	38	MARTIN	**000-45** SERIAL #6866-71866	66,959	**49,521**	42,546	35,571
GUITAR	39	MARTIN	**000-45** SERIAL #71867-74061	62,204	**46,005**	39,525	33,045
GUITAR	40	MARTIN	**000-45** SERIAL #74062-76734	62,195	**45,998**	39,520	33,041
GUITAR	41	MARTIN	**000-45** BRAZILIAN ROSEWOOD, ADIRONDACK TOP, PREWAR	38,400	**28,400**	24,400	20,400
GUITAR	70	MARTIN	**000-45** INDIAN ROSEWOOD, SERIAL #256004-271633	7,492	**5,541**	4,761	3,980
GUITAR	11	MARTIN	**1-17** SERIAL #11204-11413	939	**695**	597	499
GUITAR	31	MARTIN	**1-17**	765	**565**	486	406
GUITAR	32	MARTIN	**1-17** SERIAL #49590-52590	762	**563**	484	404
GUITAR	29	MARTIN	**1-17P** PLECTRUM, SERIAL #37569-40843	762	**563**	484	404
GUITAR	30	MARTIN	**1-17P** PLECTRUM, SERIAL #40844-45317	770	**570**	489	409
GUITAR	31	MARTIN	**1-17P** PLECTRUM, SERIAL #45318-49589	743	**549**	472	394
GUITAR	18	MARTIN	**1-18** SERIAL #12989-13450	752	**556**	478	399
GUITAR	20	MARTIN	**1-18**	1,637	**1,211**	1,040	870
GUITAR	26	MARTIN	**1-18** SERIAL #24117-28689	743	**549**	472	394
GUITAR	19	MARTIN	**1-18K HAWAIIAN** KOA WOOD, SERIAL #13451-14512	747	**553**	475	397
GUITAR	20	MARTIN	**1-21** SERIAL #14513-15848	1,682	**1,244**	1,069	894
GUITAR	25	MARTIN	**1-21** SERIAL #22009-24116	1,665	**1,231**	1,058	884
GUITAR	34	MARTIN	**1-21** SERIAL #55085-58679	1,877	**1,388**	1,193	997
GUITAR	15	MARTIN	**1-28** SERIAL #12048-12209	1,776	**1,314**	1,129	944
GUITAR	19	MARTIN	**1-28** SERIAL #13451-14512	1,659	**1,227**	1,054	881
GUITAR	29	MARTIN	**1-28P** PLECTRUM, SERIAL #37569-40843	893	**661**	567	474
GUITAR	02	MARTIN	**1-42** SERIAL #9311-9528	3,353	**2,480**	2,130	1,781
GUITAR	17	MARTIN	**2 1/2-17** SERIAL #12391-12988	715	**528**	454	379
GUITAR	41	MARTIN	**2 1/2-17** SERIAL #76735-80013	719	**531**	456	381
GUITAR	70	MARTIN	**2 1/2-17 (1870)**	3,360	**2,485**	2,135	1,785
GUITAR	42	MARTIN	**2 1/2-18** SERIAL #80014-83107	980	**747**	635	485
GUITAR	09	MARTIN	**2 1/2-26** HARDSHELL CASE, SERIAL #11002	3,460	**2,559**	2,199	1,838
GUITAR	09	MARTIN	**2 1/2-28** SERIAL #11002	3,456	**2,556**	2,196	1,836
GUITAR	22	MARTIN	**2-17** SERIAL #16759-17839	890	**658**	566	473
GUITAR	23	MARTIN	**2-17** SERIAL #17840-19891	835	**617**	530	443
GUITAR	25	MARTIN	**2-17** SERIAL #22009-24116	798	**590**	507	424
GUITAR	26	MARTIN	**2-17** SERIAL #24117-28689	816	**603**	518	433
GUITAR	27	MARTIN	**2-17** SERIAL #28690-34435	813	**601**	516	431
GUITAR	28	MARTIN	**2-17** SERIAL #34436-37568	787	**582**	500	418

TYPE	YR	MFG	PRICES--BASED ON 100% ORIGINAL MODEL	SELL EXC	SELL AVG	BUY EXC	BUY AVG
GUITAR	29	MARTIN	**2-17** SERIAL #37569-40843	768	**568**	488	408
GUITAR	30	MARTIN	**2-17** SERIAL #40844-45317	753	**557**	478	400
GUITAR	31	MARTIN	**2-17** SERIAL #45318-49589	723	**535**	459	384
GUITAR	29	MARTIN	**2-17K HAWAIIAN** KOA WOOD, SERIAL #37569-40843	645	**477**	409	342
GUITAR	41	MARTIN	**2-18** SERIAL #76735-80013	705	**521**	448	374
GUITAR	28	MARTIN	**2-18T** TENOR, SERIAL #34436-37568	826	**611**	525	439
GUITAR	29	MARTIN	**2-18T** TENOR, SERIAL #37569-40843	883	**653**	561	469
GUITAR	30	MARTIN	**2-18T** TENOR, SERIAL #40844-45317	883	**653**	561	469
GUITAR	36	MARTIN	**2-20**	1,783	**1,319**	1,133	947
GUITAR	50	MARTIN	**2-20 INTRO 1850's**	1,593	**1,178**	1,012	846
GUITAR	91	MARTIN	**2-21 (1891)**	3,168	**2,343**	2,013	1,683
GUITAR	03	MARTIN	**2-27**	3,840	**2,840**	2,440	2,040
GUITAR	29	MARTIN	**2-28T** TENOR, SERIAL #37569-40843	1,927	**1,425**	1,224	1,024
GUITAR	30	MARTIN	**2-44 OLCOTT BIKFORD MODEL** SERIAL #40844-45317	3,664	**2,710**	2,328	1,946
GUITAR	60	MARTIN	**3-17 (1860 - 1870)** CUSTOM WOOD AND METAL CASE	2,032	**1,503**	1,291	1,079
GUITAR	90	MARTIN	**3-17 (1890'S)** BRAZILIAN ROSEWOOD	2,047	**1,514**	1,301	1,087
GUITAR	96	MARTIN	**3-17 (1896)**	2,126	**1,572**	1,351	1,129
GUITAR	27	MARTIN	**5-15T** TENOR, SERIAL #28690-34435	722	**534**	459	384
GUITAR	50	MARTIN	**5-15T** TENOR, SERIAL #112962-117961	711	**526**	452	377
GUITAR	52	MARTIN	**5-15T** TENOR, SERIAL #122800-128436	709	**524**	450	376
GUITAR	55	MARTIN	**5-15T** TENOR, SERIAL #141346-147328	705	**521**	448	374
GUITAR	58	MARTIN	**5-15T** TENOR	598	**442**	380	317
GUITAR	62	MARTIN	**5-16** SPRUCE TOP, SERIAL #181298-187384	714	**528**	453	379
GUITAR	27	MARTIN	**5-17T** TENOR, SERIAL #28690-34435	710	**525**	451	377
GUITAR	28	MARTIN	**5-17T** TENOR	598	**442**	380	317
GUITAR	29	MARTIN	**5-17T** TENOR	601	**445**	382	319
GUITAR	30	MARTIN	**5-17T** TENOR, SERIAL #40844-45317	539	**399**	342	286
GUITAR	37	MARTIN	**5-17T** TENOR, SERIAL #65177-68865	616	**455**	391	327
GUITAR	37	MARTIN	**5-18**	1,195	**883**	759	634
GUITAR	45	MARTIN	**5-18** SERIAL #90150-93623	965	**714**	613	513
GUITAR	46	MARTIN	**5-18** SERIAL #93624-98158	962	**712**	611	511
GUITAR	48	MARTIN	**5-18** SERIAL #103469-108269	980	**724**	622	520
GUITAR	50	MARTIN	**5-18** SERIAL #112962-117961	826	**611**	525	439
GUITAR	56	MARTIN	**5-18** SERIAL #147329-152775	821	**607**	522	436
GUITAR	57	MARTIN	**5-18**	956	**707**	607	507
GUITAR	58	MARTIN	**5-18** SERIAL #159062-165576	816	**604**	519	434
GUITAR	60	MARTIN	**5-18**	822	**608**	522	437
GUITAR	68	MARTIN	**5-18** SERIAL #230096-241925	847	**626**	538	450
GUITAR	72	MARTIN	**5-18** SERIAL #294271-313302	720	**532**	457	382
GUITAR	73	MARTIN	**5-18** SERIAL #313303-333873	716	**529**	455	380
GUITAR	75	MARTIN	**5-18** SERIAL #353388-371828	715	**528**	454	379
GUITAR	77	MARTIN	**5-18** SERIAL #389235	713	**527**	453	378
GUITAR	70	MARTIN	**5-18S** SERIAL #256004-271633	715	**528**	454	379
GUITAR	55	MARTIN	**5-18T** TENOR, SERIAL #141346-147328	711	**526**	452	377
GUITAR	27	MARTIN	**5-21** SERIAL #28690-34435	715	**528**	454	379

TYPE	YR	MFG	PRICES--BASED ON 100% ORIGINAL MODEL	SELL EXC	SELL AVG	BUY EXC	BUY AVG
GUITAR	27	MARTIN	**5-21T** TENOR, SERIAL #28690-34435	1,076	**795**	683	571
GUITAR	39	MARTIN	**5-28T** TENOR, SERIAL #71867-74061	710	**525**	451	377
GUITAR	21	MARTIN	**5-45** PEARL INLAY, SERIAL #15849-16758	9,453	**6,991**	6,006	5,021
GUITAR	32	MARTIN	**C-1** ARCHTOP, SERIAL #49590-52590	1,335	**987**	848	709
GUITAR	34	MARTIN	**C-1** ARCHTOP, F-HOLES, SERIAL #55085-58679	1,331	**984**	846	707
GUITAR	35	MARTIN	**C-1** ARCHTOP, F-HOLES, SERIAL #58680-61947	1,329	**983**	844	706
GUITAR	36	MARTIN	**C-1** ARCHTOP, SERIAL #61948-65176	1,295	**957**	822	687
GUITAR	42	MARTIN	**C-1** ARCHTOP, F-HOLES, SERIAL #80014-83107	1,289	**953**	819	684
GUITAR	32	MARTIN	**C-1P** PLECTRUM, SERIAL #49590-52590	1,337	**989**	849	710
GUITAR	33	MARTIN	**C-1P** PLECTRUM, SERIAL #52591-55084	1,333	**986**	847	708
GUITAR	33	MARTIN	**C-1T** TENOR, SERIAL #52591-55084	1,332	**985**	846	707
GUITAR	34	MARTIN	**C-1T** TENOR, SERIAL #55085-58679	1,328	**982**	844	705
GUITAR	31	MARTIN	**C-2** ARCHTOP, ROUND HOLE, SERIAL #45318-49589	2,146	**1,587**	1,363	1,140
GUITAR	32	MARTIN	**C-2** ARCHTOP, ROUND HOLE, SERIAL #49590-52590	2,138	**1,581**	1,359	1,136
GUITAR	34	MARTIN	**C-2** ARCHTOP, F-HOLES, SERIAL #55085-58679	2,135	**1,579**	1,356	1,134
GUITAR	35	MARTIN	**C-2** ARCHTOP	2,091	**1,547**	1,329	1,111
GUITAR	36	MARTIN	**C-2** SUNBURST, ARCHTOP, F-HOLES, SERIAL #61948-65176	2,138	**1,581**	1,359	1,136
GUITAR	37	MARTIN	**C-2** ARCHTOP, F-HOLES, SERIAL #65177-68865	2,137	**1,581**	1,358	1,135
GUITAR	39	MARTIN	**C-2** ARCHTOP, F-HOLES, SERIAL #71867-74061	2,135	**1,579**	1,356	1,134
GUITAR	32	MARTIN	**C-2T** TENOR, SERIAL #49590-52590	1,475	**1,091**	937	783
GUITAR	32	MARTIN	**C-3** ARCHTOP, ROUND HOLE, SERIAL #49590-52590	2,897	**2,142**	1,840	1,539
GUITAR	33	MARTIN	**C-3** ARCHTOP, SERIAL #52591-55084	2,956	**2,186**	1,878	1,570
GUITAR	34	MARTIN	**C-3** ARCHTOP, SERIAL #55085-58679 F-HOLES	2,987	**2,209**	1,898	1,587
GUITAR	72	MARTIN	**D-12-18** 12-STRING	822	**608**	522	437
GUITAR	75	MARTIN	**D-12-18** 12-STRING	677	**501**	430	360
GUITAR	64	MARTIN	**D-12-20** 12-STRING	1,001	**740**	636	531
GUITAR	65	MARTIN	**D-12-20**	1,035	**766**	658	550
GUITAR	66	MARTIN	**D-12-20** 12-STRING, SERIAL #207031-217215	935	**691**	594	496
GUITAR	67	MARTIN	**D-12-20** 12-STRING, SERIAL #217216-230095	954	**705**	606	506
GUITAR	68	MARTIN	**D-12-20** 12-STRING, SERIAL #230096-241925	916	**678**	582	487
GUITAR	69	MARTIN	**D-12-20** 12-STRING, SERIAL #241926-256003	912	**674**	579	484
GUITAR	70	MARTIN	**D-12-20** 12-STRING, SERIAL #256004-271633	899	**665**	571	477
GUITAR	70	MARTIN	**D-12-20** 12-STRING, LEFT-HANDED	981	**725**	623	521
GUITAR	71	MARTIN	**D-12-20** 12-STRING, SERIAL #271634-294270	894	**661**	568	475
GUITAR	72	MARTIN	**D-12-20** 12-STRING, SERIAL #294271-313302	788	**582**	500	418
GUITAR	75	MARTIN	**D-12-20**	796	**589**	506	423
GUITAR	68	MARTIN	**D-12-28** INDIAN ROSEWOOD, 12-STRING	949	**702**	603	504
GUITAR	73	MARTIN	**D-12-28** NATURAL TOP, 12-STRING	871	**644**	553	463
GUITAR	75	MARTIN	**D-12-28** 12-STRING, SERIAL #353388-371828	851	**629**	541	452
GUITAR	66	MARTIN	**D-12-35** 12-STRING, SERIAL #207031-217215	1,866	**1,380**	1,185	991
GUITAR	67	MARTIN	**D-12-35** 12-STRING, SERIAL #217216-230095	1,863	**1,378**	1,184	989
GUITAR	68	MARTIN	**D-12-35** 12-STRING, SERIAL #230096-241925	1,657	**1,226**	1,053	880
GUITAR	69	MARTIN	**D-12-35** 12-STRING, SERIAL #241926-256003	1,656	**1,224**	1,052	879

TYPE	YR	MFG	PRICES--BASED ON 100% ORIGINAL MODEL	SELL EXC	SELL AVG	BUY EXC	BUY AVG
GUITAR	70	MARTIN	**D-12-35** 12-STRING, SERIAL #256004-271633	888	**657**	564	472
GUITAR	71	MARTIN	**D-12-35** 12-STRING, SERIAL #271634-294270	862	**637**	547	457
GUITAR	72	MARTIN	**D-12-35** 12-STRING, SERIAL #294271-313302	858	**634**	545	455
GUITAR	73	MARTIN	**D-12-35** 12-STRING, SERIAL #313303-333873	855	**632**	543	454
GUITAR	74	MARTIN	**D-12-35** 12-STRING, SERIAL #333874-353387	852	**630**	541	452
GUITAR	75	MARTIN	**D-12-35** 12-STIRNG, SERIAL #353388-371828	851	**629**	541	452
GUITAR	70	MARTIN	**D-12-41** 12-STRING, SERIAL #256004-271633	1,711	**1,265**	1,087	909
GUITAR	70	MARTIN	**D-12-45** 12-STRING, SERIAL #256004-271633	1,754	**1,297**	1,115	932
GUITAR	32	MARTIN	**D-18**	14,958	**11,063**	9,505	7,946
GUITAR	33	MARTIN	**D-18** SERIAL #52591-55084	14,955	**11,061**	9,503	7,945
GUITAR	34	MARTIN	**D-18** SERIAL #55085-58679	14,950	**11,056**	9,499	7,942
GUITAR	35	MARTIN	**D-18** SERIAL #58680-61947	12,808	**9,472**	8,138	6,804
GUITAR	36	MARTIN	**D-18** SERIAL #61948-65176	9,599	**7,099**	6,099	5,099
GUITAR	37	MARTIN	**D-18** SERIAL #65177-68865	9,060	**6,700**	5,757	4,813
GUITAR	38	MARTIN	**D-18** SERIAL #68866-71866	9,598	**7,098**	6,098	5,098
GUITAR	39	MARTIN	**D-18** SERIAL #71867-74061	10,423	**7,709**	6,623	5,537
GUITAR	40	MARTIN	**D-18** SERIAL #74062-76734	9,597	**7,097**	6,098	5,098
GUITAR	41	MARTIN	**D-18** SERIAL #76735-80013	13,920	**10,295**	8,845	7,395
GUITAR	42	MARTIN	**D-18** SERIAL #80014-83107	6,440	**4,763**	4,092	3,421
GUITAR	43	MARTIN	**D-18** SERIAL #83108-86724	6,443	**4,765**	4,094	3,423
GUITAR	44	MARTIN	**D-18** SERIAL #86725-90149	7,992	**5,911**	5,078	4,246
GUITAR	45	MARTIN	**D-18** SERIAL #90150-93623	4,448	**3,290**	2,826	2,363
GUITAR	46	MARTIN	**D-18** SERIAL #93624-98158	4,443	**3,286**	2,823	2,360
GUITAR	47	MARTIN	**D-18** SERIAL #98159-103468	4,060	**3,003**	2,580	2,157
GUITAR	48	MARTIN	**D-18** SERIAL #103469-108269	4,056	**2,999**	2,577	2,154
GUITAR	49	MARTIN	**D-18** SERIAL #108270-112961	4,052	**2,996**	2,574	2,152
GUITAR	51	MARTIN	**D-18** SERIAL #117962-122799	3,428	**2,535**	2,178	1,821
GUITAR	52	MARTIN	**D-18** SERIAL #122800-128436	3,045	**2,252**	1,934	1,617
GUITAR	53	MARTIN	**D-18** SERIAL #128437-134501	2,229	**1,648**	1,416	1,184
GUITAR	54	MARTIN	**D-18** SERIAL #134502-141345	3,624	**2,680**	2,303	1,925
GUITAR	55	MARTIN	**D-18** SERIAL #141346-147328	2,280	**1,686**	1,449	1,211
GUITAR	56	MARTIN	**D-18** SERIAL #147329-152775	2,071	**1,532**	1,316	1,100
GUITAR	57	MARTIN	**D-18** SERIAL #152776-159061	2,055	**1,520**	1,306	1,091
GUITAR	58	MARTIN	**D-18** SERIAL #159062-165576	2,054	**1,519**	1,305	1,091
GUITAR	59	MARTIN	**D-18** SERIAL #165577-171047	2,049	**1,515**	1,302	1,088
GUITAR	60	MARTIN	**D-18** SERIAL #171048-175689	1,941	**1,435**	1,233	1,031
GUITAR	61	MARTIN	**D-18** SERIAL #175690-181297	1,938	**1,433**	1,231	1,029
GUITAR	62	MARTIN	**D-18** SERIAL #181298-187384	1,642	**1,214**	1,043	872
GUITAR	63	MARTIN	**D-18**	1,640	**1,213**	1,042	871
GUITAR	64	MARTIN	**D-18** SERIAL #193328-199626	1,633	**1,208**	1,038	868
GUITAR	65	MARTIN	**D-18** TORTOISE PICKGUARD	1,652	**1,221**	1,049	877
GUITAR	66	MARTIN	**D-18**	1,358	**1,004**	863	721
GUITAR	67	MARTIN	**D-18** SERIAL #217216-230095	1,254	**927**	797	666

TYPE	YR	MFG	PRICES--BASED ON 100% ORIGINAL MODEL	SELL EXC	SELL AVG	BUY EXC	BUY AVG
GUITAR	68	MARTIN	**D-18** SERIAL #230096-241925	1,264	**935**	803	671
GUITAR	69	MARTIN	**D-18** SERIAL #241926-256003	1,250	**925**	794	664
GUITAR	70	MARTIN	**D-18** SERIAL #256004-271633	1,252	**926**	796	665
GUITAR	71	MARTIN	**D-18** SERIAL #271634-294270	1,119	**827**	711	594
GUITAR	72	MARTIN	**D-18** SERIAL #294271-313302	1,029	**761**	653	546
GUITAR	73	MARTIN	**D-18** SERIAL #313303-333873	1,009	**746**	641	536
GUITAR	74	MARTIN	**D-18** SERIAL #333874-353387	1,201	**888**	763	638
GUITAR	75	MARTIN	**D-18** SERIAL #353388-371828	1,033	**764**	656	549
GUITAR	67	MARTIN	**D-18S** SERIAL #217216-230095	1,326	**981**	843	704
GUITAR	69	MARTIN	**D-18S** SERIAL #241926-256003	1,438	**1,063**	913	763
GUITAR	70	MARTIN	**D-18S** SERIAL #256004-271633	1,039	**768**	660	552
GUITAR	71	MARTIN	**D-18S**	1,037	**767**	659	551
GUITAR	73	MARTIN	**D-18S**	1,034	**765**	657	549
GUITAR	56	MARTIN	**D-21** SERIAL #147329-152775	3,137	**2,320**	1,993	1,666
GUITAR	58	MARTIN	**D-21**	3,223	**2,384**	2,048	1,712
GUITAR	60	MARTIN	**D-21** SERIAL #171048-175689	3,216	**2,379**	2,044	1,709
GUITAR	61	MARTIN	**D-21** SERIAL #175690-181297	3,137	**2,320**	1,993	1,666
GUITAR	63	MARTIN	**D-21** SERIAL# 187385-193327	2,239	**1,656**	1,423	1,189
GUITAR	64	MARTIN	**D-21** SERIAL #193328-199626	2,233	**1,652**	1,419	1,186
GUITAR	65	MARTIN	**D-21** SERIAL #199627-207030	2,231	**1,650**	1,417	1,185
GUITAR	66	MARTIN	**D-21** SERIAL #207031-217215	2,138	**1,581**	1,359	1,136
GUITAR	67	MARTIN	**D-21** SERIAL #217216-230095	3,216	**2,378**	2,043	1,708
GUITAR	68	MARTIN	**D-21** SERIAL #230096-241925	3,218	**2,380**	2,045	1,710
GUITAR	69	MARTIN	**D-21** SERIAL #241926-256003	3,846	**2,844**	2,444	2,043
GUITAR	31	MARTIN	**D-28**	43,200	**31,950**	27,450	22,950
GUITAR	32	MARTIN	**D-28** SERIAL #49590-52590	36,489	**26,987**	23,186	19,385
GUITAR	33	MARTIN	**D-28** SERIAL #52591-55084	31,208	**23,081**	19,830	16,579
GUITAR	34	MARTIN	**D-28** SERIAL #55085-58679	30,644	**22,663**	19,471	16,279
GUITAR	35	MARTIN	**D-28** SERIAL #58680-61947	28,456	**21,045**	18,081	15,117
GUITAR	36	MARTIN	**D-28** SERIAL #61948-65176	35,448	**26,216**	22,524	18,831
GUITAR	37	MARTIN	**D-28** SERIAL #65177-68865	36,018	**26,638**	22,886	19,134
GUITAR	38	MARTIN	**D-28** SERIAL #68866-71866	9,600	**7,100**	6,100	5,100
GUITAR	38	MARTIN	**D-28** HERRINGBONE	11,184	**8,271**	7,106	5,941
GUITAR	39	MARTIN	**D-28** SERIAL #71867-74061	27,579	**20,397**	17,524	14,651
GUITAR	40	MARTIN	**D-28** SERIAL #74062-76734	20,063	**14,838**	12,748	10,658
GUITAR	41	MARTIN	**D-28** SERIAL #76735-80013	19,339	**14,302**	12,288	10,273
GUITAR	42	MARTIN	**D-28** SERIAL #80014-83107	18,169	**13,438**	11,545	9,652
GUITAR	43	MARTIN	**D-28** SERIAL #83108-86724	19,714	**14,580**	12,526	10,473
GUITAR	44	MARTIN	**D-28** SERIAL #86725-90149	16,921	**12,515**	10,752	8,989
GUITAR	45	MARTIN	**D-28** SERIAL #90150-93623	10,831	**8,010**	6,882	5,754
GUITAR	46	MARTIN	**D-28** SERIAL #93624-98158	8,533	**6,311**	5,422	4,533
GUITAR	47	MARTIN	**D-28** SERIAL #98159-103468	6,556	**4,849**	4,166	3,483
GUITAR	48	MARTIN	**D-28** SERIAL #103469-108269	6,916	**5,115**	4,395	3,674
GUITAR	49	MARTIN	**D-28** SERIAL #108270-112961	6,418	**4,747**	4,078	3,409

TYPE	YR	MFG	MODEL	SELL EXC	SELL AVG	BUY EXC	BUY AVG
GUITAR	50	MARTIN	D-28 SERIAL #112962-117961	6,451	4,771	4,099	3,427
GUITAR	51	MARTIN	D-28 SERIAL #117962-122799	6,175	4,567	3,924	3,280
GUITAR	52	MARTIN	D-28 SERIAL #122800-128436	7,296	5,396	4,636	3,876
GUITAR	53	MARTIN	D-28 SERIAL #128437-134501	6,353	4,698	4,036	3,375
GUITAR	54	MARTIN	D-28 SERIAL #134502-141345	4,752	3,514	3,019	2,524
GUITAR	55	MARTIN	D-28 SERIAL #141346-147328	6,247	4,620	3,969	3,319
GUITAR	56	MARTIN	D-28 SERIAL #147329-152775	5,651	4,179	3,591	3,002
GUITAR	57	MARTIN	D-28 SERIAL #152776-159061	5,744	4,248	3,650	3,051
GUITAR	58	MARTIN	D-28 SERIAL #159062-165576	5,152	3,810	3,273	2,737
GUITAR	59	MARTIN	D-28 SERIAL #165577-171047	4,917	3,636	3,124	2,612
GUITAR	60	MARTIN	D-28 SERIAL #171048-175689	5,373	3,973	3,414	2,854
GUITAR	61	MARTIN	D-28 SERIAL #175690-181297	5,366	3,968	3,409	2,850
GUITAR	62	MARTIN	D-28 SERIAL #181298-187384	5,358	3,963	3,405	2,846
GUITAR	63	MARTIN	D-28 SERIAL #187385-193327	5,354	3,960	3,402	2,844
GUITAR	64	MARTIN	D-28 SERIAL #193328-199626	5,348	3,955	3,398	2,841
GUITAR	65	MARTIN	D-28 SERIAL #199627-207030	5,344	3,952	3,395	2,839
GUITAR	66	MARTIN	D-28 SERIAL #207031-217215	3,052	2,257	1,939	1,621
GUITAR	67	MARTIN	D-28 SERIAL #217216-230095	3,931	2,907	2,497	2,088
GUITAR	68	MARTIN	D-28 SERIAL #230096-241925	3,641	2,693	2,313	1,934
GUITAR	69	MARTIN	D-28 LEFT-HANDED, SERIAL #241926-256003	3,250	2,404	2,065	1,726
GUITAR	69	MARTIN	D-28 SERIAL #241926-256003	3,627	2,683	2,305	1,927
GUITAR	70	MARTIN	D-28 SERIAL #256004-271633	1,195	883	759	634
GUITAR	71	MARTIN	D-28 SERIAL #271634-294270	1,185	876	753	629
GUITAR	72	MARTIN	D-28 SERIAL #294271-313302	1,173	867	745	623
GUITAR	73	MARTIN	D-28 SERIAL #313303-333873	1,169	864	742	621
GUITAR	74	MARTIN	D-28 SERIAL #333874-353387	1,165	861	740	619
GUITAR	75	MARTIN	D-28 LEFT-HANDED	1,157	856	735	615
GUITAR	75	MARTIN	D-28 SERIAL #353388-371828	1,162	859	738	617
GUITAR	76	MARTIN	D-28	1,911	1,413	1,214	1,015
GUITAR	78	MARTIN	D-28	2,097	1,551	1,332	1,114
GUITAR	79	MARTIN	D-28	2,092	1,547	1,329	1,111
GUITAR	34	MARTIN	D-28H SERIAL #56435	16,560	12,247	10,522	8,797
GUITAR	65	MARTIN	D-28S SERIAL #199627-207030	4,507	3,333	2,863	2,394
GUITAR	66	MARTIN	D-28S SERIAL #207031-217215	4,498	3,327	2,858	2,389
GUITAR	67	MARTIN	D-28S LEFT-HANDED	4,041	2,989	2,568	2,147
GUITAR	67	MARTIN	D-28S SERIAL #217216-230095	4,492	3,322	2,854	2,386
GUITAR	68	MARTIN	D-28S SERIAL #230096-241925	4,483	3,315	2,848	2,381
GUITAR	70	MARTIN	D-28S SERIAL#263662	1,371	1,014	871	728
GUITAR	71	MARTIN	D-28S SERIAL #271634-294270	1,816	1,343	1,154	964
GUITAR	72	MARTIN	D-28S SERIAL #294271-313302	1,369	1,013	870	727
GUITAR	74	MARTIN	D-28S SERIAL #333874-353387	1,363	1,008	866	724
GUITAR	75	MARTIN	D-28S SERIAL #353388-371828	1,354	1,001	860	719
GUITAR	65	MARTIN	D-35 SERIAL #199627-207030	3,486	2,578	2,215	1,852

TYPE	YR	MFG	PRICES--BASED ON 100% ORIGINAL MODEL	SELL EXC	SELL AVG	BUY EXC	BUY AVG
GUITAR	66	MARTIN	D-35 SERIAL #210490	3,388	2,506	2,153	1,800
GUITAR	67	MARTIN	D-35 SERIAL #217216-230095	3,281	2,426	2,084	1,743
GUITAR	68	MARTIN	D-35 SERIAL #230096-241925	3,039	2,247	1,931	1,614
GUITAR	69	MARTIN	D-35 SITKA TOP, BRAZILIAN SIDES/CENTER OF BACK	3,264	2,414	2,074	1,734
GUITAR	70	MARTIN	D-35 SERIAL #256004-271633	1,713	1,267	1,088	910
GUITAR	71	MARTIN	D-35 SERIAL #271634-294270	1,341	991	852	712
GUITAR	72	MARTIN	D-35 SERIAL #294271-313302	1,488	1,101	946	791
GUITAR	73	MARTIN	D-35 SERIAL #313303-333873	1,377	1,018	875	731
GUITAR	74	MARTIN	D-35 SERIAL #333874-353387	1,196	884	760	635
GUITAR	75	MARTIN	D-35 SERIAL #353388-371828	1,262	933	802	670
GUITAR	67	MARTIN	D-35-12 12-STRING	1,867	1,380	1,186	991
GUITAR	70	MARTIN	D-35-12 NATURAL, 12-STRING	1,045	773	664	555
GUITAR	67	MARTIN	D-35S SERIAL #217216-230095	3,442	2,546	2,187	1,828
GUITAR	69	MARTIN	D-35S SERIAL #2431100	1,775	1,312	1,127	942
GUITAR	70	MARTIN	D-35S SERIAL #256004-271633	1,312	970	833	697
GUITAR	72	MARTIN	D-35S	1,295	957	822	687
GUITAR	73	MARTIN	D-35S SERIAL #313303-333873	1,263	934	802	671
GUITAR	74	MARTIN	D-35S SERIAL #333874-353387	1,231	910	782	654
GUITAR	75	MARTIN	D-35S SERIAL #353388-371828	1,067	789	678	567
GUITAR	69	MARTIN	D-41 BRAZILIAN ROSEWOOD, SERIAL #241926-256003	5,252	3,884	3,337	2,790
GUITAR	70	MARTIN	D-41 SERIAL #256004-271633	1,687	1,248	1,072	896
GUITAR	72	MARTIN	D-41 SERIAL #294271-313302	1,397	1,033	888	742
GUITAR	73	MARTIN	D-41 SERIAL #313303-333873	1,643	1,215	1,044	873
GUITAR	74	MARTIN	D-41 SERIAL #333874-353387	1,351	999	858	718
GUITAR	36	MARTIN	D-45 SNOWFLAKE, SERIAL #61948-65176	141,224	104,447	89,736	75,025
GUITAR	38	MARTIN	D-45 BRAZILIAN ROSEWOOD, SNOWFLAKE	121,868	90,131	77,437	64,742
GUITAR	39	MARTIN	D-45 SERIAL #71867-74061	76,717	56,738	48,747	40,756
GUITAR	40	MARTIN	D-45 SERIAL #74062-76734	142,410	105,324	90,489	75,655
GUITAR	41	MARTIN	D-45 SERIAL #76735-80013	141,475	104,632	89,895	75,158
GUITAR	42	MARTIN	D-45 SERIAL #80014-83107	135,441	100,170	86,061	71,953
GUITAR	68	MARTIN	D-45 BRAZILIAN ROSEWOOD, 12-STRING, SERIAL #230096-241925	15,307	11,320	9,726	8,131
GUITAR	69	MARTIN	D-45 BRAZILIAN ROSEWOOD, SERIAL #241926-256003	15,302	11,317	9,723	8,129
GUITAR	70	MARTIN	D-45 INIDAN ROSEWOOD, SERIAL #256004-271633	4,189	3,098	2,662	2,225
GUITAR	71	MARTIN	D-45 SERIAL #271634-294270	3,840	2,840	2,440	2,040
GUITAR	75	MARTIN	D-45 SERIAL #353388-371828	3,116	2,304	1,980	1,655
GUITAR	83	MARTIN	D-45 150th ANNIVERSARY CUSTOM, MARK LEAF CASE	15,830	11,707	10,058	8,409
GUITAR	69	MARTIN	D-45S BRAZILIAN ROSEWOOD	19,186	14,190	12,191	10,192
GUITAR	76	MARTIN	D-76 BICENTENNIAL EDITION SERIAL #371829-388800	2,331	1,724	1,481	1,238
GUITAR	21	MARTIN	DITSON STYLE 2 MAHOGANY BACK/SIDES, SERIAL #15849-16758	890	658	566	473
GUITAR	40	MARTIN	F- 1 ARCHTOP, SERIAL #74062-76734	1,171	866	744	622
GUITAR	41	MARTIN	F- 1 ARCHTOP, SERIAL #76735-80013	890	658	566	473
GUITAR	41	MARTIN	F- 2 ARCHTOP, SERIAL #76735-80013	892	660	567	474

TYPE	YR	MFG	PRICES--BASED ON 100% ORIGINAL MODEL	SELL EXC	SELL AVG	BUY EXC	BUY AVG
GUITAR	42	MARTIN	**F- 2** ARCHTOP, SERIAL #80014-83107	891	**659**	566	473
GUITAR	35	MARTIN	**F- 7** ARCHTOP, SERIAL #58680-61947	2,948	**2,180**	1,873	1,566
GUITAR	35	MARTIN	**F- 7** BRAZILIAN ROSEWOOD, FLATTOP	11,531	**8,528**	7,327	6,126
GUITAR	36	MARTIN	**F- 7** ARCHTOP, SERIAL #61948-65176	2,971	**2,197**	1,887	1,578
GUITAR	37	MARTIN	**F- 7** ARCHTOP, SERIAL #65177-68865	2,981	**2,205**	1,894	1,584
GUITAR	38	MARTIN	**F- 7** ARCHTOP, SERIAL #68866-71866	2,976	**2,201**	1,891	1,581
GUITAR	35	MARTIN	**F- 9** ARCHTOP, SERIAL #58680-61947	4,921	**3,640**	3,127	2,614
GUITAR	15	MARTIN	**FODEN SPECIAL STYLE D**	8,400	**6,212**	5,337	4,462
GUITAR	75	MARTIN	**HD-28** INDIAN ROSEWOOD	1,095	**810**	696	581
GUITAR	86	MARTIN	**HD-28 CUSTOM**	5,814	**4,300**	3,694	3,089
GUITAR	79	MARTIN	**HD-28L** LEFT-HANDED	1,600	**1,183**	1,016	850
GUITAR	79	MARTIN	**HD-38**	1,076	**795**	683	571
GUITAR	88	MARTIN	**J-40MC** THINLINE PU, SERIAL #483825-	1,534	**1,134**	974	814
GUITAR	77	MARTIN	**M-38** SERIAL #388801-399625	1,353	**1,001**	860	719
GUITAR	78	MARTIN	**M-38** SERIAL #399626-407800	1,404	**1,038**	892	746
GUITAR	79	MARTIN	**M-38**	1,316	**973**	836	699
GUITAR	68	MARTIN	**N-10 CLASSICAL** SERIAL #230096-241925	691	**511**	439	367
GUITAR	69	MARTIN	**N-10 CLASSICAL** SERIAL #241926-256003	688	**509**	437	365
GUITAR	70	MARTIN	**N-10 CLASSICAL** SERIAL #256004-271633	684	**506**	434	363
GUITAR	69	MARTIN	**N-20 CLASSICAL** SERIAL #241926-256004	1,657	**1,226**	1,053	880
GUITAR	71	MARTIN	**N-20 CLASSICAL**	704	**521**	447	374
GUITAR	72	MARTIN	**N-20 CLASSICAL** SERIAL #294271-313302	688	**509**	437	365
GUITAR	76	MARTIN	**N-20 CLASSICAL**	837	**619**	531	444
GUITAR	34	MARTIN	**OM-000-18 TRANSITIONAL** SERIAL #55083-58679	5,351	**3,957**	3,400	2,842
GUITAR	30	MARTIN	**OM-18** SERIAL #40844-45317	4,661	**3,447**	2,962	2,476
GUITAR	31	MARTIN	**OM-18** SERIAL #45318-49589	4,656	**3,443**	2,958	2,473
GUITAR	32	MARTIN	**OM-18** SERIAL #49590-52590	4,653	**3,441**	2,956	2,471
GUITAR	33	MARTIN	**OM-18** SERIAL #52591-55084	4,632	**3,425**	2,943	2,460
GUITAR	34	MARTIN	**OM-18**	4,685	**3,465**	2,977	2,489
GUITAR	31	MARTIN	**OM-18P** PLECTRUM, SERIAL #45318-49589	4,359	**3,224**	2,770	2,315
GUITAR	41	MARTIN	**OM-18P** PLECTRUM, SERIAL #76735-80013	4,794	**3,545**	3,046	2,546
GUITAR	29	MARTIN	**OM-28** SERIAL #37569-40843	16,890	**12,491**	10,732	8,972
GUITAR	30	MARTIN	**OM-28** SERIAL #40844-45317	16,879	**12,483**	10,725	8,967
GUITAR	31	MARTIN	**OM-28** SERIAL #45318-49589	18,589	**13,748**	11,812	9,875
GUITAR	32	MARTIN	**OM-28** SERIAL #49590-52590	19,715	**14,581**	12,527	10,473
GUITAR	33	MARTIN	**OM-28** SERIAL #52591-55084	18,759	**13,874**	11,920	9,965
GUITAR	31	MARTIN	**OM-45** SERIAL #45318-49589	116,088	**85,856**	73,764	61,671
GUITAR	32	MARTIN	**OM-45** SERIAL #49590-52590	116,084	**85,853**	73,761	61,669
GUITAR	77	MARTIN	**OM-45** SERIAL #388801-399625	7,265	**5,373**	4,616	3,859
GUITAR	30	MARTIN	**OM-45 DLX** SERIAL #40844-45317	144,849	**107,128**	92,039	76,951
GUITAR	35	MARTIN	**R-17** MAHOGANY, ARCHTOP, SERIAL #58680-61947	888	**656**	564	471
GUITAR	37	MARTIN	**R-17** MAHOGANY, ARCHTOP, SERIAL #65177-68865	884	**653**	561	469
GUITAR	40	MARTIN	**R-17** MAHOGANY, ARCHTOP, SERIAL #74062-76734	1,032	**763**	655	548
GUITAR	32	MARTIN	**R-18** ARCHTOP	1,517	**1,122**	964	806
GUITAR	33	MARTIN	**R-18** ARCHTOP, SERIAL #52591-55084	1,058	**783**	672	562

TYPE	YR	MFG	MODEL	SELL EXC	SELL AVG	BUY EXC	BUY AVG
GUITAR	34	MARTIN	R-18 ARCHTOP, SERIAL #55085-58679	826	611	525	439
GUITAR	35	MARTIN	R-18 ARCHTOP, SERIAL #58680-61947	1,069	790	679	568
GUITAR	37	MARTIN	R-18 ARCHTOP	1,036	766	658	550
GUITAR	38	MARTIN	R-18 ARCHTOP, SERIAL #68866-71866	888	656	564	471
GUITAR	37	MARTIN	R-18T TENOR, ARCHTOP, SERIAL #65177-68865	888	657	564	472
GUITAR	40	MARTIN	R-18T TENOR, ARCHTOP, SERIAL #74062-76734	883	653	561	469
GUITAR	70	MARTIN	SO-18 T8	889	658	565	472
GUITAR	77	MARTIN	SOM-45 SERIAL #388801-399625	4,571	3,381	2,904	2,428
GUITAR	33	MARTIN	STAUFFER STYLE (1830's)	20,053	14,831	12,742	10,653
GUITAR	80	MARTIN	STYLE 1-21 (1880's) BRAZILIAN ROSEWOOD BACK/SIDES	1,474	1,090	936	783
MANDOLIN 12	MARTIN		00 BOWL BACK, SERIAL #3431-3847	468	346	297	248
MANDOL	14	MARTIN	00 BRAZILIAN ROSEWOOD RIBS, BOWL BACK	463	342	294	246
MANDOL	17	MARTIN	00 BOWL BACK	480	355	305	255
MANDOL	18	MARTIN	00 BOWL BACK, SERIAL# 5753-6370	468	346	297	248
MANDOL	14	MARTIN	000 MAHOGANY BOWL	478	353	303	253
MANDOL	27	MARTIN	1 SERIAL #28690-34435	747	553	475	397
MANDOL	14	MARTIN	2 BOWL BACK	475	351	301	252
MANDOL	20	MARTIN	2 BOWL BACK	468	346	297	248
MANDOL	40	MARTIN	2-15 SUNBURST, CARVED TOP/BACK	1,104	817	702	587
MANDOL	46	MARTIN	2-15	876	648	556	465
MANDOL	48	MARTIN	2-15 CARVED TOP/BACK, SERIAL #18304-19078	1,000	739	635	531
MANDOL	49	MARTIN	2-15 CARVED TOP/BACK	962	712	611	511
MANDOL	51	MARTIN	2-15 CARVED TOP/BACK, SERIAL #20066-20496	958	708	608	508
MANDOL	53	MARTIN	2-15 CARVED TOP/BACK	887	656	563	471
MANDOL	55	MARTIN	2-15 SUNBURST	982	726	624	521
MANDOL	63	MARTIN	2-15 CARVED TOP/BACK	766	566	486	406
MANDOL	64	MARTIN	2-15 CARVED TOP/BACK	747	553	475	397
MANDOL	64	MARTIN	2-15	757	560	481	402
MANDOL	65	MARTIN	2-15 CARVED TOP/BACK, SERIAL #24340-24439	696	514	442	369
MANDOL	29	MARTIN	2-20 ARCHED TOP/BACK	2,287	1,691	1,453	1,215
MANDOL	36	MARTIN	2-20 CARVED TOP/BACK	1,876	1,388	1,192	997
MANDOL	37	MARTIN	2-20 CARVED TOP/BACK	1,582	1,170	1,005	840
MANDOL	40	MARTIN	2-20 CARVED TOP/BACK, SERIAL #16748-16957	2,227	1,647	1,415	1,183
MANDOL	38	MARTIN	2-30 CARVED TOP/BACK, SERIAL #16438-16580	1,784	1,319	1,133	948
MANDOL	42	MARTIN	2-30 CARVED TOP/BACK, SERIAL #17264-17405	1,779	1,316	1,130	945
MANDOL	17	MARTIN	3 BOWL BACK, SERIAL #5008-5752	510	377	324	271
MANDOL	19	MARTIN	3 BOWL BACK, SERIAL #6371-7237	749	554	476	398
MANDOL	98	MARTIN	3 (1898) BOWL BACK, SERIAL #156-359	760	562	483	403
MANDOL	01	MARTIN	4 (1901) BOWL BACK, SERIAL #801-881	1,076	795	683	571
MANDOL	08	MARTIN	4 (1908) BOWL BACK, SERIAL #2358-2510	1,026	758	652	545
MANDOL	05	MARTIN	5 BOWL BACK	3,034	2,244	1,928	1,612
MANDOL	09	MARTIN	5 BOWL BACK	3,005	2,223	1,909	1,596
MANDOL	19	MARTIN	6 SNOWFLAKE INLAY	2,390	1,767	1,518	1,269
MANDOL	19	MARTIN	6A BOWL BACK	2,386	1,765	1,516	1,267

TYPE	YR	MFG	MODEL	PRICES--BASED ON 100% ORIGINAL	SELL EXC	SELL AVG	BUY EXC	BUY AVG
MANDOL	10	MARTIN	**7** BOWL BACK		3,360	**2,485**	2,135	1,785
MANDOL	20	MARTIN	**A**		557	**412**	354	296
MANDOL	22	MARTIN	**A** SERIAL #9628-10196		617	**456**	392	327
MANDOL	23	MARTIN	**A** SERIAL #10197-11020		579	**428**	368	308
MANDOL	26	MARTIN	**A** SERIAL #12521-13359		577	**427**	367	307
MANDOL	28	MARTIN	**A**		596	**440**	378	316
MANDOL	30	MARTIN	**A** SERIAL #14631-14892		590	**436**	375	313
MANDOL	34	MARTIN	**A** SERIAL #15529-15729		1,198	**886**	761	636
MANDOL	37	MARTIN	**A** SERIAL #16157-16437		586	**433**	372	311
MANDOL	38	MARTIN	**A**		583	**431**	370	310
MANDOL	39	MARTIN	**A** SERIAL #16581-16747		588	**435**	373	312
MANDOL	47	MARTIN	**A** SERIAL #17642-18303		594	**439**	377	315
MANDOL	50	MARTIN	**A**		549	**406**	348	291
MANDOL	51	MARTIN	**A** SERIAL #20066-20496		532	**394**	338	283
MANDOL	54	MARTIN	**A** SERIAL #21453-21952		536	**396**	340	285
MANDOL	55	MARTIN	**A** SERIAL #21953-22254		533	**394**	339	283
MANDOL	57	MARTIN	**A** SERIAL #22630-22985		536	**396**	340	285
MANDOL	60	MARTIN	**A**		540	**399**	343	287
MANDOL	61	MARTIN	**A**		533	**394**	339	283
MANDOL	66	MARTIN	**A** SERIAL #24440-24564		546	**403**	347	290
MANDOL	67	MARTIN	**A** SERIAL #25465-24639		546	**403**	347	290
MANDOL	72	MARTIN	**A**		518	**383**	329	275
MANDOL	73	MARTIN	**A**		514	**380**	326	273
MANDOL	74	MARTIN	**A** SERIAL #12589		541	**400**	344	287
MANDOL	75	MARTIN	**A** SERIAL #25680-25895		456	**337**	290	242
MANDOL	76	MARTIN	**A** SERIAL #25896-26045,259996-260020		533	**394**	339	283
MANDOL	77	MARTIN	**A** SERIAL #26046-26101		530	**392**	337	282
MANDOL	23	MARTIN	**A-K** KOA WOOD, SERIAL #10197-11020		728	**538**	462	387
MANDOL	25	MARTIN	**A-K** KOA WOOD, SERIAL #11810-12520		649	**480**	412	345
MANDOL	26	MARTIN	**A-K** KOA WOOD, SERIAL #12521-13359		613	**453**	389	325
MANDOL	27	MARTIN	**A-K** KOA WOOD, SERIAL #13360-13833		606	**448**	385	322
MANDOL	31	MARTIN	**A-K** KOA WOOD, SERIAL #14893-15290		535	**396**	340	284
MANDOL	19	MARTIN	**B** BRAZILIAN ROSEWOOD		553	**409**	351	294
MANDOL	20	MARTIN	**B** HERRINGBONE TRIM, SERIAL #7238-8761		536	**396**	340	285
MANDOL	22	MARTIN	**B** BRAZILIAN ROSEWOOD		637	**471**	405	338
MANDOL	23	MARTIN	**B** HERRINGBONE TRIM		796	**589**	506	423
MANDOL	25	MARTIN	**B** HERRINGBONE TRIM		557	**412**	354	296
MANDOL	31	MARTIN	**B** HERRINGBONE TRIM, SERIAL #14893-15290		536	**396**	340	285
MANDOL	41	MARTIN	**B** HERRINGBONE TRIM, SERIAL #16958-17263		532	**394**	338	283
MANDOL	20	MARTIN	**BB** BRAZILIAN ROSEWOOD		882	**652**	560	468
MANDOL	15	MARTIN	**C** ABALONE SOUNDHOLE RING, SERIAL #4463-4767		1,309	**968**	832	695
MANDOL	19	MARTIN	**C**		1,338	**989**	850	710
MANDOL	20	MARTIN	**C** PEARL BIND TOP/SOUNDBOARD		1,195	**883**	759	634
MANDOL	17	MARTIN	**E** ROSEWOOD		3,120	**2,307**	1,982	1,657
MANDOL	20	MARTIN	**E**		6,497	**4,805**	4,128	3,451
MANDOL	25	MARTIN	**T-18** ORGINAL CANVAS CASE, SERIAL #26437		1,215	**898**	772	645

TYPE	YR	MFG	PRICES--BASED ON 100% ORIGINAL MODEL	SELL EXC	SELL AVG	BUY EXC	BUY AVG
MANDOL	26	MARTIN	**T-18** TIPLE	1,227	**908**	780	652
MANDOL	68	MARTIN	**T-18** BRAZILIAN ROSEWOOD, SERIAL #239362	1,127	**833**	716	598
MANDOL	68	MARTIN	**T-28**, BRAZILIAN ROSEWOOD TIPLE, BRAZILIAN ROSEWOOD	1,638	**1,211**	1,041	870
UKULELE	20	MARTIN	**0**	462	**342**	294	245
UKE	27	MARTIN	**0** FRICTION PEGS, SERIAL #28690-34435	653	**483**	415	347
UKE	30	MARTIN	**0** SERIAL #40844-45317	425	**314**	270	225
UKE	35	MARTIN	**0** MAHOGANY, TANG FRETS	384	**284**	244	204
UKE	40	MARTIN	**0**	443	**328**	281	235
UKE	50	MARTIN	**0** SERIAL #112962-117961	444	**328**	282	236
UKE	53	MARTIN	**0**	489	**362**	311	260
UKE	55	MARTIN	**0** SERIAL #141346-147328	300	**222**	190	159
UKE	56	MARTIN	**0**	435	**322**	276	231
UKE	57	MARTIN	**0**	432	**319**	274	229
UKE	64	MARTIN	**0**	390	**288**	248	207
UKE	65	MARTIN	**0**	491	**363**	312	261
UKE	66	MARTIN	**0**	384	**284**	244	204
UKE	25	MARTIN	**1** SOPRANO, SERIAL #22009-24116	726	**537**	461	386
UKE	26	MARTIN	**1** SOPRANO, SERIAL #24117-28689	619	**457**	393	328
UKE	27	MARTIN	**1** SOPRANO	578	**428**	367	307
UKE	30	MARTIN	**1** SOPRANO, SERIAL #40844-45317	523	**386**	332	277
UKE	40	MARTIN	**1** SOPRANO, SERIAL #74062-76734	428	**316**	272	227
UKE	50	MARTIN	**1** SOPRANO, SERIAL #112962-117961	470	**347**	298	249
UKE	54	MARTIN	**1** SOPRANO	513	**379**	326	272
UKE	18	MARTIN	**1 TAROPATCH** 8-STRING	1,593	**1,178**	1,012	846
UKE	20	MARTIN	**1 TAROPATCH** MAHOGANY, 8-STRING	1,195	**883**	759	634
UKE	30	MARTIN	**1C CONCERT** MAHOGANY, SERIAL #40844-45317	649	**480**	412	345
UKE	35	MARTIN	**1C CONCERT** MAHOGANY	518	**383**	329	275
UKE	20	MARTIN	**1K** KOA WOOD, SERIAL #14513-15848	612	**452**	389	325
UKE	25	MARTIN	**1K** KOA WOOD	528	**391**	336	281
UKE	30	MARTIN	**1K** KOA WOOD	500	**369**	317	265
UKE	35	MARTIN	**1K** KOA WOOD	504	**372**	320	267
UKE	40	MARTIN	**1K** KOA WOOD, SERIAL #74062-76734	524	**387**	333	278
UKE	50	MARTIN	**1K** KOA WOOD, SERIAL #112962-117961	721	**533**	458	383
UKE	29	MARTIN	**1T** TENOR, SERIAL #37569-40843	738	**545**	469	392
UKE	33	MARTIN	**1T** TENOR, SERIAL #52591-55084	649	**480**	412	345
UKE	40	MARTIN	**1T** TENOR, SERIAL #74062-76734	560	**414**	356	297
UKE	50	MARTIN	**1T** TENOR, SERIAL #112962-117961	533	**394**	339	283
UKE	55	MARTIN	**1T** TENOR	525	**388**	333	278
UKE	60	MARTIN	**1T** TENOR, SERIAL #171048-175689	542	**401**	344	288
UKE	62	MARTIN	**1T** TENOR	518	**383**	329	275
UKE	58	MARTIN	**1T BARITONE**	432	**319**	274	229
UKE	28	MARTIN	**2** SERIAL #34436-37568	982	**726**	624	521
UKE	35	MARTIN	**2** MAHOGANY, BOUND	478	**353**	303	253
UKE	50	MARTIN	**2** MAHOGANY	637	**471**	405	338
UKE	55	MARTIN	**2** SERIAL #141346-147328	531	**393**	337	282
UKE	18	MARTIN	**2 TAROPATCH** 8-STRING	1,593	**1,178**	1,012	846

TYPE	YR	MFG	PRICES--BASED ON 100% ORIGINAL MODEL	SELL EXC	SELL AVG	BUY EXC	BUY AVG
UKE	27	MARTIN	**2K** SOPRANO, KOA WOOD	605	**448**	384	321
UKE	30	MARTIN	**2K** KOA WOOD, SERIAL #40844-45317	535	**396**	340	284
UKE	27	MARTIN	**2M** SERIAL #28690-34435	534	**395**	339	284
UKE	20	MARTIN	**3** MAHOGANY, HEADSTOCK INLAY	796	**589**	506	423
UKE	50	MARTIN	**3** MAHOGANY	716	**529**	455	380
UKE	18	MARTIN	**3 TAROPATCH** 8-STRING	1,633	**1,208**	1,038	868
UKE	21	MARTIN	**3K** KOA WOOD	1,968	**1,455**	1,250	1,045
UKE	25	MARTIN	**3K** KOA WOOD, SERIAL #22009-24116	1,018	**753**	647	541
UKE	33	MARTIN	**3K** KOA WOOD	1,474	**1,090**	936	783
UKE	30	MARTIN	**3M** SERIAL #40844-45317	710	**525**	451	377
UKE	55	MARTIN	**3M** SOPRANO, DOT NECK INLAY	621	**459**	394	329
UKE	25	MARTIN	**5** KOA, PEARL TRIM	4,320	**3,195**	2,745	2,295
UKE	41	MARTIN	**5** SERIAL #40844-45317	4,118	**3,045**	2,616	2,187
UKE	30	MARTIN	**5K** SOPRANO, KOA WOOD, SERIAL #40844-45317	4,207	**3,111**	2,673	2,235
UKE	30	MARTIN	**5K** HAWAIIAN KOA, FIGURED	5,423	**4,010**	3,445	2,880
UKE	32	MARTIN	**5K** SOPRANO, KOA WOOD	3,840	**2,840**	2,440	2,040
UKE	35	MARTIN	**5K** SOPRANO, KOA WOOD	1,961	**1,494**	1,270	971
UKE	51	MARTIN	**51** BARITONE, SERIAL #117962-122799	625	**462**	397	332
UKE	52	MARTIN	**51** BARITONE	717	**530**	455	380
UKE	60	MARTIN	**51** BARITONE, SERIAL #171048-175689	642	**474**	408	341
UKE	61	MARTIN	**51** BARITONE	677	**501**	430	360
UKE	62	MARTIN	**51** BARITONE	757	**560**	481	402
UKE	63	MARTIN	**51** BARITONE	717	**530**	455	380
UKE	64	MARTIN	**51** BARITONE	709	**524**	450	376
UKE	70	MARTIN	**51** BARITONE	677	**501**	430	360
UKE	70	MARTIN	**BARITONE** MAHOGANY	965	**714**	613	513
UKE	50	MARTIN	**T-15 TIPLE** MAHOGANY	502	**371**	319	266
UKE	17	MARTIN	**T-17 TIPLE**	714	**528**	453	379
UKE	28	MARTIN	**T-17 TIPLE**	624	**461**	396	331
UKE	31	MARTIN	**T-17 TIPLE**	557	**412**	354	296
UKE	40	MARTIN	**T-17 TIPLE**	637	**471**	405	338
UKE	23	MARTIN	**T-18 TIPLE** SERIAL #17840-19891	1,122	**829**	713	596
UKE	26	MARTIN	**T-18 TIPLE** SERIAL #24117-28689	511	**378**	325	271
UKE	27	MARTIN	**T-18 TIPLE**	497	**367**	315	264
UKE	35	MARTIN	**T-18 TIPLE**	438	**324**	278	233
UKE	55	MARTIN	**T-18 TIPLE** SPRUCE & MAHOGANY	465	**344**	295	247
UKE	27	MARTIN	**T-28 TIPLE** HERRINGBONE TRIM, SERIAL #28690-34435	996	**736**	633	529
UKE	50	MARTIN	**T-28 TIPLE** INDIAN ROSEWOOD, SPRUCE TOP	1,005	**743**	638	533
UKE	68	MARTIN	**T-28 TIPLE** BRAZILIAL ROSEWOOD, 10-STRING	1,035	**766**	658	550
UKE	71	MARTIN	**T-28 TIPLE** INDIAN ROSEWOOD	758	**560**	481	402
UKE	74	MARTIN	**T-28 TIPLE** INDIAN ROSEWOOD	693	**512**	440	368

McINTOSH LABS

TYPE	YR	MFG	MODEL	SELL EXC	SELL AVG	BUY EXC	BUY AVG
PRE	02	MCINTOSH	**AE-2 VACUUM MONO TUBE**	143	**105**	90	75
PRE	50	MCINTOSH	**C- 4 VACUUM MONO TUBE**	123	**91**	78	65
PRE	54	MCINTOSH	**C- 4P MONO TUBE**	133	**98**	84	70
PRE	55-59	MCINTOSH	**C- 8 VACUUM MONO TUBE**	266	**197**	169	141

TYPE	YR	MFG	PRICES--BASED ON 100% ORIGINAL MODEL	SELL EXC	SELL AVG	BUY EXC	BUY AVG
PRE	55-59	MCINTOSH	C- 8P MONO TUBE POWER SUPPLY	223	**165**	142	118
PRE	58-60	MCINTOSH	C- 8S VACUUM STEREO TUBE	354	**261**	225	188
PRE	61-63	MCINTOSH	C- 11 VACUUM STEREO TUBE	686	**507**	436	364
PRE	59-63	MCINTOSH	C- 20 STEREO TUBE	675	**499**	429	359
PRE	63-68	MCINTOSH	C- 22 VACUUM STEREO TUBE	1,515	**1,121**	963	805
PRE	52-55	MCINTOSH	C-104 VACUUM MONO TUBE	165	**122**	104	87
PRE	53-55	MCINTOSH	C-108 VACUUM MONO TUBE	125	**93**	79	66
PRE	62	MCINTOSH	MX-110 TUBE PREAMP/TUNER	447	**330**	284	237
PRE	71	MCINTOSH	MX-115 SOLID STATE PREAMP/TUNER	543	**401**	345	288
PWR	49	MCINTOSH	15W-1 VACUUM MONO TUBE	171	**127**	109	91
PWR	51	MCINTOSH	20W-2 MONO TUBE 20 WATTS	235	**173**	149	124
PWR	49	MCINTOSH	50W-1 VACUUM MONO TUBE	287	**212**	182	152
PWR	51	MCINTOSH	50W-2 MONO TUBE 50 WATTS	383	**283**	243	203
PWR	53-55	MCINTOSH	A-116 MONO TUBE 30 WATTS	269	**199**	171	143
PWR	54-62	MCINTOSH	MC- 30 VACUUM MONO TUBE 30 WATTS	659	**487**	419	350
PWR	59	MCINTOSH	MC- 30A MONO TUBE	454	**335**	288	241
PWR	62-69	MCINTOSH	MC- 40 VACUUM MONO TUBE 40 WATTS	630	**466**	400	335
PWR	69-70	MCINTOSH	MC- 50 SOLID STATE MONO	281	**208**	178	149
PWR	55-61	MCINTOSH	MC- 60 VACUUM MONO TUBE 60 WATTS	852	**630**	541	452
PWR	59	MCINTOSH	MC- 60A MONO TUBE	990	**732**	629	526
PWR	61-70	MCINTOSH	MC- 75 VACUUM MONO TUBE	960	**710**	610	510
PWR	70	MCINTOSH	MC- 100 SOLID STATE MONO	357	**264**	226	189
PWR	61-70	MCINTOSH	MC- 225 VACUUM STEREO TUBE 25 WATTS	609	**450**	387	323
PWR	60-69	MCINTOSH	MC- 240 VACUUM STEREO TUBE 40 WATTS	984	**727**	625	522
PWR	67	MCINTOSH	MC- 250 TRANSISTOR 50 WATTS	358	**264**	227	190
PWR	67	MCINTOSH	MC- 250E TRANSISTOR 50 WATTS	476	**352**	302	252
PWR	61-70	MCINTOSH	MC- 275 VACUUM STEREO TUBE 75 WATTS	2,257	**1,669**	1,434	1,199
PWR	67	MCINTOSH	MC-2105 SOLID STATE 105 WATTS	518	**383**	329	275
PWR	67	MCINTOSH	MC-2505 50Wpc METERED	443	**328**	281	235
PWR	68	MCINTOSH	MC-3500 MONO TUBE	3,298	**2,439**	2,095	1,752
PWR	60	MCINTOSH	MK-30 KIT MONO TUBE 30 WATTS	248	**183**	157	132
TEST	64	MCINTOSH	MI-3 STEREO OSCILLOSCOPE	240	**177**	152	127
TEST	73	MCINTOSH	MPI-4 DUAL TRACE OSCILLOSCOPE	630	**466**	400	335
TUNER	57	MCINTOSH	MR- 55 TUBE	161	**119**	102	85
TUNER	59	MCINTOSH	MR- 55A AM/FM MONO TUBE	150	**111**	95	80
TUNER	60-62	MCINTOSH	MR- 65 VACUUM MONO TUBE	258	**190**	164	137
TUNER	62-64	MCINTOSH	MR- 65B VACUUM MONO TUBE	324	**239**	206	172
TUNER	60	MCINTOSH	MR- 66 AM/FM TUBE	137	**101**	87	72
TUNER	63-68	MCINTOSH	MR- 67 VACUUM STEREO TUBE	458	**339**	291	243
TUNER	63-69	MCINTOSH	MR- 71 VACUUM TUBE	569	**421**	361	302
TUNER	69	MCINTOSH	MR- 73 AM/FM SOLID STATE	347	**257**	220	184
TUNER	70-78	MCINTOSH	MR- 77 FM STEREO SOLID STATE	473	**350**	300	251
TUNER	62	MCINTOSH	MX-110 FM TUBE TUNER/PREAMP	465	**344**	295	247
TUNER	71	MCINTOSH	MX-113 AM/FM STEREO TUNER/PREAMP	424	**313**	269	225
TUNER	69	MCINTOSH	MX-114 AM/FM SS TUNER/PREAMP	307	**227**	195	163
XOVER	55	MCINTOSH	3 MONO TUBE	1,853	**1,371**	1,177	984

MELLOTRON

TYPE	YR	MFG	MODEL	SELL EXC	SELL AVG	BUY EXC	BUY AVG
SYNTHESIZER	64	MELLOTRON	MELLOTRON MARK II	3,835	**2,836**	2,436	2,037
SYNTH	68	MELLOTRON	MELLOTRON MODEL 300	4,368	**3,230**	2,775	2,320
SYNTH	70	MELLOTRON	MELLOTRON MODEL 400	719	**531**	456	381

MESSANGER by MUSIC CRAFT

TYPE	YR	MFG	MODEL	SELL EXC	SELL AVG	BUY EXC	BUY AVG
ELEC. GUITAR	67	MESSANGER	HOLLOW BODY ALUMINUM BODY/NECK	2,390	**1,767**	1,518	1,269
ELGUIT	68	MESSANGER	SOLID BODY NATURAL ON FLAME MAPLE	4,320	**3,195**	2,745	2,295

MICROFRET

TYPE	YR	MFG	MODEL	SELL EXC	SELL AVG	BUY EXC	BUY AVG
ELEC. GUITAR	71	MICROFRET	BARITONE SIGNATURE DOUBLE CUTAWAY	446	**330**	283	237
ELGUIT	72	MICROFRET	BARITONE STAGE II DOUBLE CUTAWAY, 2 PU's	412	**305**	262	219
ELGUIT	69	MICROFRET	CALIBRA BROWN	438	**324**	278	233
ELGUIT	70	MICROFRET	CALIBRA BROWN	467	**345**	297	248

TYPE	YR	MFG	PRICES--BASED ON 100% ORIGINAL MODEL	SELL EXC	SELL AVG	BUY EXC	BUY AVG
ELGUIT	69	MICROFRET	**CALIBRA I**	480	**355**	305	255
ELGUIT	70	MICROFRET	**CALIBRA I** RED	462	**342**	294	245
ELGUIT	72	MICROFRET	**CALIBRA I** RED	424	**313**	269	225
ELGUIT	72	MICROFRET	**COVINGTON**	677	**501**	430	360
ELGUIT	68	MICROFRET	**GOLDEN COMET**	537	**397**	341	285
ELGUIT	69	MICROFRET	**GOLDEN COMET**	438	**324**	278	233
ELGUIT	71	MICROFRET	**GOLDEN MELODY** SUNBURST	518	**383**	329	275
ELGUIT	69	MICROFRET	**HUNTINGTON**	504	**372**	320	267
ELGUIT	74	MICROFRET	**HUNTINGTON**	500	**369**	317	265
ELGUIT	70	MICROFRET	**HUSKY BASS** RED	288	**213**	183	153
ELGUIT	68	MICROFRET	**ORBITER** TRIPLE CUTAWAY	557	**412**	354	296
ELGUIT	67	MICROFRET	**PLAINSMAN** TOBACCO SUNBURST	565	**418**	359	300
ELGUIT	70	MICROFRET	**RENDEZVOUS BASS** ORANGE SUNBURST, 1 PU	432	**319**	274	229
ELGUIT	79	MICROFRET	**SABRE BASS** NATURAL	956	**707**	607	507
ELGUIT	69	MICROFRET	**SIGNATURE** DOUBLE CUTAWAY, 2 PU's	478	**353**	303	253
ELGUIT	69	MICROFRET	**SIGNATURE BASS** NATURAL	478	**353**	303	253
ELGUIT	71	MICROFRET	**SIGNATURE BASS** SUNBURST	470	**347**	298	249
ELGUIT	72	MICROFRET	**SIGNATURE BASS** BARITONE, SUNBURST	452	**334**	287	240
ELGUIT	69	MICROFRET	**SPACETONE** DOUBLE CUTAWAY, 2 PU's	478	**353**	303	253
ELGUIT	69	MICROFRET	**SPACETONE**	557	**412**	354	296
ELGUIT	68	MICROFRET	**STAGE II BASS**	478	**353**	303	253
ELGUIT	70	MICROFRET	**STAGE II BASS** BROWN	469	**347**	298	249
ELGUIT	71	MICROFRET	**STAGE II BASS**	480	**355**	305	255
ELGUIT	73	MICROFRET	**STAGE II BASS**	468	**346**	297	248
ELGUIT	70	MICROFRET	**STAGE VII BASS** SUNBURST	438	**324**	278	233
ELGUIT	71	MICROFRET	**SWINGER**	498	**368**	316	264
ELGUIT	70	MICROFRET	**THUNDERMASTER BASS** SUNBURST	417	**308**	265	221
ELGUIT	70	MICROFRET	**WANDERER**	481	**356**	306	256

MONTERREY

TYPE	YR	MFG	MODEL	SELL EXC	SELL AVG	BUY EXC	BUY AVG
GUITAR (ACOUSTIC)	36	MONTERREY	**12-STRING**	1,434	**1,060**	911	761
GUITAR	39	MONTERREY	**12-STRING**	1,354	**1,001**	860	719
GUITAR	39	MONTERREY	**CUSTOM** 12-STRING	1,832	**1,355**	1,164	973
GUITAR	47	MONTERREY	**DELUXE** ARCHTOP	2,151	**1,591**	1,367	1,142
GUITAR	48	MONTERREY	**DELUXE** ARCHTOP	1,992	**1,473**	1,265	1,058
GUITAR	47	MONTERREY	**F-70 FLATTOP**	2,310	**1,708**	1,468	1,227

MOOG MUSICAL INSTRUMENTS

TYPE	YR	MFG	MODEL	SELL EXC	SELL AVG	BUY EXC	BUY AVG
EQUAL	78	MOOG	**SPGE-1 SIG** GRAPHIC	599	**443**	380	318
EQUAL	78	MOOG	**SPPE-1 PARA**	1,037	**767**	659	551
GUITAR AMP	63	MOOG	**MR- 71 VACUUM STEREO TUBE**	731	**541**	464	388
SIGNAL PROCESSOR	79	MOOG	**SPVP-1** 12 STAGE PHASER	525	**388**	333	278
SYNTHESIZER	70	MOOG	**MINIMOOG ANALOG**	893	**661**	567	474
SYNTH	75	MOOG	**POLYMOOG ANALOG**	399	**295**	253	212
SYNTH	77	MOOG	**POLYSYNTH** POLYPEDAL	1,195	**883**	759	634
SYNTH	74	MOOG	**SATELLITE**	192	**142**	122	102
SYNTH	74	MOOG	**SONIC-SIX**	637	**471**	405	338

MOONSTONE

TYPE	YR	MFG	MODEL	SELL EXC	SELL AVG	BUY EXC	BUY AVG
ELEC. GUITAR	78	MOON	**ECLIPSE DELUXE**	928	**686**	589	493
ELGUIT	78	MOON	**ECLIPSE STANDARD**	816	**604**	519	434
ELGUIT	81	MOON	**EXPLODER**	907	**670**	576	481
ELGUIT	78	MOON	**M-80**	1,558	**1,152**	990	827
ELGUIT	81	MOON	**TREMOLO V**	957	**707**	608	508
ELGUIT	78	MOON	**VULCAN DELUXE**	1,133	**838**	720	602
ELGUIT	78	MOON	**VULCAN STANDARD**	878	**649**	558	466

MOSRITE

TYPE	YR	MFG	MODEL	SELL EXC	SELL AVG	BUY EXC	BUY AVG
BANJO	65	MOSRITE	**DOBRO** ELECTRIC, 12-STRING	555	**411**	353	295

TYPE	YR	MFG	PRICES--BASED ON 100% ORIGINAL MODEL	SELL EXC	SELL AVG	BUY EXC	BUY AVG
BANJO	67	MOSRITE	**DOBRO** NATURAL, STYLE C RESONATOR	536	**396**	340	285
BANJO	68	MOSRITE	**DOBRO** NATURAL, MAHOGANY, 12-STRING	494	**365**	314	262
BANJO	68	MOSRITE	**DOBRO** BROWN, RESONATOR	618	**457**	392	328
ELEC. GUITAR	69	MOSRITE	**BASS** SUNBURST, VENTURES BODY STYLE	610	**451**	387	324
ELGUIT	70	MOSRITE	**BASS** SUNBURST, VENTURES BODY STYLE, 2 PU's	601	**445**	382	319
ELGUIT	70	MOSRITE	**BASS** BLUE METALLIC, VENTURES BODY STYLE, 2 PU's	601	**445**	382	319
ELGUIT	70	MOSRITE	**BASS** SOLID MAHOGANY, 1 PU	605	**448**	384	321
ELGUIT	76	MOSRITE	**BRASS RAIL** BLACK	1,099	**812**	698	583
ELGUIT	76	MOSRITE	**BRASS RAIL**	1,119	**827**	711	594
ELGUIT	77	MOSRITE	**BRASS RAIL** BLACK	990	**732**	629	526
ELGUIT	77	MOSRITE	**BRASS RAIL**	1,076	**795**	683	571
ELGUIT	69	MOSRITE	**CALIFORNIAN** MAROON, DOUBLE CUTAWAY, 2 PU's	828	**631**	536	410
ELGUIT	65	MOSRITE	**CELEBRITY** SUNBURST, TRAPEZE TAIL PIECE	652	**482**	414	346
ELGUIT	67	MOSRITE	**CELEBRITY** SUNBURST	607	**449**	386	322
ELGUIT	68	MOSRITE	**CELEBRITY** SUNBURST, DOUBLE CUTAWAY, 2 PU's	579	**428**	368	308
ELGUIT	70	MOSRITE	**CELEBRITY** RED, VIBRATO, 2 PU's	485	**359**	308	258
ELGUIT	70	MOSRITE	**CELEBRITY** SUNBURST	499	**369**	317	265
ELGUIT	70	MOSRITE	**CELEBRITY** RED & BLACK SUNBURST, 12-STRING	561	**415**	356	298
ELGUIT	70	MOSRITE	**CELEBRITY** GREEN, 12-STRING	562	**416**	357	298
ELGUIT	72	MOSRITE	**CELEBRITY** RED & BLACK SUNBURST, 12-STRING	504	**372**	320	267
ELGUIT	72	MOSRITE	**CELEBRITY** RED, VIBROLA	530	**392**	337	282
ELGUIT	74	MOSRITE	**CELEBRITY** AMBER SUNBURST	527	**389**	334	279
ELGUIT	70	MOSRITE	**CELEBRITY BASS** RED & BLACK SUNBURST	569	**421**	361	302
ELGUIT	68	MOSRITE	**CELEBRITY 3** SUNBURST, 2 PU's	565	**418**	359	300
ELGUIT	70	MOSRITE	**CELEBRITY 3** SUNBURST, 12-STRING	562	**416**	357	298
ELGUIT	67	MOSRITE	**CELEBRITY 3 BASS**	645	**477**	409	342
ELGUIT	68	MOSRITE	**CELEBRITY 3 BASS**	574	**424**	364	304
ELGUIT	70	MOSRITE	**CELEBRITY 3 BASS** CHERRY RED	562	**416**	357	298
ELGUIT	70	MOSRITE	**CELEBRITY 3 BASS** TRANSLUCENT BLUE, SERIAL #Z0477	562	**416**	357	298
ELGUIT	69	MOSRITE	**CELEBRITY I** ORANGE SUNBURST,MOSLEY TREMOLO,DUAL HB's	637	**471**	405	338
ELGUIT	68	MOSRITE	**COMBO** SUNBURST, 12-STRING	501	**370**	318	266
ELGUIT	68	MOSRITE	**COMBO** RED, TREMOLO	680	**503**	432	361
ELGUIT	66	MOSRITE	**COMBO MARK I** CHERRY SUNBURST	637	**471**	405	338
ELGUIT	56	MOSRITE	**CUSTOM** SUNBURST, LEFT-HANDED, CARVED SOLID MAHOGANY	3,415	**2,526**	2,170	1,814
ELGUIT	66	MOSRITE	**D-100 CALIFORNIAN** CANDY APPLE RED, ELECTRONIC RESONATOR,2 PU's	709	**524**	450	376
ELGUIT	64	MOSRITE	**MAPHIS** DOUBLE NECK	2,993	**2,213**	1,901	1,590
ELGUIT	67	MOSRITE	**MAPHIS** SUNBURST, DOUBLE NECK	1,452	**1,074**	922	771
ELGUIT	67	MOSRITE	**MAPHIS** CANDY APPLE RED, DOUBLE NECK	1,680	**1,242**	1,067	892
ELGUIT	68	MOSRITE	**MAPHIS** SUNBURST, DOUBLE NECK	1,779	**1,316**	1,130	945
ELGUIT	65	MOSRITE	**MAPHIS MARK I**	888	**656**	564	471
ELGUIT	66	MOSRITE	**MAPHIS MARK I**	912	**674**	579	484
ELGUIT	67	MOSRITE	**MAPHIS MARK I**	888	**656**	564	471
ELGUIT	68	MOSRITE	**MAPHIS MARK I**	864	**639**	549	459
ELGUIT	67	MOSRITE	**MAPHIS MARK X**	602	**445**	383	320
ELGUIT	68	MOSRITE	**MAPHIS MARK XII**	648	**479**	412	344
ELGUIT	67	MOSRITE	**MAPHIS MARK XVIII** LAKE PLACID BLUE	2,272	**1,680**	1,443	1,207

TYPE	YR	MFG	PRICES--BASED ON 100% ORIGINAL MODEL	SELL EXC	SELL AVG	BUY EXC	BUY AVG
ELGUIT	70	MOSRITE	**RAMBO PREMIER** BLOND, DOUBLE CUTAWAY	497	**367**	315	264
ELGUIT	73	MOSRITE	**V-11** SUNBURST	501	**370**	318	266
ELGUIT	63	MOSRITE	**VENTURES** SUNBURST	3,213	**2,376**	2,041	1,706
ELGUIT	64	MOSRITE	**VENTURES** SUNBURST	2,388	**1,766**	1,517	1,268
ELGUIT	64	MOSRITE	**VENTURES** VIBRAMUTE	3,501	**2,589**	2,224	1,859
ELGUIT	64	MOSRITE	**VENTURES** PEARL WHITE	3,888	**2,876**	2,471	2,066
ELGUIT	65	MOSRITE	**VENTURES** SUNBURST, 12-STRING, VIBRATO	1,213	**897**	771	644
ELGUIT	65	MOSRITE	**VENTURES** SUNBURST	2,370	**1,752**	1,506	1,259
ELGUIT	66	MOSRITE	**VENTURES** SUNBURST, 12-STRING	1,211	**896**	769	643
ELGUIT	66	MOSRITE	**VENTURES** CANDY APPLE RED	2,013	**1,488**	1,279	1,069
ELGUIT	66	MOSRITE	**VENTURES** FIESTA RED	3,824	**2,828**	2,430	2,031
ELGUIT	67	MOSRITE	**VENTURES** SUNBURST, 12-STRING	1,209	**894**	768	642
ELGUIT	67	MOSRITE	**VENTURES** WHITE, 12-STRING	1,211	**896**	769	643
ELGUIT	67	MOSRITE	**VENTURES** SUNBURST	2,285	**1,690**	1,452	1,214
ELGUIT	67	MOSRITE	**VENTURES** METALLIC BLUE	3,782	**2,797**	2,403	2,009
ELGUIT	68	MOSRITE	**VENTURES** CANDY APPLE RED	1,923	**1,422**	1,222	1,022
ELGUIT	60	MOSRITE	**VENTURES BASS** RED	1,440	**1,065**	915	765
ELGUIT	66	MOSRITE	**VENTURES BASS** METALLIC BLUE	1,193	**882**	758	633
ELGUIT	68	MOSRITE	**VENTURES BASS** METALLIC BLUE	916	**678**	582	487
ELGUIT	68	MOSRITE	**VENTURES BASS** SUNBURST	997	**737**	633	529
ELGUIT	67	MOSRITE	**VENTURES II** SUNBURST, MOSE VIBRATO	816	**603**	518	433
ELGUIT	74	MOSRITE	**VENTURES II**	610	**451**	387	324
ELGUIT	66	MOSRITE	**VENTURES MARK I**	1,257	**930**	799	668
ELGUIT	67	MOSRITE	**VENTURES MARK I** SUNBURST	1,222	**903**	776	649
ELGUIT	65	MOSRITE	**VENTURES MARK V** SUNBURST,MOSELEY TREM,TRUSS ROD ADJUST AT BODY END OF NECK	1,026	**758**	652	545
ELGUIT	66	MOSRITE	**VENTURES MARK V** BLUE	1,030	**761**	654	547
ELGUIT	66	MOSRITE	**VENTURES MARK V** MAHOGANY	1,032	**763**	655	548
ELGUIT	68	MOSRITE	**VENTURES MARK V** SUNBURST	893	**661**	567	474
ELGUIT	64	MOSRITE	**VENTURES MARK X BASS**	478	**353**	303	253
ELGUIT	65	MOSRITE	**VENTURES MARK XII** 12-STRING	599	**443**	380	318
ELGUIT	66	MOSRITE	**VENTURES MARK XVIII** SUNBURST	1,844	**1,363**	1,171	979
GUITAR (ACOUSTIC)	66	MOSRITE	**CELEBRITY MARK I** ARCHTOP	489	**362**	311	260
GUITAR	67	MOSRITE	**CELEBRITY MARK I-T** ARCHTOP	409	**303**	260	217
GUITAR	67	MOSRITE	**CELEBRITY MARK XII** ARCHTOP	496	**367**	315	263
GUITAR	67	MOSRITE	**D- 3 3/4-SIDE** BLOND TOP	520	**384**	330	276
GUITAR	65	MOSRITE	**D- 8**	599	**443**	380	318
GUITAR	66	MOSRITE	**D- 8**	537	**397**	341	285
GUITAR	66	MOSRITE	**D- 12** ALL MAHOGANY, 12-STRING	513	**379**	326	272
GUITAR	65	MOSRITE	**D- 40** SUNBURST	480	**355**	305	255
GUITAR	66	MOSRITE	**D- 40** SUNBURST	652	**482**	414	346
GUITAR	64	MOSRITE	**D- 40S** SUNBURST	603	**446**	383	320
GUITAR	64	MOSRITE	**D- 50** MAHOGANY	455	**336**	289	241
GUITAR	66	MOSRITE	**D- 50S** SQUARE NECK	665	**492**	422	353
GUITAR	67	MOSRITE	**D- 65** MAPLE TOP, MAHOGANY BODY	574	**424**	364	304

TYPE	YR	MFG	PRICES--BASED ON 100% ORIGINAL MODEL	SELL EXC	SELL AVG	BUY EXC	BUY AVG
GUITAR	68	MOSRITE	D- 65	635	470	403	337
GUITAR	68	MOSRITE	D- 65E	484	358	308	257
GUITAR	60	MOSRITE	D-100 SUNBURST, DOUBLE CUTAWAY, RESONATOR	812	600	516	431
GUITAR	67	MOSRITE	D-100 DOUBLE CUTAWAY, THIN BODY	611	452	388	324
GUITAR	68	MOSRITE	D-100	428	316	272	227

MOSSMAN

TYPE	YR	MFG	MODEL	SELL EXC	SELL AVG	BUY EXC	BUY AVG
ELEC. GUITAR	77	MOSSMAN	STINGRAY II NATURAL	438	324	278	233
GUITAR (ACOUSTIC)	73	MOSSMAN	D ROSEWOOD BACK/SIDES	909	672	577	482
GUITAR	73	MOSSMAN	DAVID CHRISTIANSON ROSEWOOD	956	707	607	507
GUITAR	74	MOSSMAN	FLINT HILLS	954	705	606	506
GUITAR	75	MOSSMAN	FLINT HILLS	840	621	533	446
GUITAR	76	MOSSMAN	FLINT HILLS ROSWOOD BACK/SIDES	731	541	464	388
GUITAR	73	MOSSMAN	GREAT PLAINS BRAZILIAN ROSEWOOD	1,195	883	759	634
GUITAR	76	MOSSMAN	GREAT PLAINS	1,216	899	772	646
GUITAR	77	MOSSMAN	GREAT PLAINS	996	736	633	529
GUITAR	75	MOSSMAN	SOUTHWIND ABALONE TRIM TOP	1,035	766	658	550
GUITAR	75	MOSSMAN	TENNESSEE 12-STRING	598	442	380	317
GUITAR	76	MOSSMAN	WINTER WHEAT 12-STRING	1,032	763	655	548
GUITAR	76	MOSSMAN	WINTER WHEAT ABALONE TOP	1,273	942	809	676

MUSIC MAN/ERNIE BALL

TYPE	YR	MFG	MODEL	SELL EXC	SELL AVG	BUY EXC	BUY AVG
ELEC. GUITAR	80	MUSICMAN	CUTLASS I BASS NATURAL, ASH GRAPHITE, STRING-THRU	796	589	506	423
ELGUIT	78	MUSICMAN	SABRE BASS BROWN	478	353	303	253
ELGUIT	78	MUSICMAN	SABRE BASS NATURAL	478	353	303	253
ELGUIT	78	MUSICMAN	SABRE I SUNBURST	518	383	329	275
ELGUIT	76	MUSICMAN	STINGRAY BASS SUNBURST, STRING-THRU	637	471	405	338
ELGUIT	78	MUSICMAN	STINGRAY BASS SUNBURST	495	366	314	263
ELGUIT	73	MUSICMAN	STINGRAY I 6-STRING	557	412	354	296
ELGUIT	76	MUSICMAN	STINGRAY I NATURAL	544	402	345	289
ELGUIT	77	MUSICMAN	STINGRAY I NATURAL	537	397	341	285
ELGUIT	78	MUSICMAN	STINGRAY I SUNBURST	518	383	329	275
ELGUIT	76	MUSICMAN	STINGRAY II	456	337	289	242
GUITAR AMP	74	MUSICMAN	410 65 AMP	384	284	244	204
GTAMP	75	MUSICMAN	HD-212 130 AMP	336	248	213	178
GTAMP	75	MUSICMAN	RD- 50 HEAD 50 WATT, TUBE	268	198	170	142
GTAMP	79	MUSICMAN	Z 2x12" SPEAKERS	354	261	225	188

NATIONAL RESO-PHONIC GUITARS, INC

TYPE	YR	MFG	MODEL	SELL EXC	SELL AVG	BUY EXC	BUY AVG
ELEC. GUITAR	64	NATIONAL	AIRLINE BLACK-RED SUNBURST, 2 PU's	239	176	151	126
ELGUIT	61	NATIONAL	BASS 85 RESOGLASS	456	337	289	242
ELGUIT	55	NATIONAL	BEL-AIRE	538	398	342	286
ELGUIT	56	NATIONAL	BEL-AIRE SUNBURST, ARCHTOP, SINGLE CUTAWAY	361	267	229	192
ELGUIT	57	NATIONAL	BEL-AIRE SUNBURST, ARCHTOP, CUTAWAY	468	346	297	248
ELGUIT	57	NATIONAL	BOLERO SUNBURST	468	346	297	248
ELGUIT	45	NATIONAL	BOSTONIAN RED SUNBURST, CUTAWAY	469	347	298	249
ELGUIT	59	NATIONAL	DEBONAIR SUNBURST, SINGLE PU, CUTAWAY, ARCHTOP	598	442	380	317
ELGUIT	56	NATIONAL	DUAL TONE SUNBURST, BOUND TOP	409	303	260	217
ELGUIT	38	NATIONAL	ERIC JOHNSON LAP VIBRATO	469	347	298	249

TYPE	YR	MFG	MODEL	SELL EXC	SELL AVG	BUY EXC	BUY AVG
ELGUIT	65	NATIONAL	**GLENWOOD 95** RED RESOGLASS	1,358	**1,004**	863	721
ELGUIT	62	NATIONAL	**GLENWOOD 98** BLACK, SEMI-HOLLOW	1,407	**1,040**	894	747
ELGUIT	50	NATIONAL	**L-7** SUNBURST, SINGLE CUTAWAY, 2 PU's	206	**152**	131	109
ELGUIT	64	NATIONAL	**NATIONAL 85** RED	619	**457**	393	328
ELGUIT	38-40	NATIONAL	**NEW YORKER** SUNBURST, NO F HOLES	677	**501**	430	360
ELGUIT	64	NATIONAL	**RESOPHONIC** BLACK, 1 PU	548	**405**	348	291
ELGUIT	64	NATIONAL	**STEREO-MATIC** SUNBURST	216	**159**	137	114
ELGUIT	64	NATIONAL	**STUDENT 1033**	238	**181**	154	118
ELGUIT	59	NATIONAL	**STUDENT 1133**	412	**305**	262	219
ELGUIT	64	NATIONAL	**STUDIO 66** BLACK, RESOGLASS	240	**177**	152	127
ELGUIT	65	NATIONAL	**STUDIO 66** BLACK, RESOGLASS	230	**170**	146	122
ELGUIT	60	NATIONAL	**VAL PRO 82** RED, MAP SHAPED	948	**701**	602	503
ELGUIT	62	NATIONAL	**VAL PRO 82** RED, MAP SHAPED	874	**646**	555	464
ELGUIT	62	NATIONAL	**VAL PRO 84** WHITE, MAP SHAPED	1,069	**790**	679	568
ELGUIT	61	NATIONAL	**VAL PRO 85 BASS** WHITE, RESOGLASS	516	**381**	328	274
ELGUIT	63	NATIONAL	**VAL PRO 85 BASS** WHITE, RESOGLASS	494	**365**	314	262
ELGUIT	62	NATIONAL	**VAL PRO 88**	1,115	**825**	708	592
ELGUIT	63	NATIONAL	**VAL PRO 88** BLACK, RESOGLASS	1,277	**945**	811	678
ELGUIT	60	NATIONAL	**VAL TROL** CREAM, 1 HB PU, SERIAL #T27573	356	**263**	226	189
ELGUIT	62	NATIONAL	**WESTWOOD 72**	944	**698**	600	501
ELGUIT	63	NATIONAL	**WESTWOOD 72**	792	**586**	503	421
ELGUIT	65	NATIONAL	**WESTWOOD 72**	599	**443**	380	318
ELGUIT	62	NATIONAL	**WESTWOOD 75** WHITE BLOCK INLAYS	524	**387**	333	278
ELGUIT	63	NATIONAL	**WESTWOOD 75**	457	**338**	290	243
ELGUIT	64	NATIONAL	**WESTWOOD 75**	463	**342**	294	246
ELGUIT	63	NATIONAL	**WESTWOOD 77**	1,231	**910**	782	654
ELGUIT	64	NATIONAL	**WESTWOOD 77** CHERRY RED	1,115	**825**	708	592
ELGUIT	65	NATIONAL	**WESTWOOD 77**	841	**622**	534	447
GUITAR AMP	48	NATIONAL	**1200** TAN, 12" SPEAKERS, 6 TUBES	312	**230**	198	165
GTAMP	62	NATIONAL	**1260 VAL-VERB** 20 WATT, 2x10"	369	**273**	234	196
GTAMP	40	NATIONAL	**B** BLACK, 20 WATT, 12" SPEAKER	313	**232**	199	166
GTAMP	40	NATIONAL	**NEW YORKER**	467	**345**	297	248
GTAMP	56	NATIONAL	**TREMOTONE** YELLOW TWEED	144	**106**	91	76
GUITAR (ACOUSTIC)	59	NATIONAL	**1155** NATURAL, ROSEWOOD BRIDGE	956	**707**	607	507
GUITAR	41	NATIONAL	**ARISTOCRAT**	956	**707**	607	507
GUITAR	53	NATIONAL	**ARISTOCRAT**	598	**442**	380	317
GUITAR	54	NATIONAL	**ARISTOCRAT**	521	**385**	331	276
GUITAR	57	NATIONAL	**BEL-AIRE**	796	**589**	506	423
GUITAR	64	NATIONAL	**BLUEGRASS 35** WHITE, RESOGLASS	637	**471**	405	338
GUITAR	65	NATIONAL	**BLUEGRASS 35** RESOGLASS	637	**471**	405	338
GUITAR	51	NATIONAL	**CALIFORNIA** NATURAL, ARCHTOP	578	**428**	367	307
GUITAR	52	NATIONAL	**CALIFORNIA**	531	**404**	344	263
GUITAR	53	NATIONAL	**CLUB COMBO**	691	**511**	439	367
GUITAR	42	NATIONAL	**COLLEGIAN** YELLOW, MAPLE, ROUND NECK	2,316	**1,713**	1,471	1,230
GUITAR	52	NATIONAL	**COSMOPOLITAN**	384	**284**	244	204
GUITAR	31	NATIONAL	**DON #1**	4,320	**3,195**	2,745	2,295
GUITAR	35	NATIONAL	**DON #2** GEOMETRIC ENGRAVINGS	7,307	**5,404**	4,643	3,882
GUITAR	36	NATIONAL	**DON #3**	5,760	**4,260**	3,660	3,060
GUITAR	30	NATIONAL	**DUOLIAN**	1,331	**984**	846	707
GUITAR	30	NATIONAL	**DUOLIAN** GRAY, ROUND NECK, RESONATOR	1,760	**1,302**	1,118	935
GUITAR	30	NATIONAL	**DUOLIAN** 12-FRET, RESONATOR	2,162	**1,599**	1,374	1,149

TYPE	YR	MFG	PRICES--BASED ON 100% ORIGINAL MODEL	SELL EXC	SELL AVG	BUY EXC	BUY AVG
GUITAR	31	NATIONAL	**DUOLIAN** 12-FRET, ROUND NECK	1,992	**1,473**	1,265	1,058
GUITAR	32	NATIONAL	**DUOLIAN** GRAY CRYSTAL	1,380	**1,020**	877	733
GUITAR	34	NATIONAL	**DUOLIAN** 14-FRET	1,336	**988**	849	709
GUITAR	35	NATIONAL	**DUOLIAN** GRAY, ROUND NECK, 14-FRET	1,669	**1,234**	1,060	886
GUITAR	37	NATIONAL	**DUOLIAN** GRAY, ROUND NECK, 14-FRET	1,195	**883**	759	634
GUITAR	38	NATIONAL	**DUOLIAN** BROWN, 14-FRET	1,231	**910**	782	654
GUITAR	35	NATIONAL	**DUOLIAN HAWAIIAN** SQUARE NECK	1,222	**903**	776	649
GUITAR	36	NATIONAL	**DUOLIAN HAWAIIAN** SQUARE NECK	1,195	**883**	759	634
GUITAR	37	NATIONAL	**DUOLIAN HAWAIIAN** SQUARE NECK	1,191	**881**	757	632
GUITAR	30	NATIONAL	**DUOLIAN SPANISH**	1,721	**1,273**	1,093	914
GUITAR	31	NATIONAL	**DUOLIAN SPANISH**	1,745	**1,290**	1,108	927
GUITAR	32	NATIONAL	**DUOLIAN SPANISH**	1,440	**1,065**	915	765
GUITAR	34	NATIONAL	**DUOLIAN SPANISH**	1,584	**1,171**	1,006	841
GUITAR	35	NATIONAL	**DUOLIAN SPANISH**	1,418	**1,049**	901	753
GUITAR	40	NATIONAL	**DUOLIAN SPANISH**	1,394	**1,031**	886	741
GUITAR	54	NATIONAL	**DYNAMIC 1125** SUNBURST, F-HOLES	309	**236**	200	153
GUITAR	30	NATIONAL	**ESTRELITA**	796	**589**	506	423
GUITAR	58	NATIONAL	**GLENWOOD** RESOGLASS	1,329	**983**	844	706
GUITAR	63	NATIONAL	**GLENWOOD 95** RESOGLASS	1,327	**981**	843	705
GUITAR	64	NATIONAL	**GLENWOOD 98** RESOGLASS	2,041	**1,510**	1,297	1,084
GUITAR	64	NATIONAL	**GLENWOOD 99** SURF GREEN, MAP SHAPE	1,394	**1,031**	886	741
GUITAR	64	NATIONAL	**GLENWOOD 99** RESOGLASS	2,189	**1,619**	1,391	1,163
GUITAR	59	NATIONAL	**GLENWOOD DELUXE**	796	**589**	506	423
GUITAR	40	NATIONAL	**HAVANA** NATURAL, SPRUCE TOP	960	**710**	610	510
GUITAR	41	NATIONAL	**HAVANA** SUNBURST, SPRUCE TOP	796	**589**	506	423
GUITAR	54	NATIONAL	**JUMBO** SUNBURST, FLATTOP	458	**349**	297	227
GUITAR	67	NATIONAL	**N-720 DREADNOUGHT** NATURAL	477	**352**	303	253
GUITAR	68	NATIONAL	**N-720 DREADNOUGHT** SPRUCE TOP, MAHOGANY BACK/SIDES	468	**346**	297	248
GUITAR	68	NATIONAL	**N-730** SUNBURST, NATURAL, SPRUCE BACK/SIDES	468	**346**	297	248
GUITAR	64	NATIONAL	**NEWPORT 82** RED, MAP SHAPE, 1 PU	709	**524**	450	376
GUITAR	65	NATIONAL	**NEWPORT 82** RESOGLASS	663	**490**	421	352
GUITAR	64	NATIONAL	**NEWPORT 84** SEAFOAM GREEN	876	**648**	556	465
GUITAR	66	NATIONAL	**NEWPORT 84** RESOGLASS	663	**490**	421	352
GUITAR	64	NATIONAL	**NEWPORT 88** RESOGLASS	994	**735**	631	528
GUITAR	61	NATIONAL	**RESONATOR TOWN & COUNTY** BLACK, RESOGLASS	771	**570**	490	410
GUITAR	50	NATIONAL	**RESOPHONIC** GRAY, PEARLOID BODY	518	**383**	329	275
GUITAR	56	NATIONAL	**RESOPHONIC** BLACK	624	**462**	397	332
GUITAR	58	NATIONAL	**RESOPHONIC** RESONATOR	796	**589**	506	423
GUITAR	59	NATIONAL	**RESOPHONIC** GRAY	842	**623**	535	447
GUITAR	60	NATIONAL	**RESOPHONIC** GRAY, PEARLOID, RESONATOR	796	**589**	506	423
GUITAR	61	NATIONAL	**RESOPHONIC** WHITE PEARLOID	796	**589**	506	423
GUITAR	66	NATIONAL	**RESOPHONIC** WHITE PEARLOID	796	**589**	506	423
GUITAR	56	NATIONAL	**RESOPHONIC 3/4** GREEN-WHITE	872	**645**	554	463
GUITAR	30	NATIONAL	**ROSITA** SUNBURST	653	**483**	415	347
GUITAR	35	NATIONAL	**ROSITA**	717	**530**	455	380
GUITAR	30	NATIONAL	**STYLE 0** 12-FRET, SQUARE NECK	1,215	**898**	772	645

TYPE	YR	MFG	PRICES--BASED ON 100% ORIGINAL MODEL	SELL EXC	SELL AVG	BUY EXC	BUY AVG
GUITAR	30	NATIONAL	STYLE 0 BRASS	3,120	2,307	1,982	1,657
GUITAR	30	NATIONAL	STYLE 0 EBONY, 14-FRET, ROUND NECK	3,204	2,369	2,036	1,702
GUITAR	30	NATIONAL	STYLE 0 12-FRET,CHROME-PLATED STEEL BODY, ETCHED HAWAIIAN SCENES	3,217	2,379	2,044	1,709
GUITAR	32	NATIONAL	STYLE 0 TENOR	1,112	822	706	591
GUITAR	32	NATIONAL	STYLE 0 12-FRET, ROUND NECK	1,992	1,473	1,265	1,058
GUITAR	32	NATIONAL	STYLE 0	3,654	2,702	2,322	1,941
GUITAR	33	NATIONAL	STYLE 0 HAWAIIAN SCENES ON BODY	2,109	1,559	1,340	1,120
GUITAR	34	NATIONAL	STYLE 0 12-FRET, SQUARE NECK	1,593	1,178	1,012	846
GUITAR	34	NATIONAL	STYLE 0 14-FRET, ROUND NECK	2,151	1,591	1,367	1,142
GUITAR	35	NATIONAL	STYLE 0 ROUND NECK	2,024	1,497	1,286	1,075
GUITAR	35	NATIONAL	STYLE 0 14-FRET, SQUARE NECK	2,064	1,527	1,312	1,097
GUITAR	35	NATIONAL	STYLE 0 14-FRET, ROUND NECK	3,213	2,376	2,041	1,706
GUITAR	36	NATIONAL	STYLE 0 METAL BODY, SQUARE NECK	1,584	1,172	1,007	842
GUITAR	37	NATIONAL	STYLE 0 TENOR	1,108	820	704	589
GUITAR	37	NATIONAL	STYLE 0 CHROME-PLATED BODY	3,428	2,535	2,178	1,821
GUITAR	38	NATIONAL	STYLE 0 14-FRET, ROUND NECK	2,219	1,641	1,410	1,179
GUITAR	40	NATIONAL	STYLE 0 SQUARE NECK	1,751	1,295	1,112	930
GUITAR	40	NATIONAL	STYLE 0 14-FRET, ROUND NECK	1,992	1,473	1,265	1,058
GUITAR	31	NATIONAL	STYLE 0 CUSTOM CHROME-PLTD BDY,STYLE #3 LILY OF THE VLLY ENGRVNG ON BODY	5,760	4,260	3,660	3,060
GUITAR	38	NATIONAL	STYLE 0 HAWAIIAN SQUARE NECK	1,329	983	844	706
GUITAR	43	NATIONAL	STYLE 0 HAWAIIAN 14-FRET, ROUND NECK	3,552	2,627	2,257	1,887
GUITAR	32	NATIONAL	STYLE 0 SPANISH 12-FRET, SLOT HEAD, ROUND NECK	2,190	1,620	1,392	1,163
GUITAR	35	NATIONAL	STYLE 0 SPANISH	2,163	1,600	1,374	1,149
GUITAR	36	NATIONAL	STYLE 0 SPANISH	2,219	1,641	1,410	1,179
GUITAR	39	NATIONAL	STYLE 0 SPANISH	2,218	1,640	1,409	1,178
GUITAR	30	NATIONAL	STYLE 2 ROUND NECK	7,397	5,471	4,700	3,930
GUITAR	36	NATIONAL	STYLE 3 PLECTRUM	1,407	1,040	894	747
GUITAR	38	NATIONAL	STYLE 3 TENOR	1,378	1,019	875	732
GUITAR	28	NATIONAL	STYLE 0 ROUND NECK, ROSE PATTERN	9,595	7,096	6,096	5,097
GUITAR	32	NATIONAL	STYLE N NICKEL	2,390	1,767	1,518	1,269
GUITAR	27	NATIONAL	TRICONE STYLE 1 SQUARE NECK	2,221	1,642	1,411	1,180
GUITAR	28	NATIONAL	TRICONE STYLE 1 TENOR	1,560	1,153	991	828
GUITAR	28	NATIONAL	TRICONE STYLE 1 SQUARE NECK	3,223	2,384	2,048	1,712
GUITAR	28	NATIONAL	TRICONE STYLE 1 ROUND NECK	4,925	3,643	3,129	2,616
GUITAR	29	NATIONAL	TRICONE STYLE 1 SQUARE NECK	2,937	2,172	1,866	1,560
GUITAR	30	NATIONAL	TRICONE STYLE 1 TENOR	1,109	820	705	589
GUITAR	30	NATIONAL	TRICONE STYLE 1 SQUARE NECK	2,915	2,156	1,852	1,548
GUITAR	30	NATIONAL	TRICONE STYLE 1 ROUND NECK	4,896	3,621	3,111	2,601
GUITAR	32	NATIONAL	TRICONE STYLE 1 TENOR	1,197	885	760	635
GUITAR	32	NATIONAL	TRICONE STYLE 1 ROUND NECK	4,800	3,550	3,050	2,550
GUITAR	40	NATIONAL	TRICONE STYLE 1 SQUARE NECK	2,390	1,767	1,518	1,269
GUITAR	31	NATIONAL	TRICONE STYLE 1 HAWAIIAN	2,905	2,149	1,846	1,543
GUITAR	29	NATIONAL	TRICONE STYLE 1 SPANISH	5,001	3,699	3,178	2,657
GUITAR	27	NATIONAL	TRICONE STYLE 2 ROUND NECK	8,008	5,922	5,088	4,254

TYPE	YR	MFG	PRICES--BASED ON 100% ORIGINAL MODEL	SELL EXC	SELL AVG	BUY EXC	BUY AVG
GUITAR	28	NATIONAL	**TRICONE STYLE 2** ROUND NECK	4,320	**3,195**	2,745	2,295
GUITAR	28	NATIONAL	**TRICONE STYLE 2** SQUARE NECK	4,331	**3,203**	2,752	2,301
GUITAR	29	NATIONAL	**TRICONE STYLE 2** SQUARE NECK	5,280	**3,905**	3,355	2,805
GUITAR	30	NATIONAL	**TRICONE STYLE 2** SQUARE NECK	4,320	**3,195**	2,745	2,295
GUITAR	30	NATIONAL	**TRICONE STYLE 2** ROUND NECK	5,280	**3,905**	3,355	2,805
GUITAR	31	NATIONAL	**TRICONE STYLE 2** SQUARE NECK	3,334	**2,465**	2,118	1,771
GUITAR	32	NATIONAL	**TRICONE STYLE 2** ROSE PATTERN ENGRAVING	7,138	**5,279**	4,535	3,792
GUITAR	30	NATIONAL	**TRICONE STYLE 2 HAWAIIAN**	3,139	**2,321**	1,994	1,667
GUITAR	30	NATIONAL	**TRICONE STYLE 2 SPANISH**	7,002	**5,178**	4,449	3,719
GUITAR	28	NATIONAL	**TRICONE STYLE 2.5** SQUARE NECK	3,483	**2,576**	2,213	1,850
GUITAR	27	NATIONAL	**TRICONE STYLE 3**	19,198	**14,198**	12,198	10,198
GUITAR	28	NATIONAL	**TRICONE STYLE 3** PLECTRUM	2,050	**1,516**	1,302	1,089
GUITAR	28	NATIONAL	**TRICONE STYLE 3**	24,000	**17,750**	15,250	12,750
GUITAR	29	NATIONAL	**TRICONE STYLE 3** ROUND NECK	9,430	**6,974**	5,992	5,009
GUITAR	30	NATIONAL	**TRICONE STYLE 3** SQUARE NECK	6,000	**4,437**	3,812	3,187
GUITAR	30	NATIONAL	**TRICONE STYLE 3** ROUND NECK	9,764	**7,221**	6,204	5,187
GUITAR	31	NATIONAL	**TRICONE STYLE 3** ROUND NECK	9,918	**7,335**	6,302	5,269
GUITAR	31	NATIONAL	**TRICONE STYLE 3 HAWAIIAN** SQUARE NECK	6,032	**4,461**	3,833	3,204
GUITAR	29	NATIONAL	**TRICONE STYLE 3 SPANISH**	9,538	**7,054**	6,060	5,067
GUITAR	29	NATIONAL	**TRICONE STYLE 4** SQUARE NECK	7,301	**5,400**	4,639	3,879
GUITAR	30	NATIONAL	**TRICONE STYLE 4** SQUARE NECK	7,201	**5,326**	4,576	3,826
GUITAR	33	NATIONAL	**TRICONE STYLE 4** ROUND NECK	19,200	**14,200**	12,200	10,200
GUITAR	39	NATIONAL	**TRICONE STYLE 4** SQUARE NECK	6,480	**4,792**	4,117	3,442
GUITAR	35	NATIONAL	**TRICONE STYLE 4 HAWAIIAN**	7,380	**5,458**	4,689	3,920
GUITAR	37	NATIONAL	**TRICONE STYLE 4 SPANISH**	13,749	**10,168**	8,736	7,304
GUITAR	39	NATIONAL	**TRICONE STYLE 35 HAWAIIAN**	1,561	**1,155**	992	829
GUITAR	38	NATIONAL	**TRICONE STYLE 35 SPANISH**	3,217	**2,379**	2,044	1,709
GUITAR	37	NATIONAL	**TRICONE STYLE 92 SPANISH**	2,313	**1,711**	1,470	1,229
GUITAR	38	NATIONAL	**TRICONE STYLE 97 HAWAIIAN**	3,712	**2,745**	2,358	1,972
GUITAR	28	NATIONAL	**TRIOLIAN** BROWN SUNBURST, ARCHTOP	1,394	**1,031**	886	741
GUITAR	28	NATIONAL	**TRIOLIAN**	1,482	**1,096**	941	787
GUITAR	28	NATIONAL	**TRIOLIAN** YELLOW, RESONATOR	2,283	**1,689**	1,451	1,213
GUITAR	29	NATIONAL	**TRIOLIAN** TENOR	1,021	**755**	649	542
GUITAR	29	NATIONAL	**TRIOLIAN** BROWN SUNBURST, 12-FRET, SLOT HEAD, ROUND NECK	1,538	**1,138**	977	817
GUITAR	29	NATIONAL	**TRIOLIAN** YELLOW	2,266	**1,676**	1,440	1,204
GUITAR	30	NATIONAL	**TRIOLIAN** PLECTRUM, SUNBURST	762	**563**	484	404
GUITAR	30	NATIONAL	**TRIOLIAN** TENOR, YELLOW	996	**736**	633	529
GUITAR	30	NATIONAL	**TRIOLIAN** RESONATOR	1,551	**1,147**	985	824
GUITAR	30	NATIONAL	**TRIOLIAN** BROWN SUNBURST, YELLOW, 12-FRET	1,647	**1,218**	1,046	875
GUITAR	30	NATIONAL	**TRIOLIAN** YELLOW	2,248	**1,662**	1,428	1,194
GUITAR	31	NATIONAL	**TRIOLIAN** BROWN SUNBURST	1,479	**1,094**	940	785
GUITAR	31	NATIONAL	**TRIOLIAN** YELLOW	2,216	**1,639**	1,408	1,177
GUITAR	32	NATIONAL	**TRIOLIAN** TENOR, SUNBURST, RESONATOR	937	**693**	595	498
GUITAR	32	NATIONAL	**TRIOLIAN** TENOR, YELLOW	1,000	**739**	635	531
GUITAR	32	NATIONAL	**TRIOLIAN** SUNBURST, ROUND NECK	1,155	**854**	734	614
GUITAR	32	NATIONAL	**TRIOLIAN** BROWN SUNBURST, MEATL BODY	1,356	**1,003**	861	720
GUITAR	32	NATIONAL	**TRIOLIAN** SUNBURST, ROUND NECK	1,426	**1,055**	906	757

TYPE	YR	MFG	PRICES--BASED ON 100% ORIGINAL MODEL	SELL EXC	SELL AVG	BUY EXC	BUY AVG
GUITAR	33	NATIONAL	**TRIOLIAN** TENOR	876	**648**	556	465
GUITAR	33	NATIONAL	**TRIOLIAN** BROWN SUNBURST, 12-FRET	1,780	**1,317**	1,131	946
GUITAR	34	NATIONAL	**TRIOLIAN** BROWN SUNBURST	1,517	**1,122**	964	806
GUITAR	35	NATIONAL	**TRIOLIAN** BROWN SUNBURST, METAL BODY	1,332	**985**	846	707
GUITAR	35	NATIONAL	**TRIOLIAN** BROWN SUNBURST, YELLOW	1,397	**1,033**	888	742
GUITAR	35	NATIONAL	**TRIOLIAN** SUNBURST, 14-FRET	1,752	**1,296**	1,113	931
GUITAR	36	NATIONAL	**TRIOLIAN** TENOR, CRYSTAL FINISH	598	**442**	380	317
GUITAR	36	NATIONAL	**TRIOLIAN** METAL BODY, 14-FRET, ROUND NECK	1,310	**969**	832	696
GUITAR	36	NATIONAL	**TRIOLIAN** ROSEWOOD, METAL BODY	1,315	**972**	835	698
GUITAR	36	NATIONAL	**TRIOLIAN**	2,890	**2,137**	1,836	1,535
GUITAR	37	NATIONAL	**TRIOLIAN** 14-FRET, SQUARE NECK	1,035	**766**	658	550
GUITAR	37	NATIONAL	**TRIOLIAN** WOOD GRAIN, METAL BODY	1,200	**888**	763	638
GUITAR	37	NATIONAL	**TRIOLIAN** BROWN SUNBURST, 14-FRET	1,313	**971**	834	697
GUITAR	30	NATIONAL	**TRIOLIAN HAWAIIAN**	1,469	**1,087**	933	780
GUITAR	29	NATIONAL	**TRIOLIAN HAWAIIAN GIRL** YELLOW	2,236	**1,654**	1,421	1,188
GUITAR	30	NATIONAL	**TRIOLIAN SPANISH**	1,221	**903**	775	648
GUITAR	35	NATIONAL	**TRIOLIAN SPANISH**	1,222	**903**	776	649
GUITAR	30	NATIONAL	**TRIOLIAN UKE** BROWN SUNBURST, METAL BODY	1,353	**1,001**	860	719
GUITAR	28	NATIONAL	**TRIPLATE STYLE 2** TENOR, 4-STRING	1,430	**1,057**	908	759
GUITAR	30	NATIONAL	**TRIPLATE STYLE 2** SQUARE NECK	2,905	**2,149**	1,846	1,543
GUITAR	30	NATIONAL	**TRIPLATE STYLE 3** ROUND NECK	8,897	**6,580**	5,653	4,726
GUITAR	30	NATIONAL	**TRIPLATE STYLE 4** SQUARE NECK	6,844	**5,062**	4,349	3,636
GUITAR	30	NATIONAL	**TRIPLATE STYLE 4** ROUND NECK	11,160	**8,254**	7,091	5,929
GUITAR	30	NATIONAL	**TROJAN** WOOD BODY. 14-FRET, SQUARE NECK, RESONATOR	715	**528**	454	379
GUITAR	30	NATIONAL	**TROJAN** WOOD BODY, 14-FRET, ROUND NECK	1,095	**810**	696	581
GUITAR	33	NATIONAL	**TROJAN** WOOD BODY	1,145	**847**	727	608
GUITAR	35	NATIONAL	**TROJAN** SUNBURST, WOOD BODY	1,010	**747**	642	537
GUITAR	38	NATIONAL	**TROJAN** WOOD BODY	1,010	**747**	642	537
GUITAR	45	NATIONAL	**TROJAN** SUNBURST, ROUND NECK w/BINDING	539	**399**	342	286
GUITAR	34	NATIONAL	**TROJAN HAWAIIAN** WOOD BODY	619	**457**	393	328
GUITAR	29	NATIONAL	**TROJAN SPANISH** WOOD BODY	958	**708**	608	508
GUITAR	36	NATIONAL	**TROJAN SPANISH** WOOD BODY	590	**449**	382	292
GUITAR	62	NATIONAL	**WESTWOOD 75** MAP SHAPED	518	**383**	329	275
GUITAR	65	NATIONAL	**WESTWOOD 77** CHERRY	537	**397**	341	285
MANDOLIN	51	NATIONAL	**1135** ICE TEA SUNBURST,GIBSON L-7 BODY,SPLIT HALF CIRCLE INLAY	636	**470**	404	338
MANDOL	39	NATIONAL	**SILVO** CHROME-PLATED METAL BODY	1,076	**795**	683	571
MANDOL	30	NATIONAL	**STYLE 0**	1,593	**1,178**	1,012	846
MANDOL	29	NATIONAL	**STYLE 1** SHINY FINISH	1,474	**1,090**	936	783
MANDOL	30	NATIONAL	**STYLE 2**	1,593	**1,178**	1,012	846
MANDOL	29	NATIONAL	**TRIOLIAN** SUNBURST	1,408	**1,041**	894	748
MANDOL	30	NATIONAL	**TRIOLIAN** SUNBURST	1,155	**854**	734	614
STEEL GUITAR	40	NATIONAL	**6-STRING LAP STEEL** BROWN	336	**249**	214	179
STGUIT	40	NATIONAL	**CHICAGO LAP STEEL** MAHOGANY SUNBURST	388	**287**	247	206
STGUIT	48	NATIONAL	**CHICAGO LAP STEEL** GRAY PEARLOID, 1 PU	264	**195**	167	140
STGUIT	53	NATIONAL	**CHICAGO LAP STEEL**	240	**177**	152	127

TYPE	YR	MFG	PRICES--BASED ON 100% ORIGINAL MODEL	SELL EXC	SELL AVG	BUY EXC	BUY AVG
STGUIT	60	NATIONAL	CHICAGO LAP STEEL GRAY	264	**195**	167	140
STGUIT	39	NATIONAL	CONSOLE BLACK & WHITE, 2 8-STRING NECKS	499	**369**	317	265
STGUIT	51	NATIONAL	DOUBLE-8 LAP STEEL WHITE	645	**477**	409	342
STGUIT	48	NATIONAL	DYNAMIC LAP STEEL	288	**213**	183	153
STGUIT	52	NATIONAL	DYNAMIC LAP STEEL BLACK & WHITE ART DECO	300	**222**	190	159
STGUIT	62	NATIONAL	DYNAMIC LAP STEEL RED, WHITE & BLACK, 6-STRING. 3 LEGS	384	**284**	244	204
STGUIT	42	NATIONAL	DYNAMIC NEW YORK STYLE BLACK & WHITE	399	**295**	253	212
STGUIT	48	NATIONAL	GRAND CONSOLE COPPER. 2 8-STRING NECKS	428	**316**	272	227
STGUIT	49	NATIONAL	GRAND CONSOLE COPPER, 2 8-STRING NECKS	501	**370**	318	266
STGUIT	50	NATIONAL	GRAND CONSOLE COPPER, 2 8-STRING NECKS	497	**367**	315	264
STGUIT	36	NATIONAL	NEW YORKER BLACK & WHITE ART DECO	424	**313**	269	225
STGUIT	38	NATIONAL	NEW YORKER BLACK & WHITE ART DECO	401	**296**	254	213
STGUIT	39	NATIONAL	NEW YORKER	432	**319**	274	229
STGUIT	40	NATIONAL	NEW YORKER NATURAL	399	**295**	253	212
STGUIT	41	NATIONAL	NEW YORKER NATURAL	384	**284**	244	204
STGUIT	42	NATIONAL	NEW YORKER BLACK & WHITE ART DECO	372	**275**	236	197
STGUIT	42	NATIONAL	NEW YORKER NATURAL, SPANISH SPRUCE TOP	658	**487**	418	349
STGUIT	47	NATIONAL	NEW YORKER BLACK & WHITE ART DECO	351	**259**	223	186
STGUIT	49	NATIONAL	NEW YORKER BLACK/WHITE	384	**284**	244	204
STGUIT	54	NATIONAL	NEW YORKER NATURAL	392	**290**	249	208
STGUIT	55	NATIONAL	NEW YORKER NATURAL	387	**286**	246	206
STGUIT	48	NATIONAL	PRINCESS STEEL WHITE PEROLOID	384	**284**	244	204
STGUIT	33	NATIONAL	PROFESSIONAL HAWAIIAN LAP STEEL	478	**353**	303	253
STGUIT	58	NATIONAL	ROCKET ONE BLACK, 10-STRING	480	**355**	305	255
STGUIT	58	NATIONAL	ROCKET ONE TEN BLACK & WHITE	447	**330**	284	237
STGUIT	64	NATIONAL	ROCKET ONE TEN WHITE, ROCKET SHAPE	366	**271**	233	194
STGUIT	50	NATIONAL	TRAILBLAZER CREAM	264	**195**	167	140
STGUIT	50	NATIONAL	TRIPLEX 1088 NATURAL, MAPLE	336	**248**	213	178
STGUIT	50	NATIONAL	TRIPLEX CHORD CHANGER LAP STEEL	360	**266**	228	191
UKULELE	33	NATIONAL	STYLE 1	3,130	**2,315**	1,989	1,663

NEUMANN

TYPE	YR	MFG	MODEL	SELL EXC	SELL AVG	BUY EXC	BUY AVG
MIC	28	NEUMANN	CMV-3 "NEUMANN BOTTLE" TUBE	3,840	**2,840**	2,440	2,040
MIC	49	NEUMANN	CMV-5B CONDENSER, M7 CAPSULE	1,992	**1,473**	1,265	1,058
MIC	53	NEUMANN	KM- 53i	1,554	**1,149**	987	825
MIC	53	NEUMANN	KM- 54iA BLACK, CONDENSER	1,217	**900**	773	646
MIC	54	NEUMANN	KM- 54iA SILVER, CONDENSER	1,217	**900**	773	646
MIC	55	NEUMANN	KM- 56i	1,948	**1,441**	1,238	1,035
MIC	64-71	NEUMANN	KM- 64i TUBE	879	**650**	558	467
MIC	66	NEUMANN	KM- 83i OMNI FET	730	**540**	464	388
MIC	66	NEUMANN	KM- 84i XLR CARDIOID FET-80	730	**540**	464	388
MIC	66	NEUMANN	KM- 85i XLR CARDIOID LOW FREQUENCY	730	**540**	464	388
MIC	98	NEUMANN	KM-100 OUTPUT STAGE MODULE	417	**308**	265	221
MIC	63	NEUMANN	KM-254i LARGE DIAPHRAGM TUBE	1,230	**910**	782	653
MIC	66	NEUMANN	KM-264i	1,013	**749**	644	538
MIC	51	NEUMANN	M- 49 LARGE DIAPHRAGM TUBE	7,680	**5,680**	4,880	4,080
MIC	54	NEUMANN	M- 49B	7,872	**5,822**	5,002	4,182

TYPE	YR	MFG	PRICES--BASED ON 100% ORIGINAL MODEL	SELL EXC	SELL AVG	BUY EXC	BUY AVG
MIC	55	NEUMANN	**M- 49C** MONO, TUBE CONDESNER	7,680	**5,680**	4,880	4,080
MIC	51	NEUMANN	**M- 50** OMNIDIRECTIONAL TUBE	8,544	**6,319**	5,429	4,539
MIC	60	NEUMANN	**M-249** LARGE DIAPHRAGM TUBE	8,544	**6,319**	5,429	4,539
MIC	62	NEUMANN	**M-269** LARGE DIAPHRAGM TUBE	8,639	**6,389**	5,489	4,589
MIC	74	NEUMANN	**QM-69** QUAD	5,990	**4,430**	3,806	3,182
MIC	57	NEUMANN	**SM- 2**	2,592	**1,917**	1,647	1,377
MIC	57	NEUMANN	**SM- 2 STEREO**	3,123	**2,310**	1,984	1,659
MIC	61	NEUMANN	**SM-23**	3,168	**2,343**	2,013	1,683
MIC	64	NEUMANN	**SM-69** STEREO TUBE, LARGE DIAPHRAGM, FET	4,215	**3,117**	2,678	2,239
MIC	65	NEUMANN	**SM-69** STEREO TUBE	4,056	**2,999**	2,577	2,154
MIC	49	NEUMANN	**U-47** VF-14 TUBE	6,624	**4,899**	4,209	3,519
MIC	49	NEUMANN	**U-47** LONG, CHROME	7,200	**5,325**	4,575	3,825
MIC	69	NEUMANN	**U-47 fet** CARDIOID FET-80	1,650	**1,220**	1,048	876
MIC	57	NEUMANN	**U-48** LARGE DIAPHRAGM TUBE	6,720	**4,970**	4,270	3,570
MIC	60	NEUMANN	**U-67** 3 PATTERN LARGE DIAPHRAGM TUBE w/POWER SUPPLY	4,224	**3,124**	2,684	2,244
MIC	67	NEUMANN	**U-87i** 3 PATTERN FET-80	2,390	**1,767**	1,518	1,269

OAHU

TYPE	YR	MFG	MODEL	SELL EXC	SELL AVG	BUY EXC	BUY AVG
ELEC. GUITAR	49	OAHU	**OAHU** SUPRO STYLE PU	240	**177**	152	127
ELGUIT	51	OAHU	**OAHU** 2-6-STRING NECKS	240	**177**	152	127
GUITAR AMP	49	OAHU	**TUNEMASTER**	345	**255**	219	183
GTAMP	50	OAHU	**TUNEMASTER**	240	**177**	152	127
STEEL GUITAR	30	OAHU	**HAWAIIAN LAP STEEL** SUNBURST, SQUARE NECK	288	**213**	183	153
STGUIT	50	OAHU	**LOLANA DUAL** 6-STRING, GOLD HARDWARE	480	**355**	305	255
STGUIT	52	OAHU	**LOLANA DUAL 6 LAP STEEL**	504	**372**	320	267

OLDKRAFT

TYPE	YR	MFG	MODEL	SELL EXC	SELL AVG	BUY EXC	BUY AVG
ELEC. GUITAR	58	OLDKRAFT	**THIN TWIN JIMMY REED**	438	**324**	278	233
ELGUIT	60	OLDKRAFT	**THIN TWIN JIMMY REED**	480	**355**	305	255
GUITAR (ACOUSTIC)	36	OLDKRAFT	**16" WIDE** SUNBURST, CURLY MAPLE	796	**589**	506	423
GUITAR	38	OLDKRAFT	**OLD KRAFTSMAN** METAL BODY	888	**656**	564	471

ORANGE

TYPE	YR	MFG	MODEL	SELL EXC	SELL AVG	BUY EXC	BUY AVG
GUITAR AMP	75	ORANGE	**BASS 113** CABINET, 2x15", 120 WATT	880	**651**	559	467
GTAMP	74	ORANGE	**BASS 114** 1x15", 60 WATT, CABINET	541	**400**	344	287
GTAMP	76	ORANGE	**COMBO 5** 2x12", 120 WATT	991	**733**	630	526
GTAMP	78	ORANGE	**GRAPHIC 112** OVERDRIVE HEAD	557	**412**	354	296
GTAMP	76	ORANGE	**GRAPHIC 120**	737	**545**	468	391

OVATION INSTRUMENTS

TYPE	YR	MFG	MODEL	SELL EXC	SELL AVG	BUY EXC	BUY AVG
ELEC. GUITAR	75	OVATION	**BREADWINNER** BLACK, 2 PU's	292	**216**	186	155
ELGUIT	74	OVATION	**CLASSICAL ELECTRIC FLATTOP**	488	**361**	310	259
ELGUIT	70	OVATION	**DEACON** 12-STRING	397	**293**	252	211
ELGUIT	70	OVATION	**H 218** BLACK, DOUBLE CUTAWAY, THIN BODY	452	**334**	287	240
ELGUIT	67	OVATION	**HURRICANE** SUNBURST, 12-STRING	837	**619**	531	444
ELGUIT	68	OVATION	**HURRICANE** SUNBURST, 12-STRING	916	**678**	582	487
ELGUIT	78	OVATION	**MAGNUM BASS I 1261** VINTAGE CHERRY, SOLID BODY	480	**355**	305	255
ELGUIT	68	OVATION	**MONSOON** BURGUNDY, CHERRY, DOUBLE CUTAWAY, 2 PU's	434	**321**	276	231
ELGUIT	68	OVATION	**MONSOON 1272** BURGUNDY, CHERRY, DOUBLE CUTAWAY, 2 PU's	455	**336**	289	241
ELGUIT	70	OVATION	**PREACHER**	346	**256**	220	184
ELGUIT	72	OVATION	**PREACHER** SERIAL #7000	385	**285**	245	205

TYPE	YR	MFG	PRICES--BASED ON 100% ORIGINAL MODEL	SELL EXC	SELL AVG	BUY EXC	BUY AVG
ELGUIT	74	OVATION	**PREACHER** RED MAHOGANY	476	**352**	302	252
ELGUIT	78	OVATION	**PREACHER 1281** SOLID BODY	384	**284**	244	204
ELGUIT	76	OVATION	**PREACHER DELUXE** SERIAL #67000-86000	403	**298**	256	214
ELGUIT	68	OVATION	**TORNADO** BURGUNDY, DOUBLE CUTAWAY, 2 PU's	452	**334**	287	240
ELGUIT	70	OVATION	**TORNADO 1260**	408	**301**	259	216
ELGUIT	70	OVATION	**TYPHOON BASS** RED	204	**151**	129	108
ELGUIT	77	OVATION	**UK-II** SUNBURST	526	**389**	334	279
ELGUIT	78	OVATION	**UK-II** GRAY SUNBURST, ABALONE INLAY, SERIAL #114001-157000	481	**356**	306	256
ELGUIT	80	OVATION	**UK-II** BLACK,K ABALONE INLAY	431	**318**	273	228
ELGUIT	74	OVATION	**VIPER**	336	**248**	213	178
ELGUIT	77	OVATION	**VIPER** SERIAL #86000-114000	377	**279**	239	200
GUITAR AMP	78	OVATION	**MAGNUM II BASS** PREAMP, EQUALIZER	336	**248**	213	178
GUITAR (ACOUSTIC)	75	OVATION	**1112-1** SUNBURST, DIAMOND INLAYS	479	**354**	304	254
GUITAR	66	OVATION	**1115** BLACK, 12-STRING	553	**409**	351	294
GUITAR	74	OVATION	**1115-1** SUNBURST, 12-STRING	461	**341**	293	245
GUITAR	66	OVATION	**1115-4** BLACK	569	**421**	361	302
GUITAR	78	OVATION	**1612-4** NATURAL	471	**348**	299	250
GUITAR	75	OVATION	**1617 ACOUSTIC/ELECTRIC** SUNBURST	424	**313**	269	225
GUITAR	75	OVATION	**1617 BALLADEER** RED TOP	446	**330**	283	237
GUITAR	77	OVATION	**ADAMAS** GRAY-BEIGE	796	**589**	506	423
GUITAR	78	OVATION	**ADAMAS** BLUE	598	**442**	380	317
GUITAR	78	OVATION	**ADAMAS** YELLOW AND BLUE SUNBURST	598	**442**	380	317
GUITAR	70	OVATION	**ADAMAS II** BROWN	816	**604**	519	434
GUITAR	67	OVATION	**BALLADEER** IVORY	1,094	**809**	695	581
GUITAR	68	OVATION	**BALLADEER** IVORY	876	**648**	556	465
GUITAR	69	OVATION	**BALLADEER** IVORY	677	**501**	430	360
GUITAR	72	OVATION	**BALLADEER** NATURAL	621	**459**	394	329
GUITAR	77	OVATION	**BALLADEER** IVORY	642	**474**	408	341
GUITAR	78	OVATION	**BALLADEER** IVORY	644	**476**	409	342
GUITAR	61	OVATION	**BALLADEER (1861)** SUNBURST	1,007	**744**	639	534
GUITAR	68	OVATION	**BALLADEER DELUXE** NATURAL	424	**313**	269	225
GUITAR	77	OVATION	**BALLADEER DELUXE** SUNBURST	577	**427**	367	307
GUITAR	79	OVATION	**CELEBRITY CC-65 ACOUS/ELECT** NATURAL	223	**165**	142	118
GUITAR	74	OVATION	**COUNTRY ARTIST** NYLON STRING	518	**383**	329	275
GUITAR	76	OVATION	**CUSTOM LEGEND**	800	**592**	508	425
GUITAR	68	OVATION	**ELITE** NATURAL, SINGLE CUTAWAY, SHALLOW BOWL	811	**599**	515	430
GUITAR	69	OVATION	**GLEN CAMPBELL**	967	**715**	614	514
GUITAR	71	OVATION	**GLEN CAMPBELL**	892	**660**	567	474
GUITAR	72	OVATION	**GLEN CAMPBELL**	865	**640**	550	460
GUITAR	75	OVATION	**GLEN CAMPBELL SIGNATURE** 12-STRING	1,115	**825**	708	592
GUITAR	68	OVATION	**JOSH WHITE**	441	**326**	280	234
GUITAR	36	OVATION	**M-2** SUNBURST, L-50 SIZE	513	**379**	326	272
GUITAR	40	OVATION	**M-2** SUNBURST	438	**324**	278	233
GUITAR	70	OVATION	**THUNDERHEAD** SEMI-HOLLOW	399	**295**	253	212

TYPE	YR	MFG	MODEL	SELL EXC	SELL AVG	BUY EXC	BUY AVG

PARAMOUNT

TYPE	YR	MFG	MODEL	SELL EXC	SELL AVG	BUY EXC	BUY AVG
BANJO	28	PARAMOUNT	**ARISTOCRAT** TENOR	1,310	**969**	832	696
BANJO	30	PARAMOUNT	**ARTIST SUPREME** PLECTRUM	6,916	**5,115**	4,395	3,674
BANJO	33	PARAMOUNT	**ARTIST SUPREME** PLECTRUM	6,091	**4,504**	3,870	3,235
BANJO	28	PARAMOUNT	**BANNER BLUE** TENOR, WALNUT, RESONATOR	468	**346**	297	248
BANJO	25	PARAMOUNT	**LEADER** TENOR, ROSEWOOD NECK/RESONATOR	939	**695**	597	499
BANJO	27	PARAMOUNT	**LEADER** TENOR, 19-FRET	798	**590**	507	424
BANJO	25	PARAMOUNT	**LEADER POT** ROSEWOOD NECK, 5-STRING	1,316	**973**	836	699
BANJO	28	PARAMOUNT	**LEADER SPECIAL** TENOR, BRAZILIAN ROSEWOOD	2,135	**1,579**	1,356	1,134
BANJO	25	PARAMOUNT	**PAL** TENOR	569	**421**	361	302
BANJO	25	PARAMOUNT	**STYLE 1** TENOR	1,175	**869**	746	624
BANJO	22	PARAMOUNT	**STYLE A** PLECTRUM	1,249	**924**	794	664
BANJO	24	PARAMOUNT	**STYLE A** TENOR	1,056	**781**	671	561
BANJO	25	PARAMOUNT	**STYLE A** TENOR	817	**604**	519	434
BANJO	25	PARAMOUNT	**STYLE A** PLECTRUM	1,274	**942**	810	677
BANJO	27	PARAMOUNT	**STYLE A** TENOR	771	**570**	490	410
BANJO	28	PARAMOUNT	**STYLE A** PLECTRUM	748	**553**	475	397
BANJO	28	PARAMOUNT	**STYLE A** TENOR	775	**573**	492	412
BANJO	22	PARAMOUNT	**STYLE B** TENOR, NATURAL	1,124	**831**	714	597
BANJO	23	PARAMOUNT	**STYLE B** TENOR	1,087	**804**	691	577
BANJO	25	PARAMOUNT	**STYLE B** TENOR	1,172	**866**	744	622
BANJO	26	PARAMOUNT	**STYLE B** TENOR	717	**530**	455	380
BANJO	20	PARAMOUNT	**STYLE C** TENOR	1,407	**1,040**	894	747
BANJO	25	PARAMOUNT	**STYLE C** TENOR, 19-FRET, SERIAL #2781	1,151	**851**	731	611
BANJO	26	PARAMOUNT	**STYLE C** TENOR	984	**727**	625	522
BANJO	27	PARAMOUNT	**STYLE C** TENOR	1,140	**843**	724	605
BANJO	29	PARAMOUNT	**STYLE C** TENOR	912	**675**	580	485
BANJO	25	PARAMOUNT	**STYLE D** PLECTRUM	2,060	**1,523**	1,309	1,094
BANJO	28	PARAMOUNT	**STYLE D** TENOR	2,294	**1,696**	1,457	1,218
BANJO	26	PARAMOUNT	**STYLE E** TENOR, HOLLY NECK/RESONATOR	1,558	**1,152**	990	827
BANJO	22	PARAMOUNT	**STYLE F** TENOR	4,183	**3,094**	2,658	2,222
BANJO	25	PARAMOUNT	**STYLE F** TENOR	3,393	**2,509**	2,156	1,802
BANJO	27	PARAMOUNT	**STYLE F** TENOR, GOLD-PLATED, ENGRAVED	4,521	**3,344**	2,873	2,402
BANJO	28	PARAMOUNT	**STYLE F** TENOR	2,969	**2,196**	1,886	1,577
BANJO	29	PARAMOUNT	**STYLE F** TENOR	3,545	**2,622**	2,252	1,883
BANJO	31	PARAMOUNT	**STYLE X** 5-STRING	1,263	**934**	802	671
BANJO	30	PARAMOUNT	**SUPER PARAMOUNT PROFESSIONAL** TENOR	4,320	**3,195**	2,745	2,295
BANJO	33	PARAMOUNT	**SUPER PARAMOUNT PROFESSIONAL** TENOR	2,887	**2,200**	1,870	1,430

PARK

TYPE	YR	MFG	MODEL	SELL EXC	SELL AVG	BUY EXC	BUY AVG
GUITAR AMP	68	PARK	**MODEL 75 AMP HEAD** 2xKT88, SMALL BOX PLEXI	1,115	**825**	708	592

PEAVEY

TYPE	YR	MFG	MODEL	SELL EXC	SELL AVG	BUY EXC	BUY AVG
BASS AMP	83	PEAVEY	**MAX BASS FC @ 4 OHM**	347	**257**	220	184

TYPE		YR	MFG	PRICES--BASED ON 100% ORIGINAL MODEL	SELL EXC	SELL AVG	BUY EXC	BUY AVG
ELEC. GUITAR		83	PEAVEY	T-15 NATURAL, MAPLE	165	122	104	87
	ELGUIT	79	PEAVEY	T-25 SUNBURST, SYNTHETIC BODY, 2 PU's	110	81	70	58
	ELGUIT	79	PEAVEY	T-27 LTD	182	134	115	96
	ELGUIT	78	PEAVEY	T-60 ASH BODY, DOUBLE CUTAWAY, 2 HB PU's	127	94	81	67
GUITAR AMP		75	PEAVEY	ARTIST VT 1x12", 120 WATT, 3-BAND EQ	129	95	82	68
	GTAMP	77	PEAVEY	BACKSTAGE	73	54	46	39
	GTAMP	74	PEAVEY	CLASSIC BLACK, 2x12", TUBE, REVERB	162	119	103	86
	GTAMP	80	PEAVEY	DEUCE 2-12" SPEAKERS, 120 WATT	172	127	109	91
	GTAMP	78	PEAVEY	HERITAGE PHASE SHIFT	245	181	156	130
	GTAMP	75	PEAVEY	LTD	127	94	81	67

PHILLIPS

TYPE		YR	MFG	MODEL	SELL EXC	SELL AVG	BUY EXC	BUY AVG
MIC		38	PHILLIPS	TORPEDO (AUSTRALIAN)	158	117	100	84

PIMENTEL

TYPE		YR	MFG	MODEL	SELL EXC	SELL AVG	BUY EXC	BUY AVG
GUITAR (ACOUSTIC)		76	PIMENTEL	001-A MAHOGANY BACK/SIDES	743	549	472	394

POLLMAN

TYPE		YR	MFG	MODEL	SELL EXC	SELL AVG	BUY EXC	BUY AVG
UPRIG		73	POLLMAN	4-STRING LION'S HEAD	12,960	9,585	8,235	6,885
	UPRIGHT	73	POLLMAN	5-STRING BASS HIGHLY FLAMED	13,188	9,753	8,380	7,006

POLYTONE

TYPE		YR	MFG	MODEL	SELL EXC	SELL AVG	BUY EXC	BUY AVG
GUITAR AMP		77	POLYTONE	MINIBRITE III	432	319	274	229

PPG

TYPE		YR	MFG	MODEL	SELL EXC	SELL AVG	BUY EXC	BUY AVG
SYNTHESIZER		80	PPG	PPG 2.2	587	434	373	312
	SYNTH	80	PPG	PPG 2.2 MIDI	796	589	506	423
	SYNTH	80	PPG	PPG 2.3	784	580	498	416

PREMIER

TYPE		YR	MFG	MODEL	SELL EXC	SELL AVG	BUY EXC	BUY AVG
GUITAR AMP		65	PREMIER	B-160 CLUB BASS 6V6 TUBES	288	213	183	153
	GTAMP	69	PREMIER	B-160 CLUB BASS	288	213	183	153
	GTAMP	57	PREMIER	MODEL 50 1x10" SPEAKER, COMBO	182	134	115	96
	GTAMP	65	PREMIER	MODEL 90 REVERB	283	209	179	150
	GTAMP	66	PREMIER	TWIN 8 2x8" COMBO	288	213	183	153
GUITAR (ACOUSTIC)		68	PREMIER	A-300 DREADNOUGHT SUNBURST	384	284	244	204
	GUITAR	65	PREMIER	E-781 SCROLL BODY, 2 PU's	446	330	283	237

PRESCOTT

TYPE		YR	MFG	MODEL	SELL EXC	SELL AVG	BUY EXC	BUY AVG
UPRIG		60	PRESCOTT	4-STRING BASS (1860) BIRD'S EYE MAPLE	34,560	25,560	21,960	18,360
	UPRIGHT	20	PRESCOTT	BIRD'S EYE MAPLE (1820) SPRUCE TOP, VIOLIN CORNERS	17,280	12,780	10,980	9,180

PRS/PAUL REED SMITH GUITARS

TYPE		YR	MFG	MODEL	SELL EXC	SELL AVG	BUY EXC	BUY AVG
ELEC. GUITAR		86	PRS	BASS-5	976	722	620	518
	ELGUIT	86	PRS	CURLY BASS-4	1,194	883	758	634
	ELGUIT	86	PRS	CURLY BASS-5	1,454	1,075	924	772
	ELGUIT	85	PRS	CUSTOM BIRD INLAY	6,229	4,607	3,958	3,309
	ELGUIT	88	PRS	SIGNATURE	4,680	3,461	2,973	2,486

QUAD U.S.A.

TYPE		YR	MFG	MODEL	SELL EXC	SELL AVG	BUY EXC	BUY AVG
PRE		62	QUAD	22 STEREO TUBE	251	186	159	133
PWR		73	QUAD	II MONO TUBE 15 WATT	463	342	294	246
TUNER		73	QUAD	FM 2 STEREO HYBRID	201	149	128	107

RAMIREZ GUITARS, DIST by DAVID PERRY GUITAR IMPORTS

TYPE		YR	MFG	MODEL	SELL EXC	SELL AVG	BUY EXC	BUY AVG
GUITAR (ACOUSTIC)		66	RAMIREZ	1a CLASSICAL BRAZILIAN ROSEWOOD BACK/SIDES	2,971	2,197	1,887	1,578
	GUITAR	69	RAMIREZ	1a CLASSICAL FLAMINGO CYPRESS BACK/SIDES	3,726	2,756	2,368	1,979
	GUITAR	70	RAMIREZ	1a CLASSICAL FLAMINGO CYPRESS BACK/SIDES	3,403	2,516	2,162	1,807
	GUITAR	72	RAMIREZ	1a CLASSICAL INDIAN ROSEWOOD BACK/SIDES	1,614	1,194	1,026	857
	GUITAR	72	RAMIREZ	1a CLASSICAL BRAZILIAN ROSEWOOD BACK/SIDES	2,341	1,731	1,487	1,243

TYPE	YR	MFG	PRICES--BASED ON 100% ORIGINAL MODEL	SELL EXC	SELL AVG	BUY EXC	BUY AVG
GUITAR	73	RAMIREZ	**1a CLASSICAL** BRAZILIAN ROSEWOOD BACK/SIDES	2,390	**1,767**	1,518	1,269
GUITAR	76	RAMIREZ	**1a CLASSICAL** INDIAN ROSEWOOD BACK/SIDES	1,888	**1,396**	1,199	1,003
GUITAR	76	RAMIREZ	**1a CLASSICAL** BRAZILIAN ROSEWOOD BACK/SIDES	2,341	**1,731**	1,487	1,243
GUITAR	78	RAMIREZ	**1a CLASSICAL** INDIAN ROSEWOOD BACK/SIDES	2,199	**1,626**	1,397	1,168
GUITAR	72	RAMIREZ	**2 CLASSICAL** INDIAN ROSEWOOD BACK/SIDES	795	**588**	505	422
GUITAR	70	RAMIREZ	**2a CLASSICAL** FLAMINGO CYPRESS BACK/SIDES	748	**553**	475	397
GUITAR	71	RAMIREZ	**2a CLASSICAL** FLAMINGO CYPRESS BACK/SIDES	1,017	**752**	646	540
GUITAR	75	RAMIREZ	**SEGOVIA MODEL** INDIAN ROSEWOOD BACK/SIDES	1,614	**1,194**	1,026	857
GUITAR	65	RAMIREZ	**STYLE A CLASSICAL** BRAZILIAN ROSEWOOD	3,142	**2,323**	1,996	1,669

RCA

TYPE	YR	MFG	MODEL	SELL EXC	SELL AVG	BUY EXC	BUY AVG
MIC	34	RCA	**30A** LAPEL RIBBON	336	**248**	213	178
MIC	31	RCA	**44A** BI DIRECTIONAL RIBBON, DIAMOND SHAPED	3,072	**2,272**	1,952	1,632
MIC	32	RCA	**44A**	1,506	**1,113**	957	800
MIC	48	RCA	**44B** BI DIRECTIONAL, DIAMOND SHAPED	1,591	**1,177**	1,011	845
MIC	32	RCA	**44BX** BI DIRECTIONAL, DIAMOND SHAPED	1,752	**1,296**	1,113	931
MIC	49	RCA	**44BX** STRIPES ALL AROUND	523	**386**	332	277
MIC	36	RCA	**74B** JUNIOR DIAMOND SHAPED	1,195	**883**	759	634
MIC	36	RCA	**77** UNIDIRECTIONAL, RIBBON	3,292	**2,435**	2,092	1,749
MIC	32	RCA	**77A** LARGE, ORIGINAL	3,360	**2,485**	2,135	1,785
MIC	37	RCA	**77B** UNIDIRECTIONAL, DOUBLE RIBBON	2,389	**1,767**	1,518	1,269
MIC	36	RCA	**77B1** UNIDIRECTIONAL,	2,178	**1,660**	1,411	1,079
MIC	38	RCA	**77C** 3 PATTERN EXTERNAL SWITCH, DOUBLE RIBBON	2,390	**1,767**	1,518	1,269
MIC	38	RCA	**77C1** 3 PATTERN INTERNAL SWITCH, DOUBLE RIBBON	2,390	**1,767**	1,518	1,269
MIC	40	RCA	**77D** POLYDIRECTIONAL, ROUND PATTERN SELECTOR PLATE	1,673	**1,237**	1,063	888
MIC	47	RCA	**77D**	2,074	**1,534**	1,318	1,102
MIC	47	RCA	**77DX** POLYDIRECTIONAL, DIAMOND PATTERN SELECTOR PLATE	2,209	**1,634**	1,404	1,174
MIC	70	RCA	**BK- 5** UNIAXIAL RIBBON	847	**626**	538	450
MIC	70	RCA	**BK- 5B** UNIAXIAL RIBBON	796	**589**	506	423
MIC	70	RCA	**BK- 6** LAVALIER MIC's, NON DIRECTIONAL	788	**582**	500	418
MIC	56	RCA	**BK- 6B** LAVALIER MIC's, NON DIRECTIONAL	871	**664**	564	431
MIC	52	RCA	**BK- 7A**	866	**641**	550	460
MIC	53	RCA	**BK-11** BIDIRECTIONAL, RIBBON	1,274	**942**	810	677
MIC	49	RCA	**KU-3A** UNIDIRECTIONAL RIBBON	1,991	**1,472**	1,265	1,057
MIC	70	RCA	**KU3A** UNIDIRECTIONAL	2,472	**1,828**	1,570	1,313
MIC	70	RCA	**MI-10001** UNIDIRECTIONAL	2,472	**1,828**	1,570	1,313
MIC	47	RCA	**MI-11001** UNIDIRECTIONAL RIBBON	331	**244**	210	175
MIC	56	RCA	**SK45B**	637	**471**	405	338
MIC	55	RCA	**SK46**	288	**213**	183	153

RECORDING KING by GIBSON GUITAR CORP

TYPE	YR	MFG	MODEL	SELL EXC	SELL AVG	BUY EXC	BUY AVG
GUITAR (ACOUSTIC)	36	RECORDKIN	**ARCHTOP** TENOR, ROSEWOOD, PEARL INLAYS	478	**353**	303	253
GUITAR	35	RECORDKIN	**CARSON ROBINSON** SUNBURST	945	**699**	600	502
GUITAR	36	RECORDKIN	**CARSON ROBINSON** SUNBURST, SERIAL #93500	938	**694**	596	498
GUITAR	40	RECORDKIN	**CARSON ROBINSON** SUNBURST	932	**689**	592	495
GUITAR	36	RECORDKIN	**M-2**	502	**371**	319	

TYPE	YR	MFG	PRICES--BASED ON 100% ORIGINAL MODEL	SELL EXC	SELL AVG	BUY EXC	BUY AVG
GUITAR	40	RECORDKIN	**M-2** SUNBURST	438	**324**	278	233
GUITAR	35	RECORDKIN	**M-3** SUNBURST	750	**555**	477	398
GUITAR	36	RECORDKIN	**M-3** SUNBURST	730	**540**	464	388
GUITAR	39	RECORDKIN	**M-3** SUNBURST	674	**499**	428	358
GUITAR	40	RECORDKIN	**M-3** SUNBURST	655	**484**	416	348
GUITAR	36	RECORDKIN	**M-5** SUNBURST	1,232	**911**	783	654
GUITAR	37	RECORDKIN	**M-5** SUNBURST	1,157	**856**	735	615
GUITAR	38	RECORDKIN	**M-5** SUNBURST	1,083	**801**	688	575
GUITAR	39	RECORDKIN	**M-5** SUNBURST	1,009	**746**	641	536
GUITAR	35	RECORDKIN	**ROY SMECK** SUNBURST	841	**622**	534	447
GUITAR	36	RECORDKIN	**WARD** SUNBURST, ARCHTOP, SERIAL #93500	409	**303**	260	217
STEEL GUITAR	40	RECORDKIN	**MODEL D LAP STEEL** BROWN	453	**335**	287	240
STGUIT	38	RECORDKIN	**ROY SMECK LAP STEEL** SUNBURST	471	**348**	299	250
STGUIT	39	RECORDKIN	**ROY SMECK LAP STEEL** SUNBURST	468	**346**	297	248
STGUIT	43	RECORDKIN	**ROY SMECK LAP STEEL** SUNBURST	384	**284**	244	204

REGAL by DOBRO

TYPE	YR	MFG	MODEL	SELL EXC	SELL AVG	BUY EXC	BUY AVG
BANJO	35	REGAL	**27** SUNBURST, SCREEN HOLES	996	**736**	633	529
BANJO	35	REGAL	**27** SUNBURST, RESONATOR, SQUARE NECK	1,216	**899**	772	646
BANJO	30	REGAL	**45** SQUARE NECK	1,155	**854**	734	614
BANJO	35	REGAL	**45** NATURAL, SPRUCE TOP, F-HOLES	938	**694**	596	498
BANJO	30	REGAL	**BANJO-UKE** WALNUT NECK/RESONATOR	280	**207**	178	148
BANJO	30	REGAL	**COLLEGIATE** TENOR, RESONATOR	467	**345**	297	248
BANJO	75	REGAL	**NASHVILLE** SUNBURST, MAHOGANY, SQUARE NECK	637	**471**	405	338
BANJO	30	REGAL	**TENOR** 17-FRET, OPEN BACK	450	**332**	286	239
BANJO	30	REGAL	**TENOR** RESONATOR	457	**338**	290	243
BANJO	30	REGAL	**TENOR** 19-FRET, MAPLE RESONATOR	468	**346**	297	248
BANJO	25	REGAL	**UB-1 BANJO-UKE** FLAT RESONATOR	286	**211**	181	151
GUITAR (ACOUSTIC)	35	REGAL	**00** ROSEWOOD, EBONY FINGERBOARD, FLATTOP, SERIAL # 5700-7600	480	**355**	305	255
GUITAR	41	REGAL	**00** SUNBURST TOP, ROSEWOOD, FLATTOP	438	**324**	278	233
GUITAR	38	REGAL	**14 M** NICKEL PLATED, BRASS BODY	1,200	**888**	763	638
GUITAR	25	REGAL	**B&J SERENADER** BLACK, 2-POINT BODY	452	**334**	287	240
GUITAR	40	REGAL	**BASSO**	458	**349**	297	227
GUITAR	76	REGAL	**BICENTENNIAL DREADNOUGHT** RED, WHITE AND BLUE	451	**333**	286	239
GUITAR	36	REGAL	**BOBCAT** SERIAL # 5700-7600	481	**356**	306	256
GUITAR	36	REGAL	**BOLERO** PIN BRIDGE, FLATTOP, SERIAL # 5700-7600	385	**285**	245	205
GUITAR	36	REGAL	**BROMAN ACE** SUNBURST, (EQUIVALENT TO DOBRO MODEL 37), SERIAL # 5700-7600	996	**736**	633	529
GUITAR	30	REGAL	**DOBRO** MAHOGANY, SERIAL a# 3000-	1,153	**853**	733	613
GUITAR	32	REGAL	**DOBRO** BROWN, SUNBURST BACK, ROUND NECK	1,139	**842**	724	605
GUITAR	33	REGAL	**DOBRO** SPRUCE TOP, MAHOGANY BACK/SIDES, BOUND	1,043	**771**	663	554
GUITAR	38	REGAL	**DOBRO** 12-FRET, SQUARE NECK, SOLID PEGHEAD, SCREEN HOLES	1,274	**942**	810	677
GUITAR	35	REGAL	**DOBRO HAWAIIAN** SUNBURST,12-FRET,ROUND NECK,POINSETTIA PATTERN COVER PLATE	939	**695**	597	499
GUITAR	33	REGAL	**DOBRO STYLE 37**	796	**589**	506	423

TYPE	YR	MFG	PRICES--BASED ON 100% ORIGINAL MODEL	SELL EXC	SELL AVG	BUY EXC	BUY AVG
GUITAR	34	REGAL	**DOBRO STYLE 37**	876	**648**	556	465
GUITAR	30	REGAL	**DOBRO STYLE 45** SPRUCE TOP, SQUARE NECK, RESONATOR	1,155	**854**	734	614
GUITAR	40	REGAL	**DOBRO STYLE 47**	935	**691**	594	496
GUITAR	17	REGAL	**HARP GUITAR** MAHOGANY, DOUBLE NECK	1,408	**1,041**	894	748
GUITAR	34	REGAL	**HAWAIIAN** PLECTRUM,DARK,BOUND FNGRBOARD,12-FRET,SLOT HEAD,ROUND NECK	677	**501**	430	360
GUITAR	34	REGAL	**LE DOMINO BIG BOY** SUNBURST	480	**355**	305	255
GUITAR	40	REGAL	**M-19**	470	**347**	298	249
GUITAR	25	REGAL	**MARTELLE** SUNBURST, 2-POINT BODY	451	**333**	286	239
GUITAR	35	REGAL	**OLD KRAFTSMAN** SUNBURST, ARCHTOP	450	**332**	286	239
GUITAR	37	REGAL	**R- 6 HAWAIIAN** RESONATOR	750	**555**	477	398
GUITAR	36	REGAL	**R-25** RESONATOR	499	**369**	317	265
GUITAR	37	REGAL	**R-25** TENOR, RESONATOR	623	**460**	395	330
GUITAR	39	REGAL	**R-25 HAWAIIAN** RESONATOR	621	**459**	394	329
GUITAR	38	REGAL	**R-27 HAWAIIAN** RESONATOR	728	**538**	462	387
GUITAR	37	REGAL	**R-32**	933	**690**	592	495
GUITAR	38	REGAL	**R-32 HAWAIIAN**	637	**471**	405	338
GUITAR	35	REGAL	**R-37** RESONATOR	777	**575**	494	413
GUITAR	36	REGAL	**R-45** RESONATOR	1,183	**875**	752	628
GUITAR	37	REGAL	**R-45** RESONATOR	1,095	**810**	696	581
GUITAR	38	REGAL	**R-45** RESONATOR	1,025	**758**	651	544
GUITAR	39	REGAL	**R-45** RESONATOR	933	**690**	592	495
GUITAR	39	REGAL	**R-46**	926	**685**	588	492
GUITAR	36	REGAL	**R-55** RESONATOR	1,017	**752**	646	540
GUITAR	35	REGAL	**R-60** RESONATOR	1,416	**1,047**	899	752
GUITAR	37	REGAL	**R-62** NICKEL-PLATED	1,569	**1,160**	997	833
GUITAR	38	REGAL	**R-62 HAWAIIAN** NICKEL-PLATED	775	**591**	502	384
GUITAR	36	REGAL	**R-65** RESONATOR	2,255	**1,667**	1,432	1,197
GUITAR	38	REGAL	**R-75** WALNUT	1,201	**888**	763	638
GUITAR	39	REGAL	**R-75 HAWAIIAN** WALNUT	897	**663**	570	476
GUITAR	37	REGAL	**RADIO TONE**	369	**281**	239	183
GUITAR	35	REGAL	**REGAL PRINCE**	619	**457**	393	328
GUITAR	70	REGAL	**T-242 DREADNOUGHT** 12-STRING, FLATTOP	394	**291**	250	209
GUITAR	76	REGAL	**T-376 BICENTENNIAL** RED, WHITE AND BLUE	339	**251**	215	180
GUITAR	76	REGAL	**T-476 BICENTENNIAL DREADNOUGHT** RED, WHITE AND BLUE	395	**292**	251	210
GUITAR	30	REGAL	**TENOR** SUNBURST, SERIAL # 3000-	240	**177**	152	127
MANDOLIN	28	REGAL	**MANDOLA** BLACK	450	**332**	286	239
MANDOL	30	REGAL	**MB-1 MANDOLIN-BANJO** MAPLE, RESONATOR	415	**316**	269	205
MANDOL	30	REGAL	**OCTOFONE** TEARDROP SHAPED OCTAVE	392	**290**	249	208
MANDOL	35	REGAL	**STYLE A** MAHOGANY	191	**141**	121	101
STEEL GUITAR	40	REGAL	**DOUBLENECK** BROWN, 2 8-STRING NECKS	467	**345**	297	248
STGUIT	70	REGAL	**LAP STEEL**	240	**177**	152	127
UKULELE	30	REGAL	**TIPLE**	240	**177**	152	127
UKE	50	REGAL	**TIPLE**	192	**142**	122	102
UKE	30	REGAL	**UKE** MAHOGANY BOUND	120	**88**	76	63

B. C. RICH INTERNATIONAL, INC

TYPE	YR	MFG	MODEL	SELL EXC	SELL AVG	BUY EXC	BUY AVG
ELEC. GUITAR	79	RICH	**DOUBLE EAGLE BASS** MAHOGANY	674	**499**	428	358
ELGUIT	77	RICH	**EAGLE ACTIVE** FLAMED KOA	873	**646**	555	464

TYPE	YR	MFG	PRICES--BASED ON 100% ORIGINAL MODEL	SELL EXC	SELL AVG	BUY EXC	BUY AVG
ELGUIT	77	RICH	**EAGLE BASS** KOA BODY, VARI-TONE	776	**574**	493	412
ELGUIT	77	RICH	**EAGLE SUPREME**	876	**648**	556	465
ELGUIT	76	RICH	**GULL** WHITE, SOLID BODY, 2 PU's	602	**445**	383	320
ELGUIT	96	RICH	**INNOVATOR BASS 4-STRING** BOLT-ON	601	**445**	382	319
ELGUIT	96	RICH	**INNOVATOR BASS 5-STRING** BOLT-ON	593	**438**	376	315
ELGUIT	76	RICH	**MOCKINGBIRD** MAPLE BODY	876	**648**	556	465
ELGUIT	76	RICH	**MOCKINGBIRD** KOA BODY	1,115	**825**	708	592
ELGUIT	77	RICH	**MOCKINGBIRD** PURPLE, SOLID BODY	1,059	**783**	673	563
ELGUIT	77	RICH	**MOCKINGBIRD** KOA BODY	1,106	**818**	703	588
ELGUIT	78	RICH	**MOCKINGBIRD** KOA BODY	1,035	**766**	658	550
ELGUIT	80	RICH	**MOCKINGBIRD** BLACK, SOLID BODY	1,017	**752**	646	540
ELGUIT	82	RICH	**MOCKINGBIRD** KOA BODY	876	**648**	556	465
ELGUIT	83	RICH	**MOCKINGBIRD** MAPLE BODY	757	**560**	481	402
ELGUIT	83	RICH	**MOCKINGBIRD** KOA BODY	796	**589**	506	423
ELGUIT	84	RICH	**MOCKINGBIRD** MAPLE BODY	750	**555**	477	398
ELGUIT	85	RICH	**MOCKINGBIRD** MAPLE BODY	677	**501**	430	360
ELGUIT	87	RICH	**MOCKINGBIRD** MAPLE BODY	696	**515**	442	370
ELGUIT	60	RICH	**MOCKINGBIRD BASS** RED, BOLT ON NECK	757	**560**	481	402
ELGUIT	76	RICH	**MOCKINGBIRD SPECIAL** NATURAL	1,049	**776**	666	557
ELGUIT	77	RICH	**MOCKINGBIRD SUPREME** RED	1,115	**825**	708	592
ELGUIT	80	RICH	**NIGHTHAWK** BOLT-ON NECK	598	**442**	380	317
ELGUIT	79	RICH	**PHOENIX** MAHOGANY, 2 PU's	480	**355**	305	255
ELGUIT	80	RICH	**PHOENIX** BOLT-ON NECK	478	**353**	303	253
ELGUIT	75	RICH	**SEAGULL** WHITE, SINGLE CUTAWAY, SOLIDBODY,NECK-THRU,2 HB	796	**589**	506	423
ELGUIT	78	RICH	**SEAGULL** CHERRY RED	785	**580**	498	417
ELGUIT	76	RICH	**SEAGULL II** DOUBLE CUTAWAY, SOLIDBODY, NECK-THRU, 2 HB	677	**501**	430	360
ELGUIT	82	RICH	**WARLOCK**	637	**471**	405	338
ELGUIT	80	RICH	**WARLOCK BASS**	734	**543**	466	390
GUITAR (ACOUSTIC)	71	RICH	**B-28** ROSEWOOD BACK/SIDES, HERRINGBONE	903	**668**	574	479
GUITAR	72	RICH	**B-28** ROSEWOOD BACK/SIDES, HERRINGBONE TRIM	728	**538**	462	387
GUITAR	73	RICH	**B-28** ROSEWOOD BACK/SIDES, HERRINGBONE TRIM	677	**501**	430	360
GUITAR	67	RICH	**B-30** NATURAL, MAPLE BACK/SIDES, HERRINGBONE TRIM	956	**707**	607	507
GUITAR	70	RICH	**B-30** NATURAL, MAPLE BACK/SIDES, HERRINGBONE TRIM	761	**563**	483	404
GUITAR	75	RICH	**B-38** FIGURED BACK/SIDES, HERRINGBONE	895	**662**	569	475
GUITAR	76	RICH	**B-38** FIGURED BACK/SIDES, HERRINGBONE TRIM	796	**589**	506	423
GUITAR	79	RICH	**B-38** FIGURED BACK/SIDES, HERRINGBONE	785	**580**	498	417

RICKENBACKER INTERNATIONAL CORP.

TYPE	YR	MFG	MODEL	SELL EXC	SELL AVG	BUY EXC	BUY AVG
BANJO	69	RICKENBAC	**BANJOLINE**	937	**693**	595	498
BANJO	67	RICKENBAC	**BANTAR**	1,216	**899**	772	646
BANJO	67	RICKENBAC	**BANTAR DELUXE** NATURAL	1,491	**1,103**	947	792
BANJO	69	RICKENBAC	**ELECTRIC** PLECTRUM, FIREGLO	1,111	**822**	706	590
ELEC. GUITAR	66	RICKENBAC	**310** MAPLEGLO, 3/4 SCALE, 2 PU's	726	**537**	461	386
ELGUIT	67	RICKENBAC	**315** FIREGLO, 3/4 SCALE, VIBRTO, 2 PU's	1,205	**891**	766	640
ELGUIT	75	RICKENBAC	**320** FIREGLO, 3/4 SCALE, 3 PU's	600	**444**	381	319

TYPE	YR	MFG	PRICES--BASED ON 100% ORIGINAL MODEL	SELL EXC	SELL AVG	BUY EXC	BUY AVG
ELGUIT	77	RICKENBAC	**320**	717	**530**	455	380
ELGUIT	64	RICKENBAC	**325 1996 ROSE MORRIS**	1,216	**899**	772	646
ELGUIT	90	RICKENBAC	**325JL JOHN LENNON LIMITED EDITION** PAPERS	1,034	**765**	657	549
ELGUIT	63	RICKENBAC	**330** MAPLE, STANDARD, FULL SCALE, 2 PU's	504	**372**	320	267
ELGUIT	65	RICKENBAC	**330**	803	**594**	510	426
ELGUIT	67	RICKENBAC	**330** SUNBURST, 2 PU's	707	**523**	449	375
ELGUIT	67	RICKENBAC	**330** FIREGLO	1,350	**998**	858	717
ELGUIT	66	RICKENBAC	**330-12** FIREGLO, 12-STRING, 2 PU's	548	**405**	348	291
ELGUIT	67	RICKENBAC	**330-12**	480	**355**	305	255
ELGUIT	64	RICKENBAC	**330-12 1993 ROSE MORRIS** BLACK	2,372	**1,754**	1,507	1,260
ELGUIT	70	RICKENBAC	**331** LIGHT SHOW, 2 PU's	4,874	**3,605**	3,097	2,589
ELGUIT	71	RICKENBAC	**331** LIGHT SHOW, 2 PU's	4,892	**3,618**	3,108	2,598
ELGUIT	59	RICKENBAC	**335** FIREGLO, VIBRATO, 2 PU's	3,059	**2,262**	1,944	1,625
ELGUIT	65	RICKENBAC	**335** FIREGLO	1,271	**940**	807	675
ELGUIT	67	RICKENBAC	**335** MAPLEGLO, VIBRATO, 2 PU's	817	**604**	519	434
ELGUIT	64	RICKENBAC	**335 1997 ROSE MORRIS**	1,287	**980**	833	637
ELGUIT	66	RICKENBAC	**335 1997 ROSE MORRIS** FIREGLO, 2 PU's	1,264	**963**	818	626
ELGUIT	67	RICKENBAC	**336-12** FIREGLO, 12-STRING, 2 PU's	2,172	**1,606**	1,380	1,154
ELGUIT	66	RICKENBAC	**340** JETGLO, 12-STRING, 3 PU's	1,505	**1,113**	956	799
ELGUIT	68	RICKENBAC	**340** BLACK, 12-STRING, 3 PU's	1,292	**955**	821	686
ELGUIT	64	RICKENBAC	**345 1998 ROSE MORRIS**	1,168	**864**	742	620
ELGUIT	57	RICKENBAC	**360** CAPRI, FULL SIZE DELUXE	3,622	**2,678**	2,301	1,924
ELGUIT	59	RICKENBAC	**360** CAPRI FIREGLO	2,186	**1,617**	1,389	1,161
ELGUIT	59	RICKENBAC	**360** CARPI SUNBURST	2,271	**1,679**	1,443	1,206
ELGUIT	60	RICKENBAC	**360** CAPRI FIREGLO	2,214	**1,637**	1,407	1,176
ELGUIT	63	RICKENBAC	**360** MAPLEGLO	3,246	**2,401**	2,063	1,724
ELGUIT	64	RICKENBAC	**360** FIREGLO	1,673	**1,237**	1,063	888
ELGUIT	65	RICKENBAC	**360** MAPLEGLO	1,779	**1,316**	1,130	945
ELGUIT	65	RICKENBAC	**360** FIREGLO	1,824	**1,349**	1,159	969
ELGUIT	66	RICKENBAC	**360** MAPLEGLO	1,619	**1,197**	1,029	860
ELGUIT	66	RICKENBAC	**360** FIREGLO	1,655	**1,224**	1,051	879
ELGUIT	67	RICKENBAC	**360** MAPLEGLO	1,162	**859**	738	617
ELGUIT	67	RICKENBAC	**360** FIREGLO	1,389	**1,027**	882	737
ELGUIT	68	RICKENBAC	**360** FIREGLO	831	**614**	528	441
ELGUIT	68	RICKENBAC	**360** JETGLO, LEFT-HANDED	1,810	**1,339**	1,150	961
ELGUIT	69	RICKENBAC	**360** BURGUNDYGLO	1,421	**1,051**	903	755
ELGUIT	70	RICKENBAC	**360** FIREGLO	747	**553**	475	397
ELGUIT	72	RICKENBAC	**360** FIREGLO	621	**459**	394	329
ELGUIT	76	RICKENBAC	**360** BURGUNDYGLO	609	**450**	387	323
ELGUIT	79	RICKENBAC	**360**	796	**589**	506	423
ELGUIT	65	RICKENBAC	**360-12** FIREGLO, 12-STRING	2,038	**1,507**	1,295	1,082
ELGUIT	66	RICKENBAC	**360-12** FIREGLO, 12-STRING	2,073	**1,533**	1,317	1,101
ELGUIT	66	RICKENBAC	**360-12** MAPLEGLO, 12-STRING	2,073	**1,533**	1,317	1,101
ELGUIT	67	RICKENBAC	**360-12** MAPLEGLO, 12-STRING	1,434	**1,060**	911	761
ELGUIT	67	RICKENBAC	**360-12** FIREGLO, 12-STRING	2,199	**1,626**	1,397	1,168

TYPE	YR	MFG	PRICES--BASED ON 100% ORIGINAL MODEL	SELL EXC	SELL AVG	BUY EXC	BUY AVG
ELGUIT	67	RICKENBAC	**360-12** JETGLO, 12-STRING	2,289	**1,693**	1,454	1,216
ELGUIT	68	RICKENBAC	**360-12** MAPLEGLO, 12-STRING	1,354	**1,001**	860	719
ELGUIT	71	RICKENBAC	**360-12**	1,274	**942**	810	677
ELGUIT	74	RICKENBAC	**360-12** JETGLO, 12-STRING	836	**618**	531	444
ELGUIT	74	RICKENBAC	**360-12** MAPLEGLO, 12-STRING	1,134	**839**	721	602
ELGUIT	75	RICKENBAC	**360-12** FIREGLO, 12-STRING	637	**471**	405	338
ELGUIT	76	RICKENBAC	**360-12** MAPLEGLO, 12-STRING	626	**463**	398	333
ELGUIT	65	RICKENBAC	**360-12 1993 ROSE MORRIS**	2,212	**1,636**	1,406	1,175
ELGUIT	59	RICKENBAC	**360-F** MAPLEGLO, CAPRI SINGLE CUT	3,947	**2,919**	2,508	2,097
ELGUIT	59	RICKENBAC	**365** FIREGLO, VIBRATO	2,255	**1,667**	1,432	1,197
ELGUIT	61	RICKENBAC	**365** FIREGLO, VIBRATO	2,187	**1,618**	1,390	1,162
ELGUIT	65	RICKENBAC	**365** MAPLEGLO, VIBRATO	2,086	**1,542**	1,325	1,108
ELGUIT	65	RICKENBAC	**365** FIREGLO, VIBRATO	2,227	**1,647**	1,415	1,183
ELGUIT	66	RICKENBAC	**365** FIREGLO, VIBRATO	2,008	**1,485**	1,276	1,066
ELGUIT	66	RICKENBAC	**365** MAPLEGLO, VIBRATO	2,015	**1,490**	1,280	1,070
ELGUIT	67	RICKENBAC	**365** FIREGLO, VIBRATO	1,933	**1,429**	1,228	1,027
ELGUIT	68	RICKENBAC	**365** JETGLO, VIBRATO	1,736	**1,284**	1,103	922
ELGUIT	68	RICKENBAC	**365** FIREGLO, VIBRATO	1,741	**1,287**	1,106	925
ELGUIT	68	RICKENBAC	**365** MAPLEGLO, VIBRATO	1,796	**1,328**	1,141	954
ELGUIT	66	RICKENBAC	**366-12** MAPLEGLO, 12-STRING	1,547	**1,144**	983	822
ELGUIT	67	RICKENBAC	**366-12** FIREGLO, 12-STRING	1,784	**1,319**	1,133	948
ELGUIT	68	RICKENBAC	**366-12** BLUE, 12-STRING	1,752	**1,296**	1,113	931
ELGUIT	58	RICKENBAC	**370** BROWN SUNBURST, 3 PU's	1,814	**1,341**	1,152	963
ELGUIT	67	RICKENBAC	**370** MAPLEGLO, 3 PU's	1,832	**1,355**	1,164	973
ELGUIT	68	RICKENBAC	**370** FIREGLO, 3 PU's	1,545	**1,143**	982	821
ELGUIT	68	RICKENBAC	**370** MAPLEGLO, 3 PU's	1,574	**1,164**	1,000	836
ELGUIT	73	RICKENBAC	**370** FIREGLO, 3 PU's	1,135	**839**	721	603
ELGUIT	69	RICKENBAC	**370-12** FIREGLO, 12-STRING, 3 PU's	2,179	**1,611**	1,384	1,157
ELGUIT	73	RICKENBAC	**370-12** MAPLEGLO, 12-STRING	1,872	**1,385**	1,190	995
ELGUIT	88	RICKENBAC	**370-12 ROGER MGUINN LTD EDITION** CHECKED BINDING,3 VINTAGE PU's,CUSTOM ACTIVE ELECTRONICS	1,035	**766**	658	550
ELGUIT	58	RICKENBAC	**375** BROWN SUNBURST, VIBRATO, 3 PU's	3,327	**2,460**	2,114	1,767
ELGUIT	61	RICKENBAC	**375** MAPLEGLO, VIBRATO, 3 PU's	1,614	**1,194**	1,026	857
ELGUIT	65	RICKENBAC	**375** FIREGLO, VIBRATO, 3 PU's	1,451	**1,073**	922	771
ELGUIT	67	RICKENBAC	**375** MAPLEGLO, VIBRATO, 3 PU's	1,416	**1,047**	899	752
ELGUIT	67	RICKENBAC	**375** JETGLO, VIBRATO, 3 PU's	1,536	**1,136**	976	816
ELGUIT	69	RICKENBAC	**381** SUNBURST, 2 PU's	1,577	**1,166**	1,002	837
ELGUIT	70	RICKENBAC	**381** JETGLO, RICKO-SOUND, 2 PU's	2,073	**1,533**	1,317	1,101
ELGUIT	63	RICKENBAC	**425** FIREGLO	933	**690**	592	495
ELGUIT	73	RICKENBAC	**425**	598	**442**	380	317
ELGUIT	60	RICKENBAC	**450-12** FIREGLO, 12-STRING	1,404	**1,038**	892	746
ELGUIT	65	RICKENBAC	**450-12** MAPLEGLO, 12-STRING	1,121	**829**	712	595
ELGUIT	66	RICKENBAC	**450-12** FIREGLO, 12-STRING	1,338	**989**	850	710
ELGUIT	66	RICKENBAC	**450-12** BLACK, 12-STRING	1,407	**1,040**	894	747

TYPE	YR	MFG	PRICES--BASED ON 100% ORIGINAL MODEL	SELL EXC	SELL AVG	BUY EXC	BUY AVG
ELGUIT	66	RICKENBAC	**450-12** MAPLEGLO, 12-STRING	1,443	**1,067**	917	767
ELGUIT	67	RICKENBAC	**450-12** FIREGLO, 12-STRING	1,167	**863**	741	620
ELGUIT	67	RICKENBAC	**450-12** MAPLEGLO, 12-STRING	1,219	**901**	774	647
ELGUIT	74	RICKENBAC	**450-12** BLACK, 12-STRING	783	**579**	497	416
ELGUIT	67	RICKENBAC	**456-12** 12-STRING	1,326	**981**	843	704
ELGUIT	68	RICKENBAC	**456-12** 12-STRING	1,195	**883**	759	634
ELGUIT	64	RICKENBAC	**460**	876	**648**	556	465
ELGUIT	73	RICKENBAC	**480** PURPLE, 2 PU's	703	**520**	447	373
ELGUIT	73	RICKENBAC	**480** NATURAL, 2 PU's	710	**525**	451	377
ELGUIT	73	RICKENBAC	**480** BLUE, 2 PU's	738	**545**	469	392
ELGUIT	76	RICKENBAC	**480** WALNUT, 2 PU's	699	**517**	444	371
ELGUIT	76	RICKENBAC	**481** BLACK, 2 HB PU's	671	**496**	426	356
ELGUIT	77	RICKENBAC	**481** RED, 2 HB PU's	657	**486**	417	349
ELGUIT	64	RICKENBAC	**615**	876	**648**	556	465
ELGUIT	75	RICKENBAC	**620** RED, 2 PU's	598	**442**	380	317
ELGUIT	77	RICKENBAC	**620**	677	**501**	430	360
ELGUIT	63	RICKENBAC	**625** VIBRATO, 2 PU's	1,368	**1,012**	869	727
ELGUIT	68	RICKENBAC	**625** MAPLEGLO, VIBRATO, 2 PU's	956	**707**	607	507
ELGUIT	76	RICKENBAC	**625** MAPLEGLO, VIBRATO, 2 PU's	829	**613**	527	440
ELGUIT	63	RICKENBAC	**900** BABY BLUE, 1 PU	629	**465**	400	334
ELGUIT	67	RICKENBAC	**1997 PETE TOWNSEND EXPORT** SUNBURST	1,912	**1,414**	1,215	1,015
ELGUIT	73	RICKENBAC	**2001 BASS** BLACK	600	**443**	381	318
ELGUIT	76	RICKENBAC	**3000 BASS** BROWN SUNBURST, 1 PU	557	**412**	354	296
ELGUIT	76	RICKENBAC	**3000 BASS** NATURAL	694	**513**	441	368
ELGUIT	76	RICKENBAC	**3001** MAROON, 1 PU	702	**519**	446	373
ELGUIT	76	RICKENBAC	**3001** ROSEWOOD, DOT NECK, 1 PU	702	**519**	446	373
ELGUIT	76	RICKENBAC	**3001 BASS** WINE RED	557	**412**	354	296
ELGUIT	57	RICKENBAC	**4000 BASS** HORSESHOE MAGNET	4,206	**3,111**	2,673	2,234
ELGUIT	58	RICKENBAC	**4000 BASS**	3,288	**2,431**	2,089	1,746
ELGUIT	59	RICKENBAC	**4000 BASS** AUTUMNGLO	1,513	**1,119**	961	804
ELGUIT	59	RICKENBAC	**4000 BASS** MAPLEGLO, GOLD GUARDS	2,215	**1,638**	1,407	1,177
ELGUIT	60	RICKENBAC	**4000 BASS** FIREGLO, GOLD GUARDS	3,360	**2,485**	2,135	1,785
ELGUIT	63	RICKENBAC	**4000 BASS** BLACK	2,166	**1,602**	1,376	1,151
ELGUIT	65	RICKENBAC	**4000 BASS** FIREGLO, LONG HEAD	3,648	**2,698**	2,318	1,938
ELGUIT	67	RICKENBAC	**4000 BASS** FIREGLO, 1 PU	1,581	**1,169**	1,004	839
ELGUIT	70	RICKENBAC	**4000 BASS** 1 PU	1,211	**896**	769	643
ELGUIT	70	RICKENBAC	**4000 BASS** AUTUMNGLO	1,338	**989**	850	710
ELGUIT	72	RICKENBAC	**4000 BASS** FIREGLO, 1 PU, CHECKERBOARD BINDING	1,680	**1,242**	1,067	892
ELGUIT	74	RICKENBAC	**4000 BASS** MAPLEGLO	796	**589**	506	423
ELGUIT	61	RICKENBAC	**4001 BASS** FIREGLO	2,072	**1,532**	1,316	1,101
ELGUIT	63	RICKENBAC	**4001 BASS** FIREGLO	1,742	**1,288**	1,107	925
ELGUIT	64	RICKENBAC	**4001 BASS** FIREGLO	1,396	**1,033**	887	742
ELGUIT	67	RICKENBAC	**4001 BASS** FIREGLO	1,356	**1,003**	861	720
ELGUIT	68	RICKENBAC	**4001 BASS** MAPLEGLO	1,108	**820**	704	589

TYPE	YR	MFG	PRICES--BASED ON 100% ORIGINAL MODEL	SELL EXC	SELL AVG	BUY EXC	BUY AVG
ELGUIT	68	RICKENBAC	4001 BASS FIREGLO	1,173	867	745	623
ELGUIT	69	RICKENBAC	4001 BASS FIREGLO	960	710	610	510
ELGUIT	70	RICKENBAC	4001 BASS MAPLEGLO	782	578	497	415
ELGUIT	70	RICKENBAC	4001 BASS LEFT-HANDED	1,307	967	830	694
ELGUIT	71	RICKENBAC	4001 BASS SUNBURST	720	532	457	382
ELGUIT	71	RICKENBAC	4001 BASS BLACK	891	659	566	473
ELGUIT	72	RICKENBAC	4001 BASS BLACK	879	650	558	467
ELGUIT	72	RICKENBAC	4001 BASS FIREGLO	984	728	625	523
ELGUIT	72	RICKENBAC	4001 BASS MAPLEGLO	1,281	947	814	680
ELGUIT	72	RICKENBAC	4001 BASS NATURAL	1,284	949	816	682
ELGUIT	72	RICKENBAC	4001 BASS NATURAL, CHECKERBOARD, LEFT-HANDED	1,572	1,162	999	835
ELGUIT	73	RICKENBAC	4001 BASS BLACK	804	594	511	427
ELGUIT	73	RICKENBAC	4001 BASS BROWN	812	600	516	431
ELGUIT	73	RICKENBAC	4001 BASS FIREGLO, LEFT-HANDED	919	680	584	488
ELGUIT	73	RICKENBAC	4001 BASS WINE RED	949	702	603	504
ELGUIT	73	RICKENBAC	4001 BASS BLUE	990	732	629	526
ELGUIT	73	RICKENBAC	4001 BASS MAPLEGLO	1,171	866	744	622
ELGUIT	74	RICKENBAC	4001 BASS BLACK	799	591	508	424
ELGUIT	74	RICKENBAC	4001 BASS WHITE	1,067	789	678	567
ELGUIT	74	RICKENBAC	4001 BASS WHITE, LEFT-HANDED	1,229	909	781	653
ELGUIT	75	RICKENBAC	4001 BASS BLACK	726	537	461	386
ELGUIT	75	RICKENBAC	4001 BASS FIREGLO, FRETLESS	931	688	591	494
ELGUIT	75	RICKENBAC	4001 BASS WHITE, LEFT-HANDED	1,170	865	743	621
ELGUIT	76	RICKENBAC	4001 BASS BLACK	727	538	462	386
ELGUIT	76	RICKENBAC	4001 BASS BLACK, FRETLESS	727	538	462	386
ELGUIT	76	RICKENBAC	4001 BASS BLUE	800	592	508	425
ELGUIT	76	RICKENBAC	4001 BASS WINE RED	949	702	603	504
ELGUIT	76	RICKENBAC	4001 BASS WHITE, LEFT-HANDED	1,165	861	740	619
ELGUIT	76	RICKENBAC	4001 BASS MAPLEGLO	1,171	866	744	622
ELGUIT	76	RICKENBAC	4001 BASS WHITE	1,171	866	744	622
ELGUIT	76	RICKENBAC	4001 BASS NATURAL	1,172	866	744	622
ELGUIT	77	RICKENBAC	4001 BASS CREAM	450	332	286	239
ELGUIT	77	RICKENBAC	4001 BASS WHITE	788	582	500	418
ELGUIT	77	RICKENBAC	4001 BASS AUTUMNGLO	876	648	556	465
ELGUIT	77	RICKENBAC	4001 BASS NATURAL	1,172	866	744	622
ELGUIT	78	RICKENBAC	4001 BASS CLEAR DEEP RED	628	465	399	334
ELGUIT	78	RICKENBAC	4001 BASS BLUE	635	470	403	337
ELGUIT	78	RICKENBAC	4001 BASS MAPLEGLO	641	474	407	340
ELGUIT	78	RICKENBAC	4001 BASS AUTUMNGLO	653	483	415	347
ELGUIT	78	RICKENBAC	4001 BASS WHITE	680	503	432	361
ELGUIT	78	RICKENBAC	4001 BASS BLACK	727	538	462	386
ELGUIT	78	RICKENBAC	4001 BASS CREAM	737	545	468	391

TYPE	YR	MFG	PRICES--BASED ON 100% ORIGINAL MODEL	SELL EXC	SELL AVG	BUY EXC	BUY AVG
ELGUIT	79	RICKENBAC	**4001 BASS** NATURAL	538	**398**	342	286
ELGUIT	79	RICKENBAC	**4001 BASS** BLOND	547	**404**	347	290
ELGUIT	79	RICKENBAC	**4001 BASS** MAPLEGLO	556	**411**	353	295
ELGUIT	79	RICKENBAC	**4001 BASS** AUTUMNGLO	576	**426**	366	306
ELGUIT	79	RICKENBAC	**4001 BASS** WHITE	593	**438**	376	315
ELGUIT	79	RICKENBAC	**4001 BASS** BLACK	611	**452**	388	324
ELGUIT	79	RICKENBAC	**4001 BASS** BLACK, LEFT-HANDED, FRETLESS	620	**458**	394	329
ELGUIT	81	RICKENBAC	**4001 BASS**	872	**645**	554	463
ELGUIT	86	RICKENBAC	**4001 BASS** FIREGLO	796	**589**	506	423
ELGUIT	80	RICKENBAC	**4001S BASS** JETGLO	806	**596**	512	428
ELGUIT	65	RICKENBAC	**4005 BASS** MAPLEGLO	2,957	**2,187**	1,879	1,571
ELGUIT	67	RICKENBAC	**4005 BASS** NATURAL, 2 PU's	3,009	**2,225**	1,912	1,598
ELGUIT	67	RICKENBAC	**4005 BASS** CRUSHED PEARL, DOUBLE BOUND	3,010	**2,226**	1,912	1,599
ELGUIT	67	RICKENBAC	**4005 BASS** FIREGLO, 2 PU's	3,026	**2,238**	1,923	1,608
ELGUIT	68	RICKENBAC	**4005 BASS** BLACK, 2 PU's	2,003	**1,481**	1,273	1,064
ELGUIT	68	RICKENBAC	**4005 BASS** FIREGLO, 2 PU's	3,497	**2,586**	2,222	1,857
ELGUIT	76	RICKENBAC	**4005 BASS** FIREGLO	1,394	**1,031**	886	741
ELGUIT	78	RICKENBAC	**4005 BASS** BLACK, 2 PU's	2,002	**1,481**	1,272	1,063
ELGUIT	79	RICKENBAC	**4005 BASS** FIREGLO, 2 PU's	1,408	**1,041**	894	748
ELGUIT	66	RICKENBAC	**4005-6 BASS** MAPLEGLO, DOUBLE BOUND	2,390	**1,767**	1,518	1,269
ELGUIT	67	RICKENBAC	**4005-8 BASS** FIREGLO, 8-STRING	1,752	**1,296**	1,113	931
ELGUIT	67	RICKENBAC	**4005WB BASS** BLACK, 2 PU's	1,731	**1,280**	1,100	920
ELGUIT	67	RICKENBAC	**4005WB BASS** MAPLEGLO, DOUBLE BOUND	1,742	**1,288**	1,107	925
ELGUIT	78	RICKENBAC	**4080 BASS** MAPLEGLO, DOUBLE NECK	1,720	**1,272**	1,093	913
ELGUIT	37	RICKENBAC	**B-6** BLACK & CHROME, BAKELITE NECK & BODY, ORIGINAL KAUFFMAN VIB	688	**509**	437	365
ELGUIT	38	RICKENBAC	**B-6** BLACK & WHITE	681	**504**	433	362
ELGUIT	48	RICKENBAC	**B-6** BLACK & WHITE	656	**485**	417	348
ELGUIT	50	RICKENBAC	**B-6** BLACK & WHITE	576	**426**	366	306
ELGUIT	56	RICKENBAC	**COMBO 400**	1,127	**833**	716	598
ELGUIT	57	RICKENBAC	**COMBO 400** BLACK	1,090	**806**	692	579
ELGUIT	57	RICKENBAC	**COMBO 400** GREEN/TULIP SHAPE	1,593	**1,178**	1,012	846
ELGUIT	62	RICKENBAC	**COMBO 420** FIREGLO	475	**351**	301	252
ELGUIT	66	RICKENBAC	**COMBO 420** FIREGLO	457	**338**	290	243
ELGUIT	72	RICKENBAC	**COMBO 420** MAPLEGLO	432	**319**	274	229
ELGUIT	63	RICKENBAC	**COMBO 425** FIREGLO	658	**487**	418	349
ELGUIT	64	RICKENBAC	**COMBO 425**	709	**524**	450	376
ELGUIT	58	RICKENBAC	**COMBO 450** SUNBURST	1,410	**1,042**	896	749
ELGUIT	59	RICKENBAC	**COMBO 450**	867	**641**	551	461
ELGUIT	60	RICKENBAC	**COMBO 450**	1,000	**739**	635	531
ELGUIT	61	RICKENBAC	**COMBO 450**	996	**736**	633	529
ELGUIT	65	RICKENBAC	**COMBO 450**	909	**672**	577	482
ELGUIT	66	RICKENBAC	**COMBO 450** MAPLEGLO	796	**589**	506	423
ELGUIT	67	RICKENBAC	**COMBO 450** FIREGLO	865	**640**	550	460
ELGUIT	74	RICKENBAC	**COMBO 450** BURGUNDY	596	**440**	378	316
ELGUIT	78	RICKENBAC	**COMBO 450** BLACK	563	**416**	358	299

TYPE	YR	MFG	MODEL	SELL EXC	SELL AVG	BUY EXC	BUY AVG
			PRICES--BASED ON 100% ORIGINAL				
ELGUIT	63	RICKENBAC	**COMBO 460**	886	**655**	563	470
ELGUIT	64	RICKENBAC	**COMBO 460**	704	**521**	447	374
ELGUIT	66	RICKENBAC	**COMBO 460**	677	**501**	430	360
ELGUIT	67	RICKENBAC	**COMBO 460** FIREGLO	677	**501**	430	360
ELGUIT	56	RICKENBAC	**COMBO 600**	677	**516**	438	335
ELGUIT	64	RICKENBAC	**COMBO 615**	757	**560**	481	402
ELGUIT	65	RICKENBAC	**COMBO 615**	499	**369**	317	265
ELGUIT	63	RICKENBAC	**COMBO 625**	619	**457**	393	328
ELGUIT	57	RICKENBAC	**COMBO 650**	633	**482**	410	313
ELGUIT	56	RICKENBAC	**COMBO 800** BLOND	1,211	**896**	769	643
ELGUIT	57	RICKENBAC	**COMBO 800**	1,115	**825**	708	592
ELGUIT	57	RICKENBAC	**COMBO 850**	1,454	**1,075**	924	772
ELGUIT	58	RICKENBAC	**COMBO 850**	1,222	**903**	776	649
ELGUIT	57	RICKENBAC	**COMBO 900**	1,680	**1,243**	1,068	893
ELGUIT	66	RICKENBAC	**COMBO 950**	1,681	**1,243**	1,068	893
ELGUIT	60	RICKENBAC	**COMBO 1000**	1,687	**1,248**	1,072	896
ELGUIT	64	RICKENBAC	**COMBO 1000** FIREGLO	1,777	**1,314**	1,129	944
ELGUIT	67	RICKENBAC	**COMBO 1000**	1,682	**1,244**	1,069	894
ELGUIT	71	RICKENBAC	**CONVERTIBLE** NATURAL, 12-STRING	1,131	**837**	719	601
ELGUIT	63	RICKENBAC	**CW-6** NATURAL WALNUT, 6-STRING	457	**338**	290	243
ELGUIT	50	RICKENBAC	**D-16** METAL w/2 8-STRING NECKS	478	**353**	303	253
ELGUIT	50	RICKENBAC	**DC-12** METAL w/2 6-STRING NECKS	557	**412**	354	296
ELGUIT	50	RICKENBAC	**DC-16** METAL & BRONZE w/2 8-STRING NECKS	518	**383**	329	275
ELGUIT	57	RICKENBAC	**DW** DOUBLE NECK STEEL w/2 6-STRING NECKS	495	**366**	314	263
ELGUIT	38	RICKENBAC	**ELECTRO**	1,097	**811**	697	582
ELGUIT	65	RICKENBAC	**ELECTRO** 6-STRING	478	**353**	303	253
ELGUIT	67	RICKENBAC	**ELECTRO** 6-STRING	929	**687**	590	493
ELGUIT	65	RICKENBAC	**ELECTRO 3/4** 1 PU, SERIAL #2230-	478	**353**	303	253
ELGUIT	62	RICKENBAC	**ELECTRO 102** RED	466	**345**	296	247
ELGUIT	63	RICKENBAC	**ELECTRO BASS** FIREGLO, 1 PU	384	**284**	244	204
ELGUIT	65	RICKENBAC	**ELECTRO BASS** SOLID, 1 PU, SERIAL #2601-	482	**357**	306	256
ELGUIT	64	RICKENBAC	**ELECTRO ES-16**	482	**357**	306	256
ELGUIT	65	RICKENBAC	**ELECTRO ES-17** FIREGLO	478	**353**	303	253
ELGUIT	46	RICKENBAC	**ELECTRO ITALIAN**	511	**378**	325	271
ELGUIT	47	RICKENBAC	**ELECTRO ITALIAN**	516	**381**	328	274
ELGUIT	48	RICKENBAC	**ELECTRO NS** METAL & GREY	468	**346**	297	248
ELGUIT	33	RICKENBAC	**ELECTRO SPANISH**	1,000	**739**	635	531
ELGUIT	35	RICKENBAC	**ELECTRO SPANISH**	717	**530**	455	380
ELGUIT	37	RICKENBAC	**ELECTRO SPANISH**	704	**521**	447	374
ELGUIT	38	RICKENBAC	**ELECTRO SPANISH** BLACK	689	**509**	437	366
ELGUIT	47	RICKENBAC	**ELECTRO SPANISH**	498	**368**	316	264
ELGUIT	33	RICKENBAC	**FRYING PAN A-25 ELECTRIC STEEL**	3,124	**2,311**	1,985	1,660
ELGUIT	35	RICKENBAC	**FRYING PAN A-25 ELECTRIC STEEL**	3,116	**2,304**	1,980	1,655
ELGUIT	50	RICKENBAC	**SD** METAL & COPPER	468	**346**	297	248
ELGUIT	37	RICKENBAC	**SILVER HAWAIIAN** CHROME-PLATED BODY	384	**284**	244	204
GUITAR AMP	55	RICKENBAC	**8ME** GRAY, 8" SPEAKER	240	**177**	152	127
GTAMP	40	RICKENBAC	**ELECTRO** 1x12", 10 WATT	336	**248**	213	178
GTAMP	55	RICKENBAC	**M-88** GRAY TOLEX	315	**240**	204	156
GTAMP	78	RICKENBAC	**TR- 75G** 2x12" SPEAKERS, 75 WATT	240	**177**	152	127
GTAMP	78	RICKENBAC	**TR- 75SG** 1x10" AND 1x15" SPEAKERS	225	**166**	143	119
GTAMP	78	RICKENBAC	**TR-100G** 4x12" SPEAKERS, 100 WATT	364	**269**	231	193
GTAMP	68	RICKENBAC	**TRANSONIC** 2x12" REV	309	**228**	196	164
GTAMP	68	RICKENBAC	**TRANSONIC BASS** 1x18"	409	**303**	260	217

TYPE	YR	MFG	PRICES--BASED ON 100% ORIGINAL MODEL	SELL EXC	SELL AVG	BUY EXC	BUY AVG
GUITAR (ACOUSTIC)	60	RICKENBAC	310 THIN HOLLOW BODY	851	648	551	421
GUITAR	64	RICKENBAC	315 THIN HOLLOW BODY	698	516	444	371
GUITAR	67	RICKENBAC	320 THIN HOLLOW BODY	1,586	1,173	1,008	843
GUITAR	58	RICKENBAC	325 THIN HOLLOW BODY	3,623	2,679	2,302	1,924
GUITAR	64	RICKENBAC	325 THIN HOLLOW BODY	2,272	1,680	1,443	1,207
GUITAR	66	RICKENBAC	325 THIN HOLLOW BODY	1,678	1,241	1,066	891
GUITAR	70	RICKENBAC	325 BLACK, 3 PU's, THIN HOLLOW BODY	1,107	819	703	588
GUITAR	60	RICKENBAC	330F THIN HOLLOW BODY	1,017	752	646	540
GUITAR	61	RICKENBAC	330F THIN HOLLOW BODY	1,495	1,106	950	794
GUITAR	66	RICKENBAC	330F FIREGLO, THIN HOLLOW BODY	1,413	1,045	897	750
GUITAR	68	RICKENBAC	330F THIN HOLLOW BODY	1,200	888	763	638
GUITAR	72	RICKENBAC	331 LIGHT SHOW	4,080	3,017	2,592	2,167
GUITAR	60	RICKENBAC	335F THIN HOLLOW BODY	1,097	811	697	582
GUITAR	66	RICKENBAC	335F THIN HOLLOW BODY	824	609	523	438
GUITAR	68	RICKENBAC	336-12 FIREGLO, THIN HOLLOW BODY	817	604	519	434
GUITAR	66	RICKENBAC	340F THIN HOLLOW BODY	820	607	521	436
GUITAR	61	RICKENBAC	345F THIN FULL BODY	1,017	752	646	540
GUITAR	66	RICKENBAC	345F THIN HOLLOW BODY	1,254	927	797	666
GUITAR	59	RICKENBAC	360 AUTUMNGLO	2,927	2,164	1,859	1,554
GUITAR	67	RICKENBAC	360 MAPLEGLO	1,044	772	663	554
GUITAR	71	RICKENBAC	360 NATURAL	1,195	883	759	634
GUITAR	65	RICKENBAC	360-12 MAPLEGLO	1,684	1,246	1,070	895
GUITAR	66	RICKENBAC	360-12 MAPLEGLO	1,155	854	734	614
GUITAR	67	RICKENBAC	360-12 FIREGLO, SERIAL #GC1417	1,473	1,089	936	782
GUITAR	72	RICKENBAC	360-12 FIREGLO	938	694	596	498
GUITAR	66	RICKENBAC	360-12F THIN FULL BODY	1,394	1,031	886	741
GUITAR	65	RICKENBAC	360-12WB FIREGLO, SERIAL #EJ967	1,656	1,224	1,052	879
GUITAR	59	RICKENBAC	360F THIN FULL BODY	3,296	2,438	2,094	1,751
GUITAR	60	RICKENBAC	360F THIN FULL BODY	2,340	1,730	1,487	1,243
GUITAR	68	RICKENBAC	360F THIN FULL BODY	1,529	1,131	971	812
GUITAR	59	RICKENBAC	365 NATURAL	1,520	1,124	966	807
GUITAR	60	RICKENBAC	365 FIREGLO	1,394	1,031	886	741
GUITAR	66	RICKENBAC	365 FIREGLO	778	575	494	413
GUITAR	60	RICKENBAC	365F NATURAL	1,742	1,328	1,128	863
GUITAR	68	RICKENBAC	365WB FIREGLO	1,548	1,180	1,003	767
GUITAR	64	RICKENBAC	366 CONVERTIBLE 6 & 12-STRING	1,988	1,470	1,263	1,056
GUITAR	68	RICKENBAC	366-12 BURGUNDY	1,433	1,060	910	761
GUITAR	69	RICKENBAC	366-12 BLACK	1,624	1,201	1,032	862
GUITAR	66	RICKENBAC	370-12 MAPLEGLO	1,654	1,223	1,051	878
GUITAR	68	RICKENBAC	370F THIN FULL BODY	1,216	899	772	646
GUITAR	68	RICKENBAC	370WB FIREGLO	1,548	1,180	1,003	767
GUITAR	59	RICKENBAC	375 CAPRI	2,351	1,738	1,493	1,248

TYPE	YR	MFG	PRICES--BASED ON 100% ORIGINAL MODEL	SELL EXC	SELL AVG	BUY EXC	BUY AVG
GUITAR	61	RICKENBAC	**375** CAPRI	2,237	**1,655**	1,421	1,188
GUITAR	67	RICKENBAC	**375** CAPRI	1,397	**1,033**	888	742
GUITAR	60	RICKENBAC	**375F** THIN FULL BODY	3,222	**2,383**	2,047	1,712
GUITAR	59	RICKENBAC	**381** THICK BODY	2,345	**1,734**	1,490	1,245
GUITAR	69	RICKENBAC	**381** FIREGLO, THICK BODY	1,527	**1,129**	970	811
GUITAR	70	RICKENBAC	**381** THICK BODY	1,636	**1,210**	1,040	869
GUITAR	58	RICKENBAC	**385** THICK BODY, FLATTOP	2,342	**1,732**	1,488	1,244
GUITAR	67	RICKENBAC	**385** D SHAPE, THICK BODY	1,216	**899**	772	646
GUITAR	68	RICKENBAC	**385S** JUMBO FLATTOP, THICK BODY	1,350	**998**	858	717
GUITAR	63	RICKENBAC	**390** THICK BODY	2,210	**1,635**	1,404	1,174
GUITAR	76	RICKENBAC	**360MG** MAPLE GLO	792	**586**	503	421
GUITAR	40	RICKENBAC	**PATRICIAN** ARCHTOP	936	**692**	594	497
STEEL GUITAR	56	RICKENBAC	**100** BROWN, 6-STRING	336	**248**	213	178
STGUIT	32	RICKENBAC	**A-22** 22 1/2" SCALE	1,035	**766**	658	550
STGUIT	46	RICKENBAC	**ACADEMY** BAKELITE, STUDENT MODEL	432	**319**	274	229
STGUIT	47	RICKENBAC	**ACADEMY** BAKELITE, STUDENT MODEL	417	**308**	265	221
STGUIT	48	RICKENBAC	**ACADEMY** BAKELITE, STUDENT MODEL	312	**230**	198	165
STGUIT	50	RICKENBAC	**BD** BLACK, 6-STRING	456	**337**	290	242
STGUIT	53	RICKENBAC	**BD** BLACK, 6-STRING	379	**280**	240	201
STGUIT	50	RICKENBAC	**BRONSON** BROWN, MODEL 52	480	**355**	305	255
STGUIT	60	RICKENBAC	**CW-6** WALNUT, 6-STRING, 3 LEGS	478	**353**	303	253
STGUIT	60	RICKENBAC	**CW-6** WALNUT, 6-STRING	566	**418**	359	300
STGUIT	40	RICKENBAC	**ELECTRO** LAP STEEL, DOUBLE NECK	766	**566**	486	406
STGUIT	42	RICKENBAC	**ELECTRO** 2 8-STRING NECKS, DOUBLE NECK	610	**451**	387	324
STGUIT	43	RICKENBAC	**ELECTRO** 2 8-STRING NECKS, DOUBLE NECK	592	**438**	376	314
STGUIT	45	RICKENBAC	**ELECTRO** 2 8-STRING NECKS, DOUBLE NECK	539	**399**	342	286
STGUIT	34	RICKENBAC	**ELECTRO B** BAKELITE, 6-STRING	1,096	**810**	696	582
STGUIT	36	RICKENBAC	**ELECTRO B** 6-STRING	964	**713**	613	512
STGUIT	37	RICKENBAC	**ELECTRO B** 6-STRING	956	**707**	607	507
STGUIT	38	RICKENBAC	**ELECTRO B** 6-STRING	944	**698**	600	501
STGUIT	38	RICKENBAC	**ELECTRO B** 8-STRING	1,195	**883**	759	634
STGUIT	39	RICKENBAC	**ELECTRO B** 6-STRING	896	**663**	569	476
STGUIT	40	RICKENBAC	**ELECTRO B** 6-STRING	868	**642**	552	461
STGUIT	40	RICKENBAC	**ELECTRO B** 8-STRING	1,115	**825**	708	592
STGUIT	41	RICKENBAC	**ELECTRO B** 8-STRING	1,045	**796**	677	517
STGUIT	46	RICKENBAC	**ELECTRO B** 8-STRING	484	**358**	308	257
STGUIT	49	RICKENBAC	**ELECTRO B** 6-STRING	504	**372**	320	267
STGUIT	48	RICKENBAC	**ELECTRO DOUBLE NECK**	518	**383**	329	275
STGUIT	48	RICKENBAC	**ELECTRO NS** GRAY, 6-STRING	384	**284**	244	204
STGUIT	49	RICKENBAC	**ELECTRO NS** GRAY, 6-STRING	371	**274**	236	197
STGUIT	52	RICKENBAC	**ELECTRO SD** TAN 2-TONE, 6-STRING	360	**266**	228	191
STGUIT	53	RICKENBAC	**ELECTRO SD** TAN, 6-STRING	475	**351**	301	252
STGUIT	54	RICKENBAC	**G DELUXE HAWAIIAN STEEL**	518	**383**	329	275

TYPE		YR	MFG	PRICES--BASED ON 100% ORIGINAL MODEL	SELL EXC	SELL AVG	BUY EXC	BUY AVG
STGUIT		64	RICKENBAC	**LAP STEEL** FIREGLO, WOOD BODY	387	**286**	246	206
STGUIT		46	RICKENBAC	**MODEL S** GRAY SPARKLE, 6-STRING, PU	432	**319**	274	229
STGUIT		48	RICKENBAC	**MODEL S** GRAY SUNBURST, METAL BODY	481	**356**	306	256
STGUIT		49	RICKENBAC	**MODEL S** GRAY, 6-STRING, METAL BODY	384	**284**	244	204
STGUIT		49	RICKENBAC	**MODEL SD** COPPER FINISH, 6-STRING	408	**301**	259	216

RIDGELAND

BANJO		81	RIDGE	**B-200 5-STRING** 16-BRACKET	60	**44**	38	32
BANJO		81	RIDGE	**B-200R 5-STRING** 16-BRACKET	61	**45**	39	32
BANJO		81	RIDGE	**B-200WR 5-STRING** 16-BRACKET	61	**45**	39	32
BANJO		81	RIDGE	**B-230 5-STRING** 30-BRACKET	62	**46**	39	33
BANJO		81	RIDGE	**B-230R 5-STRING** 30-BRACKET	61	**45**	39	32
BANJO		81	RIDGE	**B-230RC 5-STRING** 30-BRACKET	62	**46**	39	33
BANJO		81	RIDGE	**BK-160 5-STRING** 16-BRACKET	56	**41**	35	30
BANJO		81	RIDGE	**BK-160R** TENOR, 16-BRACKET	61	**45**	39	32
BANJO		81	RIDGE	**BK-160R 5-STRING** 16-BRACKET	60	**44**	38	32
BANJO		81	RIDGE	**BT-200** TENOR, 16-BRACKET	61	**45**	39	32
BANJO		81	RIDGE	**BT-200R** TENOR	62	**46**	39	33
BANJO		81	RIDGE	**BT-230R** TENOR, 30-BRACKET	60	**44**	38	32

ROLAND CORPORATION

EFFECTS		74	ROLAND	**AF- 60 BEE GEE FUZZ**	120	**88**	76	63
	EFFECTS	75	ROLAND	**AF-100 BEE BAA FUZZ TREBLE BASS**	216	**159**	137	114
GUITAR AMP		78	ROLAND	**CUBE- 20** ORANGE	168	**124**	106	89
	GTAMP	78	ROLAND	**CUBE- 40**	216	**159**	137	114
	GTAMP	82	ROLAND	**CUBE- 40** ORANGE	282	**208**	179	149
	GTAMP	79	ROLAND	**CUBE- 60** ORANGE, 1 SPEAKER	288	**213**	183	153
	GTAMP	78	ROLAND	**CUBE- 60B BASS** 1 SPEAKER	240	**177**	152	127
	GTAMP	79	ROLAND	**CUBE- 60B BASS**	230	**170**	146	122
SIGNAL PROCESSOR		70	ROLAND	**MI-11001**	2,366	**1,750**	1,503	1,257
	SGNPRO	79	ROLAND	**SDD-320 DIMENSION D**	787	**582**	500	418
	SGNPRO	79	ROLAND	**SRE-556 CHORUS ECHO**	1,243	**919**	789	660
	SGNPRO	79	ROLAND	**SVC-350 VOCODER**	1,243	**919**	789	660
SYNTHESIZER		75	ROLAND	**GR-500 GUITAR/MODULE** 3 PU's	478	**353**	303	253
	SYNTH	78	ROLAND	**RS-09** ORGAN, STRING	216	**159**	137	114
	SYNTH	78	ROLAND	**SH 7** ANALOG	479	**354**	304	254

SELMER CO, INC

GUITAR AMP		67	SELMER	**BASSMASTER HEAD**	757	**560**	481	402
	GTAMP	65	SELMER	**CONSTELLATION 20**	1,115	**825**	708	592
	GTAMP	64	SELMER	**EXTENSION CAB 2x12"**	744	**550**	473	395
	GTAMP	64	SELMER	**THUNDERBIRD** 50 WATT	677	**501**	430	360
	GTAMP	62	SELMER	**TRUE VOICE BASS** 50 WATT	438	**324**	278	233
	GTAMP	63	SELMER	**TRUE VOICE LEAD** 30 WATT	288	**213**	183	153
	GTAMP	65	SELMER	**ZODIAC** 100 WATT HEAD	480	**355**	305	255
	GTAMP	66	SELMER	**ZODIAC** 50 WATT	677	**501**	430	360
SAXOPHONE		79	SELMER	**55 BARITONE**	1,744	**1,290**	1,108	926
	SAX	79	SELMER	**55A BARITONE** LOW A	2,954	**2,185**	1,877	1,569

SENNHEISER ELECTRONICS CORPORATION

MIC		85	SENN	**MD- 21N DYNAMIC**	270	**200**	172	143
	MIC	65	SENN	**MD-211 DYNAMIC**	480	**355**	305	255

TYPE	YR	MFG	PRICES--BASED ON 100% ORIGINAL MODEL	SELL EXC	SELL AVG	BUY EXC	BUY AVG
			SEQUENTIAL CIRCUITS				
SYNTHESIZER	81	SEQU	**100 PRO-ONE** MONO ANALOG	785	**580**	498	417
SYNTH	78	SEQU	**1000 PROPHET- 5** REV. 1 or 2	445	**329**	283	236
SYNTH	79	SEQU	**1000 PROPHET- 5** REV. 3, MIDI	772	**571**	491	410
SYNTH	80	SEQU	**1010 PROPHET-10** MIDI	969	**717**	616	515
			SHURE BROTHERS, INC.				
MIC	39	SHURE	**55B "ELVIS"**	216	**159**	137	114
MIC	75	SHURE	**330 UNI RIBOON**	438	**324**	278	233
MIC	38	SHURE	**555B DYNAMIC**	240	**177**	152	127
MIC	46	SHURE	**556S UNIDYNE**	187	**138**	118	99
MIC	67	SHURE	**BROWN BULLET**	96	**71**	61	51
MIC	67	SHURE	**GREEN BULLET**	374	**276**	237	198
MIC	69	SHURE	**PE 53V SPHERE-O-DYNE**	144	**106**	91	76
MIC	57	SHURE	**PE 566 UNISPHERE I** GOLD-PLATED	120	**88**	76	63
MIC	81	SHURE	**SM 33 UNI RIBBON**	470	**347**	298	249
MIC	78	SHURE	**SM 76 OMNI DYNAMIC**	432	**319**	274	229
TEST	73	SHURE	**II-QUAD CLASSIC MONO TUBE**	189	**139**	120	100
TEST	62	SHURE	**S-3000 II**	144	**107**	92	77
			SILVERTONE by DANELECTRO				
ELEC. GUITAR	58	SILVERTON	**BASS** BROWN, WHITE SIDES, SINGLE CUTAWAY, 1 PU	413	**306**	262	219
ELGUIT	59	SILVERTON	**BASS** BROWN, WHITE SIDES, SINGLE CUTAWAY, 1 PU	285	**210**	181	151
ELGUIT	60	SILVERTON	**BASS** SUNBURST, SINGLE CUTAWAY, 1 PU	279	**206**	177	148
ELGUIT	63	SILVERTON	**BASS** RED SUNBURST, 2 PU's	268	**198**	170	142
ELGUIT	64	SILVERTON	**BASS** BLACK, SINGLE CUTAWAY, 1 PU	249	**184**	158	132
ELGUIT	64	SILVERTON	**BASS** RED SPARKLE, 2 PU's	429	**317**	272	227
ELGUIT	60	SILVERTON	**BASS IV** 1 LIPSTICK PU	436	**323**	277	232
ELGUIT	58	SILVERTON	**DAN ELECTRO** WHITE, SINGLE CUTAWAY, 1 PU	213	**157**	135	113
ELGUIT	58	SILVERTON	**DAN ELECTRO** BROWN, SINGLE CUTAWAY, 1 PU	288	**213**	183	153
ELGUIT	64	SILVERTON	**DAN ELECTRO** RED SPARKLE, 2 PU's	196	**145**	125	104
ELGUIT	63	SILVERTON	**ESPANADA** BLACK, 2 PU's	384	**284**	244	204
ELGUIT	64	SILVERTON	**ESPANADA**	361	**267**	229	192
ELGUIT	55	SILVERTON	**JIMMY REED MODEL** SUNBURST	618	**457**	392	328
ELGUIT	55	SILVERTON	**METEOR** SUNBURST, SINGLE CUTAWAY, 1 PU	192	**142**	122	102
ELGUIT	64	SILVERTON	**STANDARD** BRONZE, SINGLE CUTAWAY, 1 PU	221	**164**	140	117
GUITAR AMP	65	SILVERTON	**1 x 12"** TREMOLO	146	**108**	93	78
GTAMP	40	SILVERTON	**1304** RED	336	**248**	213	178
GTAMP	55	SILVERTON	**1331**	240	**177**	152	127
GTAMP	59	SILVERTON	**1459** BLACK, 2x12" TUBES	187	**138**	118	99
GTAMP	61	SILVERTON	**1472** TREMOLO, 12" JENSEN	96	**71**	61	51
GTAMP	63	SILVERTON	**1472**	192	**142**	122	102
GTAMP	63	SILVERTON	**1481**	134	**99**	85	71
GTAMP	64	SILVERTON	**1481** 1x6" SPEAKER	102	**75**	65	54
GTAMP	67	SILVERTON	**1481** GRAY, 1x8", TUBE	96	**71**	61	51
GTAMP	60	SILVERTON	**1482** 1x12" SPEAKER	124	**92**	79	66
GTAMP	61	SILVERTON	**1482** TREMOLO, 6V6GT TUBES	120	**88**	76	63
GTAMP	62	SILVERTON	**1482** 1x12" SPEAKER	96	**71**	61	51
GTAMP	63	SILVERTON	**1482** TREMOLO, 12" JENSEN	102	**75**	65	54
GTAMP	64	SILVERTON	**1483** 50 WATT	105	**78**	67	56

TYPE		YR	MFG	PRICES--BASED ON 100% ORIGINAL MODEL	SELL EXC	SELL AVG	BUY EXC	BUY AVG
GTAMP		64	SILVERTON	**1484** 2x12" JENSENS	192	**142**	122	102
GTAMP		66	SILVERTON	**1484** 2X12" SPEAKER	184	**136**	117	97
GTAMP		65	SILVERTON	**1485** 6x12" JENSENS	336	**248**	213	178
GTAMP		64	SILVERTON	**TWIN 12**	266	**197**	169	141
GUITAR (ACOUSTIC)		60	SILVERTON	**1448** BLACK SPRAKLE, FORMICA TOP	144	**106**	91	76
GUITAR		58	SILVERTON	**JUMBO** BLOND, SPRUCE TOP, FLATTOP	326	**241**	207	173
GUITAR		58	SILVERTON	**K-11** BLOND, SPRUCE TOP, MAPLE BACK/SIDES	336	**248**	213	178
MANDOLIN		59	SILVERTON	**1417L** COPPER FINISH, LIPSTICK PU, DOLPHIN HEADSTOCK	363	**269**	231	193
MANDOL		64	SILVERTON	**1457L** RED SPARKLE,2 PU's,CONCENTRIC CONTROLS,AMP,CASE	383	**283**	243	203
STEEL GUITAR		50	SILVERTON	**6-STRING LAP STEEL**	93	**68**	59	49

SLINGERLAND

TYPE		YR	MFG	MODEL	SELL EXC	SELL AVG	BUY EXC	BUY AVG
BANJO		24	SLINGER	**BANJO-UKE**	249	**184**	158	132
BANJO		20	SLINGER	**MANDOLIN-BANJO**	243	**180**	154	129
BANJO		25	SLINGER	**MAYBELL** PLECTRUM, WALNUT, RESONATOR	468	**346**	297	248
BANJO		30	SLINGER	**MAYBELL** PLECTRUM, WALNUT, RESONATOR	461	**341**	293	245
BANJO		23	SLINGER	**MAYBELL BANJO-UKE**	432	**319**	274	229
BANJO		30	SLINGER	**MAYBELL QUEEN** TENOR	459	**340**	292	244
BANJO		28	SLINGER	**MAYBELL RECORDING SONGSTER** TENOR	477	**352**	303	253
BANJO		30	SLINGER	**MAYBELL RECORDING SONGSTER** TENOR	468	**346**	297	248
BANJO		28	SLINGER	**MAYBELL TENOR** 17-FRET	499	**369**	317	265
BANJO		27	SLINGER	**PRO-TONE MODEL 20 BANJO-UKE**	379	**280**	240	201
BANJO		28	SLINGER	**TROUBADOUR** TENOR, BRAZILIAN ROSEWOOD	438	**324**	278	233
GUITAR (ACOUSTIC)		37	SLINGER	**GOLDEN HAWAIIAN** SUNBURST, BIRCH BODY	287	**212**	182	152
GUITAR		30	SLINGER	**MAYBELL** TENOR, NATURAL, MAHOGANY BACK/SIDES	451	**333**	286	239
GUITAR		33	SLINGER	**MAYBELL** SUNBURST, MAHOGANY BACK/SIDES, VIOLIN CRAFT	502	**371**	319	266
GUITAR		35	SLINGER	**MAYBELL** SUNBURST, ARCHTOP, MAHOGANY BACK/SIDES	469	**347**	298	249
GUITAR		35	SLINGER	**MAYBELL** SUNBURST, ARCHTOP, F-HOLES	471	**348**	299	250
GUITAR		37	SLINGER	**MAYBELL** SUNBURST, ARCHTOP	478	**353**	303	253
GUITAR		38	SLINGER	**NIGHTHAWK** SUNBURST, ARCHTOP, MAPLE BACK/SIDES	451	**333**	286	239
GUITAR		38	SLINGER	**SILVERHAWK** SUNBURST, ARCHTOP, MAPLE BACK/SIDES	456	**337**	289	242
GUITAR		37	SLINGER	**SONGSTER** SUNBURST, DOT INLAYS	468	**346**	297	248

SOLANO

TYPE		YR	MFG	MODEL	SELL EXC	SELL AVG	BUY EXC	BUY AVG
UPRIG		80	SOLANO	**PANORMO** FLAT BLACK	21,120	**15,620**	13,420	11,220
UPRIGHT		80	SOLANO	**PRESCOTT CARVED BASS**	25,440	**18,815**	16,165	13,515

SONY PRO AUDIO

TYPE		YR	MFG	MODEL	SELL EXC	SELL AVG	BUY EXC	BUY AVG
MIC		73	SONYP	**C -77 SHOTGUN FET CONDENSER**	1,434	**1,060**	911	761
MIC		59	SONYP	**C- 37A TUBE**	1,800	**1,331**	1,143	956
MIC		71	SONYP	**C- 37P FIXED CARDIOD OMNI**	899	**665**	571	477
MIC		78	SONYP	**C- 38B FIXED**	828	**612**	526	440
MIC		71	SONYP	**C-500 S/B OMNI-DIRECTIONAL ECM**	1,435	**1,061**	911	762
MIC		89	SONYP	**ECM-77 S/B OMNIDIRECTIONAL ECM**	1,624	**1,201**	1,032	862

SOUNDCITY

TYPE		YR	MFG	MODEL	SELL EXC	SELL AVG	BUY EXC	BUY AVG
GUITAR AMP		74	SOUNDCITY	**CONCORD COMBO**	472	**360**	306	233
GTAMP		72	SOUNDCITY	**TUBE GUITAR HEAD** 100 WATT	477	**364**	309	236

STEINBERGER SOUND by GIBSON MUSICAL INST

TYPE		YR	MFG	MODEL	SELL EXC	SELL AVG	BUY EXC	BUY AVG
ELEC. GUITAR		n/a	STEINBERG	**SPIRIT GU DELUXE** DBL CUTAWAY MAPLE, HEADLESS MAPLE NECK, HSH EMG SELECT PU's	271	**200**	172	144

STEINER SYNTHESIZERS

TYPE		YR	MFG	MODEL	SELL EXC	SELL AVG	BUY EXC	BUY AVG
SYNTHESIZER		79	STEINER	**BASIC STUDIO SYNTHACON ANALOG**	1,434	**1,060**	911	761
SYNTH		79	STEINER	**KEYBOARDLESS SYNTHACON ANALOG**	956	**707**	607	507
SYNTH		79	STEINER	**MULTIPHONIC SYNTHACON ANALOG**	1,593	**1,178**	1,012	846

	TYPE	YR	MFG	MODEL (PRICES--BASED ON 100% ORIGINAL)	SELL EXC	SELL AVG	BUY EXC	BUY AVG
	SYNTH	79	STEINER	**SYNTHACON ANALOG**	1,115	**825**	708	592
	SYNTH	79	STEINER	**SYNTHACON II ANALOG**	1,434	**1,060**	911	761
	SYNTH	79	STEINER	**SYNTHACON SYSTEM ANALOG**	2,071	**1,532**	1,316	1,100

STELLA

	TYPE	YR	MFG	MODEL	SELL EXC	SELL AVG	BUY EXC	BUY AVG
BANJO		65	STELLA	**TENOR**	209	**160**	136	104
GUITAR (ACOUSTIC)		31	STELLA	**6-STRING AUDITORIUM SIZE**	394	**291**	250	209
	GUITAR	26	STELLA	**12-STRING** LEAD BELLY MODEL	730	**540**	464	388
	GUITAR	27	STELLA	**12-STRING** LEAD BELLY MODEL	5,030	**3,720**	3,196	2,672
	GUITAR	30	STELLA	**12-STRING** LEAD BELLY MODEL	4,800	**3,550**	3,050	2,550
	GUITAR	32	STELLA	**12-STRING** LEAD BELLY MODEL	4,560	**3,372**	2,897	2,422
	GUITAR	33	STELLA	**12-STRING** LEAD BELLY MODEL	4,516	**3,340**	2,870	2,399
	GUITAR	55	STELLA	**12-STRING**	715	**528**	454	379
	GUITAR	30	STELLA	**TENOR** WALNUT, BIRCH BODY	216	**159**	137	114
	GUITAR	50	STELLA	**TENOR** SUNBURST, 4-STRING	257	**190**	163	136
UKULELE		20	STELLA	**UKE** BIRCH	119	**88**	75	63

S. S. STEWART

	TYPE	YR	MFG	MODEL	SELL EXC	SELL AVG	BUY EXC	BUY AVG
BANJO		89	STEWART	**1889 SPECIAL** IVORY TUNERS, DECORATIVE	976	**722**	620	518
	BANJO	89	STEWART	**1889 SPECIAL THOROUGHBRED** OPEN BACK, 5-STRING	929	**687**	590	493
	BANJO	25	STEWART	**OPEN BACK** CURVED NECK	360	**266**	228	191

STROMBERG

	TYPE	YR	MFG	MODEL	SELL EXC	SELL AVG	BUY EXC	BUY AVG
BANJO		20	STROMBERG	**BOSTON TENOR** OPEN BACK	933	**690**	592	495
	BANJO	30	STROMBERG	**MARIMBA TENOR**	1,228	**908**	780	652
GUITAR (ACOUSTIC)		51	STROMBERG	**APPRENTICE 100** SUNBURST, FULL BODY	19,552	**14,460**	12,423	10,387
	GUITAR	48	STROMBERG	**APPRENTICE 200** BLOND, FULL BODY	24,353	**18,011**	15,474	12,937
	GUITAR	35	STROMBERG	**DELUXE** SUNBURST, ARCHTOP	19,191	**14,193**	12,194	10,195
	GUITAR	47	STROMBERG	**DELUXE** SUNBURST, 17" FULL BODY	14,963	**11,066**	9,508	7,949
	GUITAR	50	STROMBERG	**DELUXE** SUNBURST, CUTAWAY	19,185	**14,189**	12,190	10,192
	GUITAR	40	STROMBERG	**G-1**	6,441	**4,764**	4,093	3,422
	GUITAR	48	STROMBERG	**G-1** ARCHTOP	5,328	**3,941**	3,386	2,831
	GUITAR	37	STROMBERG	**G-3** SUNBURST, 17" SPLIT F-HOLES	4,521	**3,344**	2,873	2,402
	GUITAR	48	STROMBERG	**MASTER 300** BLOND, FULL BODY	27,233	**20,141**	17,304	14,467
	GUITAR	50	STROMBERG	**MASTER 300** SUNBURST, CUTAWAY	24,162	**17,869**	15,353	12,836
	GUITAR	51	STROMBERG	**MASTER 300** SUNBURST, FULL BODY	23,392	**17,300**	14,863	12,427
	GUITAR	50	STROMBERG	**MASTER 400** SUNBURST	40,209	**29,738**	25,549	21,361
	GUITAR	52	STROMBERG	**MASTER 400** NATURAL, ARCHTOP	64,899	**47,998**	41,238	34,478
	GUITAR	54	STROMBERG	**MASTER 400** BLOND, CUTAWAY	111,530	**82,486**	70,868	59,250

SUPERTONE

	TYPE	YR	MFG	MODEL	SELL EXC	SELL AVG	BUY EXC	BUY AVG
BANJO		25	SUPER	**ORPHEUM #2 TENOR** WALNUT NECK, RESONATOR	619	**457**	393	328
ELEC. GUITAR		37	SUPER	**S-39 TREBLE CLEF DESIGN V-NECK**	216	**159**	137	114
GUITAR (ACOUSTIC)		35	SUPER	**BRADLEY KINKAID HOUND DOG** MAHOGANY BACK/SIDES	192	**142**	122	102
	GUITAR	40	SUPER	**BRADLEY KINKAID HOUND DOG**	225	**166**	143	119
	GUITAR	32	SUPER	**GENE AUTRY** STENCILED COWBOY SCENE	217	**161**	138	115
	GUITAR	37	SUPER	**S-39** TREBLE CLEF DESIGN, V-NECK	216	**159**	137	114
	GUITAR	35	SUPER	**SUPERTONE GENE AUTRY by REGAL** TRIPLE BINDING AROUND EDGE OF TOP AND SOUND HOLE	262	**200**	170	130
UKULELE		27	SUPER	**UKE** KOA	144	**106**	91	76

SUPRO by NATIONAL

	TYPE	YR	MFG	MODEL	SELL EXC	SELL AVG	BUY EXC	BUY AVG
ELEC. GUITAR		50	SUPRO	**BELMONT** RED	504	**372**	320	267

TYPE	YR	MFG	PRICES--BASED ON 100% ORIGINAL MODEL	SELL EXC	SELL AVG	BUY EXC	BUY AVG
ELGUIT	63	SUPRO	**BELMONT** RED RESOGLASS, 1 PU	242	**179**	154	129
ELGUIT	60	SUPRO	**CORONADO** BLACK RESOGLASS	393	**291**	250	209
ELGUIT	65	SUPRO	**CORONADO S482**	175	**129**	111	93
ELGUIT	56	SUPRO	**DEBONAIRE** CREAM, ARCHTOP	457	**338**	290	243
ELGUIT	50	SUPRO	**DUAL-TONE** 2 PU's	439	**325**	279	233
ELGUIT	55	SUPRO	**DUAL-TONE** WHITE, 2 PU's	432	**319**	274	229
ELGUIT	56	SUPRO	**DUAL-TONE** WHITE, 2 PU's	450	**332**	286	239
ELGUIT	57	SUPRO	**DUAL-TONE** WHITE, SINGLE CUTAWAY	451	**333**	286	239
ELGUIT	58	SUPRO	**DUAL-TONE** WHITE, 3 PU's	453	**335**	287	240
ELGUIT	60	SUPRO	**DUAL-TONE** WHITE RESOGLASS, 2 PU's	285	**210**	181	151
ELGUIT	63	SUPRO	**DUAL-TONE**	262	**193**	166	139
ELGUIT	53	SUPRO	**EL CAPITAN** SUNBURST	338	**250**	215	180
ELGUIT	58	SUPRO	**GAUCHO** BLUE, FLOATING PU	272	**201**	173	144
ELGUIT	63	SUPRO	**HOLIDAY** WHITE, 1 PU	254	**188**	161	135
ELGUIT	63	SUPRO	**KINGSTON** SAND BUFF RESOGLASS, 1 PU	264	**195**	167	140
ELGUIT	59	SUPRO	**KORD KING** 2 PU's	677	**501**	430	360
ELGUIT	65	SUPRO	**MARTINIQUE** ERMINE WHITE RESOGLASS	419	**310**	266	222
ELGUIT	66	SUPRO	**MARTINIQUE**	290	**221**	188	144
ELGUIT	52	SUPRO	**OZARK** NON-CUTAWAY	284	**210**	180	150
ELGUIT	65	SUPRO	**OZARK**	131	**97**	83	69
ELGUIT	60	SUPRO	**POCKET BASS** BLACK, 2 PU's	470	**347**	298	249
ELGUIT	64	SUPRO	**POCKET BASS** BLACK, 2 PU's	504	**372**	320	267
ELGUIT	66	SUPRO	**POCKET BASS** BLACK, 2 PU's	462	**342**	294	245
ELGUIT	55	SUPRO	**RANCHERO** SUNBURST, FLOATING PU	265	**196**	168	141
ELGUIT	66	SUPRO	**S-535** SHADED	264	**195**	167	140
ELGUIT	64	SUPRO	**SAHARA 70** BLUE RESOGLASS	360	**266**	228	191
ELGUIT	66	SUPRO	**SAHARA 70**	304	**225**	193	161
ELGUIT	59	SUPRO	**SUPER TWIN** IVORY-BLACK SUNBURST	518	**383**	329	275
ELGUIT	63	SUPRO	**SUPERSONIC** RED, 1 PU	158	**117**	100	84
ELGUIT	65	SUPRO	**SUPERSONIC 30**	132	**97**	84	70
ELGUIT	67	SUPRO	**SUPRO** SUNBURST, 12-STRING, SOLID, 2 PU's	172	**127**	109	91
ELGUIT	58	SUPRO	**TONEMASTER** GOLD HARDWARE	450	**332**	286	239
ELGUIT	62	SUPRO	**TONEMASTER** BLACK, DUAL TONE BODY	287	**212**	182	152
ELGUIT	63	SUPRO	**TONEMASTER** 2 PU's	312	**230**	198	165
ELGUIT	63	SUPRO	**TREMO-LECTRIC** BLUE RESOGLASS, 2 PU's	438	**324**	278	233
ELGUIT	64	SUPRO	**TREMO-LECTRIC** BLUE RESOGLASS	419	**310**	266	222
GUITAR AMP	59	SUPRO	**1616T** GRAY 2-TONE, 6x9" SPEAKER, VIB	95	**70**	60	50
GTAMP	64	SUPRO	**BANTAM** RED TOLEX, TUBE, 6" SPEAKER	76	**56**	48	40
GTAMP	64	SUPRO	**BANTAM** RED AND GOLD 8" JENSEN	80	**59**	51	42
GTAMP	60	SUPRO	**SUPER**	265	**196**	168	141
GTAMP	52	SUPRO	**SUPREME** 10" SPEAKER	96	**71**	61	51
GTAMP	52	SUPRO	**TB SUPREME** 10" SPEAKER	96	**71**	61	51
GTAMP	60	SUPRO	**THUNDERBOLT** 1x15" SPEAKER	177	**131**	112	94
GTAMP	64	SUPRO	**THUNDERBOLT** GRAY, 1x15" SPEAKER	170	**126**	108	90
GTAMP	65	SUPRO	**THUNDERBOLT** LIGHTNING BOLT LOGO	245	**181**	156	130

TYPE	YR	MFG	PRICES--BASED ON 100% ORIGINAL MODEL	SELL EXC	SELL AVG	BUY EXC	BUY AVG
GTAMP	66	SUPRO	**VIBROVERB** 2X12" JENSENS	204	**151**	129	108
GUITAR (ACOUSTIC)	38	SUPRO	**ARCADIA** WOOD BODY, RESONATOR	409	**303**	260	217
GUITAR	58	SUPRO	**FOLKSTAR**	612	**452**	389	325
GUITAR	60	SUPRO	**FOLKSTAR** RED RESOGLASS, RESONATOR	463	**342**	294	246
GUITAR	62	SUPRO	**FOLKSTAR** RED RESOGLASS, RESONATOR	433	**320**	275	230
GUITAR	64	SUPRO	**FOLKSTAR** RED RESOGLASS, RESONATOR	511	**378**	325	271
GUITAR	67	SUPRO	**FOLKSTAR** RED RESOGLASS, RESONATOR	466	**345**	296	247
GUITAR	64	SUPRO	**HOLIDAY** WHITE	185	**141**	120	92
STEEL GUITAR	40	SUPRO	**6-STRING LAP STEEL** IVORY	339	**251**	215	180
STGUIT	41	SUPRO	**6-STRING LAP STEEL** CREAM	341	**260**	221	169
STGUIT	50	SUPRO	**6-STRING LAP STEEL** GREY	351	**259**	223	186
STGUIT	54	SUPRO	**6-STRING LAP STEEL** PEARLOID	340	**252**	216	181
STGUIT	61	SUPRO	**6-STRING LAP STEEL** CREAM	346	**256**	220	184
STGUIT	57	SUPRO	**60** ROSEWOOD NECK, 1 PU	345	**255**	219	183
STGUIT	58	SUPRO	**60** WHITE, 1 PU	338	**250**	215	180
STGUIT	43	SUPRO	**CLIPPER LAP STEEL**	240	**177**	152	127
STGUIT	60	SUPRO	**COMET** PEARLOID	293	**217**	186	156
STGUIT	58	SUPRO	**CONSOLE** BLACK & WHITE, 8-STRING	336	**248**	213	178
STGUIT	36	SUPRO	**ELECTRIC HAWAIIAN** CAST ALUMINUM	432	**319**	274	229
STGUIT	62	SUPRO	**JET AIRLINER** 8-STRING	336	**248**	213	178
STGUIT	63	SUPRO	**JET AIRLINER** 8-STRING	297	**220**	189	158
STGUIT	64	SUPRO	**JET AIRLINER**	240	**177**	152	127
STGUIT	50	SUPRO	**PROFESSIONAL LAP STEEL**	294	**217**	187	156
STGUIT	51	SUPRO	**SPECTATOR**	288	**213**	183	153
STGUIT	52	SUPRO	**STUDENT DELUXE LAP STEEL**	277	**205**	176	147
STGUIT	50	SUPRO	**TWIN LAP STEEL** DOUBLE NECK	412	**305**	262	219

TANNOY

TYPE	YR	MFG	MODEL	SELL EXC	SELL AVG	BUY EXC	BUY AVG
RAW	73	TANNOY	**10 GOLD**	365	**270**	232	194
RAW	73	TANNOY	**12 GOLD**	435	**322**	276	231
RAW	73	TANNOY	**15 GOLD**	424	**313**	269	225
SPKR	73	TANNOY	**AUTOGRAPH PRO**	1,727	**1,277**	1,097	917
SPKR	74	TANNOY	**AUTOGRAPH TUDOR**	1,262	**933**	802	670
SPKR	64	TANNOY	**BELVEDERE 10"**	371	**274**	236	197
SPKR	64	TANNOY	**BELVEDERE 12"**	624	**461**	396	331
SPKR	64	TANNOY	**BELVEDERE 15"**	624	**461**	396	331
SPKR	64	TANNOY	**CADET 10"**	609	**450**	387	323
SPKR	68	TANNOY	**CHATSWORTH 12"**	460	**340**	292	244
SPKR	68	TANNOY	**LANCASTER 12"**	698	**516**	444	371
SPKR	69	TANNOY	**MALLORCAN**	452	**334**	287	240
SPKR	74	TANNOY	**TUDOR AUTOGRAPH**	1,152	**852**	732	612
SPKR	68	TANNOY	**WINDSOR GRF**	1,817	**1,344**	1,154	965

TATAY

TYPE	YR	MFG	MODEL	SELL EXC	SELL AVG	BUY EXC	BUY AVG
GUITAR (ACOUSTIC)	70	TATAY	**7R**	5,156	**3,813**	3,276	2,739
GUITAR	47	TATAY	**VINCENTE** SPRUCE, MAHOGANY BACK/SIDES	1,874	**1,428**	1,213	928
STEEL GUITAR	70	TATAY	**7R CLASSICAL** ROSEWOOD, SPRUCE	6,015	**4,448**	3,822	3,195

TEISCO DEL RAY

TYPE	YR	MFG	MODEL	SELL EXC	SELL AVG	BUY EXC	BUY AVG
ELEC. GUITAR	60	TEISCO	**EG-27** SUNBURST, 2 PU's	193	**143**	123	103
ELGUIT	66	TEISCO	**EP-200B BASS** SEMI-HOLLOW	159	**117**	101	84
ELGUIT	64	TEISCO	**KL-4**	176	**130**	112	93
ELGUIT	67	TEISCO	**SPECTRUM II** 2 PU's	266	**197**	169	141
ELGUIT	66	TEISCO	**SPECTRUM V** CANDY APPLE RED	287	**212**	182	152
ELGUIT	67	TEISCO	**SPECTRUM V** METALLIC BLUE	276	**204**	175	146

	TYPE	YR	MFG	MODEL	SELL EXC	SELL AVG	BUY EXC	BUY AVG
				PRICES--BASED ON 100% ORIGINAL				

TELEFUNKEN BY NEUMANN

	TYPE	YR	MFG	MODEL	SELL EXC	SELL AVG	BUY EXC	BUY AVG
MIC		65	TELE	**ELAM 250** TUBE BY AKG	14,701	**10,872**	9,341	7,810

TRAVIS BEAN

	TYPE	YR	MFG	MODEL	SELL EXC	SELL AVG	BUY EXC	BUY AVG
ELEC. GUITAR		78	TRAVIS	**TB- 500** BLACK	637	**471**	405	338
	ELGUIT	74	TRAVIS	**TB-1000** NATURAL, KOA BODY, 2 PU's	876	**648**	556	465
	ELGUIT	78	TRAVIS	**TB-1000S** WHITE, 2 PU's	996	**736**	633	529
	ELGUIT	77	TRAVIS	**TB-2000 BASS** NATURAL, ALUMINUM NECK	737	**545**	468	391
	ELGUIT	77	TRAVIS	**TB-3000 WEDGE** PEARL RED	1,076	**795**	683	571
	ELGUIT	76	TRAVIS	**TB-4000 WEDGE BASS** PEARL RED	1,035	**766**	658	550
	ELGUIT	78	TRAVIS	**WEDGE BASS** WHITE, 2 PU's	1,992	**1,473**	1,265	1,058

UNIVOX

	TYPE	YR	MFG	MODEL	SELL EXC	SELL AVG	BUY EXC	BUY AVG
ELEC. GUITAR		68	UNIVOX	**MOSRITE COPY**	168	**124**	106	89
	ELGUIT	74	UNIVOX	**STATOCASTER COPY** WHITE, 3 HB PU's	144	**106**	91	76
GUITAR AMP		76	UNIVOX	**U-130B BASS**	77	**57**	49	41
	GTAMP	76	UNIVOX	**U-130L LEAD**	96	**71**	61	51
	GTAMP	65	UNIVOX	**U-305R** SINGLE JENSEN	120	**88**	76	63

VALCO

	TYPE	YR	MFG	MODEL	SELL EXC	SELL AVG	BUY EXC	BUY AVG
ELEC. GUITAR		60	VALCO	**AIRLINE** SUNBURST, 2 PU's, F-HOLE	336	**248**	213	178
	ELGUIT	60	VALCO	**AIRLINE** BLACK, 6-STRING	424	**313**	269	225
	ELGUIT	61	VALCO	**AIRLINE** CANDY APPLE RED, WOOD BODY	300	**222**	190	159
	ELGUIT	61	VALCO	**AIRLINE** SUNBURST, DOUBLE CUTAWAY, 1 PU	399	**295**	253	212
	ELGUIT	62	VALCO	**AIRLINE** SUNBURST, 1 PU	399	**295**	253	212
	ELGUIT	62	VALCO	**AIRLINE** BLACK RESOGLASS, RESONATOR	484	**358**	308	257
	ELGUIT	62	VALCO	**AIRLINE** RED RESOGLASS, 2 PU's, VIBRATO	499	**369**	317	265
	ELGUIT	63	VALCO	**AIRLINE** RED & BLACK SUNBURST, 2 PU's	485	**359**	308	258
	ELGUIT	64	VALCO	**AIRLINE** CHERRY RED, 3 PU's	467	**345**	297	248
	ELGUIT	64	VALCO	**AIRLINE** BLACK RES-O-GLA, 2 SOUNDHOLES	494	**365**	314	262
	ELGUIT	65	VALCO	**AIRLINE** RESOGLASS, SINGLE CUTAWAY, 2 PU's	518	**383**	329	275
	ELGUIT	66	VALCO	**AIRLINE** RED RESOGLASS, 2 PU's	499	**369**	317	265
	ELGUIT	60	VALCO	**CUSTOM KRAFT** RED, 1 PU	237	**175**	150	125
	ELGUIT	57	VALCO	**DUAL-TONE** WHITE	432	**319**	274	229
	ELGUIT	64	VALCO	**SUPRO GOLD** 2 PU's	232	**171**	147	123
	ELGUIT	55	VALCO	**TONEMASTER** YELLOW, ENGLISH ELECTRIC	288	**213**	183	153
	ELGUIT	62	VALCO	**TONEMASTER** BLACK RESOGLASS	219	**162**	139	116
GUITAR AMP		59	VALCO	**AIRLINE 67** 2 CHANNEL, 12" JENSEN	288	**213**	183	153
	GTAMP	48	VALCO	**FULL-TONE** TWEED, TUBE 6x6"	312	**230**	198	165
	GTAMP	40	VALCO	**SUPRO** GREY CABINET	225	**166**	143	119
	GTAMP	66	VALCO	**SUPRO 1606** GREY, 8" JENSEN	216	**159**	137	114
	GTAMP	63	VALCO	**VALCO** TWEED, 1x10", 6 WATT	192	**142**	122	102
GUITAR (ACOUSTIC)		65	VALCO	**AIRLINE AUTO HARP by OSCAR SCHMIDT**	192	**142**	122	102
	GUITAR	66	VALCO	**AIRLINE AUTO HARP by OSCAR SCHMIDT**	182	**134**	115	96
	GUITAR	67	VALCO	**AIRLINE AUTO HARP by OSCAR SCHMIDT**	168	**124**	106	89
STEEL GUITAR		50	VALCO	**AIRLINE STUDENT** 6-STRING	192	**142**	122	102
	STGUIT	64	VALCO	**ROCKET** 6-STRING	432	**319**	274	229

TYPE	YR	MFG	PRICES--BASED ON 100% ORIGINAL MODEL	SELL EXC	SELL AVG	BUY EXC	BUY AVG
			VEGA				
BANJO	26	VEGA	**ARTIST** TENOR	1,216	**899**	772	646
BANJO	27	VEGA	**ARTIST** TENOR	1,195	**883**	759	634
BANJO	27	VEGA	**ARTIST** PLECTRUM, INDIVIDUAL FLANGES	1,868	**1,381**	1,187	992
BANJO	29	VEGA	**ARTIST** TENOR, INDIVIDUAL FLANGES	1,097	**811**	697	582
BANJO	14	VEGA	**CUSTOM 9** ABALONE INLAY	5,760	**4,260**	3,660	3,060
BANJO	24	VEGA	**DELUXE** PLECTRUM	5,167	**3,821**	3,283	2,745
BANJO	26	VEGA	**DELUXE** TENOR, CURLY MAPLE, RESONATOR	3,600	**2,662**	2,287	1,912
BANJO	30	VEGA	**DELUXE** PLECTRUM	2,969	**2,196**	1,886	1,577
BANJO	32	VEGA	**DELUXE** PLECTRUM	2,390	**1,767**	1,518	1,269
BANJO	24	VEGA	**DELUXE TUBAPHONE** PLECTRUM	3,696	**2,734**	2,349	1,964
BANJO	65	VEGA	**EARL SCRUGGS MODEL**	1,244	**920**	790	660
BANJO	36	VEGA	**ELECTRIC** TENOR, BLACK, HUMBUCKING HORSESHOE PU	1,589	**1,175**	1,010	844
BANJO	17	VEGA	**FAIRBANKS 2 SPECIAL**	1,161	**859**	738	617
BANJO	14	VEGA	**FAIRBANKS 2 TUBAPHONE** 5-STRING, OPEN BACK	1,394	**1,031**	886	741
BANJO	10	VEGA	**FAIRBANKS 3 TUBAPHONE** FLOWERPOT	2,191	**1,620**	1,392	1,164
BANJO	24	VEGA	**FAIRBANKS 3 TUBAPHONE** 5-STRING	1,373	**1,016**	872	729
BANJO	30	VEGA	**FAIRBANKS 3 TUBAPHONE**	1,195	**883**	759	634
BANJO	22	VEGA	**FAIRBANKS 9 TUBAPHONE** 5-STRING, ELABORATE ENGRVD INLAY, CARVED HEEL,11.5"HEAD	4,517	**3,341**	2,870	2,400
BANJO	23	VEGA	**FAIRBANKS 9 TUBAPHONE** CARVED HEEL	4,251	**3,144**	2,701	2,258
BANJO	09	VEGA	**FAIRBANKS ELEC "O" POT** 5-STRING	1,017	**752**	646	540
BANJO	14	VEGA	**FAIRBANKS IMPERIAL ELECTRIC**	1,235	**913**	785	656
BANJO	20	VEGA	**FAIRBANKS LITTLE WONDER** BANJO/MANDOLIN, OPEN BACK	288	**213**	183	153
BANJO	03	VEGA	**FAIRBANKS REGENT**	996	**736**	633	529
BANJO	14	VEGA	**FAIRBANKS REGENT**	979	**724**	622	520
BANJO	15	VEGA	**FAIRBANKS REGENT**	837	**619**	531	444
BANJO	19	VEGA	**FAIRBANKS REGENT**	617	**456**	392	327
BANJO	11	VEGA	**FAIRBANKS SENATOR**	741	**548**	470	393
BANJO	27	VEGA	**FAIRBANKS SENATOR**	616	**455**	391	327
BANJO	29	VEGA	**FAIRBANKS SENATOR**	592	**438**	376	314
BANJO	31	VEGA	**FAIRBANKS SENATOR**	844	**624**	536	448
BANJO	09	VEGA	**FAIRBANKS SENATOR 1**	598	**442**	380	317
BANJO	22	VEGA	**FAIRBANKS STYLE X 9** CRVD HEEL,11 13/16"HD,17-FRET CLEAR OF RIM,4-FRET EXTENSION	1,229	**909**	781	653
BANJO	23	VEGA	**FAIRBANKS STYLE X 9**	1,222	**903**	776	649
BANJO	19	VEGA	**FAIRBANKS TUBAPHONE STYLE M**	1,161	**859**	738	617
BANJO	22	VEGA	**FAIRBANKS TUBAPHONE STYLE M** TENOR	1,170	**865**	743	621
BANJO	65	VEGA	**FOLK RANGER** OPEN BACK	422	**312**	268	224
BANJO	68	VEGA	**FOLK RANGER** OPEN BACK	463	**342**	294	246
BANJO	62	VEGA	**FOLK RANGER FR-5** OPEN BACK	479	**354**	304	254
BANJO	63	VEGA	**FOLK WONDER FW-5**	367	**280**	238	182
BANJO	65	VEGA	**FOLKLORE** SUNBURST, 5-STRING, LONG NECK	537	**397**	341	285
BANJO	67	VEGA	**FOLKLORE SS-5**	577	**427**	367	307
BANJO	22	VEGA	**IMPERIAL ELECTRIC**	996	**736**	633	529
BANJO	24	VEGA	**IMPERIAL ELECTRIC** 5-STRING, OPEN BACK	873	**646**	555	464
BANJO	14	VEGA	**LITTLE WONDER** TENOR	430	**318**	273	228
BANJO	19	VEGA	**LITTLE WONDER** TENOR	467	**345**	297	248
BANJO	21	VEGA	**LITTLE WONDER** TENOR, OPEN BACK	478	**353**	303	253
BANJO	22	VEGA	**LITTLE WONDER** TENOR	397	**293**	252	211
BANJO	23	VEGA	**LITTLE WONDER** TENOR, OPEN BACK, 11 13/16" HEAD	391	**289**	248	208

TYPE	YR	MFG	PRICES--BASED ON 100% ORIGINAL MODEL	SELL EXC	SELL AVG	BUY EXC	BUY AVG
BANJO	24	VEGA	**LITTLE WONDER** TENOR	403	**298**	256	214
BANJO	25	VEGA	**LITTLE WONDER** TENOR	475	**351**	301	252
BANJO	26	VEGA	**LITTLE WONDER** TENOR, 17-FRET	452	**334**	287	240
BANJO	30	VEGA	**LITTLE WONDER** TENOR	446	**330**	283	237
BANJO	31	VEGA	**LITTLE WONDER** TENOR	441	**326**	280	234
BANJO	50	VEGA	**LITTLE WONDER** TENOR, SUNBURST	360	**266**	228	191
BANJO	58	VEGA	**LITTLE WONDER** TENOR	336	**248**	213	178
BANJO	65	VEGA	**LITTLE WONDER** TENOR	325	**240**	206	172
BANJO	27	VEGA	**LITTLE WONDER BANJO-GUITAR** TENOR	434	**321**	276	231
BANJO	19	VEGA	**LITTLE WONDER BANJO-MANDOLIN** TENOR	408	**301**	259	216
BANJO	23	VEGA	**LITTLE WONDER BANJO-MANDOLIN** TENOR	394	**291**	250	209
BANJO	32	VEGA	**MODERNE** TENOR	1,394	**1,031**	886	741
BANJO	63	VEGA	**PETE SEEGER** 5-STRING, LONG NECK	3,340	**2,470**	2,122	1,774
BANJO	64	VEGA	**PETE SEEGER** 5-STRING	2,255	**1,667**	1,432	1,197
BANJO	65	VEGA	**PETE SEEGER** 5-STRING, LONG NECK	2,103	**1,555**	1,336	1,117
BANJO	66	VEGA	**PETE SEEGER** 5-STRING, LONG NECK	3,360	**2,485**	2,135	1,785
BANJO	69	VEGA	**PETE SEEGER** 5-STRING, LONG NECK	1,455	**1,076**	924	773
BANJO	67	VEGA	**PRO II** PLECTRUM	578	**428**	367	307
BANJO	69	VEGA	**PRO II** PLECTRUM	615	**455**	391	326
BANJO	25	VEGA	**PROFESSIONAL** TENOR	598	**442**	380	317
BANJO	26	VEGA	**PROFESSIONAL** TENOR	575	**425**	365	305
BANJO	28	VEGA	**PROFESSIONAL** TENOR	557	**412**	354	296
BANJO	29	VEGA	**PROFESSIONAL** PLECTRUM	996	**736**	633	529
BANJO	30	VEGA	**PROFESSIONAL** PLECTRUM	956	**707**	607	507
BANJO	31	VEGA	**PROFESSIONAL** TENOR	563	**416**	358	299
BANJO	09	VEGA	**REGENT** 5-STRING, OPEN BACK	1,640	**1,213**	1,042	871
BANJO	12	VEGA	**REGENT** 5-STRING, OPEN BACK	1,572	**1,162**	999	835
BANJO	16	VEGA	**REGENT** 5-STRING, OPEN BACK	1,512	**1,118**	960	803
BANJO	25	VEGA	**REGENT** 5-STRING, OPEN BACK	1,689	**1,249**	1,073	897
BANJO	27	VEGA	**REGENT** 5-STRING, OPEN BACK	1,310	**969**	832	696
BANJO	28	VEGA	**SOLOIST** TENOR	1,040	**769**	661	552
BANJO	29	VEGA	**SOLOIST** TENOR, RESONATOR	1,218	**900**	774	647
BANJO	30	VEGA	**SOLOIST** TENOR, GOLD, 15/16" HEAD, 19 FRETS	848	**627**	539	450
BANJO	21	VEGA	**STYLE 2 SPECIAL** OPEN BACK	621	**459**	394	329
BANJO	21	VEGA	**STYLE 3 TUBAPHONE** PLECTRUM	1,522	**1,160**	986	754
BANJO	26	VEGA	**STYLE 3 TUBAPHONE** PLECTRUM	1,111	**822**	706	590
BANJO	28	VEGA	**STYLE 3 TUBAPHONE** PLECTRUM	876	**648**	556	465
BANJO	30	VEGA	**STYLE 3 TUBAPHONE** PLECTRUM	813	**601**	516	431
BANJO	23	VEGA	**STYLE 9 TUBAPHONE** PLECTRUM	3,902	**2,886**	2,479	2,073
BANJO	12	VEGA	**STYLE 40** TENOR	457	**338**	290	243
BANJO	23	VEGA	**STYLE F** TENOR	615	**455**	391	326
BANJO	26	VEGA	**STYLE F** TENOR	609	**450**	387	323

TYPE	YR	MFG	PRICES--BASED ON 100% ORIGINAL MODEL	SELL EXC	SELL AVG	BUY EXC	BUY AVG
BANJO	30	VEGA	**STYLE F** TENOR, RESONATOR	593	**438**	376	315
BANJO	31	VEGA	**STYLE F** TENOR	577	**427**	367	307
BANJO	19	VEGA	**STYLE K MANDOLIN-BANJO**	676	**500**	430	359
BANJO	22	VEGA	**STYLE K MANDOLIN-BANJO**	564	**417**	358	299
BANJO	24	VEGA	**STYLE K MANDOLIN-BANJO**	598	**442**	380	317
BANJO	30	VEGA	**STYLE K MANDOLIN-BANJO**	584	**432**	371	310
BANJO	17	VEGA	**STYLE L MANDOLIN-BANJO**	1,114	**824**	708	592
BANJO	20	VEGA	**STYLE M** TENOR	654	**484**	416	347
BANJO	26	VEGA	**STYLE M** TENOR	472	**360**	306	233
BANJO	26	VEGA	**STYLE M** 5-STRING	598	**442**	380	317
BANJO	28	VEGA	**STYLE M** 5-STRING	877	**648**	557	466
BANJO	13	VEGA	**STYLE N** TENOR	487	**360**	309	259
BANJO	14	VEGA	**STYLE N** TENOR	478	**353**	303	253
BANJO	22	VEGA	**STYLE N** TENOR	561	**415**	356	298
BANJO	23	VEGA	**STYLE N** TENOR	557	**412**	354	296
BANJO	24	VEGA	**STYLE N** TENOR	554	**410**	352	294
BANJO	27	VEGA	**STYLE N** TENOR	422	**312**	268	224
BANJO	28	VEGA	**STYLE N** TENOR	448	**331**	284	238
BANJO	21	VEGA	**STYLE R** TENOR	693	**512**	440	368
BANJO	24	VEGA	**STYLE R** TENOR	656	**485**	417	348
BANJO	22	VEGA	**STYLE X 9** TENOR	1,191	**881**	757	632
BANJO	23	VEGA	**STYLE X 9** TENOR	1,108	**820**	704	589
BANJO	26	VEGA	**STYLE X 9** TENOR	1,006	**744**	639	534
BANJO	30	VEGA	**STYLE X 9** TENOR	920	**680**	584	489
BANJO	31	VEGA	**SUPER PARAMOUNT ARTIST** TENOR, PROFESSIONAL	4,320	**3,195**	2,745	2,295
BANJO	27	VEGA	**TUBAPHONE** 4-STRING	935	**691**	594	496
BANJO	10	VEGA	**TUBAPHONE 3**	3,471	**2,567**	2,205	1,844
BANJO	16	VEGA	**TUBAPHONE 3**	3,640	**2,692**	2,313	1,933
BANJO	21	VEGA	**TUBAPHONE 3**	3,535	**2,614**	2,246	1,878
BANJO	23	VEGA	**TUBAPHONE 3**	3,478	**2,572**	2,210	1,847
BANJO	25	VEGA	**TUBAPHONE 3**	3,360	**2,485**	2,135	1,785
BANJO	26	VEGA	**TUBAPHONE 3**	2,973	**2,198**	1,889	1,579
BANJO	30	VEGA	**TUBAPHONE 3** 5-STRING	1,976	**1,461**	1,255	1,050
BANJO	23	VEGA	**TUBAPHONE 9**	3,360	**2,485**	2,135	1,785
BANJO	25	VEGA	**TUBAPHONE 9** PLECTRUM, OPEN BACK, SERIAL #65708	3,122	**2,309**	1,984	1,659
BANJO	26	VEGA	**TUBAPHONE 9** CARVED HEEL	5,760	**4,260**	3,660	3,060
BANJO	11	VEGA	**TUBAPHONE BANJARINE** 21" SCALE	1,545	**1,143**	982	821
BANJO	29	VEGA	**TUBAPHONE GUITAR-BANJO**	796	**589**	506	423
BANJO	12	VEGA	**TUBAPHONE MANDOLIN-BANJO**	1,539	**1,138**	978	818
BANJO	10	VEGA	**TUBAPHONE STYLE M** TENOR	1,399	**1,035**	889	743
BANJO	17	VEGA	**TUBAPHONE STYLE M** TENOR	1,289	**953**	819	684
BANJO	19	VEGA	**TUBAPHONE STYLE M**	713	**527**	453	378
BANJO	21	VEGA	**TUBAPHONE STYLE M** TENOR, NATURAL	959	**709**	609	509
BANJO	23	VEGA	**TUBAPHONE STYLE M** 11-3/4" HEAD	936	**692**	594	497
BANJO	24	VEGA	**TUBAPHONE STYLE M** TENOR	937	**693**	595	498
BANJO	27	VEGA	**VEGAPHONE** TENOR	748	**553**	475	397
BANJO	30	VEGA	**VEGAPHONE** TENOR	751	**555**	477	399
BANJO	30	VEGA	**VEGAPHONE DELUXE** TENOR, 4-PC FLNGE,STAR INLD BK RESONATOR/ENGRVD IVRY SIDES	4,260	**3,150**	2,707	2,263

TYPE	YR	MFG	MODEL	SELL EXC	SELL AVG	BUY EXC	BUY AVG
			PRICES--BASED ON 100% ORIGINAL				
BANJO	29	VEGA	**VEGAPHONE PROFESSIONAL** TENOR, RESONATOR	585	**433**	372	311
BANJO	30	VEGA	**VEGAPHONE PROFESSIONAL** PLECTRUM	558	**413**	355	296
BANJO	29	VEGA	**VEGAVOX** TENOR	936	**692**	594	497
BANJO	30	VEGA	**VEGAVOX I** TENOR	2,153	**1,592**	1,368	1,143
BANJO	31	VEGA	**VEGAVOX I** PLECTRUM	1,716	**1,269**	1,090	911
BANJO	36	VEGA	**VEGAVOX I** TENOR	4,089	**3,024**	2,598	2,172
BANJO	56	VEGA	**VEGAVOX I** PLECTRUM	1,404	**1,038**	892	746
BANJO	62	VEGA	**VEGAVOX I** PLECTRUM	999	**739**	635	530
BANJO	65	VEGA	**VEGAVOX I** TENOR	938	**694**	596	498
BANJO	67	VEGA	**VEGAVOX I** TENOR	930	**687**	591	494
BANJO	68	VEGA	**VEGAVOX I** TENOR	924	**683**	587	491
BANJO	31	VEGA	**VEGAVOX II** TENOR	1,056	**781**	671	561
BANJO	59	VEGA	**VEGAVOX III** TENOR	1,200	**888**	763	638
BANJO	70	VEGA	**VEGAVOX III** TENOR	956	**707**	607	507
BANJO	31	VEGA	**VEGAVOX IV** PLECTRUM	4,176	**3,089**	2,654	2,219
BANJO	64	VEGA	**VEGAVOX IV** TENOR	1,520	**1,124**	966	807
BANJO	65	VEGA	**VEGAVOX IV** TENOR	1,645	**1,216**	1,045	874
BANJO	64	VEGA	**VEGAVOX IV DELUXE** TENOR	2,390	**1,767**	1,518	1,269
BANJO	01	VEGA	**WHYTE LAYDIE** 5-STRING	4,511	**3,336**	2,866	2,396
BANJO	09	VEGA	**WHYTE LAYDIE** 26" SCALE, SERIAL #25443	1,612	**1,192**	1,024	856
BANJO	19	VEGA	**WHYTE LAYDIE** 5-STRING	1,932	**1,429**	1,227	1,026
BANJO	20	VEGA	**WHYTE LAYDIE**	1,350	**998**	858	717
BANJO	31	VEGA	**WHYTE LAYDIE** 5-STRING	809	**598**	514	429
BANJO	03	VEGA	**WHYTE LAYDIE 2**	2,976	**2,201**	1,891	1,581
BANJO	06	VEGA	**WHYTE LAYDIE 2**	2,386	**1,765**	1,516	1,267
BANJO	08	VEGA	**WHYTE LAYDIE 2**	2,253	**1,666**	1,431	1,196
BANJO	10	VEGA	**WHYTE LAYDIE 2** 5-STRING	1,848	**1,367**	1,174	982
BANJO	11	VEGA	**WHYTE LAYDIE 2** OPEN BACK	1,385	**1,024**	880	735
BANJO	11	VEGA	**WHYTE LAYDIE 2** OPEN BACK	1,474	**1,090**	936	783
BANJO	21	VEGA	**WHYTE LAYDIE 2** 5-STRING	2,081	**1,539**	1,322	1,105
BANJO	22	VEGA	**WHYTE LAYDIE 2** PLECTRUM, 5-STRING, SERIAL #48215	1,578	**1,167**	1,002	838
BANJO	23	VEGA	**WHYTE LAYDIE 2** 5-STRING	1,990	**1,471**	1,264	1,057
BANJO	24	VEGA	**WHYTE LAYDIE 2** PLECTRUM	1,408	**1,041**	894	748
BANJO	24	VEGA	**WHYTE LAYDIE 2** 5-STRING	1,948	**1,441**	1,238	1,035
BANJO	26	VEGA	**WHYTE LAYDIE 2** 5-STRING	1,867	**1,380**	1,186	991
BANJO	26	VEGA	**WHYTE LAYDIE 2** FIBERSKYN HEAD, SERIAL #68755	3,542	**2,619**	2,250	1,881
BANJO	28	VEGA	**WHYTE LAYDIE 2** 5-STRING	1,824	**1,349**	1,159	969
BANJO	39	VEGA	**WHYTE LAYDIE 2** 5-STRING	1,621	**1,199**	1,030	861
BANJO	09	VEGA	**WHYTE LAYDIE 7**	7,680	**5,680**	4,880	4,080
BANJO	21	VEGA	**WHYTE LAYDIE 7** CARVED HEEL	6,789	**5,021**	4,313	3,606
BANJO	22	VEGA	**WHYTE LAYDIE 7**	6,720	**4,970**	4,270	3,570
BANJO	24	VEGA	**WHYTE LAYDIE 7** 5-STRING	7,200	**5,325**	4,575	3,825
BANJO	25	VEGA	**WHYTE LAYDIE 7** 5-STRING, 27" SCALE	6,606	**4,886**	4,198	3,509
BANJO	26	VEGA	**WHYTE LAYDIE 7** 5-STRING, OPEN BACK	6,427	**4,753**	4,083	3,414

TYPE	YR	MFG	PRICES--BASED ON 100% ORIGINAL MODEL	SELL EXC	SELL AVG	BUY EXC	BUY AVG
BANJO	27	VEGA	**WHYTE LAYDIE 7** 5-STRING, OPEN BACK	6,315	**4,671**	4,013	3,355
BANJO	21	VEGA	**WHYTE LAYDIE GUITAR-BANJO**	1,032	**763**	655	548
BANJO	16	VEGA	**WHYTE LAYDIE STYLE R** 5-STRING	1,461	**1,080**	928	776
BANJO	18	VEGA	**WHYTE LAYDIE STYLE R** 5-STRING	1,262	**933**	802	670
BANJO	22	VEGA	**WHYTE LAYDIE STYLE R** TENOR	480	**355**	305	255
BANJO	23	VEGA	**WHYTE LAYDIE STYLE R** TENOR	657	**486**	417	349
BANJO	26	VEGA	**WHYTE LAYDIE STYLE R** TENOR	565	**418**	359	300
BANJO	30	VEGA	**WHYTE LAYDIE STYLE R** TENOR	596	**440**	378	316
ELEC. GUITAR	45	VEGA	**COMMANDER** BLACK & WHITE, 6-STRING	239	**176**	151	126
GUITAR (ACOUSTIC)	40	VEGA	**C-26**	426	**315**	270	226
GUITAR	40	VEGA	**C-56** SUNBURST	796	**589**	506	423
GUITAR	35	VEGA	**C-60**	415	**307**	264	220
GUITAR	37	VEGA	**C-66**	287	**212**	182	152
GUITAR	39	VEGA	**C-66** BLOND, ARCHTOP	280	**207**	178	148
GUITAR	38	VEGA	**C-70** FANCY PEGHEAD AND INLAY	541	**400**	344	287
GUITAR	40	VEGA	**C-80**	596	**440**	378	316
GUITAR	50	VEGA	**DUO-TRON** SUNBURST, FULL BODY, 1 PU	326	**241**	207	173
GUITAR	64	VEGA	**FT-J** MAHOGANY BACK/SIDES	743	**549**	472	394
GUITAR	20	VEGA	**LUTE** TENOR, 2 POINT BODY SHAPE	434	**321**	276	231
GUITAR	53	VEGA	**R-26** SUNBURST, NON-CUTAWAY	598	**442**	380	317
GUITAR	20	VEGA	**VEGA 12-F** BRAZILIAN ROSEWOOD BACK/SIDES, WHITE TRIM, 13 5/8" WIDE	1,408	**1,041**	894	748
MANDOLIN	00	VEGA	**1900 BOWL BACK** ABALONE SOUNDHOLE	937	**693**	595	498
MANDOL	31	VEGA	**PROFESSIONAL MANDOLIN-BANJO** FLAME	737	**545**	468	391
MANDOL	16	VEGA	**STYLE K MANDOLIN-BANJO**	480	**355**	305	255
MANDOL	22	VEGA	**STYLE K MANDOLIN-BANJO**	478	**353**	303	253
MANDOL	26	VEGA	**STYLE K MANDOLIN-BANJO**	379	**280**	240	201
MANDOL	30	VEGA	**STYLE K MANDOLIN-BANJO**	336	**248**	213	178
MANDOL	21	VEGA	**STYLE L MANDOLIN-BANJO**	438	**324**	278	233
MANDOL	24	VEGA	**STYLE L MANDOLIN-BANJO**	480	**355**	305	255
MANDOL	13	VEGA	**STYLE X TUBAPHONE MANDOLIN-BANJO**	677	**501**	430	360
STEEL GUITAR	48	VEGA	**DOUBLE 8 STEEL** NATURAL, MAHOGANY	527	**389**	334	279
STGUIT	30	VEGA	**LAP STEEL**	240	**177**	152	127
STGUIT	49	VEGA	**LAP STEEL**	216	**159**	137	114
UKULELE	50	VEGA	**ARTHUR GODFREY** BARITONE	264	**195**	167	140
UKE	55	VEGA	**ARTHUR GODFREY** BARITONE	301	**222**	191	160
UKE	60	VEGA	**ARTHUR GODFREY** BARITONE	236	**174**	150	125

VEILLETTE-CITRON

TYPE	YR	MFG	MODEL	SELL EXC	SELL AVG	BUY EXC	BUY AVG
ELEC. GUITAR	77	VEILL	**ELECTRIC 12-STRING** BLUE-BLACK	1,693	**1,252**	1,076	899
ELGUIT	78	VEILL	**ELECTRIC BASS** TIGER STRIPED MAPLE, GOLD HARDWARE, TRIPLE IMPEDENCE PU's	1,554	**1,149**	987	825
ELGUIT	78	VEILL	**STANDARD BASS** TIGER-STRIPED MAPLE	1,195	**883**	759	634

VILLER & NELSON

TYPE	YR	MFG	MODEL	SELL EXC	SELL AVG	BUY EXC	BUY AVG
ELEC. GUITAR	55	VILLER	**EXCEL** MAPLE BACK/SIDES, 16", 1 PU	956	**707**	607	507

VIVI-TONE

TYPE	YR	MFG	MODEL	SELL EXC	SELL AVG	BUY EXC	BUY AVG
ELEC. GUITAR	35	VIVI-TONE	**ELECTRIC SOLID**	1,216	**899**	772	646
GUITAR (ACOUSTIC)	35	VIVI-TONE	**ACOUSTIC (LOAR)**	2,178	**1,660**	1,411	1,079
GUITAR	34	VIVI-TONE	**LOAR ARCHTOP SIGNED LABEL**	7,680	**5,680**	4,880	4,080
GUITAR	35	VIVI-TONE	**PARLOR SIZE B. JOSEPH SIGNED LABEL**	1,474	**1,090**	936	783

VOX AMPLIFICATION

TYPE	YR	MFG	MODEL	SELL EXC	SELL AVG	BUY EXC	BUY AVG
EFFECTS	67	VOX	**CLYCE MCCOY** WAH-WAH PEDAL, NON PICTURE FACE	429	**317**	272	227
EFFECTS	65	VOX	**CLYDE MCCOY** WAH-WAH PEDAL	533	**394**	339	283

TYPE	YR	MFG	PRICES--BASED ON 100% ORIGINAL MODEL	SELL EXC	SELL AVG	BUY EXC	BUY AVG
EFFECTS	67	VOX	**ECHO REVERB UNIT** SOLID STATE	384	**284**	244	204
EFFECTS	67	VOX	**V-807 ECHO-REVERB**	480	**355**	305	255
EFFECTS	66	VOX	**V-828 TONE BENDER** GREY, FUZZ	240	**177**	152	127
EFFECTS	67	VOX	**V-837 ECHO DELUXE** TAPE ECHO	216	**159**	137	114
EFFECTS	68	VOX	**V-846 WAH**	336	**248**	213	178
EFFECTS	63	VOX	**VOLUME PEDAL**	109	**80**	69	58
GUITAR AMP	68	VOX	**1x18" BASS CABINET**	403	**298**	256	214
GTAMP	63	VOX	**1x18" FOUNDATION CABINET**	567	**432**	367	280
GTAMP	63	VOX	**2x12" EXTENSION CABINET**	757	**560**	481	402
GTAMP	69	VOX	**75 WATT** PLEXI	796	**589**	506	423
GTAMP	70	VOX	**75 WATT** STEEL FRONT	1,928	**1,426**	1,225	1,024
GTAMP	68	VOX	**6120** 100 WATTS, REVERB, HEAD, HYBRED	1,195	**883**	759	634
GTAMP	68	VOX	**7120 BASS** 100 WATTS, HEAD, HYBRED	1,186	**877**	753	630
GTAMP	68	VOX	**9120 BASS** 200 WATTS, HEAD, HYBRED	1,215	**898**	772	645
GTAMP	62	VOX	**AC- 4**	324	**239**	206	172
GTAMP	63	VOX	**AC- 4**	300	**222**	190	159
GTAMP	64	VOX	**AC- 4** BLACK, 1x8"	288	**213**	183	153
GTAMP	62	VOX	**AC- 4 COMBO** SMOOTH GREY VINYL	319	**236**	203	169
GTAMP	61	VOX	**AC- 10** TAN	796	**589**	506	423
GTAMP	66	VOX	**AC- 10**	757	**560**	481	402
GTAMP	64	VOX	**AC- 10 HEAD** 2x10" CABINET	1,433	**1,060**	910	761
GTAMP	59	VOX	**AC- 10 TWIN** WHITE TV, 2x10"	938	**694**	596	498
GTAMP	64	VOX	**AC- 10 TWIN**	757	**560**	481	402
GTAMP	65	VOX	**AC- 10VG**	663	**490**	421	352
GTAMP	58	VOX	**AC- 15** WHITE, BLACK PANEL, TV FRONT	3,153	**2,332**	2,003	1,675
GTAMP	62	VOX	**AC- 15** RED PANEL, 2x10", SERIAL #2820	757	**560**	481	402
GTAMP	63	VOX	**AC- 15** BROWN GRILL, GRAY TOLEX, 1x12"	1,294	**957**	822	687
GTAMP	64	VOX	**AC- 15** BLACK, 1x12"	642	**474**	408	341
GTAMP	64	VOX	**AC- 15 BASS** BLACK, GRAY PANEL, 1x15"	704	**521**	447	374
GTAMP	62	VOX	**AC- 15 COMBO** BEIGE, RED PANEL	806	**596**	512	428
GTAMP	64	VOX	**AC- 15 TWIN** BLACK STAND, 2x12"	891	**659**	566	473
GTAMP	66	VOX	**AC- 15 TWIN** 12x12"	803	**594**	510	426
GTAMP	67	VOX	**AC- 15 TWIN COMBO** 2x12"	1,780	**1,317**	1,131	946
GTAMP	60	VOX	**AC- 30**	2,985	**2,208**	1,897	1,586
GTAMP	62	VOX	**AC- 30** RED PANEL, 2x12", SERIAL #4261	1,522	**1,126**	967	808
GTAMP	62	VOX	**AC- 30** GRAY PANEL, 2x12", SERIAL #4077	1,676	**1,239**	1,065	890
GTAMP	62	VOX	**AC- 30** FAWN	3,915	**2,896**	2,488	2,080
GTAMP	63	VOX	**AC- 30** BLACK, 2x12" SPEAKERS	977	**722**	620	519
GTAMP	63	VOX	**AC- 30** GRAY TOLEX	1,315	**972**	835	698
GTAMP	64	VOX	**AC- 30**	1,635	**1,209**	1,039	869
GTAMP	65	VOX	**AC- 30** GRAY PANEL, TOP BOOST	1,992	**1,473**	1,265	1,058
GTAMP	66	VOX	**AC- 30** TOP BOOST	1,783	**1,319**	1,133	947
GTAMP	67	VOX	**AC- 30** SILVER, TOP BOOST	1,593	**1,178**	1,012	846
GTAMP	68	VOX	**AC- 30**	1,474	**1,090**	936	783
GTAMP	60	VOX	**AC- 30 COMBO** RED PANEL, SERIAL #0001-4561	1,125	**832**	714	597
GTAMP	61	VOX	**AC- 30 COMBO** BEIGE, RED PANEL, 2x12"	2,365	**1,749**	1,503	1,256
GTAMP	62	VOX	**AC- 30 COMBO** RED PANEL, SERIAL #0001-4561	1,125	**832**	714	597
GTAMP	62	VOX	**AC- 30 COMBO** BEIGE, TOP BOOST	2,153	**1,592**	1,368	1,143

TYPE	YR	MFG	PRICES--BASED ON 100% ORIGINAL MODEL	SELL EXC	SELL AVG	BUY EXC	BUY AVG
GTAMP	63	VOX	AC- 30 COMBO BLACK, TOP BOOST, FACTORY, SERIAL #4406-4600	1,408	**1,041**	894	748
GTAMP	64	VOX	AC- 30 COMBO BLACK, BLACK PANEL, 2x12"	1,155	**854**	734	614
GTAMP	64	VOX	AC- 30 COMBO TOP BOOST, BULLDOG SPEAKERS, SERIAL #46000	1,268	**937**	805	673
GTAMP	65	VOX	AC- 30 COMBO BROWN GRILL	1,272	**940**	808	675
GTAMP	65	VOX	AC- 30 COMBO BLACK, TOP BOOST, FACTORY, 2x12", SERIAL #15770-16	1,274	**942**	810	677
GTAMP	67	VOX	AC- 30 COMBO SILVER	939	**695**	597	499
GTAMP	79	VOX	AC- 30 COMBO 2x12"	959	**709**	609	509
GTAMP	62	VOX	AC- 30 HEAD	967	**715**	614	514
GTAMP	63	VOX	AC- 30 HEAD BLACK TOLEX	956	**707**	607	507
GTAMP	64	VOX	AC- 30 HEAD BROWN GRILL, 2x12" CABINET	2,216	**1,639**	1,408	1,177
GTAMP	64	VOX	AC- 30 HEAD COPPER	2,389	**1,767**	1,518	1,269
GTAMP	65	VOX	AC- 30 HEAD GRAY, SQUARE BOX, JMI	1,125	**832**	714	597
GTAMP	63	VOX	AC- 30 TWIN BLACK, TOP BOOST, REVERB	1,408	**1,041**	894	748
GTAMP	64	VOX	AC- 30 TWIN TOP BOOST. SERIAL #46000	1,436	**1,062**	912	762
GTAMP	65	VOX	AC- 30 TWIN BLACK, TOP BOOST, 2x12"	1,356	**1,003**	861	720
GTAMP	66	VOX	AC- 30 TWIN	1,513	**1,119**	961	804
GTAMP	63	VOX	AC- 30HF BLACK, GRAY PANEL, 2x12" CELESTION	1,492	**1,104**	948	793
GTAMP	63	VOX	AC- 30HG BLACK, RED PANEL, 2x12"	1,521	**1,125**	966	808
GTAMP	64	VOX	AC- 50 BLACK, SERIAL #56001	982	**726**	624	521
GTAMP	65	VOX	AC- 50 BLACK, REVERB	977	**722**	620	519
GTAMP	65	VOX	AC- 50 BLACK, TOP BOOST	977	**722**	620	519
GTAMP	65	VOX	AC- 50 GRAY PANEL	1,195	**883**	759	634
GTAMP	60	VOX	AC- 50 HEAD JMI MODEL	799	**591**	508	424
GTAMP	64	VOX	AC- 50 HEAD	757	**560**	481	402
GTAMP	66	VOX	AC- 50 HEAD	747	**553**	475	397
GTAMP	70	VOX	AC- 50 HEAD VSL MODEL	248	**183**	157	132
GTAMP	63	VOX	AC- 50 TWIN BLACK, GRAY PANEL	1,133	**838**	720	602
GTAMP	64	VOX	AC- 50 TWIN BLACK, TOP BOOST, REV	937	**693**	595	498
GTAMP	65	VOX	AC- 50 TWIN BLACK, GRAY PANEL, 2x12"	1,535	**1,135**	975	815
GTAMP	63	VOX	AC-100 GRAY PANEL, 4x12", SERIAL #48574	1,101	**814**	699	584
GTAMP	64	VOX	AC-100 BLACK, BLACK PANEL, HEAD ONLY	956	**707**	607	507
GTAMP	64	VOX	AC-100 BLACK, REV, 4x12"	1,115	**825**	708	592
GTAMP	65	VOX	AC-100 BLACK, 4x12"	1,211	**896**	769	643
GTAMP	64	VOX	AC-100 TWIN REVERB, 4x12"	1,449	**1,072**	921	770
GTAMP	65	VOX	AC-100 TWIN BLACK, BLACK PANEL, 4x15"	1,195	**883**	759	634
GTAMP	66	VOX	CAMBRIDGE REVERB V102 TUBE, 18 WATT, 1x18"	514	**380**	326	273
GTAMP	67	VOX	CAMBRIDGE REVERB TRANSISTOR, 30 WATT, 2 CHANNEL	360	**266**	228	191
GTAMP	68	VOX	CAMBRIDGE REVERB	456	**337**	289	242
GTAMP	67	VOX	CONQUEROR HEAD	598	**442**	380	317
GTAMP	66	VOX	CONQUEROR TWIN 30 WATT, SOLID STATE, 2x12"	484	**358**	308	257
GTAMP	67	VOX	DEFIANT 50 WATT, SOLID STATE, 1 HORN, 2x12"	717	**530**	455	380
GTAMP	67	VOX	DEFIANT HEAD	384	**284**	244	204
GTAMP	66	VOX	DEFIANT TWIN 50 WATT, SOLID STATE, 2x12"	240	**177**	152	127
GTAMP	65	VOX	DOMINO GRAY/BLUE	696	**515**	442	370
GTAMP	66	VOX	DYNAMIC BASS 50 WATT, SOLID STATE, 1x15"	478	**353**	303	253

TYPE	YR	MFG	PRICES--BASED ON 100% ORIGINAL MODEL	SELL EXC	SELL AVG	BUY EXC	BUY AVG
GTAMP	63	VOX	**FOUNDATION BASS** COVER, 1x18"	578	**428**	367	307
GTAMP	64	VOX	**FOUNDATION BASS** BLACK COVER, 1x18"	539	**399**	342	286
GTAMP	64	VOX	**FOUNDATION BASS** 2x15"	656	**485**	417	348
GTAMP	65	VOX	**FOUNDATION BASS** BLACK COVER, 1x18"	373	**276**	237	198
GTAMP	67	VOX	**FOUNDATION CABINET**	408	**301**	259	216
GTAMP	68	VOX	**FOUNDATION HEAD**	438	**324**	278	233
GTAMP	62	VOX	**REVERB TANK** BEIGE	1,195	**883**	759	634
GTAMP	64	VOX	**REVERB UNIT** RICHARD MODEL	193	**143**	123	103
GTAMP	65	VOX	**REVERB UNIT** BLACK, ALL TUBE	1,035	**766**	658	550
GTAMP	67	VOX	**SCORPION V116** 60 WATT, SOLID STATE, REV, 4x10"	367	**271**	233	195
GTAMP	67	VOX	**SOVEREIGN BASS V117 TWIN** 60 WATT, 4x12"	439	**325**	279	233
GTAMP	64	VOX	**STUDENT** BLACK, 1x6" BULLDOG	216	**159**	137	114
GTAMP	64	VOX	**STUDENT** GRAY TOLEX, 1x6" BULLDOG	409	**303**	260	217
GTAMP	66	VOX	**SUPREME** 100 WATT, SOLID STATE, 4x12"	478	**353**	303	253
GTAMP	67	VOX	**SUPREME HEAD**	598	**442**	380	317
GTAMP	63	VOX	**T- 60** RED PANEL, STAND, SERIAL #1450	1,097	**811**	697	582
GTAMP	62	VOX	**T- 60 BASS** BLACK, RED PANEL, 2x12"	967	**715**	614	514
GTAMP	62	VOX	**T- 60 BASS** BEIGE, RED PANEL, STAND, SERIAL #00100-00500	1,073	**793**	681	570
GTAMP	63	VOX	**T- 60 BASS** BLACK, STAND, SERIAL #45265	1,017	**752**	646	540
GTAMP	64	VOX	**T- 60 BASS** BLACK	938	**694**	596	498
GTAMP	64	VOX	**T- 60 BASS** BLACK, GRAY PANEL, STAND	942	**697**	599	500
GTAMP	65	VOX	**T- 60 BASS** BLACK, BLACK PANEL, 1x12"	932	**689**	592	495
GTAMP	70	VOX	**TONE BENDER** BLACK	192	**142**	122	102
GTAMP	66	VOX	**TRAVELER** 20 WATT, SOLID STATE	339	**251**	215	180
GTAMP	68	VOX	**TREBLE-BASS** BOOSTER	168	**124**	106	89
GTAMP	70	VOX	**V-15 VSL** TUBE BOOST, COMBO, 2x10"	431	**318**	273	228

VOX/JMI, LTD

TYPE	YR	MFG	MODEL	SELL EXC	SELL AVG	BUY EXC	BUY AVG
ELEC. GUITAR	61	VOX/JMI	**ACE** RED, SOLID BODY, 2 PU's	313	**232**	199	166
ELGUIT	67	VOX/JMI	**ASTRO IV** SUNBURST, HOLLOW BODY	538	**398**	342	286
ELGUIT	61	VOX/JMI	**BASSMASTER** WHITE, SOLID BODY, 2 PU's, SERIAL #1B-000/1B-320	451	**333**	286	239
ELGUIT	63	VOX/JMI	**BOUZOUKI** SOLID BODY, 12-STRING, 3 PU's, TREM	703	**520**	447	373
ELGUIT	62	VOX/JMI	**CLUBMAN** RED, 2 PU's	337	**249**	214	179
ELGUIT	62	VOX/JMI	**CLUBMAN BASS** RED, 1 PU	409	**303**	260	217
ELGUIT	66	VOX/JMI	**CLUBMAN BASS** RED	384	**284**	244	204
ELGUIT	63	VOX/JMI	**CLUBMAN DELUXE** RED, 3 PU's	366	**271**	233	194
ELGUIT	62	VOX/JMI	**CONSORT** WHITE, SOLID BODY, 3 PU's	313	**232**	199	166
ELGUIT	66	VOX/JMI	**COUGAR 335** SUNBURST, 2 PU's	518	**383**	329	275
ELGUIT	60	VOX/JMI	**DELTA IV BASS**	419	**310**	266	222
ELGUIT	62	VOX/JMI	**FOLK 12** FLATTOP	384	**284**	244	204
ELGUIT	60	VOX/JMI	**HARLEM**	217	**161**	138	115
ELGUIT	70	VOX/JMI	**HAWK IV** CREAM	283	**209**	179	150
ELGUIT	70	VOX/JMI	**HAWK IV BASS** CREAM	451	**333**	286	239
ELGUIT	67	VOX/JMI	**INVADER** BUILT-IN EFFECTS	637	**471**	405	338
ELGUIT	60	VOX/JMI	**MANDO**	366	**271**	233	194
ELGUIT	60	VOX/JMI	**MARK IV BASS**	492	**364**	312	261

TYPE	YR	MFG	PRICES--BASED ON 100% ORIGINAL MODEL	SELL EXC	SELL AVG	BUY EXC	BUY AVG
ELGUIT	63	VOX/JMI	**MARK IV BASS**	510	**377**	324	271
ELGUIT	60	VOX/JMI	**MARK IX**	791	**585**	502	420
ELGUIT	62	VOX/JMI	**MARK IX**	747	**553**	475	397
ELGUIT	65	VOX/JMI	**MARK IX** BLACK, TEARDROP	681	**504**	433	362
ELGUIT	63	VOX/JMI	**MARK VI** TEARDROP	595	**440**	378	316
ELGUIT	64	VOX/JMI	**MARK VI** TEARDROP	658	**487**	418	349
ELGUIT	63	VOX/JMI	**MARK XII** TEARDROP, 12-STRING	764	**565**	485	405
ELGUIT	66	VOX/JMI	**MARK XII** TEARDROP, 12-STRING	850	**629**	540	451
ELGUIT	67	VOX/JMI	**MARK XII** TEARDROP, 12-STRING	625	**462**	397	332
ELGUIT	60	VOX/JMI	**METEOR**	336	**249**	214	179
ELGUIT	60	VOX/JMI	**NEW ORLEANS** HOLLOW BODY	342	**253**	217	182
ELGUIT	62	VOX/JMI	**PANTHER BASS** 1 PU	442	**327**	281	235
ELGUIT	65	VOX/JMI	**PANTHER BASS**	484	**358**	308	257
ELGUIT	68	VOX/JMI	**PANTHER BASS** SUNBURST	456	**337**	289	242
ELGUIT	68	VOX/JMI	**PHANTOM GEMINI BASS** WHITE	801	**592**	509	425
ELGUIT	65	VOX/JMI	**PHANTOM IV BASS**	815	**602**	517	432
ELGUIT	67	VOX/JMI	**PHANTOM IV BASS**	658	**487**	418	349
ELGUIT	62	VOX/JMI	**PHANTOM VI**	831	**614**	528	441
ELGUIT	65	VOX/JMI	**PHANTOM VI** WHITE	803	**594**	510	426
ELGUIT	63	VOX/JMI	**PHANTOM XII**	991	**733**	630	526
ELGUIT	65	VOX/JMI	**PHANTOM XII** BLACK, 12-STRING	671	**496**	426	356
ELGUIT	67	VOX/JMI	**PHANTOM XII** BLACK, 12-STRING	713	**527**	453	378
ELGUIT	68	VOX/JMI	**PHANTOM XII** WHITE, 12-STRING	716	**529**	455	380
ELGUIT	69	VOX/JMI	**PHANTOM XII** 12-STRING, SOLID BODY	663	**490**	421	352
ELGUIT	67	VOX/JMI	**SATURN IV BASS** SUNBURST, SINGLE CUTAWAY, 1 PU	495	**366**	314	263
ELGUIT	68	VOX/JMI	**SATURN IV BASS** 3-TONE SUNBURST, SINGLE CUTAWAY	492	**364**	312	261
ELGUIT	61	VOX/JMI	**SHADOW** BLACK, SOLID BODY, TREMOLO, 2 PU's	265	**196**	168	141
ELGUIT	60	VOX/JMI	**SIDEWINDER IV BASS**	559	**413**	355	297
ELGUIT	65	VOX/JMI	**SIDEWINDER IV BASS**	518	**383**	329	275
ELGUIT	67	VOX/JMI	**SIDEWINDER IV BASS**	598	**442**	380	317
ELGUIT	68	VOX/JMI	**SIDEWINDER IV BASS** SUNBURST, 2 PU's	475	**351**	301	252
ELGUIT	61	VOX/JMI	**SOUNDCASTER** RED, SOLID BODY, 3 PU's, TREM	350	**259**	222	186
ELGUIT	62	VOX/JMI	**SPITFIRE**	392	**290**	249	208
ELGUIT	68	VOX/JMI	**SPITFIRE** SUNBURST	353	**261**	224	187
ELGUIT	69	VOX/JMI	**SPITFIRE** SUNBURST	346	**256**	220	184
ELGUIT	61	VOX/JMI	**STROLLER** WHITE, SOLID BODY, 1 PU, SERIAL #1-250/1-500	265	**196**	168	141
ELGUIT	60	VOX/JMI	**STUDENT PRINCE** HOLLOW BODY	291	**215**	185	155
ELGUIT	61	VOX/JMI	**SUPER ACE** WHITE, 3 PU's	368	**272**	234	195
ELGUIT	62	VOX/JMI	**SUPER ACE** RED, 3 PU's	344	**254**	218	183
ELGUIT	63	VOX/JMI	**SUPER LYNX DELUXE**	471	**348**	299	250
ELGUIT	68	VOX/JMI	**SUPER LYNX DELUXE**	480	**355**	305	255
ELGUIT	66	VOX/JMI	**SUPER LYNX V-243** 2 SC PU's	438	**324**	278	233
ELGUIT	60	VOX/JMI	**SUPER METEOR**	487	**360**	309	259
ELGUIT	68	VOX/JMI	**SUPER METEOR**	437	**323**	278	232
ELGUIT	60	VOX/JMI	**TORNADO** SEMI-HOLLOW BODY	468	**346**	297	248
ELGUIT	67	VOX/JMI	**TORNADO** SUNBURST	267	**198**	170	142
ELGUIT	60	VOX/JMI	**TYPHOON** HOLLOW BODY	474	**350**	301	251
ELGUIT	68	VOX/JMI	**TYPHOON** HOLLOW BODY	288	**213**	183	153
ELGUIT	67	VOX/JMI	**TYPHOON JAZZ** RED, SEMI-HOLLOW BODY	496	**367**	315	263

TYPE	YR	MFG	PRICES--BASED ON 100% ORIGINAL MODEL	SELL EXC	SELL AVG	BUY EXC	BUY AVG
ELGUIT	62	VOX/JMI	**VICTO** HOLLOW BODY, DOUBLE CUTAWAY, 2 PU's	456	**337**	290	242
ELGUIT	68	VOX/JMI	**VIOLIN BASS** SUNBURST, HOLLOW BODY 2 PU's	518	**383**	329	275
ELGUIT	66	VOX/JMI	**WYMAN BASS** SUNBURST	889	**658**	565	472

VOX/THOMAS

TYPE	YR	MFG	MODEL	SELL EXC	SELL AVG	BUY EXC	BUY AVG
GUITAR AMP	64	VOX/THOM	**BEATLE** 4x12"	935	**691**	594	496
GTAMP	68	VOX/THOM	**BEATLE** 4x12"	1,176	**870**	747	625
GTAMP	65	VOX/THOM	**BERKLEY** 2x10", SOLID STATE	340	**252**	216	181
GTAMP	69	VOX/THOM	**BERKLEY II**	367	**280**	238	182
GTAMP	67	VOX/THOM	**BERKLEY III** 2x10", 32 WATT, SOLID STATE	433	**320**	275	230
GTAMP	68	VOX/THOM	**BERKLEY III** 2x10", BOTTOM	478	**353**	303	253
GTAMP	65	VOX/THOM	**BERKLEY SUPER REVERB** 2x10", TUBE	698	**516**	444	371
GTAMP	64	VOX/THOM	**BUCKINGHAM**	476	**352**	302	252
GTAMP	68	VOX/THOM	**ECHO UNIT CO 3**	480	**355**	305	255
GTAMP	70	VOX/THOM	**ESCORT** PORTABLE	169	**125**	107	90
GTAMP	65	VOX/THOM	**ESSEX BASS** STAND	354	**261**	225	188
GTAMP	66	VOX/THOM	**ESSEX BASS**	239	**176**	151	126
GTAMP	64	VOX/THOM	**KENSINGTON BASS** 1x12"	372	**275**	236	197
GTAMP	68	VOX/THOM	**KENSINGTON BASS** TOLEX	438	**324**	278	233
GTAMP	67	VOX/THOM	**KENSINGTON BASS V** 22 WATT, SOLID STATE	499	**369**	317	265
GTAMP	60	VOX/THOM	**PACEMAKER** TUBE	481	**356**	306	256
GTAMP	64	VOX/THOM	**PACEMAKER**	467	**345**	297	248
GTAMP	65	VOX/THOM	**PACEMAKER** TUBE	408	**301**	259	216
GTAMP	68	VOX/THOM	**PACEMAKER** 10" SPEAKER, SINGLE CHANNEL	390	**288**	248	207
GTAMP	66	VOX/THOM	**PACEMAKER V102** TUBE, 18 WATT, 1x10"	433	**320**	275	230
GTAMP	65	VOX/THOM	**PATHFINDER** TUBE	240	**177**	152	127
GTAMP	66	VOX/THOM	**PATHFINDER** V101 TUBE, 1x8"	288	**213**	183	153
GTAMP	64	VOX/THOM	**ROYAL GUARDSMAN** 4x12"	478	**353**	303	253
GTAMP	67	VOX/THOM	**ROYAL GUARDSMAN** 2x12" CABINET	434	**321**	276	231
GTAMP	71	VOX/THOM	**ROYAL GUARDSMAN** SOLID STATE	334	**247**	212	177
GTAMP	68	VOX/THOM	**SUPER BEATLE 1141**	562	**416**	357	298
GTAMP	72	VOX/THOM	**SUPER BEATLE 1143** HEAD ONLY	480	**355**	305	255
GTAMP	64	VOX/THOM	**SUPER BEATLE 1144** 4x12"	817	**604**	519	434
GTAMP	67	VOX/THOM	**VISCOUNT V1154** 2x12", 35 WATT, SOLID STATE	240	**177**	152	127
GTAMP	64	VOX/THOM	**WESTMINSTER** 1x18"	313	**232**	199	166
GTAMP	65	VOX/THOM	**WESTMINSTER BASS** 2x15"	468	**346**	297	248
GTAMP	67	VOX/THOM	**WESTMINSTER BASS V1182 TWIN** 120 WATT, SOLID STATE	499	**369**	317	265
GUITAR (ACOUSTIC)	60	VOX/THOM	**COUNTRY WESTERN** FLATTOP, DREADNOUGHT	386	**286**	245	205
GUITAR	65	VOX/THOM	**COUNTRY WESTERN** FLATTOP, DREADNOUGHT	451	**333**	286	239
GUITAR	60	VOX/THOM	**FOLK 12** FLATTOP, DREADNOUGHT	387	**286**	246	206
MANDOLIN	67	VOX/THOM	**MANDO GUITAR** 12-STRING	956	**707**	607	507

VOX/THOMAS by EKO

TYPE	YR	MFG	MODEL	SELL EXC	SELL AVG	BUY EXC	BUY AVG
ELEC. GUITAR	64	VOX/THOME	**BOBCAT** HOLLOW BODY	467	**345**	297	248
ELGUIT	66	VOX/THOME	**BOBCAT** TREMOLO, 3 SC PU's	432	**319**	274	229
ELGUIT	60	VOX/THOME	**BULLDOG** SUNBURST	811	**599**	515	430
ELGUIT	63	VOX/THOME	**BULLDOG** SUNBURST	805	**595**	511	427

TYPE	YR	MFG	PRICES--BASED ON 100% ORIGINAL MODEL	SELL EXC	SELL AVG	BUY EXC	BUY AVG
ELGUIT	68	VOX/THOME	**BULLDOG** SUNBURST	765	**565**	486	406
ELGUIT	63	VOX/THOME	**COUGAR BASS**	396	**293**	251	210
ELGUIT	63	VOX/THOME	**GUITORGAN** w/TRANSFORMER ONLY	872	**645**	554	463
ELGUIT	63	VOX/THOME	**HURRICANE** VIBRATO, 2 PU's	274	**203**	174	145
ELGUIT	68	VOX/THOME	**HURRICANE** SUNBURST	385	**285**	245	205
ELGUIT	68	VOX/THOME	**LYNX** SUNBURST, 2 PU's	313	**232**	199	166
ELGUIT	63	VOX/THOME	**SERENADER** FLATTOP	212	**156**	134	112
ELGUIT	67	VOX/THOME	**STEREO PHANTOM 12** BOOK BOUND, EBONY FINGERBOARD	637	**471**	405	338
ELGUIT	68	VOX/THOME	**STINGER IV BASS** SUNBURST, 2 PU's	457	**338**	290	243
ELGUIT	64	VOX/THOME	**TEMPEST XII**	275	**203**	175	146
ELGUIT	68	VOX/THOME	**TEMPEST XII** SUNBURST, 12-STRING	251	**186**	159	133
ELGUIT	64	VOX/THOME	**V-250 BASS** SUNBURST, VIOLIN SHAPE	380	**281**	241	201
ELGUIT	67	VOX/THOME	**V-250 BASS** SUNBURST, VIOLIN SHAPE	480	**355**	305	255
ELGUIT	63	VOX/THOME	**VIOLIN BASS** SUNBURST	798	**590**	507	424
ELGUIT	67	VOX/THOME	**VIOLIN BASS** SUNBURST, VIOLIN BODY	752	**556**	478	399
ELGUIT	68	VOX/THOME	**VIOLIN BASS** SUNBURST, SEMI-HOLLOW BODY	863	**638**	548	458
ELGUIT	64	VOX/THOME	**WYMAN BASS**	822	**608**	522	437

WASHBURN INTERNATIONAL, INC.

TYPE	YR	MFG	MODEL	SELL EXC	SELL AVG	BUY EXC	BUY AVG
BANJO	00	WASHBURN	**1900 BANJO 25.5"SCLE 11"HD OPEN BK** MTAL CLAD RIM,AFRICAN TURBO SNL INLAY,/ENGRVD FNGRBRD DOTS	792	**586**	503	421
BANJO	20	WASHBURN	**MANDOLIN-BANJO** OPEN BACK	192	**142**	122	102
BANJO	20	WASHBURN	**PLECTRUM** MAHOGANY, RESONATOR	384	**284**	244	204
BANJO	20	WASHBURN	**STYLE C** TENOR	336	**248**	213	178
BANJO	23	WASHBURN	**STYLE C** TENOR	283	**209**	179	150
BANJO	10	WASHBURN	**STYLE D** OPEN BACK	504	**372**	320	267
BANJO	10	WASHBURN	**WASHBURN** TENOR, OPEN BACK	382	**282**	242	202
BANJO	20	WASHBURN	**WASHBURN PARLOR**	377	**279**	239	200
ELEC. GUITAR	74	WASHBURN	**TB-2000 BASS** NATURAL, ALUMINUM NECK	796	**589**	506	423
GUITAR (ACOUSTIC)	96	WASHBURN	**1896 PARLOR GUITAR**	993	**734**	631	527
GUITAR	98	WASHBURN	**1898** BRAZILIAN ROSEWOOD BACK/SIDES, 13" WIDE	637	**471**	405	338
GUITAR	35	WASHBURN	**COLLEGIAN**	468	**346**	297	248
GUITAR	78	WASHBURN	**D-50S** ROSEWOOD INLAYS	456	**337**	289	242
GUITAR	38	WASHBURN	**INSPIRATION**	337	**249**	214	179
GUITAR	37	WASHBURN	**JUNIOR**	452	**334**	287	240
GUITAR	35	WASHBURN	**SOLO**	290	**221**	188	144
GUITAR	38	WASHBURN	**SOLO DELUXE**	361	**267**	229	192
GUITAR	00	WASHBURN	**STYLE 217** ROSEWOOD BACK/SIDES	489	**362**	311	260
GUITAR	15	WASHBURN	**STYLE E** BRAZILIAN ROSEWOOD	513	**379**	326	272
GUITAR	37	WASHBURN	**SUPERB** SUNBURST, PEARL STRIPE INLAY	751	**555**	477	399
GUITAR	10	WASHBURN	**WASHBURN # 80** BRAZILIAN ROSEWOOD	1,201	**888**	763	638
GUITAR	01	WASHBURN	**WASHBURN # 101** ROSEWOOD BACK/SIDES	710	**525**	451	377
GUITAR	00	WASHBURN	**WASHBURN # 111**	409	**312**	265	202
GUITAR	05	WASHBURN	**WASHBURN # 112**	479	**354**	304	254
GUITAR	01	WASHBURN	**WASHBURN # 115** BRAZILIAN ROSEWOOD BACK/SIDES	561	**415**	356	298
GUITAR	01	WASHBURN	**WASHBURN # 211**	478	**353**	303	253
GUITAR	00	WASHBURN	**WASHBURN # 225**	1,239	**916**	787	658
GUITAR	11	WASHBURN	**WASHBURN # 312**	492	**364**	312	261
GUITAR	14	WASHBURN	**WASHBURN # 345**	478	**353**	303	253
GUITAR	24	WASHBURN	**WASHBURN # 350** ARTIST SPECIAL	432	**319**	274	229
GUITAR	10	WASHBURN	**WASHBURN # 388**	459	**340**	292	244
GUITAR	12	WASHBURN	**WASHBURN # 399**	546	**416**	353	270

	TYPE	YR	MFG	PRICES--BASED ON 100% ORIGINAL MODEL	SELL EXC	SELL AVG	BUY EXC	BUY AVG
	GUITAR	14	WASHBURN	WASHBURN # 423	337	249	214	179
	GUITAR	26	WASHBURN	WASHBURN # 425 INLAID G. HART & SON	518	383	329	275
	GUITAR	20	WASHBURN	WASHBURN #1118 ROSEWOOD, "0" SIZE	435	332	282	215
	GUITAR	30	WASHBURN	WASHBURN #5237 ROSEWOOD BACK/SIDES, 12-FRET	640	473	406	340
	GUITAR	30	WASHBURN	WASHBURN #5238 HERRINGBONE TRIM, GOLD FLORAL	1,992	1,473	1,265	1,058
	GUITAR	35	WASHBURN	WASHBURN #5250 MAHOGANY BACK/SIDES, ARCHTOP	467	345	297	248
MANDOLIN		35	WASHBURN	0-18 SPRUCE TOP	383	283	243	203
	MANDOL	30	WASHBURN	00-28 BRAZILIAN ROSEWOOD, HERRINGBONE	1,035	766	658	550
	MANDOL	00	WASHBURN	BOWL BACK ROSEWOOD	438	324	278	233
	MANDOL	92	WASHBURN	STYLE 80 (1892)	956	707	607	507
	MANDOL	00	WASHBURN	STYLE 115 BRAZILIAN ROSEWOOD, BOWL BACK	609	450	387	323
	MANDOL	01	WASHBURN	STYLE 115 ROSEWOOD BACK, BOWL BACK, 9 RIBS	462	342	294	245
	MANDOL	90	WASHBURN	STYLE 122 (1890) BOWL BACK	462	342	294	245
	MANDOL	97	WASHBURN	STYLE 175 (1897) SPRUCE, ABALONE	1,035	766	658	550
	MANDOL	20	WASHBURN	STYLE A BRAZILIAN ROSEWOOD	480	355	305	255
	MANDOL	15	WASHBURN	STYLE E BRAZILIAN ROSEWOOD	498	368	316	264
	MANDOL	23	WASHBURN	STYLE E BRAZILIAN ROSEWOOD	379	280	240	201
	MANDOL	20	WASHBURN	WASHBURN PROF A-SERIES MAPLE BACK/SIDES	1,216	899	772	646
STEEL GUITAR		26	WASHBURN	TONK BROTHERS 00-28 ROSEWOOD, HERRINGBONE	2,051	1,517	1,303	1,089
UKULELE		30	WASHBURN	MODEL 701 ROSEWOOD, MAHOGANY	360	266	228	191

WEBSTER

	TYPE	YR	MFG	MODEL	SELL EXC	SELL AVG	BUY EXC	BUY AVG
MIC		42	WEBSTER	W-1248 L RIBBON BAKELITE BODY	1,513	1,119	961	804

WEISSENBORN

	TYPE	YR	MFG	MODEL	SELL EXC	SELL AVG	BUY EXC	BUY AVG
GUITAR (ACOUSTIC)		25	WEISSENBO	STYLE 1 HAWAIIAN	1,762	1,303	1,119	936
	GUITAR	26	WEISSENBO	STYLE 1 HAWAIIAN	1,647	1,218	1,046	875
	GUITAR	28	WEISSENBO	STYLE 1 HAWAIIAN	1,473	1,089	936	782
	GUITAR	32	WEISSENBO	STYLE 1 HAWAIIAN	1,309	968	832	695
	GUITAR	34	WEISSENBO	STYLE 1 HAWAIIAN	1,384	1,023	879	735
	GUITAR	35	WEISSENBO	STYLE 1 HAWAIIAN	1,302	963	827	692
	GUITAR	20	WEISSENBO	STYLE 2 HAWAIIAN	1,195	883	759	634
	GUITAR	25	WEISSENBO	STYLE 2 HAWAIIAN	1,368	1,012	869	727
	GUITAR	33	WEISSENBO	STYLE 2 HAWAIIAN	1,258	930	799	668
	GUITAR	20	WEISSENBO	STYLE 3 HAWAIIAN FLATTOP	1,451	1,073	922	771
	GUITAR	25	WEISSENBO	STYLE 3 HAWAIIAN	1,642	1,214	1,043	872
	GUITAR	35	WEISSENBO	STYLE 3 HAWAIIAN	1,327	981	843	705
	GUITAR	20	WEISSENBO	STYLE 4 HAWAIIAN	3,840	2,840	2,440	2,040
	GUITAR	25	WEISSENBO	STYLE 4 HAWAIIAN	3,079	2,277	1,956	1,636
	GUITAR	27	WEISSENBO	STYLE 4 HAWAIIAN	2,885	2,134	1,833	1,533
	GUITAR	35	WEISSENBO	STYLE 4 HAWAIIAN	2,057	1,521	1,307	1,092
	GUITAR	32	WEISSENBO	STYLE A SPANISH NECK	1,832	1,355	1,164	973
UKULELE		20	WEISSENBO	SOPRANO KOAWOOD BODY	192	142	122	102
	UKE	30	WEISSENBO	UKE ROPE BINDING	254	188	161	135
	UKE	60	WEISSENBO	UKE #2	288	213	183	153

WEYMANN

	TYPE	YR	MFG	MODEL	SELL EXC	SELL AVG	BUY EXC	BUY AVG
BANJO		10	WEYMANN	KEYSTONE STATE TENOR	288	213	183	153
	BANJO	24	WEYMANN	KEYSTONE STATE TENOR	251	186	159	133
	BANJO	25	WEYMANN	STYLE 1 TENOR	1,239	916	787	658
	BANJO	26	WEYMANN	STYLE 1 TENOR	1,195	883	759	634
	BANJO	27	WEYMANN	STYLE 1 TENOR	1,171	866	744	622
	BANJO	28	WEYMANN	STYLE 1 TENOR	1,118	827	710	594
	BANJO	20	WEYMANN	STYLE 2 TENOR, CURLY MAPLE	704	521	447	374

TYPE	YR	MFG	MODEL	SELL EXC	SELL AVG	BUY EXC	BUY AVG
BANJO	25	WEYMANN	STYLE 2 TENOR, MAPLE NECK	677	501	430	360
BANJO	28	WEYMANN	STYLE 2 TENOR, RESONATOR, FLANGE	778	575	494	413
BANJO	28	WEYMANN	STYLE 2 PLECTRUM, CURLY MAPLE	796	589	506	423
BANJO	25	WEYMANN	STYLE 30 TENOR	462	342	294	245
BANJO	30	WEYMANN	STYLE 30 TENOR, MAHOGANY, RESONATOR	467	345	297	248
BANJO	28	WEYMANN	STYLE 85 TENOR	482	357	306	256
BANJO	25	WEYMANN	STYLE 180 TENOR	565	418	359	300
BANJO	23	WEYMANN	STYLE 1500 TENOR, 19-FRET	713	527	453	378
BANJO	25	WEYMANN	STYLE A TENOR, MAHOGANY, RESONATOR	468	346	297	248
MANDOLIN	00	WEYMANN	1900 PRESENTAION SPRUCE, ENGRAVED BORDER	1,015	751	645	539
MANDOL	10	WEYMANN	BOWL ROSEWOOD AND BIRDSEYE MAPLE BACK	265	196	168	141
MANDOL	12	WEYMANN	MANDOCELLO ARCHED SPRUCE TOP	675	514	437	334
MANDOL	22	WEYMANN	MANDOLUTE NATURAL, MAPLE BACK/SIDES	313	232	199	166
MANDOL	30	WEYMANN	MANDOLUTE MAPLE, FLAME, EBONY BOARD	193	143	123	103
MANDOL	20	WEYMANN	MANDOLUTE 30 CURLY MAPLE BACK/SIDES	440	325	279	234
MANDOL	20	WEYMANN	STYLE 40 CURLY MAPLE BACK/SIDES/NECK	401	296	254	213
UKULELE	25	WEYMANN	SOPRANO MAHOGANY BODY	201	149	128	107
UKE	31	WEYMANN	SOPRANO KOAWOOD BODY, PEARL INLAY	737	545	468	391

YAMAHA CORPORATION OF AMERICA

TYPE	YR	MFG	MODEL	SELL EXC	SELL AVG	BUY EXC	BUY AVG
ELEC. GUITAR	80	YAMAHA	B-800 BURGUNDY	198	146	126	105
ELGUIT	80	YAMAHA	BB-350F BASS FRETLESS BOLT-ON NECK	198	146	126	105
ELGUIT	80	YAMAHA	SA-2000 TOBACCO SUNBURST, 2 PU's	504	372	320	267
ELGUIT	72	YAMAHA	SBG-2100	347	257	220	184
ELGUIT	67	YAMAHA	SG-2 JAZZMASTER 1 SINGLE COIL, 1 HUMBUCKER	273	202	173	145
ELGUIT	68	YAMAHA	SG-3 BASS BLUE	160	118	101	85
ELGUIT	66	YAMAHA	SG-5 SUNBURST, SOLID BODY, MAPLE, 3 PU's	183	135	116	97
GUITAR AMP	80	YAMAHA	JX-20A BASS 30 WATT	189	139	120	100
GTAMP	80	YAMAHA	JX-30B BASS 30 WATT	189	139	120	100
GUITAR (ACOUSTIC)	81	YAMAHA	CJ-818SB FOLK CJ JUMBO 6-STRING	192	142	122	102
GUITAR	78	YAMAHA	ETERNA	280	207	178	148
GUITAR	72	YAMAHA	FG-75	95	70	60	50
GUITAR	75	YAMAHA	FG-160 DREADNOUGHT	108	80	68	57
GUITAR	79	YAMAHA	FG-336 SUNBURST	137	101	87	72
GUITAR	73	YAMAHA	FG-1500 BRAZILIAN ROSEWOOD	390	288	248	207
GUITAR	77	YAMAHA	G-255-S CLASSICAL INDIAN ROSEWOOD	253	187	161	134
SYNTHESIZER	77	YAMAHA	CS-80 ANALOG	1,482	1,096	941	787

ZORKO

TYPE	YR	MFG	MODEL	SELL EXC	SELL AVG	BUY EXC	BUY AVG
UPRIG	48	ZORKO	ELECTRIC UPRIGHT	2,952	2,183	1,875	1,568

2004 Orion Blue Book Survey Form

Orion Research Corporation

14555 N. Scottsdale Rd. suite #330
Scottsdale, AZ 85254
voice: 480.951.1114
fax: 800.375.1315
email: sales@orionbluebook.com

You can receive a **$20 coupon** toward your next purchase of an Orion Blue Book. Simply return this form completely filled out (45 items in section 1 and 5 items each in sections 2 and 3). Mail or fax completed surveys to the address above. Please mark which book this survey is for:

☐ AUDIO   ☐ CAMERA   ☐ CAR STEREO

☐ COMPUTER   ☐ COPIER   ☐ GUN

☐ GUITARS & MUSICAL INSTRUMENTS   ☐ COMPUTER   ☐ POWER TOOL

☐ PROFESSIONAL SOUND   ☐ VIDEO & TELEVISION   ☐ VINTAGE GUITARS & COLLECTIBLES

Name: _____ Company: _____

Address: _____ Phone: _____

City: _____ State: _____ Zip: _____

1. List 45 Products you have taken into your inventory of used equipment:

Product type	Mfg.	Model	Amount Given	Selling Price	Days to sell
1.					
2.					
3.					
4.					
5.					
6.					
7.					
8.					
9.					
10.					
11.					
12.					
13.					
14.					
15.					
16.					
17.					
18.					
19.					
20.					
21.					
22.					
23.					
24.					
25.					
26.					

Orion Research reserves the right to refuse any survey
because of incomplete information

1. Continued:

Product type	Mfg.	Model	Amount Given	Selling Price	Days to sell
27.					
28.					
29.					
30.					
31.					
32.					
33.					
34.					
35.					
36.					
37.					
38.					
39.					
40.					
41.					
42.					
43.					
44.					
45.					

2. List 5 products that have gone up in value over the last year:

Product type	Mfg.	Model	Amount Given	Selling Price	Days to sell
1.					
2.					
3.					
4.					
5.					

3. List 5 products that have dramatically decreased in value over the last year:

Product type	Mfg.	Model	Amount Given	Selling Price	Days to sell
1.					
2.					
3.					
4.					
5.					

Orion Research Corporation
voice: 480.951.1114   fax: 800.375.1315